DISTRIBUTED SYSTEMS

Fourth edition

Version 4.01

(January 2023)

Maarten van Steen

Andrew S. Tanenbaum

Cover art by Max van Steen

To Mariëlle, Max, and Elke
– MvS
To Suzanne, Barbara, Marvin, Aron, Nathan, Olivia, and Mirte
– AST

CONTENTS

Preface   xi

1 Introduction   1
  1.1 From networked systems to distributed systems   3
    1.1.1 Distributed versus decentralized systems   3
    1.1.2 Why making the distinction is relevant   7
    1.1.3 Studying distributed systems   8
  1.2 Design goals 10
    1.2.1 Resource sharing 10
    1.2.2 Distribution transparency 11
    1.2.3 Openness 15
    1.2.4 Dependability 18
    1.2.5 Security 21
    1.2.6 Scalability 24
  1.3 A simple classification of distributed systems 32
    1.3.1 High-performance distributed computing 32
    1.3.2 Distributed information systems 37
    1.3.3 Pervasive systems 43
  1.4 Pitfalls 52
  1.5 Summary 53

2 Architectures   55
  2.1 Architectural styles 56
    2.1.1 Layered architectures 57
    2.1.2 Service-oriented architectures 62
    2.1.3 Publish-subscribe architectures 68
  2.2 Middleware and distributed systems 73
    2.2.1 Middleware organization 74
    2.2.2 Modifiable middleware 78
  2.3 Layered-system architectures 78
    2.3.1 Simple client-server architecture 79
    2.3.2 Multitiered Architectures 80
    2.3.3 Example: The Network File System 83
    2.3.4 Example: The Web 85
  2.4 Symmetrically distributed system architectures 88
    2.4.1 Structured peer-to-peer systems 90
    2.4.2 Unstructured peer-to-peer systems 92

2.4.3   Hierarchically organized peer-to-peer networks   95
2.4.4   Example: BitTorrent   96
2.5   Hybrid system architectures   98
2.5.1   Cloud computing   98
2.5.2   The edge-cloud architecture   100
2.5.3   Blockchain architectures   104
2.6   Summary   108

3   Processes   111
3.1   Threads   112
3.1.1   Introduction to threads   113
3.1.2   Threads in distributed systems   122
3.2   Virtualization   127
3.2.1   Principle of virtualization   127
3.2.2   Containers   133
3.2.3   Comparing virtual machines and containers   138
3.2.4   Application of virtual machines to distributed systems .   139
3.3   Clients   141
3.3.1   Networked user interfaces   141
3.3.2   Virtual desktop environment   144
3.3.3   Client-side software for distribution transparency   148
3.4   Servers   149
3.4.1   General design issues   149
3.4.2   Object servers   154
3.4.3   Example: The Apache Web server   159
3.4.4   Server clusters   161
3.5   Code migration   167
3.5.1   Reasons for migrating code   167
3.5.2   Models for code migration   171
3.5.3   Migration in heterogeneous systems   174
3.6   Summary   177

4   Communication   181
4.1   Foundations   183
4.1.1   Layered Protocols   183
4.1.2   Types of Communication   190
4.2   Remote procedure call   192
4.2.1   Basic RPC operation   192
4.2.2   Parameter passing   197
4.2.3   RPC-based application support   201
4.2.4   Variations on RPC   205
4.3   Message-oriented communication   208
4.3.1   Simple transient messaging with sockets   208
4.3.2   Advanced transient messaging   213

        4.3.3   Message-oriented persistent communication 220
        4.3.4   Example: Advanced Message Queuing Protocol (AMQP) 227
   4.4 Multicast communication 232
        4.4.1   Application-level tree-based multicasting 232
        4.4.2   Flooding-based multicasting 236
        4.4.3   Gossip-based data dissemination 240
   4.5 Summary 245

5 Coordination   247
   5.1 Clock synchronization 249
        5.1.1   Physical clocks 250
        5.1.2   Clock synchronization algorithms 253
   5.2 Logical clocks 260
        5.2.1   Lamport's logical clocks 260
        5.2.2   Vector clocks 266
   5.3 Mutual exclusion 272
        5.3.1   Overview 272
        5.3.2   A centralized algorithm 273
        5.3.3   A distributed algorithm 274
        5.3.4   A token-ring algorithm 276
        5.3.5   A decentralized algorithm 277
        5.3.6   Example: Simple locking with ZooKeeper 280
   5.4 Election algorithms 283
        5.4.1   The bully algorithm 283
        5.4.2   A ring algorithm 285
        5.4.3   Example: Leader election in ZooKeeper 286
        5.4.4   Example: Leader election in Raft 289
        5.4.5   Elections in large-scale systems 290
        5.4.6   Elections in wireless environments 294
   5.5 Gossip-based coordination 297
        5.5.1   Aggregation 297
        5.5.2   A peer-sampling service 298
        5.5.3   Gossip-based overlay construction 299
        5.5.4   Secure gossiping 303
   5.6 Distributed event matching 306
        5.6.1   Centralized implementations 307
        5.6.2   Secure publish-subscribe solutions 313
   5.7 Location systems 315
        5.7.1   GPS: Global Positioning System 315
        5.7.2   When GPS is not an option 317
        5.7.3   Logical positioning of nodes 318
   5.8 Summary 322

6 Naming   325

6.1   Names, identifiers, and addresses 326
6.2   Flat naming 329
      6.2.1   Simple solutions 329
      6.2.2   Home-based approaches 331
      6.2.3   Distributed hash tables 333
      6.2.4   Hierarchical approaches 338
      6.2.5   Secure flat naming 343
6.3   Structured naming 344
      6.3.1   Name spaces 344
      6.3.2   Name resolution 347
      6.3.3   The implementation of a name space 352
      6.3.4   Example: The Domain Name System 359
      6.3.5   Example: The Network File System 369
6.4   Attribute-based naming 375
      6.4.1   Directory services 375
      6.4.2   Hierarchical implementations: LDAP 376
      6.4.3   Decentralized implementations 380
6.5   Named-data networking 385
      6.5.1   Basics 385
      6.5.2   Routing 387
      6.5.3   Security in named-data networking 388
6.6   Summary 389

7   Consistency and replication   391
7.1   Introduction 392
      7.1.1   Reasons for replication 393
      7.1.2   Replication as scaling technique 394
7.2   Data-centric consistency models 395
      7.2.1   Consistent ordering of operations 396
      7.2.2   Eventual consistency 406
      7.2.3   Continuous consistency 410
7.3   Client-centric consistency models 415
      7.3.1   Monotonic reads 417
      7.3.2   Monotonic writes 418
      7.3.3   Read your writes 420
      7.3.4   Writes follow reads 421
      7.3.5   Example: client-centric consistency in ZooKeeper . . . 422
7.4   Replica management 423
      7.4.1   Finding the best server location 424
      7.4.2   Content replication and placement 426
      7.4.3   Content distribution 430
      7.4.4   Managing replicated objects 434
7.5   Consistency protocols 437
      7.5.1   Sequential consistency: Primary-based protocols 438

	7.5.2	Sequential consistency: Replicated-write protocols	. . .	440
	7.5.3	Cache-coherence protocols		443
	7.5.4	Implementing continuous consistency		446
	7.5.5	Implementing client-centric consistency		448
7.6		Example: Caching and replication in the Web		451
7.7		Summary		458

8 Fault tolerance   **461**

8.1		Introduction to fault tolerance		462
	8.1.1	Basic concepts		463
	8.1.2	Failure models		466
	8.1.3	Failure masking by redundancy		470
8.2		Process resilience		471
	8.2.1	Resilience by process groups		472
	8.2.2	Failure masking and replication		474
	8.2.3	Consensus in faulty systems with crash failures		475
	8.2.4	Example: Paxos		479
	8.2.5	Consensus in faulty systems with arbitrary failures	. . .	491
	8.2.6	Consensus in blockchain systems		502
	8.2.7	Some limitations on realizing fault tolerance		503
	8.2.8	Failure detection		506
8.3		Reliable client-server communication		508
	8.3.1	Point-to-point communication		508
	8.3.2	RPC semantics in the presence of failures		509
8.4		Reliable group communication		515
	8.4.1	Introduction		515
	8.4.2	Scalability in reliable multicasting		518
	8.4.3	Atomic multicast		522
8.5		Distributed commit		528
8.6		Recovery		536
	8.6.1	Introduction		536
	8.6.2	Checkpointing		538
	8.6.3	Message logging		541
8.7		Summary		543

9 Security   **545**

9.1		Introduction to security		546
	9.1.1	Security threats, policies, and mechanisms		547
	9.1.2	Design issues		548
9.2		Cryptography		555
	9.2.1	Basics		555
	9.2.2	Symmetric and asymmetric cryptosystems		557
	9.2.3	Hash functions		560
	9.2.4	Key management		562

9.3   Authentication 571
    9.3.1   Introduction to authentication 571
    9.3.2   Authentication protocols 572
9.4   Trust in distributed systems 585
    9.4.1   Trust in the face of Byzantine failures 586
    9.4.2   Trusting an identity 586
    9.4.3   Trusting a system 591
9.5   Authorization 593
    9.5.1   General issues in access control 593
    9.5.2   Attribute-based access control 598
    9.5.3   Delegation 601
    9.5.4   Decentralized authorization: an example 605
9.6   Monitoring 609
    9.6.1   Firewalls 609
    9.6.2   Intrusion detection: basics 611
    9.6.3   Collaborative intrusion detection 612
9.7   Summary 613

Index   **615**

Bibliography   **631**

Glossary   **665**

PREFACE

This is the fourth edition of "Distributed Systems." We have stayed close to the setup of the third edition, including examples of (part of) existing distributed systems close to where general principles are discussed. For example, we have included material on blockchain systems, and discuss their various components throughout the book. We have, again, used special boxed sections for material that can be skipped at first reading.

The text has been thoroughly reviewed, revised, and updated. In particular, all the Python code has been updated to Python3, while at the same time the channel package has been almost completely revised and simplified. The coding examples in the book leave out many details for readability, but the complete examples are available through the book's Website, hosted at www.distributed-systems.net. We have made sure that virtually all examples can be instantly executed through a simple script. However, it will be necessary to download and install special packages, such as Redis.

As before, the Website also contains slides in PDF and PPT, as well as the sources for producing slides using LaTeX with the Beamer class. All figures, now including those for tables and coding examples, are available in PDF and PNG formats.

Like the previous edition, the book can be (freely) downloaded, making it much easier to use hyperlinks where appropriate. At the same time, we are offering a printed version through Amazon.com, available at minimal costs.

The book being fully digital allows us to incorporate updates when needed. We plan to run updates on a yearly basis, while keeping previous versions digitally available, as well as the original printed version. Running frequent updates is not always the right thing to do from the perspective of teaching, but yearly updates and maintaining previous versions seems a good compromise. Updates generally consist of small corrections, the kind that usually pop up in errata lists. Next to that, the book now also contains an index section, as well as a glossary section. These are typically sections that generally take a huge time to compile, but are also sections that typically grow as the book is being used. Likewise, we may find ways to improve how hyperlinks have been incorporated. Such matters do not affect the main text, while potentially improving the usability of the digital version.

Acknowledgements

Many teachers and students have helped with spotting the inevitable errors in the third edition, and we owe them many thanks, but in any case Michael May, Linh Phan, Juan Abadie, and Christian Zirpins. For the fourth edition, a handful of colleagues were so kind to review parts of the material. In particular, we wish to thank Armin Stocker, Hermann de Meer, Pim Otte, Johan Pouwelse, Michael P. Anderson, Ivo Varenhorst, Aditya Pappu, and Alexander Iosup. A special thanks goes to Hein Meling of Stavanger University. Not only did he help us tremendously in understanding how Paxos works (already for the third edition), we have gratefully adopted, and adapted, his LaTeX style file for generating message-sequence charts. These figures are now much more consistent. We thank Max van Steen for designing the cover.

Maarten van Steen
Andrew S. Tanenbaum

01

INTRODUCTION

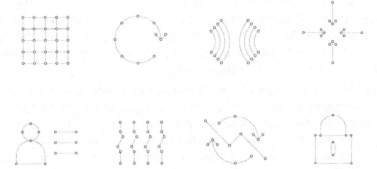

The pace at which computer systems change was, is, and continues to be overwhelming. From 1945, when the modern computer era began, until about 1985, computers were large and expensive. Moreover, lacking a way to connect them, these computers operated independently of one another.

Starting in the mid-1980s, however, two advances in technology began to change that situation. The first was the development of powerful microprocessors. Initially, these were 8-bit machines, but soon 16-, 32-, and 64-bit CPUs became common. With powerful multicore CPUs, we now are again facing the challenge of adapting and developing programs to exploit parallelism. In any case, the current generation of machines have the computing power of the mainframes deployed 30 or 40 years ago, but for 1/1000th of the price or less.

The second development was the invention of high-speed computer networks. **Local-area networks** or **LANs** allow thousands of machines within a building to be connected in such a way that small amounts of information can be transferred in a few microseconds or so. Larger amounts of data can be moved between machines at rates of billions of *bits per second* (**bps**). **Wide-area network** or **WANs** allow hundreds of millions of machines all over the earth to be connected at speeds varying from tens of thousands to hundreds of millions bps and more.

Parallel to the development of increasingly powerful and networked machines, we have also been able to witness miniaturization of computer systems, with perhaps the smartphone as the most impressive outcome. Packed with sensors, lots of memory, and a powerful multicore CPU, these devices are nothing less than full-fledged computers. Of course, they also have networking capabilities. Along the same lines, so-called **nano computers** have become readily available. These small, single-board computers, often the size of a credit card, can easily offer near-desktop performance. Well-known examples include Raspberry Pi and Arduino systems.

And the story continues. As digitalization of our society continues, we become increasingly aware of how many computers are actually being used, regularly embedded into other systems such as cars, airplanes, buildings, bridges, the power grid, and so on. This awareness is, unfortunately, increased when such systems suddenly turn out to be hackable. For example, in 2021, a fuel pipeline in the United States was effectively shut down by a ransomware attack. In this case, the computer system consisted of a mix of sensors, actuators, controllers, embedded computers, servers, etc., all brought together into a single system. What many of us do not realize, is that vital infrastructures, such as fuel pipelines, are monitored and controlled by **networked computer systems**. Along the same lines, it may be time to start realizing that a modern car is actually an autonomously operating, mobile networked computer. In this case, instead of the mobile computer being carried by a person, we need to deal with the mobile computer carrying people.

The size of a networked computer system may vary from a handful of devices, to millions of computers. The interconnection network may be wired, wireless, or a combination of both. Moreover, these systems are often highly dynamic, in the sense that computers can join and leave, with the topology and performance of the underlying network almost continuously changing.

It is difficult to think of computer systems that are *not* networked. And as a matter of fact, most networked computer systems can be accessed from any place in the world because they are hooked up to the Internet. Studying to understand these systems can easily become exceedingly complex. In this chapter, we start with shedding some light on what needs to be understood to build up the bigger picture without getting lost.

1.1 From networked systems to distributed systems

Before we dive into various aspects of distributed systems, let us first consider what distribution, or decentralization, actually entails.

1.1.1 Distributed versus decentralized systems

When considering various sources, there are quite a few opinions on distributed versus decentralized systems. Often, the distinction is illustrated by three different organizations of networked computer systems, as shown in Figure 1.1, where each node represents a computer system and an edge a communication link between two nodes.

To what extent such distinctions are useful remains to be seen, especially when discussions open on the pros and cons of each organization. For example, it is often stated that centralized organizations do not scale well. Likewise, distributed organizations are said to be more robust against failures. As we shall see, none of these claims are generally true.

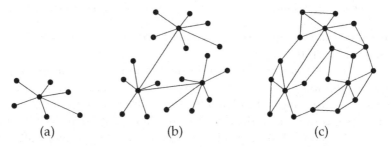

(a)   (b)   (c)

Figure 1.1: The organization of a (a) centralized, (b) decentralized, and (c) distributed system, according to various popular sources. We take a different approach, as figures such as these are really not that meaningful.

We take a different approach. If we think of a networked computer system as a collection of computers connected in a network, we can ask ourselves how these computers even became connected to each other in the first place. There are roughly two views that one can take.

The first, **integrative view**, is that there was a need to connect existing (networked) computer systems to each other. Typically, this happens when services running on a system need to be made available to users and applications that were not thought of before. This may happen, for example, when integrating financial services with project management services, as is often the case within a single organization. In the scientific-research domain, we have seen efforts to connect a myriad of often expensive resources (special-purpose computers, supercomputers, very large database systems, etc.) into what came to be known as a grid computer.

The second, **expansive view** is that an existing system required an extension through additional computers. This view is the one most often related to the field of distributed systems. It entails expanding a system with computers to hold resources close to where those resources are needed. An expansion may also be driven by the need to improve dependability: if one computer fails, then there are others who can take over. An important type of expansion is when a service needs to be made available for remote users and applications, for example, by offering a Web interface or a smartphone application. This last example also shows that the distinction between an integrative and an expansive view is not a clear-cut.

In both cases, we see that the networked system runs services, where each service is implemented as a collection of processes and resources spread across multiple computers. The two views lead to a natural distinction between two types of networked computer systems:

- A **decentralized system** is a networked computer system in which processes and resources are **necessarily** spread across multiple computers.

- A **distributed system** is a networked computer system in which processes and resources are **sufficiently** spread across multiple computers.

Before we discuss why this distinction is important, let us look at a few examples of each type of system.

Decentralized systems are mainly related to the integrative view of networked computer systems. They come to being because we want to connect systems, yet may be hindered by administrative boundaries. For example, many applications in the artificial-intelligence domain require massive amounts of data for building reliable predictive models. Normally, data is brought to the high-performance computers that literally train models before they can be used. But when data needs to stay within the perimeter of an organization (and there can be many reasons why this is necessary), we need to bring the training to the data. The result is known as **federated learning,** and is implemented by a decentralized system, where the need for spreading processes and resources is dictated by administrative policies.

Another example of a decentralized system is that of **distributed ledger**, also known as a **blockchain**. In this case, we need to deal with the situation that participating parties do not trust each other enough to set up simple schemes for collaboration. Instead, what they do is essentially make transactions among each other fully public (and verifiable) by an extend-only ledger that keeps records of those transactions. The ledger itself is fully spread across the participants, and the participants are the ones who validate transactions (of others) before admitting them to the ledger. The result is a decentralized system in which processes and resources are, indeed, *necessarily* spread across multiple computers, in this case due to lack of trust.

As a last example of a decentralized system, consider systems that are naturally geographically dispersed. This occurs typically with systems in which an actual location needs to be monitored, for example, in the case of a power plant, a building, a specific natural environment, and so on. The system, controlling the monitors and where decisions are made, may easily be placed somewhere else than the location being monitored. One obvious example is monitoring and controlling of satellites, but also more mundane situations as monitoring and controlling traffic, trains, etc. In these examples, the necessity for spreading processes and resources comes from a spatial argument.

As we mentioned, distributed systems are mainly related to the expansive view of networked computer systems. A well-known example is making use of e-mail services, such as Google Mail. What often happens is that a user logs into the system through a Web interface to read and send mails. More often, however, is that users configure their personal computer (such as a laptop) to make use of a specific mail client. To that end, they need to configure a few settings, such as the incoming and outgoing server. In the case of Google Mail, these are imap.gmail.com and smtp.gmail.com, respectively. Logically, it seems as if these two servers will handle all your mail. However, with an estimate of close to 2 billion users as of 2022, it is unlikely that only two computers can handle all their e-mails (which was estimated to be more than 300 billion per year, that is, some 10,000 mails *per second*). Behind the scenes, of course, the entire Google Mail service has been implemented and spread across many computers, jointly forming a distributed system. That system has been set up to make sure that so many users can process their mails (i.e., ensures scalability), but also that the risk of losing mail because of failures, is minimal (i.e., the system ensures fault tolerance). To the user, however, the image of just two servers is kept up (i.e., the distribution itself is highly transparent to the user). The distributed system implementing an e-mail service, such as Google Mail, typically expands (or shrinks) as dictated by dependability requirements, in turn, dependent on the number of its users.

An entirely different type of distributed system is formed by the collection of so-called **Content Delivery Networks**, or **CDNs** for short. A well-known example is Akamai with, in 2022, over 400,000 servers worldwide. We will discuss the principle working of CDNs later in Chapter 3. What it boils down to, is that the content of an actual Website, is copied and spread across various servers of the CDN. When visiting a Website, the user is transparently redirected to a nearby server that holds all or part of the content of that Website. The choice for which server to direct a user to may depend on many things, but surely when dealing with streaming content, a server is selected for which good performance in terms of latency and bandwidth can be guaranteed. The CDN dynamically ensures that the selected server will have the required content readily available, as well as update that content when needed, or remove it from the server when there are no or very few users to service there. Meanwhile, the user knows nothing about what is going on behind the scenes (which, again, is a form of distribution transparency). We also see in this example, that content is not copied to all servers, yet only to where it makes sense, that is, *sufficiently*, and for reasons of performance. CDNs also copy content to multiple servers to provide high levels of dependability.

As a final, much smaller distributed system, consider a setup based on a **Network-Attached Storage device**, also called a **NAS**. For domestic use, a typical NAS consists of 2–4 slots for internal hard disks. The NAS operates as a file server: it is accessible through a (generally wireless) network for any authorized device, and as such can offer services like shared storage, automated backups, streaming media, and so on. The NAS itself can best be seen as a single computer optimized for storing files, and offering the ability to easily share those files. The latter is important, and together with multiple users, we essentially have a setup of a distributed system. The users will be working with a set of files that are locally (i.e., from their laptop) easily accessible (in fact, seemingly integrated into the local file system), while also directly accessible by and for other users. Again, where and how the shared files are stored is hidden (i.e., the distribution is transparent). Assuming that sharing files is the goal, then we see that indeed a NAS can provide sufficient spreading of processes and resources.

Note 1.1 (More information: Are centralized solutions bad?)
There appears to be a stubborn misconception that centralized solutions cannot scale. Moreover, they are almost always associated with introducing a single point of failure. Both reasons are often seen to be enough to dismiss centralized solutions as being a good choice when designing distributed systems.

What many people forget is that a difference should be made between logical and physical designs. A logically centralized solution can be implemented in a highly scalable distributed manner. An excellent example is the **Domain Name System (DNS)**, which we discuss extensively in Chapter 6. Logically, DNS is organized as a huge tree, where each path from the root to a leaf node represents a fully qualified name, such as www.distributed-systems.net. It would be a mistake to think that the root node is implemented by just a single server. In fact, the root node is implemented by 13 different root servers, each server, in turn, implemented as a large cluster computer. The physical organization of DNS also shows that the root is *not* a single point of failure. Being highly replicated, it would take serious efforts to bring that root down and so far, all attempts to do so have failed.

Centralized solutions are not bad just because they seem to be centralized. In fact, as we shall encounter many times throughout this book, (logically, and even physically) centralized solutions are often much better than distributed counterparts for the simple reason that there *is* a single point of failure. It makes them much easier to manage, for example, and certainly in comparison where there may be multiple points of failures. Moreover, that single point of failure can be hardened against many kinds of failures as well as many kinds of security attacks. When it comes to being a performance bottleneck, we will also see that many things can be done to ensure that even that cannot be held against centralization.

In this sense, let us not forget that centralized solutions have even proven to be extremely scalable and robust. They are called cloud-based solutions. Again, their implementations can make use of very sophisticated distributed solutions, yet even then, we shall see that even those solutions may sometimes need to rely on a small set of physical machines, if only to guarantee performance.

1.1.2 Why making the distinction is relevant

Why do we make this distinction between decentralized and distributed systems? It is important to realize that centralized solutions are generally much simpler, and also simpler along different criteria. Decentralization, that is, the act of spreading the implementation of a service across multiple computers because we believe it is *necessary*, is a decision that needs to be considered carefully. Indeed, distributed and decentralized solutions are inherently difficult:

- There are many, often unexpected, dependencies that hinder understanding the behavior of these systems.

- Distributed and decentralized systems suffer almost continuously from **partial failures**: some process or resource, somewhere at one of the participating computers, is not operating according to expectations. Discovering that failure may actually take some time, while also such failures are preferably masked (i.e., they go unnoticed for users and applications), including the recovery from failures.

- Much related to partial failures is the fact that in many networked computer systems, participating nodes, processes, resources, and so on, come and go. This makes these systems highly dynamic, in turn requiring forms of automated management and maintenance, in turn increasing the complexity.

- The fact that distributed and decentralized systems are networked, used by many users and applications, and often cross multiple administrative boundaries, make them particularly vulnerable to security attacks. Therefore, understanding these systems and their behavior, requires that we understand how they can be, and are secured. Unfortunately, understanding security is not that easy.

Our distinction is one between *sufficiency* and *necessity* for spreading processes and resources across multiple computers. Throughout this book, we take the standpoint that decentralization can never be a goal in itself, and that it should focus on the *sufficiency* for spreading processes and resources across computers. In principle, the less spreading, the better. Yet at the same time, we need to realize that spreading is sometimes truly necessary, as illustrated by the examples of decentralized systems. From this point of sufficiency, the book is truly about distributed systems and where appropriate, we shall speak of decentralized systems.

Along the same lines, considering that distributed and decentralized systems are inherently complex, it is equally important to consider solutions that are as simple as possible. Therefore, we shall hardly discuss optimizations to solutions, firmly believing that the impact of their negative contribution to increased complexity outweighs the importance of their positive contribution to an increase of any type of performance.

1.1.3   Studying distributed systems

Considering that distributed systems are inherently difficult, it is important to take a systematic approach toward studying them. One of our major concerns is that there are so many explicit and implicit dependencies in distributed systems. For example, there is no such thing as a separate communication module, or a separate security module. Our approach is to take a look at distributed systems from a limited number, yet different perspectives. Each perspective is considered in a separate chapter.

- There are many ways in which distributed systems are organized. We start our discussion by taking the **architectural perspective**: what are common organizations, what are common styles? The architectural perspective will help in getting a first grip on how various components of existing systems interact and depend on each other.

- Distributed systems are all about processes. The **process perspective** is all about understanding the different forms of processes that occur in distributed systems, be they threads, their virtualization of hardware processes, clients, servers, and so on. Processes form the software backbone of distributed systems, and their understanding is essential for understanding distributed systems.

- Obviously, with multiple computers at stake, communication between processes is essential. The **communication perspective** concerns the facilities that distributed systems provide to exchange data between processes. It essentially entails mimicking procedure calls across multiple computers, high-level message passing with a wealth of semantic options, and various sorts of communication between sets of processes.

- To make distributed systems work, what happens under the hood on top of which applications are executed, is that processes coordinate things. They jointly coordinate, for example, to compensate for the lack of global clock, for realizing mutual exclusive access to shared resources, and so on. The **coordination perspective** describes a number of fundamental coordination tasks that need to be carried out as part of most distributed systems.

- To access processes and resources, we need naming. In particular, we need naming schemes that, when used, will lead to the process, resources, or whatever other type of entity that is being named. As simple as this may seem, naming not only turns out to be crucial in distributed systems, there are also many ways in which naming is supported. The **naming perspective** focuses entirely on resolving a name to the access point of the named entity.

- A critical aspect of distributed systems is that they perform well in terms of efficiency and in terms of dependability. The key instrument for both aspects is replicating resources. The only problem with replication is that updates may happen, implying that all copies of a resource need to be updated as well. It is here, that keeping up the appearance of a nondistributed system becomes challenging. The **consistency and replication perspective** essentially concentrates on the trade-offs between consistency, replication, and performance.

- We already mentioned that distributed systems are subject to partial failures. The **perspective of fault tolerance** dives into the means for masking failures and their recovery. It has proven to be one of the toughest perspectives for understanding distributed systems, mainly because there are so many trade-offs to be made, and also because completely masking failures and their recovery is provably impossible.

- As also mentioned, there is no such thing as a nonsecured distributed system. The **security perspective** focuses on how to ensure authorized access to resources. To that end, we need to discuss trust in distributed systems, along with authentication, namely verifying a claimed identity. The security perspective comes last, yet later in this chapter we shall discuss a few basic instruments that are needed to understand the role of security in the previous perspectives.

1.2   Design goals

Just because it is possible to build distributed systems does not necessarily mean that it is a good idea. In this section, we discuss four important goals that should be met to make building a distributed system worth the effort. A distributed system should make resources easily accessible; it should hide the fact that resources are distributed across a network; it should be open; and it should be scalable.

1.2.1   Resource sharing

An important goal of a distributed system is to make it easy for users (and applications) to access and share remote resources. Resources can be virtually anything, but typical examples include peripherals, storage facilities, data, files, services, and networks, to name just a few. There are many reasons for wanting to share resources. One obvious reason is that of economics. For example, it is cheaper to have a single high-end reliable storage facility be shared than having to buy and maintain storage for each user separately.

Connecting users and resources also makes it easier to collaborate and exchange information, as is illustrated by the success of the Internet with its simple protocols for exchanging files, mail, documents, audio, and video. The connectivity of the Internet has allowed geographically widely dispersed groups of people to work together by all kinds of **groupware**, that is, software for collaborative editing, teleconferencing, and so on, as is illustrated by multinational software-development companies that have outsourced much of their code production to Asia, but also the myriad of collaboration tools that became (more easily) available due to the COVID-19 pandemic.

Resource sharing in distributed systems is also illustrated by the success of file-sharing peer-to-peer networks like **BitTorrent**. These distributed systems make it simple for users to share files across the Internet. Peer-to-peer networks are often associated with distribution of media files such as audio and video. In other cases, the technology is used for distributing large amounts of data, as in the case of software updates, backup services, and data synchronization across multiple servers.

Seamless integration of resource-sharing facilities in a networked environment is also now commonplace. A group of users can simply place files into a special shared folder that is maintained by a third party somewhere on the Internet. Using special software, the shared folder is barely distinguishable from other folders on a user's computer. In effect, these services replace the use of a shared directory on a local distributed file system, making data available to users independent of the organization they belong to, and independent of where they are. The service is offered for different operating systems. Where exactly data are stored is completely hidden from the end user.

1.2.2 Distribution transparency

An important goal of a distributed system is to hide the fact that its processes and resources are physically distributed across multiple computers, possibly separated by large distances. In other words, it tries to make the distribution of processes and resources **transparent**, that is, invisible, to end users and applications. As we shall discuss more extensively in Chapter 2, achieving distribution transparency is realized through what is known as **middleware**, sketched in Figure 1.2 (see Gazis and Katsiri [2022] for a first introduction).

In essence, what applications get to see is the same interface everywhere, whereas behind that interface, where and how processes and resources are and how they are accessed is kept transparent. There are different types of transparency, which we discuss next.

Types of distribution transparency

The concept of transparency can be applied to several aspects of a distributed system, of which the most important ones are listed in Figure 1.3. We use the term *object* to mean either a process or a resource.

Access transparency deals with hiding differences in data representation and the way that objects can be accessed. At a basic level, we want to hide differences in machine architectures, but more important is that we reach

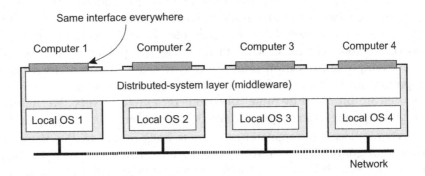

Figure 1.2: Realizing distribution transparency through a middleware layer.

Transparency	Description
Access	Hide differences in data representation and how an object is accessed
Location	Hide where an object is located
Relocation	Hide that an object may be moved to another location while in use
Migration	Hide that an object may move to another location
Replication	Hide that an object is replicated
Concurrency	Hide that an object may be shared by several independent users
Failure	Hide the failure and recovery of an object

Figure 1.3: Different forms of transparency in a distributed system (see ISO [1995]). An object can be a resource or a process.

agreement on how data is to be represented by different machines and operating systems. For example, a distributed system may have computer systems that run different operating systems, each having their own file-naming conventions. Differences in naming conventions, differences in file operations, or differences in how low-level communication with other processes is to take place, are examples of access issues that should preferably be hidden from users and applications.

An important group of transparency types concerns the location of a process or resource. **Location transparency** refers to the fact that users cannot tell where an object is physically located in the system. Naming plays an important role in achieving location transparency. In particular, location transparency can often be achieved by assigning only logical names to resources, that is, names in which the location of a resource is not secretly encoded. An example of a such a name is the **uniform resource locator (URL)** https://www.distributed-systems.net/, which gives no clue about the actual location of the Web server where this book is offered. The URL also gives no clue whether files at that site have always been at their current location or were recently moved there. For example, the entire site may have been moved from one data center to another, yet users should not notice. The latter is an example of **relocation transparency**, which is becoming increasingly important in the context of **cloud computing**: the phenomenon by which services are provided by huge collections of remote servers. We return to cloud computing in subsequent chapters, and, in particular, in Chapter 2.

Where relocation transparency refers to *being* moved by the distributed system, **migration transparency** is offered by a distributed system when it supports the mobility of processes and resources initiated by users, without affecting ongoing communication and operations. A typical example is communication between mobile phones: regardless whether two people are actually moving, mobile phones will allow them to continue their conversation. Other examples that come to mind include online tracking and tracing of goods as they are being transported from one place to another, and teleconferencing (partly) using devices that are equipped with mobile Internet.

As we shall see, replication plays an important role in distributed systems. For example, resources may be replicated to increase availability or to improve performance by placing a copy close to the place where it is accessed. **Replication transparency** deals with hiding the fact that several copies of a resource exist, or that several processes are operating in some form of lockstep mode so that one can take over when another fails. To hide replication from users, it is necessary that all replicas have the same name. Consequently, a system that supports replication transparency should generally support location transparency as well, because it would otherwise be impossible to refer to replicas at different locations.

We already mentioned that an important goal of distributed systems is to allow sharing of resources. In many cases, sharing resources is done cooperatively, as in the case of communication channels. However, there are also many examples of competitive sharing of resources. For example, two independent users may each have stored their files on the same file server or may be accessing the same tables in a shared database. In such cases, it is important that each user does not notice that the other is making use of the same resource. This phenomenon is called **concurrency transparency**. An important issue is that concurrent access to a shared resource leaves that resource in a consistent state. Consistency can be achieved through locking mechanisms, by which users are, in turn, given exclusive access to the desired resource. A more refined mechanism is to make use of transactions, but these may be difficult to implement in a distributed system, notably when scalability is an issue.

Last, but certainly not least, it is important that a distributed system provides **failure transparency**. This means that a user or application does not notice that some piece of the system fails to work properly, and that the system subsequently (and automatically) recovers from that failure. Masking failures is one of the hardest issues in distributed systems and is even impossible when certain apparently realistic assumptions are made, as we will discuss in Chapter 8. The main difficulty in masking and transparently recovering from failures lies in the inability to distinguish between a dead process and a painfully slowly responding one. For example, when contacting a busy Web server, a browser will eventually time out and report that the Web page is unavailable. At that point, the user cannot tell whether the server is actually down or that the network is badly congested.

Degree of distribution transparency

Although distribution transparency is generally considered preferable for any distributed system, there are situations in which blindly attempting to hide all distribution aspects from users is not a good idea. A simple example is requesting your electronic newspaper to appear in your mailbox before 7 AM local time, as usual, while you are currently at the other end of the world living in a different time zone. Your morning paper will not be the morning paper you are used to.

Likewise, a wide-area distributed system that connects a process in San Francisco to a process in Amsterdam cannot be expected to hide the fact that Mother Nature will not allow it to send a message from one process to the other in less than approximately 35 milliseconds. Practice shows that it actually takes several hundred milliseconds using a computer network. Signal transmission is not only limited by the speed of light, but also by limited processing capacities and delays in the intermediate switches.

There is also a trade-off between a high degree of transparency and the performance of a system. For example, many Internet applications repeatedly try to contact a server before finally giving up. Consequently, attempting to mask a transient server failure before trying another one may slow down the system as a whole. In such a case, it may have been better to give up earlier, or at least let the user cancel the attempts to make contact.

Another example is where we need to guarantee that several replicas, located on different continents, must be consistent all the time. In other words, if one copy is changed, that change should be propagated to all copies before allowing any other operation. A single update operation may now even take seconds to complete, something that cannot be hidden from users.

Finally, there are situations in which it is not at all obvious that hiding distribution is a good idea. As distributed systems are expanding to devices that people carry around and where the very notion of location and context awareness is becoming increasingly important, it may be best to actually *expose* distribution rather than trying to hide it. An obvious example is making use of location-based services, which can often be found on mobile phones, such as finding a nearest shop or any nearby friends.

There are other arguments against distribution transparency. Recognizing that full distribution transparency is simply impossible, we should ask ourselves whether it is even wise to *pretend* that we can achieve it. It may be much better to make distribution explicit so that the user and application developer are never tricked into believing that there is such a thing as transparency. The result will be that users will much better understand the (sometimes unexpected) behavior of a distributed system, and are thus much better prepared to deal with this behavior.

The conclusion is that aiming for distribution transparency may be a nice goal when designing and implementing distributed systems, but that it should be considered together with other issues such as performance and comprehensibility. The price for achieving full transparency may be surprisingly high.

Note 1.2 (Discussion: Against distribution transparency)

Several researchers have argued that hiding distribution will lead to only further complicating the development of distributed systems, exactly for the reason that full distribution transparency can never be achieved. A popular technique for achieving access transparency is to extend procedure calls to remote servers. However, Waldo et al. [1997] already pointed out that attempting to hide distribution by such remote procedure calls can lead to poorly understood semantics, for the simple reason that a procedure call *does* change when executed over a faulty communication link.

As an alternative, various researchers and practitioners are now arguing for less transparency, for example, by more explicitly using message-style communication, or more explicitly posting requests to, and getting results from remote machines, as is done on the Web when fetching pages. Such solutions will be discussed in detail in the next chapter.

A somewhat radical standpoint was taken by Wams [2012] by stating that partial failures preclude relying on the successful execution of a remote service. If such reliability cannot be guaranteed, it is then best to always perform only local executions, leading to the **copy-before-use** principle. According to this principle, data can be accessed only after they have been transferred to the machine of the process wanting that data. Moreover, modifying a data item should not be done. Instead, it can only be updated to a new version. It is not difficult to imagine that many other problems will surface. However, Wams shows that many existing applications can be retrofitted to this alternative approach without sacrificing functionality.

1.2.3 Openness

Another important goal of distributed systems is openness. An **open distributed system** is essentially a system that offers components that can easily be used by, or integrated into other systems. At the same time, an open distributed system itself will often consist of components that originate from elsewhere.

Interoperability, composability, and extensibility

To be open means that components should adhere to standard rules that describe the syntax and semantics of what those components have to offer (i.e., which service they provide). A general approach is to define services through **interfaces** using an **Interface Definition Language** (**IDL**). Interface definitions written in an IDL nearly always capture only the syntax of services. In other words, they specify precisely the names of the functions that are available together with types of the parameters, return values, possible exceptions that can be raised, and so on. The hard part is specifying precisely what those services do, that is, the semantics of interfaces. In practice, such specifications are given in an informal way by natural language.

If properly specified, an interface definition allows an arbitrary process that needs a certain interface, to talk to another process that provides that interface. It also allows two independent parties to build entirely different implementations of those interfaces, leading to two separate components that operate in exactly the same way.

Proper specifications are complete and neutral. Complete means that everything that is necessary to make an implementation has indeed been specified. However, many interface definitions are not at all complete, so that it is necessary for a developer to add implementation-specific details. Just as important is the fact that specifications do not prescribe what an implementation should look like; they should be neutral.

As pointed out in Blair and Stefani [1998], completeness and neutrality are important for interoperability and portability. **Interoperability** characterizes the extent by which two implementations of systems or components from different manufacturers can co-exist and work together by merely relying on each other's services as specified by a common standard. **Portability** characterizes to what extent an application developed for a distributed system A can be executed, without modification, on a different distributed system B that implements the same interfaces as A.

Another important goal for an open distributed system is that it should be easy to configure the system out of different components (possibly from different developers). Moreover, it should be easy to add new components or replace existing ones without affecting those components that stay in place. In other words, an open distributed system should also be **extensible**. For example, in an extensible system, it should be relatively easy to add parts that run on a different operating system, or even to replace an entire file system. Relatively simple examples of extensibility are plug-ins for Web browsers, but also those for Websites, such as the ones used for WordPress.

Note 1.3 (Discussion: Open systems in practice)
Of course, what we have just described is an ideal situation. Practice shows that many distributed systems are not as open as we would like, and that still a lot of effort is needed to put various bits and pieces together to make a distributed system. One way out of the lack of openness is to simply reveal all the gory details of a component and to provide developers with the actual source code. This approach is becoming increasingly popular, leading to so-called open-source projects, where large groups of people contribute to improving and debugging systems. Admittedly, this is as open as a system can get, but whether it is the best way is questionable.

Separating policy from mechanism

To achieve flexibility in open distributed systems, it is crucial that the system be organized as a collection of relatively small and easily replaceable or adaptable components. This implies that we should provide definitions of not only the highest-level interfaces, that is, those seen by users and applications, but also definitions for interfaces to internal parts of the system and describe how those parts interact. This approach is relatively new. Many older and even contemporary systems are constructed using a monolithic approach in which components are only logically separated but implemented as one, huge program. This approach makes it hard to replace or adapt a component without affecting the entire system. Monolithic systems thus tend to be closed instead of open.

The need for changing a distributed system is often caused by a component that does not provide the optimal policy for a specific user or application. As an example, consider caching in Web browsers. There are many different parameters that need to be considered:

Storage: Where is data to be cached? Typically, there will be an in-memory cache next to storage on disk. In the latter case, the exact position in the local file system needs to be considered.

Exemption: When the cache fills up, which data is to be removed so that newly fetched pages can be stored?

Sharing: Does each browser make use of a private cache, or is a cache to be shared among browsers of different users?

Refreshing: When does a browser check if cached data is still up-to-date? Caches are most effective when a browser can return pages without having to contact the original Website. However, this bears the risk of returning stale data. Note also that refresh rates are highly dependent on which data is actually cached: whereas timetables for trains hardly change, this is not the case for Web pages showing current highway-traffic conditions, or worse yet, stock prices.

What we need is a separation between **policy** and **mechanism**. In the case of Web caching, for example, a browser should ideally provide facilities for only storing documents (i.e., a mechanism) and at the same time allow users to decide which documents are stored and for how long (i.e., a policy). In practice, this can be implemented by offering a rich set of parameters that the user can set (dynamically). When taking this a step further, a browser may even offer facilities for plugging in policies that a user has implemented as a separate component.

Note 1.4 (Discussion: Is a strict separation really what we need?)
In theory, strictly separating policies from mechanisms seems to be the way to go. However, there is an important trade-off to consider: the stricter the separation, the more we need to make sure that we offer the appropriate collection of mechanisms. In practice, this means that a rich set of features is offered, in turn leading to many configuration parameters. As an example, the popular Firefox browser comes with a few hundred configuration parameters. Just imagine how the configuration space explodes when considering large distributed systems consisting of many components. In other words, strict separation of policies and mechanisms may lead to highly complex configuration problems.

One option to alleviate these problems is to provide reasonable defaults, and this is what often happens in practice. An alternative approach is one in which the system observes its own usage and dynamically changes parameter settings. This leads to what are known as **self-configurable systems**. Nevertheless, the fact alone that many mechanisms need to be offered to support a wide range of policies often makes coding distributed systems very complicated. Hard-coding policies into a distributed system may reduce complexity considerably, but at the price of less flexibility.

1.2.4 Dependability

As its name suggests, **dependability** refers to the degree that a computer system can be relied upon to operate as expected. In contrast to single-computer systems, dependability in distributed systems can be rather intricate due to **partial failures**: somewhere there is a component failing while the system as a whole still seems to be living up to expectations (up to a certain point or moment). Although single-computer systems can also suffer from failures that do not appear immediately, having a potentially large collection of networked computer systems complicates matters considerably. In fact, one should assume that at any time, there are always partial failures occurring. An important goal of distributed systems is to mask those failures, as well as mask the recovery from those failures. This masking is the essence of being able to tolerate faults, accordingly referred to as **fault tolerance**.

Basic concepts

Dependability is a term that covers several useful requirements for distributed systems, including the following [Kopetz and Verissimo, 1993]:

- Availability
- Reliability
- Safety
- Maintainability

Availability is defined as the property that a system is ready to be used immediately. In general, it refers to the probability that the system is operating correctly at any given moment and is available to perform its functions on behalf of its users. In other words, a highly available system is one that will most likely be working at a given instant in time.

Reliability refers to the property that a system can run continuously without failure. In contrast to availability, reliability is defined in terms of a time interval instead of an instant in time. A highly reliable system is one that will most likely continue to work without interruption during a relatively long period of time. This is a subtle but important difference when compared to availability. If a system goes down on average for one, seemingly random millisecond every hour, it has an availability of more than 99.9999 percent, but is still unreliable. Similarly, a system that never crashes but is shut down for two specific weeks every August has high reliability but only 96 percent availability. The two are not the same.

Safety refers to the situation that when a system temporarily fails to operate correctly, no catastrophic event happens. For example, many process-control systems, such as those used for controlling nuclear power plants or sending people into space, are required to provide a high degree of safety. If such control systems temporarily fail for only a very brief moment, the effects could be disastrous. Many examples from the past (and probably many more yet to come) show how hard it is to build safe systems.

Finally, **maintainability** refers to how easily a failed system can be repaired. A highly maintainable system may also show a high degree of availability, especially if failures can be detected and repaired automatically. However, as we shall see, automatically recovering from failures is easier said than done.

Traditionally, fault-tolerance has been related to the following three metrics:

- **Mean Time To Failure** (*MTTF*): The average time until a component fails.

- **Mean Time To Repair** (*MTTR*): The average time needed to repair a component.

- **Mean Time Between Failures** (*MTBF*): Simply *MTTF* + *MTTR*.

Note that these metrics make sense only if we have an accurate notion of what a failure actually is. As we will encounter in Chapter 8, identifying the occurrence of a failure may actually not be so obvious.

Faults, errors, failures

A system is said to **fail** when it cannot meet its promises. In particular, if a distributed system is designed to provide its users with several services, the system has failed when one or more of those services cannot be (completely) provided. An **error** is a part of a system's state that may lead to a failure. For example, when transmitting packets across a network, it is to be expected that some packets have been damaged when they arrive at the receiver. Damaged in this context means that the receiver may incorrectly sense a bit value (e.g., reading a 1 instead of a 0), or may even be unable to detect that something has arrived.

The cause of an error is called a **fault**. Clearly, finding out what caused an error is important. For example, a wrong or bad transmission medium may easily cause packets to be damaged. In this case, it is relatively easy to remove the fault. However, transmission errors may also be caused by bad weather conditions, such as in wireless networks. Changing the weather to reduce or prevent errors is a bit trickier.

As another example, a crashed program is clearly a failure, which may have happened because the program entered a branch of code containing a programming bug (i.e., a programming error). The cause of that bug is typically a programmer. In other words, the programmer is the cause of the error (programming bug), in turn leading to a failure (a crashed program).

Building dependable systems closely relates to controlling faults. As explained by Avizienis et al. [2004], a distinction can be made between preventing, tolerating, removing, and forecasting faults. For our purposes, the most important issue is **fault tolerance**, meaning that a system can provide its services even in the presence of faults. For example, by applying error-correcting codes for transmitting packets, it is possible to tolerate, to a certain extent, relatively poor transmission lines and reducing the probability that an error (a damaged packet) may lead to a failure.

Faults are generally classified as transient, intermittent, or permanent. **Transient faults** occur once and then disappear. If the operation is repeated, the fault goes away. A bird flying through the beam of a microwave transmitter may cause lost bits on some network (not to mention a roasted bird). If the transmission times out and is retried, it will probably work the second time.

An **intermittent fault** occurs, then vanishes on its own accord, then reappears, and so on. A loose contact on a connector will often cause an intermittent fault. Intermittent faults cause a great deal of aggravation because they are difficult to diagnose. Typically, when the fault doctor shows up, the system works fine.

A **permanent fault** is one that continues to exist until the faulty component is replaced. Burnt-out chips, software bugs, and disk-head crashes are examples of permanent faults.

Dependable systems are also required to provide security, especially in terms of confidentiality and integrity. **Confidentiality** is the property that information is disclosed only to authorized parties, while **integrity** relates to ensuring that alterations to various assets can be made only in an authorized way. Indeed, can we speak of a dependable system when confidentiality and integrity are not in place? We return to security next.

1.2.5 Security

A distributed system that is not secure, is not dependable. As mentioned, special attention is needed to ensure confidentiality and integrity, both of which are directly coupled to authorized disclosure and access of information and resources. In any computer system, **authorization** is done by checking whether an identified entity has proper access rights. In turn, this means that the system should know it is indeed dealing with the proper entity. For this reason, **authentication** is essential: verifying the correctness of a claimed identity. Equally important is the notion of **trust**. If a system can positively authenticate a person, what is that authentication worth if the person cannot be trusted? For this reason alone, proper authorization is important, as it may be used to limit any damage that a person, who could in hindsight not be trusted, can cause. For example, in financial systems, authorization may limit the amount of money a person is allowed to transfer between various accounts. We will discuss trust, authentication, and authorization at length in Chapter 9.

Key elements needed to understand security

An essential technique to making distributed systems secure is cryptography. This is not the place in this book to extensively discuss cryptography (which we also defer until Chapter 9), yet to understand how security fits into various perspectives in the following chapters, we informally introduce some of its basic elements.

Keeping matters simple, security in distributed systems is all about **encrypting** and **decrypting** data using **security keys**. The easiest way of considering a security key K is to see it as a function operating on some data data. We use the notation $K(\text{data})$ to express the fact that the key K operates on data.

There are two ways of encrypting and decrypting data. In a **symmetric cryptosystem**, encryption and decryption takes place with a single key. Denoting by $E_K(\text{data})$ the encryption of data using key E_K, and likewise $D_K(\text{data})$ for decryption with key D_K, then in a symmetric cryptosystem, the same key is used for encryption and decryption, i.e.,

$$\textit{if } \text{data} = D_K(E_K(\text{data})) \textit{ then } D_K = E_K.$$

Note that in a symmetric cryptosystem, the key will need to be kept secret by all parties that are authorized to encrypt or decrypt data. In an **asymmetric cryptosystem**, the keys used for encryption and decryption are different. In particular, there is a **public key** PK that can be used by anyone, and a **secret key** SK that is, as its name suggests, to be kept secret. Asymmetric cryptosystems are also called **public-key systems**.

Encryption and decryption in public-key systems can be used in two, fundamentally different ways. First, if Alice wants to encrypt data that can be decrypted only by Bob, she should use Bob's public key, PK_B, leading to the encrypted data $PK_B(\text{data})$. Only the holder of the associated secret key can decrypt this information, i.e., Bob, who will apply the operation $SK_B(PK_B(\text{data}))$, which returns data.

A second, and widely applied use case, is that of realizing **digital signatures**. Suppose Alice makes some data available for which it is important that any party, but let us assume it is Bob, needs to know for sure that it comes from Alice. In that case, Alice can encrypt the data with her secret key SK_A, leading to $SK_A(\text{data})$. If it can be assured that the associated public key PK_A indeed belongs to Alice, then successfully decrypting $SK_A(\text{data})$ to data, is proof that Alice knows about data: she is the only one holding the secret key SK_A. Of course, we need to make the assumption that Alice is indeed the only one who holds SK_A. We return to some of these assumptions in Chapter 9.

As it turns out, proving that an entity has seen, or knows about some data, returns frequently in secured distributed systems. Practical placement of digital signatures is generally more efficient by a **hash function**. A hash function H has the property that when operating on some data, i.e., $H(\text{data})$, it returns a fixed-length string, regardless of the length of data. Any change of data to data* will lead to a different hash value $H(\text{data}^*)$. Moreover, given a hash value h, it is computationally impossible in practice, to discover the original data. What this all means, is that for placing a digital signature, Alice computes sig $= SK_A(H(\text{data}))$ as her signature, and tells Bob about data, H and sig. Bob, in turn, can then verify that signature by computing $PK_A(\text{sig})$ and verifying that it matches the value $H(\text{data})$.

Using cryptography in distributed systems

The application of cryptography in distributed systems comes in many forms. Besides its general use for encryption and digital signatures, cryptography forms the basis for realizing a **secure channel** between two communicating parties. Such channels basically let two parties know for sure that they are indeed communicating to the entities that they expected to communicate with. In other words, a communication channel that supports mutual authentication. A practical example of a secure channel is using https when accessing Websites. Now, many browsers demand that Websites support this protocol, and at the very least will warn the user when this is not the case. In general, using cryptography is necessary to realize authentication (and authorization) in distributed systems.

Cryptography is also used to realize secure distributed data structures. A well-known example is that of a **blockchain**, which is, literally, a chain of blocks. The basic idea is simple: hash the data in a block B_i, and place that hash value as part of the data in its succeeding block B_{i+1}. Any change in

B_i (for example, as the result of an attack), will require that the attacker also changes the stored hash value in B_{i+1}. However, because the successor of B_{i+1} contains the hash computed over the data in B_{i+1}, and thus including the *original* hash value of B_i, the attacker will also have to change the new has value of B_i as stored in B_{i+1}. Yet changing that value, also means changing the hash value of B_{i+1}, and thus the value stored in B_{i+2}, in turn, requiring that a new hash value is to be computed for B_{i+2}, and so on. In other words, by securely linking blocks into a chain, any successful change to a block requires that *all* successive blocks be modified as well. These modifications should go unnoticed, which is virtually impossible.

Cryptography is also used for another important mechanism in distributed systems: delegating access rights. The basic idea is that Alice may want to delegate some rights to Bob, who, in turn, may want to pass some of those rights on to Chuck. Using appropriate means (which we discuss in Chapter 9, a service can securely check that Chuck has indeed been authorized to perform certain operations, without the need for that service to check with Alice whether the delegation is in place. Note that delegation is something we are now used to: many of us delegate access rights that we have as a user to specific applications, such as an e-mail client.

An upcoming distributed application of cryptography is so-called **multi-party computation**: the means for two or three parties to compute a value for which the data of those parties is needed, but without having to actually share that data. An often-used example is computing the number of votes without having to know who voted for whom.

We will see many more examples of security in distributed systems in the following chapters. With the brief explanations of the cryptographic basis, it should suffice to see how security is applied. We shall consistently use the notations as shown in Figure 1.4. Alternatively, security examples can be skipped until having studied Chapter 9.

Notation	Description
$K_{A,B}$	Secret key shared by A and B
PK_A	Public key of A
SK_A	Private (secret) key of A
$E_K(data)$	Encryption of data using key E_K (or key K)
$D_K(data)$	Decryption of (encrypted) data using key D_K (or key K)
$H(data)$	The hash of data computed using function H

Figure 1.4: Notations for cryptosystems used in this book.

1.2.6   Scalability

For many of us, worldwide connectivity through the Internet is as common as being able to send a package to anyone anywhere around the world. Moreover, where until recently, we were used to having relatively powerful desktop computers for office applications and storage, we are now witnessing that such applications and services are being placed in what has been coined "the cloud," in turn leading to an increase of much smaller networked devices such as tablet computers or even cloud-only laptops such as Google's Chromebook. With this in mind, scalability has become one of the most important design goals for developers of distributed systems.

Scalability dimensions

Scalability of a system can be measured along at least three different dimensions (see [Neuman, 1994]):

Size scalability: A system can be scalable regarding its size, meaning that we can easily add more users and resources to the system without any noticeable loss of performance.

Geographical scalability: A geographically scalable system is one in which the users and resources may lie far apart, but the fact that communication delays may be significant is hardly noticed.

Administrative scalability: An administratively scalable system is one that can still be easily managed even if it spans many independent administrative organizations.

Let us take a closer look at each of these three scalability dimensions.

Size scalability   When a system needs to scale, very different types of problems need to be solved. Let us first consider scaling regarding size. If more users or resources need to be supported, we are often confronted with the limitations of centralized services, although often for very different reasons. For example, many services are centralized in the sense that they are implemented by a single **server** running on a specific machine in the distributed system. In a more modern setting, we may have a group of collaborating servers co-located on a cluster of tightly coupled machines physically placed at the same location. The problem with this scheme is obvious: the server, or group of servers, can simply become a bottleneck when it needs to process an increasing number of requests. To illustrate how this can happen, let us assume that a service is implemented on a single machine. In that case, there are essentially three root causes for becoming a bottleneck:

- The computational capacity, limited by the CPUs

- The storage capacity, including the I/O transfer rate

- The network between the user and the centralized service

Let us first consider the computational capacity. Just imagine a service for computing optimal routes taking real-time traffic information into account. It is not difficult to imagine that this may be primarily a compute-bound service, requiring several (tens of) seconds to complete a request. If there is only a single machine available, then even a modern high-end system will eventually run into problems if the number of requests increases beyond a certain point.

Likewise, but for different reasons, we will run into problems when having a service that is mainly I/O bound. A typical example is a poorly designed centralized search engine. The problem with content-based search queries is that we essentially need to match a query against an entire data set. Even with advanced indexing techniques, we may still face the problem of having to process a huge amount of data exceeding the main-memory capacity of the machine running the service. As a consequence, much of the processing time will be determined by the relatively slow disk accesses and transfer of data between disk and main memory. Simply adding more or higher-speed disks will prove not to be a sustainable solution as the number of requests continues to increase.

Finally, the network between the user and the service may also be the cause of poor scalability. Just imagine a video-on-demand service that needs to stream high-quality video to multiple users. A video stream can easily require a bandwidth of 8 to 10 Mbps, meaning that if a service sets up point-to-point connections with its customers, it may soon hit the limits of the network capacity of its own outgoing transmission lines.

There are several solutions to attack size scalability, which we discuss below after having looked into geographical and administrative scalability.

Note 1.5 (Advanced: Analyzing size scalability)

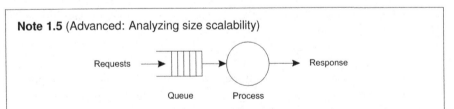

Figure 1.5: A simple model of a service as a queuing system.

Size scalability problems for centralized services can be formally analyzed using queuing theory and making a few simplifying assumptions. At a conceptual level, a centralized service can be modeled as the simple queuing system shown in Figure 1.5: requests are submitted to the service, where they are queued until further notice. As soon as the process can handle a next request, it fetches it from the queue, does its work, and produces a response. We largely follow Menasce and Almeida [2002] in explaining the performance of a centralized service.

Often, we may assume that the queue has an infinite capacity, meaning that there is no restriction on the number of requests that can be accepted for further processing. Strictly speaking, this means that the arrival rate of requests is not influenced by what is currently in the queue or being processed. Assuming that the arrival rate of requests is λ requests per second, and that the processing capacity of the service is μ requests per second, one can compute that the fraction of time p_k that there are k requests in the system is equal to:

$$p_k = \left(1 - \frac{\lambda}{\mu}\right)\left(\frac{\lambda}{\mu}\right)^k$$

If we define the **utilization** U of a service as the fraction of time that it is busy, then clearly,

$$U = \sum_{k>0} p_k = 1 - p_0 = \frac{\lambda}{\mu} \Rightarrow p_k = (1 - U)U^k$$

We can then compute the average number $\overline{N}$ of requests in the system as

$$\overline{N} = \sum_{k \geq 0} k \cdot p_k = \sum_{k \geq 0} k \cdot (1 - U)U^k = (1 - U) \sum_{k \geq 0} k \cdot U^k = \frac{(1 - U)U}{(1 - U)^2} = \frac{U}{1 - U}.$$

What we are truly interested in, is the response time R: how long does it take before the service to process a request, including the time spent in the queue. To that end, we need the average throughput X. Considering that the service is "busy" when at least one request is being processed, and that this then happens with a throughput of μ requests per second, and during a fraction U of the total time, we have:

$$X = \underbrace{U \cdot \mu}_{\text{server at work}} + \underbrace{(1 - U) \cdot 0}_{\text{server idle}} = \frac{\lambda}{\mu} \cdot \mu = \lambda$$

Using Little's formula [Trivedi, 2002], we can then derive the response time as

$$R = \frac{\overline{N}}{X} = \frac{S}{1 - U} \Rightarrow \frac{R}{S} = \frac{1}{1 - U}$$

where $S = \frac{1}{\mu}$, the actual service time. Note that if U is small, the response-to-service time ratio is close to 1, meaning that a request is virtually instantly processed, and at the maximum speed possible. However, as soon as the utilization comes closer to 1, we see that the response-to-server time ratio quickly increases to very high values, effectively meaning that the system is coming close to a grinding halt. This is where we see scalability problems emerge. From this simple model, we can see that the only solution is bringing down the service time S. We leave it as an exercise to the reader to explore how S may be decreased.

Geographical scalability   Geographical scalability has its own problems. One of the main reasons why it is still difficult to scale existing distributed systems that were designed for local-area networks is that many of them are based on **synchronous communication**. In this form of communication, a party requesting a service, generally referred to as a **client**, blocks until a reply is sent back from the **server** implementing the service. More specifically, we often see a communication pattern consisting of many client-server interactions, as may be the case with database transactions. This approach generally works fine in LANs, where communication between two machines is often at worst a few hundred microseconds. However, in a wide-area system, we need to consider that interprocess communication may be hundreds of milliseconds, three orders of magnitude slower. Building applications using synchronous communication in wide-area systems requires a great deal of care (and not just a little patience), notably with a rich interaction pattern between client and server.

Another problem that hinders geographical scalability is that communication in wide-area networks is inherently much less reliable than in local-area networks. In addition, we generally also need to deal with limited bandwidth. The effect is that solutions developed for local-area networks cannot always be easily ported to a wide-area system. A typical example is streaming video. In a home network, even when having only wireless links, ensuring a stable, fast stream of high-quality video frames from a media server to a display is quite simple. Simply placing that same server far away and using a standard TCP connection to the display will surely fail: bandwidth limitations will instantly surface, but also maintaining the same level of reliability can easily cause headaches.

Yet another issue that pops up when components lie far apart is the fact that wide-area systems generally have only very limited facilities for multipoint communication. In contrast, local-area networks often support efficient broadcasting mechanisms. Such mechanisms have proven to be extremely useful for discovering components and services, which is essential from a management perspective. In wide-area systems, we need to develop separate services, such as naming and directory services, to which queries can be sent. These support services, in turn, need to be scalable as well and often no obvious solutions exist as we will encounter in later chapters.

Administrative scalability Finally, a difficult, and often open, question is how to scale a distributed system across multiple, independent administrative domains. A major problem that needs to be solved is that of conflicting policies regarding resource usage (and payment), management, and security. To illustrate, for many years, scientists have been looking for solutions to share their (often expensive) equipment in what is known as a **computational grid**. In these grids, a global decentralized system is constructed as a federation of local distributed systems, allowing a program running on a computer at an organization A to directly access resources at the organization B.

Many components of a distributed system that reside within a single domain can often be trusted by users that operate within that same domain. In such cases, system administration may have tested and certified applications, and may have taken special measures to ensure that such components cannot be tampered with. In essence, the users trust their system administrators. However, this trust does not expand naturally across domain boundaries.

If a distributed system expands to another domain, two types of security measures need to be taken. First, the distributed system has to protect itself against malicious attacks from the new domain. For example, users from the new domain may have only read access to the file system in its original domain. Likewise, facilities such as expensive image setters or high-performance computers may not be made available to unauthorized users. Second, the new domain has to protect itself against malicious attacks from the distributed system. A typical example is that of downloading programs, such as in the case of federated learning. Basically, the new domain does not know what to expect from such foreign code. The problem, as we shall see in Chapter 9, is how to enforce those limitations.

As a counterexample of distributed systems spanning multiple administrative domains that apparently *do not* suffer from administrative scalability problems, consider modern file-sharing peer-to-peer networks. In these cases, end users simply install a program implementing distributed search and download functions and within minutes can start downloading files. Other examples include peer-to-peer applications for telephony over the Internet such as older Skype systems [Baset and Schulzrinne, 2006], and (again older) peer-assisted audio-streaming applications such as Spotify [Kreitz and Niemelä, 2010]. A more modern application (that has yet to prove itself in terms of scalability) are blockchains. What these decentralized systems have in common is that *end users*, and not administrative entities, collaborate to keep the system up and running. At best, underlying administrative organizations such as **Internet Service Providers (ISPs)** can police the network traffic that these peer-to-peer systems cause.

Scaling techniques

Having discussed some scalability problems brings us to the question of how those problems can generally be solved. In most cases, scalability problems in distributed systems appear as performance problems caused by limited capacity of servers and network. Simply improving their capacity (e.g., by increasing memory, upgrading CPUs, or replacing network modules) is often a solution, referred to as **scaling up**. When it comes to **scaling out**, that is, expanding the distributed system by essentially deploying more machines, there are basically only three techniques we can apply: hiding communication latencies, distribution of work, and replication (see also Neuman [1994]).

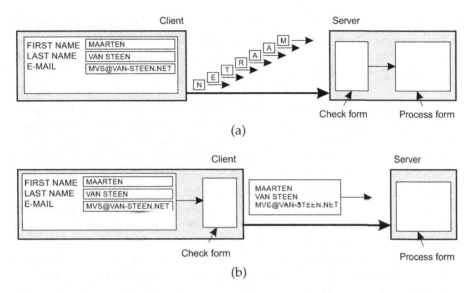

Figure 1.6: The difference between letting (a) a server or (b) a client check forms as they are being filled.

Hiding communication latencies Hiding communication latencies is applicable in the case of geographical scalability. The basic idea is simple: try to avoid waiting for responses to remote-service requests as much as possible. For example, when a service has been requested at a remote machine, an alternative to waiting for a reply from the server is to do other useful work at the requester's side. Essentially, this means constructing the requesting application in such a way that it uses only **asynchronous communication**. When a reply comes in, the application is interrupted and a special handler is called to complete the previously issued request. Asynchronous communication can often be used in batch-processing systems and parallel applications, in which independent tasks can be scheduled for execution while another task is waiting for communication to complete. Alternatively, a new thread of control can be started to perform the request. Although it blocks waiting for the reply, other threads in the process can continue.

However, there are many applications that cannot make effective use of asynchronous communication. For example, in interactive applications when a user sends a request, she will generally have nothing better to do than to wait for the answer. In such cases, a much better solution is to reduce the overall communication, for example, by moving part of the computation that is normally done at the server to the client process requesting the service. A typical case where this approach works is accessing databases using forms. Filling in forms can be done by sending a separate message for each field and waiting for an acknowledgment from the server, as shown in Figure 1.6(a). For example, the server may check for syntactic errors before accepting an entry.

A much better solution is to ship the code for filling in the form, and possibly checking the entries, to the client, and have the client return a completed form, as shown in Figure 1.6(b). This approach of shipping code is widely supported by the Web through JavaScript.

Partitioning and distribution   Another important scaling technique is partitioning and distribution, which involves taking a component or other resource, splitting it into smaller parts, and subsequently spreading those parts across the system. A good example of partitioning and distribution is the Internet Domain Name System (DNS). The DNS name space is hierarchically organized into a tree of **domains**, which are divided into nonoverlapping **zones**, as shown for the original DNS in Figure 1.7. The names in each zone are handled by a single name server. Without going into too many details now (we return to DNS extensively in Chapter 6), one can think of each path name being the name of a host on the Internet, and is thus associated with a network address of that host. Basically, resolving a name means returning the network address of the associated host. Consider, for example, the name flits.cs.vu.nl. To resolve this name, it is first passed to the server of zone Z1 (see Figure 1.7) which returns the address of the server for zone Z2, to which the rest of the name, flits.cs.vu, can be handed. The server for Z2 will return the address of the server for Z3, which is capable of handling the last part of the name, and will return the address of the associated host.

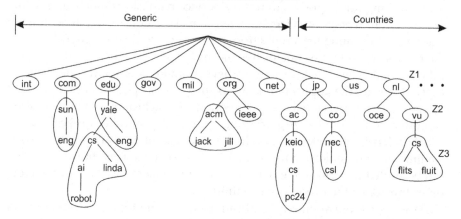

Figure 1.7: An example of dividing the (original) DNS name space into zones.

These examples illustrate how the **naming service** as provided by DNS, is distributed across several machines, thus avoiding that a single server has to deal with all requests for name resolution.

As another example, consider the World Wide Web. To most users, the Web appears to be an enormous document-based information system, in which each document has its own unique name in the form of a URL. Conceptually, it may even appear as if there is only a single server. However, the Web is physically partitioned and distributed across *a few hundreds of millions* of servers, each handling often a number of Websites, or parts of Websites. The name of the server handling a document is encoded into that document's URL. It is only because of this distribution of documents that the Web has been capable of scaling to its current size. Yet, note that finding out how many servers provide Web-based services is virtually impossible: A Website today is so much more than a few static Web documents.

Replication   Considering that scalability problems often appear in the form of performance degradation, it is generally a good idea to actually replicate components or resources, etc., across a distributed system. Replication not only increases availability, but also helps to balance the load between components, leading to better performance. Moreover, in geographically widely dispersed systems, having a copy nearby can hide much of the communication latency problems mentioned before.

Caching is a special form of replication, although the distinction between the two is often hard to make or even artificial. As in the case of replication, caching results in making a copy of a resource, generally in the proximity of the client accessing that resource. However, in contrast to replication, caching is a decision made by the client of a resource and not by the owner of a resource.

There is one serious drawback to caching and replication that may adversely affect scalability. Because we now have multiple copies of a resource, modifying one copy makes that copy different from the others. Consequently, caching and replication leads to **consistency** problems.

To what extent inconsistencies can be tolerated depends on the usage of a resource. For example, many Web users find it acceptable that their browser returns a cached document of which the validity has not been checked for the last few minutes. However, there are also many cases in which strong consistency guarantees need to be met, such as in the case of electronic stock exchanges and auctions. The problem with strong consistency is that an update must be immediately propagated to all other copies. Moreover, if two updates happen concurrently, it is often also required that updates are processed in the same order everywhere, introducing a global ordering problem. To make things worse, combining consistency with desirable properties such as availability may simply be impossible, as we discuss in Chapter 8.

Replication therefore often requires some global synchronization mechanism. Unfortunately, such mechanisms are extremely hard or even impossible to implement in a scalable way, if alone because network latencies have a natural lower bound. Consequently, scaling by replication may introduce other, inherently nonscalable solutions. We return to replication and consistency extensively in Chapter 7.

Discussion   When considering these scaling techniques, one could argue that size scalability is the least problematic from a technical perspective. Often, increasing the capacity of a machine will save the day, although perhaps there is a high monetary cost to pay. Geographical scalability is a much tougher problem, as network latencies are naturally bound from below. As a consequence, we may be forced to copy data to locations close to where clients are, leading to problems of maintaining copies consistent. Practice shows that combining distribution, replication, and caching techniques with different forms of consistency generally leads to acceptable solutions. Finally, administrative scalability seems to be the most difficult problem to solve, partly because we need to deal with nontechnical issues, such as politics of organizations and human collaboration. The introduction and now widespread use of peer-to-peer technology has successfully demonstrated what can be achieved if end users are put in control [Lua et al., 2005; Oram, 2001]. However, peer-to-peer networks are obviously not the universal solution to all administrative scalability problems.

1.3   A simple classification of distributed systems

We have discussed distributed versus decentralized systems, yet it is also useful to classify distributed systems according to what they are being developed and used for. We make a distinction between systems that are developed for (high performance) computing, for general information processing, and those that are developed for pervasive computing, i.e., for the "Internet of Things." As with many classifications, the boundaries between these three types are not strict and combinations can easily be thought of.

1.3.1   High-performance distributed computing

An important class of distributed systems is the one used for high-performance computing tasks. Roughly speaking, one can make a distinction between two subgroups. In **cluster computing** the underlying hardware consists of a collection of similar compute nodes, interconnected by a high-speed network, often alongside a more common local-area network for controlling the nodes. In addition, each node generally runs the same operating system.

The situation becomes very different in the case of **grid computing**. This subgroup consists as decentralized systems that are often constructed as a federation of computer systems, where each system may fall under a different administrative domain, and may be very different when it comes to hardware, software, and deployed network technology.

Note 1.6 (More information: Parallel processing)

High-performance computing more or less started with the introduction of **multi-processor machines**. In this case, multiple CPUs are organized in such a way that they all have access to the same physical memory, as shown in Figure 1.8(a). In contrast, in a **multicomputer system** several computers are connected through a network and there is no sharing of main memory, as shown in Figure 1.8(b). The shared-memory model turned out to be highly convenient for improving the performance of programs, and it was relatively easy to program.

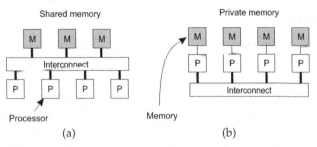

Figure 1.8: A comparison between (a) multiprocessor and (b) multicomputer architectures.

Its essence is that multiple threads of control are executing at the same time, while all threads have access to shared data. Access to that data is controlled through well-understood synchronization mechanisms like semaphores (see Ben-Ari [2006] or Herlihy et al. [2021] for more information on developing parallel programs). Unfortunately, the model does not easily scale: so far, machines have been developed in which only a few tens (and sometimes hundreds) of CPUs have efficient access to shared memory. To a certain extent, we are seeing the same limitations for multicore processors.

To overcome the limitations of shared-memory systems, high-performance computing moved to distributed-memory systems. This shift also meant that many programs had to make use of message passing instead of modifying shared data as a means of communication and synchronization between threads. Unfortunately, message-passing models have proven to be much more difficult and error-prone compared to the shared-memory programming models. For this reason, there has been significant research in attempting to build so-called **distributed shared-memory multicomputers**, or simply **DSM systems** [Amza et al., 1996].

In essence, a DSM system allows a processor to address a memory location at another computer as if it were local memory. This can be achieved using existing techniques available to the operating system, for example, by mapping all main-memory pages of the various processors into a single virtual address space. Whenever a processor A addresses a page located at another processor B, a page fault occurs at A allowing the operating system at A to fetch the content of the referenced page at B in the same way that it would normally fetch it locally from disk. At the same time, the processor B would be informed that the page is currently not accessible.

Mimicking shared-memory systems using multicomputers eventually had to be abandoned because performance could never meet the expectations of programmers, who would rather resort to far more intricate, yet better (predictably) performing message-passing models. An important side effect of exploring the hardware-software boundaries of parallel processing is a thorough understanding of consistency models, to which we return extensively in Chapter 7.

Cluster computing

Cluster computing systems became popular when the price/performance ratio of personal computers and workstations improved. At a certain point, it became financially and technically attractive to build a supercomputer using off-the-shelf technology by simply hooking up a collection of relatively simple computers in a high-speed network. In virtually all cases, cluster computing is used for parallel programming, in which a single (compute intensive) program is run in parallel on multiple machines. The principle of this organization is shown in Figure 1.9.

This type of high-performance computing has evolved considerably. As discussed extensively by Gerofi et al. [2019], the developments of supercomputers organized as clusters have reached a point where we see clusters with more than 100,000 CPUs, with each CPU having 8 or 16 cores. There are multiple networks. Most important is a network formed by dedicated high-speed interconnects between the various nodes (in other words, there is often no such thing as a shared high-speed network for computations). A separate management network, as well as nodes, are used to monitor and control

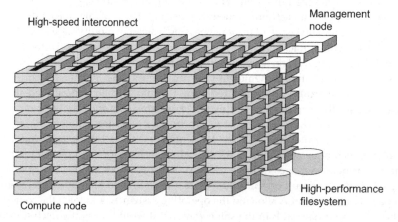

Figure 1.9: An example of a cluster computing system (adapted from [Gerofi et al., 2019].)

the organization and performance of the system as a whole. In addition, a special high-performance file system or database is used, again with its own local, dedicated network. Figure 1.9 does not show additional equipment, notably high-speed I/O as well as networking facilities for remote access and communication.

A management node is generally responsible for collecting jobs from users, to subsequently distribute the associated tasks among the various compute nodes. In practice, several management nodes are used when dealing with very large clusters. As such, a management node actually runs the software needed for the execution of programs and management of the cluster, while the compute nodes are equipped with a standard operating system extended with typical functions for communication, storage, fault tolerance, and so on.

An interesting development, as explained in Gerofi et al. [2019], is the role of the operating system. There has been a clear trend to minimize the operating system to lightweight kernels, essentially ensuring the least possible overhead. A drawback is that such operating systems become highly specialized and fine-tuned toward the underlying hardware. This specialization affects compatibility, or openness. To compensate, we are now gradually seeing so-called multikernel approaches, in which a full-fledged operating system operates next to a lightweight kernel, thus achieving the best of two worlds. This combination is also necessary given increasingly more often, a high-performance compute node is required to run multiple, independent jobs simultaneously. At present, 95% of all high-performance computers run Linux-based systems; multikernel approaches are developed for multicore CPUs, with most cores running a lightweight kernel and the other running a regular Linux system. In this way, new developments such as containers (which we discuss in Chapter 3) can also be supported. The effects for computing performance still needs to be seen.

Grid computing

A characteristic feature of traditional cluster computing is its homogeneity. In most cases, the computers in a cluster are largely the same, have the same operating system, and are all connected through the same network. However, as we just discussed, there is a continuous trend toward more hybrid architectures in which nodes are specifically configured for certain tasks. This diversity is even more prevalent in **grid-computing systems**: no assumptions are made concerning similarity of hardware, operating systems, networks, administrative domains, security policies, etc. [Rajaraman, 2016].

A key issue in a grid-computing system is that resources from different organizations are brought together to allow the collaboration of a group of people from different institutions, indeed forming a federation of systems. Such a collaboration is realized in the form of a **virtual organization**. The processes belonging to the same virtual organization have access rights to the

resources that are provided to that organization. Typically, resources consist of
compute servers (including supercomputers, possibly implemented as cluster
computers), storage facilities, and databases. In addition, special networked
devices such as telescopes, sensors, etc., can be provided as well.

Given its nature, much of the software for realizing grid computing evolves
around providing access to resources from different administrative domains,
and to only those users and applications that belong to a specific virtual
organization. For this reason, focus is often on architectural issues. An
architecture initially proposed by Foster et al. [2001] is shown in Figure 1.10,
which still forms the basis for many grid computing systems.

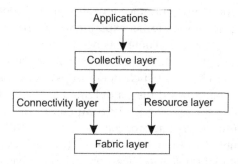

Figure 1.10: A layered architecture for grid computing systems.

The architecture consists of four layers. The lowest **fabric layer** provides
interfaces to local resources at a specific site. Note that these interfaces are
tailored to allow sharing of resources within a virtual organization. Typically,
they will provide functions for querying the state and capabilities of a resource,
along with functions for actual resource management (e.g., locking resources).

The **connectivity layer** consists of communication protocols for supporting
grid transactions that span the usage of multiple resources. For example,
protocols are needed to transfer data between resources, or to simply access
a resource from a remote location. In addition, the connectivity layer will
contain security protocols to authenticate users and resources. Note that in
many cases, human users are not authenticated; instead, programs acting on
behalf of the users are authenticated. In this sense, delegating rights from
a user to programs is an important function that needs to be supported in
the connectivity layer. We return to delegation when discussing security in
distributed systems in Chapter 9.

The **resource layer** is responsible for managing a single resource. It uses the
functions provided by the connectivity layer and calls directly the interfaces
made available by the fabric layer. For example, this layer will offer functions
for obtaining configuration information on a specific resource, or, in general,
to perform specific operations such as creating a process or reading data. The

resource layer is thus seen to be responsible for access control, and hence will rely on the authentication performed as part of the connectivity layer.

The next layer in the hierarchy is the **collective layer**. It deals with handling access to multiple resources and typically consists of services for resource discovery, allocation and scheduling of tasks onto multiple resources, data replication, and so on. Unlike the connectivity and resource layer, each consisting of a relatively small, standard collection of protocols, the collective layer may consist of many protocols reflecting the broad spectrum of services it may offer to a virtual organization.

Finally, the **application layer** consists of the applications that operate within a virtual organization and which make use of the grid computing environment.

Typically, the collective, connectivity, and resource layer form the heart of what could be called a grid middleware layer. These layers jointly provide access to and management of resources that are potentially dispersed across multiple sites.

An important observation from a middleware perspective is that in grid computing, the notion of a site (or administrative unit) is common. This prevalence is emphasized by the gradual shift toward a **service-oriented architecture** in which sites offer access to the various layers through a collection of Web services [Joseph et al., 2004]. This, by now, has led to the definition of an alternative architecture known as the **Open Grid Services Architecture (OGSA)** [Foster et al., 2006]. OGSA is based upon the original ideas as formulated by Foster et al. [2001], yet having gone through a standardization process makes it complex, to say the least. OGSA implementations generally follow Web service standards.

1.3.2 Distributed information systems

Another important class of distributed systems is found in organizations that were confronted with a wealth of networked applications, but for which interoperability turned out to be a painful experience. Many of the existing middleware solutions are the result of working with an infrastructure in which it was easier to integrate applications into an enterprise-wide information system [Alonso et al., 2004; Bernstein, 1996; Hohpe and Woolf, 2004].

We can distinguish several levels at which integration can take place. Often, a networked application simply consists of a server running that application (often including a database) and making it available to remote programs, called **clients**. Such clients send a request to the server for executing a specific operation, after which a response is sent back. Integration at the lowest level allows clients to wrap several requests, possibly for different servers, into a single larger request and have it executed as a **distributed transaction**. The key idea is that all, or none of the requests are executed.

As applications became more sophisticated and were gradually separated into independent components (notably distinguishing database components from processing components), it became clear that integration should also take place by letting applications communicate directly with each other. This has now led to an industry on **enterprise application integration** (**EAI**).

Distributed transaction processing

To clarify our discussion, we concentrate on database applications. In practice, operations on a database are carried out in the form of **transactions**. Programming using transactions requires special primitives that must either be supplied by the underlying distributed system or by the language runtime system. Typical examples of transaction primitives are shown in Figure 1.11. The exact list of primitives depends on what kinds of objects are being used in the transaction [Gray and Reuter, 1993; Bernstein and Newcomer, 2009]. In a mail system, there might be primitives to send, receive, and forward mail. In an accounting system, they might be quite different. READ and WRITE are typical examples, however. Ordinary statements, procedure calls, and so on, are also allowed inside a transaction. In particular, **remote procedure calls** (**RPC**), that is, procedure calls to remote servers, are often also encapsulated in a transaction, leading to what is known as a **transactional RPC**. We discuss RPCs extensively in Section 4.2.

Primitive	Description
BEGIN_TRANSACTION	Mark the start of a transaction
END_TRANSACTION	Terminate the transaction and try to commit
ABORT_TRANSACTION	Kill the transaction and restore the old values
READ	Read data from a file, a table, or otherwise
WRITE	Write data to a file, a table, or otherwise

Figure 1.11: Example primitives for transactions.

BEGIN_TRANSACTION and END_TRANSACTION are used to delimit the scope of a transaction. The operations between them form the body of the transaction. The characteristic feature of a transaction is either all of these operations are executed or none are executed. These may be system calls, library procedures, or bracketing statements in a language, depending on the implementation.

This all-or-nothing property of transactions is one of the four characteristic properties that transactions have. More specifically, transactions adhere to the so-called **ACID** properties:

- **Atomic**: To the outside world, the transaction happens indivisibly

- **Consistent**: The transaction does not violate system invariants

- **Isolated**: Concurrent transactions do not interfere with each other
- **Durable**: Once a transaction commits, the changes are permanent

In distributed systems, transactions are often constructed as a number of subtransactions, jointly forming a **nested transaction** as shown in Figure 1.12. The top-level transaction may fork off children that run in parallel with one another, on different machines, to gain performance or simplify programming. Each of these children may also execute one or more subtransactions, or fork off its own children.

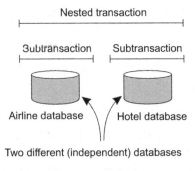

Figure 1.12: A nested transaction.

Subtransactions give rise to a subtle, but important, problem. Imagine that a transaction starts several subtransactions in parallel, and one of these commits, making its results visible to the parent transaction. After further computation, the parent aborts, restoring the entire system to the state it had before the top-level transaction started. Consequently, the results of the subtransaction that committed must nevertheless be undone. Thus, the permanence referred to above applies only to top-level transactions.

Since transactions can be nested arbitrarily deep, considerable administration is needed to get everything right. The semantics are clear, however. When any transaction or subtransaction starts, it is conceptually given a private copy of all data in the entire system for it to manipulate as it wishes. If it aborts, its private universe just vanishes, as if it had never existed. If it commits, its private universe replaces the parent's universe. Thus, if a subtransaction commits and then later a new subtransaction is started, the second one sees the results produced by the first one. Likewise, if an enclosing (higher level) transaction aborts, all its underlying subtransactions have to be aborted as well. And if several transactions are started concurrently, the result is as if they ran sequentially in some unspecified order.

Nested transactions are important in distributed systems, for they provide a natural way of distributing a transaction across multiple machines. They follow a *logical* division of the work of the original transaction. For example, a transaction for planning a trip by which three different flights need to be reserved can be logically split up into three subtransactions. Each of these subtransactions can be managed separately and independently.

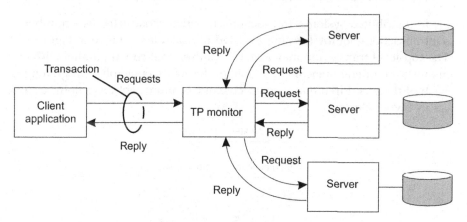

Figure 1.13: The role of a TP monitor in distributed systems.

Ever since the early days of enterprise middleware systems, the component that handles distributed (or nested) transactions belongs to the core for integrating applications at the server or database level. This component is called a **transaction-processing monitor** or **TP monitor** for short. Its main task is to allow an application to access multiple server/databases by offering it a transactional programming model, as shown in Figure 1.13. Essentially, the TP monitor coordinates the commitment of subtransactions following a standard protocol known as **distributed commit**, which we discuss in detail in Section 8.5.

An important observation is that applications wanting to coordinate several subtransactions into a single transaction do not have to implement this coordination themselves. By simply making use of a TP monitor, this coordination is done for them. This is precisely where middleware comes into play: it implements services that are useful for many applications, avoiding that such services have to be reimplemented over and over again by application developers.

Enterprise application integration

As mentioned, the more applications became decoupled from the databases they were built upon, the more evident it became that facilities were needed to integrate applications independently of their databases. In particular, application components should be able to communicate directly with each other and not merely by means of the request/reply behavior that was supported by transaction processing systems.

This need for interapplication communication led to many communication models. The main idea was that existing applications could directly exchange information, as shown in Figure 1.14.

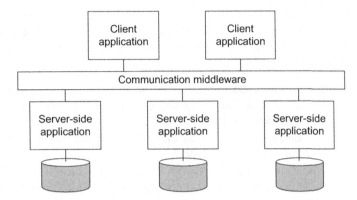

Figure 1.14: Middleware as a communication facilitator in enterprise application integration.

Several types of communication middleware exist. With **remote procedure calls (RPC)**, an application component can effectively send a request to another application component by doing a local procedure call, which results in the request being packaged as a message and sent to the callee. Likewise, the result will be sent back and returned to the application as the result of the procedure call.

As the popularity of object technology increased, techniques were developed to allow calls to remote objects, leading to what is known as **remote method invocations (RMI)**. An RMI is essentially the same as an RPC, except that it operates on objects instead of functions.

RPC and RMI have the disadvantage that the caller and callee both need to be up and running at the time of communication. In addition, they need to know exactly how to refer to each other. This tight coupling is often experienced as a serious drawback, and has led to what is known as **message-oriented middleware**, or simply **MOM**. In this case, applications send messages to logical contact points, often described by a subject. Likewise, applications can indicate their interest for a specific type of message, after which the communication middleware will take care that those messages are delivered to those applications. These so-called **publish-subscribe** systems form an important and expanding class of distributed systems.

Note 1.7 (More information: On integrating applications)

Supporting enterprise application integration is an important goal for many middleware products. In general, there are four ways to integrate applications [Hohpe and Woolf, 2004]:

File transfer: The essence of integration through file transfer, is that an application produces a file containing shared data that is subsequently read by other applications. The approach is technically simple, making it appealing. The drawback, however, is that there are numerous things that need to be agreed upon:

- File format and layout: text, binary, its structure, and so on. Nowadays, the **extended markup language** (**XML**) has become popular as its files are, in principle, self-describing.
- File management: where are they stored, how are they named, who is responsible for deleting files?
- Update propagation: When an application produces a file, there may be several applications that need to read that file to provide the view of a single coherent system. As a consequence, sometimes separate programs need to be implemented that notify applications of file updates.

Shared database: Many of the problems associated with integration through files are alleviated when using a shared database. All applications will have access to the same data, and often through a high-level database language such as SQL. Furthermore, it is easy to notify applications when changes occur, as triggers are often part of modern databases. There are, however, two major drawbacks. First, there is still a need to design a common data schema, which may be far from trivial if the set of applications that need to be integrated is not completely known in advance. Second, when there are many reads and updates, a shared database can easily become a performance bottleneck.

Remote procedure call: Integration through files or a database implicitly assumes that changes by one application can easily trigger other applications to act. However, practice shows that sometimes small changes should actually trigger many applications to take actions. In such cases, it is not really the change of data that is important, but the execution of a series of actions.

Series of actions are best captured through the execution of a procedure (which may, in turn, lead to all kinds of changes in shared data). To prevent that every application needs to know all the internals of those actions (as implemented by another application), standard encapsulation techniques should be used, as deployed with traditional procedure calls or object invocations. For such situations, an application can best offer a procedure to other applications in the form of a remote procedure call, or RPC. In essence, an RPC allows an application A to make use of the information available only to the application B, without giving A direct access to that information. There are many advantages and disadvantages to remote procedure calls, which are discussed in depth in Chapter 4.

Messaging: A main drawback of RPCs is that caller and callee need to be up and running at the same time in order for the call to succeed. However, in many scenarios, this simultaneous activity is often difficult or impossible to guarantee. In such cases, offering a messaging system carrying requests from the application A to perform an action at the application B, is what is needed. The messaging system ensures that eventually the request is delivered, and if needed, that a response is eventually returned as well. Obviously, messaging is not the panacea for application integration: it also introduces problems concerning data formatting and layout, it requires an application to know where to send a message to, there need to be scenarios for dealing with lost messages, and so on. Like RPCs, we will be discussing these issues extensively in Chapter 4.

What these four approaches tell us, is that application integration will generally not be simple. Middleware (in the form of a distributed system), however, can significantly help in integration by providing the right facilities such as support for RPCs or messaging. As said, enterprise application integration is an important target field for many middleware products.

1.3.3 Pervasive systems

The distributed systems discussed so far are largely characterized by their stability: nodes are fixed and have a more or less permanent and high-quality connection to a network. To a certain extent, this stability is realized through the various techniques for achieving distribution transparency. For example, there are many ways how we can create the illusion that only occasionally components may fail. Likewise, there are all kinds of means to hide the actual network location of a node, effectively allowing users and applications to believe that nodes stay put.

However, matters have changed since the introduction of mobile and embedded computing devices, leading to what are generally referred to as **pervasive systems**. As its name suggests, pervasive systems are intended to blend into our environment naturally. Many of their components are *necessarily* spread across multiple computers, making them arguably a type of decentralized system in our view. At the same time, most pervasive systems have many components that are *sufficiently* spread throughout the system, for example, to handle failures and such. In this sense, they are also arguably distributed systems. The seemingly strict separation between decentralized and distributed systems is thus seen to be less strict than one could initially imagine.

What makes them unique, in comparison to the computing and information systems described so far, is that the separation between users and system components is much more blurred. There is often no single dedicated interface, such as a screen/keyboard combination. Instead, a pervasive system is often equipped with many **sensors** that pick up various aspects of a user's behavior. Likewise, it may have a myriad of **actuators** to provide information and feedback, often even purposefully aiming to *steer* behavior.

Many devices in pervasive systems are characterized by being small, battery-powered, mobile, and having only a wireless connection, although not all these characteristics apply to all devices. These are not necessarily restrictive characteristics, as is illustrated by smartphones [Roussos et al., 2005] and their role in what is now coined as the **Internet of Things** [Mattern and Floerkemeier, 2010; Stankovic, 2014]. Nevertheless, notably, the fact that we often need to deal with the intricacies of wireless and mobile communication, will require special solutions to make a pervasive system as transparent or unobtrusive as possible.

In the following, we make a distinction between three different types of pervasive systems, although there is considerable overlap between the three types: ubiquitous computing systems, mobile systems, and sensor networks. This distinction allows us to focus on different aspects of pervasive systems.

Ubiquitous computing systems

So far, we have been talking about pervasive systems to emphasize that its elements have spread through in many parts of our environment. In a ubiquitous computing system, we go one step further: the system is pervasive and continuously present. The latter means that a user will be continuously interacting with the system, often not even being aware that interaction is taking place. Poslad [2009] describes the core requirements for a **ubiquitous computing system** roughly as follows:

1. (**Distribution**) Devices are networked, distributed, and accessible transparently

2. (**Interaction**) Interaction between users and devices is highly unobtrusive

3. (**Context awareness**) The system is aware of a user's context to optimize interaction

4. (**Autonomy**) Devices operate autonomously without human intervention, and are thus highly self-managed

5. (**Intelligence**) The system as a whole can handle a wide range of dynamic actions and interactions

Let us consider these requirements from a distributed-systems perspective.

Ad. 1: Distribution   As mentioned, a ubiquitous computing system is an example of a distributed system: the devices and other computers forming the nodes of a system are simply networked and work together to form the illusion of a single, coherent system. Distribution also comes naturally: there will be devices close to users (such as sensors and actuators), connected to computers hidden from view and perhaps even operating remotely in a cloud. Most, if not all, of the requirements regarding distribution transparency mentioned in Section 1.2.2, should therefore hold.

Ad. 2: Interaction When it comes to interaction with users, ubiquitous computing systems differ a lot in comparison to the systems we have been discussing so far. End users play a prominent role in the design of ubiquitous systems, meaning that special attention needs to be paid to how the interaction between users and core system takes place. For ubiquitous computing systems, much of the interaction by humans will be implicit, with an **implicit action** being defined as one "that is not primarily aimed to interact with a computerized system but which such a system understands as input" [Schmidt, 2000]. In other words, a user could be mostly unaware of the fact that input is being provided to a computer system. From a certain perspective, ubiquitous computing can be said to seemingly *hide* interfaces.

A simple example is where the settings of a car's driver's seat, steering wheel, and mirrors are fully personalized. If Bob takes a seat, the system will recognize that it is dealing with Bob and subsequently makes the appropriate adjustments. The same happens when Alice uses the car, while an unknown user will be steered toward making his or her own adjustments (to be remembered for later). This example already illustrates an important role of sensors in ubiquitous computing, namely as input devices that are used to identify a situation (a specific person apparently wanting to drive), whose input analysis leads to actions (making adjustments). In turn, the actions may lead to natural reactions, for example that Bob slightly changes the seat settings. The system will have to take all (implicit and explicit) actions by the user into account and react accordingly.

Ad. 3: Context awareness Reacting to the sensory input, but also the explicit input from users, is more easily said than done. What a ubiquitous computing system needs to do, is to take the **context** in which interactions take place into account. Context awareness also differentiates ubiquitous computing systems from the more traditional systems we have been discussing before, and is described by Dey and Abowd [2000] as "any information that can be used to characterize the situation of entities (i.e., whether a person, place, or object) that are considered relevant to the interaction between a user and an application, including the user and the application themselves." In practice, context is often characterized by location, identity, time, and activity: the *where*, *who*, *when*, and *what*. A system will need to have the necessary (sensory) input to determine one or several of these context types. As discussed by Alegre et al. [2016], developing context-aware systems is difficult, if only for the reason that the notion of context is difficult to grasp.

What is important, from a distributed-systems perspective, is that raw data as collected by various sensors is lifted to a level of abstraction that can be used by applications. A concrete example is detecting where a person is, for example in terms of GPS coordinates, and subsequently mapping that information to an actual location, such as the corner of a street, or a specific shop or other known facility. The question is where this processing of sensory input takes place: is all data collected at a central server connected to a database with detailed information on a city, or is it the user's smartphone where the mapping is done? Clearly, there are trade-offs to be considered.

Dey [2010] discusses more general approaches toward building context-aware applications. When it comes to combining flexibility and potential distribution, so-called **shared data spaces** in which processes are decoupled in time and space are attractive, yet as we shall see in later chapters, suffer from scalability problems. A survey on context-awareness and its relation to middleware and distributed systems is provided by Baldauf et al. [2007].

Ad. 4: Autonomy   An important aspect of most ubiquitous computing systems is that explicit systems management has been reduced to a minimum. In a ubiquitous computing environment, there is simply no room for a systems administrator to keep everything up and running. As a consequence, the system as a whole should be able to act autonomously, and automatically react to changes. This requires a myriad of techniques, of which several will be discussed throughout this book. To give a few simple examples, think of the following:

Address allocation: In order for networked devices to communicate, they need an IP address. Addresses can be allocated automatically using protocols like the **Dynamic Host Configuration Protocol (DHCP)** [Droms, 1997] (which requires a server) or **Zeroconf** [Guttman, 2001].

Adding devices: It should be easy to add devices to an existing system. A step towards automatic configuration is realized by the **Universal Plug and Play protocol (UPnP)** [UPnP Forum, 2008]. Using UPnP, devices can discover each other and make sure that they can set up communication channels between them.

Automatic updates: Many devices in a ubiquitous computing system should be able to regularly check through the Internet if their software should be updated. If so, they can download new versions of their components and ideally continue where they left off.

Admittedly, these are simple examples, but the picture should be clear that manual intervention is to be kept to a minimum. We will be discussing many techniques related to self-management in detail throughout the book.

Ad. 5: Intelligence   Finally, Poslad [2009] mentions that ubiquitous computing systems often use methods and techniques from the field of artificial intelligence. What this means, is that often a wide range of advanced algorithms and models need to be deployed to handle incomplete input, quickly react to a changing environment, handle unexpected events, and so on. The extent to which this can or should be done in a distributed fashion is crucial from the perspective of distributed systems. Unfortunately, distributed solutions for many problems in the field of artificial intelligence are yet to be found, meaning that there may be a natural tension between the first requirement of networked and distributed devices, and advanced distributed information processing.

Mobile computing systems

As mentioned, mobility often forms an important component of pervasive systems, and many, if not all aspects that we have just discussed also apply to **mobile computing**. There are several issues that set mobile computing aside to pervasive systems in general (see also Adelstein et al. [2005] and Tarkoma and Kangasharju [2009]).

First, the devices that form part of a (distributed) mobile system may vary widely. Typically, mobile computing is done with devices such as smartphones and tablet computers. However, entirely different types of devices are now using the Internet Protocol (IP) to communicate, placing mobile computing in a different perspective. Such devices include remote controls, pagers, active badges, car equipment, various GPS-enabled devices, and so on. A characteristic feature of all these devices is that they use wireless communication. Mobile implies wireless, so it seems (although there are exceptions to the rules).

Second, in mobile computing, the location of a device is assumed to change over time. A changing location has its effects on many issues. For example, if the location of a device changes regularly, so will perhaps the services that are locally available. As a consequence, we may need to pay special attention to dynamically discovering services, but also letting services announce their presence. In a similar vein, we often also want to know where a device actually is. This may mean that we need to know the actual geographical coordinates of a device such as in tracking and tracing applications, but it may also require that we can simply detect its network position (as in mobile IP [Perkins, 2010; Perkins et al., 2011].

Changing locations may also have a profound effect on communication. For some time, researchers in mobile computing have been concentrating on what are known as **mobile ad hoc networks**, also known as **MANETs**. The basic idea was that a group of local mobile computers would jointly set up a local, wireless network and to subsequently share resources and services. The idea never really became popular. Along the same lines, there are researchers who believe that end users are willing to share their local resources for another user's compute, storage, or communication requirements (see, e.g., Ferrer et al. [2019]). Practice has shown over and over again that voluntarily making resources available is not something users are willing to do, even if they have resources in abundance. The effect is that in the case of mobile computing, we generally see single mobile devices setting up connections to stationary servers. Changing locations then simply means that those connections need to be handed over by routers on the path from the mobile device to the server. Mobile computing is then brought back to its essence: a mobile device connected to a server (and nothing else). In practice, this means that mobile computing is all about mobile devices making use of cloud-based services, as sketched in Figure 1.15(a).

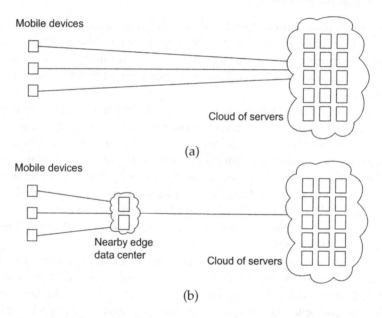

Figure 1.15: (a) Mobile Cloud Computing versus (b) Mobile Edge Computing.

Despite the conceptual simplicity of this model of mobile computing, the mere fact that so many devices make use of remote services has led to what is known as **Mobile Edge Computing**, or simply **MEC** [Abbas et al., 2018], in contrast to **Mobile Cloud Computing** (**MCC**). As we shall discuss further in Chapter 2, (mobile) edge computing, as sketched in Figure 1.15(b), is becoming increasingly important in those cases where latency, but also computational issues play a role for the mobile device. Typical example applications that require short latencies *and* computational resources include augmented reality, interactive gaming, real-time sports monitoring, and various health applications [Dimou et al., 2022]. In these examples, the combination of monitoring, analyses, and immediate feedback in general make it difficult to rely on servers that may be placed thousands of miles from the mobile devices.

Sensor networks

Our last example of pervasive systems is **sensor networks**. These networks in many cases form part of the enabling technology for pervasiveness, and we see that many solutions for sensor networks return in pervasive applications. What makes sensor networks interesting from a distributed system's perspective is that they are more than just a collection of input devices. Instead, as we shall see, sensor nodes often collaborate to process the sensed data efficiently in an application-specific manner, making them very different from, for example, traditional computer networks. Akyildiz et al. [2002] and Akyildiz et al. [2005] provide an overview from a networking perspective. A more systems-oriented introduction to sensor networks is given by Zhao and Guibas [2004], but also [Hahmy, 2021] will show to be useful.

A sensor network generally consists of tens to hundreds or thousands of relatively small nodes, each equipped with one or more sensing devices. In addition, nodes can often act as actuators [Akyildiz and Kasimoglu, 2004], a typical example being the automatic activation of sprinklers when a fire has been detected. Many sensor networks use wireless communication, and the nodes are often battery powered. Their limited resources, restricted communication capabilities, and constrained power consumption demand that efficiency is high on the list of design criteria.

When zooming into an individual node, we see that, conceptually, they do not differ a lot from "normal" computers: above the hardware there is a software layer akin to what traditional operating systems offer, including low-level network access, access to sensors and actuators, memory management, and so on. Normally, support for specific services is included, such as localization, local storage (think of additional flash devices), and convenient communication facilities such as messaging and routing. However, similar to other networked computer systems, additional support is needed to effectively deploy sensor network *applications*. In distributed systems, this takes the form of middleware. For sensor networks, we can, in principle, follow a similar approach in those cases that sensor nodes are sufficiently powerful and that energy consumption is not a hindrance for running a more elaborate software stack. Various approaches are possible (see also [Zhang et al., 2021b]).

From a programming perspective, and extensively surveyed by Mottola and Picco [2011], it is important to take the scope of communication primitives into account. This scope can vary between addressing the physical neighborhood of a node, and providing primitives for systemwide communication. In addition, it may also be possible to address a specific group of nodes. Likewise, computations may be restricted to an individual node, a group of nodes, or affect all nodes. To illustrate, Welsh and Mainland [2004] use so-called **abstract regions** allowing a node to identify a neighborhood from where it can, for example, gather information:

```
1     region  = k_nearest_region.create(8);
2     reading = get_sensor_reading();
3     region.putvar(reading_key, reading);
4     max_id  = region.reduce(OP_MAXID, reading_key);
```

In line 1, a node first creates a region of its eight nearest neighbors, after which it fetches a value from its sensor(s). This reading is subsequently written to the previously defined region to be defined using the key reading_key. In line 4, the node checks whose sensor reading in the defined region was the largest, which is returned in the variable max_id.

When considering that sensor networks produce data, one can also focus on the data-access model. This can be done directly by sending messages to and between nodes, or either moving code between nodes to locally access data. More advanced is to make remote data directly accessible, as if variables and such were available in a shared data space. Finally, and also quite popular, is to let the sensor network provide a view of a single database. Such a view is easy to understand when realizing that many sensor networks are deployed for measurement and surveillance applications [Bonnet et al., 2002]. In these cases, an operator would like to extract information from (a part of) the network by simply issuing queries such as "What is the northbound traffic load on highway 1 at Santa Cruz?" Such queries resemble those of traditional databases. In this case, the answer will probably need to be provided through collaboration of many sensors along highway 1, while leaving other sensors untouched.

To organize a sensor network as a distributed database, there are essentially two extremes, as shown in Figure 1.16. First, sensors do not cooperate but simply send their data to a centralized database located at the operator's site. The other extreme is to forward queries to relevant sensors and to let each compute an answer, requiring the operator to aggregate the responses.

Neither of these solutions is very attractive. The first one requires that sensors send all their measured data through the network, which may waste network resources and energy. The second solution may also be wasteful, as it discards the aggregation capabilities of sensors, which would allow much fewer data to be returned to the operator. What is needed are facilities for **in-network data processing**, similar to the previous example of abstract regions.

In-network processing can be done in numerous ways. One obvious way is to forward a query to all sensor nodes along a tree encompassing all nodes and to subsequently aggregate the results as they are propagated back to the root, where the initiator is located. Aggregation will take place where two or more branches of the tree come together. As simple as this scheme may sound, it introduces difficult questions:

- How do we (dynamically) set up an efficient tree in a sensor network?

- How does aggregation of results take place? Can it be controlled?

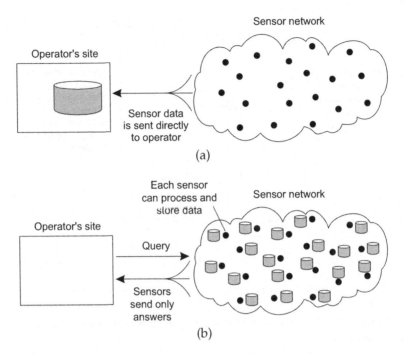

Figure 1.16: Organizing a sensor network database, while storing and processing data (a) only at the operator's site or (b) only at the sensors.

- What happens when network links fail?

These questions have been partly addressed in TinyDB, which implements a declarative (database) interface to wireless sensor networks [Madden et al., 2005]. In essence, TinyDB can use any tree-based routing algorithm. An intermediate node will collect and aggregate the results from its children, along with its own findings, and send that toward the root. To make matters efficient, queries span a period of time, allowing for careful scheduling of operations so that network resources and energy are optimally consumed.

However, when queries can be initiated from different points in the network, using single-rooted trees such as in TinyDB may not be efficient enough. As an alternative, sensor networks may be equipped with special nodes where results are forwarded to, as well as the queries related to those results. To give a simple example, queries and results related to temperature readings may be collected at a different location than those related to humidity measurements. This approach corresponds directly to the notion of publish-subscribe systems.

The interesting aspect of sensor networks, as discussed along these lines, is that we really need to concentrate on the organization of sensor *nodes*, and not the sensors themselves. Likewise, many sensor nodes will be equipped with **actuators**, i.e., devices that directly influence an environment. A typical

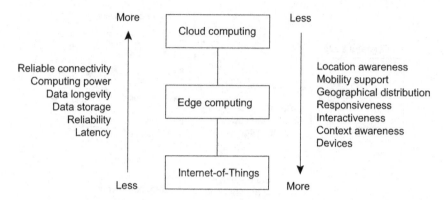

Figure 1.17: A hierarchical view from clouds to devices (adapted from Yousef-pour et al. [2019]).

actuator is one that controls the temperature in a room, or switches devices on or off. By viewing and organizing the network as a distributed system, an operator is provided with a higher level of abstraction to monitor and control a situation.

Cloud, edge, things

As may have become clear by now, distributed systems span a huge range of different networked computer systems. Many of such systems operate in a setting in which the various computers are connected through a local-area network. Yet with the growth of the Internet-of-Things and the connectivity with remote services offered through cloud-based systems, new organizations across wide-area networks are emerging. Figure 1.17 presents this more hierarchical approach.

Typically, higher up the hierarchy we see that typical qualities of distributed systems improve: they become more reliable, have more capacity, and, in general, perform better. Lower in the hierarchy, we see that location-related aspects are easier facilitated, as well as performance qualities related to latencies. At the same time, the lower parts show in an increase in the number of devices and computers, whereas higher up, the number of computers becomes less.

1.4   Pitfalls

It should be clear by now that developing a distributed system is a formidable task. As we will see many times throughout this book, there are so many issues to consider, while it seems that only complexity can be the result.

Nevertheless, by following several design principles, distributed systems can be developed that strongly adhere to the goals we set out in this chapter.

Distributed systems differ from traditional software because components are dispersed across a network. Not taking this dispersion into account during design time is what makes so many systems needlessly complex and results in flaws that need to be patched later on. Peter Deutsch, at the time working at Sun Microsystems, formulated these flaws as the following false assumptions that many make when developing a distributed application for the first time:

- The network is reliable
- The network is secure
- The network is homogeneous
- The topology does not change
- Latency is zero
- Bandwidth is infinite
- Transport cost is zero
- There is one administrator

Note how these assumptions relate to properties that are unique to distributed systems: reliability, security, heterogeneity, and topology of the network; latency and bandwidth; transport costs; and finally administrative domains. When developing nondistributed applications, most of these issues will most likely not show up.

Most of the principles we discuss in this book relate immediately to these assumptions. In all cases, we will be discussing solutions to problems that are caused by the fact that one or more assumptions are false. For example, reliable networks simply do not exist and lead to the impossibility of achieving failure transparency. We devote an entire chapter to deal with the fact that networked communication is inherently insecure. We have already argued that distributed systems need to be open and take heterogeneity into account. Likewise, when discussing replication for solving scalability problems, we are essentially tackling latency and bandwidth problems. We will also touch upon management issues at various points throughout this book.

1.5 Summary

A distributed system is a collection of networked computer systems in which processes and resources are spread across different computers. We make a distinction between *sufficiently* and *necessarily* spread, where the latter relates to decentralized systems. This distinction is important to make, as spreading processes and resources cannot be considered to be a goal by itself. Instead,

most choices for coming to a distributed system come from the need to improve the performance of a single computer system in terms of, for example,
reliability, scalability, and efficiency. However, considering that most centralized systems are still much easier to manage and maintain, one should
think twice before deciding to spread processes and resources. There are also
cases when there is simply no choice, for example when connecting systems
belonging to different organizations, or when computers simply operate from
different locations (as in mobile computing).

Design goals for distributed systems include sharing resources and ensuring openness. Increasingly important is designing secure distributed systems.
In addition, designers aim at hiding many of the intricacies related to the
distribution of processes, data, and control. However, this distribution transparency not only comes at a performance price, in practical situations it can
never be fully achieved. The fact that trade-offs need to be made between
achieving various forms of distribution transparency is inherent to the design
of distributed systems, and can easily complicate their understanding. One
specific difficult design goal that does not always blend well with achieving
distribution transparency is scalability. This is particularly true for geographical scalability, in which case hiding latencies and bandwidth restrictions can
turn out to be difficult. Likewise, administrative scalability, by which a system
is designed to span multiple administrative domains, may easily conflict with
goals for achieving distribution transparency.

Different types of distributed systems exist which can be classified as
being oriented toward supporting computations, information processing, and
pervasiveness. Distributed computing systems are typically deployed for
high-performance applications, often originating from the field of parallel
computing. A field that emerged from parallel processing was initially grid
computing with a strong focus on worldwide sharing of resources, in turn
leading to what is now known as cloud computing. Cloud computing goes
beyond high-performance computing and also supports distributed systems
found in traditional office environments, where we see databases playing
an important role. Typically, transaction processing systems are deployed
in these environments. Finally, an emerging class of distributed systems is
where components are small, the system is composed in an ad hoc fashion,
but most of all is no longer managed through a system administrator. This last
class is typically represented by pervasive computing environments, including
mobile-computing systems as well as sensor-rich environments.

Matters are further complicated by the fact that many developers initially
make assumptions about the underlying network that are fundamentally
wrong. Later, when assumptions are dropped, it may turn out to be difficult
to mask unwanted behavior. A typical example is assuming that network
latency is not significant. Other pitfalls include assuming that the network is
reliable, static, secure, and homogeneous.

ARCHITECTURES

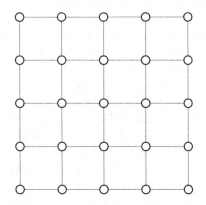

Distributed systems are often complex pieces of software, of which the components are by definition dispersed across multiple machines. To master their complexity, it is crucial that these systems be properly organized. There are different ways on how to view the organization of a distributed system, but an obvious one is to make a distinction between, on the one hand, the logical organization of the collection of software components, and on the other hand the actual physical realization.

The organization of distributed systems is mostly about the software components that constitute the system. These **software architectures** tell us how the various software components are to be organized and how they should interact. In this chapter, we will first pay attention to some commonly applied architectural styles toward organizing (distributed) computer systems.

An important goal of distributed systems is to separate applications from underlying platforms by providing a so-called middleware layer. Adopting such a layer is an important architectural decision, and its main purpose is to provide distribution transparency. However, trade-offs need to be made to achieve transparency, which has led to various techniques to adjust the middleware to the needs of the applications that make use of it. We discuss some of the more commonly applied techniques, as they affect the organization of the middleware itself.

The actual realization of a distributed system requires that we instantiate and place software components on real machines. There are many choices that can be made in doing so. The final instantiation of a software architecture is also referred to as a **system architecture**. In this chapter, we will look into traditional centralized architectures in which a single server implements most of the software components (and thus functionality), while remote clients can access that server using simple communication means. In addition, we consider decentralized peer-to-peer architectures in which all nodes more or less play equal roles. Many real-world distributed systems are often organized in a hybrid fashion, combining elements from centralized and decentralized architectures. We discuss several examples that illustrate the complexity of many real-world distributed systems.

2.1 Architectural styles

We start our discussion on architectures by first considering the logical organization of a distributed system into software components, also referred to as its **software architecture** [Bass et al., 2021; Richards and Ford, 2020]. Research on software architectures has matured considerably, and it is now commonly accepted that designing or adopting an architecture is crucial for the successful development of large software systems.

For our discussion, the notion of an **architectural style** is important. Such a style is formulated in terms of components, the way that components are connected to each other, the data exchanged between components, and finally, how these elements are jointly configured into a system. A **component** is a modular unit with well-defined required and provided **interfaces** that is *replaceable* within its environment [OMG, 2004]. That a component can be replaced, and, in particular, while a system continues to operate, is important. This is because often it is not an option to shut down a system for maintenance. At best, only parts of it may be put temporarily out of order. Replacing a component can be done only if its interfaces remain untouched. In practice, we see that replacing or updating a component means that a part of a system (such as a server), runs a regular update and switches to the refreshed components once their installation has finished. Special measures may need to be taken when a part of the distributed system does need to be restarted to let the updates take effect. Such measures may include having replicated standbys that take over while the partial restart is taking place.

A somewhat more difficult concept to grasp is that of a **connector**, which is generally described as a mechanism that mediates communication, coordination, or cooperation among components [Bass et al., 2021]. For example, a connector can be formed by the facilities for (remote) procedure calls, message passing, or streaming data. In other words, a connector allows for the flow of control and data between components.

Using components and connectors, we can come to various configurations, which, in turn, have been classified into architectural styles. Several styles have by now been identified, of which the most important ones for distributed systems are:

- Layered architectures
- Service-oriented architectures
- Publish-subscribe architectures

In the following, we discuss each of these styles separately. We note in advance that in most real-world distributed systems, many styles are combined. Notably, following an approach by which a system is subdivided into several (logical) layers is such a universal principle that it is generally combined with most other architectural styles.

2.1.1 Layered architectures

The basic idea for the layered style is simple: components are organized in a **layered fashion** where a component at layer L_j can make a **downcall** to a component at a lower-level layer L_i (with $i < j$) and generally expects a response. Only in exceptional cases will an **upcall** be made to a higher-level component. The three common cases are shown in Figure 2.1.

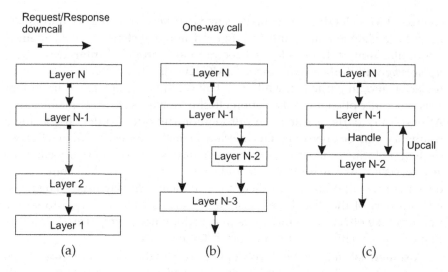

Figure 2.1: (a) Pure layered organization. (b) Mixed layered organization. (c) Layered organization with upcalls (adopted from [Krakowiak, 2009]).

Figure 2.1(a) shows a standard organization in which only downcalls to the next lower layer are made. This organization is commonly deployed in the case of network communication.

In many situations, we also encounter the organization shown in Figure 2.1(b). Consider, for example, an application A that makes use of a library L_{OS} to interface to an operating system. At the same time, the application uses a specialized mathematical library L_{math} that has been implemented by also making use of L_{OS}. In this case, referring to Figure 2.1(b), A is implemented at layer $N - 1$, L_{math} at layer $N - 2$, and L_{OS} which is common to both of them, at layer $N - 3$.

Finally, a special situation is shown in Figure 2.1(c). In some cases, it is convenient to have a lower layer do an upcall to its next higher layer. A typical example is when an operating system signals the occurrence of an event, to which end it calls a user-defined operation for which an application had previously passed a reference (typically referred to as a **handle**).

Layered communication protocols

A well-known and ubiquitously applied layered architecture is that of **communication-protocol stacks**. We will concentrate here on the global picture only and defer a detailed discussion to Section 4.1.1.

In communication-protocol stacks, each layer implements one or several, **communication services** allowing data to be sent from a destination to one or several targets. To this end, each layer offers an **interface** specifying the

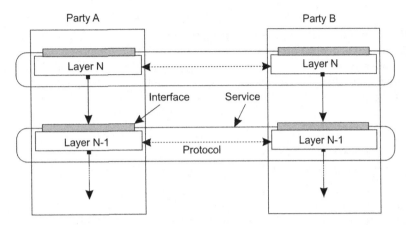

Figure 2.2: A layered communication-protocol stack, showing the difference between a service, its interface, and the protocol it deploys.

functions that can be called. In principle, the interface should completely hide the actual implementation of a service. Another important concept in the case of communication is that of a **(communication) protocol**, which describes the rules that parties will follow to exchange information. It is important to understand the difference between a service offered by a layer, the interface by which that service is made available, and the protocol that a layer implements to establish communication. This distinction is shown in Figure 2.2.

To make this distinction clear, consider a reliable, connection-oriented service, which is provided by many communication systems. In this case, a communicating party first needs to set up a connection to another party before the two can send and receive messages. Being reliable means that strong guarantees will be given that sent messages will indeed be delivered to the other side, even when there is a high risk that messages may be lost (as, for example, may be the case when using a wireless medium). In addition, such services generally also ensure that messages are delivered in the same order as that they were sent.

This kind of service is realized in the Internet by the **Transmission Control Protocol (TCP)**. The protocol specifies which messages are to be exchanged for setting up or tearing down a connection, what needs to be done to preserve the ordering of transferred data, and what both parties need to do to detect and correct data that was lost during transmission. The service is made available in the form of a relatively simple programming interface, containing calls to set up a connection, send and receive messages, and to tear down the connection again. In fact, there are different interfaces available, often dependent on the operating system or programming language used. Likewise, there are many implementations of the protocol and its interfaces. (All the gory details can be found in [Stevens, 1994; Wright and Stevens, 1995].)

Note 2.1 (Example: Two communicating parties)
To make this distinction between service, interface, and protocol more concrete, consider the following two communicating parties, also known as a **client** and a **server**, respectively, expressed in Python (note that some code has been removed for clarity).

```
1  from socket  import *
2
3  s = socket(AF_INET, SOCK_STREAM)
4  (conn, addr) = s.accept()  # returns new socket and addr. client
5  while True:                # forever
6    data = conn.recv(1024)   # receive data from client
7    if not data: break       # stop if client stopped
8    msg = data.decode()+"*"  # process the incoming data into a response
9    conn.send(msg.encode())  # return the response
10 conn.close()               # close the connection
```

(a) A simple server

```
1  from socket  import *
2
3  s = socket(AF_INET, SOCK_STREAM)
4  s.connect((HOST, PORT)) # connect to server (block until accepted)
5  msg = "Hello World"     # compose a message
6  s.send(msg.encode())    # send the message
7  data = s.recv(1024)     # receive the response
8  print(data.decode())    # print the result
9  s.close()               # close the connection
```

(b) A client

Figure 2.3: Two communicating parties.

In this example, a server is created that makes use of a **connection-oriented service** as offered by the socket library available in Python. This service allows two communicating parties to reliably send and receive data over a connection. The main functions available in its interface are:

- socket(): to create an object representing the connection
- accept(): a blocking call to wait for incoming connection requests; if successful, the call returns a new socket for a separate connection
- connect(): to set up a connection to a specified party
- close(): to tear down a connection
- send(), recv(): to send and receive data over a connection, respectively

The combination of constants AF_INET and SOCK_STREAM is used to specify that the TCP protocol should be used in the communication between the two parties. These two constants can be seen as part of the interface, whereas making use of TCP is part of the offered service. *How* TCP is implemented, or for that matter, any part of the communication service, is hidden completely from the applications.

> Finally, also note that these two programs implicitly adhere to an application-level protocol: apparently, if the client sends some data, the server will return it. Indeed, it operates as an echo server, where the server adds an asterisk to the data sent by the client.

Application layering

Let us now turn our attention to the logical layering of applications. Considering that a large class of distributed applications is targeted toward supporting users or applications access to databases, many people have advocated a distinction between three logical levels, essentially following a layered architectural style:

- The application-interface level
- The processing level
- The data level

In line with this layering, we see that applications can often be constructed from roughly three different pieces: a part that handles interaction with a user or some external application, a part that operates on a database or file system, and a middle part that generally contains the core functionality of the application. This middle part is logically placed at the processing level. In contrast to user interfaces and databases, there are not many aspects common to the processing level. Therefore, we shall give several examples to make this level clearer.

As a first example, consider a simple Internet search engine, for example one dedicated to buying houses. Such search engines appear as seemingly simple Websites through which someone can provide descriptors such as a city or region, a price range, the type of house, etc. The back end consists of a huge database of houses currently for sale. The processing layer does nothing else but transform the provided descriptors into a collection of database queries, retrieves the answers and post-processes these answers by, for example, ranking the output by relevance and subsequently generating an HTML page. Figure 2.4 shows this organization.

As another example, consider the organization of this book's Website, in particular, the interface that allows someone to get a personalized digital copy of the book in PDF. In this case, the interface consists of a WordPress-based Web server that merely collects the user's e-mail address (and some information on exactly which version of the book is being requested). This information is internally appended to a file requests.txt. The data layer is simple: it merely consists of a collection of LaTeX files and figures that jointly constitute the entire book.

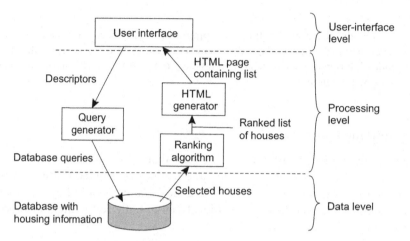

Figure 2.4: The simplified organization of an Internet search engine for housing, into three different layers.

Making a personalized copy consists of embedding the user's e-mail address into each of the figures. To this end, once every five minutes a separate process is started that takes the list of requests and one-by-one adds the requester's e-mail address into each bitmapped figure, generates a fresh copy of the book, stores the generated PDF in a special location (accessible through a unique URL), and sends the requester an e-mail that the copy is available for download. This process continues until all requests have been handled. In this example, we thus see that the processing layer outweighs the data layer or the application-interface layer in terms of computational efforts and actions to take.

2.1.2 Service-oriented architectures

Although the layered architectural style is popular, one of its major drawbacks is the often strong dependency between different layers. Good examples where these potential dependencies have been carefully considered are found in designing communication protocol stacks. Bad examples include applications that have essentially been designed and developed as compositions of existing components without much concern for the stability of interfaces or the components themselves, let alone the overlap of functionality between different components. (A compelling example is given by Kucharski [2020], who describes the dependency on a simple component that pads a given string with zeroes or spaces. The author withdrew the component from the NPM library, leaving thousands of programs affected.)

Such direct dependencies to specific components have led to an architectural style reflecting a more loose organization into a collection of separate, independent entities. Each entity encapsulates a service. Whether they are called **services**, **objects**, or **microservices**, they have in common that the service is executed as a separate process (or thread). Of course, running separate entities does not necessarily lower dependencies in comparison to a layered architectural style.

Object-based architectural style

Taking the object-based approach as an example, we have a logical organization as shown in Figure 2.5. In essence, each object corresponds to what we have defined as a component, and these components are connected through a procedure call mechanism. In the case of distributed systems, a procedure call can also take place over a network, that is, the calling object need not be executed on the same machine as the called object. In fact, *where* exactly the called object is located can be transparent to the caller: the called object may equally well run as a separate process on the same machine.

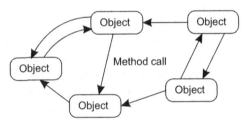

Figure 2.5: An object-based architectural style.

Object-based architectures are attractive because they provide a natural way of **encapsulating** data (called an object's **state**) and the operations that can be performed on that data (which are referred to as an object's **methods**) into a single entity. The **interface** offered by an object conceals implementation details, essentially meaning that we, in principle, can consider an object completely independent of its environment. As with components, this also means that if the interface is clearly defined and left otherwise untouched, an object should be replaceable with one having the same interface.

This separation between interfaces and the objects implementing these interfaces allows us to place an interface at one machine, while the object itself resides on another machine. This organization, which is shown in Figure 2.6 is commonly referred to as a **distributed object**, or every so often a **remote object**.

When a client **binds** to a distributed object, an implementation of the object's interface, called a **proxy**, is then loaded into the client's address space. A proxy is analogous to a so-called **client stub** in RPC systems. The only thing it does is pack method invocations into messages and unpack reply messages to return the result of the method invocation to the client. The actual object

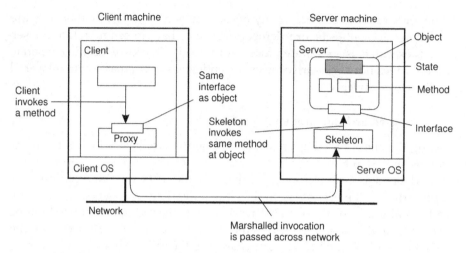

Figure 2.6: Common organization of a remote object with client-side proxy.

resides at a server machine, where it offers the same interface as it does on the client machine. Incoming invocation requests are first passed to a server stub, which unpacks them to make method invocations at the object's interface at the server. The server stub is also responsible for packing return values into a message, and forwarding these reply messages to the client-side proxy.

The server-side stub is often referred to as a **skeleton** as it provides the bare means for letting the server middleware access the user-defined objects. In practice, it often contains incomplete code in the form of a language-specific class that needs to be further specialized by the developer.

A characteristic, but somewhat counterintuitive, feature of most distributed objects is that their state is *not* distributed: it resides at a single machine. Only the interfaces implemented by the object are made available on other machines. Such objects are also referred to as **remote objects**. In a general distributed object, the state itself may be physically distributed across multiple machines, but this distribution is also hidden from clients behind the object's interfaces.

Microservice architectural style

One could argue that object-based architectures form the foundation of encapsulating services into independent units. **Encapsulation** is the keyword here: the service as a whole is realized as a self-contained entity, although it can possibly make use of other services. By clearly separating various services such that they can operate independently, we are paving the road toward **service-oriented architectures**, generally abbreviated as **SOAs**.

Stimulated by object-oriented designs and inspired by the Unix approach in which many, many small and mutually independent programs can be easily composed to form larger programs, software architects have been working on what are called **microservices**. Essential is that each microservice runs as a separate (network) process. The implementation of a microservice could be in the form of a remote object, but this is not a requirement. Furthermore, despite that people speak of *micro*services, there is no common agreement on what the size of such a service should be. Most important, however, is that a microservice truly represents a separate, independent service. In other words, modularization is key to designing microservices [Wolff, 2017].

Nevertheless, size does matter. By already stating that microservices run as separate networked processes, we are also given a choice *where* to place a microservice. As we shall see later in this chapter, in the advent of edge and fog infrastructures, discussions have started on the **orchestration** of deploying distributed applications across different layers. In other words, where do we place what.

Coarse-grained service composition

In a service-oriented architecture, a distributed application or system is essentially constructed as a composition of many services. A difference (although not strict) with microservices is that not all of these services may belong to the same administrative organization. We already came across this phenomenon when discussing cloud computing: it may very well be that an organization running its business application makes use of storage services offered by a cloud provider. These storage services are logically completely encapsulated into a single unit, of which an interface is made available to customers.

Of course, storage is a rather basic service, but more sophisticated situations easily come to mind. Consider, for example, a Web shop selling goods such as e-books. A simple implementation, following the application layering we discussed previously, may consist of an application for processing orders, which, in turn, operates on a local database containing the e-books. Order processing typically involves selecting items, registering and checking the delivery channel (perhaps by making use of e-mail), but also making sure that a payment takes place. The latter can be handled by a separate service, run by a different organization, to which a purchasing customer is redirected for the payment, after which the e-book organization is notified so that it can complete the transaction. This example also illustrates that where microservices are considered to be relatively small, a general service may be expected to be relatively large. In fact, it is not uncommon to implement a service as a collection of microservices.

In this way, we see that the problem of developing a distributed system is partly one of *service composition*, and making sure that those services operate in harmony. Indeed, this problem is completely analogous to the enterprise application integration issues discussed in Section 1.3.2. Crucial is, and remains, that each service offers a well-defined (programming) interface. In practice, this also means that each service offers *its own* interface, in turn, possibly making the composition of services far from trivial.

Resource-based architectures

As an increasing number of services became available over the Web and the development of distributed systems through service composition became more important, researchers started to rethink the architecture of mostly Web-based distributed systems. One of the problems with service composition is that connecting various components can easily turn into an integration nightmare.

As an alternative, one can also view a distributed system as a huge collection of resources that are individually managed by components. Resources may be added or removed by (remote) applications, and likewise can be retrieved or modified. This approach has now been widely adopted for the Web and is known as **Representational State Transfer** (**REST**) [Fielding, 2000]. There are four key characteristics of what are known as **RESTful architectures** [Pautasso et al., 2008]:

1. Resources are identified through a single naming scheme

2. All services offer the same interface, consisting of at most four operations, as shown in Figure 2.7

3. Messages sent to or from a service are fully self-described

4. After executing an operation at a service, that component forgets everything about the caller

The last property is also referred to as a **stateless execution**, a concept to which we return in Chapter 3.

Operation	Description
PUT	Modify a resource by transferring a new state
POST	Create a new resource
GET	Retrieve the state of a resource in some representation
DELETE	Delete a resource

Figure 2.7: The four operations available in RESTful architectures.

To illustrate how RESTful can work in practice, consider a cloud storage service, such as Amazon's **Simple Storage Service** (**Amazon S3**). Amazon S3, described in [Murty, 2008] and more recently in [Culkin and Zazon, 2022], supports two resources: *objects*, which are essentially the equivalent of files, and *buckets*, the equivalent of directories. There is no concept of placing buckets into buckets. An object named ObjectName contained in a bucket BucketName is referred to by the following **Uniform Resource Identifier** (**URI**):

`https://s3.amazonaws.com/BucketName/ObjectName`

To create a bucket, or an object for that matter, an application would essentially send a PUT request with the URI of the bucket/object. In principle, the protocol that is used with the service is HTTP. In other words, it is just another HTTP request, which will subsequently be correctly interpreted by S3. If the bucket or object already exists, an HTTP error message is returned.

Similarly, to know which objects are contained in a bucket, an application would send a GET request with the URI of that bucket. S3 will return a list of object names, again as an ordinary HTTP response.

The RESTful architecture has become popular because of its simplicity. Pautasso et al. [2008] have compared RESTful services to service-specific interfaces, and, as to be expected, they both have their advantages and disadvantages. In particular, the simplicity of RESTful architectures can easily prohibit easy solutions to intricate communication schemes. One example is where distributed transactions are needed, which generally requires that services keep track of the state of execution. On the other hand, there are many examples in which RESTful architectures match perfectly a simple integration scheme of services, yet where the myriad of service interfaces will complicate matters.

Note 2.2 (Advanced: On interfaces)
Clearly, a service cannot be made easier or more difficult just because of the particular interface it offers. A service offers functionality, and at best the way that the service is accessed is determined by the interface. Indeed, one could argue that the discussion on RESTful versus service-specific interfaces is much about access transparency. To better appreciate why so many people are paying attention to this issue, let us zoom in on the **Amazon S3** service, which offers a REST interface as well as a more traditional interface (referred to as the SOAP interface). The fact that the latter has been deprecated out says a lot.

Bucket operations	Object operations
ListAllMyBuckets	PutObjectInline
CreateBucket	PutObject
DeleteBucket	CopyObject
ListBucket	GetObject
GetBucketAccessControlPolicy	GetObjectExtended
SetBucketAccessControlPolicy	DeleteObject
GetBucketLoggingStatus	GetObjectAccessControlPolicy
SetBucketLoggingStatus	SetObjectAccessControlPolicy

Figure 2.8: The operations in Amazon's S3 SOAP interface, by now deprecated.

The SOAP interface consists of approximately 16 operations, listed in Figure 2.8. However, if we were to access Amazon S3 using the Python boto3 library, we would have more than 100 operations available. In contrast, the REST interface offers only very few operations, essentially those listed in Figure 2.7. Where do these differences come from? The answer is, of course, in the parameter space. In the case of RESTful architectures, an application will need to provide all that it wants through the parameters it passes by one of the operations. In Amazon's SOAP interface, the number of parameters per operation is generally limited, and this is certainly the case if we were to use the Python boto3 library.

Sticking to principles (so that we can avoid the intricacies of real code), suppose that we have an interface bucket that offers an operation create, requiring an input string such as mybucket, for creating a bucket with name "mybucket." Normally, the operation would be called roughly as follows:

```
import bucket
bucket.create("mybucket")
```

However, in a RESTful architecture, the call would need to be essentially encoded as a single string, such as

```
PUT "https://mybucket.s3.amazonsws.com/"
```

The difference is striking. For example, in the first case, many syntactical errors can often already be caught during compile time, whereas in the second case, checking needs to be deferred until runtime. Secondly, one can argue that specifying the semantics of an operation is much easier with specific interfaces than with ones that offer only generic operations. On the other hand, with generic operations, changes are much easier to accommodate, as they would generally involve changing the layout of strings that encode what is actually required.

2.1.3 Publish-subscribe architectures

As systems continue to grow and processes can more easily join or leave, it becomes important to have an architecture in which dependencies between processes become as loose as possible. A large class of distributed systems have adopted an architecture in which there is a strong separation between *processing* and *coordination*. The idea is to view a system as a collection of autonomously operating processes. In this model, **coordination** encompasses the communication and cooperation between processes. It forms the glue that binds the activities performed by processes into a whole [Gelernter and Carriero, 1992].

Cabri et al. [2000] provide a taxonomy of coordination models that can be applied equally to many types of distributed systems. Slightly adapting their terminology, we make a distinction between models along two different dimensions, temporal and referential, as shown in Figure 2.9.

When processes are temporally and referentially coupled, coordination takes place directly, referred to as **direct coordination**. The referential coupling generally appears in the form of explicit referencing in communication. For example, a process can communicate only if it knows the name or identifier of

	Temporally coupled	Temporally decoupled
Referentially coupled	Direct	Mailbox
Referentially decoupled	Event-based	Shared data space

Figure 2.9: Examples of different forms of coordination.

the other processes it wants to exchange information with. Temporal coupling means that processes that are communicating will both have to be up and running. In real life, talking over cell phones (and assuming that a cell phone has only one owner), is an example of direct communication.

A different type of coordination occurs when processes are temporally decoupled, but referentially coupled, which we refer to as **mailbox coordination**. In this case, there is no need for two communicating processes to be active at the same time to let communication take place. Instead, communication takes place by putting messages in a (possibly shared) mailbox. Because it is necessary to explicitly address the mailbox that will hold the messages that are to be exchanged, there is a referential coupling.

The combination of referentially decoupled and temporally coupled systems form the group of models for **event-based coordination**. In referentially decoupled systems, processes do not know each other explicitly. The only thing a process can do is **publish** a **notification** describing the occurrence of an event (e.g., that it wants to coordinate activities, or that it just produced some interesting results). Assuming that notifications come in all sorts and kinds, processes may **subscribe** to a specific kind of notification (see also [Mühl et al., 2006]). In an ideal event-based coordination model, a published notification will be delivered exactly to those processes that have subscribed to it. However, it is generally required that the subscriber is up-and-running at the time the notification was published.

A well-known coordination model is the combination of referentially and temporally decoupled processes, leading to what is known as a **shared data space**. The key idea is that processes communicate entirely through **tuples**, which are structured data records consisting of several fields, very similar to a row in a database table. Processes can put any type of tuple into the shared data space. To retrieve a tuple, a process provides a search pattern that is matched against the tuples. Any tuple that matches is returned.

Shared data spaces are thus seen to implement an associative search mechanism for tuples. When a process wants to extract a tuple from the data space, it specifies (some of) the values of the fields it is interested in. Any tuple that matches that specification is then removed from the data space and passed to the process.

Shared data spaces are often combined with event-based coordination: a process subscribes to certain tuples by providing a search pattern; when a process inserts a tuple into the data space, matching subscribers are notified. In both cases, we are dealing with a **publish-subscribe** architecture, and indeed, the key characteristic feature is that processes have no explicit reference to each other. The difference between a pure event-based architectural style , and that of a shared data space, is shown in Figure 2.10. We have also shown an abstraction of the *mechanism* by which publishers and subscribers are matched, known as an **event bus**.

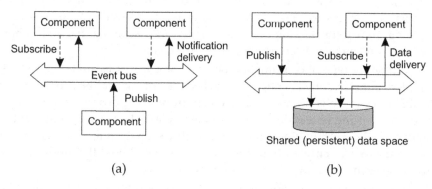

Figure 2.10: The (a) event-based and (b) shared data-space architectural style.

Note 2.3 (Example: Linda tuple spaces)

To make matters a bit more concrete, we take a closer look at **Linda**, a programming model developed in the 1980s [Carriero and Gelernter, 1989]. The shared data space in Linda is known as a **tuple space**, which supports three operations:

- in(t): remove a tuple that matches the template t
- rd(t): obtain a copy of a tuple that matches the template t
- out(t): add the tuple t to the tuple space

Note that if a process would call out(t) twice in a row, we would find that two copies of tuple t would have been stored. Formally, a tuple space is therefore always modeled as a *multiset*. Both in and rd are *blocking* operations: the caller will be blocked until a matching tuple is found, or has become available.

Consider a simple microblog application in which messages are tagged with the name of its poster and a topic, followed by a short string. Each message is modeled as a tuple <string,string,string> where the first string names the poster, the second string represents the topic, and the third one is the actual content. Assuming that we have created a shared data space called MicroBlog, Figure 2.11 shows how Alice and Bob can post messages to that space, and how

Chuck can pick a (randomly selected) message. We have omitted some code for clarity. Note that neither Alice nor Bob knows who will read their postings.

```
1  blog = linda.universe._rd(("MicroBlog",linda.TupleSpace))[1]
2
3  blog._out(("bob","distsys","I am studying chap 2"))
4  blog._out(("bob","distsys","The linda example's pretty simple"))
5  blog._out(("bob","gtcn","Cool book!"))
```

(a) Bob's code for creating a microblog and posting three messages.

```
1  blog = linda.universe._rd(("MicroBlog",linda.TupleSpace))[1]
2
3  blog._out(("alice","gtcn","This graph theory stuff is not easy"))
4  blog._out(("alice","distsys","I like systems more than graphs"))
```

(b) Alice's code for creating a microblog and posting two messages.

```
1  blog = linda.universe._rd(("MicroBlog",linda.TupleSpace))[1]
2
3  t1 = blog._rd(("bob","distsys",str))
4  t2 = blog._rd(("alice","gtcn",str))
5  t3 = blog._rd(("bob","gtcn",str))
```

(c) Chuck reading a message from Bob's and Alice's microblog.

Figure 2.11: A simple example of using a shared data space.

In the first line of each code fragment, a process looks up the tuple space named "MicroBlog." Bob posts three messages: two on topic distsys, and one on gtcn. Alice posts two messages, one on each topic. Chuck, finally, reads three messages: one from Bob on distsys and one on gtcn, and one from Alice on gtcn.

Obviously, there is much room for improvement. For example, we should ensure that Alice cannot post messages under Bob's name. However, the important issue to note now, is that by providing only tags, a reader such as Chuck will be able to pick up messages without needing to directly reference the poster. In particular, Chuck could also read a randomly selected message on topic distsys through the statement

```
t = blog_rd((str,"distsys",str))
```

We leave it as an exercise to the reader to extend the code fragments such that a *next* message will be selected instead of a random one.

An important aspect of publish-subscribe systems is that communication takes place by describing the events that a subscriber is interested in. As a consequence, naming plays a crucial role. We return to naming later, but for now, the important issue is that often, data items are not explicitly identified by senders and receivers.

Let us first assume that events are described by a series of **attributes**. A notification describing an event is said to be **published** when it is made available for other processes to read. To that end, a **subscription** needs to be passed to the middleware, containing a description of the event that the subscriber is interested in. Such a description typically consists of some (*attribute, value*) pairs, which is common for so-called **topic-based publish-subscribe systems**.

As an alternative, in **content-based publish-subscribe systems**, a subscription may also consist of (*attribute, range*) pairs. In this case, the specified attribute is expected to take on values within a specified range. Descriptions can sometimes be given using all kinds of predicates formulated over the attributes, very similar in nature to SQL-like queries in the case of relational databases. Obviously, the more expressive a description is allowed to be, the more difficult it will be to test whether an event matches a description.

We are now confronted with a situation in which subscriptions need to be **matched** against notifications, as shown in Figure 2.12. Often, an event actually corresponds to data becoming available. In that case, when matching succeeds, there are two possible scenarios. In the first case, the middleware may decide to forward the published notification, along with the associated data, to its current set of subscribers, that is, processes with a matching subscription. As an alternative, the middleware can also forward only a notification, at which point subscribers can execute a read operation to retrieve the data item.

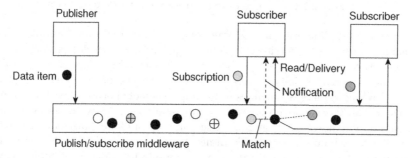

Figure 2.12: The principle of exchanging data items between publishers and subscribers.

In those cases, in which data associated with an event are immediately forwarded to subscribers, the middleware will generally not offer storage of data. Storage is either explicitly handled by a separate service, or is the responsibility of subscribers. In other words, we have a referentially decoupled, but temporally coupled system.

This situation is different when notifications are sent so that subscribers need to explicitly read the associated data. Necessarily, the middleware will have to store data items. In these situations, there are additional operations for data management. It is also possible to attach a **lease** to a data item such that when the lease expires that the data item is automatically deleted.

Events can easily complicate the processing of subscriptions. To illustrate, consider a subscription such as "notify when room ZI.1060 is unoccupied and the door is unlocked." Typically, a distributed system supporting such subscriptions can be implemented by placing independent sensors for monitoring room occupancy (e.g., motion sensors) and those for registering the status of a door lock. Following the approach sketched so far, we would need to *compose* such primitive events into a publishable data item, to which processes can then subscribe. Event composition turns out to be a difficult task, notably when the primitive events are generated from sources dispersed across the distributed system.

Clearly, in publish-subscribe systems such as these, the crucial issue is the efficient and scalable implementation of matching subscriptions to notifications. From the outside, the publish-subscribe architecture provides lots of potential for building very large-scale distributed systems due to the strong decoupling of processes. On the other hand, devising scalable implementations without losing this independence is not a trivial exercise, notably in the case of content-based publish-subscribe systems. In this sense, although many claim that the publish-subscribe style offers the path toward scalable architectures, the fact is that implementations may easily form a bottleneck, certainly when security and privacy is at stake, as we will discuss in Chapter 9 and later in Chapter 5.

2.2 Middleware and distributed systems

To assist the development of distributed applications, distributed systems are often organized to have a separate layer of software that is logically placed on top of the respective operating systems of the computers that are part of the

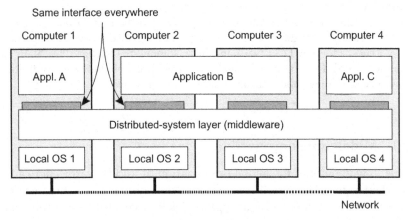

Figure 2.13: A distributed system organized in a middleware layer, which extends over multiple machines, offering each application the same interface.

system. This organization is shown in Figure 2.13, leading to what is known as **middleware** [Bernstein, 1996].

Figure 2.13 shows four networked computers and three applications, of which application B is distributed across computers 2 and 3. Each application is offered the same interface. The distributed system provides the means for components of a single distributed application to communicate with each other, but also to let different applications communicate. At the same time, it hides, as best and reasonably as possible, the differences in hardware and operating systems from each application.

In a sense, middleware is the same to a distributed system as what an operating system is to a computer: a manager of resources offering its applications to efficiently share and deploy those resources across a network. Next to resource management, it offers services that can also be found in most operating systems, including:

- Facilities for interapplication communication.
- Security services.
- Accounting services.
- Masking of and recovery from failures.

The main difference with their operating-system equivalents, is that middleware services are offered in a networked environment. Note also that most services are useful to many applications. In this sense, middleware can also be viewed as a container of commonly used components and functions that now no longer have to be implemented by applications separately.

Note 2.4 (Historical note: The term middleware)
Although the term middleware became popular in the mid 1990s, it was most likely mentioned for the first time in a report on a NATO software engineering conference, edited by Peter Naur and Brian Randell in October 1968 [Naur and Randell, 1968]. Indeed, middleware was placed precisely between applications and service routines (the equivalent of operating systems).

2.2.1   Middleware organization

Let us now zoom into the actual organization of middleware. There are two important types of *design patterns* that are often applied to the organization of middleware: wrappers and interceptors. Each targets different problems, yet addresses the same goal for middleware: achieving openness (as we discussed in Section 1.2.3).

Wrappers

When building a distributed system out of existing components, we immediately bump into a fundamental problem: the interfaces offered by the legacy component are most likely not suitable for all applications. In Section 1.3.2 we discussed how enterprise application integration could be established through middleware as a communication facilitator, but there we still implicitly assumed that, in the end, components could be accessed through their native interfaces.

A **wrapper** or **adapter** is a special component that offers an interface acceptable to a client application, of which the functions are transformed into those available at the component. In essence, it solves the problem of incompatible interfaces (see also Gamma et al. [1994]).

Although originally narrowly defined in the context of object-oriented programming, in the context of distributed systems wrappers are much more than simple interface transformers. For example, an **object adapter** is a component that allows applications to invoke remote objects, although those objects may have been implemented as a combination of library functions operating on the tables of a relational database.

As another example, reconsider Amazon's S3 storage service. As mentioned, there are two types of interfaces available, one adhering to a RESTful architecture, another following a more traditional approach. For the RESTful interface, clients will be using the HTTP protocol, essentially communicating with a traditional Web server which now acts as an adapter to the actual storage service, by partly dissecting incoming requests and subsequently handing them off to specialized servers internal to S3.

Wrappers have always played an important role in extending systems with existing components. Extensibility, which is crucial for achieving openness, used to be addressed by adding wrappers as needed. In other words, if an application A managed data that was needed by an application B, one approach would be to develop a wrapper specific for B so that it could have access to A's data. Clearly, this approach does not scale well: with N applications we would, in theory, need to develop $N \times (N-1) = \mathcal{O}(N^2)$ wrappers.

Again, facilitating a reduction of the number of wrappers is typically done through middleware. One way of doing this is implementing a so-called **broker**, which is logically a centralized component that handles all the accesses between different applications. An often-used type is a **message broker** of which we discuss the technicalities in Section 4.3.3. In the case of a message broker, applications simply send requests to the broker containing information on what they need. The broker, having knowledge of all relevant applications, contacts the appropriate applications, possibly combines and transforms the responses and returns the result to the initial application. In principle, because a broker offers a single interface to each application, we

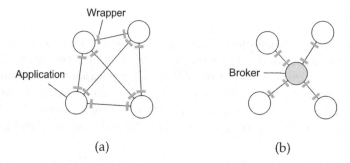

Figure 2.14: (a) Requiring each application to have a wrapper for each other application. (b) Reducing the number of wrappers by making use of a broker.

now need at most $2N = \mathcal{O}(N)$ wrappers instead of $\mathcal{O}(N^2)$. This situation is sketched in Figure 2.14.

Interceptors

Conceptually, an **interceptor** is nothing but a software construct that will break the usual flow of control and allow other (application specific) code to be executed. Interceptors are a primary means for adapting middleware to the specific needs of an application. As such, they play an important role in making middleware open. To make interceptors generic may require a substantial implementation effort, as illustrated by Schmidt et al. [2000], and it is unclear whether in such cases generality should be preferred over restricted applicability and simplicity. Furthermore, often having only limited interception facilities will improve management of the software and the distributed system as a whole.

To make matters concrete, consider interception as supported in many object-based distributed systems. The basic idea is simple: an object A can call a method that belongs to an object B, while the latter resides on a different machine than A. As we explain in detail later in the book, such a remote-object invocation is carried out in three steps:

1. Object A is offered a local interface that is the same as the interface offered by object B. A calls the method available in that interface.

2. The call by A is transformed into a generic object invocation, made possible through a general object-invocation interface offered by the middleware at the machine where A resides.

3. Finally, the generic object invocation is transformed into a message that is sent through the transport-level network interface as offered by A's local operating system.

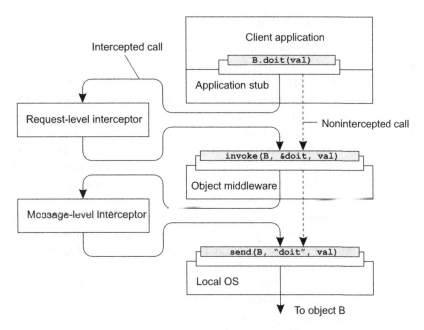

Figure 2.15: Using interceptors to handle remote-object invocations.

This scheme is shown in Figure 2.15. After the first step, the call B.doit(val) is transformed into a generic call, such as invoke(B,&doit,val) with a reference to B's method and the parameters that go along with the call. Now imagine that object B is replicated. In that case, each replica should actually be invoked. This is a clear point where interception can help. What the **request-level interceptor** will do, is simply call invoke(B,&doit,val) for each of the replicas. The beauty of this all is that the object A need not be aware of the replication of B, but also the object middleware need not have special components that deal with this replicated call. Only the request-level interceptor, which may be *added* to the middleware, needs to know about B's replication.

In the end, a call to a remote object will have to be sent over the network. In practice, this means that the messaging interface as offered by the local operating system will need to be invoked. At that level, a **message-level interceptor** may assist in transferring the invocation to the target object. For example, imagine that the parameter val actually corresponds to a huge array of data. In that case, it may be wise to fragment the data into smaller parts to have it assembled again at the destination. Such a fragmentation may improve performance or reliability. Again, the middleware need not be aware of this fragmentation; the lower-level interceptor will transparently handle the rest of the communication with the local operating system.

2.2.2   Modifiable middleware

What wrappers and interceptors offer are means to extend and adapt the middleware. The need for adaptation comes from the fact that the environment in which distributed applications are executed changes continuously. Changes include those resulting from mobility, a strong variance in the quality-of-service of networks, failing hardware, and battery drainage, among others. Rather than making applications responsible for reacting to changes, this task is placed in the middleware. Moreover, as the size of a distributed system increases, changing its parts can rarely be done by temporarily shutting it down. What is needed is being able to make changes on-the-fly.

These strong influences from the environment have brought many designers of middleware to consider the construction of *adaptive software*. We follow Parlavantzas and Coulson [2007] in speaking of **modifiable middleware** to express that middleware may not only need to be adaptive, but that we should be able to purposefully modify it without bringing it down. In this context, interceptors can be thought of offering a means to adapt the standard flow of control. Replacing software components at runtime is an example of modifying a system. And indeed, perhaps one of the most popular approaches toward modifiable middleware is that of dynamically constructing middleware from components.

Component-based design focuses on supporting modifiability through composition. A system may either be configured statically at design time, or dynamically at runtime. The latter requires support for late binding, a technique that has been successfully applied in programming language environments, but also for operating systems where modules can be loaded and unloaded at will. Automatically selecting the best implementation of a component during runtime is by now well understood [Yellin, 2003] but again, the process remains complex for distributed systems, especially when considering that replacement of one component requires to know exactly what the effect of that replacement on other components will be. Often, components are less independent as one may think.

The bottom line is that to accommodate dynamic changes to the software that makes up middleware, we need at least basic support to load and unload components at runtime. In addition, for each component explicit specifications of the interfaces it offers, as well the interfaces it requires, are needed. If state is maintained between calls to a component, then further special measures are needed. By-and-large, it should be clear that organizing middleware to be modifiable requires special attention.

2.3   Layered-system architectures

Let us now take a look at how many distributed systems are actually organized by considering where software components are placed. Deciding on software components, their interaction, and their placement leads to an instance of a software architecture, also known as a **system architecture** [Bass et al., 2021]. We start with discussing layered architectures. Other forms follow later.

Despite the lack of consensus on many distributed systems issues, there is one issue that many researchers and practitioners agree upon: thinking in terms of *clients* that request services from *servers* helps to understand and manage the complexity of distributed systems [Saltzer and Kaashoek, 2009]. In the following, we first consider a simple layered organization, followed by looking at multi-layered organizations.

2.3.1 Simple client-server architecture

In the basic client-server model, processes in a distributed system are divided into two (possibly overlapping) groups. A **server** is a process implementing a specific service, for example, a file system service or a database service. A **client** is a process that requests a service from a server by sending it a request and subsequently waiting for the server's reply. This client-server interaction, also known as **request-reply behavior** is shown in Figure 2.16.

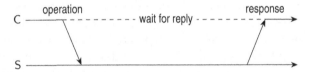

Figure 2.16: General interaction between a client C and a server S. C sends the operation oper and waits for the response from S.

Communication between a client and a server can be implemented by a simple connectionless protocol when the underlying network is fairly reliable, as in many local-area networks. In these cases, when a client requests a service, it simply packages a message for the server, identifying the service it wants, along with the necessary input data. The message is then sent to the server. The latter, in turn, will always wait for an incoming request, subsequently process it, and package the results in a reply message that is then sent to the client.

Using a connectionless protocol has the obvious advantage of being efficient. As long as messages do not get lost or corrupted, the request/reply protocol just sketched works fine. Unfortunately, making the protocol resistant to occasional transmission failures is not trivial. The only thing we can do is possibly let the client resend the request when no reply message comes in. The problem, however, is that the client cannot detect whether the original request message was lost, or that transmission of the reply failed. If the reply was lost, then resending a request may result in performing the operation twice. If the operation was something like "transfer $10,000 from my bank account," then clearly, it would have been better that we simply reported an error instead. On the other hand, if the operation was "tell me how much money I have left," it would be perfectly acceptable to resend the request. When an operation can be repeated multiple times without harm, it is said to be **idempotent**. Since some requests are idempotent and others are not, it should be clear that there is no single solution for dealing with lost messages. We defer a detailed discussion on handling transmission failures to Section 8.3.

As an alternative, many client-server systems use a reliable connection-oriented protocol. Although this solution is not entirely appropriate in a local-area network due to relatively low performance, it works perfectly fine in wide-area systems in which communication is inherently unreliable. For example, virtually all Internet application protocols are based on reliable TCP/IP connections. In this case, whenever a client requests a service, it first sets up a connection to the server before sending the request. The server generally uses that same connection to send the reply message, after which the connection is torn down. The trouble may be that setting up and tearing down a connection is relatively costly, especially when the request and reply messages are small.

The client-server model has been subject to many debates and controversies over the years. One of the main issues was how to draw a clear distinction between a client and a server. Not surprisingly, there is often no clear distinction. For example, a server for a distributed database may continuously act as a client because it is forwarding requests to different file servers responsible for implementing the database tables. In such a case, the database server itself only processes the queries.

2.3.2 Multitiered Architectures

The distinction into three logical levels, as discussed so far, suggests several possibilities for physically distributing a client-server application across several machines. The simplest organization is to have only two types of machines:

1. A client machine containing only the programs implementing (part of) the user-interface level

2. A server machine containing the rest, that is, the programs implementing the processing and data level

In this organization everything is handled by the server while the client is essentially no more than a dumb terminal, possibly with only a convenient graphical interface. There are, however, many other possibilities. As explained in Section 2.1.1, many distributed applications are divided into three layers: (1) a user-interface layer, (2) a processing layer, and (3) a data layer. One approach for organizing clients and servers is then to distribute these layers across different machines, as shown in Figure 2.17 (see also Umar [1997]). As a first step, we make a distinction between only two kinds of machines: client machines and server machines, leading to what is also referred to as a **(physically) two-tiered architecture**.

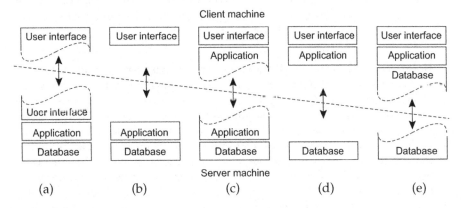

Figure 2.17: Client-server organizations in a two-tiered architecture.

One possible organization is to have only the terminal-dependent part of the user interface on the client machine, as shown in Figure 2.17(a), and give the applications remote control over the presentation of their data. An alternative is to place the entire user-interface software on the client side, as shown in Figure 2.17(b). In such cases, we essentially divide the application into a graphical front end, which communicates with the rest of the application (residing at the server) through an application-specific protocol. In this model, the front end (the client software) does no processing other than necessary for presenting the application's interface.

Continuing along this line of reasoning, we may also move part of the application to the front end, as shown in Figure 2.17(c). An example where this makes sense is where the application makes use of a form that needs to be filled in entirely before it can be processed. The front end can then check the correctness and consistency of the form, and where necessary interact with the user. Another example of the organization of Figure 2.17(c), is that of a word processor in which the basic editing functions execute on the client side where they operate on locally cached, or in-memory data, but where the advanced support tools such as checking the spelling and grammar execute on the server side.

In many client-server environments, the organizations shown in Figure 2.17(d) and Figure 2.17(e) are particularly popular. These organizations are used where the client machine is a PC or workstation, connected through a network to a distributed file system or database. Essentially, most of the application is running on the client machine, but all operations on files or database entries go to the server. For example, many banking applications run on an end-user's machine, where the user prepares transactions and such. Once finished, the application contacts the database on the bank's server and uploads the transactions for further processing. Figure 2.17(e) represents the situation where the client's local disk contains part of the data. For example, when browsing the Web, a client can gradually build a huge cache on local disk of most recent inspected Web pages.

Note 2.5 (More information: Is there something like the best organization?)
We note that there has been a strong trend to move away from the configurations shown in Figure 2.17(d) and Figure 2.17(e) in those cases, that client software is placed at end-user machines. Instead, most of the processing and data storage is handled at the server side. The reason for this is simple: although client machines do a lot, they are also more problematic to manage. Having more functionality on the client machine means that a wide range of end users will need to be able to handle that software. This implies that more effort needs to be spent on making software resilient to end-user behavior. In addition, client-side software is dependent on the client's underlying platform (i.e., operating system and resources), which can easily mean that multiple versions will need to be maintained. From a systems-management perspective, having what are called **fat clients** is not optimal. Instead, the **thin clients** as represented by the organizations shown in Figure 2.17(a)–(c) are much easier, perhaps at the cost of less sophisticated user interfaces and client-perceived performance.

Does this mean the end of fat clients? Not in the least. For one thing, there are many applications for which a fat-client organization is often still the best. We already mentioned office suites, but also many multimedia applications require that processing is done on the client's side. Moreover, when end users need to operate offline, we see that installing applications will be necessary. Second, with the advent of advanced Web browsing technology, it is now much easier to dynamically place and manage client-side software by simply uploading (the sometimes very sophisticated) scripts to the client. Combined with the fact that this type of client-side software runs in well-defined commonly deployed environments, and thus that platform dependency is much less of an issue, we see that the counter-argument of management complexity is often no longer valid. This has led to the deployment of **virtual desktop environments**, which we discuss further in Chapter 3.

Finally, note that moving away from fat clients does not imply that we no longer need distributed systems. On the contrary, what we continue to see is that server-side solutions are becoming increasingly more distributed as a single server is being replaced by multiple servers running on different machines. Cloud computing is a good example in this case: the complete server side is being executed in data centers, and generally on multiple servers.

When distinguishing only client and server machines as we did so far, we miss the point that a server may sometimes need to act as a client, as shown in Figure 2.18, leading to a **(physically) three-tiered architecture**.

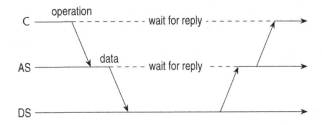

Figure 2.18: An example of an application server AS acting as client for a database server DS.

In this architecture, traditionally programs that form part of the processing layer are executed by a separate server, but may additionally be partly distributed across the client and server machines. A typical example of where a three-tiered architecture is used is in transaction processing. A separate process, called the transaction processing monitor, coordinates all transactions across possibly different data servers.

Another, but very different example where we often see a three-tiered architecture is in the organization of Websites. In this case, a Web server acts as an entry point to a site, passing requests to an application server where the actual processing takes place. This application server, in turn, interacts with a database server. We already came across such an organization when discussing this book's Website and the facilities for generating and downloading a personalized copy.

2.3.3 Example: The Network File System

Many distributed files systems are organized like client-server architectures, with Sun Microsystem's **Network File System (NFS)** being one of the most widely deployed ones for Unix systems [Callaghan, 2000; Haynes, 2015; Noveck and Lever, 2020].

The basic idea behind NFS is that each file server provides a standardized view of its local file system. In other words, it should not matter how that local file system is implemented; each NFS server supports the same model. This approach has been adopted for other distributed files systems as well. NFS comes with a communication protocol that allows clients to access the files stored on a server, thus allowing a heterogeneous collection of processes, possibly running on different operating systems and machines, to share a common file system.

The model underlying NFS and similar systems is that of a **remote file service**. In this model, clients are offered transparent access to a file system that is managed by a remote server. However, clients are normally unaware of the actual location of files. Instead, they are offered an interface to a file system that is similar to the interface offered by a conventional local file system. In particular, the client is offered only an interface containing various file operations, but the server is responsible for implementing those operations. This model is therefore also referred to as the **remote access model**. It is shown in Figure 2.19(a).

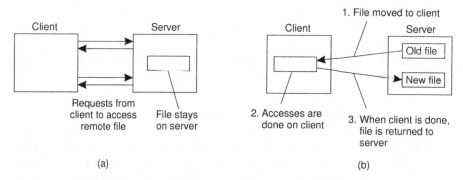

Figure 2.19: (a) The remote access model. (b) The upload/download model.

In contrast, in the **upload/download model** a client accesses a file locally after having downloaded it from the server, as shown in Figure 2.19(b) When the client is finished with the file, it is uploaded back to the server again so that it can be used by another client. The Internet's FTP service can be used this way when a client downloads a complete file, modifies it, and then puts it back.

NFS has been implemented for numerous operating systems, although the Unix versions are predominant. For virtually all modern Unix systems, NFS is generally implemented following the architecture shown in Figure 2.20.

A client accesses the file system using the system calls provided by its local operating system. However, the local Unix file system interface is replaced by an interface to the **Virtual File System** (**VFS**), which by now is a de facto standard for interfacing to different (distributed) file systems [Kleiman, 1986]. Virtually all modern operating systems provide VFS, and not doing so more or less forces developers to largely reimplement huge parts of an operating system when adopting a new file-system structure. With NFS, operations on the VFS interface are either passed to a local file system, or passed to a separate component known as the **NFS client**, which takes care of handling access to files stored at a remote server. In NFS, all client-server communication is done through so-called **remote procedure calls** (**RPCs**). As mentioned before, an RPC is essentially a standardized way to let a client on a machine A make an ordinary call to a procedure that is implemented on another machine B. We discuss RPCs extensively in Chapter 4. The NFS client implements the NFS file system operations as remote procedure calls to the server. Note that the operations offered by the VFS interface can be different from those offered by

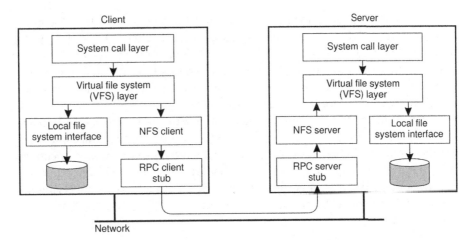

Figure 2.20: The basic NFS architecture for Unix systems.

the NFS client. The whole idea of the VFS is to hide the differences between various file systems.

On the server side, we see a similar organization. The **NFS server** is responsible for handling incoming client requests. The RPC component at the server converts incoming requests to regular VFS file operations that are subsequently passed to the VFS layer. Again, the VFS is responsible for implementing a local file system in which the actual files are stored.

An important advantage of this scheme is that NFS is largely independent of local file systems. It does not matter whether the operating system at the client or server uses a Unix file system, a Windows file system, or even an old MS-DOS file system. The only important issue is that these file systems are compliant with the file system model offered by NFS. For example, MS-DOS with its short file names cannot be used to implement an NFS server in a fully transparent way.

2.3.4   Example: The Web

The architecture of Web-based distributed systems is not fundamentally different from other distributed systems. However, it is interesting to see how the initial idea of supporting distributed documents has evolved since its inception in the 1990s. Documents turned from being purely static and passive to dynamically generated content. Furthermore, recently, many organizations have begun supporting services instead of just documents.

Simple Web-based systems

Many Web-based systems are still organized as relatively simple client-server architectures. The core of a Web site is formed by a process that has access to a local file system storing documents. The simplest way to refer to a document is by a reference called a **uniform resource locator (URL)**. It specifies where a document is located by embedding the DNS name of its associated server along with a file name by which the server can look up the document in its local file system. Furthermore, a URL specifies the application-level protocol for transferring the document across the network.

A client interacts with Web servers through a **browser**, which is responsible for properly displaying a document. Furthermore, a browser accepts input from a user mostly by letting the user select a reference to another document, which it then subsequently fetches and displays. The communication between a browser and Web server is standardized: they both adhere to the **HyperText Transfer Protocol (HTTP)**. This leads to the overall organization shown in Figure 2.21.

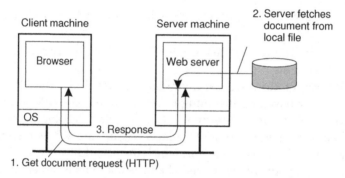

Figure 2.21: The overall organization of a traditional Web site.

Let us zoom in a bit into what a document actually is. Perhaps the simplest form is a standard text file. In that case, the server and browser have barely anything to do: the server copies the file from the local file system and transfers it to the browser. The latter, in turn, merely displays the content of the file ad verbatim without further ado.

More interesting are Web documents that have been marked up, which is usually done in the **HyperText Markup Language**, or simply **HTML**. In that case, the document includes various instructions expressing how its content should be displayed, similar to what one can expect from any decent word-processing system (although those instructions are normally hidden from the end user). For example, instructing text to be emphasized is done by the following markup:

```
<emph>Emphasize this text</emph>
```

There are many more of such markup instructions. The point is that the browser understands these instructions and will act accordingly when displaying the text.

Documents can contain much more than just markup instructions. In particular, they can have complete programs embedded, of which **JavaScript** is the one most often deployed. In this case, the browser is warned that there is some code to execute as in:

```
<script type="text/javascript">....</script>
```

and as long as the browser has an appropriate embedded interpreter for the specified language, everything between "`<script>`" and "`</script>`" will be executed as any other program. The main benefit of including scripts is that it allows for much better interaction with the end user, including sending information back to the server. (The latter, by the way, has always been supported in HTML through **forms**.)

Much more can be said about Web documents, but this is not the place to do so. A good introduction on how to build Web-based applications can be found in [Sebesta, 2015].

Multitiered architectures

The Web started out as the relatively simple two-tiered client-server system shown in Figure 2.21. By now, this simple architecture has been extended to support much more sophisticated means of documents. In fact, one could justifiably argue that the term "document" is no longer appropriate. For one, most things that we get to see in our browser has been generated on the spot as the result of sending a request to a Web server. Content is stored in a database at the server's side, along with client-side scripts and such, to be composed on-the-fly into a document which is then subsequently sent to the client's browser. Documents have thus become completely dynamic.

One of the first enhancements to the basic architecture was support for simple user interaction by the **Common Gateway Interface** or simply **CGI**. CGI defines a standard way by which a Web server can execute a program taking user data as input. Usually, user data come from an HTML form; it specifies the program that is to be executed at the server side, along with parameter values that are filled in by the user. Once the form has been completed, the program's name and collected parameter values are sent to the server, as shown in Figure 2.22.

When the server sees the request, it starts the program named in the request and passes it the parameter values. At that point, the program simply does its work and generally returns the results in the form of a document that is sent back to the user's browser to be displayed.

CGI programs can be as sophisticated as a developer wants. For example, as shown in Figure 2.22 many programs operate on a database local to the Web server. After processing the data, the program generates an HTML document and returns that document to the server. The server will then pass the document to the client. An interesting observation is that to the server,

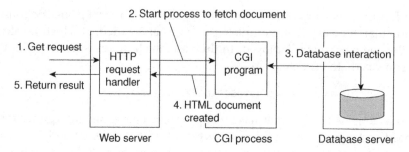

Figure 2.22: The principle of using server-side CGI programs.

it appears as if it is asking the CGI program to fetch a document. In other words, the server does nothing but delegate the fetching of a document to an external program.

The main task of a server used to be handling client requests by simply fetching documents. With CGI programs, fetching a document could be delegated in such a way that the server would remain unaware of whether a document had been generated on the fly, or actually read from the local file system. Note that we have just described a two-tiered organization of server-side software.

However, servers nowadays do much more than just fetching documents. One of the most important enhancements is that servers can also process a document before passing it to the client. In particular, a document may contain a **server-side script**, which is executed by the server when the document has been fetched locally. The result of executing a script is sent along with the rest of the document to the client. The script itself is not sent. In other words, using a server-side script changes a document by essentially replacing the script with the results of its execution. To make matters concrete, take a look at a simple example of dynamically generating a document. Assume a file is stored at the server with the following content:

```
<strong> <?php echo $_SERVER['REMOTE_ADDR']; ?> </strong>
```

The server will examine the file and subsequently process the PHP code (between "<?php" and "?>") replacing the code with the address of the requesting client. Much more sophisticated settings are possible, such as accessing a local database and subsequently fetching content from that database to be combined with other dynamically generated content.

2.4 Symmetrically distributed system architectures

Multitiered client-server architectures are a direct consequence of dividing distributed applications into a user interface, processing components, and data-management components. The different tiers correspond directly with the logical organization of applications. In many business environments, distributed processing is equivalent to organizing a client-server application as a multitiered architecture. We refer to this type of distribution as **vertical distribution**. The characteristic feature of vertical distribution is that it is achieved by placing logically different components on different machines. The term is related to the concept of *vertical fragmentation* as used in distributed relational databases, where it means that tables are split columnwise, and subsequently distributed across multiple machines [Özsu and Valduriez, 2020].

Again, from a systems-management perspective, having a vertical distribution can help: functions are logically and physically split across multiple machines, where each machine is tailored to a specific group of functions. However, vertical distribution is only one way of organizing client-server applications. In modern architectures, it is often the distribution of the clients and the servers that counts, which we refer to as **horizontal distribution**. In this type of distribution, a client or server may be physically split up into logically equivalent parts, but each part is operating on its own share of the complete data set, thus balancing the load. In this section, we will take a look at a class of modern system architectures that support horizontal distribution, known as **peer-to-peer systems**.

From a high-level perspective, the processes that constitute a peer-to-peer system are all equal. This means that the functions that need to be carried out are represented by every process that constitutes the distributed system. As a consequence, much of the interaction between processes is symmetric: each process will act as a client and a server at the same time (which is also referred to as acting as a **servant**).

Given this symmetric behavior, peer-to-peer architectures revolve around the question of how to organize the processes in an **overlay network** [Tarkoma, 2010]: a network in which the nodes are formed by the processes and the links represent the possible communication channels (which are often realized as TCP connections). A node may not be able to communicate directly with an arbitrary other node, but is required to send messages through the available communication channels. Two types of overlay networks exist: those that are structured and those that are not. These two types are surveyed extensively in Lua et al. [2005] along with numerous examples. Buford and Yu [2010] additionally includes an extensive list of various peer-to-peer systems. Aberer et al. [2005] provide a reference architecture that allows for a more formal comparison of the different types of peer-to-peer systems. A survey taken from the perspective of content distribution is provided by Androutsellis-Theotokis and Spinellis [2004]. Finally, Buford et al. [2009], Tarkoma [2010] and Vu et al. [2010] go beyond the level of surveys and form adequate textbooks for initial or further study.

2.4.1 Structured peer-to-peer systems

As its name suggests, in a **structured peer-to-peer system** the nodes (i.e.,
processes) are organized in an overlay that adheres to a specific, deterministic
topology: a ring, a binary tree, a grid, etc. This topology is used to efficiently
look up data. Characteristic for structured peer-to-peer systems, is that they
are generally based on using a so-called semantic-free index. What this means
is that each data item that is to be maintained by the system, is uniquely
associated with a key, and that this key is subsequently used as an index. To
this end, it is common to use a hash function so that we get:

$$key(data\ item) = hash(data\ item's\ value).$$

The peer-to-peer system as a whole is now responsible for storing (*key*,*value*)
pairs. To this end, each node is assigned an identifier from the same set
of all possible hash values, and each node is made responsible for storing
data associated with a specific subset of keys. In essence, the system is
thus seen to implement a **distributed hash table**, generally abbreviated to a
DHT [Balakrishnan et al., 2003].

   Following this approach now reduces the essence of structured peer-to-
peer systems to being able to look up a data item by its key. That is, the
system provides an efficient implementation of a function *lookup* that maps a
key to an *existing* node:

$$existing\ node = lookup(key).$$

This is where the topology of a structured peer-to-peer system plays a crucial
role. Any node can be asked to look up a given key, which then boils down to
efficiently *routing* that lookup request to the node responsible for storing the
data associated with the given key.

   To clarify these matters, let us consider a simple peer-to-peer system with
a *fixed* number of nodes, organized into a hypercube. A **hypercube** is an
n-dimensional cube. The hypercube shown in Figure 2.23 is four-dimensional.
It can be thought of as two ordinary cubes, each with 8 vertices and 12 edges.
To expand the hypercube to five dimensions, we would add another set of
two interconnected cubes to the figure, connect the corresponding edges in
the two halves, and so on.

   For this (admittedly naive) system, each data item is associated with one
of the 16 nodes. This can be achieved by hashing the value of a data item to a
key $k \in \{0, 1, 2, \ldots, 2^4 - 1\}$. Now suppose that the node with identifier 0111
is requested to look up the data having key 14, corresponding to the binary
value 1110. In this example, we assume that the node with identifier 1110 is
responsible for storing all data items that have key 14. What node 0111 can
simply do, is forward the request to a neighbor who is closer to node 1110. In
this case, this is either node 0110 or node 1111. If it picks a node 0110, that

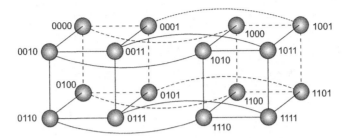

Figure 2.23: A simple peer-to-peer system organized as a four-dimensional hypercube.

node will then forward the request directly to a node 1110 from where the data can be retrieved.

Note 2.6 (Example: The Chord system)

The previous example illustrates two things: (1) the use of a hashing function to identify the node responsible for storing some data item, and (2) the routing along the topology of a peer-to-peer system when looking up a data item given its key. However, it is not a very realistic example, if only for the reason that we assumed that the total set of nodes is fixed. Let us therefore consider a more realistic example of a structured peer-to-peer system that is considered as belonging to the foundations for many other such systems.

In the **Chord system** [Stoica et al., 2003] the nodes are logically organized in a ring such that a data item with an m-bit key k is mapped to the node with the smallest (again, also m bit) identifier id $\geq k$. This node is referred to as the **successor** of key k and denoted as $succ(k)$. Keys and identifiers are typically 128 or 160 bits long. Figure 2.24 shows a much smaller Chord ring, where $m = 5$ and with nine nodes $\{1, 4, 9, 11, 14, 18, 20, 21, 28\}$. The successor of key 7 is equal to 9. Likewise, $succ(5) = 9$, but also $succ(9) = 9$. In Chord, each node maintains shortcuts to other nodes. A shortcut appears as a directed edge from one node to another. How these shortcuts are constructed is explained in Chapter 6. The construction is done in such a way that the length of the shortest path between any pair of nodes is of order $\mathcal{O}(\log N)$, where N is the total number of nodes.

To look up a key, a node will try to forward the request "as far as possible," but without passing it beyond the node responsible for that key. To clarify, suppose that in our example Chord ring, node 9 is asked to look up the node responsible for key 3 (which is node 4). Node 9 has four shortcuts: to nodes 11, 14, 18, and 28, respectively. As the node 28 is the farthest node 9 knows about and still preceding the one responsible for key 3, it will get the lookup request. Node 28 has three shortcuts: to nodes 1, 4, and 14, respectively. Note that node 28 has no knowledge about the existence of nodes between nodes 1 and 4. For this reason, the best what it can do is forward the request to the node 1. The latter knows that its successor in the ring is node 4, and thus that this is the node responsible for the key 3, to which it will subsequently forward the request.

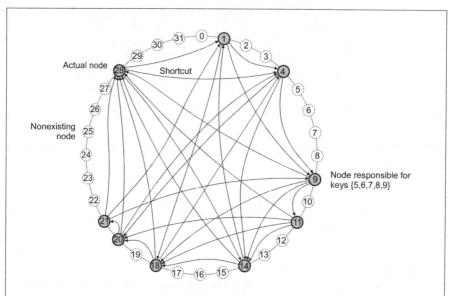

Figure 2.24: The organization of nodes and data items in Chord.

Now suppose that a node, with the unique identifier u, wants to join a Chord overlay. To that end, it contacts an arbitrary node and requests it to look up *u*, that is, return the value v= *succ(u)*. At that point, node u will simply need to insert itself between the predecessor of v and v itself, thus becoming the new predecessor of v. During this process, shortcuts from u to other nodes will be established, but also some existing ones previously directed toward v will now be adjusted to point to u (again, details are deferred until later chapters). Obviously, any data item with key *k* stored at v but for which *succ(k)* is now equal to u is transferred from v to u. Leaving is just as simple: node u informs its departure to its predecessor and successor, and transfers its data items to *succ(u)*.

We return to Chord in more detail in Section 6.2.3 when discussing the resolution of random bit strings to network addresses.

2.4.2   Unstructured peer-to-peer systems

Structured peer-to-peer systems attempt to maintain a specific, deterministic overlay network. In contrast, in an **u**nstructured peer-to-peer system, each node maintains an ad hoc list of neighbors. The resulting overlay resembles what is known as a **random graph**: a graph in which an edge $\langle u, v \rangle$ between two nodes u and v exists only with a certain probability $\mathbb{P}[\langle u, v \rangle]$. Ideally, this probability is the same for all pairs of nodes, but in practice a wide range of distributions is observed.

In an unstructured peer-to-peer system, when a node joins, it often contacts a well-known node to obtain a starting list of other peers in the system. This list can then be used to find more peers, and perhaps ignore others, and so on. In practice, a node generally changes its local list almost continuously. For example, a node may discover that a neighbor is no longer responsive and that it needs to be replaced. There may be other reasons, which we will describe shortly.

Unlike structured peer-to-peer systems, looking up data cannot follow a predetermined route when lists of neighbors are constructed in an ad hoc fashion. Instead, in an unstructured peer-to-peer systems, we really need to resort to *searching* for data [Risson and Moors, 2006]. Let us look at two extremes and consider the case in which we are requested to search for specific data (e.g., identified by keywords).

Flooding: In the case of **flooding**, an issuing node u simply passes a request for a data item to all its neighbors. A request will be ignored when its receiving node, say v, had seen it before. Otherwise, v searches locally for the requested data item. If v has the required data, it can either respond directly to the issuing node u, or send it back to the original forwarder, who will then return it to *its* original forwarder, and so on. If v does not have the requested data, it forwards the request to all of its own neighbors.

Obviously, flooding can be expensive, for which reason a request often has an associated **time-to-live** or **TTL** value, giving the maximum number of hops a request is allowed to be forwarded. Choosing the right TTL value is crucial: too small means that a request will stay close to the issuer and may thus not reach a node having the data. Too large incurs high communication costs.

As an alternative to setting TTL values, a node can also start a search with an initial TTL value of 1, meaning that it will first query only its neighbors. If no, or not enough results are returned, the TTL is increased, and a new search is initiated.

Random walks: At the other end of the search spectrum, an issuing node u can simply try to find a data item by asking a randomly chosen neighbor, say v. If v does not have the data, it forwards the request to one of its randomly chosen neighbors, and so on. The result is known as a **random walk** [Gkantsidis et al., 2006; Lv et al., 2002]. Obviously, a random walk imposes much less network traffic, yet it may take much longer before a node is reached that has the requested data. To decrease the waiting time, an issuer can simply start n random walks simultaneously. Indeed, studies show that in this case, the time it takes before reaching a node that has the data drops approximately by a factor n. Lv et al. [2002] reports that relatively small values of n, such as 16 or 64, turn out to be effective.

A random walk also needs to be stopped. To this end, we can either again use a TTL, or alternatively, when a node receives a lookup request, check with the issuer whether forwarding the request to another randomly selected neighbor is still needed.

Note that neither method relies on a specific comparison technique to decide when requested data has been found. For structured peer-to-peer systems, we assumed the use of keys for comparison; for the two approaches just described, any comparison technique would suffice.

Between flooding and random walks lie **policy-based search methods**. For example, a node may decide to keep track of peers who responded positively, effectively turning them into preferred neighbors for succeeding queries. Likewise, we may want to restrict flooding to fewer neighbors, but in any case give preference to neighbors having many neighbors themselves.

Note 2.7 (Advanced: Flooding versus random walks)

When giving the matter some thought, it may come as a surprise that people have even considered a random walk as an alternative way to search. At first instance, it would seem like a technique resembling the search for a needle in a haystack. However, we need to realize that in practice we are dealing with *replicated* data, and even for minimal replication factors and different replication distributions, studies show that deploying random walks is not only effective, it can also be much more efficient in comparison to flooding.

To see why, we closely follow the model described in Lv et al. [2002] and Cohen and Shenker [2002]. Assume there are a total of N nodes and that each data item is replicated across r randomly chosen nodes. A search consists of repeatedly selecting a node at random until the item is found. If $\mathbb{P}[k]$ is the probability that the item is found after k attempts, we have

$$\mathbb{P}[k] = \frac{r}{N}(1 - \frac{r}{N})^{k-1}.$$

Let the average search size S be the expected number of nodes that need to be probed before finding the requested data item:

$$S = \sum_{k=1}^{N} k \cdot \mathbb{P}[k] = \sum_{k=1}^{N} k \cdot \frac{r}{N}(1 - \frac{r}{N})^{k-1} \approx N/r \text{ for } 1 \ll r \leq N.$$

By simply replicating every data item to each node, $S = 1$ and it is clear that a random walk will always outperform flooding even for TTL values of 1. More realistically, however, is to assume that r/N is relatively low, such as 0.1%, meaning that the average search size would be approximately 1000 nodes.

To compare this to flooding, assume that each node, on average, forwards a request to d randomly selected neighbors. After one step, the request will have arrived at d nodes, each of who will forward it to another $d - 1$ nodes (assuming that the node from where the request came is skipped), and so on. In other words, after k steps, and considering that a node can receive the request more than once, we will have reached (at most) the following number of nodes:

$$R(k) = d(d - 1)^{k-1}$$

Various studies show that $R(k)$ is a good estimate for the actual number of nodes reached, as long as we have only a few number of flooding steps. Of these nodes, we can expect a fraction of r/N to have the requested data item, meaning that when $\frac{r}{N} \cdot R(k) \geq 1$, we will most likely have found a node that has the data item.

To illustrate, let $r/N = 0.001 = 0.1\%$, which means that $S \approx 1000$. With flooding to, on average, $d = 10$ neighbors, we would require at least 4 flooding steps, reaching some 7290 nodes, which is considerably more than the 1000 nodes required when using a random walk. Only with $d = 33$ will we need to contact approximately also 1000 nodes in $k = 2$ flooding steps and having $r/N \cdot R(k) \geq 1$.

The obvious drawback of deploying random walks, is that it may take much longer before an answer is returned.

2.4.3 Hierarchically organized peer-to-peer networks

Notably in unstructured peer-to-peer systems, locating relevant data items can become problematic as the network grows. The reason for this scalability problem is simple: as there is no deterministic way of routing a lookup request to a specific data item, essentially the only technique a node can resort to is *searching* for the request by flooding or randomly walking through the network. As an alternative, many peer-to-peer systems have proposed to make use of special nodes that maintain an index of data items.

There are other situations in which abandoning the symmetric nature of peer-to-peer systems is sensible. Consider a collaboration of nodes that offer resources to each other. For example, in a collaborative **Content Delivery Network** (CDN), nodes may offer storage for hosting copies of Web documents allowing Web clients to access pages nearby, and thus to access them quickly. What is needed is a means to find out where documents can be stored best. In that case, making use of a **broker** that collects data on resource usage and availability for several nodes that are in each other's proximity allows selecting a node quickly with sufficient resources.

Nodes such as those maintaining an index or acting as a broker are generally referred to as **super peers**. As the name suggests, super peers are often also organized in a peer-to-peer network, leading to a hierarchical organization, as explained in Yang and Garcia-Molina [2003]. A simple example of such an organization is shown in Figure 2.25. In this organization, every regular peer, now referred to as a **weak peer**, is connected as a client to a super peer. All communication from and to a weak peer proceeds through that peer's associated super peer.

Often, the association between a weak peer and its super peer is fixed: whenever a weak peer joins the network, it attaches to one of the super peers and remains attached until it leaves the network. Obviously, it is expected that super peers are long-lived processes with high availability. To compensate for potential unstable behavior of a super peer, backup schemes can be deployed,

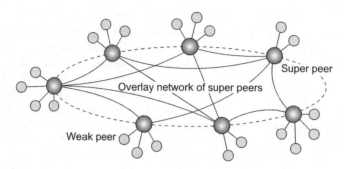

Figure 2.25: A hierarchical organization of nodes into a super-peer network.

such as pairing every super peer with another one and requiring weak peers to attach to both.

Having a fixed association with a super peer may not always be the best solution. For example, in the case of file-sharing networks, it may be better for a weak peer to attach to a super peer that maintains an index of files that the weak peer is currently interested in. In that case, chances are bigger that when a weak peer is looking for a specific file, its super peer will know where to find it. Garbacki et al. [2010] describe a relatively simple scheme in which the association between weak peer and strong peer can change as weak peers discover better super peers to associate with. In particular, a super peer returning the result of a lookup operation is given preference over other super peers.

As we have seen, peer-to-peer networks offer a flexible means for nodes to join and leave the network. However, with super-peer networks a new problem is introduced, namely how to select the nodes that are eligible to become super peer. This problem is closely related to the **leader-election problem**, which we discuss in Section 5.4.

2.4.4 Example: BitTorrent

Let us consider the widely popular **BitTorrent** file-sharing system [Cohen, 2003] as an example of a (largely) unstructured peer-to-peer system. BitTorrent is a file-downloading system. Its principle working is shown in Figure 2.26. The basic idea is that when an end user is looking for a file, she downloads chunks of the file from other users until the downloaded chunks can be assembled, yielding the complete file. An important design goal was to ensure collaboration. In most file-sharing systems, a significant fraction of participants merely download files but otherwise contribute close to nothing [Adar and Huberman, 2000; Saroiu et al., 2003; Yang et al., 2005], a phenomenon referred to as **free riding**. To prevent this situation, in BitTorrent a file can

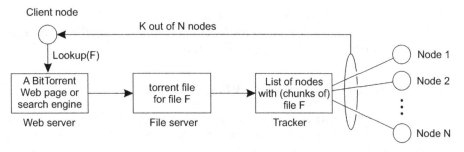

Figure 2.26: The principle working of BitTorrent [adapted with permission from Pouwelse et al. [2005].

be downloaded only when the downloading client is providing content to someone else.

To download a file, a user needs to access a global directory, which is generally just one of a few well-known Websites. Such a directory contains references to what are called torrent files. A **torrent file** contains the information that is needed to download a specific file. In particular, it contains a link to what is known as a **tracker**, which is a server that is keeping an accurate account of *active* nodes that have (chunks of) the requested file. An active node is one that is currently downloading the file as well. Obviously, there will be many trackers, although there will generally be only a single tracker per file (or collection of files).

Once the nodes have been identified from where chunks can be downloaded, the downloading node effectively becomes active. At that point, it will be forced to help others, for example by providing chunks of the file it is downloading that others do not yet have. This enforcement comes from a simple rule: if a node P notices that a node Q is downloading more than it is uploading, P can decide to decrease the rate at which it sends data to Q. This scheme works well, provided P has something to download from Q. For this reason, nodes are often supplied with references to many other nodes, putting them in a better position to trade data.

Clearly, BitTorrent combines centralized with decentralized solutions. As it turns out, the bottleneck of the system is easily formed by the trackers. In an alternative implementation of BitTorrent, a node also joins a separate structured peer-to-peer system (i.e., a DHT) to assist in tracking file downloads. In effect, a central tracker's load is now distributed across the participating nodes, with each node acting as a tracker for a relatively small set of torrent files. The original function of the tracker coordinating the collaborative downloading of a file is retained. However, we note that in many BitTorrent systems used today, the tracking functionality has actually been minimized to a one-time provisioning of peers currently involved in downloading the file. From that moment on, the newly participating peer will communicate only with those peers and no longer with the initial tracker. The initial tracker for the requested file is looked up in the DHT through a so-called **magnet link**. We return to DHT-based lookups in Section 6.2.3.

2.5 Hybrid system architectures

Real-world distributed systems are complex in the sense that they combine a myriad of architectures: centralized features are combined with peer-to-peer features are combined with hierarchical organizations, etc. The complexity is aggravated by the fact that many distributed systems cross organizational boundaries, leading to truly decentralized solutions in which even no single organization can take responsibility for a system's operation. In this section, we will take a closer look into these complex, hybrid system architectures.

2.5.1 Cloud computing

Organizations in charge of running data centers have been seeking ways for opening up their resources to customers. Eventually, this led to the concept of **utility computing** by which a customer could upload tasks to a data center and be charged on a per-resource basis. Utility computing formed the basis for what is now commonly referred to as **cloud computing**.

Following Vaquero et al. [2008], cloud computing is characterized by an easily usable and accessible pool of *virtualized* resources. Which and how resources are used can be configured dynamically, providing the basis for scalability: if more work needs to be done, a customer can simply acquire more resources. The link to utility computing is formed by the fact that cloud computing is generally based on a pay-per-use model in which guarantees are offered by customized **service-level agreements** (**SLAs**). Keeping it simple, clouds are organized into four layers, as shown in Figure 2.27.

Hardware: The lowest layer is formed by the means to manage the necessary hardware: processors, routers, but also power and cooling systems. It is generally implemented at data centers and contains the resources that customers normally never get to see directly.

Infrastructure: This is an important layer forming the backbone for most cloud computing platforms. It deploys virtualization techniques (discussed in Section 3.2) to provide customers an infrastructure consisting of virtual storage and computing resources. Indeed, nothing is what it seems: cloud computing evolves around allocating and managing virtual storage devices and virtual servers.

Platform: One could argue that the platform layer provides to a cloud-computing customer what an operating system provides to application developers, namely the means to easily develop and deploy applications that need to run in a cloud. In practice, an application developer is offered a vendor-specific API, which includes calls to uploading and executing a program in that vendor's cloud. In a sense, this is comparable to the Unix exec family of system calls, which take an executable file as a parameter and pass it to the operating system to be executed.

Furthermore, like operating systems, the platform layer provides higher-level abstractions for storage and such. For example, as we discussed, the **Amazon S3 storage system** [Murty, 2008; Culkin and Zazon, 2022] is offered to the application developer in the form of an API allowing (locally created) files to be organized and stored in **buckets**. By storing a file in a bucket, that file is automatically uploaded to the Amazon cloud.

Application: Actual applications run in this layer and are offered to users for further customization. Well-known examples include those found in office suites (text processors, spreadsheet applications, presentation applications, and so on). It is important to realize that these applications are again executed in the vendor's cloud. As before, they can be compared to the traditional suite of applications that are shipped when installing an operating system.

Cloud-computing providers offer these layers to their customers through various interfaces (including command-line tools, programming interfaces, and Web interfaces), leading to three different types of services:

- **Infrastructure-as-a-Service** (**IaaS**) covering the hardware and infrastructure layer.

- **Platform-as-a-Service** (**PaaS**) covering the platform layer.

- **Software-as-a-Service** (**SaaS**) in which their applications are covered.

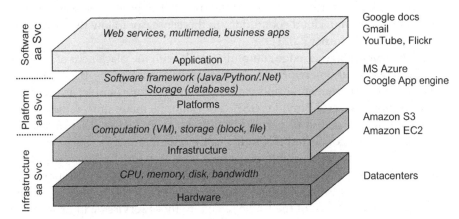

Figure 2.27: The organization of clouds (adapted from Zhang et al. [2010]).

As of now, making use of clouds is relatively easy, and we discuss in later chapters more concrete examples of interfaces to cloud providers. As a consequence, cloud computing as a means for outsourcing local computing infrastructures has become a serious option for many enterprises.

From the perspective of a system architecture, which deals with configuring (micro)services across some infrastructure, one may argue that in the case of cloud computing, we are dealing with a highly advanced client-server architecture. However, let it be noted that the actual implementation of a server is generally completely hidden from the client: it is often unclear *where* the server actually is, and even whether the server is actually implemented in a fully distributed manner (which it often is). To further illustrate this point, the notion of a **Function-as-a-Service**, or simply **Faas**, allows a client to execute code without bothering even with starting a server to handle the code (see also Shahrad et al. [2019]).

2.5.2   The edge-cloud architecture

In the advent of increasingly more network-connected devices and the emergence of the **Internet-of-Things (IoT)** many became aware of the fact that we may need more than just cloud computing. **Edge computing** was born. There is a lot to say about edge computing, and much has already been said. And as is the case with so many topics in distributed systems, it simply takes a few years before things settle down a bit. In this section, we take a look at edge computing from an architectural perspective and will return to various elements throughout the book, often without even explicitly mentioning edge computing. An excellent overview of edge computing is given by Yousefpour et al. [2019] and the interested reader is referred to that paper to get a better grip on its nomenclature. We deliberately take a simplified and broad view of edge computing, using it as a general term for most of the things sitting between the devices that comprise the Internet-of-Things and the services typically offered through cloud computing. In this sense, we follow the discussion as presented by Horner [2021].

As its name suggests, edge computing deals with the placement of services "at the edge" of the network. This edge is often formed by the boundary between enterprise networks and the actual Internet, for example, as provided by an **Internet Service Provider (ISP)**. For example, many universities reside on a campus consisting of various buildings, each having their own local network, in turn connected through a campuswide network. As part of the campus, there may be multiple on-premise services for storage, computing, security, lectures, and so on. On-premise means that the local IT department is responsible for hosting those services on servers directly hooked up to the campus network. Much of the traffic related to those services will never leave the campus network, and the network together with its servers and services form a typical **edge infrastructure**.

At the same time, such servers may be connected to those of other universities and perhaps even making use of, again, other servers. In other words, instead of setting up connections between universities in a peer-to-peer fashion, we also see configurations in which various universities share services through a logically centralized infrastructure. Such an infrastructure may be situated "in the cloud," but it may equally well have been set up through a regional infrastructure using locally available data centers. As we move closer to cloud infrastructures, the term **fog computing** is often used. We thus see an overall picture emerge as the one shown in Figure 2.28, where the boundaries between cloud and edge are becoming blurred.

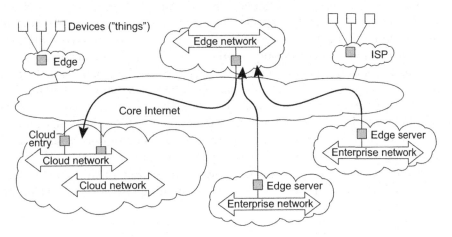

Figure 2.28: A collection of infrastructures involving edge devices, edge infrastructures and cloud infrastructures, and a possible setup between two enterprise edge infrastructures, an intermediate edge infrastructure, and a cloud infrastructure.

Many configurations for an edge infrastructure easily come to mind, ranging from infrastructures needed to keep track of your activities, layered video-streaming infrastructures, gaming infrastructures, etc. What all of these have in common is that there is some smart end device that one way or the other needs to (eventually) connect to a service hosted somewhere in the cloud. The question then pops up why an edge infrastructure is needed at all. Logically, it seems much simpler to just connect to the cloud service directly using existing and often excellent networking facilities. Let us take a critical look at a few arguments.

Latency and bandwidth What should have become clear from our examples is that edge infrastructures are considered to be close to the end devices. Closeness can be measured in terms of latency and often also bandwidth. Throughout the decades, bandwidth, or actually lack of bandwidth, has always been used as an argument for introducing solutions close to specific devices. However, if anything has become clear all this time, is that available bandwidth continues to increase, now reaching the point that one should seriously question how problematic it actually is, and whether installing and maintaining edge infrastructures for having insufficient bandwidth is a good reason. Nevertheless, there are situations in which closeness to end devices is actually needed to guarantee quality of service. The canonical example is formed by video services: the closer the video sources are, the better bandwidth guarantees can be given, reducing issues such as jitter.

More problematic is when Mother Nature gets in our way. This may easily happen when dealing with latency. It may take 100 ms to reach a cloud, rendering many interactive applications quite useless. One such important application is (semi-)autonomous driving. A car will need to continuously observe its environment through a myriad of sensors and react accordingly. Having to coordinate its movements through the cloud is not acceptable from a real-time aspect alone. This example also illustrates that cars may need to detect each other beyond the capabilities of their sensors, for example, when heading toward a junction with clear visibility. In a real-time system, cars may be able to provide their current position to a local edge infrastructure and reveal themselves to each other when approaching the junction.

Other examples in which latency plays a crucial role easily come to mind. Overcoming latency is one of the most compelling reasons for developing edge infrastructures.

Reliability   Many argue that cloud connectivity is simply not reliable enough for many applications, for which reason edge infrastructures should be deployed. To what extent this is a valid argument remains to be seen. The fact is that for many networked applications, connectivity is generally good and reliable, if not excellent. Of course, there are situations in which relying on 24/7 reliability is not an option. This may be the case for hospitals, factories, and other critical settings in general. Yet, in those cases, measures have been traditionally already taken and to what extent edge computing brings in anything new is not always clear.

Security and privacy   Finally, many argue that edge solutions enhance security and privacy. It all depends. One could argue that if a cloud solution is not secure, then there is no reason why an edge solution would be. An implicit assumption that many people make is that an edge infrastructure is owned by a specific organization and operates within the (protected) network boundaries of that organization. In that case, it often does indeed become simpler to protect data and operations, yet one should ask whether such protection is sufficient. As we shall discuss in Chapter 9, simply trying to protect assets by developing a secure wall around an organization does not help against insider attacks, whether they are intended or not. A same reasoning holds for privacy: if we cannot protect personal data in the cloud, then why would an edge infrastructure suffice for privacy? A thorough discussion on the role and position of privacy in the edge and edge devices is given by Hong [2017]. From that discussion, it is clear that there is still considerable work to be done.

However, there may be another reason related to security and privacy why edge infrastructures are needed. In many cases, organizations are simply not allowed, for whatever regulatory reasons, to place data in the cloud or have data be processed by a cloud service. For example, medical records may have to be kept on premise on certified servers and with strict audit procedures in place. In this case, an organization will have to resort to maintaining an edge infrastructure.

Introducing additional layers between end devices and cloud infrastructures opens a whole can of worms compared to the relatively simple situation of just having to deal with cloud computing. For the latter, one can argue that the cloud provider to a considerable extent decides where and how a service is actually implemented. In practice, we will be dealing with a data center in which the (micro)services that make up the entire service are distributed across multiple machines.

Matters become more intricate in the case of edge computing. In this case, the client organization will now have to make informed decisions on what to do where. Which services need to be placed on premise on a local edge infrastructure, and which can be moved to the cloud? To what extent does an edge infrastructure offer facilities for virtual resources, akin to the facilities offered in cloud computing? Moreover, where we may be able to assume that computational and storage resources are in abundance when dealing with a cloud, this is not necessarily the case for an edge infrastructure. In practice, the latter simply have less hardware resources available, but often also offer less flexibility in terms of available platforms.

By and large, allocating resources in the case of edge computing appears to be much more challenging in comparison to clouds. As summarized by Hong and Varghese [2019], we are dealing with limitations when it comes to resources, higher degrees of hardware heterogeneity, and much more dynamic workloads, which, when taken together, have led to a higher demand of **orchestration**. Moreover, where from a client's perspective the cloud appears to be hiding many of its internal intricacies, this is necessarily no longer the case, making it much more difficult to do the orchestration [Bittencourt et al., 2018]. Orchestration boils down to the following (see also Taleb et al. [2017]):

- **Resource allocation**: specific services require specific resources. The question is then to guarantee the availability of the resources required to perform a service. Typically, resources amount to CPU, storage, memory, and networking facilities.

- **Service placement**: regardless the availability of resources, it is important to decide *when* and *where* to place a service. This is notably relevant for mobile applications, for in that case finding the edge infrastructure that is closest to that application may be crucial. A typical use case is that of video conferencing, for which the encoding is often not done on the mobile device, but at an edge infrastructure. In practice, one needs to decide at which edges the service should be installed. An extensive overview of service placement in the case of edge computing is provided by Salaht et al. [2020].

- **Edge selection**: related to service placement is deciding which edge infrastructure should be used when the service needs to be offered. It may seem logical to use the edge infrastructure closest to the end device, but all kinds of circumstances may ask for an alternative solution, for example the connectivity of that edge to the cloud provider.

Other issues play a role as well, but it should be clear by now that the edge-cloud architecture is much more demanding than one might initially think it to be. Moreover, the different perspectives on how the continuum between end devices and the cloud should be filled with edge components and solutions has still to converge [Antonini et al., 2019].

2.5.3   Blockchain architectures

An upcoming and much debated type of distributed system is that of so-called **blockchains**. Blockchain systems enable the registration of transactions, for which reason they are also referred to as **distributed ledgers**. The latter is actually more accurate, with blockchains forming one of different ways for implementing distributed ledgers.

The key issue in transaction systems is that a transaction is validated, effectuated, and subsequently stored for various auditing purposes. For example, Alice may decide to create a transaction stating that she transfers $10 to Bob's account. Normally, she would go to a bank, where she would have to sign the transaction to prove that she really wants it to be carried out. Whether this all happens physically or digitally does not really matter. The bank will check whether she has enough credit, whether Bob is eligible for receiving the money, and assuming everything is fine, will subsequently transfer the money. A record of the transaction is kept for all kinds of auditing purposes. Note that transactions in blockchains systems are taken very broad. Besides monetary transactions, systems have been developed for registering identification documents, registering resource usage and allocation, electronic voting, and sharing health records, to name a few.

The bank operates as a **trusted third party**. An important design assumption for blockchains is that participating parties can, in principle, not be trusted. This also excludes having a trusted third party that handles all transactions. We will return to trust in Section 9.4, and concentrate on the implications lack of trust has for the architecture of a system.

In the case of blockchains, we assume there is a (potentially very large) set of participants who jointly register transactions among them in a publicly available ledger. In this way, any participant can see what has happened and also verify the validity of a transaction. For example, in a blockchain system for digital coins, each having a unique and unforgeable ID, any participant should be able to check whether a coin has already been spent by checking all transactions that have taken place since the beginning.

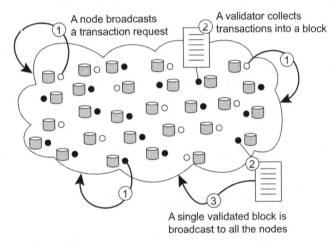

Figure 2.29: The principle operation of a blockchain.

To this end, when Alice wants to transfer $10 to Bob, she essentially tells all the participants in the blockchain system about this intent, thus allowing volunteers to validate the intended transaction. This is shown as Step 1 in Figure 2.29. To avoid having to check every transaction separately one-by-one as they are submitted, a validator groups several transactions into a block to increase efficiency, shown as Step 2 in Figure 2.29. If everything goes well, i.e., the transactions in the block are considered to be valid, the validator securely protects the block against any modifications, and appends the now immutable block to the chain of other blocks with validated transactions. It does so by broadcasting the validated block to all participants, shown as Step 3 in Figure 2.29.

An important observation is that there is logically only a single chain of blocks with validated transactions. Each block is immutable, in the sense that if an adversary decides to modify any transaction from any block in that chain, the modification can never go unnoticed. Securely protecting blocks of transactions against modifications, but also securely appending a block to an existing list, are well-understood techniques, which we will explain further in Section 9.4.3. The immutability of a block makes it an ideal fit for massive replication: it will never be changed anyway, so someone may just as well store it locally to make verification as simple as possible. Effectively, the logically single chain of immutable blocks may be physically massively replicated across the Internet among all participating parties. This is precisely what happens: each block is broadcast to every participating node in a blockchain, as we just explained.

What differentiates so many blockchain systems from each other is deciding on which node(s) may actually carry out validation tasks. In other words, we need to figure out who is allowed to append a block of validated transactions to the existing chain. Appending such a block means that there is global consensus on fulfilled transactions. It is therefore important that we also reach consensus on which validator can move ahead. All others will have to do their validation over again, as their transactions may be affected by the newly appended ones and thus may need to be revisited.

Deciding on which validator can move ahead requires **(distributed) consensus**. In principle, there are three options:

1. A centralized solution, in which a trusted third party validates transactions as before.

2. A distributed solution, in which a small, preselected group of processes takes over the role of a trusted third party.

3. A fully decentralized solution, in which, in principle, all participating nodes in the blockchain jointly reach consensus without any (distributed) third party.

These three options are shown in Figure 2.30. As mentioned, each node participating in the blockchain is assumed to have a full copy locally available.

Obviously, a centralized architecture for a blockchain does not fit its design goals, which state that there is essentially no place for a trusted third party. The distributed architecture is an interesting one. In this case, there is a relatively small group of nodes that are *permissioned* to validate transactions. For blockchains, it is important to realize that none of these permissioned nodes are assumed to be trusted, yet they are assumed to run a consensus protocol that can withstand malicious behavior. Specifically, if there are n permissioned nodes, then it is assumed that at most $k \leq (n-1)/3$ will fail and perhaps act maliciously. One problem with such so-called **permissioned blockchains** is that n is quite limited, in practice, to less than a few tens of nodes.

Finally, in so-called **permissionless blockchains** all nodes collectively participate to validate transactions. In practice, this means that all nodes who want to validate transactions are engaged in a process called **leader election**. The process elected as leader appends a block to the current chain (and is

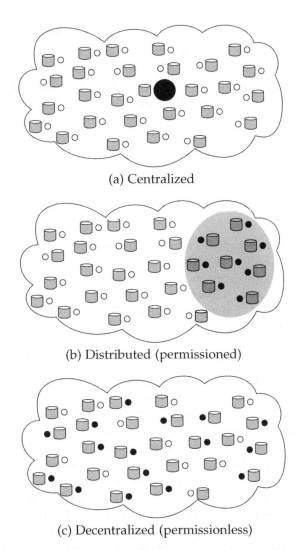

(a) Centralized

(b) Distributed (permissioned)

(c) Decentralized (permissionless)

Figure 2.30: The three different organizations of blockchains: (a) centralized, (b) distributed, (c) fully decentralized. Filled nodes represent validators; other nodes are participants not engaged in validation.

often rewarded for that). In practice, not all participating nodes will want to act as validator, if only because the leader-election algorithm is costly in terms of resources. We return to leader elections in Section 5.4.

The architecture of a blockchain system is thus seen to be quite complex. In a permissioned system, we have a few tens of nodes for validating transactions. None of these nodes needs to be individually trusted beforehand, yet it may be argued that they form a centralized, fault-tolerant distributed group. Trust is needed in so far that we need to assume that not too many of those nodes act maliciously or collude against any decisions they should make. On the other hand, permissionless blockchains may be viewed as being fully decentralized, but here we see that special measures are needed to guarantee some form of fairness among willing validators. In fact, through the dynamics of permissionless blockchains, we often see that, in practice, only a relatively few number of nodes can carry out validation tasks, effectively also leading to a more centralized system. An overview of the various settings in blockchains from the perspective of architectures is given by Xu et al. [2017].

2.6 Summary

Distributed systems can be organized in many ways. We can make a distinction between software architecture and system architecture. The latter considers where the components that constitute a distributed system are placed across the various machines. The former is more concerned about the logical organization of the software: how do components interact, in what ways can they be structured, how can they be made independent, and so on?

A keyword when talking about architectures is architectural style. A style reflects the basic principle that is followed in organizing the interaction between the software components comprising a distributed system. Important styles include layering, service-oriented styles, and styles in which handling events are prominent, exemplified by are known as publish-subscribe styles.

There are many organizations of distributed systems. An important class is where machines are divided into clients and servers. A client sends a request to a server, who will then produce a result that is returned to the client. The client-server architecture reflects the traditional way of modularizing software, in which a module calls the functions available in another module. By placing different components on different machines, we obtain a natural physical distribution of functions across a collection of machines.

Client-server architectures are often highly centralized. In decentralized architectures, we often see an equal role played by the processes that constitute a distributed system, also known as peer-to-peer systems. In peer-to-peer systems, the processes are organized into an overlay network, which is a logical network in which every process has a local list of other peers that it can communicate with. The overlay network can be structured, in which case deterministic schemes can be deployed for routing messages between processes. In unstructured networks, the list of peers is more or less random, implying that search algorithms need to be deployed for locating data or other processes.

In hybrid architectures, elements from centralized and decentralized organizations are combined. A typical example is that of cloud computing, which logically follows a client-server architecture, but where the server is generally completely distributed across a data center. In the last decade, we have seen a strong emergence of what is known as edge computing. Edge infrastructures form several steps between end devices and clouds and are demanding from the view point of organizing and configuring distributed systems. Finally, as an example in which decentralization plays a prominent role, the increasing popular blockchain architecture illustrates yet another class of hybrid system architectures.

03

PROCESSES

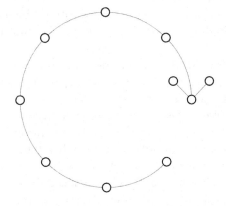

In this chapter, we take a closer look at how the different types of processes play a crucial role in distributed systems. The concept of a process originates from the field of operating systems, where it is generally defined as a program in execution. From an operating-system perspective, the management and scheduling of processes are perhaps the most important issues to deal with. However, when it comes to distributed systems, other issues turn out to be equally or more important.

We start with extensively discussing threads and their role in distributed systems. As it turns out, threads play a crucial role in obtaining performance in multicore and multiprocessor environments, but also help in structuring clients and servers. There are many cases where we see threads being replaced by processes and using the underlying operating system for guaranteeing protection and facilitating communication. Nevertheless, when performance is at stake, threads continue to play an important role.

Since a few years, the concept of virtualization has regained much popularity. Virtualization allows an application, and possibly also its complete environment including the operating system, to run concurrently with other applications, but highly independent of the underlying hardware and platforms, leading to a high degree of portability. Moreover, virtualization helps in isolating failures caused by errors or security problems. It is an important concept for distributed systems, and we pay attention to it in a separate section.

Client-server organizations are important in distributed systems. In this chapter, we take a closer look at typical organizations of both clients and servers. We also pay attention to general design issues for servers, including those typically used in object-based distributed systems. A widely used Web server is Apache, to which we pay separate attention. The organization of server clusters remains important, especially when they need to collaboratively provide the illusion of a single system. we will discuss examples of how to achieve this perspective, including wide-area servers like PlanetLab.

An important issue, especially in wide-area distributed systems, is moving processes between different machines. Process migration or more specifically, code migration, can help in achieving scalability, but can also help to configure clients and servers dynamically. What is actually meant by code migration and what its implications are is also discussed in this chapter.

3.1   Threads

Although processes form a building block in distributed systems, practice indicates that the granularity of processes as provided by the operating systems on which distributed systems are built is not sufficient. Instead, it turns out that having a finer granularity in the form of multiple threads of control per process makes it much easier to build distributed applications and to get better performance. In this section, we take a closer look at the role of threads in distributed systems and explain why they are so important. More on threads and how they can be used to build applications can be found in [Lewis and Berg, 1998; Stevens, 1999; Robbins and Robbins, 2003]. Herlihy and Shavit [2008] is highly recommended to learn more about multithreaded concurrent programming in general.

3.1.1 Introduction to threads

To understand the role of threads in distributed systems, it is important to understand what a process is, and how processes and threads relate. To execute a program, an operating system creates a number of **virtual processors**, each one for running a different program. To keep track of these virtual processors, the operating system has a **process table**, containing entries to store CPU register values, memory maps, open files, accounting information, privileges, etc. Jointly, these entries form a **process context**.

A process context can be viewed as the software analog of the hardware's **processor context**. The latter consists of the minimal information that is automatically stored by the hardware to handle an interrupt, and to later return to where the CPU left off. The processor context contains at least the program counter, but sometimes also other register values such as the stack pointer.

A **process** is often defined as a program in execution, that is, a program that is currently being executed on one of the operating system's virtual processors. An important issue is that the operating system takes great care to ensure that independent processes cannot maliciously or inadvertently affect the correctness of each other's behavior. In other words, the fact that multiple processes may be concurrently sharing the same CPU and other hardware resources is made transparent. Usually, the operating system requires hardware support to enforce this separation.

This concurrency transparency comes at a price. For example, each time a process is created, the operating system must create a complete independent address space. Allocation can mean initializing memory segments by, for example, zeroing a data segment, copying the associated program into a text segment, and setting up a stack for temporary data. Likewise, switching the CPU between two processes may require some effort as well. Apart from saving the data as currently stored in various registers (including the program counter and stack pointer), the operating system will also have to modify registers of the **Memory Management Unit** (**MMU**) and invalidate address translation caches, such as in the **Translation Lookaside Buffer** (**TLB**). In addition, if the operating system supports more processes than it can simultaneously hold in main memory, it may have to swap processes between main memory and disk before the actual switch can take place.

Like a process, a thread executes its own piece of code, independently of other threads. However, in contrast to processes, no attempt is made to achieve a high degree of concurrency transparency if this would result in performance degradation. Therefore, a thread system generally maintains only the minimum information to allow a CPU to be shared by several threads. In particular, a **thread context** often consists of nothing more than the processor context, along with some other information for thread management. For example, a thread system may keep track of the fact that a thread is currently blocked on a mutex variable, so as not to select it for execution. Information that is not strictly necessary to manage multiple threads is generally ignored. For this reason, protecting data against inappropriate access by threads within a single process is left entirely to application developers. We thus see that a processor context is contained in a thread context, and that, in turn, a thread context is contained in a process context.

There are two important implications of deploying threads, as we just sketched. First, the performance of a multithreaded application need hardly ever be worse than that of its single-threaded counterpart. In fact, often, multithreading even leads to a performance gain. Second, because threads are not automatically protected against each other the way processes are, development of multithreaded applications requires additional intellectual effort. Proper design and keeping things simple, as usual, help a lot. Unfortunately, current practice does not demonstrate that this principle is equally well understood.

Thread usage in nondistributed systems

Before discussing the role of threads in distributed systems, let us first consider their usage in traditional, nondistributed systems. There are several benefits to multithreaded processes that have increased the popularity of using thread systems.

The most important benefit comes from the fact that in a single-threaded process, whenever a blocking system call is executed, the process as a whole is blocked. To illustrate, consider an application such as a spreadsheet program, and assume that a user continuously and interactively wants to change values. An important property of a spreadsheet program is that it maintains the functional dependencies between different cells, often from different spreadsheets. Therefore, whenever a cell is modified, all dependent cells are automatically updated. When a user changes the value in a single cell, such a modification can trigger a large series of computations. If there is only a single thread of control, computation cannot proceed while the program is waiting for input. Likewise, it may be difficult to provide input while dependencies are being calculated. The easy solution is to have at least two threads of control: one for handling interaction with the user and one for updating the spreadsheet. Meanwhile, a third thread could be used for backing up the spreadsheet to disk while the other two are doing their work.

Another advantage of multithreading is that it becomes possible to exploit parallelism when executing the program on a multiprocessor or multicore system. In that case, each thread is assigned to a different CPU or core, while shared data are stored in shared main memory. When properly designed, such parallelism can be transparent: the process will run equally well on a uniprocessor system, albeit slower. Multithreading for parallelism is becoming increasingly important with the availability of relatively cheap multiprocessor and multicore computers. Such computer systems are typically used for running servers in client-server applications, but are by now also extensively used in devices such as smartphones.

Multithreading is also useful in the context of large applications Such applications are often developed as a collection of cooperating programs, each to be executed by a separate process. This approach is typical for a Unix environment. Cooperation between programs is implemented through **interprocess communication (IPC)** mechanisms. For Unix systems, these mechanisms typically include (named) pipes, message queues, and shared memory segments (see also Stevens and Rago [2005]). The major drawback of all IPC mechanisms is that communication often requires relatively extensive context switching, shown at three different points in Figure 3.1.

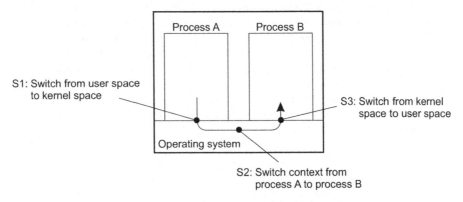

Figure 3.1: Context switching as the result of IPC.

Because IPC requires kernel intervention, a process will generally first have to switch from user mode to kernel mode, shown as $S1$ in Figure 3.1. This requires changing the memory map in the MMU, as well as flushing the TLB. Within the kernel, a process context switch takes place ($S2$ in the figure), after which the other party can be activated by switching from kernel mode to user mode again ($S3$ in Figure 3.1). The latter switch again requires changing the MMU map and flushing the TLB.

Instead of using processes, an application can also be constructed such that different parts are executed by separate threads. Communication between those parts is entirely dealt with by using shared data. Thread switching can sometimes be done entirely in user space, although in other implementations, the kernel is aware of threads and schedules them. The effect can be a dramatic improvement in performance.

Finally, there is also a pure software engineering reason to use threads: many applications are simply easier to structure as a collection of cooperating threads. Think of applications that need to perform several (more or less independent) tasks, like our spreadsheet example discussed previously.

Note 3.1 (Advanced: The cost of a context switch)

There have been many studies on measuring the performance effects of context switches. As in so many cases with measuring computer systems, finding the ground truth is not easy. Tsafrir [2007] notes that handling clock ticks has become more or less ubiquitous in operating systems, making it an excellent candidate to measure overheads. A clock handler is activated once every T milliseconds by a clock interrupt. Common values for T range between 0.5 and 20 milliseconds, corresponding to interrupt frequencies of 2000 Hz and 50 Hz, respectively. The handler typically assists in realizing various timing and CPU usage services, sends alarm signals, and assists in preempting running tasks for fair CPU sharing. By simply varying the frequency by which the hardware generates an interrupt, one can easily get an impression of the incurred overhead.

To measure the performance effects of an interrupt, a distinction is made between **direct overhead** and **indirect overhead**. The direct overhead consists of the time it takes to do the actual context switch, along with the time it takes for the handler to do its work and subsequently switching back to the interrupted task. The indirect overhead is everything else, and is mainly caused by cache perturbations (to which we will return shortly). For various Intel processors, Tsafrir [2007] found that the time to switch context is in the order of 0.5–1 microsecond, and that the handler itself takes in the order of 0.5–7 microseconds to do its work, depending strongly on the implementation.

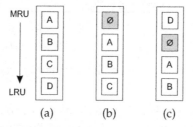

Figure 3.2: The organization of the cache when dealing with interrupts: (a) before the context switch, (b) after the context switch, and (c) after accessing block D. (Adapted from Liu and Solihin [2010].)

However, it turns out that the direct overhead is not really that influential. In a complimentary study, Liu and Solihin [2010] make clear that context switching can greatly perturbate the cache, resulting in a loss of performance in comparison to the situation before an interrupt occurred. In fact, for the simple case of clock

---

interrupts, Tsafrir [2007] measured an indirect overhead of approximately 80%. To understand what is going on, consider the data organizations as sketched in Figure 3.2. Assume the cache is organized such that a least-recently used block of data is removed from the cache when room is needed for a fresh data block.

Figure 3.2(a) shows the situation before the interrupt occurs. After the interrupt has been handled, block D may have been evicted from the cache, leaving a hole as shown in Figure 3.2(b). Accessing block D will copy it back into the cache, possibly evicting block C, and so on. In other words, even a simple interrupt may cause a considerable, and relatively long-lasting reorganization of the cache, in turn, affecting the overall performance of an application.

```
1  from multiprocessing import Process
2  from time import *
3  from random import *
4
5  def sleeper(name):
6      t = gmtime()
7      s = randint(1,20)
8      txt = str(t.tm_min)+':'+str(t.tm_sec)+' '+name+' is going to sleep for '+str(s)+' seconds'
9      print(txt)
10     sleep(s)
11     t = gmtime()
12     txt = str(t.tm_min)+':'+str(t.tm_sec)+' '+name+' has woken up'
13     print(txt)
14
15 if __name__ == '__main__':
16     p = Process(target=sleeper, args=('eve',))
17     q = Process(target=sleeper, args=('bob',))
18     p.start(); q.start()
19     p.join(); q.join()
```

(a)

```
40:23 eve is going to sleep for 14 seconds
40:23 bob is going to sleep for 4 seconds
40:27 bob has woken up
40:37 eve has woken up
```

(b)

Figure 3.3: (a) A simple example in which two processes are started, and (b) the output after a run.

A simple example in Python

To make matters more concrete, let us look at a simple example in Python, also to illustrate the differences between processes and threads. Consider the code shown in Figure 3.3(a), which shows how we start to separate processes

in Python using the multiprocessing package. The core of the example is
formed by the function sleeping which simply puts the calling process to
sleep for a randomly chosen number of seconds.

```
 1  from multiprocessing import Process
 2  from threading import Thread
 3
 4  shared_x = random.randint(10,99)
 5
 6  def sleeping(name):
 7      global shared_x
 8      s = randint(1,20)
 9      sleep(s)
10      shared_x = shared_x + 1
11
12  def sleeper(name):
13      sleeplist = list()
14      for i in range(3):
15          subsleeper = Thread(target=sleeping, args=(name+' '+str(i),))
16          sleeplist.append(subsleeper)
17
18      for s in sleeplist: s.start()
19      for s in sleeplist: s.join()
```

(a)

```
eve sees shared x being 71
53:21 eve 0 is going to sleep for 20 seconds
bob sees shared x being 84
53:21 eve 1 is going to sleep for 15 seconds
53:21 eve 2 is going to sleep for 3 seconds
53:21 bob 0 is going to sleep for 8 seconds
53:21 bob 1 is going to sleep for 16 seconds
53:21 bob 2 is going to sleep for 8 seconds
53:24 eve 2 has woken up, seeing shared x being 72
53:29 bob 0 has woken up, seeing shared x being 85
53:29 bob 2 has woken up, seeing shared x being 86
53:36 eve 1 has woken up, seeing shared x being 73
53:37 bob 1 has woken up, seeing shared x being 87
bob sees shared x being 87
53:41 eve 0 has woken up, seeing shared x being 74
eve sees shared x being 74
```

(b)

Figure 3.4: (a) A multithreading example in which two processes are started,
each with three threads, and (b) the output after a run.

To create two processes, we call the operation Process in lines 16 and 17,
respectively, to subsequently start each of them. The join operation tells the

main process to wait until the newly created processes have finished. A possible output is shown in Figure 3.3(b), indicating the time in "minutes:seconds" format when each process outputs some text.

The differences between threads and processes can be observed when we extend our example as shown in Figure 3.4 (where we have left out many statements for recording time and printing text). In this case, we again start two processes, named eve and bob (the code is the same as lines 15–19 in Figure 3.3 and has been omitted for clarity). Each process subsequently starts three threads, each, in turn, executing the function sleeping. The main difference is that there is now a shared variable shared_x. (To keep matters simple, we incorrectly assume that the assignment in line 10 is atomic. We explain atomic operations in detail in Chapter 5). What the output in Figure 3.4 shows is that this is a variable shared among the threads in a single process, but *not* shared between the two processes eve and bob. In other words, each *process* has its own instance of shared_x.

The output also shows that the sleep operation works at the thread level as well as the process level. In this case, each thread is suspended for a few seconds, yet the process hosting that thread is not blocked when sleep is called. Instead, another thread is scheduled (who subsequently also calls sleep). How this has been implemented is transparent to the programmer. Likewise, it is also transparent to what extent different threads are executed on different cores, if available, of the used CPU. If we had started 1000 threads per process, we would still see accurate timing. However, if we would replace the call to sleep with a busy waiting loop, such as in:

```
c = s * 26000000
for i in range(c):
    x = x + 1.0
```

we would see that the thread execution may be completely serialized *per process*, whereas each process would be assigned to a separate core and thus run in parallel. What exactly is done, depends on the underlying operating system and the used Python runtime system. The standard implementations of Python assign all threads within a single process to just one core.

Thread implementation

Threads are often provided in the form of a thread package. Such a package contains operations to create and destroy threads, as well as operations on synchronization variables such as mutexes and condition variables. There are basically two approaches to implement a thread package. The first approach is to construct a thread library that is executed entirely in user space. The second approach is to have the kernel be aware of threads and schedule them.

A user-level thread library has several advantages. First, it is cheap to create and destroy threads. Because all thread administration is kept in the user's address space, the price of creating a thread is primarily determined by the cost for allocating memory to set up a thread stack. Analogously, destroying a thread mainly involves freeing memory for the stack, which is no longer used. Both operations are cheap.

A second advantage of user-level threads is that switching thread context can often be done in just a few instructions. Basically, only the values of the CPU registers need to be stored and subsequently reloaded with the previously stored values of the thread to which it is being switched. There is no need to change memory maps, flush the TLB, do CPU accounting, and so on. Switching thread context is done when two threads need to synchronize, for example, when entering a section of shared data. However, as discussed in Note 3.1, much of the overhead of context switching is caused by perturbing memory caches.

A major drawback of user-level threads comes from deploying the **many-to-one threading model**: multiple threads are mapped to a single schedulable entity. We already saw this with our simple multithreaded Python example in Figure 3.4. As a consequence, the invocation of a blocking system call will immediately block the entire process to which the thread belongs, and thus also all the other threads in that process. As we explained, threads are particularly useful to structure large applications into parts that could be logically executed at the same time. In that case, blocking on I/O should not prevent other parts to be executed in the meantime. For such applications, user-level threads are of no help.

These problems can be mostly circumvented by implementing threads in the operating system's kernel, leading to what is known as the **one-to-one threading model** in which every thread is a schedulable entity. The price to pay is that every thread operation (creation, deletion, synchronization, etc.), will have to be carried out by the kernel, requiring a system call. Switching thread contexts may now become as expensive as switching process contexts. However, because the performance of context switching is generally dictated by ineffective use of memory caches, and not by the distinction between the many-to-one or one-to-one threading model, many operating systems now offer the latter model, if only for its simplicity.

Note 3.2 (Advanced: Many-to-many threading model)
An alternative to the two threading extremes is a hybrid form of user-level and kernel-level threads, a so-called **many-to-many threading model**. In the following, we simplify our terminology and speak of user threads and kernel threads. A kernel thread runs in the context of a single process, and there can be several kernel threads per process. In addition to managing kernel threads, a runtime system also offers a user-level thread package, offering applications the usual operations for creating and destroying threads. In addition, the package provides facilities for thread synchronization, such as mutexes and condition variables. The

important issue is that the thread package is implemented entirely in user space: all operations on threads are carried out without intervention of the kernel.

The thread package can be shared by multiple kernel threads, as shown in Figure 3.5. This means that each kernel thread can be running its own (user level) thread. Multithreaded applications are constructed by creating user and kernel threads, and subsequently assigning each user thread to a kernel thread.

The combination of user threads and kernel threads works as follows. The thread package has a single routine to schedule the next thread. When creating a kernel thread (which is done through a system call), the kernel thread is given its own stack, and is instructed to execute the scheduling routine searching for a user thread to execute. If there are several kernel threads, then each of them executes the scheduler. The thread table, which is used to keep track of the current set of threads, is thus shared by the kernel threads. Protecting this table to guarantee mutually exclusive access is done through mutexes that are implemented entirely in user space. In other words, synchronization between kernel threads does not require any kernel support. A thread table is often implemented as a ready queue.

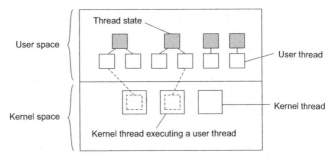

Figure 3.5: Combining kernel-level and user-level threads.

When a kernel thread finds a runnable user thread, it switches context to that thread. Meanwhile, other kernel threads may be looking for other runnable user threads as well. If a user thread needs to block on a mutex or condition variable, it does the necessary administration and eventually calls the scheduling routine. When another runnable user thread has been found, a context switch is made to that thread. The beauty of all this is that the kernel thread executing the user thread need not be informed: the context switch is implemented completely in user space and appears to the kernel thread as normal program code.

Now let us see what happens when a user thread does a blocking system call. In that case, execution changes from user mode to kernel mode, but still continues in the context of the current kernel thread. At the point where the current kernel thread can no longer continue, the operating system may decide to switch context to another kernel thread, which also implies that a context switch is made back to user mode. The selected kernel thread will simply continue where it had previously left off.

There are several advantages to using kernel threads with a user-level thread package. First, creating, destroying, and synchronizing threads is relatively cheap and involves no kernel intervention at all. Second, provided that a process has enough kernel threads, a blocking system call will not suspend the entire process. Third, there is no need for an application to know about the kernel threads. All it sees are user threads. Fourth, kernel threads can be easily used in multiprocessing environments by executing different kernel threads on different CPUs or different cores. This multiprocessing can be hidden entirely from the application.

The approach just sketched is actually the general form of combining user and kernel threads. This approach has been implemented in the Go programming language [Donovan and Kernighan, 2015]. The libfibre runtime system described and evaluated by Karsten and Barghi [2020] is also exemplary for the many-to-many threading model. A slightly different approach can be found in Arachne [Qin et al., 2018]. Arachne hides the kernel threads from applications, but instead assumes that an application can get full insight in the cores that have been assigned. It assigns one kernel thread per allocated core. An important consequence is that Arachne does not provide support for blocking I/O calls.

As a final note, it is important to realize that using threads is one way of organizing simultaneous and concurrent executions within an application. In practice, we often see that applications are constructed as a collection of concurrent *processes*, jointly making use of the interprocess facilities offered by an operating system (see also [Robbins and Robbins, 2003; Stevens, 1999]). A good example of this approach is the organization of the Apache Web server, which, by default, starts with a handful of processes for handling incoming requests. Each process forms a single-threaded instantiation of the server, yet is capable of communicating with other instances through standard means.

As argued by Srinivasan [2010], using processes instead of threads has the important advantage of separating the data space: each process works on its own part of data and is protected from interference from others through the operating system. The advantage of this separation should not be underestimated: thread programming is considered to be notoriously difficult because the developer is fully responsible for managing concurrent access to shared data. Using processes, data spaces, in the end, are protected by hardware support. If a process attempts to access data outside its allocated memory, the hardware will raise an exception, which is then further processed by the operating system. No such support is available for threads concurrently operating within the same process.

3.1.2 Threads in distributed systems

An important property of threads is that they can provide a convenient means of allowing blocking system calls without blocking the entire process in which the thread is running (assuming we do not have a **many-to-one threading model**). This property makes threads particularly attractive to use in distributed systems, as it makes it much easier to express communication in the form of maintaining multiple logical connections at the same time. We illustrate this point by taking a closer look at multithreaded clients and servers, respectively.

Multithreaded clients

To establish a high degree of distribution transparency, distributed systems that operate in wide-area networks may need to conceal long interprocess message propagation times. The round-trip delay in a wide-area network can easily be in the order of hundreds of milliseconds, or sometimes even seconds.

The usual way to hide communication latencies is to initiate communication and immediately proceed with something else. A typical example where this happens is in Web browsers. Often, a Web document consists of an HTML file containing plain text along with a collection of images, icons, etc. To fetch each element of a Web document, the browser has to set up a TCP/IP connection, read the incoming data, and pass it to a display component. Setting up a connection as well as reading incoming data are inherently blocking operations. When dealing with long-haul communication, we also have the disadvantage that the time for each operation to complete may be long.

A Web browser often starts with fetching the HTML page and subsequently displays it. To hide communication latencies as much as possible, some browsers start displaying data while it is still coming in. While the text is made available to the user, including the facilities for scrolling and such, the browser continues with fetching other files that make up the page, such as the images. The latter are displayed as they are brought in. The user need thus not wait until all the components of the entire page are fetched before the page is made available.

In effect, it is seen that the Web browser is doing several tasks simultaneously. As it turns out, developing the browser as a multithreaded client simplifies matters considerably. As soon as the main HTML file has been fetched, separate threads can be activated to take care of fetching the other parts. Each thread sets up a separate connection to the server and pulls in the data. Setting up a connection and reading data from the server can be programmed using the standard (blocking) system calls, assuming that a blocking call does not suspend the entire process. As is also illustrated in [Stevens, 1998], the code for each thread is the same and, above all, simple. Meanwhile, the user notices only delays in the display of images and such, but can otherwise browse through the document.

There is another important benefit to using multithreaded Web browsers, in which several connections can be opened simultaneously. In the previous example, several connections were set up to the same server. If that server is heavily loaded, or just plain slow, no real performance improvements will be noticed compared to pulling in the files that make up the page strictly one after the other.

However, often, Web servers have been replicated across multiple machines, where each server provides the same set of Web documents. The replicated servers are located at the same site, and are known under the same name. When a request for a Web page comes in, the request is forwarded to one of the servers, often using a round-robin strategy or some other load-balancing technique. When using a multithreaded client, connections may be set up to different replicas, allowing data to be transferred in parallel, effectively establishing that the entire Web document is fully displayed in a much shorter time than with a nonreplicated server. This approach is possible only if the client can handle truly parallel streams of incoming data. Threads are ideal for this purpose.

Note 3.3 (Advanced: Exploiting client-side threads for performance)

Although there are obvious opportunities for using threads to reach high performance, it is interesting to see whether multithreading is effectively exploited. In a study to see to what extent multiple threads put a multicore processor to work, Blake et al. [2010] looked at the execution of various applications on modern architectures. Browsers, like many other client-side applications, are interactive innately, for which reason the expected processor idle time may be quite high. To properly measure to what extent a multicore processor is being used, Blake et al. used a metric known as **thread-level parallelism** (**TLP**). Let c_i denote the fraction of time that exactly i threads are being executed simultaneously. Thread-level parallelism is then defined as:

$$TLP = \frac{\sum_{i=1}^{N} i \cdot c_i}{1 - c_0}$$

where N is the maximum number of threads that (can) execute at the same time. In their study, a typical Web browser at that time had a TLP value between 1.5 and 2.5, meaning that to effectively exploit parallelism, the client machine should have two or three cores, or likewise, 2–3 processors.

These results are interesting when considering that modern Web browsers create hundreds of threads, and that tens of threads are active at the same time (note that an active thread is not necessarily running; it may be blocked waiting for an I/O request to complete). We thus see that multithreading is used to organize an application, but that this multithreading is not leading to dramatic performance improvements through hardware exploitation. That browsers can be effectively designed for exploiting parallelism is shown, for example, by Meyerovich and Bodik [2010]. By adapting existing algorithms, the authors manage to establish several-fold speedups.

Multithreaded servers

Although there are important benefits to multithreaded clients, the main use of multithreading in distributed systems is found at the server side. Practice shows that multithreading not only simplifies server code considerably, but also makes it much easier to develop servers that exploit parallelism to attain high performance, even on uniprocessor systems. However, with modern multicore processors, multithreading for parallelism is an obvious path to follow.

To understand the benefits of threads for writing server code, consider the organization of a file server that occasionally has to block waiting for the disk. The file server normally waits for an incoming request for a file operation, subsequently carries out the request, and then sends back the reply. One possible, and particularly popular, organization is shown in Figure 3.6. Here, one thread, the **dispatcher**, reads incoming requests for a file operation. The requests are sent by clients to a well-known end point for this server. After examining the request, the server chooses an idle (i.e., blocked) **worker thread** and hands it the request.

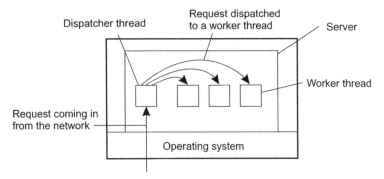

Figure 3.6: A multithreaded server organized in a dispatcher/worker model.

The worker proceeds by performing a blocking read on the *local* file system, which may cause the thread to be suspended until the data are fetched from disk. If the thread is suspended, another thread is selected to be executed. For example, the dispatcher may be selected to acquire more work. Alternatively, another worker thread can be selected that is now ready to run.

Now consider how the file server might have been written without threads. One possibility is to have it operate as a single thread. The main loop of the file server gets a request, examines it, and carries it out to completion before getting the next one. While waiting for the disk, the server is idle and does not process any other requests. Consequently, requests from other clients cannot be handled. In addition, if the file server is running on a dedicated machine, as is commonly the case, the CPU is simply idle while the file server is waiting for the disk. The net result is that many fewer requests per time unit can be processed. Thus threads gain considerable performance, but each thread is programmed sequentially, in the usual way.

So far, we have seen two possible designs: a multithreaded file server and a single-threaded file server. A third alternative is to run the server as a big single-threaded finite-state machine. When a request comes in, the one and only thread examines it. If it can be satisfied from the in-memory cache, fine, but if not, the thread must access the disk. However, instead of issuing a blocking disk operation, the thread schedules an asynchronous (i.e., nonblocking) disk operation for which it will be later interrupted by the operating system. To make this work, the thread will record the status of the request (namely, that it has a pending disk operation), and continues to see if there were any other incoming requests that require its attention.

Once a pending disk operation has been completed, the operating system will notify the thread, who will then, in due time, look up the status of the associated request and continue processing it. Eventually, a response will be sent to the originating client, again using a nonblocking call to send a message over the network.

In this design, the "sequential process" model that we had in the first two cases is lost. Every time the thread needs to do a blocking operation, it needs to record exactly where it was in processing the request, possibly also storing additional state. Once that has been done, it can start the operation and continue with other work. Other work means processing newly arrived requests, or post-processing requests for which a previously started operation has completed. Of course, if there is no work to be done, the thread may indeed block. In effect, we are simulating the behavior of multiple threads and their respective stacks the hard way. The process is being operated as a finite-state machine that gets an event and then reacts to it, depending on what is in it.

Model	Characteristics
Multithreading	Parallelism, blocking system calls
Single-threaded process	No parallelism, blocking system calls
Finite-state machine	Parallelism, nonblocking system calls

Figure 3.7: Three ways to construct a server.

It should now be clear what threads have to offer. They make it possible to retain the idea of sequential processes that make blocking system calls and still achieve parallelism. Blocking system calls make programming easier as they appear as just normal procedure calls. In addition, multiple threads allow for parallelism and thus performance improvement. The single-threaded server retains the ease and simplicity of blocking system calls, but may severely hinder performance in terms of number of requests that can be handled per time unit. The finite-state machine approach achieves high performance through parallelism, but uses nonblocking calls, which are generally hard to program and thus to maintain. These models are summarized in Figure 3.7.

Again, note that instead of using threads, we can also use multiple processes to organize a server (leading to the situation that we actually have a multiprocess server). The advantage is that the operating system can offer more protection against accidental access to shared data. However, if processes need to communicate a lot, we may see a noticeable adverse effect on performance in comparison to using threads.

3.2 Virtualization

Threads and processes can be seen as a way to do more things at the same time. In effect, they allow us to build (pieces of) programs that appear to be executed simultaneously. On a single-processor (single core) computer, this simultaneous execution is, of course, an illusion. As there is only a single CPU, only an instruction from a single thread or process will be executed at a time. By rapidly switching between threads and processes, the illusion of parallelism is created.

This separation between having a single CPU and being able to pretend there are more can be extended to other resources as well, leading to what is known as **resource virtualization**. This virtualization has been applied for many decades, but has received renewed interest as (distributed) computer systems have become more commonplace and complex, leading to the situation that application software is mostly always outliving its underlying systems software and hardware.

3.2.1 Principle of virtualization

In practice, every (distributed) computer system offers a programming interface to higher-level software, as shown in Figure 3.8(a). There are many types of interfaces, ranging from the basic instruction set as offered by a CPU to the vast collection of application programming interfaces that are shipped with many current middleware systems. In its essence, **virtualization** deals with extending or replacing an existing interface to mimic the behavior of another system, as shown in Figure 3.8(b). We will come to discuss technical details on virtualization shortly, but let us first concentrate on why virtualization is important.

Virtualization and distributed systems

One of the most important reasons for introducing virtualization, back in the 1970s, was to allow legacy software to run on expensive mainframe hardware. The software not only included various applications, but in fact also the operating systems they were developed for. This approach toward supporting legacy software has been successfully applied on the IBM 370 mainframes (and

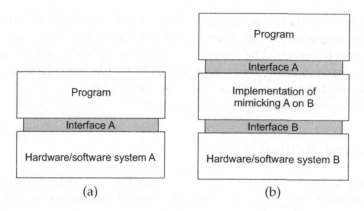

Figure 3.8: (a) General organization between a program, interface, and system. (b) General organization of virtualizing system A on top of B.

their successors) that offered a virtual machine to which different operating systems had been ported.

As hardware became cheaper, computers became more powerful, and the number of different operating system flavors was reducing, virtualization became less of an issue. However, matters have changed again since the late 1990s. First, while hardware and low-level systems software change reasonably fast, software at higher levels of abstraction (e.g., middleware and applications), are often much more stable. In other words, we are facing the situation that legacy software cannot be maintained in the same pace as the platforms it relies on. Virtualization can help here by porting the legacy interfaces to the new platforms, and thus immediately opening up the latter for large classes of existing programs.

Equally important is the fact that networking has become completely pervasive. It is hard to imagine that a modern computer is not connected to a network. In practice, this connectivity requires that system administrators maintain a large and heterogeneous collection of server computers, each one running very different applications, which can be accessed by clients. At the same time, the various resources should be easily accessible to these applications. Virtualization can help a lot: the diversity of platforms and machines can be reduced by essentially letting each application run on its own virtual machine, possibly including the related libraries *and* operating system, which, in turn, run on a common platform.

This last type of virtualization provides a high degree of portability and flexibility. For example, in order to realize content delivery networks that can easily support replication of dynamic content, Awadallah and Rosenblum [2002] have argued that management becomes much easier if edge servers would support virtualization, allowing a complete site, including its environment, to be dynamically copied. These arguments are still valid, and indeed, portability is perhaps the most important reason why virtualization plays such a key role in many distributed systems.

Finally, an important reason for virtualization is that it provides an additional means of isolating code, which is particularly relevant in the case of cloud computing. At the same time, virtualization also introduces new security threats.

Note 3.4 (Discussion: Stable software?)

Although there is indeed a lot of legacy software that can benefit from stable interfaces to rapidly changing underlying hardware, it is a mistake to believe that the software for widely available services hardly changes. With the increasing shift toward server-side computing in the form of **Software-as-a-Service** (SaaS), much software can be maintained for a relatively homogeneous platform, owned entirely by the organization offering the associated service. As a consequence, maintaining software products can be much easier, as there is much lesser need to distribute changes to potentially millions of customers. In fact, changes may rapidly succeed each other following changes in available hardware and platform, but without any client actually noticing downtimes [Barroso et al., 2018].

Types of virtualization

There are many ways in which virtualization can be realized. An overview of these various approaches is described by Smith and Nair [2005a]. A more recent account is described by Bugnion et al. [2017], which provides many technical details on the realization of various forms of virtualization. To understand the differences in virtualization, it is important to realize that computer systems generally offer four different types of interfaces, at three different levels:

1. An interface between the hardware and software, referred to as the **instruction set architecture** (**ISA**), forming the set of machine instructions. This set is divided into two subsets:

   - Privileged instructions, which are allowed to be executed only by the operating system.
   - General instructions, which can be executed by any program.

2. An interface consisting of **system calls** as offered by an operating system.

3. An interface consisting of library calls, generally forming what is known as an **application programming interface** (**API**). Often, the aforementioned system calls are hidden by an API.

These different types are shown in Figure 3.9. The essence of virtualization is to mimic the behavior of these interfaces.

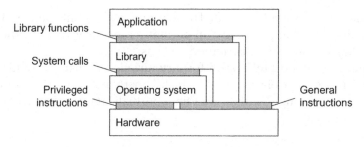

Figure 3.9: Various interfaces offered by computer systems.

Virtualization can take place in two different ways. First, we can build a runtime system that essentially provides an abstract instruction set that is to be used for executing applications. Instructions can be interpreted (as is the case for the Java runtime environment), but could also be emulated, as is done for running Windows applications on Unix platforms. Note that in the latter case, the emulator will also have to mimic the behavior of system calls, which has proven to be generally far from trivial. This type of virtualization, shown in Figure 3.10(a), leads to what Smith and Nair [2005a] call a **process virtual machine**, stressing that virtualization is only for a single process.

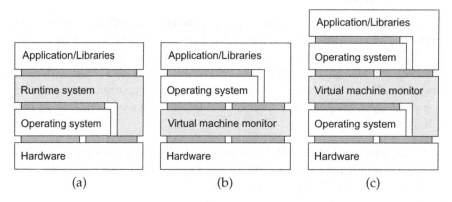

Figure 3.10: (a) A process virtual machine. (b) A native virtual machine monitor. (c) A hosted virtual machine monitor.

An alternative approach toward virtualization, shown in Figure 3.10(b), is to provide a system that is implemented as a layer shielding the original hardware, but offering the complete instruction set of that same (or other hardware) as an interface. This leads to what is known as a **native virtual machine monitor**. It is called native because it is implemented directly on top of the underlying hardware. Note that the interface offered by a virtual machine monitor can be offered *simultaneously* to different programs. As a result, it is now possible to have multiple, and different **guest operating systems** run independently and concurrently on the same platform.

A native virtual machine monitor will have to provide and regulate access to various resources, like external storage and networks. Like any operating system, this implies that it will have to implement device drivers for those resources. Rather than doing all this effort anew, a **hosted virtual machine monitor** will run on top of a trusted **host operating system** as shown in Figure 3.10(c). In this case, the virtual machine monitor can make use of existing facilities provided by that host operating system. It will generally have to be given special privileges instead of running as a user-level application. Using a hosted virtual machine monitor is highly popular in modern distributed systems such as data centers and clouds.

As argued by Rosenblum and Garfinkel [2005], virtual machines are important in the context of reliability and security for (distributed) systems. As they allow for the isolation of a complete application and its environment, a failure caused by an error or security attack need no longer affect a complete machine. In addition, as we also mentioned before, portability is greatly improved as virtual machines provide a further decoupling between hardware and software, allowing a complete environment to be moved from one machine to another. We return to migration in Section 3.5.

Note 3.5 (Advanced: On the performance of virtual machines)
Virtual machines perform surprisingly well. In fact, many studies show that modern virtual machines perform close to running applications directly on the host operating system. Let us take a closer look at what is going under the hood of virtual machines. A detailed and comprehensive account of virtual machines is provided by Smith and Nair [2005b].

Part of the answer to performance issues is shown in Figure 3.11, which forms an extension of Figure 3.10(c): a large part of the code constituting a virtual machine monitor, guest operating system, and application is running natively on the underlying hardware. In particular, all general (i.e., unprivileged) machine instructions are directly executed by the underlying machine.

This approach is not new and is founded on research by Popek and Goldberg [1974] who formalized the requirements for the efficient execution of virtual machines. In a nutshell, Popek and Goldberg assumed that the underlying machine provided at least two modes of operation (system and user mode), that a subset of the instructions could be executed only in system mode, and that memory addressing was relative (i.e., a physical address was obtained by adding a relative address to an offset found in a relocation register). A distinction was further made between two types of instructions. A **privileged instruction** is an instruction that is characterized by the fact that if and only if executed in user mode, it causes a **trap** to the operating system. **Nonprivileged instructions** are all other instructions.

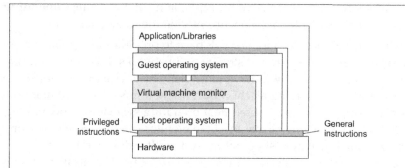

Figure 3.11: Applications, guest operating system, virtual machine monitor, and host operating system on a single hardware platform.

Given these formal assumptions, Popek and Goldberg defined two classes of special instructions. A **control-sensitive instruction** is one that may affect the configuration of a machine. A typical example is an instruction that affects the memory layout, for example, by changing the memory offset as stored in a relocation register. Another example is instructions that affect the interrupt table, containing pointers to interrupt handlers.

A **behavior-sensitive instruction** is one whose effect is partially determined by the context in which it is executed. For example, Intel x86 processors have instructions that may, or may not, affect certain registers depending on whether that instruction is executed in system mode or user mode. An example given in [Smith and Nair, 2005b] is that of the POPF instruction, which may set an interrupt-enabled flag, but only when executed in system mode.

We now have the following important result:

> *For any conventional computer, a virtual machine monitor may be constructed if the set of sensitive instructions for that computer is a subset of the set of privileged instructions.*

What this says is that as long as sensitive instructions are caught when executed in user mode, we can safely run all nonsensitive instructions natively on the underlying hardware. This also means that when designing instruction sets, if we take care that the above requirement is met, we will not be unnecessarily obstructing efficient virtualization of that instruction set.

Unfortunately, not all instruction sets have privileged-only sensitive instructions, including perhaps the most popular one, namely the Intel x86 instruction set. As it turns out, this set has 17 sensitive instructions that are not privileged [Robin and Irvine, 2000]. In other words, each of these instructions can be executed in user mode without causing a trap to the operating system, yet affect the way that the operating system is managing its resources. In these cases, there are essentially two solutions.

The first solution is to emulate all instructions. Of course, this would have a serious adverse effect on performance. To circumvent problems, an approach implemented in VMWare [Sugerman et al., 2001], is to scan the executable and to insert code around the nonprivileged sensitive instructions to divert control to the virtual machine monitor. There, appropriate emulation will take place, for example, by considering the context in which the instruction was to be executed. The effect is that full virtualization can take place, meaning that execution can take place without changing the guest operating system, nor the application itself.

An alternative solution is to apply **paravirtualization**, which requires the guest operating system to be modified. In particular, the guest operating system is modified such that all side effects of running nonprivileged sensitive instructions in user mode, which would normally be executed in system mode, are dealt with. For example, code can be rewritten such that these instructions simply no longer occur, or if they do, that their semantics are the same regardless whether being executed in user or system mode. Paravirtualization has been adopted by Xen [Barham et al., 2003, Chisnall, 2007].

3.2.2 Containers

Virtual machines offer a means to run applications relying on a specific operating environment, including its instruction set and operating system, to run independently across different platforms. As we have seen, this may require significant efforts to ensure portability and performance. However, often we see that applications are relatively stable when it comes to the used instruction set and operating system, yet do rely on specific libraries and other support software. In these cases, what we really want is to allow different applications to run side-by-side, yet each uses its own environment of support software without even noticing that there be other applications with a different environment. This is where **containers** come into the game.[1]

A container can be thought of a collection of binaries (also called images) that jointly constitute the software environment for running applications. The easiest way to think of a container is what a user would get to see when logging into, for example, a Unix system: it will consist of several standard directories containing executable programs, libraries, documentation, etc. A naive implementation of a container would be to copy an entire environment for a specific use case and install it as a subdirectory of, say, the root file system. Using a command such as chroot, the user would then be diverted to that subdirectory and run various applications, with this subdirectory now acting as the root. An application would see exactly the libraries and other dependencies it needed, while applications in other containers would have their own view on what the operating system is offering. In this sense, a container effectively virtualizes the software environment for an application.

However, this naive implementation is certainly not enough from a virtualization perspective. For one, applications and processes operating in different

---

[1]The material in this section has been inspired by Julia Evans's wonderful material at wizardzines.com.

containers need to be isolated from each other. Likewise, simply copying an entire environment is not very efficient, certainly not because we may expect that many libraries and such are the same across different containers. Finally, it is important that an operating system hosting containers has some control over the usage of its own resources. All of these aspects are handled in Unix environments (i.e., notably Linux) through three important mechanisms:

- **Namespaces**, by which a collection of processes associated with a container is given their own view of identifiers and such, independent of other containers.

- **Union file system**, which allows to, literally, combine several file systems into a layered fashion with only the highest layer allowing for write operations (and the one being part of a container).

- **Control groups**, or simply **cgroups**, by which resource restrictions can be imposed upon a collection of processes.

Let us look a bit deeper into each of these mechanisms. **Namespaces** are necessary for giving a process running inside a container the illusion that it is on its own. As such, namespaces are important for isolating containers from each other. Perhaps the one most illustrative is setting the PID namespace. As every machine has only a single init process (with PID equal to 1), every container should see its own "init" process. This is established through the Unix unshare command:

```
unshare --pid --fork --mount-proc bash
```

will bring the calling process into a new shell in which the command ps -ef yields:

```
UID        PID    PPID C STIME TTY          TIME CMD
root         1       0 0 06:27 pts/0    00:00:00 bash
root         2       1 0 06:27 pts/0    00:00:00 ps -ef
```

Indeed, we see that there now seems to be a new collection of processes with just one having PID equal to 1. All other processes have become invisible when working from this new shell.

Another important mechanism is efficient sharing of existing file systems. Many containers will be based on a common instance of an operating system, say Ubuntu 20.4. Instead of copying that entire environment and installing it as a subdirectory as explained above, we can use it as a base layer and stack other parts on top of it. For example, we may decide to replace the entire collection of subdirectories that constitute PHP7.4 for an older version by simply stacking those directories on top the ones for version 7.4. The result is that a PHP application will be using the older version. Note that this approach is very similar to mounting a file system at a directory dir. Anything that was contained in dir will no longer be visible until the file system is unmounted again. Indeed, taking the union of file systems is done through successive calls to the mount system call, with each layer being mounted in read-only mode. Only the top layer can be written to, and will need to be explicitly saved when a running container finishes.

Finally, to control what a container can actually use, Unix systems offer **cgroups**. In essence, when creating a control group, the collection of processes running in that group may be restricted to the amount of main memory that they can use, the priority when it comes to using the CPU, etc. In this way, the hosting operating system can prevent that a single container is using too much of its resources, preventing perhaps other containers to do their work.

There are many other things related to isolate containers and properly restrict what processes can do within a container. In the end, a container can be thought of an archive of files that are placed somewhere in a filesystem, together with a specific stack of common, shared, existing read-only subdirectories. Processes running inside the context of a container are presented with a view that their context is the only one (through the use of namespaces) and they have certain abilities when it comes tot using resources (through cgroups, but also restrictions when it comes to, for example, system calls). This view is summarized in Figure 3.12. Besides the material from Julia Evans at wizardzines.com, the interested reader is referred to [Pahl et al., 2019] for an overview of container technologies.

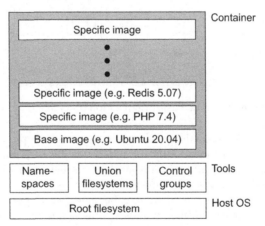

Figure 3.12: The organization of a container within a hosting environment.

Note 3.6 (Example: PlanetLab)
There are many examples of container technologies, yet at this point it is interesting to look at a specific case where the technology was used for developing a wide-area cluster of computers, even before it became popular in the context of cloud

computing. **PlanetLab** was a collaborative distributed system in which different organizations each donated one or more computers, adding up to a total of hundreds of nodes. Together, these computers formed a 1-tier server cluster, where access, processing, and storage could all take place on each node individually. Management of PlanetLab was by necessity almost entirely distributed. The project closed down in 2020.

General organization In PlanetLab, a participating organization donated one or more nodes (i.e., computers) that were subsequently shared among all PlanetLab users. Each node was organized as shown in Figure 3.13. There are two important components [Bavier et al., 2004; Peterson et al., 2006]. The first one is the virtual machine monitor (VMM), which is an enhanced Linux operating system, essentially one capable of supporting containers along the lines sketched above. The enhancements mainly comprise adjustments for supporting the second component, namely (Linux) **Vservers**. A Vserver is essentially a container in execution.

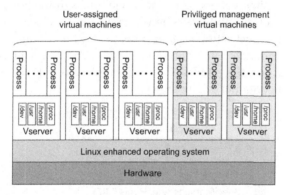

Figure 3.13: The basic organization of a PlanetLab node.

The Linux VMM ensured that Vservers were separated: processes in different Vservers are executed concurrently and independently, each making use only of the software packages and programs available in their own environment. The isolation between processes in different Vservers is strict. For example, two processes in different Vservers could have the same user ID, but this did not imply that they would stem from the same user. This separation considerably eased supporting users from different organizations that wanted to use PlanetLab as, for example, a testbed to experiment with entirely different distributed systems and applications. Note that this separation is precisely the one that is realized through the unshare command.

To support such experimentation, PlanetLab used **slices**, each slice being a set of Vservers, each Vserver running on a different node, as illustrated in Figure 3.14. A slice can thus be thought of as a virtual server cluster, implemented by a collection of containers connected through a wide-area network.

Central to managing PlanetLab resources was the **node manager**. Each node had such a manager, implemented by a separate Vserver, whose only task was to create other Vservers on the node it managed and to control resource allocation. To create a new slice, each node would also run a **slice creation service** (**SCS**), which, in turn, could contact the node manager requesting it to create a Vserver and to allocate resources. The node manager itself could not be contacted directly over a network, allowing it to concentrate only on local resource management. In turn, the SCS would not accept slice-creation requests from just anybody. Only specific **slice authorities** were eligible for requesting the creation of a slice. Each slice authority would have access rights to a collection of nodes. The simplest model was that there is only a single, centralized slice authority that is allowed to request slice creation on all nodes. In practice, we saw that this slice authority was the one used to get a user up-and-running on PlanetLab.

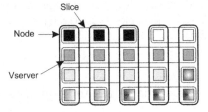

Figure 3.14: The principle of a PlanetLab slice, showing sets of associated Vservers across different nodes.

Keeping track of resources was done by a resource specification, or rspec for short. An rspec specified a time interval during which certain resources had been allocated. Resources include disk space, file descriptors, inbound and outbound network bandwidth, transport-level end points, main memory, and CPU usage. An rspec was identified through a globally unique 128-bit identifier known as a resource capability (rcap). Given an rcap, the node manager could look up the associated rspec in a local table.

Resources were bound to slices. In other words, to make use of resources, it was necessary to create a slice. Each slice was associated with a **service provider**, which can best be seen as an entity having an account on PlanetLab. Every slice could then be identified by a (principal_id, slice_tag) pair, where the principal_id identified the provider and slice_tag being an identifier chosen by the provider.

Vservers   Let us now turn our attention to PlanetLab's Vservers, which have been described and evaluated by Soltesz et al. [2007]. A Vserver was organized as a container. The primary task of a Vserver was therefore to merely support a group of processes and keep that group isolated from processes running under the jurisdiction of another Vserver.

An important advantage of the container-based approach toward virtualization, in comparison to running separate guest operating systems, is that resource allocation could generally be much simpler. In particular, it was possible to overbook resources by allowing for dynamic resource allocation, just as is done with allocating resources to normal processes. Normally, when using a guest operating system, the guest will have to be allocated a fixed number of resources in advance (notably main memory). When considering that the nodes provided by participating PlanetLab organizations were required to have only a few GByte of main memory, it is not hard to imagine that memory would be a scarce resource. It was therefore necessary to dynamically allocate memory to allow tens of containers to be running at the same time on a single node. Vservers were ideal for this type of resource management; operating systems are much harder to support in such cases. Of course, this could not prevent a Vserver from using too much memory on a busy node. The PlanetLab policy in that case was simple: the Vserver, hogging memory when swap space was almost filled, was reset.

PlanetLab status   Although the official PlanetLab closed down in 2020, a similar system is running worldwide as EdgeNet. Not surprisingly, where Vservers were containers *avant-la-lettre*, that technology has been replaced in EdgeNet by modern container technology, namely Docker in combination with Kubernetes.

3.2.3   Comparing virtual machines and containers

Ever since containers became popular, mainly caused by their introduction through Docker, an oftentimes heated debate has been going on what is better: virtual machines or containers? This debate has been hindered through the improper use of terminology, such as *lightweight* containers versus *heavyweight* virtual machines, immediately leading to often unsubstantiated performance statements (suggesting that heavyweight means slow). However, life is not so simple and understanding the technology of virtual machines as well as those of containers can help in making better judgments on when to use which technology. In this section, let us take a closer look at one specific, important aspect: performance. We return to portability later when discussing code migration.

Measuring the performance of any system requires looking at a multitude of criteria. Obvious ones include CPU and memory usage. Likewise, various I/O measurements are needed to get a good insight into how well a system is performing, in particular accessing disks and network I/O. On top of this, we need to ask ourselves how measurements are carried out. In other words, which workloads or benchmarks are used to evaluate and compare the performing systems.

A systematic study on comparing Linux containers (LXC) against Linux virtual machines (KVM) was conducted by Sharma et al. [2016]. If we just look at a baseline comparison in which an application is running either within a container or on top of a virtual machine, differences can be observed in favor of containers, yet these differences are not that big, except when it comes to I/O. In that case, we see that virtual machines perform significantly less than containers. This should not come as a surprise, as notably with traditional I/O, the operating system plays a crucial role: it has to execute many privileged instructions.

Nevertheless, even the obvious may come with surprises. In a more recent study on comparing different container technologies with virtual-machine approaches, van Rijn and Rellermeyer [2021] demonstrate that the differences between the two may often be close to negligible, even when looking at disk and network I/O. There are several reasons for this small difference, but one is that the host operating system caches results in main memory. In other words, when actually performing I/O operations, many subsequent operations are performed on in-memory data instead of data that is stored on disk. This makes benchmarking more difficult, yet also reflects realistic application-driven behavior. Furthermore, when running actual application-level benchmarks, such as those available for mysql, differences may exist, but can be small. Nevertheless, depending on the actual I/O behavior, the overall conclusion is that virtual machines do impose more overhead in comparison to containers.

Of course, it is more natural that several applications run side-by-side. The question then is to what extent the performance of one application influences that of another. In effect, this aspect boils down to the question how well scheduling resources among competitors actually is. In this case, the general trend is that containerization has more difficulty isolating independent applications and that scheduling for CPU usage as well as for disk performance is handled better through virtual machines.

What van Rijn and Rellermeyer [2021] and other recent studies show is that over the years many improvements have been made and that there is no real need for virtualization techniques to perform significantly slower in comparison to running applications directly on top of the hosting operating system.

3.2.4 Application of virtual machines to distributed systems

From the perspective of distributed systems, the most important application of virtualization lies in cloud computing. As we already mentioned in Section 1.3.1, cloud providers offer roughly three different types of services:

- **Infrastructure-as-a-Service (IaaS)** covering the basic infrastructure
- **Platform-as-a-Service (PaaS)** covering system-level services
- **Software-as-a-Service (SaaS)** containing actual applications

Virtualization plays a key role in IaaS. Instead of renting out a physical machine, a cloud provider will rent out a virtual machine (monitor) that may, or may not, be sharing a physical machine with other customers. The beauty of virtualization is that it allows for almost complete isolation between customers, who will indeed have the illusion that they have just rented a dedicated physical machine. Isolation is, however, never complete, if only for the fact that the actual physical resources are shared, in turn leading to observable lower performance.

To make matters concrete, let us consider the **Amazon Elastic Compute Cloud**, or simply **EC2**. EC2 allows one to create an environment consisting of several networked virtual servers, thus jointly forming the basis of a distributed system. To make life easy, there is a (large) number of pre-configured *machine images* available, referred to as **Amazon Machine Image**s, or simply **AMI**s. An AMI is an installable software package consisting of an operating-system kernel along with several services. An example of a simple, basic AMI is a **LAMP** image, consisting of a Linux kernel, the Apache Web server, a MySQL database system, and PHP libraries. More elaborate images containing additional software are also available, as well as images based on other Unix kernels or Windows. In this sense, an AMI is essentially the same as a boot disk (although there are a few important differences, to which we return shortly).

An EC2 customer needs to select an AMI, possibly after adapting or configuring one. An AMI can then be *launched*, resulting in what is called an **EC2 instance**: the actual virtual machine that can be used to host a customer's applications. An important issue is that a customer will hardly ever know exactly where an instance is actually being executed. Obviously, it is running on a single physical machine, but where that machine is located remains hidden. The closest one can get to pinpoint the location where an instance should run is by selecting one of a few regions provided by Amazon (US, South America, Europe, Asia).

To communicate, each instance obtains two IP addresses: a private one that can be used for internal communication between different instances, making use of EC2's internal networking facilities, and a public IP address allowing any Internet clients to contact an instance. The public address is mapped to the private one using standard **network-address translation** (**NAT**) technology. A simple way to manage an instance is to make use of an SSH connection, for which Amazon provides the means for generating the appropriate keys.

The EC2 environment in which an instance is executed provides different levels of the following services:

- **CPU**: allows selecting the number and type of core, including GPUs
- **Memory**: defines how much main memory is allocated to an instance
- **Storage**: defines how much local storage is allocated
- **Platform**: distinguishes between 32-bit or 64-bit architectures
- **Networking**: sets the bandwidth capacity that can be used

In addition, extra resources can be requested, such as an additional networking interface. The local storage that comes with an instance is *transient*: when the instance stops, all the data stored locally is lost. To prevent data loss, a customer will need to explicitly save data to a persistent store, for example, by making use of Amazon's Simple Storage Service (S3). An alternative is to attach a storage device that is mapped to Amazon's **Elastic Block Store (EBS)**. Again, this is yet another service, but one that can be used in the form of a virtual block device that is simply mounted as one would mount an additional hard disk. When an instance is stopped, all data that was stored on EBS will persist. And just as one would expect, an EBS device can be (re)mounted to any other instance as well.

It should be clear by now that, without having gone into any significant level of detail, the IaaS as offered by EC2 allows a customer to create a (potentially large) number of virtual machines, each configured with resources as needed, and capable of exchanging messages through an IP network. In addition, these virtual machines can be accessed from anywhere over the Internet (provided a client has the proper credentials). As such, Amazon EC2, like many other IaaS providers, offers the means to configure a complete distributed system consisting of networked virtual servers and running customer-supplied distributed applications. At the same time, those customers will not need to maintain any physical machine, which by itself is often already a huge gain, as we will encounter at several occasions throughout this text. One can indeed argue that virtualization lies at the core of modern cloud computing.

3.3 Clients

In the previous chapters we discussed the client-server model, the roles of clients and servers, and the ways they interact. Let us now take a closer look at the anatomy of clients and servers, respectively. We start in this section with a discussion of clients. Servers are discussed in the next section.

3.3.1 Networked user interfaces

A major task of client machines is to provide the means for users to interact with remote servers. There are roughly two ways in which this interaction can be supported. First, for each remote service, the client machine will have a separate counterpart that can contact the service over the network. A typical example is a calendar running on a user's smartphone that needs to synchronize with a remote, possibly shared calendar. In this case, an application-level protocol will handle the synchronization, as shown in Figure 3.15(a).

A second solution is to provide direct access to remote services by offering only a convenient user interface. Effectively, this means that the client machine is used only as a terminal with no need for local storage, leading to an application-neutral solution as shown in Figure 3.15(b). In the case of networked user interfaces, everything is processed and stored at the server. This **thin-client approach** has received much attention with the increase in Internet connectivity and the use of mobile devices. Thin-client solutions are also popular as they ease the task of system management.

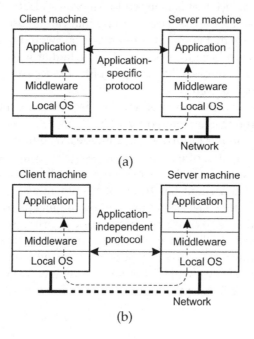

Figure 3.15: (a) A networked application with its own protocol. (b) A general solution to allow access to remote applications.

Example: The X window system

Perhaps one of the oldest and still widely used networked user interfaces is the **X Window System**. The X Window System, generally referred to simply as **X**, is used to control bit-mapped terminals, which include a monitor, keyboard, and a pointing device such as a mouse. Next to supporting traditional terminals as can be found with desktop computers and workstations, X also supports modern devices such a touchscreens on tablets and smartphones. In a sense, X can be viewed as that part of an operating system that controls the terminal. The heart of the system is formed by what we shall call the **X kernel**. It contains all the terminal-specific device drivers, and as such, is generally highly hardware dependent.

The X kernel offers a relatively low-level interface for controlling the screen, but also for capturing events from the keyboard and mouse. This interface is made available to applications as a library called Xlib. Its organization is shown in Figure 3.16. Note that Xlib is hardly ever used directly by applications, which instead deploy toolkits implemented on top of Xlib.

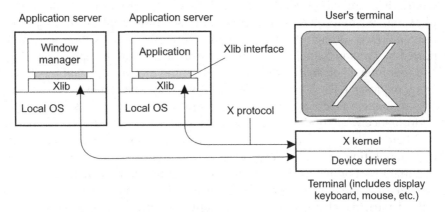

Figure 3.16: The basic organization of the X Window System.

The interesting aspect of X is that the X kernel and the X applications need not necessarily reside on the same machine. In particular, X provides the **X protocol**, which is an application-level communication protocol by which an instance of Xlib can exchange data and events with an X kernel. For example, Xlib can send requests to the X kernel for creating or killing a window, setting colors, and defining the type of cursor to display, among many other requests. In turn, the X kernel will react to local events such as keyboard and mouse input by sending event packets back to Xlib.

Several applications can communicate at the same time with the X kernel. There is one specific application that is given special rights, known as the **window manager**. This application can dictate the "look and feel" of the display as it appears to the user. For example, the window manager can prescribe how each window is decorated with extra buttons, how windows are to be placed on the display, and so on. Other applications will have to adhere to these rules. In practice, this means that much of the interaction between an application and an X terminal is redirected through a window manager.

It is interesting to note how the X window system actually fits into client-server computing. From what we have described so far, it should be clear that the X kernel receives requests to manipulate the display. It gets these requests from (possibly remote) applications. In this sense, the X kernel acts as a server, while the applications play the role of clients. This terminology has been adopted by X, and although strictly speaking it is correct, it can easily lead to confusion.

Thin-client network computing

Obviously, applications manipulate a display using the specific display commands as offered by X. These commands are generally sent over the network where they are subsequently executed by the X kernel. By its nature, applications written for X should preferably separate application logic from user-interface commands. Unfortunately, this is often not the case. As reported by Lai and Nieh [2002] it turns out that much of the application logic and user interaction are tightly coupled, meaning that an application will send many requests to the X kernel for which it will expect a response before being able to make a next step. This synchronous behavior may adversely affect performance when operating over a wide-area network with long latencies.

There are several solutions to this problem. One is to re-engineer the implementation of the X protocol, as is done with NX [Pinzari, 2003]. An important part of this work concentrates on bandwidth reduction by reducing the size of X messages. To this end, messages are considered to consist of a fixed part, which is treated as an identifier, and a variable part. Often, multiple messages will have the same identifier, in which case they will often contain similar data. This property can be used to send only the differences between messages having the same identifier. By having the sender and receiver maintain identifiers, decoding at the receiver can be readily applied. Bandwidth reductions up to a factor 1000 have been reported, which allows X to also run through low-bandwidth links of only 9600 kbps.

As an alternative to using X, researchers and practitioners have also sought to let an application *completely* control the remote display, that is, up to the pixel level. This approach is also referred to as controlling a **remote desktop**. Changes in the bitmap are then sent over the network to the display, where they are immediately transferred to the local frame buffer. A well-known example of this approach is **Virtual Network Computing** (**VNC**) [Richardson et al., 1998], which has been around ever since the late 1990s. Obviously, letting the application control the display requires sophisticated encoding techniques to prevent bandwidth availability to become a problem. For example, consider displaying a video stream at 30 frames per second on a simple 320×240 screen. If each pixel is encoded by 24 bits, then without an efficient encoding scheme, we would need a bandwidth of approximately 53 Mbps. In practice, various encoding techniques are used, yet choosing the best one is generally application dependent.

3.3.2 Virtual desktop environment

As cloud computing further matured, and notably the number of cloud applications was growing, it became opportune to actually turn the cloud into a **virtual desktop environment** for end users. The only thing needed was the client-side software to access that desktop environment. One of the first providers of this model was Google with the introduction of **Chrome OS**. The basic idea is simple: let the browser provide the local desktop interface. Next to the browser, multiple stand-alone applications can be available of which each, in principle, eventually operates with a cloud-based counterpart. In this sense, the desktop is actually akin to what is offered by modern smartphones. With an increasing trend to transform applications to browser extensions, we can see that the browser is taking over the role of an operating system's user interface.

The anatomy of a Web browser

To get a better appreciation of what is going on, let us take a closer look at the anatomy of the Chrome browser, which has been reported to be the most widely used among all browsers.[2] The Chrome browser is an intricate piece of software consisting of over 25 million lines of code, comparable to the size of the Linux kernel. Where in the beginning the Web consisted of merely simple HTML pages, we are now dealing with not only a highly advanced markup language, but also an array of tools for interaction and client-side scripting languages. A high-level overview of how the Chrome browser works is shown in Figure 3.17.

At the core, we see the resource loader, responsible for fetching content from a Web server. It generally starts with fetching an HTML file and subsequently, in parallel, sets up connections for other material referenced in that page. This is typically done through separate threads. Note that the resource loader will need to partially parse the original HTML file to discover which other content it needs to fetch. Most of the parsing, however, is done by a separate component that constructs what is known as a **Document Object Model**, or **DOM** for short. In essence, a DOM is a tree representation of the HTML file.

Where the DOM can be said to represent structure, actual styling information is provided by a separate document. For example, it may state that every paragraph should be represented in a specific color and in a specific font. This information is parsed separately and essentially added to the DOM, leading to a render tree. This tree contains all the information for the next step: determining exactly where the various elements in the tree will be displayed. In particular, geometric regions need to be computed for different parts of the DOM, but also where lines will be broken (and considering language-specific issues such as reading text from left to right, or *vice versa* as is the case with Hebrew or Arabic. Line breaking, in turn, requires exact computations for which the styling component will need to take font characteristics into account. It is not difficult to see that the process of determining the layout can become

---

[2]See gs.statcounter.com.

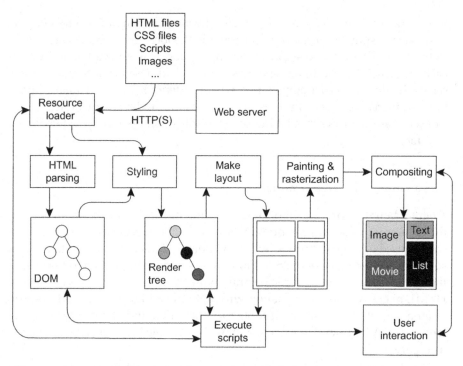

Figure 3.17: An overview of how the Chrome browser renders a Web page (adapted from Pourghassemi [2021]).

quite complex when, for example, floating images or multiple columns need to be rendered.

Once the layout has been determined, the painting component, takes the layout instructions and constructs a program consisting of paint operations, like drawRectangle(x,y,height,width). There are many of such operations, which are subsequently executed by a rasterization process which fills in all the details for every pixel on the screen, notably, of course, its color. Rasterization also takes the embedded images into account (and based on the information provided by the painting process) ensures that each pixel on an embedded image gets properly displayed. What we have not shown explicitly in Figure 3.17, is that the DOM is actually decomposed into several layers, and that each layer is eventually rasterized separately. As a result, the layers need to be composed into a final image that can be displayed. Meanwhile, the compositor can interact with the user, who may be scrolling through a page.

Last, yet certainly not least, every browser now has a separate component for handling scripts, that is, executable code. A popular scripting language for client-side Web applications is **JavaScript**, but increasingly more often we also see **WebAssembly** codes [Sletten, 2022]. The latter offer performance that can be close to executing native code, certainly in combination with actual compilations. The generated code is always restricted to the permissions the browser has, making it (relatively) safe. The power of being able to run code inside a browser cannot be underestimated. It forms the core of giving the illusion to an end user that she is indeed running an application on the local desktop. We return to this phenomenon below.

Although we have skipped many details, it should be clear that actually rendering a Web page is a highly complex endeavor. Furthermore, it is not difficult to imagine that many of the elements just described, such as rasterizing layers, can be done in parallel and perhaps even on special processors, such a GPU. This is precisely what a modern Web browser does: spawning threads and processes, not only to provide more structure and organization to this immense complex software, but also to make sure that the rendering as a whole is done efficiently.

In fact, modern Web browsers also use processes to protect various parts of their code from each other. For example, the whole rendering in Chrome is done by a separate process (i.e., the components HTML parsing, styling, making the layout, painting, and compositing are taken together), while rasterization is separated to make use of a possibly available GPU. The rasterization process communicates with the main process through message passing. Moreover, every browser tab gets its own renderer process. To improve security, each renderer is running in a separate **sandbox**: a protection mechanism that precludes direct communication with the underlying operating system. We return to sandboxes when discussing mobile code.

Browsers and applications

As we already indicated, having a browser is often sufficient for offering a virtual desktop environment. Important is the fact that browsers can execute scripts as the client-side part of an otherwise remote application. Such scripts can largely handle everything that is needed to provide the illusion that a user is working on a local machine. This is precisely what Chrome OS offers. However, things become a bit more complicated when local resources are truly needed for offering a desktop environment. The first type of resources that come to mind are related to media: camera, microphone, speakers, etc. Many Web-based applications will ask the user for permission to use those resources.

It is often also possible to run applications natively on the computer hosting the client-side desktop. In essence, this is what happens with modern smartphones. Native applications (also referred to as mobile apps) operate as any other locally executing application. Their main advantage over running Web-based applications is that, in principle, a user can work offline. However, by simply examining how many mobile apps are useful when there is no network connectivity already illustrates that working offline is not assumed to be the default.

A development that is gradually emerging is that of using **Progressive Web apps (PWA)**. These applications use the browser as their hosting environment, yet appear as an ordinary mobile app. In a nutshell, what a PWA does is move a lot of the server-side content that is not dependent on (high quality) network connectivity, to the client where it is subsequently cached. The effect is that many of these apps, which can run in the browser or even appear as a mobile app (i.e., the browser user interface itself is hidden) can be executed much faster and comparable to that of their mobile-app counterpart. Furthermore, because much less needs to be communicated with the server, many PWAs can operate well even when the quality of the network is at stake.

By and large, we see that virtual desk environments are moving extremely thin clients to ones that are hosts to much more functionality, and for which communication over the Internet has been highly optimized. As we mentioned before, a major advantage over the traditional fat clients that have mainly locally installed applications is that management of browser-based apps is much easier: the server can simply upload new parts to the client as needed.

3.3.3 Client-side software for distribution transparency

Client software comprises more than just user interfaces. Often, parts of the processing and data level in a client-server application are executed on the client side as well. A special class is formed by embedded client software, such as for automatic teller machines (ATMs), cash registers, barcode readers, TV set-top boxes, etc. In these cases, the user interface is a relatively small part of the client software, in contrast to the local processing and communication facilities.

Besides the user interface and other application-related software, client software comprises components for achieving **distribution transparency**. Ideally, a client should not be aware that it is communicating with remote processes. In contrast, distribution is often less transparent to servers for reasons of performance and correctness.

Access transparency is generally handled through the generation of a **client stub** from an interface definition of what the server has to offer. The stub provides the same interface as the one available at the server, but hides the possible differences in machine architectures, as well as the actual communication. The client stub transforms local calls to messages that are sent to the server, and *vice versa* transforms messages from the server to return values as one would expect when calling an ordinary procedure.

There are different ways to handle **location**, **migration**, and **relocation transparency** . Using a convenient naming system is crucial. Often, cooperation with client-side software is also important. For example, when a client is already bound to a server, the client can be directly informed when the server changes location. In this case, the client's middleware can hide the server's current network location from the user, and also transparently rebind to the server if necessary. At worst, the client's application may notice a temporary loss of performance.

Similarly, many distributed systems implement **replication transparency** employing client-side solutions. For example, imagine a distributed system with replicated servers, Such replication can be achieved by forwarding a request to each replica, as shown in Figure 3.18. Client-side software can transparently collect all responses and pass a single response to the client application.

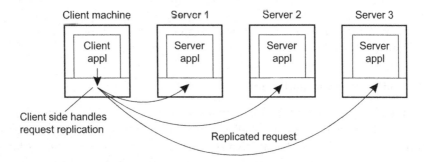

Figure 3.18: Transparent replication of a server using a client-side solution.

Regarding **failure transparency**, masking communication failures with a server is typically done through client middleware. For example, client middleware can be configured to repeatedly attempt to connect to a server, or perhaps try another server after several attempts. There are even situations in which the client middleware returns data it had cached during a previous session, as is sometimes done by Web browsers that fail to connect to a server.

Finally, **concurrency transparency** can be handled through special intermediate servers, notably transaction monitors, and requires less support from client software.

3.4 Servers

Let us now take a closer look at the organization of servers. In the following pages, we first concentrate on a number of general design issues for servers, followed by a discussion on server clusters.

3.4.1 General design issues

A server is a process implementing a specific service on behalf of a collection of clients. In essence, each server is organized in the same way: it waits for an incoming request from a client and subsequently ensures that the request is taken care of, after which it waits for the next incoming request.

Concurrent versus iterative servers

There are several ways to organize servers. In the case of an **iterative server**, the server itself handles the request and, if necessary, returns a response to the requesting client. A **concurrent server** does not handle the request itself, but passes it to a separate thread or another process, after which it immediately waits for the next incoming request. A multithreaded server is an example of a concurrent server. An alternative implementation of a concurrent server is to fork a new process for each new incoming request. This approach is followed in many Unix systems. The thread or process that handles the request is responsible for returning a response to the requesting client.

Contacting a server: end points

Another issue is where clients contact a server. In all cases, clients send requests to an **end point**, also called a **port**, at the machine where the server is running. Each server listens to a specific end point. How do clients know the end point of a service? One approach is to globally assign end points for well-known services. For example, servers that handle Internet FTP requests always listen to TCP port 21. Likewise, an HTTP server for the World Wide Web will always listen to TCP port 80. These end points have been assigned by the **Internet Assigned Numbers Authority (IANA)**, and are documented in [Reynolds and Postel, 1994]. With assigned end points, the client needs to find only the network address of the machine where the server is running. Name services can be used for that purpose.

There are many services that do not require a preassigned end point. For example, a time-of-day server may use an end point that is dynamically assigned to it by its local operating system. In that case, a client will first have to look up the end point. One solution is to have a special daemon running on each machine that runs servers. The daemon keeps track of the current end point of each service implemented by a co-located server. The daemon itself listens to a well-known end point. A client will first contact the daemon, request the end point, and then contact the specific server, as shown in Figure 3.19(a).

It is common to associate an end point with a specific service. However, actually implementing each service by means of a separate server may be a waste of resources. For example, in a typical Unix system, it is common to have many servers running simultaneously, with most of them passively waiting until a client request comes in. Instead of having to keep track of so many passive processes, it can be more efficient to have a single **superserver** listening to each end point associated with a specific service, as shown in

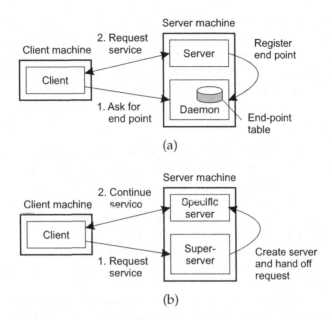

Figure 3.19: (a) Client-to-server binding using a daemon. (b) Client-to-server binding using a superserver.

Figure 3.19(b). For example, the inetd daemon in Unix listens to a number of well-known ports for Internet services. When a request comes in, the daemon forks a process to handle it. That process will exit when finished.

Interrupting a server

Another issue that needs to be considered when designing a server is whether and how a server can be interrupted. For example, consider a user who has just decided to upload a huge file to an FTP server. Then, suddenly realizing that it is the wrong file, she wants to interrupt the server to cancel further data transmission. There are several ways to do this. One approach that works only too well in the current Internet (and is sometimes the only alternative) is for the user to abruptly exit the client application (which will automatically break the connection to the server), immediately restart it, and pretend nothing happened. The server will eventually tear down the old connection, thinking the client has probably crashed.

A much better approach for handling communication interrupts is to develop the client and server such that it is possible to send **out-of-band data**, which is data that is to be processed by the server before any other data from that client. One solution is to let the server listen to a separate control end point to which the client sends out-of-band data, while at the same time listening (with a lower priority) to the end point through which the normal data passes. Another solution is to send out-of-band data across the same connection through which the client is sending the original request. In TCP, for example, it is possible to transmit urgent data. When urgent data are received at the server, the latter is interrupted (e.g., through a signal in Unix systems), after which it can inspect the data and handle them accordingly.

Stateless versus stateful servers

A final, important design issue, is whether the server is stateless. A **stateless server** does not keep information on the state of its clients, and can change its own state without having to inform any client [Birman, 2012]. A Web server, for example, is stateless. It merely responds to incoming HTTP requests, which can be either for uploading a file to the server or (most often) for fetching a file. When the request has been processed, the Web server forgets the client completely. Likewise, the collection of files that a Web server manages (possibly in cooperation with a file server), can be changed without clients having to be informed.

Note that in many stateless designs, the server actually does maintain information on its clients, but crucial is the fact that if this information is lost, it will not lead to a disruption of the service offered by the server. For example, a Web server generally logs all client requests. This information is useful, for example, to decide whether certain documents should be replicated, and where they should be replicated to. Clearly, there is no penalty, other than perhaps in the form of suboptimal performance if the log is lost.

A particular form of a stateless design is where the server maintains what is known as **soft state**. In this case, the server promises to maintain state on behalf of the client, but only for a limited time. After that time has expired, the server falls back to default behavior, thereby discarding any information it kept on account of the associated client. An example of this type of state is a server promising to keep a client informed about updates, but only for a limited time. Thereafter, the client is required to poll the server for updates. Soft-state approaches originate from protocol design in computer networks, but can be equally applied to server design [Clark, 1989; Lui et al., 2004].

In contrast, a **stateful server** generally maintains persistent information on its clients. This means that the information needs to be explicitly deleted by the server. A typical example is a file server that allows a client to keep a local copy of a file, even for performing update operations. Such a server would maintain a table containing *(client, file)* entries. Such a table allows the server to keep track of which client currently has the update permissions on which file, and thus possibly, also the most recent version of that file.

This approach can improve the performance of read and write operations as perceived by the client. Performance improvement over stateless servers is often an important benefit of stateful designs. However, the example also illustrates the major drawback of stateful servers. If the server crashes, it has to recover its table of *(client, file)* entries, or otherwise it cannot guarantee that it has processed the most recent updates on a file. In general, a stateful server needs to recover its entire state as it was just before the crash. Enabling recovery can introduce considerable complexity, as we discuss in Chapter 8. In a stateless design, no special measures need to be taken at all for a crashed server to recover. It simply starts running again, and waits for client requests to come in.

Ling et al. [2004] argue that one should actually make a distinction between (temporary) **session state** and **permanent state**. The example above is typical for session state: it is associated with a series of operations by a single user and should be maintained for some time, but not indefinitely. As it turns out, session state is often maintained in three-tiered client-server architectures, where the application server actually needs to access a database server through a series of queries before being able to respond to the requesting client. The issue here is that no real harm is done if session state is lost, provided that the client can simply re-issue the original request. This observation allows for simpler and less reliable storage of state.

What remains for permanent state is typically information maintained in databases, such as customer information, keys associated with purchased software, etc. However, for most distributed systems, maintaining session state already implies a stateful design requiring special measures when failures do happen and making explicit assumptions about the durability of state stored at the server. We will return to these matters when discussing fault tolerance.

When designing a server, the choice for a stateless or stateful design should not affect the services provided by the server. For example, if files have to be opened before they can be read from, or written to, then a stateless server should one way or the other mimic this behavior. A common solution is that the server responds to a read or write request by first opening the referred file, then does the actual read or write operation, and immediately closes the file again.

In other cases, a server may want to keep a record of a client's behavior so that it can more effectively respond to its requests. For example, Web servers sometimes offer the possibility to immediately direct a client to its favorite pages. This approach is possible only if the server has history information on that client. When the server cannot maintain state, a common solution is then to let the client send along additional information on its previous accesses. In the case of the Web, this information is transparently stored by the client's browser in what is called a **cookie**, which is a small piece of data containing client-specific information that is of interest to the server. Cookies are never executed by a browser; they are merely stored and sent to the server when accessed a next time.

The first time a client accesses a server, the latter sends a cookie along with the requested Web pages back to the browser, after which the browser safely tucks the cookie away. Each subsequent time the client accesses the server, its cookie for that server is sent along with the request.

3.4.2   Object servers

Let us take a look at the general organization of object servers needed for distributed objects. The important difference between a general object server and other (more traditional) servers is that an object server by itself does not provide a specific service. Specific services are implemented by the objects that reside in the server. Essentially, the server provides only the means to invoke local objects, based on requests from remote clients. As a consequence, it is relatively easy to change services by simply adding and removing objects.

An object server thus acts as a place where objects live. An object consists of two parts: data representing its state and the code for executing its methods. Whether these parts are separated, or whether method implementations are shared by multiple objects, depends on the object server. Furthermore, there are differences in the way an object server invokes its objects. For example, in a multithreaded server, each object may be assigned a separate thread, or a separate thread may be used for each invocation request. These and other issues are discussed next.

For an object to be invoked, the object server needs to know which code to execute, on which data it should operate, whether it should start a separate thread to take care of the invocation, and so on. A simple approach is to assume that all objects look alike and that there is only one way to invoke an object. Unfortunately, such an approach is generally inflexible and often unnecessarily constrains developers of distributed objects.

A much better approach is for a server to support different policies. Consider, for example, a **transient object**: an object that exists only as long as its server exists, but possibly for a shorter period of time. An in-memory, read-only copy of a file could typically be implemented as a transient object. Likewise, a calculator could also be implemented as a transient object. A reasonable policy is to create a transient object at the first invocation request and to destroy it as soon as no clients are bound to it anymore.

The advantage of this approach is that a transient object will need a server's resources only as long as the object is really needed. The drawback is that an invocation may take some time to complete because the object needs to be created first. Therefore, an alternative policy is sometimes to create all transient objects at the time the server is initialized, at the cost of consuming resources even when no client is making use of the object.

Similarly, a server could follow the policy that each of its objects is placed in a memory segment of its own. In other words, objects share neither code nor data. Such a policy may be necessary when an object implementation does not separate code and data, or when objects need to be separated for security reasons. In the latter case, the server will need to provide special measures, or require support from the underlying operating system, to ensure that segment boundaries are not violated.

The alternative approach is to let objects at least share their code. For example, a database containing objects that belong to the same class can be efficiently implemented by loading the class implementation only once into the server. When a request for an object invocation comes in, the server need only fetch that object's state and execute the requested method.

Likewise, there are many policies regarding threading. The simplest approach is to implement the server with only a single thread of control. Alternatively, the server may have several threads, one for each of its objects. Whenever an invocation request comes in for an object, the server passes the request to the thread responsible for that object. If the thread is currently busy, the request is temporarily queued.

The advantage of this approach is that objects are automatically protected against concurrent access: all invocations are serialized through the single thread associated with the object. Neat and simple. Of course, it is also possible to use a separate thread for each invocation request, requiring that objects should have already been protected against concurrent access. Independent of using a thread per object or thread per method is the choice of whether threads are created on demand or the server maintains a pool of threads. Generally, there is no single best policy. Which one to use depends on whether threads are available, how much performance matters, etc.

Decisions on how to invoke an object are commonly referred to as **activation policies**, to emphasize that often the object itself must first be brought into the server's address space (i.e., activated) before it can actually be invoked. What is needed then is a mechanism to group objects per policy. Such a mechanism is sometimes called an **object adapter**, or alternatively an **object wrapper**. An object adapter can best be thought of as software implementing a specific activation policy. The main issue, however, is that object adapters come as generic components to assist developers of distributed objects, and which need only to be configured for a specific policy.

An object adapter has one or more objects under its control. Because a server should be capable of simultaneously supporting objects that require different activation policies, several object adapters may reside in the same server. When an invocation request is delivered to the server, the request is first dispatched to the appropriate object adapter, as shown in Figure 3.20.

An important observation is that object adapters are unaware of the specific interfaces of the objects they control. Otherwise, they could never be generic. The only issue that is important to an object adapter is that it can extract an object reference from an invocation request, and subsequently dispatch the request to the referenced object, but now following a specific activation policy. As is also illustrated in Figure 3.20, rather than passing the request directly to the object, an adapter hands an invocation request to the server-side stub

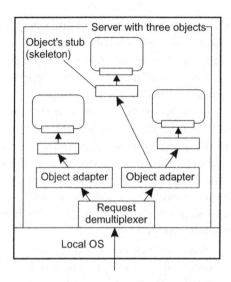

Figure 3.20: An object server supporting different activation policies.

of that object. The stub, also called a skeleton, is normally generated from the interface definitions of the object, unmarshals the request and invokes the appropriate method.

An object adapter can support different activation policies by simply configuring it at runtime. For example, in CORBA-compliant systems [OMG, 2001], it is possible to specify whether an object should continue to exist after its associated adapter has stopped. Likewise, an adapter can be configured to generate object identifiers, or to let the application provide one. An adapter can also be configured to operate in single-threaded or multithreaded mode.

Note that although in Figure 3.20 we have spoken about objects, we have said nothing about what these objects actually are. In particular, it should be stressed that as part of the implementation of such an object the server may (indirectly) access databases or call special library routines. The implementation details are hidden for the object adapter, who communicates only with a skeleton. As such, the actual implementation may have nothing to do with what we often see with language-level (i.e., compile-time) objects. For this reason, a different terminology is generally adopted. A **servant** is the general term for a piece of code that forms the implementation of an object.

Example: The Ice runtime system

Let us briefly consider the Ice distributed-object system, which has been partly developed in response to the intricacies of commercial object-based distributed systems [Henning, 2004]. An object server in Ice is nothing but an ordinary process that simply starts with initializing the Ice runtime system. The basis of the runtime environment is formed by what is called a *communicator*. A communicator is a component that manages several basic resources, of which the most important one is formed by a pool of threads. Likewise, it will have associated dynamically allocated memory, and so on. In addition, a communicator provides the means for configuring the environment. For example, it is possible to specify maximum message lengths, maximum invocation retries, and so on.

Normally, an object server would have only a single communicator. However, when different applications need to be fully separated and protected from each other, a separate communicator (with possibly a different configuration) can be created within the same process. At the very least, such an approach would separate the different thread pools so that if one application has consumed all its threads, then this would not affect the other application.

A communicator is used to create an object adapter, such as shown in Figure 3.21. In this example, we start with creating and initializing the runtime environment, which returns a communicator. Using the communicator, an object adapter is created. In this case, it is instructed to listen for incoming TCP connections on port 11000. Note that the adapter is created in the context of the just created communicator. We are now in the position to create objects and add those to the adapter. In this case, we create two objects, object1 and object2, respectively. Both are added to the adapter, yet under different names. What we see here, is that the adapter will be listening for incoming requests on a single port, yet will use an object's name to invoke the proper object. Once the objects have been added, the adapter is *activated*, meaning that, under the hood, a thread is activated that will start listening for incoming requests.

On the client side, we see that two printer objects are created, one for each of their server-side counterparts. And, indeed, after starting the server and then the client, the output on the server's side will match:

```
Object1 says: Hello World from printer1!
Object2 says: Hello World from printer2!
```

Note that if we had associated printer2 in line 9 of the client with base1, the output would have been:

```
Object1 says: Hello World from printer1!
Object1 says: Hello World from printer2!
```

In other words, printer2 would have been associated to object1 instead of object2.

This code does not yet show much differentiation in activation policies. Policies can be changed by modifying the *properties* of an adapter. One family of properties is related to maintaining an adapter-specific set of threads that are used for handling incoming requests. For example, one can specify that

```
 1  import sys, Ice
 2  import Demo
 3
 4  class PrinterI(Demo.Printer):
 5      def __init__(self, t):
 6          self.t = t
 7
 8      def printString(self, s, current=None):
 9          print(self.t, s)
10
11  communicator = Ice.initialize(sys.argv)
12
13  adapter = communicator.createObjectAdapterWithEndpoints("SimpleAdapter", "default -p 11000")
14  object1 = PrinterI("Object1 says:")
15  object2 = PrinterI("Object2 says:")
16  adapter.add(object1, communicator.stringToIdentity("SimplePrinter1"))
17  adapter.add(object2, communicator.stringToIdentity("SimplePrinter2"))
18  adapter.activate()
19
20  communicator.waitForShutdown()
```

(a)

```
 1  import sys, Ice
 2  import Demo
 3
 4  communicator = Ice.initialize(sys.argv)
 5
 6  base1 = communicator.stringToProxy("SimplePrinter1:default -p 11000")
 7  base2 = communicator.stringToProxy("SimplePrinter2:default -p 11000")
 8  printer1 = Demo.PrinterPrx.checkedCast(base1)
 9  printer2 = Demo.PrinterPrx.checkedCast(base2)
10  if (not printer1) or (not printer2):
11      raise RuntimeError("Invalid proxy")
12
13  printer1.printString("Hello World from printer1!")
14  printer2.printString("Hello World from printer2!")
15
16  communicator.waitForShutdown()
```

(b)

Figure 3.21: (a) An example of creating a simple object server in Ice, and (b) a corresponding client (slightly adapted from [ZeroC, 2022]).

there should always be only one thread, effectively serializing all accesses to objects that have been added to the adapter.

In the example above, an object is created as part of the application, after which it is added to an adapter. Effectively, this means that an adapter may need to support many objects at the same time, leading to potential scalability problems. An alternative solution is to dynamically load objects into memory when they are needed. To do this, Ice provides support for special objects known as *locators*. A locator can be viewed as a special type of servant; it is called when the adapter receives an incoming request for an object that has not been explicitly added. In that case, the request is forwarded to the locator, whose job is to further handle the request.

To make matters more concrete, suppose a locator is handed a request for an object of which the locator knows that its state is stored in a relational database system. Of course, there is no magic here: the locator has been programmed explicitly to handle such requests. In this case, the object's identifier may correspond to the key of a record in which that state is stored. The locator will then simply do a lookup on that key, fetch the state, and will then be able to further process the request.

There can be more than one locator added to an adapter. In that case, the adapter would keep track of which object identifiers would belong to the same locator. Using multiple locators allows supporting many objects by a single adapter. Of course, objects (or rather their state) would need to be loaded at runtime, but this dynamic behavior would possibly make the server itself relatively simple. More examples and detailed information on Ice can be found in [ZeroC, 2022].

3.4.3 Example: The Apache Web server

An interesting example of a server that balances the separation between policies and mechanisms is the **Apache Web server**. It is also an extremely popular server, estimated to be used to host approximately 25% of all Websites. Apache is a complex piece of software, and with the numerous enhancements to the types of documents that are now offered on the Web, it is important that the server be highly configurable and extensible, and at the same time largely independent of specific platforms.

Making the server platform independent is realized by essentially providing its own basic runtime environment, which is then subsequently implemented for different operating systems. This runtime environment, known as the **Apache Portable Runtime** (**APR**), is a library that provides a platform-independent interface for file handling, networking, locking, threads, and so on. When extending Apache, portability is largely guaranteed provided that only calls to the APR are made and none to platform-specific libraries.

From a certain perspective, Apache can be considered as a completely general server tailored to produce a response to an incoming request. Of course, there are all kinds of hidden dependencies and assumptions by which Apache turns out to be primarily suited for handling requests for Web documents. For example, as we mentioned, Web browsers and servers use HTTP as their communication protocol. HTTP is virtually always implemented on top of TCP, for which reason the core of Apache assumes that all incoming requests adhere to a TCP-based connection-oriented way of communication. Requests based on UDP cannot be handled without modifying the Apache core.

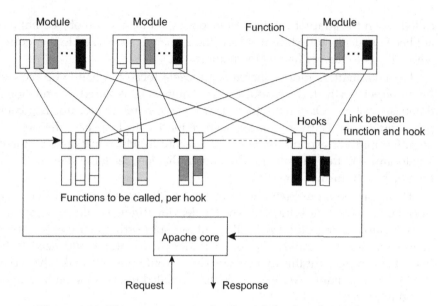

Figure 3.22: The general organization of the Apache Web server.

Otherwise, the Apache core makes few assumptions on how incoming requests should be handled. Its overall organization is shown in Figure 3.22. Fundamental to this organization are **modules**. A module consists of one, or several, functions that should be called for properly handling a request. This raises several questions:

1. How do we ensure that a function is called in the first place?

2. How do we ensure that a function is called at the right moment?

3. How do we prevent that a function is called for a request it was not supposed to handle?

The last question is actually the simplest: each function will be called (along with the request), yet each function will return the value DECLINED if the request was not meant for it.

Getting a function to be called at all is handled through a **hook**, which is a placeholder for a function. There is a hook for each function, and each module provides the Apache core with a list of hooks to its functions. By statically or dynamically linking modules to the Apache core, we establish a connection between a hook and its associated function.

For example, there is a hook to translate a URL to a local file name. Such a translation will almost certainly need to be done when processing a request. Likewise, there is a hook for writing information to a log, a hook for checking a client's identification, a hook for checking access rights, and a hook for checking which MIME type the request is related to (e.g., to make sure that the request can be properly handled). As shown in Figure 3.22, the hooks are processed in a specific order. It is here that we explicitly see that Apache enforces a specific flow of control concerning the processing of requests.

Often, functions can be processed independently of each other: they operate in perfect isolation on a request. However, this may not be generally the case, for which Apache distinguishes a number of phases. When hooking up a function to Apache, we need to specify whether that function should be called in the beginning, the middle, or the end of the total request-processing flow. If fine-grained control is necessary, one can also specify before or after which other module a function should be called. However, it is easily seen that trying to develop functions that operate in isolation (and are, in effect, stateless) contributes to a modular design.

Much more on the Apache Web server can be found in the (by now somewhat outdated) book by Laurie and Laurie [2002], as well as the developer's documentation provided by Apache itself.

3.4.4   Server clusters

In Chapter 1, we briefly discussed cluster computing as one of the many appearances of distributed systems. We now take a closer look at the organization of server clusters, along with the salient design issues. We first consider common server clusters that are organized in local-area networks. A special group is formed by wide-area server clusters, which we subsequently discuss.

Local-area clusters

Simply put, a server cluster is nothing else but a collection of machines connected through a network, where each machine runs one or more servers. The server clusters that we consider here, are the ones in which the machines are connected through a local-area network, often offering high bandwidth and low latency.

General organization   Often, a server cluster is logically organized into three tiers, as shown in Figure 3.23. The first tier consists of a (logical) switch through which client requests are routed. Such a switch can vary widely. For example, transport-layer switches accept incoming TCP connection requests and pass requests on to one of the servers in the cluster. A completely different example is a Web server that accepts incoming HTTP requests, but that partly passes requests to application servers for further processing only to later collect results from those servers and return an HTTP response.

As in any multitiered client-server architecture, many server clusters also contain servers dedicated to application processing. In cluster computing, these are typically servers running on high-performance hardware dedicated

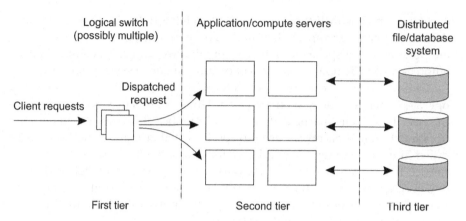

Figure 3.23: The general organization of a three-tiered server cluster.

to delivering compute power. However, in the case of enterprise server clusters, it may be the case that applications need only run on relatively low-end machines, as the required compute power is not the bottleneck, but access to storage is.

This brings us to the third tier, which consists of data-processing servers, notably file and database servers. Again, depending on the usage of the server cluster, these servers may be running on specialized machines, configured for high-speed disk access and having large server-side data caches.

Of course, not all server clusters will follow this strict separation. It is frequently the case that each machine is equipped with its own local storage, often integrating application and data processing in a single server, leading to a two-tiered architecture. For example, when dealing with streaming media using a server cluster, it is common to deploy a two-tiered system architecture, where each machine acts as a dedicated media server [Steinmetz and Nahrstedt, 2004].

When a server cluster offers multiple services, different machines may run different application servers. As a consequence, the switch will have to be able to distinguish services, or otherwise it cannot forward requests to the proper machines. As a consequence, we may find that certain machines are temporarily idle, while others are receiving an overload of requests. What would be useful is to temporarily migrate services to idle machines. A solution is to use virtual machines, allowing a relatively easy migration of services.

Request dispatching Let us now take a closer look at the first tier, consisting of the switch, also known as the **front end**. An important design goal for server clusters is to hide the fact that there are multiple servers. In other words, client applications running on remote machines should have no need to know anything about the internal organization of the cluster. This access

transparency is invariably offered through a single access point, in turn
implemented through some kind of hardware switch such as a dedicated
machine.

The switch forms the entry point for the server cluster, offering a single
network address. For scalability and availability, a server cluster may have
multiple access points, where each access point is then realized by a separate
dedicated machine. We consider only the case of a single access point.

In practice, we see two types of switches. In the case of **transport-layer
switches**, the switch accepts incoming TCP connection requests, and hands
off such connections to one of the servers. The client sets up a TCP connection
such that all requests and responses pass through the switch The switch,
in turn, will set up a TCP connection with a selected server and pass client
requests to that server, and also accept server responses (which it will pass
on to the client). In effect, the switch sits in the middle of a TCP connection
between the client and a selected server, rewriting the source and destination
addresses when passing TCP segments. This approach is a form of **network-
address translation** (NAT) [Srisuresh and Holdrege, 1999].

As an alternative, **application-layer switches** are used. As its name suggest,
an application-layer switch operates by inspecting the content of requests
instead of just looking at information available in TCP. For example, the
switch can inspect the actual URL in case of a Web server. This distinction
allows for developing server clusters in which dedicated machines can be
configured for handling, for example, video or other media, next to those
requiring access to specific databases, etc. In general, the more a switch knows
about what is being requested, the better it can decide on which server to
handle the request. An obvious drawback of application-layer switches is that
they may be slower than transport-layer switches. On the other hand, using
the right software and hardware, costs can be kept acceptable low. This is
demonstrated, for example, by the nginx server, which has been designed to
handle thousands of simultaneous connections and is used for many sites as
what is also called a **reverse proxy** [DeJonghe, 2022]. Note that the Apache
Web server can also be configured as an application-layer switch.

Note 3.7 (Example: TCP handoff)

In the days that request dispatching was relatively expensive, a simple and elegant
way of ensuring that performance criteria could still be met, was by implementing
TCP handoff. The idea is a switch can actually hand off the connection to a
selected server such that all responses are directly communicated to the client
without passing through the switch [Hunt et al., 1997; Pai et al., 1998]. The
principle working is shown in Figure 3.24.

When the switch receives a TCP connection request, it first identifies the best
server for handling that request, and forwards the request packet to that server.
The server, in turn, will send an acknowledgment back to the requesting client, but

inserting the switch's IP address as the source field of the header of the IP packet carrying the TCP segment. Note that this address rewriting is necessary for the client to continue executing the TCP protocol: it is expecting an answer back from the switch, not from some arbitrary server it has never heard of before. Clearly, a TCP-handoff implementation requires operating-system level modifications. TCP handoff is especially effective when responses are much larger than requests, as in the case of Web servers.

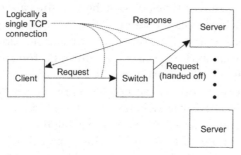

Figure 3.24: The principle of TCP handoff.

It can already be seen that the switch can play an important role in distributing the load among the various servers. By deciding where to forward a request to, the switch also decides which server is to handle further processing of the request. The simplest load-balancing policy that the switch can follow is round robin: each time it picks the next server from its list to forward a request to. Of course, the switch will have to keep track to which server it handed off a TCP connection, at least until that connection is torn down. As it turns out, maintaining this state and handing off subsequent TCP segments belonging to the same TCP connection, may actually slow down the switch.

Wide-area clusters

We came across wide-area clusters in our discussion on PlanetLab (see Note 3.6): an architecture in which participants contribute some (relatively simple) machines for hosting containers that are subsequently "sliced" across as many machines as a client needs. Thereafter, the client is on her own. Much more sophisticated and commercially deployed wide-area clusters exist today.

A straightforward version is seen with cloud providers like Amazon and Google, who manage several data centers placed at different locations worldwide. As such, they can offer an end user the ability to build a wide-area distributed system consisting of a potentially large collection of networked virtual machines, scattered across the Internet. An important reason for wanting such distributed systems is to provide locality: offering data and services that are close to clients. An example where such locality is important is streaming media: the closer a video server is located to a client, the easier it becomes to provide high-quality streams. This approach is followed by so-called cloud-based **Content Delivery Networks**, or simply CDNs, which we will discuss shortly.

An alternative is to have a single organization place servers across the Internet, effectively negotiating with local ISPs to decide how to make use of their facilities. This is the approach followed by the Akamai CDN [Dilley et al., 2002; Nygren et al., 2010], in 2022 having some 400,000 servers spread across 1350 ISPs and more than 135 countries.

The general organization of a CDN As CDNs form an important group of distributed systems that make use of wide-area clusters, let us take a closer look at how they are generally organized. We take a simplified view of the Akamai organization, shown in Figure 3.25. More information on CDNs can be found in [Passarella, 2012; Stocker et al., 2017] and [Zolfaghari et al., 2021]. The basic idea is that there is an **origin server** that hosts a Website with all its documents. As we will explain in Chapter 6, each document of such a site is referred to by a URL containing the **domain name** of the origin server, such as www.example.com. To access a document, the domain name needs to be resolved to a network address, which is done by the **Domain Name System**, which we will discuss in detail also in Chapter 6. To have the content of the origin server be hosted by a CDN, Akamai first makes sure that the domain name www.example.com is resolved to something like www.example.com.akamai.net, which, in turn, will refer to an edge server that is part of the Akamai CDN. To be able to still access the origin server, its domain name will have to be changed to, say, org-www.example.com. The principle is shown in Figure 3.25.

The client first looks up the regular domain name, but is redirected to the

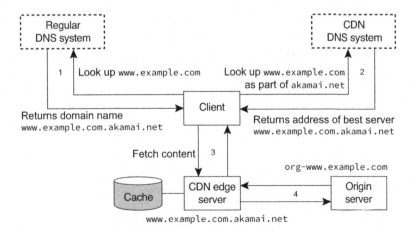

Figure 3.25: A simplified version of the working of the Akamai CDN.

akamai.net resolvers (step 1). The Akamai name resolvers will look up the best edge server to serve the client, and return its network address (step 2). This allows the client to contact the edge server (step 3), who is aware of the new name of the origin server. If the requested content is not in the edge server's cache, it fetches documents from the origin server (step 4), caches those documents and returns the requested ones to the client. More details can be found in [Su et al., 2006].

Request dispatching   This example already shows the importance of client-request redirection. In principle, by properly redirecting clients, a CDN can stay in control when it comes to client-perceived performance, but also considering global system performance by, for example, avoiding that requests are sent to heavily loaded servers. These so-called **adaptive redirection policies** can be applied when information on the system's current behavior is provided to the processes that take redirection decisions.

An important issue is whether request redirection is transparent to the client or not. In essence, there are only three redirection techniques: TCP handoff, DNS redirection, and HTTP redirection. We discussed TCP handoff in Note 3.7. This technique is applicable only for server clusters and does not scale to wide-area networks.

DNS redirection is a transparent mechanism by which the client can be kept completely unaware of where documents are located. Akamai's two-level redirection is one example of this technique. We can also directly deploy DNS to return one of several addresses. Note, however, that DNS redirection can be applied only to an entire site (or, more specifically, only at the level of a domain name): the name of individual documents does not fit into the DNS name space.

Unfortunately, DNS redirection is not perfect for two reasons. First, a client generally contacts the Domain Name System through a local DNS server that then acts as a proxy for that client. As a consequence, not the client's IP address, but that of the local DNS server, is used to identify the location of the client. Mao et al. [2002] have shown that there may be a huge additional communication cost, as the local DNS server is often not *that* local. Furthermore, even when clients are returned several options for selecting an edge server, simply picking the first on the list, which is what normally happens, may not be the best choice [Goel et al., 2015].

Secondly, depending on the scheme that is used for resolving a domain name, it may even be the case that the address of the local DNS server is not even being used. Instead, it may happen that the DNS server that is deciding on which IP address to return, may be fooled by the fact that the requester is yet another DNS server acting as an intermediate between the original client and the deciding DNS server (we will explain the details of this scheme in Chapter 6. In those cases, locality awareness has been completely lost.

Despite that DNS-based redirection may not always be very accurate, it is widely deployed if only for the fact that it is relatively easy to implement and also transparent to the client. In addition, there is no need to rely on location-aware client-side software.

HTTP redirection, finally, is a nontransparent mechanism. When a client requests a specific document, it may be given an alternative URL as part of an HTTP response message, to which it is then redirected. An important observation is that this URL is visible to the client's browser. In fact, the user may decide to bookmark the referral URL, potentially rendering the redirection policy useless.

3.5 Code migration

So far, we have been mainly concerned with distributed systems in which communication is limited to passing data. However, there are situations in which passing programs, sometimes even while they are being executed, simplifies the design of a distributed system. In this section, we take a detailed look at what code migration actually is.

3.5.1 Reasons for migrating code

Traditionally, code migration in distributed systems took place in the form of **process migration** in which an entire process was moved from one node to another [Milojicic et al., 2000]. Moving a running process to a different machine is a costly and intricate task, and there had better be a good reason for doing so. Let us first consider why one would even want to migrate code from one machine to another.

Performance   By far the most important reason for code migration has always been performance. The basic idea is that overall system performance can be improved if processes are moved from heavily loaded to lightly loaded machines. Load is often expressed in terms of the CPU queue length or CPU utilization, but other performance indicators are used as well. When completing their survey, Milojicic et al. had already come to the conclusion that process migration was no longer a viable option for improving distributed systems.

Instead of offloading machines, we can now witness that code is moved to make sure that a machine is *sufficiently* loaded. In particular, migrating complete virtual machines with their suite of applications to lightly loaded machines to minimize the total number of nodes being used is common practice in optimizing energy usage in data centers. Interestingly enough, although migrating virtual machines may require more resources, the task itself is far less intricate than migrating a process, as we discuss below.

In general, load-distribution algorithms by which decisions are made concerning the allocation and redistribution of tasks regarding a set of machines, play an important role in compute-intensive systems. However, in many modern distributed systems, optimizing computing capacity is less an issue than, for example, trying to minimize communication. Moreover, due to the heterogeneity of the underlying platforms and computer networks, performance improvement through code migration is often based on qualitative reasoning instead of mathematical models.

Consider, as an example, a client-server system in which the server manages a huge database. If a client application needs to perform many database operations involving large quantities of data, it may be better to ship part of the client application to the server and send only the results across the network. Otherwise, the network may be swamped with the transfer of data from the server to the client. In this case, code migration is assuming that it generally makes sense to process data close to where those data reside.

This same reason can be used for migrating parts of the server to the client. For example, in many interactive database applications, clients need to fill in forms that are subsequently translated into a series of database operations. Processing the form at the client side, and sending only the completed form to the server, can sometimes avoid that a relatively large number of small messages need to cross the network. The result is that the client perceives better performance, while at the same time the server spends less time on form processing and communication. In the case of smartphones, moving code to be executed at the handheld instead of the server may be the only viable solution to obtain acceptable performance, *both* for the client and the server (see Kumar et al. [2013] for a survey on offloading computations).

Support for code migration can also help improve performance by exploiting parallelism, but without the usual intricacies related to parallel programming. A typical example is searching for information in the Web. It is relatively simple to implement a search query in the form of a small mobile program, called a **mobile agent**, that moves from site to site. By making several copies of such a program, and sending each off to different sites, we may be able to achieve a linear speed-up compared to using just a single program instance. However, Carzaniga et al. [2007] conclude that mobile agents have never become successful because they did not really offer an obvious advantage over other technologies.

Privacy and security   Another reason for moving code to where the data is, has to do with security. Recently, the canonical example for this approach is found in **federated learning**. Federated learning comes from the need to train machine-learning models, notably all kinds of variants of artificial neural networks. To keep it simple, a neural network consists of a collection of nodes, organized as a series of several layers, and having weighted links between

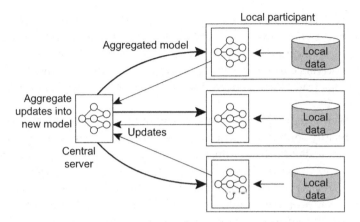

Figure 3.26: The principle of federated learning.

nodes of successive layers. Each node puts data on its outgoing links, which is the result of a (relatively simple) computation that it gets from data on its incoming links. Links have an adjustable weight. During a training phase, the weights of the links are gradually computed by feeding the network with data items for which it is known what the network should produce as a result. By systematically adjusting the weights to minimize the difference between what a network produces and what it should have produced, we eventually establish a final model. That model can then be used on unknown data items, for which we then take the produced result as a given.

A traditional approach is to collect the training data at a centralized location, often using specialized high-performance computers to construct an acceptable model. Obviously, this could mean that sensitive data, such as personal photo's and such, needed to be handed out to an organization that someone may not trust.

In such cases, a better approach is to bring the (partially) trained model to where the data is, and continue training with that local data. This will lead to an updated model (i.e., the weights have been further adjusted because of using new data). If several entities are involved in training with local data, a server can simply collect the different models, aggregate the results, and return an updated model to the local participants who can then continue with training. This iterative process, sketched in Figure 3.26 stops when the aggregated model is deemed sufficiently trained and fit for actual use.

It must be said that federated learning is easier from a code-migration perspective than, e.g., migrating processes. In general, the code involved in a neural network is relatively straightforward, which makes it easier to have it adopted by a local participant. This has been a high-level view on federated learning, of which a good introduction is given by Zhang et al. [2021a]. As described in Lyu et al. [2020], simply doing local training may not be sufficient from a privacy and security perspective.

Flexibility   There are other reasons for supporting code migration as well. An important one is that of flexibility. The traditional approach to building distributed applications is to partition the application into different parts, and decide in advance where each part should be executed. This approach, for example, has lead to different multitiered client-server applications discussed in Chapter 2.

However, if code can move between different machines, it becomes possible to dynamically configure distributed systems. For example, suppose a server implements a standardized interface to a file system. To allow remote clients to access the file system, the server makes use of a proprietary protocol. Normally, the client-side implementation of the file system interface, which is based on that protocol, would need to be linked with the client application. This approach requires that the software be readily available to the client at the time the client application is being developed.

An alternative is to let the server provide the client's implementation no sooner than is strictly necessary, that is, when the client binds to the server. At that point, the client dynamically downloads the implementation, goes through the necessary initialization steps, and subsequently invokes the server. This principle is shown in Figure 3.27 (we note that the code repository is generally located as part of the server). This model of dynamically moving code from a remote site does require that the protocol for downloading and initializing code is standardized. Furthermore, it is necessary that the downloaded code can be executed on the client's machine. Typically, scripts that run in a virtual machine embedded in, for example, a Web browser, will do the trick. Arguably, this form of code migration has been key to the success of the dynamic Web. These and other solutions are discussed below and in later chapters.

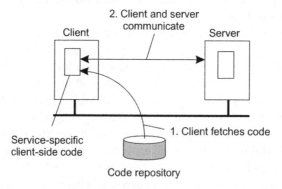

Figure 3.27: The principle of dynamically configuring a client to communicate with a server.

The important advantage of this model of dynamically downloading client-side software is that clients need not have all the software preinstalled to talk to servers. Instead, the software can be moved in as necessary, and likewise, discarded when no longer needed. Another advantage is that as long as interfaces are standardized, we can change the client-server protocol and its implementation as often as we like. Changes will not affect existing client applications that rely on the server.

There are, of course, also disadvantages. The most serious one, which we discuss in Chapter 9, has to do with security. Blindly trusting that the downloaded code implements only the advertised interface while accessing your unprotected hard disk and does not send the juiciest parts to heaven-knows-who may not always be such a good idea. Fortunately, it is well understood how to protect the client against malicious, downloaded code.

Note 3.8 (More information: Moving away from thin-client computing?)

By now, there is much more insight and expertise concerning transparent and safe dynamic migration of code to clients. As a result, the trend that we described in Note 2.5 of moving toward thin-client computing because managing client-side software often turned out to be cumbersome, has been partly reverted. By dynamically migrating client-side software, yet keeping the management of that software entirely at the server side (or rather, at its owner), having "richer" client-side software has become practically feasible. The most important domain where we see this happening is through applications running on smartphones. In fact, as soon as, for example, a bug is discovered, and update can take place. It is for this reason why many banks consider it safer to use a mobile app instead of a fixed piece of client-side software.

3.5.2 Models for code migration

Although code migration suggests that we move only code between machines, the term actually covers a much richer area. Traditionally, communication in distributed systems is concerned with exchanging data between processes. Code migration in the broadest sense deals with moving programs between machines, with the intention to have those programs be executed at the target. In some cases, as in process migration, the execution status of a program, pending signals, and other parts of the environment must be moved as well.

To get a better understanding of the different models for code migration, we use a framework proposed by Fuggetta et al. [1998]. In this framework, a process consists of three segments. The **code segment** is the part that contains the set of instructions that make up the program that is being executed. The **resource segment** contains references to external resources needed by the process, such as files, printers, devices, other processes, and so on. Finally, an **execution segment** is used to store the current execution state of a process, consisting of private data, the stack, and, of course, the program counter.

A further distinction can be made between sender-initiated and receiver-initiated migration. In **sender-initiated** migration, migration is initiated at the machine where the code currently resides or is being executed. Typically, sender-initiated migration is done when uploading programs to a compute server. Another example is sending a query, or batch of queries, to a remote database server. In **receiver-initiated** migration, the initiative for code migration is taken by the target machine. Java applets are an example of this approach.

Receiver-initiated migration is simpler than sender-initiated migration. Often, code migration occurs between a client and a server, where the client takes the initiative for migration. Securely uploading code to a server, as is done in sender-initiated migration, often requires that the client has previously been registered and authenticated at that server. In other words, the server is required to know all its clients, the reason being is that the client will presumably want access to the server's resources such as its disk. Protecting such resources is essential. In contrast, downloading code, as in the receiver-initiated case, can often be done anonymously. Moreover, the server is generally not interested in the client's resources. Instead, code migration to the client is done only for improving client-side performance. To that end, only a limited number of resources need to be protected, such as memory and network connections.

This brings us to four different paradigms for code mobility, as shown in Figure 3.28. Following Fuggetta et al. [1998], we make a distinction between simple **client-server computing**, **remote evaluation**, **code-on-demand**, and **mobile agents**. Figure 3.28 shows the situation at respectively the client and the server, before and after execution of the mobile code.

In the case of client-server computing, the code, execution state, and resource segment are all located at the server, and after execution, only the execution state at the server is generally modified. This state modification is denoted using an asterisk. With the sender-initiated **remote evaluation**, the client migrates code to the server where that code is executed and leading to a modification of the execution state at the server. **Code-on-demand** is a receiver-initiated scheme by which the client obtains code from the server, with its execution modifying the client-side execution state and operating on the client's resources. Finally, **mobile agents** typically follow a sender-initiated approach, moving code as well as execution state from the client to the server, operating on both the client's and the server's resources. Running a mobile agent will generally lead to modification of the associated execution state.

The bare minimum for code migration is to provide only **weak mobility**. In this model, it is possible to transfer only the code segment, along with perhaps some initialization data. A characteristic feature of weak mobility is that a transferred program is always started anew. This is what happens, for example, with Java applets, which start from the same initial state. In

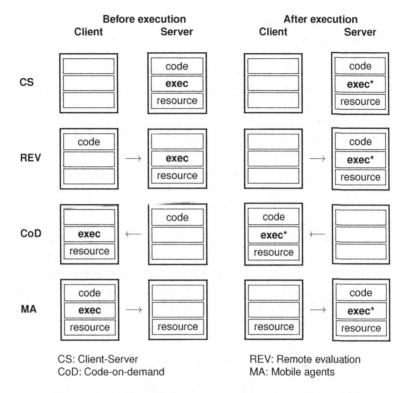

Figure 3.28: Four different paradigms for code mobility.

other words, no history from where the migrated code left off at a previous location is maintained by the underlying middleware. If such history needs to be preserved, it will have to be encoded as part of the mobile application itself. The benefit of weak mobility is its simplicity, as it requires only that the target machine can execute the code segment. In essence, this boils down to making the code portable. We return to these matters when discussing migration in heterogeneous systems.

In contrast to weak mobility, in systems that support **strong mobility** the execution segment can be transferred as well. The characteristic feature of strong mobility is that a running process can be stopped, subsequently moved to another machine, and then resume execution exactly where it left off. Clearly, strong mobility is much more general than weak mobility, but also much more difficult to implement. In particular, when migrating a process, the execution segment generally also contains data that is highly dependent on a specific *implementation* of the underlying operating system. For example, it may rely on information normally found in the operating system's process table. As a consequence, migrating to a different operating system, even one that belongs to the same family as the source, may cause plenty of headaches.

In the case of weak mobility, it also makes a difference if the migrated code is executed by the target process, or whether a separate process is started. For example, Java applets are simply downloaded by a Web browser and are executed in the browser's address space. The benefit of this approach is that there is no need to start a separate process, thereby avoiding interprocess communication at the target machine. The main drawback, obviously, is that the target process needs to be protected against malicious or inadvertent code executions, which may be reason enough to isolate the migrated code in a separate process.

Instead of moving a running process, also referred to as process migration, strong mobility can also be supported by remote cloning. In contrast to process migration, cloning yields an exact copy of the original process, but now running on a different machine. The cloned process is executed in parallel to the original process. In Unix systems, remote cloning takes place by forking off a child process and letting that child continue on a remote machine. The benefit of cloning is that the model closely resembles the one that is already used in many applications. The only difference is that the cloned process is executed on a different machine. In this sense, migration by cloning is a simple way to improve distribution transparency.

3.5.3   Migration in heterogeneous systems

So far, we have tacitly assumed that the migrated code can be easily executed at the target machine. This assumption is in order when dealing with homogeneous systems. In general, however, distributed systems are constructed on a heterogeneous collection of platforms, each having their own operating system and machine architecture.

The problems coming from heterogeneity are in many respects the same as those of portability. Not surprisingly, solutions are also very similar. For example, at the end of the 1970s, a simple solution to alleviate many of the problems of porting Pascal to different machines was to generate machine-independent intermediate code for an abstract virtual machine [Barron, 1981]. That machine, of course, would need to be implemented on many platforms, but it would then allow Pascal programs to be run anywhere. Although this simple idea was widely used for some years, it never really caught on as the general solution to portability problems for other languages, notably C.

About 25 years later, code migration in heterogeneous systems is being tackled by scripting languages and highly portable languages such as Java and Python. In essence, these solutions adopt the same approach as was done for porting Pascal. All such solutions have in common that they rely on a (process) virtual machine that either directly interprets source code (as in the case of scripting languages), or otherwise interprets intermediate code generated by a compiler (as in Java). Being in the right place at the right time is also important for language developers.

Further developments have weakened the dependency on programming languages. In particular, solutions have been proposed to migrate not only processes, but to migrate entire computing environments. The basic idea is to compartmentalize the overall environment and to provide processes in the same part their own view on their computing environment. That compartmentalization takes place in the form of virtual machine monitors running an operating system and a suite of applications.

With virtual machine migration, it becomes possible to decouple a computing environment from the underlying system and actually migrate it to another machine (see Medina and Garcia [2014] or Zhang et al. [2018] for overviews on migration mechanisms for virtual machines). A major advantage of this approach is that processes can remain ignorant of the migration itself: they need not be interrupted in their execution, nor should they experience any problems with used resources. The latter are either migrating along with a process, or the way that a process accesses a resource is left unaffected (at least, for that process).

As an example, Clark et al. [2005] concentrated on real-time migration of a virtualized operating system, typically something that would be convenient in a cluster of servers where a tight coupling is achieved through a single, shared local-area network. Under these circumstances, migration involves two major problems: migrating the entire memory image and migrating bindings to local resources.

As to the first problem, there are, in principle, three ways to handle migration (which can be combined):

1. Pushing memory pages to the new machine and resending the ones that are later modified during the migration process.

2. Stopping the current virtual machine; migrate memory, and start the new virtual machine.

3. Letting the new virtual machine pull in new pages as needed, that is, let processes start on the new virtual machine immediately and copy memory pages on demand.

The second option may lead to unacceptable downtime if the migrating virtual machine is running a live service, that is, one that offers continuous service. On the other hand, a pure on-demand approach as represented by the third option may extensively prolong the migration period, but may also lead to poor performance because it takes a long time before the working set of the migrated processes has been moved to the new machine.

As an alternative, Clark et al. [2005] propose to use a pre-copy approach which combines the first option, along with a brief stop-and-copy phase as represented by the second option. As it turns out, this combination can lead to very low service downtimes.

Concerning local resources, matters are simplified when dealing only with a cluster server. First, because there is a single network, the only thing that needs to be done is to announce the new network-to-MAC address binding, so that clients can contact the migrated processes at the correct network interface. Finally, if it can be assumed that storage is provided as a separate tier (like we showed in Figure 3.23), then migrating binding to files is similarly simple, as it effectively means reestablishing network connections.

Matters become more intricate when we need to migrate a virtual machine to another data center. Although the transfer of memory can be largely done as before, we do need to actually transfer files to the target data center. Somewhat problematic is also the network connectivity: one way or the other clients need to be able to continue contacting the virtual machine while, and after, its migration to the new destination. Zhang et al. [2018] mention various solutions. In essence, many of these either boil down to extending the local network to the target using techniques such as tunneling, or using techniques that support transparent reassigning of network addresses (meaning that a client uses dynamic rebinding to actual network addresses).

Note 3.9 (Advanced: On the performance of live virtual machine migration)
One potential problem with virtual-machine migration is that it may take considerable time. This by itself need not be bad, as long as the services that are running on the migrating virtual machine can continue to operate. An approach used in practice was briefly described above. First, memory pages are copied to the target machine, possibly sending updates of pages that were modified while copying took place (remember that copying lots of memory may take tens of seconds, even across a high-speed local network). Second, when most pages have been faithfully copied, the current machine is stopped, the remaining dirty pages are copied to the target, where the now exact copy can be started where the original left off.

The downtime in which the remaining dirty pages need to be copied depends on the applications running on the virtual machine. Clark et al. [2005] report downtimes for specific configurations between 60 milliseconds and less than 4 seconds. Voorsluys et al. [2009] come to similar values. However, what may be more interesting is to observe what the response time is of the service running on the virtual machine while the latter is being migrated. The model in this case is that the service continues to operate on the original machine until full migration has completed. However, we cannot ignore that migration itself is a resource-intensive operation, requiring considerable processing capacity as well as network bandwidth.

Voorsluys et al. [2009] have observed that a complete migration may actually take tens of seconds, leading to a ten- to twentyfold increase in response time. In addition, we need to realize that during the migration, a service will be completely unavailable (i.e., unresponsive) for perhaps 4 seconds. The good news is that the response time goes up significantly only after the downtime to complete the migration, as shown in Figure 3.29.

Often, virtual machines are migrated to optimize the usage of actual machines. However, it may also be desirable to clone a virtual machine, for example because the workload for the current machine is becoming too high. Such cloning is very similar to using multiple processes in concurrent servers, by which a dispatcher process creates worker processes to handle incoming requests. This scheme was explained in Figure 3.6 when discussing multithreaded servers.

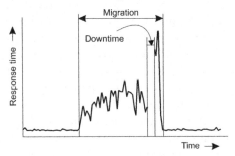

Figure 3.29: The effect on the response time of a service while migrating its underlying virtual machine. Adapted from Voorsluys et al. [2009].

When cloning for this type of performance, it often makes more sense *not* to first copy memory pages, but, in fact, start with as few pages as possible as the service running on the cloned machine will essentially start anew. Note that this behavior is very similar to the usual parent-child behavior we see when forking a Unix process. Namely, the child will start with loading its own executable, thereby effectively cleaning the memory it inherited from its parent. This analogy inspired Lagar-Cavilla et al. [2009] to develop an analogous mechanism for *forking* a virtual machine. However, unlike the mechanism used traditionally for migrating virtual machines, their **VM fork** copies pages primarily on demand. The result is an extremely efficient cloning mechanism.

It is thus seen that there is no single best way to place copies of a virtual machine on different physical machines: it very much depends on how and why a virtual machine is being deployed.

3.6 Summary

Processes play a fundamental role in distributed systems, as they form a basis for communication between different machines. An important issue is how processes are internally organized and, in particular, whether or not they support multiple threads of control. Threads in distributed systems are particularly useful to continue using the CPU when a blocking I/O operation is performed. In this way, it becomes possible to build highly efficient servers that run multiple threads in parallel, of which several may be blocking to wait until disk I/O or network communication completes. In general, threads are preferred over the use of processes when performance is at stake.

Virtualization has since long been an important field in computer science, but in the advent of cloud computing has regained tremendous attention. Popular virtualization schemes allow users to run a suite of applications on top of their favorite operating system and configure complete virtual distributed systems in the cloud. Impressively enough, performance remains close to running applications on the host operating system, unless that system is shared with other virtual machines or when the virtual machine is I/O bound. The flexible application of virtual machines has led to different types of services for cloud computing, including infrastructures, platforms, and software — all running in virtual environments. A special form of virtualization is that of containerization, which boils down to providing an application with its own environment (notably libraries and specific supporting programs) while sharing the same operating system. By sharing the same operating system, containers generally tend to perform better in the case of I/O-bound applications, yet it is fair to say that differences in performance between virtual machines and containers is diminishing.

Organizing a distributed application in terms of clients and servers has proven to be useful. Client processes generally implement user interfaces, which may range from simple displays to advanced interfaces that can handle compound documents. Client software is furthermore aimed at achieving distribution transparency by hiding details concerning the communication with servers, where those servers are currently located, and whether servers are replicated. In addition, client software is partly responsible for hiding failures and recovery from failures. An interesting phenomenon is the increasing popularity of virtual desktop environments, by which an entire desktop more or less runs in the cloud.

Servers are often more intricate than clients, but are nevertheless subject to only a relatively few design issues. For example, servers can either be iterative or concurrent, implement one or more services, and can be stateless or stateful. Other design issues deal with addressing services and mechanisms to interrupt a server after a service request has been issued and is possibly already being processed.

Special attention needs to be paid when organizing servers into a cluster. A common objective is to hide the internals of a cluster from the outside world. This means that the organization of the cluster should be shielded from applications. To this end, most clusters use a single entry point that can hand off messages to servers in the cluster. A challenging problem is to transparently replace this single entry point by a fully distributed solution.

Advanced object servers have been developed for hosting remote objects. An object server provides many services to basic objects, including facilities for storing objects, or to ensure serialization of incoming requests. Another important role is providing the illusion to the outside world that a collection of data and procedures operating on that data correspond to the concept of an object. This role is implemented by object adapters. Object-based systems have come to a point where we can build entire frameworks that can be extended for supporting specific applications. Java has proven to provide a powerful means for setting up more generic services, exemplified by the highly popular Enterprise Java Beans concept and its implementation.

An exemplary server for Web-based systems is the one from Apache. Again, the Apache server can be seen as a general solution for handling a myriad of HTTP-based queries. By offering the right hooks, we essentially obtain a flexibly configurable Web server. Apache has served as an example not only for traditional Websites, but also for setting up clusters of collaborative Web servers, even across wide-area networks.

An important development is that of content delivery networks in wide-area networks, which facilitate accessing data and other resources close to clients. An essential component is ensuring that resources from an origin server are copied to the proper edge servers transparently. To this end, the combination of client-request redirection techniques and advanced nearby caching is essential.

Another important topic for distributed systems is the migration of code between different machines. Two important reasons to support code migration are increasing performance and flexibility. When communication is expensive, we can sometimes reduce communication by shipping computations from the server to the client, and let the client do as much local processing as possible. Flexibility is increased if a client can dynamically download software needed to communicate with a specific server. The downloaded software can be specifically targeted to that server, without forcing the client to have it preinstalled. Lately, we see that also privacy and security have become reasons for migrating code, as is illustrated by federated learning.

Code migration brings along problems related to usage of local resources for which it is required that either resources are migrated as well, new bindings to local resources at the target machine are established, or for which systemwide network references are used. Another problem is that code migration requires that we take heterogeneity into account. Current practice indicates that the best solution to handle heterogeneity is to use virtual machines. These can take either the form of process virtual machines as in the case of, for example, Java, or through using virtual machine monitors that effectively allow the migration of a collection of processes along with their underlying operating system.

COMMUNICATION

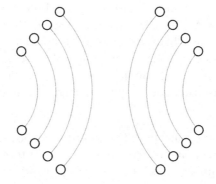

Interprocess communication is at the heart of all distributed systems. It makes no sense to study distributed systems without carefully examining the ways that processes on different machines can exchange information. Communication in distributed systems has traditionally always been based on low-level message passing as offered by the underlying network. Expressing communication through message passing is more difficult than using primitives based on shared memory, as available for nondistributed platforms. Modern distributed systems often consist of thousands or even millions of processes scattered across a network with unreliable communication, such as the Internet. Unless the primitive communication facilities of computer networks are replaced by something else, development of large-scale distributed applications is extremely difficult.

In this chapter, we start by discussing the rules that communicating processes must adhere to, known as protocols, and concentrate on structuring those protocols in the form of layers. We then look at two widely used models for communication: Remote Procedure Call (RPC), and Message-Oriented Middleware (MOM). We also discuss the general problem of sending data to multiple receivers, called multicasting.

Our first model for communication in distributed systems is the remote procedure call (RPC). An RPC aims at hiding most of the intricacies of message passing, and is ideal for client-server applications. However, realizing RPCs transparently is easier said than done. We look at several important details that cannot be ignored, while diving into actually code to illustrate to what extent distribution transparency can be realized such that performance is still acceptable.

In many distributed applications, communication does not follow the rather strict pattern of client-server interaction. In those cases, it turns out that thinking in terms of messages is more appropriate. The low-level communication facilities of computer networks are in many ways not suitable, again due to their lack of distribution transparency. An alternative is to use a high-level message-queuing model, in which communication proceeds much the same as in e-mail systems. Message-oriented communication is a subject important enough to warrant a section of its own. We look at numerous aspects, including application-level routing.

Finally, since our understanding of setting up multicast facilities has improved, novel and elegant solutions for data dissemination have emerged. We pay separate attention to this subject in the last section of this chapter, discussing traditional deterministic means of multicasting, as well as probabilistic approaches as used in flooding and gossiping. The latter have been receiving much attention over the past years due to their elegance, reliability, and simplicity.

4.1 Foundations

Before we start our discussion on communication in distributed systems, we first recapitulate some fundamental issues related to communication. In the next section, we briefly discuss network communication protocols, as these form the basis for any distributed system. Thereafter, we take a different approach by classifying the different types of communication that usually occur in distributed systems.

4.1.1 Layered Protocols

Due to the absence of shared memory, all communication in distributed systems is based on sending and receiving (low level) messages. When process P wants to communicate with process Q, it first builds a message in its own address space. Then it executes a system call that causes the operating system to send the message over the network to Q. Although this basic idea sounds simple enough, to prevent chaos, P and Q have to agree on the meaning of the bits being sent.

The OSI reference model

To make it easier to deal with the numerous levels and issues involved in communication, the International Standards Organization (ISO) developed a reference model that clearly identifies the various levels involved, gives them standard names, and points out which level should do which job. This model is called the **Open Systems Interconnection Reference Model** [Day and Zimmerman, 1983] usually abbreviated as **ISO OSI** or sometimes just the **OSI model**. It should be emphasized that the protocols that were developed as part of the OSI model were never widely used and are essentially dead. However, the underlying model itself has proved to be quite useful for understanding computer networks. Although we do not intend to give a full description of this model and all of its implications here, a brief introduction will be helpful. For more details, see [Tanenbaum et al., 2021].

The OSI model is designed to allow open systems to communicate. An open system is one that is prepared to communicate with any other open system by using standard rules that govern the format, contents, and meaning of the messages sent and received. These rules are formalized in what are called **communication protocols**. To allow a group of computers to communicate over a network, they must all agree on the protocols to be used. A protocol is said to provide a **communication service**. There are two types of such services. In the case of a **connection-oriented service**, before exchanging data the sender and receiver first explicitly establish a connection, and possibly negotiate specific parameters of the protocol they will use. When they are done, they release (terminate) the connection. The telephone is a typical connection-oriented communication service. With a **connectionless services**, no setup in advance is needed. The sender just transmits the first message when it is ready. Dropping a letter in a mailbox is an example of making use of connectionless communication service. With computers, both connection-oriented and connectionless communication are common.

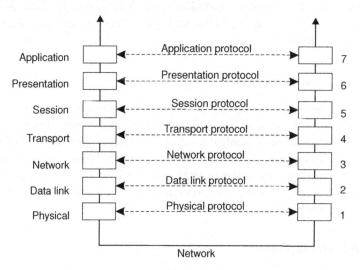

Figure 4.1: Layers, interfaces, and protocols in the OSI model.

In the OSI model, communication is divided into seven levels or layers, as shown in Figure 4.1. Each layer offers one or more specific communication services to the layer above it. In this way, the problem of getting a message from A to B can be divided into manageable pieces, each of which can be solved independently of the others. Each layer provides an **interface** to the one above it. The interface consists of a set of operations that together define the service the layer is prepared to offer. The seven OSI layers are:

Physical layer Deals with standardizing how two computers are connected and how 0s and 1s are represented.

Data link layer Provides the means to detect and possibly correct transmission errors, as well as protocols to keep a sender and receiver in the same pace.

Network layer Contains the protocols for routing a message through a computer network, as well as protocols for handling congestion.

Transport layer Mainly contains protocols for directly supporting applications, such as those that establish reliable communication, or support real-time streaming of data.

Session layer Provides support for sessions between applications.

Presentation layer Prescribes how data is represented in a way that is independent of the hosts on which communicating applications are running.

Application layer Essentially, everything else: e-mail protocols, Web access protocols, file-transfer protocols, and so on.

When a process P wants to communicate with some remote process Q, it builds a message and passes that message to the application layer as offered to it through an interface. This interface will typically appear in the form of a library procedure. The application layer software then adds a *header* to the front of the message and passes the resulting message across the layer 6/7 interface to the presentation layer. The presentation layer, in turn, adds its own header and passes the result down to the session layer, and so on. Some layers add not only a header to the front, but also a trailer to the end. When it hits the bottom, the physical layer actually transmits the message (which by now might look as shown in Figure 4.2) by putting it onto the physical transmission medium.

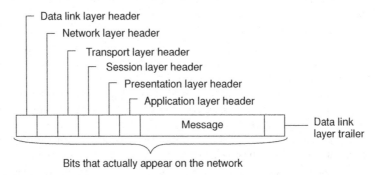

Figure 4.2: A typical message as it appears on the network.

When the message arrives at the remote machine hosting Q, it is passed upward, with each layer stripping off and examining its own header. Finally, the message arrives at the receiver, process Q, which may reply to it using the reverse path. The information in the layer-n header is used for the layer-n protocol.

In the OSI model, there are not two layers, but seven, as we saw in Figure 4.1. The collection of protocols used in a particular system is called a **protocol suite** or **protocol stack**. It is important to distinguish a *reference model* from its actual *protocols*. As said, the OSI protocols were never popular, in contrast to protocols developed for the Internet, such as TCP and IP.

Note 4.1 (More information: Protocols in the OSI model)

Let us briefly examine each of the OSI layers in turn, starting at the bottom. Instead of giving examples of OSI protocols, where appropriate, we will point out some Internet protocols used in each layer.

Lower-level protocols   The three lowest layers of the OSI protocol suite implement the basic functions that encompass a computer network.

The **physical layer** is concerned with transmitting the 0s and 1s. How many volts to use for 0 and 1, how many bits per second can be sent, and whether transmission can take place in both directions simultaneously are key issues in the physical layer. In addition, the size and shape of the network connector (plug), as well as the number of pins and meaning of each, are of concern here.

The physical layer protocol deals with standardizing the electrical, optical, mechanical, and signaling interfaces so that when one machine sends a 0 bit it is actually received as a 0 bit and not a 1 bit. Many physical layer standards have been developed (for different media), for example, the USB standard for serial communication lines.

The physical layer just sends bits. As long as no errors occur, all is well. However, real communication networks are subject to errors, so some mechanism is needed to detect and correct them. This mechanism is the main task of the **data link layer**. What it does is to group the bits into units, also called **frames**, and see that each frame is correctly received.

The data link layer does its work by putting a special bit pattern on the start and end of each frame to mark them, as well as computing a **checksum** by adding up all the bytes in the frame in a certain way. The data link layer appends the checksum to the frame. When the frame arrives, the receiver recomputes the checksum from the data and compares the result to the checksum following the frame. If the two agree, the frame is considered correct and is accepted. If they disagree, the receiver asks the sender to retransmit it. Frames are assigned sequence numbers (in the header), so everyone can tell which is which.

On a LAN, there is usually no need for the sender to locate the receiver. It just puts the message out on the network and the receiver takes it off. A wide-area network, however, consists of numerous machines, each with some number of lines to other machines, rather like a large-scale map showing major cities and roads connecting them. For a message to get from the sender to the receiver it may have to make a number of hops, at each one choosing an outgoing line to use. The question of how to choose the best path is called **routing**, and is essentially the primary task of the **network layer**.

The problem is complicated by the fact that the shortest route is not always the best route. What really matters is the amount of delay on a given route, which, in turn, is related to the amount of traffic and the number of messages queued up for transmission over the various lines. The delay can thus change over the course of time. Some routing algorithms try to adapt to changing loads, whereas others are content to make decisions based on long-term averages.

At present, the most widely used network protocol is the connectionless **IP** (**Internet Protocol**), which is part of the Internet protocol suite. An IP **packet** (the technical term for a message in the network layer) can be sent without any setup. Each IP packet is routed to its destination independent of all others. No internal path is selected and remembered.

Transport protocols   The **transport layer** forms the last part of what could be called a basic network protocol stack, in the sense that it implements all those services that are not provided at the interface of the network layer, but which are reasonably needed to build network applications. In other words, the transport layer turns the underlying network into something that an application developer can use.

Packets can be lost on the way from the sender to the receiver. Although some applications can handle their own error recovery, others prefer a reliable connection. The job of the transport layer is to provide this service. The idea is that the application layer should be able to deliver a message to the transport layer with the expectation that it will be delivered without loss.

Upon receiving a message from the application layer, the transport layer breaks it into pieces small enough for transmission, assigns each one a sequence number, and then sends them all. The discussion in the transport layer header concerns which packets have been sent, which have been received, how many more the receiver has room to accept, which should be retransmitted, and similar topics.

Reliable transport connections (which by definition are connection-oriented) can be built on top of connection-oriented or connectionless network services. In the former case all the packets will arrive in the correct sequence (if they arrive at all), but in the latter case it is possible for one packet to take a different route and arrive earlier than the packet sent before it. It is up to the transport layer software to put everything back to maintain the illusion that a transport connection is like a big tube–you put messages into it, and they come out undamaged and in the same order in which they went in. Providing this end-to-end communication behavior is an important aspect of the transport layer.

The Internet transport protocol is called **TCP (Transmission Control Protocol)** and is described in detail by Comer [2013]. The combination TCP/IP is now used as a de facto standard for network communication. The Internet protocol suite also supports a connectionless transport protocol called **UDP (Universal Datagram Protocol)**, which is essentially just IP with some minor additions. User programs that do not need a connection-oriented protocol normally use UDP.

Additional transport protocols are regularly proposed. For example, to support real-time data transfer, the **Real-time Transport Protocol (RTP)** has been defined. RTP is a framework protocol in the sense that it specifies packet formats for real-time data without providing the actual mechanisms for guaranteeing data delivery. In addition, it specifies a protocol for monitoring and controlling data transfer of RTP packets [Schulzrinne et al., 2003]. Likewise, the **Streaming Control Transmission Protocol (SCTP)** has been proposed as an alternative to

TCP [Stewart, 2007]. The main difference between SCTP and TCP is that SCTP groups data into messages, whereas TCP merely moves bytes between processes. Doing so may simplify application development.

Higher-level protocols   Above the transport layer, OSI distinguishes three additional layers. In practice, only the **application layer** is ever used. In fact, in the Internet protocol suite, everything above the transport layer is grouped together. In the face of middleware systems, we shall see that neither the OSI nor the Internet approach is really appropriate.

The **session layer** is essentially an enhanced version of the transport layer. It provides dialog control, to keep track of which party is currently talking, and it provides synchronization facilities. The latter are useful to allow users to insert checkpoints into long transfers, so that in the event of a crash, it is necessary to go back only to the last checkpoint, rather than all the way back to the beginning. In practice, few applications are interested in the session layer, and it is rarely supported. It is not even present in the Internet protocol suite. However, in the context of developing middleware solutions, the concept of a session and its related protocols has turned out to be quite relevant, notably when defining higher-level communication protocols.

Unlike the lower layers, which are concerned with getting the bits from the sender to the receiver reliably and efficiently, the **presentation layer** is concerned with the meaning of the bits. Most messages do not consist of random bit strings, but more structured information such as people's names, addresses, amounts of money, and so on. In the presentation layer, it is possible to define records containing fields like these and then have the sender notify the receiver that a message contains a particular record in a certain format. This makes it easier for machines with different internal representations to communicate with each other.

The OSI application layer was originally intended to contain a collection of standard network applications such as those for electronic mail, file transfer, and terminal emulation. By now, it has become the container for all applications and protocols that in one way or the other do not fit into one of the underlying layers. From the perspective of the OSI reference model, virtually all distributed systems are just applications.

What is missing in this model is a clear distinction between applications, application-specific protocols, and general-purpose protocols. For example, the Internet **File Transfer Protocol** (FTP) [Postel and Reynolds, 1985; Horowitz and Lunt, 1997] defines a protocol for transferring files between a client and server machine. The protocol should not be confused with the ftp program, which is an end-user application for transferring files and which also (not entirely coincidentally) happens to implement the Internet FTP.

Another example of a typical application-specific protocol is the **HyperText Transfer Protocol** (**HTTP**) [Fielding and Reschke, 2014] which is designed to remotely manage and handle the transfer of Web pages. The protocol is implemented by applications such as Web browsers and Web servers. However, HTTP is now also used by systems that are not intrinsically tied to the Web. For example,

Java's object-invocation mechanism can use HTTP to request the invocation of remote objects that are protected by a firewall.

There are also many general-purpose protocols that are useful to many applications, but which cannot be qualified as transport protocols. Often, such protocols fall into the category of middleware protocols.

Middleware protocols

Middleware is an application that logically lives (mostly) in the OSI application layer, but which contains many general-purpose protocols that warrant their own layers, independent of other, more specific applications. Let us briefly look at some examples.

The **Domain Name System (DNS)** [Liu and Albitz, 2006] is a distributed service that is used to look up a network address associated with a name, such as the address of a so-called **domain name** like www.distributed-systems.net. In terms of the OSI reference model, DNS is an application and therefore is logically placed in the application layer. However, it should be quite obvious that DNS is offering a general-purpose, application-independent service. Arguably, it forms part of the middleware.

As another example, there are various ways to establish **authentication**, that is, provide proof of a claimed identity. Authentication protocols are not closely tied to any specific application, but instead, can be integrated into a middleware system as a general service. Likewise, **authorization protocols** by which authenticated users and processes are granted access only to those resources for which they have authorization, tend to have a general, application-independent nature. Being labeled as applications in the OSI reference model, these are clear examples that belong in the middleware.

Distributed commit protocols establish that in a group of processes, possibly spread out across several machines, either all processes carry out a particular operation, or that the operation is not carried out at all. This phenomenon is also referred to as **atomicity** and is widely applied in transactions. As it turns out, commit protocols can present an interface independently of specific applications, thus providing a general-purpose transaction service. In such a form, they typically belong to the middleware and not to the OSI application layer.

As a last example, consider a **distributed locking protocol**, by which a resource can be protected against simultaneous access by a collection of processes that are distributed across multiple machines. It is not hard to imagine that such protocols can be designed in an application-independent fashion, and accessible through a relatively simple, again application-independent interface. As such, they generally belong in the middleware.

These protocol examples are not directly tied to communication, yet there

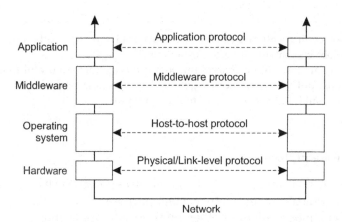

Figure 4.3: An adapted reference model for networked communication.

are also many middleware communication protocols. For example, with a so-called **remote procedure call**, a process is offered a facility to *locally* call a procedure that is effectively implemented on a *remote* machine. This communication service belongs to one of the oldest types of middleware services and is used for realizing access transparency. In a similar vein, there are high-level communication services for setting and synchronizing streams for transferring real-time data, such as needed for multimedia applications. As a last example, some middleware systems offer reliable multicast services that scale to thousands of receivers spread across a wide-area network.

Taking this approach to layering leads to the adapted and simplified reference model for communication, as shown in Figure 4.3. Compared to the OSI model, the session and presentation layer have been replaced by a single middleware layer that contains application-independent protocols. These protocols do not belong in the lower layers we just discussed. Network and transport services have been grouped into communication services as normally offered by an operating system, which, in turn, manages the specific lowest-level hardware used to establish communication.

4.1.2   Types of Communication

In the remainder of this chapter, we concentrate on high-level middleware communication services. Before doing so, there are other general criteria for distinguishing (middleware) communication. To understand the various alternatives in communication that middleware can offer to applications, we view the middleware as an additional service in client-server computing, as shown in Figure 4.4. Consider, for example, an e-mail system. In principle, the core of the mail delivery system can be seen as a middleware communication service. Each host runs a user agent allowing users to compose, send, and receive e-mail. A sending user agent passes such mail to the mail delivery system, expecting it, in turn, to eventually deliver the mail to the intended recipient. Likewise, the user agent at the receiver's side connects to the mail delivery system to see whether any mail has come in. If so, the messages are transferred to the user agent so that they can be read by the user.

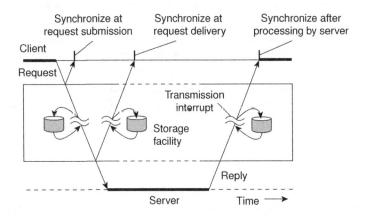

Figure 4.4: Viewing middleware as an intermediate (distributed) service in application-level communication.

An e-mail system is a typical example in which communication is persistent. With **persistent communication**, a message that has been submitted for transmission is stored by the communication middleware as long as it takes to deliver it to the receiver. In this case, the middleware will store the message at one or several of the storage facilities shown in Figure 4.4. As a consequence, it is not necessary for the sending application to continue execution after submitting the message. Likewise, the receiving application need not be executing when the message is submitted.

In contrast, with **transient communication**, a message is stored by the communication system only as long as the sending and receiving application are executing. More precisely, in terms of Figure 4.4, if the middleware cannot deliver a message due to a transmission interrupt, or because the recipient is currently not active, it will simply be discarded. Typically, all transport-level communication services offer only transient communication. In this case, the communication system consists of traditional store-and-forward routers. If a router cannot deliver a message to the next one or the destination host, it will simply drop the message.

Besides being persistent or transient, communication can also be asynchronous or synchronous. The characteristic feature of **asynchronous communication** is that a sender continues immediately after it has submitted its message for transmission. This means that the message is (temporarily) stored immediately by the middleware upon submission. With **synchronous communication**, the sender is blocked until its request is known to be accepted. There are essentially three points where synchronization can take place. First, the sender may be blocked until the middleware notifies that it will take over transmission of the request. Second, the sender may synchronize until its request has been delivered to the intended recipient. Third, synchronization may take place by letting the sender wait until its request has been fully processed, that is, up to the time that the recipient returns a response.

Various combinations of persistence and synchronization occur in practice. Popular ones are persistence in combination with synchronization at request submission, which is a common scheme for many message-queuing systems, which we discuss later in this chapter. Likewise, transient communication with synchronization after the request has been fully processed is also widely used. This scheme corresponds with remote procedure calls, which we discuss in the following section.

4.2   Remote procedure call

Many distributed systems have been based on explicit message exchange between processes. However, the operations send and receive do not conceal communication at all, which is important to achieve access transparency in distributed systems. This problem has long been known, but little was done about it until researchers in the 1980s [Birrell and Nelson, 1984] introduced an entirely different way of handling communication. Although the idea is refreshingly simple (once someone has thought of it), the implications are often subtle. In this section we will examine the concept, its implementation, its strengths, and its weaknesses.

In a nutshell, the proposal was to allow programs to call procedures located on other machines. When a process on a machine A calls a procedure on a machine B, the calling process on A is suspended, and execution of the called procedure takes place on B. Information can be transported from the caller to the callee in the parameters and can come back in the procedure result. No message passing at all is visible to the programmer. This method is known as **remote procedure call**, or often just **RPC**.

While the basic idea sounds simple and elegant, subtle problems exist. To start with because the calling and called procedures run on different machines, they execute in different address spaces, which causes complications. Parameters and results also have to be passed, which can be complicated, especially if the machines are not identical. Finally, either or both machines can crash, and each of the possible failures causes different problems. Still, most of these can be dealt with, and RPC is a widely used technique that underlies many distributed systems.

4.2.1   Basic RPC operation

The idea behind RPC is to make a remote procedure call look as much as possible as a local one. In other words, we want RPC to be transparent—the calling procedure should not be aware that the called procedure is executing on a different machine or vice versa. Suppose that a program has access to a database that allows it to append data to a stored list, after which it returns a reference to the modified list. The operation is made available to a program by a routine append:

```
newlist = append(data, dbList)
```

In a traditional (single processor) system, append is extracted from a library by the linker and inserted into the object program. In principle, it can be a short procedure, which could be implemented by a few file operations for accessing the database.

Even though append eventually does only a few basic file operations, it is called in the usual way, by pushing its parameters onto the stack. The programmer does not know the implementation details of append, and this is, of course, how it is supposed to be.

Note 4.2 (More information: Conventional procedure calls)
To understand how RPC works and some of its pitfalls, it may help to first understand how a conventional (i.e., single machine) procedure call works. Consider the operation newlist = append(data, dbList);

We assume that the purpose of this call is to take a *globally* defined list object, referred here to as dbList, and append a simple data element to it, represented by the variable data. An important observation is that in various programming languages such as C, dbList is implemented as a *reference* to a list object (i.e., a pointer), whereas data may be represented directly by its value (which we assume to be the case here). When calling append, both the representations of data and dbList are pushed onto the stack, making those representations accessible to the implementation of append. For data, this means the variable follows a **call-by-value** policy, the policy for dblist is **call-by-reference**. What happens before and during the call is shown in Figure 4.5.

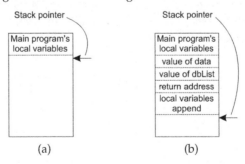

Figure 4.5: (a) Parameter passing in a local procedure call: the stack before the call to append. (b) The stack while the called procedure is active.

Several things are worth noting. For one, a value parameter, such as data, is just an initialized local variable. The called procedure may modify it, but such changes do not affect the original value at the calling side.

When a parameter like dbList is actually a pointer to a variable rather than the value of the variable, something else happens. What is pushed onto the stack is the address of the list object as stored in main memory. When the value of data is appended to the list, a call to append *does* modify the list object. The difference between call-by-value and call-by-reference is quite important for RPC.

One other parameter passing mechanism also exists, although it is not used in most programming languages. It is called **call-by-copy/restore**. It consists of having the variable copied to the stack by the caller, as in call-by-value, and then copied back after the call, overwriting the caller's original value. Under most conditions, this achieves the same effect as call-by-reference, but in some situations, such as the same parameter being present multiple times in the parameter list, the semantics are different.

The decision of which parameter passing mechanism to use is normally made by the language designers and is a fixed property of the language. Every so often, it depends on the data type being passed. In C, for example, integers and other scalar types are always passed by value, whereas arrays are always passed by reference. Some Ada compilers use copy/restore for inout parameters, but others use call-by-reference. The language definition permits either choice, which makes the semantics a bit fuzzy. In Python, all variables are passed by reference, but some actually get copied to local variables, thus mimicking the behavior of copy-by-value.

RPC achieves its transparency analogously. When append is actually a remote procedure, a different version of append, called a **client stub**, is offered to the calling client. Like the original one, it, too, is called using a normal calling sequence. However, unlike the original one, it does not perform an append operation. Instead, it packs the parameters into a message and requests that message to be sent to the server, as illustrated in Figure 4.6. Following the call to send, the client stub calls receive, blocking itself until the reply comes back.

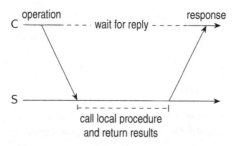

Figure 4.6: The principle of RPC between a client and server program.

When the message arrives at the server, the server's operating system passes it to a **server stub**. A server stub is the server-side equivalent of a client stub: it is a piece of code that transforms requests coming in over the network into local procedure calls. Typically, the server stub will have called receive and be blocked waiting for incoming messages. The server stub unpacks the parameters from the message and then calls the server procedure in the usual way. From the server's perspective, it is as though it is being called directly by the client—the parameters and return address are all on the stack where they belong and nothing seems unusual. The server performs its work and then returns the result to the caller (in this case the server stub) in the usual way.

When the server stub gets control back after the call has completed, it packs the result in a message and calls send to return it to the client. Thereafter, the server stub usually does a call to receive again, to wait for the next incoming request.

When the result message arrives at the client's machine, the operating system passes it through the receive operation, which had been called previously, to the client stub, and the client process is subsequently unblocked. The client stub inspects the message, unpacks the result, copies it to its caller, and returns in the usual way. When the caller gets control following the call to append, all it knows is that it appended some data to a list. It has no idea that the work was done remotely at another machine.

This blissful ignorance for the client is the beauty of the whole scheme. As far as it is concerned, remote services are accessed by making ordinary (i.e., local) procedure calls, not by calling send and receive. All the details of the message passing are hidden away in the two library procedures, just as the details of actually making system calls are hidden away in traditional libraries. To summarize, a remote procedure call occurs in the following steps:

1. The client procedure calls the client stub in the normal way.
2. The client stub builds a message and calls the local operating system.
3. The client's OS sends the message to the remote OS.
4. The remote OS gives the message to the server stub.
5. The server stub unpacks the parameter(s) and calls the server.
6. The server does the work and returns the result to the stub.
7. The server stub packs the result in a message and calls its local OS.
8. The server's OS sends the message to the client's OS.
9. The client's OS gives the message to the client stub.
10. The stub unpacks the result and returns it to the client.

The first steps are shown in Figure 4.7 for an abstract two-parameter procedure doit(a,b), where we assume that parameter a is of type type1, and b of type type2. The net effect of all these steps is to convert the local call by the client procedure to the client stub, to a local call to the server procedure,

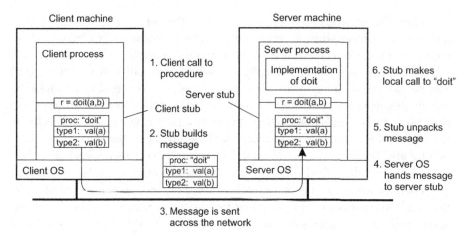

Figure 4.7: The steps involved in calling a remote procedure doit(a,b). The return path for the result is not shown.

without either client or server being aware of the intermediate steps or the existence of the network.

Note 4.3 (More information: An example in Python)

To make matters concrete, let us consider how a remote procedure call could be implemented for the operation append discussed previously. Take a look at the Python code shown in Figure 4.8 (from which we omit nonessential code fragments).

The class DBList is a simple representation of a list object, mimicking what one would expect to see in a version that would be found in a database environment. The client stub, represented by the class Client, consists of an implementation of append. When called with parameters data and dbList, the following happens. The call is transformed into a tuple (APPEND, data, dbList) containing all the information the server would need to do its work. The client stub then sends the request off to the server, and subsequently waits for the response. In the channel package, a recvFrom operation always returns a (*sender,message*) pair, allowing the caller to identify the process who had sent the message. In our case, when the response comes in, the client stub finishes the call to append by simply passing the returned message from the server to the program that initially called the stub.

On the server side, we see that in the server stub, the server waits for any incoming message, and inspects which operation it is required to call. Again, the channel package returns the identifier of the original sender (line 24). Assuming the server received a request to call append, it then simply does a *local* call to its implementation of append with the appropriate parameters as also found in the request tuple. The result is then sent back to the identified client.

Note that an actual client would simply call c.append(...) where c is an instance of the class Client. Indeed, the call truly seems to take place locally.

```
1  import channel, pickle
2
3  class DBList:
4    def append(self, data):
5      self.value.extend(data)
6      return self
7
8  class Client:
9    def append(self, data, dbList):
10     msglst = (APPEND, data, dbList)              # message payload
11     self.channel.sendTo(self.server, msglst)    # send message to server
12     msgrcv = self.channel.recvFrom(self.server) # wait for an incoming message
13
14     # A call to recvFrom returns a [senderID, message] pair
15     return msgrcv[1]                             # pass returned message to caller
16
17 class Server:
18   def append(self, data, dbList):
19     return dbList.append(data)
20
21   def run(self):
22     while True:
23       msgreq = self.channel.recvFromAny() # wait for any request
24       client = msgreq[0]                   # see who is the caller
25       msgrpc = msgreq[1]                   # fetch the actual request
26
27       # At this point, msgreq should have the form (operation, data, list)
28       if APPEND == msgrpc[0]:            # check what is being requested
29         result = self.append(msgrpc[1], msgrpc[2]) # do local call
30         self.channel.sendTo(client,result)         # return response
```

Figure 4.8: A simple RPC example for operation append.

4.2.2 Parameter passing

The function of the client stub is to take its parameters, pack them into a message, and send them to the server stub. While this sounds straightforward, it is not quite as simple as it at first appears.

Packing parameters into a message is called **parameter marshaling**. Returning to our append operation, we need to ensure that its two parameters (data and dbList) are sent over the network and correctly interpreted by the server. The thing to realize, is that the server will just be seeing a series of bytes coming in that constitute the original message sent by the client. However, no additional information on what those bytes mean is normally provided with the message. Also, we would be facing the same problem again: how should the meta-information be recognized as such by the server?

Besides this interpretation problem, we also need to handle the case that the placement of bytes in memory may differ between machine architectures. In particular, we need to account for the fact that some machines, such as Intel processors, number their bytes from right to left, whereas many others, such as the older ARM processors, number them the other way (ARM now supports both). The Intel format is called **little endian** and the (older) ARM format is called **big endian**. Byte ordering is also important for networking: also here we can witness that machines may use a different ordering when transmitting (and thus receiving) bits and bytes. However, big endian is what is normally used for transferring bytes across a network.

The solution to this problem is to transform data that is to be sent to a machine- and network-independent format, next to making sure that both communicating parties expect the same *message data type* to be transmitted. The latter can typically be solved at the level of programming languages. The former is accomplished by using machine-*dependent* routines that transform data to and from machine- and network-independent formats.

Marshaling and unmarshaling is all about this transformation to neutral formats and forms an essential part of remote procedure calls.

Note 4.4 (More information: An example in Python revisited)

```
 1  import channel, pickle
 2
 3  class Client:
 4    def append(self, data, dbList):
 5      msglst = (APPEND, data, dbList)                # message payload
 6      msgsnd = pickle.dumps(msglst)                  # wrap call
 7      self.channel.sendTo(self.server, msgsnd)       # send request to server
 8      msgrcv = self.channel.recvFrom(self.server)    # wait for response
 9      retval = pickle.loads(msgrcv[1])               # unwrap return value
10      return retval                                  # pass it to caller
11
12  class Server:
13    def run(self):
14      while True:
15        msgreq = self.channel.recvFromAny()  # wait for any request
16        client = msgreq[0]                   # see who is the caller
17        msgrpc = pickle.loads(msgreq[1])     # unwrap the call
18        if APPEND == msgrpc[0]:              # check what is being requested
19          result = self.append(msgrpc[1], msgrpc[2]) # do local call
20          msgres = pickle.dumps(result)             # wrap the result
21          self.channel.sendTo(client,msgres)        # send response
```

Figure 4.9: A simple RPC example for operation append, but now with proper marshaling.

It is not difficult to see that the solution to remote procedure calling as shown in Figure 4.8 will not work in general. Only if the client and server are operating on machines that obey the same byte-ordering rules *and* have the same machine representations for data structures, will the exchange of messages as shown lead to correct interpretations. A robust solution is shown in Figure 4.9 (where we again have omitted code for brevity).

In this example, we use the Python `pickle` library for marshaling and unmarshaling data structures. Note that the code hardly changes in comparison to what we have shown in Figure 4.8. The only changes occur just before sending, and after receiving a message. Also note that both client and server are programmed to work on the same data structures, as we discussed above.

(We do note that, behind the scene, whenever a class instance is passed as a parameter, Python generally takes care of *pickling* and later *unpickling* the instance. In this sense, our explicit use of `pickle` is, strictly speaking, not necessary.)

We now come to a difficult problem: How are pointers, or in general, references passed? The answer is: only with the greatest of difficulty, if at all. A pointer is meaningful only within the address space of the process in which it is being used. Getting back to our append example, we stated that the second parameter, dbList, is implemented through a *reference* to a list stored in a database. If that reference is just a pointer to a local data structure somewhere in the caller's main memory, we cannot simply pass it to the server. The transferred pointer value will most likely be referring to something entirely different.

One solution is just to forbid pointers and reference parameters in general. However, these are so important that this solution is highly undesirable. In fact, it is often not necessary either. First, reference parameters are often used with fixed-sized data types, such as static arrays, or with dynamic data types for which it is easy to compute their size at runtime, such as strings or dynamic arrays. In such cases, we can simply copy the entire data structure to which the parameter is referring, effectively replacing the copy-by-reference mechanism by copy-by-value/restore. Although this is semantically not always identical, it frequently is good enough. An obvious optimization is that when the client stub knows the referred data will be only read, there is no need to copy it back when the call has finished. Copy-by-value is thus good enough.

More intricate data types can often be supported as well, and certainly if a programming language supports those data types. For example, a language such as Python or Java supports user-defined classes, allowing a language system to provide fully automated marshaling and unmarshaling of those data types. Note, however, that as soon as we are dealing with large, nested, or otherwise intricate dynamic data structures, automatic (un)marshaling may not be available, or even desirable.

The problem with pointers and references, as discussed so far, is that they make sense only locally: they refer to memory locations that have meaning only to the calling process. Problems can be alleviated by using *global* references: references that are meaningful to the calling and the called process. For example, if the client and the server have access to the same file system, passing a file handle instead of a pointer may do the trick. There is one important observation: both processes need to know exactly what to do when a global reference is passed. In other words, if we consider a global reference having an associated data type, the calling and called process should have the same picture of the operations that can be performed. Moreover, both processes should have agreement on exactly what to do when a file handle is passed. Again, these are typically issues that can be solved by proper programming-language support. We will return to this subject shortly.

Note 4.5 (Advanced: Parameter passing in object-based systems)
Object-based systems often use global references. Consider the situation that all objects in the system can be accessed from remote machines. In that case, we can consistently use **object references** as parameters in method invocations. References are passed by value, and thus copied from one machine to the other. When a process is given an object reference as the result of a method invocation, it can simply bind to the object referred to when needed later (see also Section 2.1.2).

Unfortunately, using only distributed objects can be highly inefficient, especially when objects are small, such as integers, or worse yet, Booleans. Each invocation by a client that is not co-located in the same server as the object, generates a request between different address spaces or, even worse, between different machines. Therefore, references to remote objects and those to local objects are often treated differently.

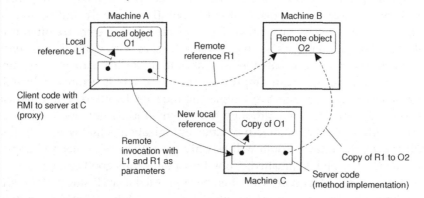

Figure 4.10: Passing an object by reference or by value.

When invoking a method with an object reference as parameter, that reference is copied and passed as a value parameter only when it refers to a remote object. In this case, the object is literally passed by reference. However, when the reference refers to a local object, that is an object in the same address space as the client, the referred object is copied as a whole and passed along with the invocation. In other words, the object is passed by value.

These two situations are illustrated in Figure 4.10 which shows a client program running on a machine A, and a server program on a machine C. The client has a reference to a local object O1 that it uses as a parameter when calling the server program on machine C. In addition, it holds a reference to a remote object O2 residing at machine B, which is also used as a parameter. When calling the server, a copy of O1 is passed to the server on machine C, along with only a copy of the reference to O2.

Note that whether we are dealing with a reference to a local object or a reference to a remote object can be highly transparent, such as in Java. In Java, the distinction is visible only because local objects are essentially of a different data type than remote objects. Otherwise, both types of references are treated very much the same (see also [Wollrath et al., 1996]). On the other hand, when using conventional programming languages such as C, a reference to a local object can be as simple as a pointer, which can never be used to refer to a remote object.

The side effect of invoking a method with an object reference as parameter is that we may be *copying* an object. Obviously, hiding this aspect is unacceptable so that we are consequently forced to make an explicit distinction between local and distributed objects. Clearly, this distinction not only violates distribution transparency, but also makes it harder to write distributed applications.

We can now also easily explain how global references can be implemented when using portable, interpreted languages such as Python or Java: use the entire client stub as a reference. The key observation is that a client stub is often just another data structure that is compiled into (portable) bytecode. That compiled code can actually be transferred across the network and executed at the receiver's side. In other words, there is no need for explicit binding anymore; simply copying the client stub to the recipient is enough to allow the latter to invoke the associated server-side object. Of course, it may be necessary to marshall that code before shipping it to the other machine, although strictly speaking, there is no reason why that other machine would work with different layouts.

4.2.3 RPC-based application support

From what we have explained so far, it is clear that hiding a remote procedure call requires that the caller and the callee agree on the format of the messages they exchange and that they follow the same steps when it comes to, for example, passing complex data structures. In other words, both sides in an RPC should follow the same protocol or the RPC will not work correctly. There are at least two ways in which RPC-based application development can be supported. The first one is to let a developer specify exactly what needs to be called remotely, from which complete client-side and server-side stubs can be generated. A second approach is to embed remote procedure calling as part of a programming-language environment.

Stub generation

Consider the function someFunction of Figure 4.11(a). It has three parameters, a character, a floating-point number, and an array of five integers. Assuming a word is four bytes, the RPC protocol might prescribe that we should transmit a character in the rightmost byte of a word (leaving the next three bytes empty), a float as a whole word, and an array as a group of words whose size is equal to the array length, preceded by a word giving the length, as shown in Figure 4.11(b). Thus given these rules, the client stub for someFunction knows that it must use the format of Figure 4.11(b), and the server stub knows that incoming messages for someFunction will have the format of Figure 4.11(b).

```
void someFunction(char x; float y; int z[5])
```

(a)

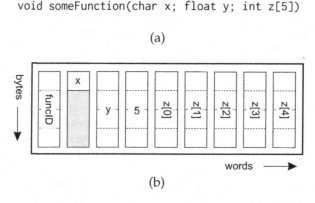

(b)

Figure 4.11: (a) A function. (b) The corresponding message, and the order in which bytes and words are sent across the network.

Defining the message format is one aspect of an RPC protocol, but it is not sufficient. What we also need is the client and the server to agree on the representation of simple data structures, such as integers, characters, Booleans, etc. For example, the protocol could prescribe that integers are represented in two's complement, characters in 16-bit Unicode, and floats in the IEEE standard #754 format, with everything stored in little endian. With this additional information, messages can be unambiguously interpreted.

With the encoding rules now pinned down to the last bit, the only thing that remains to be done is that the caller and callee agree on the actual exchange of messages. For example, it may be decided to use a connection-oriented transport service, such as TCP/IP. An alternative is to use an unreliable datagram service and let the client and server implement an error control scheme as part of the RPC protocol. In practice, several variants exist, and it is up to the developer to indicate the preferred underlying communication service.

Once the RPC protocol has been fully defined, the client and server stubs need to be implemented. Fortunately, stubs for the same protocol, but different procedures, normally differ only in their interface to the applications. An interface consists of a collection of procedures that can be called by a client, and which are implemented by a server. An interface is usually available in the same programming language as the one in which the client or server is written (although this is, strictly speaking, not necessary). To simplify matters, interfaces are often specified through an **Interface Definition Language** (IDL). An interface specified in such an IDL is then subsequently compiled into a client stub and a server stub, along with the appropriate compile-time or run-time interfaces. This process is sketched in Figure 4.12.

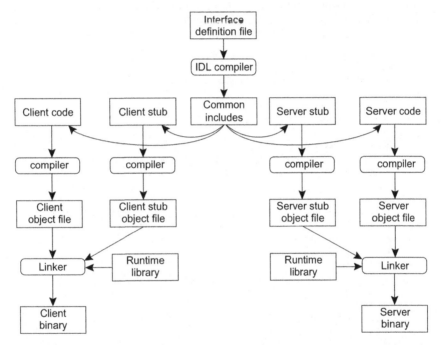

Figure 4.12: The principle of generating stubs from an interface definition file.

The figure shows the situation for compiled languages, yet it is not hard to imagine that a very similar situation holds for interpreted languages. Also note that it is possible that the client and server code are written in *different* languages. There is no principal reason why the client side cannot consist of components written in, for example, Python, while the server side is written in C. Of course, in that case, the box in Figure 4.12 representing common includes will then contain separate files for the client and server, respectively. Important in this scheme is the runtime library: it forms the interface to the actual runtime system, constituting the middleware.

Practice shows that using an interface definition language considerably simplifies client-server applications based on RPCs. Because it is easy to fully generate client and server stubs, all RPC-based middleware systems offer an IDL to support application development. In some cases, using the IDL is even mandatory.

Note 4.6 (More information: Language-based RPC in Python)
Let us see by an example of how remote procedure calling can be integrated in a language. We have been using the Python language for most of our examples, and will continue to do so now as well. In Figure 4.13 we show a simple server for our DBList data structure. In this case, it has two *exposed* operations: exposed_append for appending elements, and exposed_value to display what is currently in the list. We use the Python RPyC package for embedding RPCs.

```
 1  import rpyc
 2  from rpyc.utils.server import ForkingServer
 3
 4  class DBList(rpyc.Service):
 5    value = [] # Used to build a list of strings
 6
 7    def exposed_append(self, data):
 8      self.value.extend(str(data)) # Extend the list with the data
 9      return self.value            # Return the current list
10
11  class Server:
12    # Create a forking server at inititalization time and immediately start it.
13    # For each incoming request, the server will spawn another process to handle
14    # that request. The process that started the (main) server can simply kill
15    # it when it's time to do so.
16    def __init__(self):
17      self.server = ForkingServer(DBList, hostname=SERVER, port=PORT)
18
19    def start(self):
20      self.server.start()
21
22  class Client:
23    def run(self):
24      conn = rpyc.connect(SERVER, PORT) # Connect to the server
25      conn.root.exposed_append(2)       # Call an exposed operation,
26      conn.root.exposed_append(4)       # and append two elements
27      print(conn.root.exposed_value())  # Print the result
```

Figure 4.13: Embedding RPCs in a language

The client is also shown in Figure 4.13. When a connection is made to the server, a new instance of DBList will be created and the client can immediately append values to the list. The exposed operations are called without further ado.

Note that as the client breaks the connection to the server, the list will be lost. It is a **transient object** and special measures will need to be taken to make it a **persistent object**.

Language-based support

The approach described up until now is largely independent of a specific programming language. As an alternative, we can also embed remote procedure
calling into a language itself. The main benefit is that application development
often becomes much simpler. Furthermore, reaching a high degree of access
transparency is often simpler, as many issues related to parameter passing
can be circumvented altogether.

A well-known example in which remote procedure calling is fully embedded is Java, where an RPC is referred to as a **remote method invocation
(RMI)**. In essence, a client being executed by its own (Java) virtual machine
can invoke a method of an object managed by another virtual machine. By
simply reading an application's source code, it may be hard or even impossible
to see whether a method invocation is to a local or to a remote object.

4.2.4 Variations on RPC

As in conventional procedure calls, when a client calls a remote procedure, the
client will block until a reply is returned. This strict request-reply behavior
is unnecessary when there is no result to return, or may hinder efficiency
when multiple RPCs need to be performed. In the following, we look at two
variations on the RPC scheme we have discussed so far.

Asynchronous RPC

To support situations in which there is simply no result to return to the client,
RPC systems may provide facilities for what are called **asynchronous RPCs**.
With asynchronous RPCs, the server, in principle, immediately sends a reply
back to the client the moment the RPC request is received, after which it
locally calls the requested procedure. The reply acts as an acknowledgment
to the client that the server is going to process the RPC. The client will
continue without further blocking as soon as it has received the server's
acknowledgment. Figure 4.14(b) shows how client and server interact in the
case of asynchronous RPCs. For comparison, Figure 4.14(a) shows the normal
request-reply behavior.

Asynchronous RPCs can also be useful when a reply will be returned, but
the client is not prepared to wait for it and do nothing in the meantime. A
typical case is when a client needs to contact several servers independently.
In that case, it can send the call requests one after the other, effectively
establishing that the servers operate more or less in parallel. After all call
requests have been sent, the client can start waiting for the various results to be
returned. In cases such as these, it makes sense to organize the communication
between the client and server through an asynchronous RPC combined with a
callback, as shown in Figure 4.15. In this scheme, also referred to as **deferred
synchronous RPC**, the client first calls the server, waits for the acceptance,

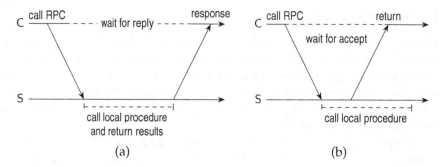

(a)   (b)

Figure 4.14: (a) The interaction between client and server in a traditional RPC. (b) The interaction using asynchronous RPC.

and continues. When the results become available, the server sends a response message that leads to a callback at the client's side. A callback is a user-defined function that is invoked when a special event happens, such as an incoming message. A straightforward implementation is to spawn a separate thread and let it block on the occurrence of the event while the main process continues. When the event occurs, the thread is unblocked and calls the function.

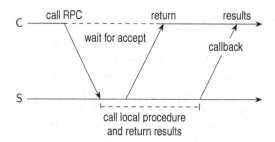

Figure 4.15: A client and server interacting through a deferred synchronous RPC.

It should be noted that variants of asynchronous RPCs exist in which the client continues executing immediately after sending the request to the server. In other words, the client does not wait for an acknowledgment of the server's acceptance of the request. We refer to such RPCs as **one-way RPCs**. The problem with this approach is that when reliability is not guaranteed, the client cannot know for sure whether its request will be processed. We return to these matters in Chapter 8. Likewise, in the case of deferred synchronous RPC, the client may poll the server to see whether the results are available yet, instead of letting the server calling back the client.

Multicast RPC

Asynchronous and deferred synchronous RPCs facilitate another alternative to remote procedure calls, namely executing multiple RPCs at the same time. Adopting the one-way RPCs (i.e., when a server does not tell the client it has accepted its call request but immediately starts processing it, while the client continues just after issuing the RPC), a **multicast RPC** boils down to sending an RPC request to a group of servers. This principle is shown in Figure 4.16. In this example, the client sends a request to two servers, who subsequently process that request independently and in parallel. When done, the result is returned to the client where a callback takes place.

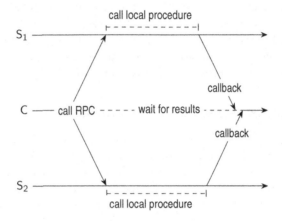

Figure 4.16: The principle of a multicast RPC.

There are several issues that we need to consider. First, as before, the client application may be unaware of the fact that an RPC is actually being forwarded to more than one server. For example, to increase fault tolerance, we may decide to have all operations executed by a backup server who can take over when the main server fails. That a server has been replicated can be completely hidden from a client application by an appropriate stub. Yet even the stub need not be aware that the server is replicated, for example because we are using a transport-level multicast address.

Second, we need to consider what to do with the responses. In particular, will the client proceed after all responses have been received, or wait just for one? It all depends. When the server has been replicated for fault tolerance, we may decide to wait for just the first response, or perhaps until a majority of the servers returns the same result. On the other hand, if the servers have been replicated to do the same work but on different parts of the input, their results may need to be merged before the client can continue. Again, such matters can be hidden in the client-side stub, yet the application developer will, at the very least, have to specify the purpose of the multicast RPC.

4.3 Message-oriented communication

Remote procedure calls and remote object invocations contribute to hiding communication in distributed systems, that is, they enhance access transparency. Unfortunately, neither mechanism is always appropriate. In particular, when it cannot be assumed that the receiving side is executing at the time a request is issued, alternative communication services are needed. Likewise, the inherent synchronous nature of RPCs, by which a client is blocked until its request has been processed, may need to be replaced by something else.

That something else is messaging. In this section, we concentrate on message-oriented communication in distributed systems by first taking a closer look at what exactly synchronous behavior is and what its implications are. Then, we discuss messaging systems that assume that parties are executing at the time of communication. Finally, we will examine message-queuing systems that allow processes to exchange information, even if the other party is not executing at the time communication is initiated.

4.3.1 Simple transient messaging with sockets

Many distributed systems and applications are built directly on top of the simple message-oriented model offered by the transport layer. To better understand and appreciate the message-oriented systems as part of middleware solutions, we first discuss messaging through transport-level sockets.

Special attention has been paid to standardizing the interface of the transport layer to allow programmers to make use of its entire suite of (messaging) protocols through a simple set of operations. Furthermore, standard interfaces make it easier to port an application to a different machine. As an example, we briefly discuss the **socket interface** as introduced in the 1970s in Berkeley Unix, and which has been adopted as a POSIX standard (with only very few adaptations).

Conceptually, a **socket** is a communication end point to which an application can write data that are to be sent out over the underlying network, and from which incoming data can be read. A socket forms an abstraction over the actual port that is used by the local operating system for a specific transport protocol. In the following text, we concentrate on the socket operations for TCP, which are shown in Figure 4.17.

Servers generally execute the first four operations, normally in the order given. When calling the socket operation, the caller creates a new communication end point for a specific transport protocol. Internally, creating a communication end point means that the local operating system reserves resources for sending and receiving messages for the specified protocol.

The bind operation associates a local address with the newly created socket. For example, a server should bind the IP address of its machine together with a (possibly well-known) port number to a socket. Binding tells the operating

Operation	Description
socket	Create a new communication end point
bind	Attach a local address to a socket
listen	Tell operating system what the maximum number of pending connection requests should be
accept	Block caller until a connection request arrives
connect	Actively attempt to establish a connection
send	Send some data over the connection
receive	Receive some data over the connection
close	Release the connection

Figure 4.17: The socket operations for TCP/IP.

system that the server wants to receive messages only on the specified address and port. In the case of connection-oriented communication, the address is used to receive incoming connection requests.

The listen operation is called only in the case of connection-oriented communication. It is a nonblocking call that allows the local operating system to reserve enough buffers for a specified maximum number of pending connection requests that the caller is willing to accept.

A call to accept blocks the caller until a connection request arrives. When a request arrives, the local operating system creates a new socket with the same properties as the original one, and returns it to the caller. This approach will allow the server to, for example, fork a process that will subsequently handle the actual communication through the new connection. The server can go back and wait for another connection request on the original socket.

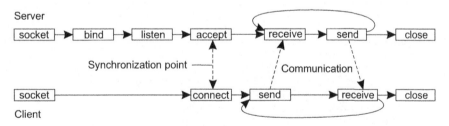

Figure 4.18: Connection-oriented communication pattern using sockets.

Let us now take a look at the client side. Here, too, a socket must first be created using the socket operation, but explicitly binding the socket to a local address is not necessary, since the operating system can dynamically allocate a port when the connection is set up. The connect operation requires that the caller specifies the transport-level address to which a connection request is to be sent. The client is blocked until a connection has been set up successfully, after which both sides can start exchanging information through the send and receive operations. Finally, closing a connection is symmetric when using sockets, and is established by having both the client and server call the close operation. Although there are many exceptions to the rule, the general pattern followed by a client and server for connection-oriented communication using sockets is as shown in Figure 4.18. Details on network programming using sockets and other interfaces in Unix can be found in [Stevens, 1998].

Note 4.7 (Example: A simple socket-based client-server system)

As an illustration of the recurring pattern in Figure 4.18, consider the simple socket-based client-server system shown in Figure 4.19 (see also Note 2.1). We see the server starting by creating a socket, and subsequently binding an address to that socket. It calls the listen operation, and waits for an incoming connection request. When the server accepts a connection, the socket library creates a separate connection, conn, which is used to receive data and send a response to the connected client. The server enters a loop receiving and sending messages, until no more data has been received. It then closes the connection.

```
1  from socket  import *
2
3  class Server:
4    def run(self):
5      s = socket(AF_INET, SOCK_STREAM)
6      s.bind((HOST, PORT))
7      s.listen(1)
8      (conn, addr) = s.accept()  # returns new socket and addr. client
9      while True:                # forever
10       data = conn.recv(1024)   # receive data from client
11       if not data: break       # stop if client stopped
12       conn.send(data+b"*")      # return sent data plus an "*"
13     conn.close()               # close the connection
```

(a)

```
1  class Client:
2    def run(self):
3      s = socket(AF_INET, SOCK_STREAM)
4      s.connect((HOST, PORT)) # connect to server (block until accepted)
5      s.send(b"Hello, world") # send same data
6      data = s.recv(1024)     # receive the response
7      print(data)             # print what you received
8      s.send(b"")             # tell the server to close
9      s.close()               # close the connection
```

(b)

Figure 4.19: A simple socket-based client-server system.

The client again follows the pattern from Figure 4.18. It creates a socket, and calls connect to request a connection with the server. Once the connection has been established, it sends a single message, waits for the response, and after printing the result, closes the connection.

Note 4.8 (Advanced: Implementing stubs as global references revisited)
To provide a more in-depth insight in the working of sockets, let us look at a more elaborate example, namely the use of stubs as global references.

```
1   class DBClient:
2     def __sendrecv(self, message):          # this is a private method
3       sock = socket()                        # create a socket
4       sock.connect((self.host, self.port))   # connect to server
5       sock.send(pickle.dumps(message))       # send some data
6       result = pickle.loads(sock.recv(1024)) # receive the response
7       sock.close()                           # close the connection
8       return result
9
10    def create(self):
11      self.listID = self.__sendrecv([CREATE])
12      return self.listID
13
14    def getValue(self):
15      return self.__sendrecv([GETVALUE, self.listID])
16
17    def appendData(self, data):
18      return self.__sendrecv([APPEND, data, self.listID])
```

(a)

```
1   class Server:
2     self.setOfLists = {}                    # init: no lists to manage
3
4   def run(self):
5     while True:
6       (conn, addr) = self.sock.accept() # accept incoming call
7       data = conn.recv(1024)            # fetch data from client
8       request = pickle.loads(data)      # unwrap the request
9
10      if request[0] == CREATE:              # create a list
11        listID = len(self.setOfLists) + 1   # allocate listID
12        self.setOfLists[listID] = []        # initialize to empty
13        conn.send(pickle.dumps(listID))     # return ID
14
15      elif request[0] == APPEND:            # append request
16        listID = request[2]                 # fetch listID
17        data   = request[1]                 # fetch data to append
18        self.setOfLists[listID].append(data) # append it to the list
19        conn.send(pickle.dumps(OK))         # return an OK
20
21      elif request[0] == GETVALUE:          # read request
22        listID = request[1]                 # fetch listID
23        result = self.setOfLists[listID]    # get the elements
24        conn.send(pickle.dumps(result))     # return the list
```

(b)

Figure 4.20: Implementing a list server in Python.

We return to our example of implementing a shared list, which we now do using a list server, implemented in the form of the Python class shown in Figure 4.20(b). Figure 4.20(a) shows the stub implementation of a shared list. Again, we have omitted code for readability.

The DBClient class represents a client-side stub that, once marshaled, can be passed between processes. It provides three operations associated with a list: create, getValue, and append, with obvious semantics. A DBClient is assumed to be associated with one specific list as managed by the server. An identifier for that list is returned when the list is created. Note how the (internal) sendrecv operation follows the client-side pattern explained in Figure 4.18.

The server maintains lists, as shown in Figure 4.20(b). Its internal data structure is a setOfLists with each element being a previously created list. The server simply waits for incoming requests, unmarshals the request, and checks which operation is being requested. Results are sent back to the requesting client (which always issues the sendrecv operation implemented as part of DBClient). Again, we see that the server follows the pattern shown in Figure 4.18: it creates a socket, binds an address to it, informs the operating system to how many connections it should listen, and then waits to accept an incoming connection request. Once a connection has been established, the server receives data, sends a response, and closes the connection again.

```
1  class Client:
2    def __init__(self, port):
3      self.host = 'localhost'              # this machine
4      self.port = port                     # port it will listen to
5      self.sock = socket()                 # socket for incoming calls
6      self.sock.bind((self.host, self.port)) # bind socket to an address
7      self.sock.listen(2)                  # max num connections
8
9    def sendTo(self, host, port, data):
10     sock = socket()
11     sock.connect((host, port))     # connect to server (blocking call)
12     sock.send(pickle.dumps(data)) # send some data
13     sock.close()
14
15   def recvAny(self):
16     (conn, addr) = self.sock.accept()
17     return conn.recv(1024)
```

Figure 4.20: (c) Implementing a list server in Python: the client.

To use a stub as a global reference, we represent each client application by the class Client shown in Figure 4.20(c). The class is instantiated in the same process running the application (exemplified by the value of self.host), and will be listening on a specific port for messages from other applications, as well as the server. Otherwise, it merely sends and receives messages, coded through the operations sendTo and recvAny, respectively.

Now consider the code shown in Figure 4.20(d), which mimics two client applications. The first one creates a new list and appends data to it. Then note how dbClient1 is simply sent to the other client. Under the hood, we now know that it is marshaled in the operation sendTo (line 12) of class Client shown in Figure 4.20(c).

```
1  def client1():
2     c1  = Client(PORTC1)              # create client
3     dbC1 = DBClient(HOSTS,PORTS)      # create reference
4     dbC1.create()                    # create new list
5     dbC1.appendData('Client 1')      # append some data
6     c1.sendTo(HOSTC2,PORTC2,dbC1)    # send to other client
7
8  def client2():
9     c2  = Client(PORTC2)             # create a new client
10    data = c2.recvAny()              # block until data is sent
11    dbC2 = pickle.loads(data)        # receive reference
12    dbC2.appendData('Client 2')      # append data to same list
```

Figure 4.20: (d) Passing stubs as references.

The second client simply waits for an incoming message (line 12), unmarshals the result, knowing that it is a DBClient instance, and subsequently appends some more data to the same list as the one the first client appended data. Indeed, an instance of DBClient is seen to be passed as a global reference, seemingly along with all the operations that go with the associated class.

4.3.2   Advanced transient messaging

The standard socket-based approach toward transient messaging is very basic and, as such, rather brittle: a mistake is easily made. Furthermore, sockets essentially support only TCP or UDP, meaning that any extra facility for messaging needs to be implemented separately by an application programmer. In practice, we do often need more advanced approaches for message-oriented communication to make network programming easier, to expand beyond the functionality offered by existing networking protocols, to make better use of local resources, and so on.

Using messaging patterns: ZeroMQ

One approach toward making network programming easier is based on the observation that many messaging applications, or their components, can be effectively organized according to a few simple communication patterns. By subsequently providing enhancements to sockets for each of these patterns, it may become easier to develop a networked, distributed application. This approach has been followed in ZeroMQ and documented in [Hintjens, 2013; Akgul, 2013].

Like in the Berkeley approach, ZeroMQ also provides sockets through which all communication takes place. Actual message transmission generally takes place over TCP connections, and like TCP, all communication is essentially connection-oriented, meaning that a connection will first be set up between a sender and receiver before message transmission can take place. However, setting up, and maintaining connections is kept mostly under the hood: an application programmer need not bother with those issues. To further simplify matters, a socket may be bound to multiple addresses, effectively allowing a server to handle messages from very different sources through a single interface. For example, a server can listen to multiple ports using a single blocking receive operation. ZeroMQ sockets can thus support *many-to-one* communication instead of just *one-to-one* communication, as is the case with standard Berkeley sockets. To complete the story: ZeroMQ sockets also support *one-to-many* communication, i.e., multicasting.

Essential to ZeroMQ is that communication is **asynchronous**: a sender will normally continue after having submitted a message to the underlying communication subsystem. An interesting side effect of combining asynchronous with connection-oriented communication, is that a process can request a connection setup, and subsequently send a message even if the recipient is not yet up-and-running and ready to accept incoming connection requests, let alone incoming messages. What happens, of course, is that a connection request and subsequent messages are queued at the sender's side, while a separate thread as part of ZeroMQ's library will take care that eventually the connection is set up and messages are transmitted to the recipient.

Simplifying matters, ZeroMQ establishes a higher level of abstraction in socket-based communication by *pairing* sockets: a specific type of socket used for sending messages is paired with a corresponding socket type for receiving messages. Each pair of socket types corresponds to a **communication pattern**. The three most important communication patterns supported by ZeroMQ are *request-reply*, *publish-subscribe*, and *pipeline*.

The **request-reply pattern** is used in traditional client-server communication, like the ones normally used for remote procedure calls. A client application uses a *request socket* (of type REQ) to send a request message to a server and expects the latter to respond with an appropriate response. The server is assumed to use a *reply socket* (of type REP). The request-reply pattern simplifies matters for developers by avoiding the need to call the listen operation, as well as the accept operation. Moreover, when a server receives a message, a subsequent call to send is automatically targeted toward the original sender. Likewise, when a client calls the recv operation (for receiving a message) after having sent a message, ZeroMQ assumes the client is waiting for a response from the original recipient. Note that this approach was effectively encoded in the local sendrecv operation of Figure 4.20(b), which we discussed in Note 4.8.

Note 4.9 (Example: The request-reply pattern)

Let us look at a simple programming example to illustrate the request-reply pattern. Figure 4.21 shows a server that appends an asterisk to a received message. As before, it creates a socket, and binds it to a combination of a protocol (in this case TCP), and a host and port. In our example, the server is willing to accept incoming connection requests on two different ports. It then waits for incoming messages. The request-reply pattern effectively ties the receipt of a message to the subsequent response. In other words, when the server calls send, it will transmit a message to the same client from which it previously had received a message. Of course, this simplicity can be achieved only if the programmer indeed abides to the request-reply pattern.

```
1   import zmq
2
3   def server():
4       context = zmq.Context()
5       socket  = context.socket(zmq.REP)        # create reply socket
6       socket.bind("tcp://*:12345")             # bind socket to address
7
8       while True:
9           message = socket.recv()              # wait for incoming message
10          if not "STOP" in str(message):       # if not to stop...
11              reply = str(message.decode())+'*' # append "*" to message
12              socket.send(reply.encode())      # send it away (encoded)
13          else:
14              break                            # break out of loop and end
15
16  def client():
17      context = zmq.Context()
18      socket  = context.socket(zmq.REQ)        # create request socket
19
20      socket.connect("tcp://localhost:12345")  # block until connected
21      socket.send(b"Hello world")              # send message
22      message = socket.recv()                  # block until response
23      socket.send(b"STOP")                     # tell server to stop
24      print(message.decode())                  # print result
```

Figure 4.21: A ZeroMQ client-server system.

The client, also shown in Figure 4.21, creates a socket and connects to the associated server. When it sends a message, it can expect to receive, from that same server, a response. By sending the string "STOP", it tells the server it is done, after which the server will actually stop.

Interestingly, the asynchronous nature of ZeroMQ allows one to start the client *before* starting the server. An implication is that if, in this example, we would start the server, then a client, and after a while a second client, that the latter will be blocked until the server is restarted. Furthermore, note that ZeroMQ does not require the programmer to specify how many bytes are expected to be received. Unlike TCP, ZeroMQ uses messages instead of byte streams.

In the case of a **publish-subscribe pattern**, clients *subscribe* to specific messages that are *published* by servers. We came across this pattern in Section 2.1.3 when discussing coordination. In effect, only the messages to which the client has subscribed will be transmitted. If a server is publishing messages to which no one has subscribed, these messages will be lost. In its simplest form, this pattern establishes multicasting messages from a server to several clients. The server is assumed to use a socket of type PUB, while each client must use SUB type sockets. Each client socket is connected to the socket of the server. By default, a client subscribes to no specific message. This means that as long as no explicit subscription is provided, a client will not receive a message published by the server.

Note 4.10 (Example: The publish-subscribe pattern)
Again, let us make this pattern more concrete through a simple example. Figure 4.22 shows an admittedly naive time server that publishes its current, local time, through a PUB socket. The local time is published every five seconds, for any interested client.

```
1   import multiprocessing
2   import zmq, time
3
4   def server():
5       context = zmq.Context()
6       socket = context.socket(zmq.PUB)          # create a publisher socket
7       socket.bind("tcp://*:12345")              # bind socket to the address
8       while True:
9           time.sleep(5)                         # wait every 5 seconds
10          t = "TIME " + time.asctime()
11          socket.send(t.encode())               # publish the current time
12
13  def client():
14      context = zmq.Context()
15      socket = context.socket(zmq.SUB)          # create a subscriber socket
16      socket.connect("tcp://localhost:12345")   # connect to the server
17      socket.setsockopt(zmq.SUBSCRIBE, b"TIME") # subscribe to TIME messages
18
19      for i in range(5):        # Five iterations
20          time = socket.recv()  # receive a message related to subscription
21          print(time.decode())  # print the result
```

Figure 4.22: A multicasting socket-based setup.

A client is equally simple, as also shown in Figure 4.22. It first creates a SUB socket which it connects to the corresponding PUB socket of the server. To receive the appropriate messages, it needs to subscribe to messages that have TIME as their tag. In our example, a client will simply print the first five messages received from the server. Note that we can have as many clients as we want: the server's message will be multicasted to all subscribers. Most important in this example, is that it illustrates that the *only* messages received through the SUB socket, are the ones the client had subscribed to.

Finally, the **pipeline pattern** is characterized by the fact that a process wants to *push out* its results, assuming that there are other processes that want to *pull in* those results. The essence of the pipeline pattern is that a pushing process does not really care which other process pulls in its results: the first available one will do just fine. Likewise, any process pulling in results from multiple other processes will do so from the first pushing process making its results available. The intention of the pipeline pattern is thus seen to keep as many processes working as possible, pushing results through a pipeline of processes as quickly as possible.

Note 4.11 (Example: The pipeline pattern)

As our last example, consider the following template for keeping a collection of worker tasks busy. Figure 4.23 shows the code for a so-called **farmer task**: a process producing tasks to be picked up by others. In this example, we simulate the task by letting the producer pick a random number modeling the duration, or load, of the work to be done. This workload is then sent to the PUSH socket, effectively being queued until another process picks it up.

```
1  def producer():
2      context = zmq.Context()
3      socket  = context.socket(zmq.PUSH)        # create a push socket
4      socket.bind("tcp://127.0.0.1:12345")      # bind socket to address
5
6      while True:
7          workload = random.randint(1, 100)     # compute workload
8          socket.send(pickle.dumps(workload))   # send workload to worker
9          time.sleep(workload/NWORKERS)         # balance production by waiting
10
11 def worker(id):
12     context = zmq.Context()
13     socket  = context.socket(zmq.PULL)        # create a pull socket
14     socket.connect("tcp://localhost:12345")   # connect to the producer
15
16     while True:
17         work = pickle.loads(socket.recv())    # receive work from a source
18         time.sleep(work)                      # pretend to work
```

Figure 4.23: A producer-worker pattern.

Such other processes are known as **worker tasks,** of which a sketch is also given in Figure 4.23. A worker task connects to a single PULL socket. Once it picks up some work, it simulates that it is actually doing something by sleeping for some time proportional to the received workload.

> The semantics of this push-pull pattern is such that the first available worker will pick up work from the producer, and likewise, if there are multiple workers ready to pick up work, each one of them will be provided with a task. How work distribution is actually done fairly requires some specific attention, which we will not discuss further here.

The Message-Passing Interface (MPI)

With the advent of high-performance multicomputers, developers have been looking for message-oriented operations that would allow them to easily write highly efficient applications. This means that the operations should be at a convenient level of abstraction (to ease application development), and that their implementation incurs only minimal overhead. Sockets were deemed insufficient for two reasons. First, they were at the wrong level of abstraction by supporting only simple send and receive operations. Second, sockets had been designed to communicate across networks using general-purpose protocol stacks such as TCP/IP. They were not considered suitable for the proprietary protocols developed for high-speed interconnection networks, such as those used in high-performance server clusters. Those protocols required an interface that could handle more advanced features, such as different forms of buffering and synchronization.

The result was that most interconnection networks and high-performance multicomputers were shipped with proprietary communication libraries. These libraries offered a wealth of high-level and generally efficient communication operations. Of course, all libraries were mutually incompatible, so that application developers now had a portability problem.

The need to be hardware and platform independent eventually lead to the definition of a standard for message passing, simply called the **Message-Passing Interface** or **MPI**. MPI is designed for parallel applications and as such is tailored to transient communication. It makes direct use of the underlying network. Furthermore, it assumes that serious failures such as process crashes or network partitions are fatal and do not require automatic recovery.

MPI assumes communication takes place within a known group of processes. Each group is assigned an identifier. Each process within a group is also assigned a (local) identifier. A (groupID, processID) pair therefore uniquely identifies the source or destination of a message, and is used instead of a transport-level address. There may be several, possibly overlapping, groups of processes involved in a computation and that are all executing at the same time.

At the core of MPI are messaging operations to support transient communication, of which the most intuitive ones are summarized in Figure 4.25. To understand their semantics, it helps to keep Figure 4.4 in mind, with the middleware formed entirely by an MPI implementation. In particular, the middleware maintains its own buffers and synchronization is often related to when the necessary data has been copied from the calling application to the middleware.

Operation	Description
MPI_BSEND	Append outgoing message to a local send buffer
MPI_SEND	Send a message and wait until copied to local or remote buffer
MPI_SSEND	Send a message and wait until transmission starts
MPI_SENDRECV	Send a message and wait for reply
MPI_ISEND	Pass reference to outgoing message, and continue
MPI_ISSEND	Pass reference to outgoing message, and wait until receipt starts
MPI_RECV	Receive a message; block if there is none
MPI_IRECV	Check if there is an incoming message, but do not block

Figure 4.24: Some of the more intuitive message-passing operations of MPI.

Transient asynchronous communication is supported by the MPI_BSEND operation. The sender submits a message for transmission, which is generally first copied to a local buffer in the MPI runtime system. When the message has been copied, the sender continues. The local MPI runtime system will remove the message from its local buffer and take care of transmission as soon as a receiver has called a receive operation.

There is also a blocking send operation, called MPI_SEND, of which the semantics are implementation dependent. The operation MPI_SEND may either block the caller until the specified message has been copied to the MPI runtime system at the sender's side, or until the receiver has initiated a receive operation. Synchronous communication by which the sender blocks until its request is accepted for further processing is available through the MPI_SSEND operation. Finally, the strongest form of synchronous communication is also supported: when a sender calls MPI_SENDRECV, it sends a request to the receiver and blocks until the latter returns a reply. Basically, this operation corresponds to a normal RPC.

Both MPI_SEND and MPI_SSEND have variants that avoid copying messages from user buffers to buffers internal to the local MPI runtime system. These variants essentially correspond to a form of asynchronous communication. With MPI_ISEND, a sender passes a pointer to the message, after which the MPI runtime system takes care of communication. The sender immediately continues. To prevent overwriting the message before communication completes, MPI offers operations to check for completion, or even to block if required. As with MPI_SEND, whether the message has actually been transferred to the receiver or that it has merely been copied by the local MPI runtime system to an internal buffer is left unspecified.

Likewise, with `MPI_ISSEND`, a sender also passes only a pointer to the MPI runtime system. When the runtime system indicates it has processed the message, the sender is then guaranteed that the receiver has accepted the message and is now working on it.

The operation `MPI_RECV` is called to receive a message; it blocks the caller until a message arrives. There is also an asynchronous variant, called `MPI_IRECV`, by which a receiver indicates that it is prepared to accept a message. The receiver can check whether a message has indeed arrived, or block until one does.

The semantics of MPI communication operations are not always straightforward, and different operations can sometimes be interchanged without affecting the correctness of a program. The official reason why so many different forms of communication are supported is that it gives implementers of MPI systems enough possibilities for optimizing performance. Cynics might say the committee could not make up its collective mind, so it threw in everything. By now, MPI is in its fourth version with over 650 operations available. Being designed for high-performance parallel applications, it is perhaps easier to understand its diversity. More on MPI can be found in [Gropp et al., 2016]. The complete MPI-4 reference can be found in [Message Passing Interface Forum, 2021].

4.3.3 Message-oriented persistent communication

We now come to an important class of message-oriented middleware services, generally known as **message-queuing systems**, or just **message-oriented middleware (MOM)**. Message-queuing systems provide extensive support for persistent asynchronous communication. The essence of these systems is that they offer intermediate-term storage capacity for messages, without requiring either the sender or receiver to be active during message transmission. An important difference with sockets and MPI is that message-queuing systems are typically targeted to support message transfers that are allowed to take minutes instead of seconds or milliseconds.

Message-queuing model

The basic idea behind a message-queuing system is that applications communicate by inserting messages in specific queues. These messages are forwarded over a series of communication servers and are eventually delivered to the destination, even if it was down when the message was sent. In practice, most communication servers are directly connected to each other. In other words, a message is generally transferred directly to a destination server. In principle, each application has its own private queue to which other applications can send messages. A queue can be read only by its associated application, but it is also possible for multiple applications to share a single queue.

An important aspect of message-queuing systems is that a sender is generally given only the guarantees that its message will eventually be inserted in the recipient's queue. No guarantees are given about when, or even if the message will actually be read, which is completely determined by the behavior of the recipient.

These semantics permit communication to be decoupled in time, as also discussed in Section 2.1.3. There is thus no need for the receiver to be executing when a message is being sent to its queue. Likewise, there is no need for the sender to be executing the moment its message is picked up by the receiver. The sender and receiver can execute completely independently of each other. In fact, once a message has been deposited in a queue, it will remain there until it is removed, irrespective of whether its sender or receiver is executing. This gives us four combinations regarding the execution mode of the sender and receiver, as shown in Figure 4.25.

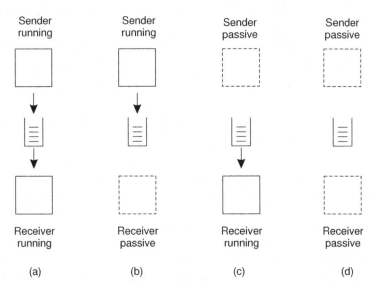

Figure 4.25: Four combinations for loosely coupled communication using queues.

In Figure 4.25(a), both the sender and receiver are in execution during the entire transmission of a message. In Figure 4.25(b), only the sender is in execution, while the receiver is passive, that is, in a state in which message delivery is not possible. Nevertheless, the sender can still send messages. The combination of a passive sender and an active receiver is shown in Figure 4.25(c). In this case, the receiver can read messages that were sent to it, but it is not necessary that their respective senders are in execution as well. Finally, in Figure 4.25(d), we see the situation that the system is storing (and possibly transmitting) messages even while sender and receiver are passive. One may argue that only if this last configuration is supported, the message-queuing system truly provides persistent messaging.

Messages can, in principle, contain any data. The only important aspect from the perspective of middleware is that messages are properly addressed. In practice, addressing is done by providing a systemwide unique name of the destination queue. In some cases, message size may be limited, although it is also possible that the underlying system takes care of fragmenting and assembling large messages in a way that is completely transparent to applications. An effect of this approach is that the basic interface offered to applications can be simple, as shown in Figure 4.26.

Operation	Description
PUT	Append a message to a specified queue
GET	Block until the specified queue is nonempty, and remove the first message
POLL	Check a specified queue for messages, and remove the first. Never block
NOTIFY	Install a handler to be called when a message is put into the specified queue

Figure 4.26: Basic interface to a queue in a message-queuing system.

The PUT operation is called by a sender to pass a message to the underlying system that is to be appended to the specified queue. As we explained, this is a nonblocking call. The GET operation is a blocking call by which an authorized process can remove the longest pending message in the specified queue. The process is blocked only if the queue is empty. Variations on this call allow searching for a specific message in the queue, for example, using a priority, or a matching pattern. The nonblocking variant is given by the POLL operation. If the queue is empty, or if a specific message could not be found, the calling process simply continues.

Finally, most queuing systems also allow a process to install a handler as a *callback function*, which is automatically invoked whenever a message is put into the queue. Arranging this scheme is handled through a NOTIFY operation. Callbacks can also be used to automatically start a process that will fetch messages from the queue if no process is currently in execution. This approach is often implemented through a daemon on the receiver's side that continuously monitors the queue for incoming messages and handles accordingly.

General architecture of a message-queuing system

Let us now take a closer look at what a general message-queuing system looks like. First, queues are managed by **queue managers**. A queue manager is either a separate process, or is implemented through a library that is linked with an application. Secondly, as a rule of thumb, an application can put messages only into a *local* queue. Likewise, getting a message is possible by extracting it from a *local* queue only. As a consequence, if a queue manager QM_A handling the queues for an application A runs as a separate process, both processes QM_A and A will generally be placed on the same machine, or at worst on the same LAN. Also note that if *all* queue managers are linked into their respective applications, we can no longer speak of a persistent asynchronous messaging system.

If applications can put messages only into local queues, then clearly each message will have to carry information concerning its destination. It is the queue manager's task to make sure that a message reaches its destination. This brings us to several issues.

In the first place, we need to consider how the destination queue is addressed. Obviously, to enhance location transparency, it is preferable that queues have logical, location-independent names. Assuming that a queue manager is implemented as a separate process, using logical names implies that each name should be associated with a **contact address**, such as a (host,port)-pair, and that the name-to-address mapping is readily available to a queue manager, as shown in Figure 4.27. In practice, a contact address carries more information, notably the protocol to be used, such as TCP or UDP. We came across such contact addresses in our examples of advanced sockets in, for example, Note 4.9.

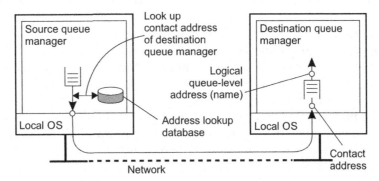

Figure 4.27: The relationship between queue-level naming and network-level addressing.

A second issue that we need to consider is how the name-to-address mapping is actually made available to a queue manager. A common approach is to simply implement the mapping as a lookup table and copy that table to all managers. Obviously, this leads to a maintenance problem, for every time that a new queue is added or named, many, if not all tables, need to be updated. There are various ways to alleviate such problems, which we will discuss in Chapter 6.

This brings us to a third issue, related to the problems of efficiently maintaining name-to-address mappings. We have implicitly assumed that if a destination queue at manager QM_B is known to queue manager QM_A, then QM_A can directly contact QM_B to transfer messages. In effect, this means that (the contact address of) each queue manager should be known to all others. Obviously, when dealing with large message-queuing systems, we will have a scalability problem. In practice, there are often special queue managers that operate as **routers**: they forward incoming messages to other queue managers. In this way, a message-queuing system may gradually grow into a complete, application-level, **overlay network**.

If only a few routers need to know about the network topology, then a source queue manager need only to know to which adjacent router, say R, it should forward a message, given a destination queue. The router R, in turn, may need to keep track only of its adjacent routers to see where to forward the message to, and so on. Of course, we still need to have name-to-address mappings for all queue managers, including the routers, but it is not difficult to imagine that such tables can be much smaller and easier to maintain.

Message brokers

An important application area of message-queuing systems is integrating existing and new applications into a single, coherent distributed information system. If we assume that communication with an application takes place through messages, then integration requires that applications can understand the messages they receive. In practice, this requires the sender to have its outgoing messages in the same format as that of the receiver, but also that its messages adhere to the same semantics as those expected by the receiver. Sender and receiver essentially need to speak the same language, that is, adhere to the same messaging protocol.

The problem with this approach is that each time an application A is added to the system having its own messaging protocol, then for each other application B that is to communicate with A we will need to provide the means for converting their respective messages. In a system with N applications, we will thus need $N \times N$ messaging-protocol converters.

An alternative is to agree on a common messaging protocol, as is done with traditional network protocols. Unfortunately, this approach will generally not work for message-queuing systems. The problem is the level of abstraction at which these systems operate. A common messaging protocol makes sense only if the collection of processes that make use of that protocol indeed have enough in common. If the collection of applications that make up a distributed information system is highly diverse (which it often is), then inventing a one-size-fits-all solution is simply not going to work.

If we focus only on the format and meaning of messages, commonality can be achieved by lifting the level of abstraction, as is done with XML messages.

In this case, messages carry information on their own organization, and what has been standardized is the way that they can describe their content. As a consequence, an application can provide information on the organization of its messages that can be automatically processed. Of course, this information is generally not enough: we also need to make sure that the *semantics* of messages are well understood.

Given these problems, the general approach is to learn to live with differences, and try to provide the means to make conversions as simple as possible. In message-queuing systems, conversions are handled by special nodes in a queuing network, known as **message brokers**. A message broker acts as an application-level gateway in a message-queuing system. Its main purpose is to convert incoming messages so that they can be understood by the destination application. Note that to a message-queuing system, a message broker is just another application, as shown in Figure 4.28. In other words, a message broker is generally not considered to be an integral part of the queuing system.

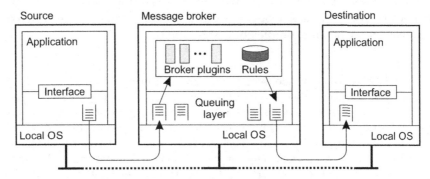

Figure 4.28: The general organization of a message broker in a message-queuing system.

A message broker can be as simple as a reformatter for messages. For example, assume an incoming message contains a table from a database in which records are separated by a special *end-of-record* delimiter and fields within a record have a known, fixed length. If the destination application expects a different delimiter between records, and also expects that fields have variable lengths, a message broker can be used to convert messages to the format expected by the destination.

In a more advanced setting, a message broker may act as an application-level gateway, in which information on the messaging protocol of several applications has been encoded. In general, for each pair of applications, we will have a separate subprogram capable of converting messages between the two applications. In Figure 4.28, this subprogram is drawn as a **plugin** to emphasize that such parts can be dynamically plugged in, or removed from a broker.

Finally, note that often a message broker is used for advanced **enterprise application integration** (**EAI**), as we discussed in Section 1.3.2. In this case, rather than (only) converting messages, a broker is responsible for *matching* applications based on the messages that are being exchanged. In such a **publish-subscribe model**, applications send messages in the form of *publishing*. In particular, they may publish a message on topic X, which is then sent to the broker. Applications that have stated their interest in messages on topic X, that is, who have *subscribed* to those messages, will then receive these messages from the broker. More advanced forms of mediation are also possible.

At the heart of a message broker lies a repository of rules for transforming a message of one type to another. The problem is defining the rules and developing the plugins. Most message-broker products come with sophisticated development tools, but the bottom line is still that the repository needs to be filled by experts. Here we see a perfect example where commercial products are often misleadingly said to provide "intelligence," where, in fact, the intelligence is to be found only in the heads of those experts. It may be better to consistently talk about "advanced" systems (but even then, we often see that this stands for complex or complicated).

Note 4.12 (More information: A note on message-queuing systems)
Considering what we have said about message-queuing systems, it would appear that they have long existed in the form of implementations for e-mail services. E-mail systems are generally implemented through a collection of mail servers that store and forward messages on behalf of the users on hosts directly connected to the server. Routing is generally left out, as e-mail systems can make direct use of the underlying transport services. For example, in the mail protocol for the Internet, SMTP [Postel, 1982], a message is transferred by setting up a direct TCP connection to the destination mail server.

What makes e-mail systems special compared to message-queuing systems is that they are primarily aimed at providing direct support for end users. This explains, for example, why several groupware applications are based directly on an e-mail system [Khoshafian and Buckiewicz, 1995]. In addition, e-mail systems may have very specific requirements such as automatic message filtering, support for advanced messaging databases (e.g., to easily retrieve previously stored messages), and so on.

General message-queuing systems are not aimed at supporting only end users. An important issue is that they are set up to enable persistent communication between processes, regardless of whether a process is running a user application, handling access to a database, performing computations, and so on. This approach leads to a different set of requirements for message-queuing systems than pure e-mail systems. For example, e-mail systems generally need not provide guaranteed message delivery, message priorities, logging facilities, efficient multicasting, load balancing, fault tolerance, and so on for general usage.

General-purpose message-queuing systems, therefore, have a wide range of applications, including e-mail, workflow, groupware, and batch processing. However, as we have stated before, the most important application area is the integration of a (possibly widely dispersed) collection of databases and applications into a federated information system [Hohpe and Woolf, 2004]. For example, a query expanding several databases may need to be split into subqueries that are forwarded to individual databases. Message-queuing systems assist by providing the basic means to package each subquery into a message and routing it to the appropriate database. Other communication facilities we have discussed in this chapter are far less appropriate.

4.3.4 Example: Advanced Message Queuing Protocol (AMQP)

An interesting observation about message-queuing systems is that they have been developed in part to allow legacy applications to interoperate, yet at the same time we see that when it comes to operations between different message-queuing systems, we often hit a wall. As a consequence, once an organization chooses to use a message-queuing system from manufacturer X, they may have to settle for solutions that only X provides. Message-queuing solutions are thus in large part proprietary solutions. So much for openness.

In 2006, a working group was formed to change this situation, which resulted in the specification of the **Advanced Message-Queuing Protocol**, or simply **AMQP**. There are different versions of AMQP, with version 1.0 being the most recent one. There are also various implementations of AMQP, notably of versions before 1.0, which by the time version 1.0 was established, had gained considerable popularity. Because a pre-1.0 version is so different from the 1.0 version, yet has also a steady user base, we may see various pre-1.0 AMQP servers exist next to (their undeniably incompatible) 1.0 servers.

In this section, we will describe AMQP, but will more or less deliberately mix the pre-1.0 and 1.0 versions, sticking to the essentials and spirit of AMQP. Details can be found in the specifications [AMQP Working Group, 2008; OASIS, 2012]. Implementations of AMQP include RabbitMQ [Roy, 2018] and Apache's ActiveMQ.

Basics

AMQP revolves around applications, queue managers, and queues. Taking an approach that is common for many networking situations, we make a distinction between AMQP as a *messaging service*, the actual *messaging protocol*, and, finally, the *messaging interface* as offered to applications. To this end, it is easiest to consider having only a single queue manager, running as a single, separate server, forming the implementation of AMQP as a service. An application communicates with this queue manager through a local interface.

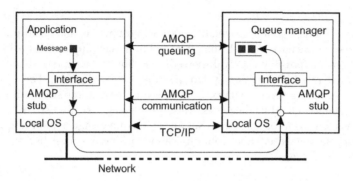

Figure 4.29: An overview of a single-server AMQP instance.

Between an application and the queue manager, communication proceeds according to the AMQP protocol.

This situation is shown in Figure 4.29 and should look familiar. The AMQP stub shields the application (as well as the queue manager) from the details concerning message transfer and communication in general. At the same time, it implements a message-queuing interface, allowing the application to make use of AMQP as a message-queuing service. Although the distinction between AMQP stub and queue manager is made explicit for queue managers, the strictness of the separation is left to an implementation. Nevertheless, if not strict, conceptually there is a distinction between handling queues and handling related communication as we shall make clear shortly.

AMQP communication

AMQP allows an application to set up a **connection** to a queue manager; a connection is a container for a number of one-way **channels**. Whereas the lifetime of a channel can be highly dynamic, connections are assumed to be relatively stable. This difference between connection and channel allows for efficient implementations, notably by using a single transport-layer TCP connection to multiplex many different channels between an application and a queue manager. In practice, AMQP assumes TCP is used for establishing AMQP connections.

Bidirectional communication is established through **sessions**: a logical grouping of two channels. A connection may have multiple sessions, but note that a channel need not necessarily be part of a session.

Finally, to actually transfer messages, a **link** is needed. Conceptually, a link, or rather its end points, keep track of the status of messages that are being transferred. It thus provides fine-grained flow control between an application and a queue manager, and, indeed, different control policies can be put simultaneously in place for different messages that are transferred through the same session or connection. Flow control is established through credits: a receiver can tell the sender how many messages it is allowed to send over a specific link.

When a message is to be transferred, the application passes it to its local AMQP stub. As mentioned, each message transfer is associated with one specific link. Message transfer normally proceeds in three steps.

1. At the sender's side, the message is assigned a unique identifier and is recorded *locally* to be in an **unsettled state**. The stub subsequently transfers the message to the server, where the AMQP stub also records it as being in an unsettled state. At that point, the server-side stub passes it to the queue manager.

2. The receiving application (in this case the queue manager), is assumed to handle the message and normally reports back to its stub that it is finished. The stub passes this information to the original sender, at which point the message at the original sender's AMQP stub enters a **settled state**.

3. The AMQP stub of the original sender now tells the stub of the original receiver that message transfer has been settled (meaning that the original sender will forget about the message from now on). The receiver's stub can now also discard anything about the message, formally recording it as being settled as well.

Note that because the receiving application can indicate to the underlying AMQP communication layer that it is done with a message, AMQP enables true end-to-end communication reliability. In particular, the application, be it a client application or an actual queue manager, can instruct the AMQP communication layer to keep hold of a message (i.e., a message stays in the unsettled state).

AMQP messaging

Messaging in AMQP logically takes place at the layer above the one handling communication. It is here that an application can indicate what needs to be done with a message, but can also see what has happened so far. Messaging formally takes place between two **nodes**, of which there are three types: a producer, a consumer, or a queue. Typically, producer and consumer nodes represent regular applications, whereas queues are used to store and forward messages. Indeed, a queue manager will typically consist of multiple queue nodes. In order for message transfer to take place, two nodes will have to establish a link between them.

The receiver can indicate to the sender whether its message was accepted (meaning that it was successfully processed), or rejected. Note that this means that a notification is returned to the original sender. AMQP also

```
 1  import rabbitpy
 2
 3  def producer():
 4    connection = rabbitpy.Connection() # Connect to RabbitMQ server
 5    channel = connection.channel()      # Create new channel on the connection
 6
 7    exchange = rabbitpy.Exchange(channel, 'exchange') # Create an exchange
 8    exchange.declare()
 9
10    queue1 = rabbitpy.Queue(channel, 'example1') # Create 1st queue
11    queue1.declare()
12
13    queue2 = rabbitpy.Queue(channel, 'example2') # Create 2nd queue
14    queue2.declare()
15
16    queue1.bind(exchange, 'example-key') # Bind queue1 to a single key
17    queue2.bind(exchange, 'example-key') # Bind queue2 to the same key
18
19    message = rabbitpy.Message(channel, 'Test message')
20    message.publish(exchange, 'example-key') # Publish the message using the key
21    exchange.delete()
```

(a)

```
 1  import rabbitpy
 2
 3  def consumer():
 4    connection = rabbitpy.Connection()
 5    channel = connection.channel()
 6
 7    queue = rabbitpy.Queue(channel, 'example1')
 8
 9    # While there are messages in the queue, fetch them using Basic.Get
10    while len(queue) > 0:
11      message = queue.get()
12      print('Message Q1: %s' % message.body.decode())
13      message.ack()
14
15    queue = rabbitpy.Queue(channel, 'example2')
16
17    while len(queue) > 0:
18      message = queue.get()
19      print('Message Q2: %s' % message.body.decode())
20      message.ack()
```

(b)

Figure 4.30: A simple (a) producer and (b) consumer for RabbitMQ, adapted from [Roy, 2018].

supports fragmentation and assembly of large messages, for which additional notifications are sent.

Of course, an important aspect of AMQP is its support for **persistent messaging**. Achieving persistence is handled through several mechanisms. First, a message can be marked as durable, indicating that the source expects any intermediate node, such as a queue, to be able to recover in the case of a failure. An intermediate node that cannot guarantee such durability will have to reject a message. Second, a source or target node can also indicate its durability: if durable, will it maintain its state, or will it also maintain the (unsettled) state of durable messages? Combining the latter with durable messages effectively establishes reliable message transfer and persistent messaging.

AMQP is truly a messaging protocol in the sense that it does not by itself support, for example, publish-subscribe primitives. It expects that such issues are handled by more advanced, proprietary queue managers, akin to the message brokers discussed in Section 4.3.3.

Finally, there is no reason why a queue manager cannot be connected to another queue manager. In fact, it is quite common to organize queue managers into an overlay network in which messages are routed from producers to their consumers. AMQP does not specify how the overlay network should be constructed and managed, and, indeed, different providers of AMQP-based systems offer different solutions. Of particular importance is specifying how messages should be routed through the network. The bottom line is that administrators will need to do a lot of this specification manually. Only in cases where overlays have regular structures, such as cycles or trees, it becomes easier to provide the necessary routing details.

AMQP in practice

One of the more popular implementations of message brokering is the RabbitMQ server, extensively described by Roy [2018]. The RabbitMQ server is based on the 0.9 version of AMQP, while also fully supporting version 1.0. An important difference between these two versions is the use of **exchanges**. Instead of directly manipulating queues, producers contact an exchange, which, in turn, places messages in one or several queues. In essence, an exchange allows a producer to use a synchronous or asynchronous RPC to a queue manager. An exchange never stores messages; it simply makes sure that a message is placed in an appropriate queue.

To illustrate this concept, consider Figure 4.30(a) showing a simple producer. As mentioned previously, AMQP embeds channels as part of more durable connections, and the first we do is create a means for communicating with the server (we are omitting various details; in this case we establish a default connection with the server). In the following lines, an exchange is created within the realm of the server, along with two queues. In Lines 16 and 17, both queues are bound to the same exchange by a simple key named `example-key`. After creating a message, the producer tells the exchange that it should publish that message to any queue bound by the specified key.

As to be expected, the exchange will place the message in both queues, which is verified by the simple consumer shown in Figure 4.30(b). In this case, the consumer simply fetches messages from either queue and prints their content.

Exchanges and queues have many options, for which we refer the interested reader to Roy [2018]. It is important to note that using systems such as RabbitMQ, but also other messaging brokers, one can generally set up advanced overlay networks for application-level message routing. At the same time, maintenance of those networks can easily become a nightmare.

4.4 Multicast communication

An important topic in communication in distributed systems is the support for sending data to multiple receivers, also known as **multicast communication**. For many years, this topic has belonged to the domain of network protocols, where numerous proposals for network-level and transport-level solutions have been implemented and evaluated [Janic, 2005; Obraczka, 1998]. A major issue in all solutions was setting up the communication paths for information dissemination. In practice, this involved a huge management effort, often requiring human intervention. In addition, as long as there is no convergence of proposals, ISPs have shown to be reluctant to support multicasting [Diot et al., 2000].

With the advent of peer-to-peer technology, and notably structured overlay management, it became easier to set up communication paths. As peer-to-peer solutions are typically deployed at the application layer, various application-level multicasting techniques have been introduced. In this section, we will take a brief look at these techniques.

Multicast communication can also be accomplished in other ways than setting up explicit communication paths. As we also explore in this section, gossip-based information dissemination provides simple (yet often less efficient) ways for multicasting.

4.4.1 Application-level tree-based multicasting

The basic idea in **application-level multicasting** is that nodes are organized into an overlay network, which is then used to disseminate information to its members. An important observation is that network routers are not involved in group membership. As a consequence, the connections between nodes in the overlay network may cross several physical links, and as such, routing messages within the overlay may not be optimal in comparison to what could have been achieved by network-level routing.

A crucial design issue is the construction of the overlay network. In essence, there are two approaches [El-Sayed et al., 2003; Hosseini et al., 2007; Allani et al., 2009]. First, nodes may organize themselves directly into a tree, meaning that there is a unique (overlay) path between every pair of nodes. An alternative approach is that nodes organize into a mesh network in which every node will have multiple neighbors and, in general, there exist multiple paths between every pair of nodes. The main difference between the two is that the latter generally provides higher robustness: if a connection breaks (e.g., because a node fails), there will still be an opportunity to disseminate information without having to immediately reorganize the entire network.

Note 4.13 (Advanced: Constructing a multicast tree in Chord)

To make matters concrete, let us consider a relatively simple scheme for constructing a multicast tree in Chord, which we described in Note 2.6. This scheme was originally proposed for Scribe [Castro et al., 2002b] which is an application-level multicasting scheme built on top of Pastry [Rowstron and Druschel, 2001]. The latter is also a DHT-based peer-to-peer system.

Assume a node wants to start a multicast session. To this end, it simply generates a multicast identifier, say, mid which is just a randomly chosen 160-bit key. It then looks up succ(mid), which is the node responsible for that key, and promotes it to become the root of the multicast tree that will be used for sending data to interested nodes. To join the tree, a node P simply executes the operation lookup(mid) having the effect that a lookup message with the request to join the multicast group mid will be routed from P to succ(mid). The routing algorithm itself will be explained in detail in Chapter 6.

On its way toward the root, the join request will pass several nodes. Assume it first reaches node Q. If Q had never seen a join request for mid before, it will become a **forwarder** for that group. At that point, P will become a child of Q whereas the latter will continue to forward the join request to the root. If the next node on the root, say, R is also not yet a forwarder, it will become one and record Q as its child and continue to send the join request.

On the other hand, if Q (or R) is already a forwarder for mid, it will also record the previous sender as its child (i.e., P or Q, respectively), but there will not be a need to send the join request to the root anymore, as Q (or R) will already be a member of the multicast tree.

Nodes such as P that have explicitly requested to join the multicast tree are, by definition, also forwarders. The result of this scheme is that we construct a multicast tree across the overlay network with two types of nodes: pure forwarders that act as helpers, and nodes that are also forwarders, but have explicitly requested to join the tree. Multicasting is now simple: a node merely sends a multicast message toward the root of the tree by again executing the lookup(mid) operation, after which that message can be sent along the tree.

We note that this high-level description of multicasting in Scribe does not do complete justice to its original design. The interested reader is encouraged to take a look at the details, which can be found in [Castro et al., 2002b].

Performance issues in overlays

From the high-level description given above, it should be clear that although building a tree by itself is not that difficult once we have organized the nodes into an overlay, building an efficient tree may be a different story. Note that in our description so far, the selection of nodes that participate in the tree does not take into account any performance metrics: it is purely based on the (logical) routing of messages through the overlay.

To understand the problem at hand, take a look at Figure 4.31 which shows a small set of five nodes that are organized in a simple overlay network, with the node A forming the root of a multicast tree. The costs for traversing a physical link are also shown. Now, whenever A multicasts a message to the other nodes, the *logical* route, i.e., at the level of the overlay, is simply $A \rightarrow B \rightarrow E \rightarrow D \rightarrow C$. The actual route crosses the network-level links in the following order: $A \rightarrow Ra \rightarrow Rb \rightarrow B \rightarrow Rb \rightarrow Ra \rightarrow Re \rightarrow E \rightarrow Re \rightarrow Rc \rightarrow Rd \rightarrow D \rightarrow Rd \rightarrow Rc \rightarrow C$. It is thus seen that this message will traverse each of the links $\langle B, Rb \rangle$, $\langle Ra, Rb \rangle$, $\langle E, Re \rangle$, $\langle Rc, Rd \rangle$, and $\langle D, Rd \rangle$ twice. The overlay network would have been more efficient if we had not constructed *overlay links* $\langle B, E \rangle$, and $\langle D, E \rangle$, but instead $\langle A, E \rangle$ and $\langle C, E \rangle$. Such a configuration would have saved the double traversal across physical links $\langle Ra, Rb \rangle$ and $\langle Rc, Rd \rangle$.

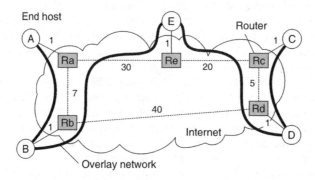

Figure 4.31: The relation between links in an overlay and network-level routes.

The quality of an application-level multicast tree is generally measured by three different metrics: link stress, stretch, and tree cost. **Link stress** is defined per link and counts how often a packet crosses the same link [Chu et al., 2002]. A link stress greater than 1 comes from the fact that although at a logical level a packet may be forwarded along two different connections, part of those connections may actually correspond to the same physical link, as we showed in Figure 4.31.

The **stretch** or **relative delay penalty (RDP)** measures the ratio of the delay between two nodes in the overlay, and the delay that those two nodes would experience in the underlying network. For example, messages from

B to C follow the route B $\rightarrow$ Rb $\rightarrow$ Ra $\rightarrow$ Re $\rightarrow$ E $\rightarrow$ Re $\rightarrow$ Rc $\rightarrow$ Rd $\rightarrow$ D $\rightarrow$ Rd $\rightarrow$ Rc $\rightarrow$ C in the overlay network, having a total cost of 73 units. However, messages would have been routed in the underlying network along the path B $\rightarrow$ Rb $\rightarrow$ Rd $\rightarrow$ Rc $\rightarrow$ C, with a total cost of 47 units, leading to a stretch of 1.55. Obviously, when constructing an overlay network, the goal is to minimize the aggregated stretch, or similarly, the average RDP measured over all node pairs.

Finally, the **tree cost** is a global metric, generally related to minimizing the aggregated link costs. For example, if the cost of a link is taken to be the delay between its two end nodes, then optimizing the tree cost boils down to finding a minimal spanning tree in which the total time for disseminating information to all nodes is minimal.

To simplify matters somewhat, assume that a multicast group has an associated and well-known node that keeps track of the nodes that have joined the tree. When a new node issues a join request, it contacts this **rendezvous node** to obtain a (potentially partial) list of members. The goal is to select the best member that can operate as the new node's parent in the tree. Who should it select? There are many alternatives, and different proposals often follow very different solutions.

Consider, for example, a multicast group with only a single source. In this case, the selection of the best node is obvious: it should be the source (because in that case, we can be assured that the stretch will be equal to 1). However, in doing so, we would introduce a star topology with the source in the middle. Although simple, it is not difficult to imagine the source may easily become overloaded. In other words, selection of a node will generally be constrained in such a way that only those nodes may be chosen who have k or fewer neighbors, with k being a design parameter. This constraint severely complicates the tree-establishment algorithm, as a suitable solution may require that part of the existing tree is reconfigured. Tan et al. [2003] provide an extensive overview and evaluation of various solutions to this problem.

Note 4.14 (Advanced: Switch-trees)
As an illustration, let us take a closer look at one specific family, known as **switch-trees** [Helder and Jamin, 2002]. The basic idea is simple. Assume we already have a multicast tree with a single source as root. In this tree, a node P can switch parents by dropping the link to its current parent in favor of a link to another node. The only constraints imposed on switching links is that the new parent can never be a member of the subtree rooted at P (as this would partition the tree and create a loop), and that the new parent will not have too many immediate children. This last requirement is needed to limit the load of forwarding messages by any single node.

There are different criteria for deciding to switch parents. A simple one is to optimize the route to the source, effectively minimizing the delay when a message is to be multicasted. To this end, each node regularly receives information on other nodes (we will explain one specific way of doing this below). At that point, the node can evaluate whether another node would be a better parent in terms of delay along the route to the source, and if so, initiates a switch.

Another criterion could be whether the delay to the potential other parent is lower than to the current parent. If every node takes this as a criterion, then the aggregated delays of the resulting tree should ideally be minimal. In other words, this is an example of optimizing the cost of the tree, as we explained above. However, more information would be needed to construct such a tree, but as it turns out, this simple scheme is a reasonable heuristic leading to a good approximation of a minimal spanning tree.

As an example, consider the case where a node P receives information on the neighbors of its parent. Note that the neighbors consist of P's grandparent, along with the other siblings of P's parent. Node P can then evaluate the delays to each of these nodes and subsequently choose the one with the lowest delay, say Q, as its new parent. To that end, it sends a switch request to Q. To prevent loops from being formed due to concurrent switching requests, a node that has an outstanding switch request will simply refuse to process any incoming requests. In effect, this leads to a situation where only completely independent switches can be carried out simultaneously. Furthermore, P will provide Q with enough information to allow the latter to conclude that both nodes have the same parent, or that Q is the grandparent.

An important problem that we have not yet addressed is node failure. In the case of switch-trees, a simple solution is proposed: whenever a node notices that its parent has failed, it attaches itself to the root. At that point, the optimization protocol can proceed as usual and will eventually place the node at a good point in the multicast tree. Experiments described in [Helder and Jamin, 2002] show that the resulting tree is indeed close to a minimal spanning one.

4.4.2 Flooding-based multicasting

So far, we have assumed that when a message is to be multicasted, it is to be received by every node in the overlay network. Strictly speaking, this corresponds to **broadcasting**. In general, multicasting refers to sending a message to a subset of all the nodes, that is, a specific *group of nodes*. A key design issue when it comes to multicasting is to minimize the use of intermediate nodes for which the message is not intended. To make this clear, if the overlay is organized as a multi-level tree, yet only the leaf nodes are the ones who should receive a multicast message, then clearly there may be quite some nodes who need to store and subsequently forward a message that is not meant for them.

One simple way to avoid such inefficiency, is to construct an overlay network *per multicast group*. As a consequence, multicasting a message m to a group G is the same as broadcasting m to G. The drawback of this solution is that a node belonging to several groups, will, in principle, need to maintain a separate list of its neighbors for each group of which it is a member.

If we assume that an overlay corresponds to a multicast group, and thus that we need to broadcast a message, a naive way of doing so is to apply **flooding**. In this case, each node simply forwards a message m to each of its neighbors, except to the one from which it received m. Furthermore, if a node keeps track of the messages it received and forwarded, it can simply ignore duplicates.

To understand the performance of flooding, we model an overlay network as a connected undirected graph $G - (V, E)$ with nodes V and links E. Let v_0 be the node that initiates flooding. In principle, every node other node than v_0 will send out the message to its neighbors once, except to the neighbor from which it had received the message. We will thus see a total of $\delta(v_0) + \sum_{v \in V - v_0}(\delta(v) - 1)$ messages, with $\delta(v)$ the number of neighbors of the node v. For any undirected graph, $\sum_{v \in V} \delta(v) = 2 \cdot |E|$, with $|E|$ denoting the total number of edges. In other words, we will see $2|E| - |V| + 1$ messages being sent, making flooding quite inefficient. Only if G is a tree, will flooding be optimal, for in that case, $|E| = |V| - 1$. In the worst case, when G is fully connected, we have $|E| = \binom{|V|}{2}$ leading to an order of $|V|^2$ messages.

Suppose now that we have no information on the structure of the overlay network and that the best we can assume is that it can be represented as a **random graph**, which (to keep it simple) is a graph having a probability p_{edge} that two vertices are joined by an edge, also known as an **Erdös-Rényi graph** [Erdös and Rényi, 1959]. Note that we are actually considering our overlay network to be an unstructured peer-to-peer network, and that we do not have any information on how it is being constructed. With a probability p_{edge} that two nodes are joined, and a total of $\binom{|V|}{2}$ edges, it is not difficult to see that we can expect our overlay to have $|E| = \frac{1}{2} \cdot p_{edge} \cdot |V| \cdot (|V| - 1)$ edges. To give an impression of what we are dealing with, Figure 4.32 shows the relationship between the number of nodes and edges for different values of p_{edge}. As can be seen, the number of edges can easily become large, even for small values of p_{edge}.

To reduce the number of messages, we can also use **probabilistic flooding** as introduced by Banaei-Kashani and Shahab [2003] and formally analyzed by Oikonomou and Stavrakakis [2007]. The idea is simple: when a node is flooding a message m and needs to forward m to a specific neighbor, it will do so with a probability p_{flood}. The effect can be dramatic: the total number of messages sent will drop linearly in p_{flood}. However, there is also a risk: the lower p_{flood}, the higher the chance that not all nodes in the network will be reached. This risk is caused by the simple fact that all neighbors of a specific node Q may have decided *not* to forward m to Q. If Q has n neighbors, then this can happen roughly with a probability of $(1 - p_{flood})^n$. Clearly, the

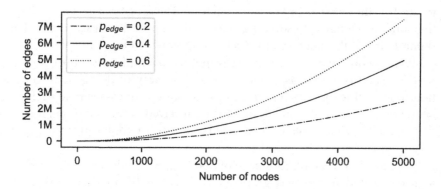

Figure 4.32: The size of a random overlay as function of the number of nodes.

number of neighbors plays an important role in deciding whether to forward a message, and, indeed, we can replace the static probability of forwarding with one that takes the degree of the neighbor into account. This has been further developed and analyzed by Sereno and Gaeta [2011]. To give an idea of the efficiency of probabilistic broadcasting: in a random network of 10,000 nodes and $p_{edge} = 0.1$, we need only set $p_{flood} = 0.01$ to establish a more than 50-fold reduction in the number of messages sent in comparison to full flooding.

When dealing with a structured overlay, that is, one having a more or less deterministic topology, designing efficient flooding schemes is simpler. As an example, consider an n-dimensional hypercube, shown in Figure 4.33 for the case $n = 4$, as also discussed in Section 2.4.1.

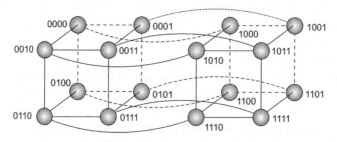

Figure 4.33: A simple peer-to-peer, four-dimensional hypercube.

A simple and efficient broadcast scheme has been designed by Schlosser et al. [2002] and relies on keeping track of neighbors *per dimension*. This is best explained by considering that every node in an n-dimensional hypercube is represented by a bit string of length n. Each edge in the overlay is labeled with its dimension. For the case $n = 4$, node 0000 will have as its neighbors the set $\{0001, 0010, 0100, 1000\}$. The edge between 0000 and 0001 is labeled

"4" corresponding to changing the 4th bit when comparing 0000 to 0001 and *vice versa*. Likewise, the edge ⟨0000, 0100⟩ is labeled "2," and so forth. A node initially broadcasts a message m to all of its neighbors, and tags m with the label of the edge over which it sends the message. In our example, if node 1001 broadcasts a message, it will send the following:

- (m,1) to 0001
- (m,2) to 1101
- (m,3) to 1011
- (m,4) to 1000

When a node receives a broadcast message, it will forward it only along edges that have a higher dimension. In other words, in our example, node 1101 will forward m only to nodes 1111 (joined to 1101 by an edge labeled "3") and 1100 (joined by an edge with label "4"). Using this scheme, it can be shown that every broadcast requires precisely $N - 1$ messages, where $N = 2^n$, that is the number of nodes in a n-dimensional hypercube. This broadcasting scheme is therefore optimal in terms of the number of messages sent.

Note 4.15 (Advanced: Ring-based flooding)

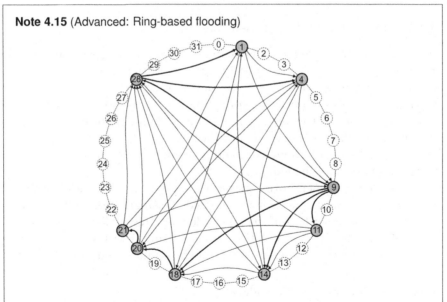

Figure 4.34: A Chord ring in which node 9 broadcasts a message.

A hypercube is a straightforward example of how we can effectively use knowledge of the structure of an overlay network to establish efficient flooding. In the case of Chord, we can follow an approach proposed by Ghodsi [2010]. Recall that in Chord each node is identified by a number p, and each resource (typically a file), is assigned a key k from the same space as used for node identifiers. The successor succ(k) of a key k is the node with the smallest identifier p $\geq$ k. Consider the small Chord ring shown in Figure 4.34 and assume that node 9 wants to flood a message to all other nodes.

In our example, node 9 divides the identifier space into four segments (one for each of its neighbors). Node 28 is requested to make sure that the message reaches all nodes with identifiers 28 $\leq$ k < 9 (recall that we are applying modulo arithmetic); node 18 takes care of nodes with identifiers 18 $\leq$ k < 28; node 14 for 14 $\leq$ k < 18; and 11 for identifiers 11 $\leq$ k < 14.

Node 28 will subsequently divide the part of the identifier space it is requested to handle into two subsegments: one for its neighboring node 1 and another for 4. Likewise, node 18, responsible for segment [18, 28) will "split" that segment into only one part: it has only one neighbor to delegate the flood to, and forwards the message to node 20, telling it that it should handle segment [20, 28).

In the last step, only node 20 has work to do. It forwards the message to node 21, telling it to forward it to nodes known to it in the segment [21, 28). As there are no such nodes anymore, the broadcast completes.

As in the case of our hypercube example, we see that flooding is done with $N - 1$ messages, with N being the number of nodes in the system.

4.4.3   Gossip-based data dissemination

An important technique for disseminating information is to rely on **epidemic behavior**, also referred to as **gossiping**. Observing how diseases spread among people, researchers have since long investigated whether simple techniques could be developed for spreading information in very large-scale distributed systems. The main goal of these **epidemic protocols** is to rapidly propagate information among a large collection of nodes using only local information. In other words, there is no central component by which information dissemination is coordinated.

To explain the general principles of these algorithms, we assume that all updates for a specific data item are initiated at a single node. In this way, we simply avoid write-write conflicts. The following presentation is based on the classical paper by Demers et al. [1987] on epidemic algorithms. An overview of epidemic information dissemination can be found in [Eugster et al., 2004].

Information dissemination models

As the name suggests, epidemic algorithms are based on the theory of epidemics, which studies the spreading of infectious diseases. In the case of large-scale distributed systems, instead of spreading diseases, they spread information. Research on epidemics for distributed systems also aims at an entirely different goal: whereas health organizations will do their best to prevent infectious diseases from spreading across large groups of people, designers of epidemic algorithms for distributed systems will try to "infect" all nodes with new information as fast as possible.

Using the terminology from epidemics, a node that is part of a distributed system is called **infected** if it holds data that it is willing to spread to other nodes. A node that has not yet seen this data is called **susceptible**. Finally, an updated node that is not willing or able to spread its data is said to have been **removed**. Note that we assume we can distinguish old from new data, for example because it has been timestamped or versioned. In this light, nodes are also said to spread updates.

A popular propagation model is that of **anti-entropy**. In this model, a node P picks another node Q at random, and subsequently exchanges updates with Q. There are three approaches to exchanging updates:

1. P only pulls in new updates from Q

2. P only pushes its own updates to Q

3. P and Q send updates to each other (i.e., a push-pull approach)

When it comes to rapidly spreading updates, only pushing updates turns out to be a bad choice. Intuitively, this can be understood as follows. First, note that in a pure push-based approach, updates can be propagated only by infected nodes. However, if many nodes are infected, the probability of each one selecting a susceptible node is relatively small. Consequently, chances are that a particular node remains susceptible for a long period simply because an infected node does not select it.

In contrast, the pull-based approach works much better when many nodes are infected. In that case, spreading updates is essentially triggered by susceptible nodes. Chances are big that such a node will contact an infected one to subsequently pull in the updates and become infected as well.

If only a single node is infected, updates will rapidly spread across all nodes using either form of anti-entropy, although push-pull remains the best strategy [Jelasity et al., 2007]. Define a **round** as spanning a period in which every node will have taken the initiative once to exchange updates with a randomly chosen other node. It can then be shown that the number of rounds to propagate a single update to all nodes is of the order $\mathcal{O}(log(N))$, where N is the number of nodes in the system. This indicates indeed that propagating updates is fast, but above all scalable.

Note 4.16 (Advanced: An analysis of anti-entropy)
A simple and straightforward analysis will give some idea on how well anti-entropy works. Consider a system with N nodes. One of these nodes initiates the spreading of a message m to all other nodes. Let p_i denote the probability that a node P has not yet received m after the ith round. We distinguish the following three cases:

- With a pure pull-based approach, $p_{i+1} = (p_i)^2$: not only had P not yet been updated in the previous round, also P contacts a node that had not yet received m.
- With a pure push-based approach, $p_{i+1} = p_i \cdot (1 - \frac{1}{N-1})^{N(1-p_i)}$: again, P should not have been updated in the previous round, but also none of the updated nodes should contact P. The probability that not a single node contacts P is $1 - \frac{1}{N-1}$; we can expect that there are $N(1 - p_i)$ updated nodes in round i.
- In a push-pull approach, we can simply combine the two: P should not contact an updated node, and should not be contacted by one.

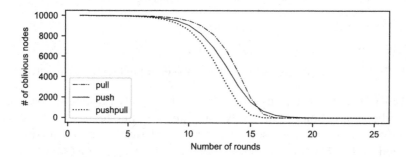

Figure 4.35: (a) The number of nodes that have not been updated as a function of the number of dissemination rounds.

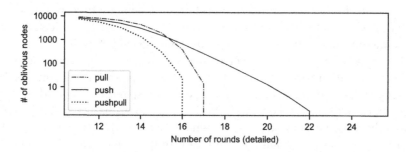

Figure 4.35: (b) Zooming in the differences between the three anti-entropy approaches when almost all nodes have been updated.

Figure 4.35(a) shows how quickly the probability of not yet being updated drops as a function of the number of rounds in a network of 10,000 nodes. After a slow start, the information is rapidly disseminated. In Figure 4.35(b) we have zoomed into what happens in the last number of rounds while also using a log scale for the y-axis. Indeed, assuming that nodes are up-and-running all the time, it turns out that an anti-entropy push-pull strategy can be an extremely effective dissemination protocol.

One specific variant of epidemic protocols is called **rumor spreading**. It works as follows. If node P has just been updated for a data item x, it contacts an arbitrary other node Q and tries to push the update to Q. However, it is possible that Q was already updated by another node. In that case, P may lose interest in spreading the update any further, say with probability p_{stop}. In other words, it then becomes removed.

Rumor spreading is gossiping as we mostly experience it in real life. When Bob has some hot news to spread around, he may phone his friend Alice, telling her all about it. Alice, like Bob, will be really excited to spread the rumor to her friends as well. However, she will become disappointed when phoning a friend, say Chuck, only to hear that the news has already reached him. Chances are that she will stop phoning other friends, for what good is it if they already know?

Rumor spreading turns out to be an excellent way of rapidly spreading news. However, it cannot guarantee that all nodes will actually be updated [Demers et al., 1987]. In fact, when there are many nodes that participate in the epidemics, the fraction s of nodes that will remain ignorant of an update, that is, remain susceptible, satisfies the equation:

$$s = e^{-(1/p_{stop}+1)(1-s)}$$

To get an idea of what this means, take a look at Figure 4.36, which shows s as a function of p_{stop}. Even for high values of p_{stop} we see that the fraction of nodes that remains ignorant is relatively low, and always less than approximately 0.2. For $p_{stop} = 0.20$ it can be shown that $s = 0.0025$. However, in those cases when p_{stop} is relatively high, additional measures will need to be taken to ensure that *all* nodes are updated.

Note 4.17 (Advanced: Analysis of rumor spreading)

To formally analyze the situation for rumor spreading, we let s denote the fraction of nodes that have not yet been updated, i.e., the fraction of susceptible nodes. Likewise, let i denote the fraction of infected nodes: the ones that have been updated and are still contacting other nodes to spread information. Finally, r is the fraction of nodes that have been updated, but have given up, i.e., they are passive and no longer play a role in disseminating information. Obviously, $s + i + r = 1$. Using theory from epidemics, it is not difficult to see the following:

$$
\begin{aligned}
(1) \quad ds/dt &= -s \cdot i \\
(2) \quad di/dt &= s \cdot i - p_{stop} \cdot (1-s) \cdot i \\
\Rightarrow \quad di/ds &= -(1 + p_{stop}) + \frac{p_{stop}}{s} \\
\Rightarrow \quad i(s) &= -(1 + p_{stop}) \cdot s + p_{stop} \cdot \ln(s) + C
\end{aligned}
$$

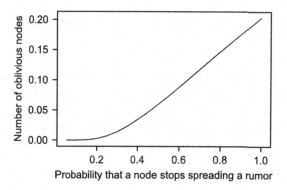

Figure 4.36: The relation between the fraction s of update-ignorant nodes and the probability p_{stop} that a node will stop gossiping once it contacts a node that has already been updated.

where we use the notation $i(s)$ to express i as a function of s. When $s = 1$, no nodes have yet been infected, meaning that $i(1) = 0$. This allows us to derive that $C = 1 + p_{stop}$, and thus

$$i(s) = (1 + p_{stop}) \cdot (1 - s) + p_{stop} \cdot \ln(s)$$

We are looking for the situation that there is no more rumor spreading, i.e., when $i(s) = 0$. Having a closed expression for $i(s)$ then leads to

$$s = e^{-(1/p_{stop}+1)(1-s)}$$

One of the main advantages of epidemic algorithms is their scalability since the number of synchronizations between processes is relatively small compared to other propagation methods. For wide-area systems, Lin and Marzullo [1999] have shown that it makes sense to take the actual network topology into account to achieve better results. In that case, nodes that are connected to only a few other nodes are contacted with a relatively high probability. The underlying assumption is that such nodes form a bridge to other remote parts of the network; therefore, they should be contacted as soon as possible. This approach is referred to as **directional gossiping** and comes in different variants.

This problem touches upon an important assumption that most epidemic solutions make, namely that a node can randomly select any other node to gossip with. This implies that, in principle, the complete set of nodes should be known to each member. In a large system, this assumption can never hold, and special measures will need to be taken to mimic such properties. We return to this issue in Section 5.5.2 when we discuss a **peer-sampling service**.

Removing data

Epidemic algorithms are fantastic for spreading updates. However, they have a rather strange side effect: spreading the *deletion* of a data item is hard. The essence of the problem lies in the fact that deletion of a data item destroys all information on that item. Consequently, when a data item is simply removed from a node, that node will eventually receive old copies of the data item and interpret those as updates on something it did not have before.

The trick is to record the deletion of a data item as just another update, and keep a record of that deletion. In this way, old copies will not be interpreted as something new, but merely treated as versions that have been updated by a delete operation. The recording of a deletion is done by spreading **death certificates**.

Of course, the problem with death certificates is that they should eventually be cleaned up, or otherwise each node will gradually build a huge local database of historical information on deleted data items that is otherwise not used. Demers et al. [1987] propose to use what are called **dormant death certificates**. Each death certificate is timestamped when it is created. If it can be assumed that updates propagate to all nodes within a known finite time, then death certificates can be removed after this maximum propagation time has elapsed.

However, to provide hard guarantees that deletions are indeed spread to all nodes, only a very few nodes maintain dormant death certificates that are never thrown away. Assume node P has such a certificate for a data item x. If by any chance an obsolete update for x reaches P, P will react by simply spreading the death certificate for x again.

4.5 Summary

Having powerful and flexible facilities for communication between processes is essential for any distributed system. In traditional network applications, communication is often based on the low-level message-passing primitives offered by the transport layer. An important issue in middleware systems is to offer a higher level of abstraction that will make it easier to express communication between processes than the support offered by the interface to the transport layer.

One of the most widely used abstractions is the Remote Procedure Call (RPC). The essence of an RPC is that a service is implemented through a procedure, of which the body is executed at a server. The client is offered only the signature of the procedure, that is, the procedure's name along with its parameters. When the client calls the procedure, the client-side implementation, called a stub, takes care of wrapping the parameter values into a message and sending that to the server. The latter calls the actual procedure and returns the results, again in a message. The client's stub extracts the result values from the return message and passes it back to the calling client application.

RPCs offer synchronous communication facilities, by which a client is blocked until the server has sent a reply. Although variations of either mechanism exist by which this strict synchronous model is relaxed, it turns out that general-purpose, high-level message-oriented models are often more convenient.

In message-oriented models, the issues are whether communication is persistent, and whether communication is synchronous. The essence of persistent communication is that a message that is submitted for transmission, is stored by the communication system as long as it takes to deliver it. In other words, neither the sender nor the receiver needs to be up and running for message transmission to take place. In transient communication, no storage facilities are offered so that the receiver must be prepared to accept the message when it is sent.

In asynchronous communication, the sender is allowed to continue immediately after the message has been submitted for transmission, possibly before it has even been sent. In synchronous communication, the sender is blocked at least until a message has been received. Alternatively, the sender may be blocked until message delivery has taken place or even until the receiver has responded, as with RPCs.

Message-oriented middleware models generally offer persistent asynchronous communication, and are used where RPCs are not appropriate. They are often used to assist the integration of (widely dispersed) collections of databases into large-scale information systems.

Finally, an important class of communication protocols in distributed systems is multicasting. The basic idea is to disseminate information from one sender to multiple receivers. We have discussed two different approaches. First, multicasting can be achieved by setting up a tree from the sender to the receivers. Considering that it is now well understood how nodes can self-organize into peer-to-peer system, solutions have also appeared to dynamically set up trees in a decentralized fashion. Second, flooding messages across the network is extremely robust, yet requires special attention if we want to avoid severe waste of resources as nodes may see messages multiple times. Probabilistic flooding, by which a node forwards a message with a certain probability, often proves to combine simplicity and efficiency, while being highly effective.

Another important class of dissemination solutions deploys epidemic protocols. These protocols have proven to be simple and extremely robust.

05

COORDINATION

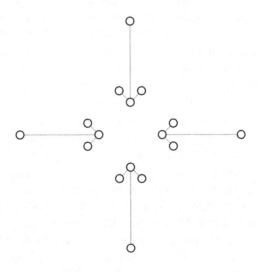

In the previous chapters, we have looked at processes and communication between processes. While communication is important, it is not the entire story. Closely related is how processes cooperate and synchronize with one another. Cooperation is partly supported by naming, which allows processes to at least share resources, or entities in general.

In this chapter, we mainly concentrate on how processes can synchronize and coordinate their actions. For example, it is important that multiple processes do not simultaneously access a shared resource, such as a file, but instead cooperate in granting each other temporary exclusive access. Another example is that multiple processes may sometimes need to agree on the ordering of events, such as whether message m_1 from process P was sent before or after message m_2 from process Q.

Synchronization and coordination are two closely related phenomena. In **process synchronization** we make sure that one process waits for another to complete its operation. When dealing with **data synchronization**, the problem is to ensure that two sets of data are the same. When it comes to **coordination**, the goal is to manage the interactions and dependencies between activities in a distributed system [Malone and Crowston, 1994]. From this perspective, one could state that coordination encapsulates synchronization.

As it turns out, coordination in distributed systems is often much more difficult compared to that in uniprocessor or multiprocessor systems. The problems and solutions that are discussed in this chapter are, by their nature, rather general, and occur in many situations in distributed systems.

We start with a discussion of the issue of synchronization based on actual time, followed by synchronization in which only relative ordering matters rather than ordering in absolute time.

Often, it is important that a group of processes can appoint one process as a coordinator, which can be done through election algorithms. We discuss various election algorithms in a separate section. Before that, we look into several algorithms for coordinating mutual exclusion to a shared resource. As a special class of coordination problems, we also dive into location systems, by which we place a process in a multidimensional plane. Such placements are useful when dealing with very large distributed systems.

We also consider three different gossip-based coordination problems: aggregation, peer sampling, and overlay construction.

Finally, we already came across publish-subscribe systems, but have not yet discussed in any detail how we actually match subscriptions to publications. There are many ways to do this, and we look at centralized as well as decentralized implementations.

Distributed algorithms come in all sorts and flavors and have been developed for different types of distributed systems. Many examples (and further references) can be found in Andrews [2000], Cachin et al. [2011], and Fokkink [2018]. More formal approaches to a wealth of algorithms can be found in textbooks from Attiya and Welch [2004], Lynch [1996], Santoro [2007], and Tel [2000].

5.1 Clock synchronization

In a centralized system, time is unambiguous. When a process wants to know the time, it simply makes a call to the operating system. If process A asks for the time, and then a little later process B asks for the time, the value that B gets will be higher than (or possibly equal to) the value A got. It will certainly not be lower. In a distributed system, achieving agreement on time is not trivial.

Just think, for a moment, about the implications of the lack of global time on the Unix make program, as a simple example. Normally, in Unix, large programs are split up into multiple source files, so that a change to one source file requires only one file to be recompiled, not all the files. If a program consists of 100 files, not having to recompile everything because one file has been changed greatly increases the speed at which programmers can work.

The way make normally works is simple. When the programmer has finished changing all the source files, she runs make, which examines the times at which all the source and object files were last modified. If the source file input.c has time 2151 and the corresponding object file input.o has time 2150, make knows that input.c has been changed since input.o was created, and thus input.c must be recompiled. On the other hand, if output.c has time 2144 and output.o has time 2145, no compilation is needed. Thus make goes through all the source files to find out which ones need to be recompiled and calls the compiler to recompile them.

Now imagine what could happen in a distributed system in which there was no global agreement on time. Suppose that output.o has time 2144 as above, and shortly thereafter output.c is modified but is assigned time 2143 because the clock on its machine is slightly behind, as shown in Figure 5.1. Make will not call the compiler. The resulting executable binary program will then contain a mixture of object files from the old sources and the new sources. It may crash, and the programmer will go crazy trying to understand what is wrong with the code.

There are many more examples where an accurate account of time is needed. The example above can easily be reformulated to file timestamps in general. In addition, think of application domains such as financial brokerage, security auditing, and collaborative sensing, and it will become clear that accurate timing is important. From a different perspective, Najafi et al. [2021] argue that accurate timing is essential for most systems research, if only to ensure that performance measurements can be properly compared. Since time is so basic to the way people think and the effect of not having all the clocks synchronized can be so dramatic, it is fitting that we begin our study of

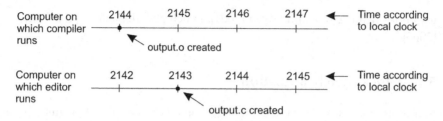

Figure 5.1: When each machine has its own clock, an event that occurred after another event may nevertheless be assigned an earlier time.

synchronization with the simple question: Would it be possible to synchronize all the clocks in a distributed system? The answer is surprisingly complicated.

5.1.1 Physical clocks

Nearly all computers often have several circuits for keeping track of time. Despite the widespread use of the word "clock" to refer to these devices, they are not actually clocks in the usual sense. **Timer** is perhaps a better word. A computer timer is usually a precisely machined quartz crystal. When kept under tension, quartz crystals oscillate at a well-defined frequency that depends on the kind of crystal, how it is cut, and the amount of tension. Associated with each crystal are two registers, a **counter** and a **holding register**. Each oscillation of the crystal decrements the counter by one. When the counter gets to zero, an interrupt is generated and the counter is reloaded from the holding register. In this way, it is possible to program a timer to generate an interrupt 60 times a second, or at any other desired frequency. Each interrupt is called one **clock tick**.

When the system is booted and initialized for the very first time, the user is asked for the current time zone, or even time, to convert time to the number of ticks after some known starting date and stored in memory. Most computers have a special battery-backed up CMOS RAM so that the date and time need not be entered on subsequent boots. At every clock tick, the interrupt service procedure adds one to the time stored in memory. In this way, the (software) clock is kept up to date.

With a single computer and a single clock, it does not matter much if this clock is off by a small amount. Since all processes on the machine use the same clock, they will still be internally consistent. For example, if the file input.c has time 2151 and file input.o has time 2150, make will recompile the source file, even if the clock is off by 2 and the true times are 2153 and 2152, respectively. All that really matters are the relative times.

As soon as multiple CPUs are introduced, each with its own clock, the situation changes radically. Although the frequency at which a crystal oscillator runs is usually fairly stable, it is impossible to guarantee that the crystals in different computers all run at the same frequency. In practice, when a system has n computers, all n crystals will run at slightly different rates, causing the (software) clocks gradually to get out of sync and give different values when read out. This difference in time values is called **clock skew**. As a consequence of this clock skew, programs that expect the time associated with a file, object, process, or message to be correct and independent of the machine on which it was generated (i.e., which clock it used) can fail, as we saw in the make example above.

In some systems (e.g., real-time systems), the actual clock time is important. Under these circumstances, external physical clocks are needed. For reasons of efficiency and redundancy, multiple physical clocks are generally considered desirable, which yields two problems: (1) how do we synchronize them with real-world clocks, and (2) how do we synchronize the clocks with each other?

Note 5.1 (More information: Determining real time)

Before answering these questions, let us digress slightly to see how time is actually measured. It is not nearly as easy as one might think, especially when high accuracy is required. Since the invention of mechanical clocks in the 17th century, time has been measured astronomically. Every day, the sun appears to rise on the eastern horizon, then climbs to a maximum height in the sky, and finally sinks in the west. The event of the sun's reaching its highest apparent point in the sky is called the **transit of the sun**. This event occurs at about noon each day. The interval between two consecutive transits of the sun is called the **solar day**. Since there are 24 hours in a day, each containing 3600 seconds, the **solar second** is defined as exactly $1/86400^{th}$ of a solar day. The geometry of the mean solar day calculation is shown in Figure 5.2.

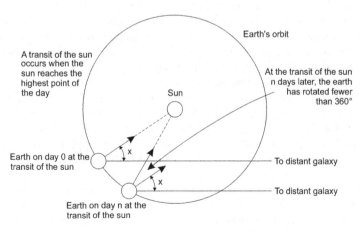

Figure 5.2: Computation of the mean solar day.

In the 1940s, it was established that the period of the earth's rotation is not constant. The earth is slowing down due to tidal friction and atmospheric drag. Based on studies of growth patterns in ancient coral, geologists now believe that 300 million years ago there were about 400 days per year. The length of the year (the time for one trip around the sun) is not thought to have changed; the day has simply become longer. In addition to this long-term trend, short-term variations in the length of the day also occur, probably caused by turbulence deep in the earth's core of molten iron. These revelations lead astronomers to compute the length of the day by measuring a large number of days and taking the average before dividing by 86,400. The resulting quantity was called the **mean solar second**.

With the invention of the atomic clock in 1948, it became possible to measure time much more accurately, and independent of the wiggling and wobbling of the earth, by counting transitions of the cesium 133 atom. The physicists took over the job of timekeeping from the astronomers and defined the second to be the time it takes the cesium 133 atom to make exactly 9,192,631,770 transitions. The choice of 9,192,631,770 was made to make the atomic second equal to the mean solar second in the year of its introduction. Currently, several laboratories around the world have cesium 133 clocks. Periodically, each laboratory tells the Bureau International de l'Heure (BIH) in Paris how many times its clock has ticked. The BIH averages these to produce **International Atomic Time**, which is abbreviated to **TAI**. Thus TAI is just the mean number of ticks of the cesium 133 clocks since midnight on Jan. 1, 1958 (the beginning of time) divided by 9,192,631,770.

Although TAI is highly stable and available to anyone who wants to go to the trouble of buying a cesium clock, there is a serious problem with it; 86,400 TAI seconds is now about 3 msec less than a mean solar day (because the mean solar day is getting longer all the time). Using TAI for keeping time would mean that over the course of the years, noon would get earlier and earlier, until it would eventually occur in the wee hours of the morning. People might notice this and we could have the same kind of situation as occurred in 1582 when Pope Gregory XIII decreed that 10 days be omitted from the calendar. This event caused riots in the streets because landlords demanded a full month's rent and bankers a full month's interest, while employers refused to pay workers for the 10 days they did not work, to mention only a few of the conflicts. The Protestant countries, as a matter of principle, refused to have anything to do with papal decrees and did not accept the Gregorian calendar for 170 years.

BIH solves the problem by introducing **leap seconds** whenever the discrepancy between TAI and solar time grows to 800 msec. The use of leap seconds is illustrated in Figure 5.3. This correction gives rise to a time system based on constant TAI seconds but which stays in phase with the apparent motion of the sun. This time system is known as **Coordinated Universal Time** abbreviated to **UTC**.

Most electric power companies synchronize the timing of their 60-Hz or 50-Hz clocks to UTC, so when BIH announces a leap second, the power companies raise their frequency to 61 Hz or 51 Hz for 60 or 50 sec, to advance all the clocks in their distribution area. Since 1 sec is a noticeable interval for a computer, an operating system that needs to keep accurate time over a period of years must have special software to account for leap seconds as they are announced (unless they use the power line for time, which is usually too crude). The total number of leap seconds introduced into UTC so far is about 30.

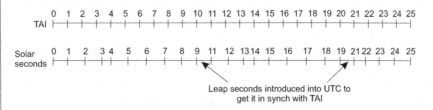

Figure 5.3: TAI seconds are of constant length, unlike solar seconds. Leap seconds are introduced when necessary to keep in phase with the sun.

The basis for keeping global time is a called **Coordinated Universal Time**, but is abbreviated as **UTC**. UTC is the basis of all modern civil timekeeping and is a worldwide standard. To provide UTC to people who need precise time, some 40 shortwave radio stations around the world broadcast a short pulse at the start of each UTC second. The accuracy of these stations is about $\pm$ 1 msec, but due to random atmospheric fluctuations that can affect the length of the signal path, in practice the accuracy is no better than $\pm$ 10 milliseconds.

Several earth satellites also offer a UTC service. The Geostationary Operational Environment Satellite can provide UTC accurately to 0.5 msec, and some other satellites do even better. By combining receptions from several satellites, ground timeservers can be built, offering an accuracy of 50 nanoseconds. UTC receivers are commercially available, and many computers are equipped with one.

5.1.2   Clock synchronization algorithms

If one machine has a UTC receiver, the goal becomes keeping all the other machines synchronized to it. If no machines have UTC receivers, each machine keeps track of its own time, and the goal is to keep all the machines together as well as possible. Many algorithms have been proposed for doing this synchronization. Surveys are provided by Ramanathan et al. [1990], Horauer [2004], Shin et al. [2011], and Levesque and Tipper [2016].

All clocks are based on some harmonic oscillator: an object that resonates at a certain frequency and from which we can subsequently derive time. Atomic clocks are based on the transitions of the cesium 133 atom, which is not only very high, but also very constant. Hardware clocks in most computers use a crystal oscillator based on quartz, which is also capable of producing a very high, stable frequency, although not as stable as that of atomic clocks. A software clock in a computer is derived from that computer's hardware clock. In particular, the hardware clock is assumed to cause an interrupt f times per second. When this timer goes off, the interrupt handler adds 1 to a counter that keeps track of the number of ticks (interrupts) since some agreed-upon time in the past. This counter acts as a software clock C, resonating at frequency F.

When the UTC time is t, denote by $C_p(t)$ the value of the software clock on machine p. The goal of **clock synchronization algorithms** is to keep the deviation between the respective clocks of any two machines in a distributed system, within a specified bound, known as the **precision** π:

$$\forall t, \forall \mathsf{p}, \mathsf{q} : |C_p(t) - C_q(t)| \leq \pi$$

Note that precision refers to the deviation of clocks only *between machines* that are part of a distributed system. When considering an external reference point, like UTC, we speak of **accuracy**, aiming to keep it bound to a value α:

$$\forall t, \forall \mathsf{p} : |C_p(t) - t| \leq \alpha$$

The whole idea of clock synchronization is that we keep clocks *precise*, referred to as **internal synchronization** or *accurate*, known as **external synchronization**. A set of clocks that are accurate within bound α, will be precise within bound $\pi = 2\alpha$. However, being precise does not allow us to conclude anything about the accuracy of clocks.

In a perfect world, we would have $C_p(t) = t$ for all p and all t, and thus $\alpha = \pi = 0$. Unfortunately, hardware clocks, and thus also software clocks, are subject to **clock drift**: because their frequency is not perfect and affected by external sources such as temperature, clocks on different machines will gradually start showing different values for time. This is known as the **clock drift rate**: the difference per unit of time from a perfect reference clock. A typical quartz-based hardware clock has a clock drift rate of some 10^{-6} seconds per second, or approximately 31.5 seconds per year. Computer hardware clocks exist that have much lower drift rates.

The specifications of a hardware clock include its maximum clock drift rate ρ. If $F(t)$ denotes the actual oscillator frequency of the hardware clock at time t and F its ideal (constant) frequency, then a hardware clock is living up to its specifications if

$$\forall t : (1 - \rho) \leq \frac{F(t)}{F} \leq (1 + \rho)$$

By using hardware interrupts we are directly coupling a software clock to the hardware clock, and thus also its clock drift rate. In particular, we have that

$$C_p(t) = \frac{1}{F} \int_0^t F(t)dt, \text{ and thus: } \frac{dC_p(t)}{dt} = \frac{F(t)}{F}$$

which brings us to our goal, namely keeping the software clock drift rate also bounded to ρ:

$$\forall t : 1 - \rho \leq \frac{dC_p(t)}{dt} \leq 1 + \rho$$

Slow, perfect, and fast clocks are shown in Figure 5.4.

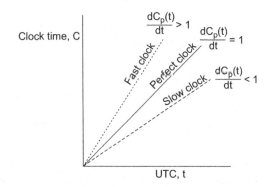

Figure 5.4: The relation between clock time and UTC when clocks tick at different rates.

If two clocks are drifting from UTC in the opposite direction, at a time Δt after they were synchronized, they may be as much as $2\rho \cdot \Delta t$ apart. If the system designers want to guarantee a precision π, that is, that no two clocks ever differ by more than π seconds, clocks must be resynchronized (in software) at least every $\pi/(2\rho)$ seconds. The various algorithms differ in precisely how this resynchronization is done.

Network Time Protocol

A common approach in many protocols, and originally proposed by Cristian [1989], is to let clients contact a timeserver. The latter can accurately provide the current time, for example because it is equipped with a UTC receiver or an accurate clock. The problem, of course, is that when contacting the server, message delays will have outdated the reported time. The trick is to find a good estimation for these delays. Consider the situation sketched in Figure 5.5.

In this case, A will send a request to B, timestamped with value T_1. B, in turn, will record the time of receipt T_2 (taken from its own local clock), and returns a response timestamped with value T_3, and piggybacking the previously recorded value T_2. Finally, A records the time of the response's arrival, T_4. Let us assume that the propagation delays from A to B is roughly the same as B to A, meaning that $\delta T_{req} = T_2 - T_1 \approx T_4 - T_3 = \delta T_{res}$. In that

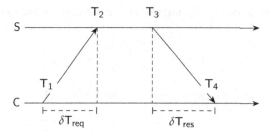

Figure 5.5: Getting the current time from a time server.

case, A can estimate its offset relative to B as

$$\theta = T_3 + \frac{(T_2 - T_1) + (T_4 - T_3)}{2} - T_4 = \frac{(T_2 - T_1) + (T_3 - T_4)}{2}$$

Of course, time is not allowed to run backward. If A's clock is fast, $\theta < 0$, meaning that A should, in principle, set its clock backward. This is not allowed as it could cause serious problems, such as an object file compiled just after the clock change having a time earlier than the source which was modified just before the clock change.

Such a change must be introduced gradually. One way is as follows. Suppose that the timer is set to generate 100 interrupts per second. Normally, each interrupt would add 10 msec to the time. When slowing down, the interrupt routine adds only 9 msec each time until the correction has been made. Similarly, the clock can be advanced gradually by adding 11 msec at each interrupt instead of jumping it forward all at once.

In the case of the **Network Time Protocol (NTP)**, this protocol is set up pairwise between servers. In other words, B will also probe A for its current time. The offset θ is computed as given above, along with the estimation δ for the delay:

$$\delta = \frac{(T_4 - T_1) - (T_3 - T_2)}{2}$$

Eight pairs of (θ, δ) values are buffered, finally taking the minimal value found for δ as the best estimation for the delay between the two servers, and subsequently the associated value θ as the most reliable estimation of the offset.

Applying NTP symmetrically should, in principle, also let B adjust its clock to that of A. However, if B's clock is known to be more accurate, then such an adjustment would be foolish. To solve this problem, NTP divides servers into strata. A server with a **reference clock** such as a UTC receiver or an atomic clock, is known to be a **stratum-1 server** (the clock itself is said to operate at stratum 0). When A contacts B, it will adjust only its time if its own stratum level is higher than that of B. Moreover, after the synchronization, A's stratum level will become one higher than that of B. In other words, if B is a stratum-k server, then A will become a stratum-$(k + 1)$ server if its original stratum level was already larger than k. Due to the symmetry of NTP, if A's stratum level was *lower* than that of B, B will adjust itself to A.

There are many important features about NTP, of which many relate to identifying and masking errors, but also security attacks (see, e.g., Malhotra et al. [2016]). Many security issues, such as also described by Levesque and Tipper [2016], can be dealt with by establishing a secure channel between a time server and its client. NTP was originally described in [Mills, 1992] and is known to achieve (worldwide) accuracy in the range of 1–50 msec. A detailed description of NTP can be found in [Mills, 2011].

Clock synchronization in wireless networks

An important advantage of more traditional distributed systems is that we can easily and efficiently deploy timeservers. Moreover, most machines can contact each other, allowing for a relatively simple dissemination of information. These assumptions are no longer valid in many wireless networks, notably sensor networks. Nodes are resource constrained, and multihop routing is expensive. In addition, it is often important to optimize algorithms for energy consumption. These and other observations have led to the design of very different clock synchronization algorithms for wireless networks. In the following, we consider one specific solution. Sivrikaya and Yener [2004] provide a brief overview of other solutions. An extensive survey can be found in [Sundararaman et al., 2005].

Reference broadcast synchronization (RBS) is a clock synchronization protocol that is quite different from other proposals [Elson et al., 2002]. First, the protocol does not assume that there is a single node with an accurate account of the actual time available. Instead of aiming to provide all nodes UTC time, it aims at merely internally synchronizing the clocks. Second, the solutions we have discussed so far are designed to bring the sender and receiver into sync, essentially following a two-way protocol. RBS deviates from this pattern by letting only the receivers synchronize, keeping the sender out of the loop.

In RBS, a sender broadcasts a reference message that allows its receivers to adjust their clocks. A key observation is that in a sensor network the time to propagate a signal to other nodes is roughly constant, provided no multi-hop routing is assumed. Propagation time in this case is measured from the moment that a message leaves the network interface of the sender. As a consequence, two important sources of variation in message transfer no longer play a role in estimating delays: the time spent to construct a message, and the time spent to access the network. This principle is shown in Figure 5.6.

Note that in protocols such as NTP, a timestamp is added to the message before it is passed on to the network interface. Furthermore, as wireless

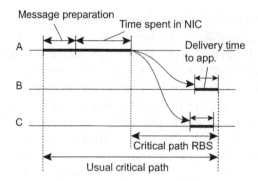

Figure 5.6: The usual critical path and the one used in RBS in determining network delays.

networks are based on a contention protocol, there is generally no saying how long it will take before a message can actually be transmitted. These factors of nondeterminism are eliminated in RBS. What remains is the delivery time at the receiver, but this time varies considerably less than the network-access time.

The idea underlying RBS is simple: when a node broadcasts a reference message m, each node p simply records the time $T_{p,m}$ that it received m. Note that $T_{p,m}$ is read from p's local clock. Ignoring clock skew, two nodes p and q can exchange each other's delivery times to estimate their mutual, relative offset:

$$Offset[p,q] = \frac{\sum_{k=1}^{M}(T_{p,k} - T_{q,k})}{M}$$

where M is the total number of reference messages sent. This information is important: node p will know the value of q's clock relative to its own value. Moreover, if it simply stores these offsets, there is no need to adjust its own clock, which saves energy.

Unfortunately, clocks can drift apart. The effect is that simply computing the average offset as done above will not work: the last values sent are simply less accurate than the first ones. Moreover, as time goes by, the offset will presumably increase. Elson et al. [2002] use a simple algorithm to compensate for this: instead of computing an average, they apply standard linear regression to compute the offset as a function:

$$Offset[p,q](t) = \alpha t + \beta$$

The constants α and β are computed from the pairs $(T_{p,k}, T_{q,k})$. This new form allows a much more accurate computation of q's current clock value by node p, and vice versa.

Note 5.2 (More information: How important is an accurate account of time?)

So why is time such a big deal for distributed systems? As we shall discuss in the remainder of this chapter, reaching consensus on a global ordering of events is what we really want, and this can be achieved without any notion of global absolute time. However, as will become clear, alternative methods for distributed coordination do not come easy.

Life would be much simpler if processes in a distributed system could time-stamp their events with infinite precision. Although infinite precision is asking too much, we can come practically close. Researchers at Google were confronted with the fact that their customers would really like to make use of a globally distributed database that supported transactions. Such a database would need to serve massive numbers of clients, rendering the use of, for example, a central transaction processing monitor as we discussed in Section 1.3.2, infeasible. Instead, for their Spanner system, Google decided to implement a true-time service, called TrueTime [Corbett et al., 2013]. This service provides three operations:

Operation	Result
TT.now()	A time interval $[T_{lwb}, T_{upb}]$ with $T_{lwb} < T_{upb}$
TT.after(t)	True if timestamp t has definitely passed
TT.before(t)	True if timestamp t has definitely not arrived

The most important aspect is that T_{lwb} and T_{upb} are *guaranteed* bounds. Of course, if $\epsilon = T_{upb} - T_{lwb}$ is large, say 1 hour, then implementing the service is relatively easy. Impressively enough, $\epsilon = 6ms$. To achieve this accuracy, the TrueTime service makes use of *time-master* machines of which there are several per data center. Time-slave daemons run on every machine in a data center and query multiple time masters, including ones from other data centers, very similar to what we described for NTP. Many time masters are equipped with accurate GPS receivers, while many others are independently equipped with atomic clocks. The result is a collection of time sources with a high degree of mutual independence (which is important for reasons of fault tolerance). Using a version of an algorithm developed by Marzullo and Owicki [1983], outliers are kept out of the computations. Meanwhile, the performance of TrueTime is continuously monitored and "bad" time machines are (manually) removed to give at least very high guarantees for the accuracy of the TrueTime service.

With a guaranteed accuracy of 6 milliseconds, building a transactional system becomes much easier: transactions can actually be timestamped, even by different servers, with the restriction that timestamping may need to be delayed for ϵ time units. More precisely, to know for sure that a transaction has committed, reading the resulting data may impose a wait for ϵ units. This is achieved by pessimistically assigning a timestamp to a transaction that writes data to the global database and making sure that clients never see any changes before the assigned timestamp (which is relatively easy to implement).

There are many details to this approach, which can be found in [Corbett et al., 2013]. As we are still dealing with a time interval, taking more traditional

> ordering mechanisms into account it is possible to improve results, as explained by Demirbas and Kulkarni [2013].

5.2   Logical clocks

Clock synchronization is naturally related to time, although it may not be necessary to have an accurate account of the real time: it may be sufficient that every node in a distributed system agrees on *a* current time. We can go one step further. For running make it is adequate that two nodes agree that input.o is outdated by a new version of input.c, for example. In this case, keeping track of each other's events (such as a producing a new version of input.c) is what matters. For these algorithms, it is conventional to speak of the clocks as **logical clocks**.

In a seminal paper, Lamport [1978] showed that although clock synchronization is possible, it need not be absolute. If two processes do not interact, it is not necessary that their clocks be synchronized because the lack of synchronization would not be observable and thus could not cause problems. Furthermore, he pointed out that what usually matters is not that all processes agree on exactly what time it is, but rather that they agree on the *order in which events occur*. In the make example, what counts is whether input.c is older or newer than input.o, not their respective absolute creation times.

5.2.1   Lamport's logical clocks

To synchronize logical clocks, Lamport defined a relation called **happens-before**. The expression $a \rightarrow b$ is read "event a happens before event b" and means that all processes agree that first event a occurs, then afterward, event b occurs. The happens-before relation can be observed directly in two situations:

1. If a and b are events in the same process, and a occurs before b, then $a \rightarrow b$ is true.

2. If a is the event of a message being sent by one process, and b is the event of the message being received by another process, then $a \rightarrow b$ is also true. A message cannot be received before it is sent, or even at the same time it is sent, since it takes a finite, nonzero amount of time to arrive.

Happens-before is a transitive relation, so if $a \rightarrow b$ and $b \rightarrow c$, then $a \rightarrow c$. If two events, x and y, happen in different processes that do not exchange messages (not even indirectly via third parties), then $x \rightarrow y$ is not true, but neither is $y \rightarrow x$. These events are said to be **concurrent**, which simply means that nothing can be said (or need be said) about when the events happened or which event happened first.

What we need is a way of measuring a notion of time such that for every event, a, we can assign it a time value $C(a)$ on which all processes agree. These time values must have the property that if $a \rightarrow b$, then $C(a) < C(b)$. To rephrase the conditions we stated earlier, if a and b are two events within the same process and a occurs before b, then $C(a) < C(b)$. Similarly, if a is the sending of a message by one process and b is the reception of that message by another process, then $C(a)$ and $C(b)$ must be assigned in such a way that everyone agrees on the values of $C(a)$ and $C(b)$ with $C(a) < C(b)$. In addition, the clock time, C, must always go forward (increasing), never backward (decreasing). Corrections to time can be made by adding a positive value, never by subtracting one.

Now let us look at the algorithm Lamport proposed for assigning times to events. Consider the three processes depicted in Figure 5.7. The processes run on different machines, each with its own clock. For the sake of argument, we assume that a clock is implemented as a software counter: the counter is incremented by a specific value every T time units. However, the value by which a clock is incremented differs per process. The clock in process P_1 is incremented by 6 units, 8 units in process P_2, and 10 units in process P_3, respectively. (Below, we explain that Lamport clocks are, in fact, **event counters**, which explains why their value may differ between processes.)

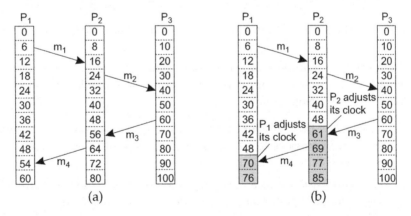

Figure 5.7: (a) Three processes, each with its own (logical) clock. The clocks run at different rates. (b) Lamport's algorithm corrects their values.

At time 6, process P_1 sends message m_1 to process P_2. How long this message takes to arrive depends on whose clock you believe. In any event, the clock in process P_2 reads 16 when it arrives. If the message carries the starting time, 6, in it, process P_2 will conclude that it took 10 ticks to make the journey. This value is certainly possible. According to this reasoning, message m_2 from P_2 to P_3 takes 16 ticks, again a plausible value.

Now consider message m_3. It leaves process P_3 at 60 and arrives at P_2 at 56. Similarly, message m_4 from P_2 to P_1 leaves at 64 and arrives at 54. These values are clearly impossible. It is this situation that must be prevented.

Lamport's solution follows directly from the happens-before relation. Since m_3 left at 60, it must arrive at 61 or later. Therefore, each message carries the sending time according to the sender's clock. When a message arrives and the receiver's clock shows a value before the time the message was sent, the receiver fast forwards its clock to be one more than the sending time. In Figure 5.7, we see that m_3 now arrives at 61. Similarly, m_4 arrives at 70.

Let us formulate this procedure more precisely. At this point, it is important to distinguish three different layers of software, as we already encountered in Section 2.2: the network, a middleware layer, and an application layer, as shown in Figure 5.8. What follows is typically part of the middleware layer.

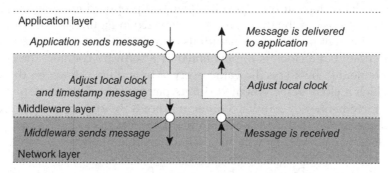

Figure 5.8: The positioning of Lamport's logical clocks in distributed systems.

To implement Lamport's logical clocks, each process P_i maintains a *local* counter C_i. These counters are updated according to the following steps [Raynal and Singhal, 1996]:

1. Before executing an event (i.e., sending a message over the network, delivering a message to an application, or some other internal event), P_i increments C_i: $C_i \leftarrow C_i + 1$.

2. When process P_i sends a message m to process P_j, it sets m's timestamp $ts(m)$ equal to C_i after having executed the previous step.

3. Upon the receipt of a message m, process P_j adjusts its own local counter as $C_j \leftarrow \max\{C_j, ts(m)\}$ after which it then executes the first step and delivers the message to the application.

In some situations, an additional requirement is desirable: no two events ever occur at the same time. To achieve this goal, we also use the unique process identifier to break ties and use tuples instead of only the counter's values. For example, an event at time 40 at process P_i will be timestamped as $\langle 40, i \rangle$. If we also have an event $\langle 40, j \rangle$ and $i < j$, then $\langle 40, i \rangle < \langle 40, j \rangle$.

Note that by assigning the event time $C(a) \leftarrow C_i(a)$ if a happened at process P_i at time $C_i(a)$, we have a distributed implementation of the global time value we were initially seeking for; we have thus constructed a **logical clock**.

Example: Totally ordered multicasting

As an application of Lamport's logical clocks, consider the situation in which a database has been replicated across several sites. For example, to improve query performance, a bank may place copies of an account database in two different cities, say New York and San Francisco. A query is always forwarded to the nearest copy. The price for a fast response to a query is partly paid in higher update costs because each update operation must be carried out at each replica.

In fact, there is a more stringent requirement regarding updates. Assume a customer in San Francisco wants to add $100 to her account, which currently contains $1,000. At the same time, a bank employee in New York initiates an update by which the customer's account is to be increased with 1 percent interest. Both updates should be carried out at both copies of the database. However, due to communication delays in the underlying network, the updates may arrive in the order as shown in Figure 5.9.

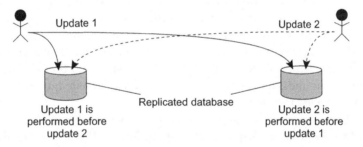

Figure 5.9: Updating a replicated database and leaving it in an inconsistent state.

The customer's update operation is performed in San Francisco before the interest update. In contrast, the copy of the account in the New York replica is first updated with the 1 percent interest, and after that with the $100 deposit. Consequently, the San Francisco database will record a total amount of $1,111, whereas the New York database records $1,110.

The problem that we are faced with is that the two update operations should have been performed in the same order at each copy. Although it makes a difference whether the deposit is processed before the interest update or the other way around, which order is followed is not essential from a consistency perspective. The important issue is that both copies should be the same after the updates have taken place. In general, situations such as these require a **totally ordered multicast**, that is, a multicast operation by which all messages are delivered in the same order to each receiver. Lamport's logical clocks can be used to implement totally ordered multicasts in a completely distributed fashion.

Consider a group of processes multicasting messages to each other. Each message is always timestamped with the current (logical) time of its sender. When a message is multicasted, it is conceptually also sent to the sender. In addition, we assume that messages from the same sender are received in the order they were sent, and that no messages are lost.

When a process receives a message, it is put into a local queue, ordered according to its timestamp. The receiver multicasts an acknowledgment to the other processes. Note that if we follow Lamport's algorithm for adjusting local clocks, the timestamp of the received message is lower than the timestamp of the acknowledgment. The interesting aspect of this approach is that all processes will eventually have the same copy of the local queue (provided no messages are removed).

A process can deliver a queued message to the application it is running only when that message is at the head of the queue and has been acknowledged by each other process. At that point, the message is removed from the queue and handed over to the application; the associated acknowledgments can simply be removed. Because each process has the same copy of the queue, all messages are delivered in the same order everywhere. In other words, we have established totally ordered multicasting. We leave it as an exercise to the reader to figure out that it is not strictly necessary that each multicast message has been explicitly acknowledged. It is sufficient that a process *reacts* to an incoming message, either by returning an acknowledgment or sending its own multicast message.

Totally ordered multicasting is an important vehicle for replicated services, where the replicas are kept consistent by letting them execute the same operations in the same order everywhere. As the replicas essentially follow the same transitions in the same finite state machine, it is also known as **state machine replication** [Schneider, 1990].

Note 5.3 (Advanced: Using Lamport clocks to achieve mutual exclusion)
To further illustrate the usage of Lamport's clocks, let us see how we can use the previous algorithm for totally ordered multicasting to establish access to what is commonly known as a **critical region**: a section of code that can be executed by at most one process at a time. This algorithm is very similar to the one for multicasting, as essentially all processes need to agree on the order by which processes are allowed to enter their critical region.

Figure 5.10(a) shows the code that each process executes when requesting, releasing, or allowing access to the critical region (again, omitting details). Each process maintains a request queue as well as a logical clock. To enter the critical region, a call to requestToEnter is made, which results in inserting an ENTER message with timestamp (clock,procID) into the local queue and sending that message to the other processes. The operation cleanupQ essentially sorts the queue. We return to it shortly.

```
 1  class Process:
 2    def __init__(self, chanID, procID, procIDSet):
 3      self.chan.join(procID)
 4      self.procID     = int(procID)
 5      self.otherProcs.remove(self.procID)
 6      self.queue      = []                       # The request queue
 7      self.clock      = 0                        # The current logical clock
 8
 9    def requestToEnter(self):
10      self.clock = self.clock + 1                            # Increment clock value
11      self.queue.append((self.clock, self.procID, ENTER)) # Append request to q
12      self.cleanupQ()                                        # Sort the queue
13      self.chan.sendTo(self.otherProcs, (self.clock, self.procID, ENTER)) # Send request
14
15    def ackToEnter(self, requester):
16      self.clock = self.clock + 1                            # Increment clock value
17      self.chan.sendTo(requester, (self.clock, self.procID, ACK)) # Permit other
18
19    def release(self):
20      tmp = [r for r in self.queue[1:] if r[2] == ENTER]  # Remove all ACKs
21      self.queue = tmp                                      # and copy to new queue
22      self.clock = self.clock + 1                           # Increment clock value
23      self.chan.sendTo(self.otherProcs, (self.clock, self.procID, RELEASE)) # Release
24
25    def allowedToEnter(self):
26      commProcs = set([req[1] for req in self.queue[1:]]) # See who has sent a message
27      return (self.queue[0][1] == self.procID and len(self.otherProcs) == len(commProcs))
```

Figure 5.10: (a) Using Lamport's logical clocks for mutual exclusion.

When a process P receives an ENTER message from process Q, it can simply acknowledge that Q can enter its critical region, even if P wants to do so as well. In the latter case, P's ENTER request will have a lower logical timestamp than the ACK message sent by P to Q, meaning that P's request will have been inserted into Q's queue *before* P's ACK message.

Finally, when a process leaves its critical region, it calls release. It cleans up its local queue by removing all received ACK messages, leaving only the ENTER requests from other processes. It then multicasts a RELEASE message.

To actually enter a critical region, a process will have to repeatedly call allowedToEnter and when returned False, will have to block on a next incoming message. The operation allowedToEnter does what is to be expected: it checks if the calling process's ENTER message is at the head of the queue, and sees if all other processes have sent a message as well. The latter is encoded through the set

commProcs, which contains the procIDs of all processes having sent a message by
inspecting all messages in the local queue from the second position and onwards.

```
1   def receive(self):
2       msg = self.chan.recvFrom(self.otherProcs)[1]        # Pick up any message
3       self.clock = max(self.clock, msg[0])                # Adjust clock value...
4       self.clock = self.clock + 1                         # ...and increment
5       if msg[2] == ENTER:
6           self.queue.append(msg)                          # Append an ENTER request
7           self.ackToEnter(msg[1])                         # and unconditionally allow
8       elif msg[2] == ACK:
9           self.queue.append(msg)                          # Append a received ACK
10      elif msg[2] == RELEASE:
11          del(self.queue[0])                              # Just remove first message
12      self.cleanupQ()                                     # And sort and cleanup
```

Figure 5.10: (b) Using Lamport's logical clocks for mutual exclusion:
handling incoming requests.

What to do when a message is received is shown in Figure 5.10(b). First,
the local clock is adjusted according to the rules for Lamport's logical clocks
explained above. When receiving an ENTER or ALLOW message, that message is
simply inserted into the queue. An entry request is always acknowledged, as we
just explained. When a RELEASE message is received, the original ENTER request is
removed. Note that this request is at the head of the queue. Thereafter, the queue
is cleaned up again.

At this point, note that if we would clean up the queue by only sorting it,
we may get into trouble. Suppose that processes P and Q want to enter their
respective critical regions at roughly the same time, but that P is allowed to go
first based on logical-clock values. P may find Q's request in its queue, along
with ENTER or ALLOW messages from other processes. If its own request is at the
head of its queue, P will proceed and enter its critical region. However, Q will
also send an ALLOW message to P as well, in addition to its original ENTER message.
That ALLOW message may arrive *after* P had already entered its critical region, but
before ENTER messages from other processes. When Q eventually enters, and leaves
its critical region, Q's RELEASE message would result in removing Q's original
ENTER message, but not the ALLOW message it had previously sent to P. By now,
that message is at the head of P's queue, effectively blocking the entrance to the
critical region of other processes in P's queue. Cleaning up the queue thus also
involves removing old ALLOW messages.

5.2.2   Vector clocks

Lamport's logical clocks lead to a situation where all events in a distributed
system are totally ordered with the property that if event a happened before
event b, then a will also be positioned in that ordering before b, that is,
$C(a) < C(b)$.

However, with Lamport clocks, nothing can be said about the relationship between two events a and b by merely comparing their time values $C(a)$ and $C(b)$, respectively. In other words, if $C(a) < C(b)$, then this does not necessarily imply that a indeed happened before b. Something more is needed for that.

To explain, consider the messages as sent by the three processes shown in Figure 5.11. Denote by $T_{snd}(m_i)$ the logical time at which message m_i was sent, and likewise, by $T_{rcv}(m_i)$ the time of its receipt. By construction, we know that for each message $T_{snd}(m_i) < T_{rcv}(m_i)$. But what can we conclude in general from $T_{rcv}(m_i) < T_{snd}(m_j)$ for different messages m_i and m_j?

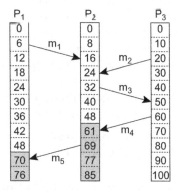

Figure 5.11: Concurrent message transmission using logical clocks.

In the case for which $m_i = m_1$ and $m_j = m_3$, we know that these values correspond to events that took place at process P_2, meaning that m_3 was indeed sent after the receipt of message m_1. This may indicate that the sending of message m_3 depended on what was received through message m_1. At the same time, we also know that $T_{rcv}(m_1) < T_{snd}(m_2)$. However, as far as we can tell from Figure 5.11, the sending of m_2 has nothing to do with the receipt of m_1.

The problem is that Lamport clocks do not capture **causality**. In practice, causality is captured by means of **vector clocks**. To better understand where these come from, we follow the explanation as given by Baquero and Preguica [2016]. In fact, tracking causality is simple if we assign each event a unique name such as the combination of a process ID and a locally incrementing counter: p_k is the kth event that happened at process P. The problem then boils down to keeping track of **causal histories**. For example, if two local events happened at process P, then the causal history $H(p_2)$ of event p_2 is $\{p_1, p_2\}$.

Now assume that process P sends a message to process Q (which is an event at P and thus recorded as p_k for some k), and that at the time of arrival (an event for Q), the most recent causal history of Q was $\{q_1\}$. To track causality, P also sends its most recent causal history (assume it was $\{p_1, p_2\}$, extended with p_3 expressing the sending of the message). Upon arrival, Q records the event (q_2), and merges the two causal histories into a new one: $\{p_1, p_2, p_3, q_1, q_2\}$.

Checking whether an event p causally precedes an event q can be done by checking whether $H(p) \subset H(q)$ (i.e., it should be a *proper* subset). In fact, with our notation, it even suffices to check whether $p \in H(q)$, assuming that q is always the last local event in $H(q)$.

The problem with causal histories, is that their representation is not very efficient. However, there is no need to keep track of all successive events from the same process: the last one will do. If we subsequently assign an index to each process, we can represent a causal history as a vector, in which the jth entry represents the number of events that happened at process P_j. Causality can then be captured by means of **vector clocks**, which are constructed by letting each process P_i maintain a vector VC_i with the following two properties:

1. $VC_i[i]$ is the number of events that have occurred so far at P_i. In other words, $VC_i[i]$ is the local logical clock at process P_i.

2. If $VC_i[j] = k$ then P_i knows that k events have occurred at P_j. It is thus P_i's knowledge of the local time at P_j.

The first property is maintained by incrementing $VC_i[i]$ at the occurrence of each new event that happens at process P_i. The second property is maintained by piggybacking vectors along with messages that are sent. In particular, the following steps are performed:

1. Before executing an event (i.e., sending a message over the network, delivering a message to an application, or some other internal event), P_i executes $VC_i[i] \leftarrow VC_i[i] + 1$. This is equivalent to recording a new event that happened at P_i.

2. When process P_i sends a message m to P_j, it sets m's (vector) timestamp $ts(m)$ equal to VC_i after having executed the previous step (i.e., it also records the sending of the message as an event that takes place at P_i).

3. Upon the receipt of a message m, process P_j adjusts its own vector by setting $VC_j[k] \leftarrow \max\{VC_j[k], ts(m)[k]\}$ for each k (which is equivalent to merging causal histories), after which it executes the first step (recording the receipt of the message) and then delivers the message to the application.

Note that if an event a has timestamp $ts(a)$, then $ts(a)[i] - 1$ denotes the number of events processed at P_i that causally precede a. As a consequence, when P_j receives a message m from P_i with timestamp $ts(m)$, it knows about the number of events that have occurred at P_i that causally preceded the sending of m. More important, however, is that P_j is also told how many events at *other* processes have taken place, known to P_i, before P_i sent message m. In other words, timestamp $ts(m)$ tells the receiver how many events in other processes have preceded the sending of m, and on which m may causally depend.

To see what this means, consider Figure 5.12 which shows three processes. In Figure 5.12(a), P_2 sends a message m_1 at logical time $VC_2 = (0,1,0)$ to process P_1. Message m_1 thus receives timestamp $ts(m_1) = (0,1,0)$. Upon its receipt, P_1 adjusts its logical time to $VC_1 \leftarrow (1,1,0)$ and delivers it. Message m_2 is sent by P_1 to P_3 with timestamp $ts(m_2) = (2,1,0)$. Before P_1 sends another message, m_3, an event happens at P_1, eventually leading to timestamping m_3 with value $(4,1,0)$. After receiving m_3, process P_2 sends message m_4 to P_3, with timestamp $ts(m_4) = (4,3,0)$.

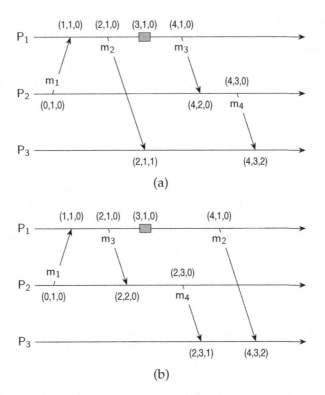

Figure 5.12: Capturing potential causality when exchanging messages.

Now consider the situation shown in Figure 5.12(b). Here, we have delayed sending message m_2 until after message m_3 has been sent, and after the event had taken place. It is not difficult to see that $ts(m_2) = (4,1,0)$, while $ts(m_4) = (2,3,0)$. Compared to Figure 5.12(a), we have the following situation:

Situation	$ts(m_2)$	$ts(m_4)$	$ts(m_2)$ $<$ $ts(m_4)$	$ts(m_2)$ $>$ $ts(m_4)$	Conclusion
Figure 5.12(a)	$(2,1,0)$	$(4,3,0)$	Yes	No	m_2 may causally precede m_4
Figure 5.12(b)	$(4,1,0)$	$(2,3,0)$	No	No	m_2 and m_4 may conflict

We use the notation $ts(a) < ts(b)$ if and only if for all k, $ts(a)[k] \leq ts(b)[k]$ and there is at least one index k' for which $ts(a)[k'] < ts(b)[k']$. Thus, by using vector clocks, process P_3 can detect whether m_4 may be causally dependent on m_2, or whether there may be a potential conflict. Note, by the way, that without knowing the actual information contained in messages, it is not possible to state with certainty that there is indeed a causal relationship, or perhaps a conflict.

Note 5.4 (Advanced: Enforcing causal communication)

Using vector clocks, it is now possible to ensure that a message is delivered only if all messages that may have causally preceded it have been received as well. To enable such a scheme, we will assume that messages are multicast within a group of processes. Note that this **causally ordered multicasting** is weaker than totally ordered multicasting. Specifically, if two messages are not in any way related to each other, we do not care in which order they are delivered to applications. They may even be delivered in different order at different locations.

For enforcing causal message delivery, we assume that clocks are adjusted only when sending and *delivering* messages (note, again, that messages are not adjusted when they are *received* by a process, but only when they are delivered to an application). In particular, only upon sending a message, will process P_i increment $VC_i[i]$ by 1. Only when it delivers a message m with timestamp $ts(m)$, will it adjust $VC_i[k]$ to $\max\{VC_i[k], ts(m)[k]\}$ for each k.

Now suppose that P_j receives a message m from P_i with (vector) timestamp $ts(m)$. The delivery of the message to the application layer will then be delayed until the following two conditions are met:

1. $ts(m)[i] = VC_j[i] + 1$
2. $ts(m)[k] \leq VC_j[k]$ for all $k \neq i$

The first condition states that m is the next message that P_j was expecting from process P_i. The second condition states that P_j has delivered all the messages that have been delivered by P_i when it sent message m. Note that there is no need for process P_j to delay the delivery of its own messages.

As an example, consider three processes P_1, P_2, and P_3 as shown in Figure 5.13. At local time $(1,0,0)$, P_1 multicasts message m to the other two processes. Note that $ts(m) = (1,0,0)$. Its receipt and subsequent delivery by P_2, will bring the logical clock at P_2 to $(1,0,0)$, effectively indicating that it has received one message from P_1, has itself sent no message so far, and has not yet delivered a message from P_3. P_2 then decides to multicast m^*, at updated time $(1,1,0)$, which arrives at P_3 *sooner* than m.

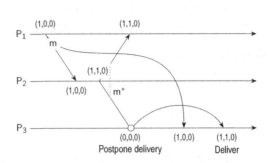

Figure 5.13: Enforcing causal communication.

When comparing the timestamp of m with its current time, which is $(0,0,0)$, P_3 concludes that it is still missing a message from P_1 which P_2 apparently had delivered before sending m^*. P_3 therefore, decides to postpone the delivery of m^* (and will also not adjust its local, logical clock). Later, after m has been received and delivered by P_3, which brings its local clock to $(1,0,0)$, P_3 can deliver message m^* and also update its clock.

A note on ordered message delivery Some middleware systems, notably ISIS and its successor Horus [Birman and van Renesse, 1994], provide support for totally ordered and causally ordered (reliable) multicasting. There has been some controversy whether such support should be provided as part of the message-communication layer, or whether applications should handle ordering (see, e.g., Cheriton and Skeen [1993]; Birman [1994]). Matters have not been settled, but more important is that the arguments still hold today.

There are two main problems with letting the middleware deal with message ordering. First, because the middleware cannot tell what a message actually contains, only *potential* causality is captured. For example, two messages from the same sender that are completely independent will always be marked as causally related by the middleware layer. This approach is overly restrictive and may lead to efficiency problems.

A second problem is that not all causality may be captured. Consider some digital chat room. Suppose Alice posts a message. If she then phones Bob telling about what she just wrote, Bob may post another message as a reaction without having seen Alice's posting. In other words, there is a causality between Bob's posting and that of Alice due to *external* communication. This causality is not captured by the chat room system.

In essence, ordering issues, like many other application-specific communication issues, can be adequately solved by looking at the application for which communication is taking place. This is also known as the **end-to-end principle** in systems design [Saltzer et al., 1984]. A drawback of having only application-level solutions is that a developer is forced to concentrate on issues that do not immediately relate to the core functionality of the application. For example, ordering may

not be the most important problem when developing a messaging system such
as the one for a chat room. In that case, having an underlying communication
layer handle ordering may turn out to be convenient. We will come across the
end-to-end argument several times.

5.3   Mutual exclusion

Fundamental to distributed systems is the concurrency and collaboration
among multiple processes. In many cases, this also means that processes
will need to simultaneously access the same resources. To prevent that such
concurrent accesses corrupt the resource, or make it inconsistent, solutions are
needed to grant mutual exclusive access by processes. In this section, we take
a look at some important and representative distributed algorithms that have
been proposed. Surveys of distributed algorithms for mutual exclusion are
provided by Saxena and Rai [2003] and Velazquez [1993]. Various algorithms
are also presented in [Kshemkalyani and Singhal, 2008].

5.3.1   Overview

Distributed mutual exclusion algorithms can be classified into two different
categories. In **token-based solutions** mutual exclusion is achieved by passing
a special message between the processes, known as a **token**. There is only one
token available, and who ever has that token is allowed to access the shared
resource. When finished, the token is passed on to a next process. If a process
having the token is not interested in accessing the resource, it passes it on.

Token-based solutions have a few important properties. First, depending
on how the processes are organized, they can fairly easily ensure that every
process will get a chance at accessing the resource. In other words, they provide guarantees for **safety** by avoiding what is known as **starvation**. Second,
deadlocks by which several processes are indefinitely waiting for each other
to proceed, can easily be avoided, contributing to their simplicity. The main
drawback of token-based solutions is a rather serious one: when the token
is lost (e.g. because the process holding it crashed), an intricate distributed
procedure needs to be started to ensure that a new token is created, but above
all, that it is also the only token.

As an alternative, many distributed mutual exclusion algorithms follow
a **permission-based approach**. In this case, a process wanting to access the
resource first requires the permission from other processes. There are many
ways toward granting such permission and in the sections that follow we will
consider a few of them.

5.3.2 A centralized algorithm

A straightforward way to achieve mutual exclusion in a distributed system is to simulate how it is done in a one-processor system. One process is elected as the coordinator. Whenever a process wants to access a shared resource, it sends a request message to the coordinator stating which resource it wants to access and asking for permission. If no other process is currently accessing that resource, the coordinator sends back a reply granting permission, as shown in Figure 5.14(a). When the reply arrives, the requester can go ahead.

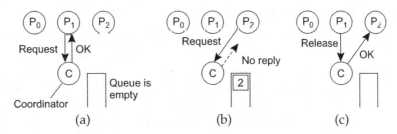

Figure 5.14: (a) Process P_1 asks for permission to access a shared resource. Permission is granted. (b) Process P_2 asks permission to access the same resource, but receives no reply. (c) When P_1 releases the resource, the coordinator replies to P_2.

Now suppose that another process, P_2 in Figure 5.14(b) asks for permission to access the resource. The coordinator knows that a different process is already at the resource, so it cannot grant permission. The exact method used to deny permission is system dependent. In Figure 5.14(b) the coordinator just refrains from replying, thus blocking process P_2, which is waiting for a reply. Alternatively, it could send a reply saying "permission denied." Either way, it queues the request from P_2 for the time being and waits for more messages.

When process P_1 is finished with the resource, it sends a message to the coordinator releasing its exclusive access, as shown in Figure 5.14(c). The coordinator takes the first item off the queue of deferred requests and sends that process a grant message. If the process was still blocked (i.e., this is the first message to it), it unblocks and accesses the resource. If an explicit message has already been sent denying permission, the process will have to poll for incoming traffic or block later. Either way, when it sees the grant, it can go ahead as well.

It is easy to see that the algorithm guarantees mutual exclusion: the coordinator lets only one process at a time access the resource. It is also fair, since requests are granted in the order in which they are received. No process ever waits forever (no starvation). The scheme is easy to implement, too, and requires only three messages per use of resource (request, grant, release). Its simplicity makes it an attractive solution for many practical situations.

The centralized approach also has shortcomings. The coordinator is a single point of failure, so if it crashes, the entire system may go down. If processes normally block after making a request, they cannot distinguish a dead coordinator from "permission denied" since in both cases no message comes back. In addition, in a large system, a single coordinator can become a performance bottleneck. Nevertheless, the benefits coming from its simplicity often outweigh the potential drawbacks. Moreover, distributed solutions are not necessarily better, as we illustrate next.

5.3.3   A distributed algorithm

Using Lamport's logical clocks, and inspired by Lamport's original solution for distributed mutual exclusion (which we discussed in Note 5.3), Ricart and Agrawala [1981] provided the following algorithm. Their solution requires a total ordering of all events in the system. That is, for any pair of events, such as messages, it must be unambiguous which one actually happened first.

The algorithm works as follows. When a process wants to access a shared resource, it builds a message containing the name of the resource, its process number, and the current (logical) time. It then sends the message to all other processes, conceptually including itself. The sending of messages is assumed to be reliable; that is, no message is lost.

When a process receives a request message from another process, the action it takes depends on its own state regarding the resource named in the message. Three different cases have to be clearly distinguished:

- If the receiver is not accessing the resource and does not want to access it, it sends back an OK message to the sender.

- If the receiver already has access to the resource, it simply does not reply. Instead, it queues the request.

- If the receiver wants to access the resource as well but has not yet done so, it compares the timestamp of the incoming message with the one contained in the message that it has sent everyone. The lowest one wins. If the incoming message has a lower timestamp, the receiver sends back an OK message. If its own message has a lower timestamp, the receiver queues the incoming request and sends nothing.

After sending out requests asking permission, a process sits back and waits until everyone else has given permission. As soon as all the permissions are in, it may go ahead. When it is finished, it sends OK messages to all processes in its queue and deletes them all from the queue. If there is no conflict, it clearly works. However, suppose that two processes try to access the resource simultaneously, as shown in Figure 5.15(a).

Process P_0 sends everyone a request with timestamp 8, while at the same time, process P_2 sends everyone a request with timestamp 12. P_1 is not

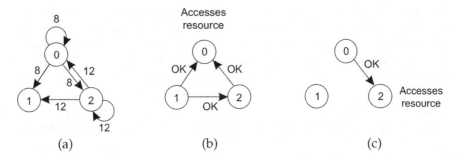

Figure 5.15: (a) Two processes want to access a shared resource at the same moment. (b) P_0 has the lowest timestamp, so it wins. (c) When process P_0 is done, it sends an OK also, so P_2 can now go ahead.

interested in the resource, so it sends OK to both senders. Processes P_0 and P_2 both see the conflict and compare timestamps. P_2 sees that it has lost, so it grants permission to P_0 by sending OK. Process P_0 now queues the request from P_2 for later processing and accesses the resource, as shown in Figure 5.15(b). When it is finished, it removes the request from P_2 from its queue and sends an OK message to P_2, allowing the latter to go ahead, as shown in Figure 5.15(c). The algorithm works because in the case of a conflict, the lowest timestamp wins and everyone agrees on the ordering of the timestamps.

With this algorithm, mutual exclusion is guaranteed without deadlock or starvation. If the total number of processes is N, then the number of messages that a process needs to send and receive before it can enter its **critical region** is $2 \cdot (N - 1)$: $N - 1$ request messages to all other processes, and subsequently $N - 1$ OK messages, one from each other process. A critical region is a series of instructions to be executed by a process, which requires mutually exclusive access.

Unfortunately, this algorithm has N points of failure. If any process crashes, it will fail to respond to requests. This silence will be interpreted (incorrectly) as denial of permission, thus blocking all subsequent attempts by all processes to enter any of their respective critical regions. The algorithm can be patched up as follows. When a request comes in, the receiver always sends a reply, either granting or denying permission. Whenever either a request or a reply is lost, the sender times out and keeps trying until either a reply comes back or the sender concludes that the destination is dead. After a request is denied, the sender should block, waiting for a subsequent OK message.

Another problem with this algorithm is that either a multicast communication primitive must be used, or each process must maintain the group membership list itself, including processes entering the group, leaving the group, and crashing. The method works best with small groups of processes that never change their group memberships. Finally, note that *all* processes are involved in *all* decisions concerning accessing the shared resource, which may impose a burden on processes running on resource-constrained machines.

Various minor improvements are possible to this algorithm. For example, getting permission from everyone is overkill. All that is needed is a method to prevent two processes from accessing the resource at the same time. The algorithm can be modified to grant permission when it has collected permission from a simple majority of the other processes, rather than from all of them.

5.3.4   A token-ring algorithm

An entirely different approach to deterministically achieving mutual exclusion in a distributed system is illustrated in Figure 5.16. In software, we construct an overlay network in the form of a logical ring in which each process is assigned a position in the ring. All that matters is that each process knows who is next in line after itself.

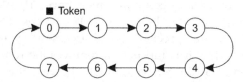

Figure 5.16: An overlay network constructed as a logical ring with a token circulating between its members.

When the ring is initialized, process P_0 is given a **token**. The token circulates around the ring. Assuming there are N processes, the token is passed from process P_k to process $P_{(k+1) \bmod N}$ in point-to-point messages. When a process acquires the token from its neighbor, it checks to see if it needs to access the shared resource. If so, the process goes ahead, does all the work it needs to, and releases the resources. After it has finished, it passes the token along the ring. It is not permitted to enter the resource immediately again using the same token.

If a process is handed the token by its neighbor and is not interested in the resource, it just passes the token along. As a consequence, when no processes need the resource, the token just circulates around the ring.

The correctness of this algorithm is easy to see. Only one process has the token at any instant, so only one process can actually get to the resource. Since the token circulates among the processes in a well-defined order, starvation cannot occur. Once a process decides it wants to have access to the resource, at worst it will have to wait for every other process to use the resource.

This algorithm has its own problems. If the token is ever lost, for example because its holder crashes or due to a lost message containing the token, it must be regenerated. In fact, detecting that it is lost may be difficult, since the amount of time between successive appearances of the token on the network is unbounded. The fact that the token has not been spotted for an hour does not mean that it has been lost; somebody may still be using it.

The algorithm also runs into trouble if a process crashes, but recovery is relatively easy. If we require a process receiving the token to acknowledge receipt, a dead process will be detected when its neighbor tries to give it the token and fails. At that point, the dead process can be removed from the group, and the token holder can throw the token over the head of the dead process to the next member down the line, or the one after that, if necessary. Of course, doing so requires that everyone maintains the current ring configuration.

5.3.5 A decentralized algorithm

Let us take a look at a fully decentralized solution. Lin et al. [2004] propose to use a voting algorithm. Each resource is assumed to be replicated N times. Every replica has its own coordinator for controlling the access by concurrent processes.

However, whenever a process wants to access the resource, it will simply need to get a majority vote from $m > N/2$ coordinators. We assume that when a coordinator does not give permission to access a resource (which it will do when it had granted permission to another process), it will tell the requester.

The assumption is that when a coordinator crashes, it recovers quickly but will have forgotten any vote it gave before it crashed. Another way of viewing this is that a coordinator resets itself at arbitrary moments. The risk that we are taking is that a reset will make the coordinator forget that it had previously granted permission to some process to access the resource. As a consequence, it may incorrectly grant this permission again to another process after its recovery.

Let $p = \Delta t / T$ be the probability that a coordinator resets during a time interval Δt, while having a lifetime of T. The probability $\mathbb{P}[k]$ that k out of m coordinators reset during the same interval is then

$$\mathbb{P}[k] = \binom{m}{k} p^k (1 - p)^{m-k}$$

If f coordinators reset, then the correctness of the voting mechanism will be violated when we have more than m other coordinators think it is okay to allocate the resource, that is, when $N - (m - f) \geq m$, or, in other words, when $f \geq 2m - N$. The probability that such a violation occurs is $\sum_{k=2m-N}^{m} \mathbb{P}[k]$. To give an impression of what this could mean, Figure 5.17 shows the probability of violating correctness for different values of N, m, and p. Note that we compute p by considering the number of seconds per hour that a coordinator resets, and also taking this value to be the average time needed to access a resource. Our values for p are considered to be (very) conservative. The conclusion is that, in general, the probability of violating correctness can be so low that it can be neglected in comparison to other types of failure.

N	m	p	Violation	N	m	p	Violation
8	5	3 sec/hour	$< 10^{-5}$	8	5	30 sec/hour	$< 10^{-3}$
8	6	3 sec/hour	$< 10^{-11}$	8	6	30 sec/hour	$< 10^{-7}$
16	9	3 sec/hour	$< 10^{-4}$	16	9	30 sec/hour	$< 10^{-2}$
16	12	3 sec/hour	$< 10^{-21}$	16	12	30 sec/hour	$< 10^{-13}$
32	17	3 sec/hour	$< 10^{-4}$	32	17	30 sec/hour	$< 10^{-2}$
32	24	3 sec/hour	$< 10^{-43}$	32	24	30 sec/hour	$< 10^{-27}$

Figure 5.17: Violation probabilities for various parameter values of decentralized mutual exclusion.

To implement this scheme, we can use a system in which a resource is replicated N times. Assume that the resource is known under its unique name rname. We can then assume that the ith replica is named rname$_i$ which is then used to compute a unique key using a known hash function. As a consequence, every process can generate the N keys given a resource's name, and subsequently look up each node responsible for a replica (and controlling access to that replica) using some commonly used naming system.

If permission to access the resource is denied (i.e., a process gets less than m votes), it is assumed that it will back off for some randomly chosen time, and make a next attempt later. The problem with this scheme is that if many nodes want to access the same resource, it turns out that the utilization rapidly drops. In that case, there are so many nodes competing to get access that eventually no one can get enough votes, leaving the resource unused. A solution to solve this problem can be found in [Lin et al., 2004].

Note 5.5 (More information: A comparison of the mutual-exclusion algorithms)
A brief comparison of the mutual exclusion algorithms we have looked at is instructive. In Figure 5.18 we have listed the algorithms and two performance properties: the number of messages required for a process to access and release a shared resource, and the delay before access can occur (assuming messages are passed sequentially over a network).

In the following, we assume only point-to-point messages (or, equivalently, count a multicast to N processes as N messages).

- The centralized algorithm is simplest and also most efficient. It requires only three messages to enter and leave a critical region: a request, a grant to enter, and a release to exit.

- The distributed algorithm requires $N - 1$ request messages, one to each of the other processes, and an additional $N - 1$ grant messages, for a total of $2(N - 1)$.

- With the token ring algorithm, the number is variable. If every process constantly wants to enter a critical region, then each token pass will result in one entry and exit, for an average of one message per critical region entered. At the other extreme, the token may sometimes circulate for hours without anyone being interested in it. In this case, the number of messages per entry into a critical region is unbounded.

- The decentralized case requires sending N messages to coordinators, and another N responses. If it does not get a majority, it will have to release (at most) $N/2$ votes. If it did get enough votes, it will have to send an additional N release messages later on. A process may need to go through $k \geq 1$ attempts.

Algorithm	Messages per entry/exit	Delay before entry (in message times)
Centralized	3	2
Distributed	$2(N - 1)$	$2(N - 1)$
Token ring	$1, \ldots, \infty$	$0, \ldots, N - 1$
Decentralized	$2kN + (k - 1)N/2 + N, k = 1, 2, \ldots$	$2kN + (k - 1)N/2$

Figure 5.18: A comparison of four mutual exclusion algorithms.

The delay from the moment a process needs to enter a critical region until its actual entry also varies. For a worst-case analysis, we assume that messages are sent one after the other (i.e., there are never two or more messages in transit at the same time), and that message transfer time is roughly the same everywhere. Delay can then be expressed in **message transfer time units**, or simply **MTTU**. Under these assumptions, when the time using a resource is short, the dominant factor in the delay is determined by the total number of messages sent through the system before access can be granted. When resources are used for a long period of time, the dominant factor is waiting for everyone else to take their turn. In Figure 5.18 we show the former case.

- It takes only two MTTUs to enter a critical region in the centralized case, caused by a request message and the subsequent grant message sent by the coordinator.

- The distributed algorithm requires sending $N - 1$ request messages, and receiving another $N - 1$ grant messages, adding up to $2(N - 1)$ MTTUs.

- For the token ring, the delay varies from 0 MTTU (in case the token had just arrived) to $N - 1$ (for when the token had just departed).

- In the case of decentralized, the delay is dependent on the number of times a process needed to return the (minority of) votes. With having to go through $k \geq 1$ attempts, a process may see $2kN + (k - 1)N/2$ MTTUs.

> Virtually all algorithms suffer badly in the event of crashes. Special measures and additional complexity must be introduced to avoid having a crash bring down the entire system. It is somewhat ironic that distributed algorithms are generally more sensitive to crashes than centralized ones. In this sense, it should not come as a surprise that, indeed, centralized mutual exclusion is widely applied: it is simple to understand the behavior, and relatively easy to increase the fault tolerance of the centralized server.

5.3.6   Example: Simple locking with ZooKeeper

For many practical reasons, mutual exclusion in distributed systems is often done with a centralized coordinator, not in the least because the behavior of these solutions is much easier to understand than many other noncentralized versions. Let us briefly look at a system that is designed for coordination tasks in distributed systems, and which is by now also widely deployed. **ZooKeeper** was developed to provide facilities for supporting various coordination tasks, including locking, leader election, monitoring, to name but just a few. It has been designed for scalability and fault tolerance. For our purposes now, we concentrate only on a relatively simple setup, namely to support locking through a single server. ZooKeeper's fault tolerance aspects are discussed in Chapter 8. The system was first described in [Hunt et al., 2010], to be later followed up with a practical description by Junqueira and Reed [2014].

ZooKeeper basics

As mentioned, ZooKeeper is designed to facilitate different coordination functions. An important design principle is its lack of blocking primitives: clients send messages to the ZooKeeper service and, in principle, are always immediately returned a response. In the case of locking, this means that a client will, for example, be informed whether it was able to grab a lock. If the lock could not be acquired, a new attempt will be necessary, as we discuss shortly.

To facilitate a range of coordination functions, ZooKeeper maintains a namespace, organized as a tree. Operations on the tree are simple: creating and deleting nodes, as well as reading and updating the data contained in a node (if any). A partial update of a node is not possible: all the node's data will be overwritten in the case of an update. In addition, a client can check with the server whether a node exists. At this point, it should be become clear how one could implement a locking service in ZooKeeper: to acquire a lock, simply let a process create a special node, say lock, but have that operation fail if the node already exists. Releasing a lock is done by merely deleting the node lock. We return to some important details below.

There are two types of nodes in ZooKeeper. Persistent nodes need to be created and deleted explicitly. In contrast, ephemeral nodes are created explicitly, but are automatically removed if the connection with the creating client closes (perhaps because of a failure), or expires. Of course, an ephemeral node can also be explicitly deleted.

An important consequence of not supporting blocking operations, is that a client will have to regularly check the status of the namespace: have nodes been added or removed, have nodes in the namespace been changed? However, polling is generally not considered to be very efficient. To this end, ZooKeeper supports a notification mechanism by which a client can subscribe to a change in a node or a branch in the tree. When a change happens, the client receives a message.

There are a few things that need to be considered to make this all work. First, suppose a client subscribes to changes at a specific node after having read the state of that node. If the node is updated twice in a row, we want to prevent that the client sees the second update before being notified, as the notification dealt with changes to the *previous* state, i.e., the state after the first update took place.

Second, it should be clear that there can be a lot of concurrency among competing clients. As we shall discuss in detail in Chapter 7, problematic are, in particular, the situations in which one client C_1 reads data to subsequently decide to update that data. If, between the read and intended update another client C_2 performs an update, client C_1 may now request an update based on out-of-date information. Such intended updates can be prevented by using version numbers, as shown in Figure 5.19.

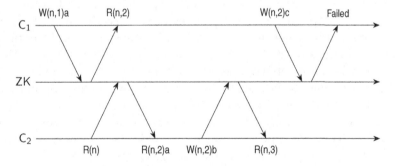

Figure 5.19: Preventing updates based on out-of-date information through versions (based on [Junqueira and Reed, 2014].

We use the notation $W(n, k)a$ to denote the request to write the value a to node n, under the assumption that its current version is k. $R(n, k)$ denotes that the current version of node n is k. The operation $R(n)$ tells that a client wants to read the current value of node n, and $R(n, k)a$ means that the value a from node n is returned with its current version k. In Figure 5.19 we see that client C_1 writes value a to node n, assuming its version is 1. If no write has ever taken place, this assumption is correct. The ZooKeeper service (ZK) returns the new version number, namely 2.

Meanwhile, client C_2 issues a read request for node n and is returned the previously written value a having version number 2. C_2 decides to update n, assuming its current version is still 2, by means of the write operation $W(n, 2)b$. ZooKeeper accepts the write, and returns the new version number 3. This concurrent update places C_1 in the position that its intended write operation $W(n, 2)c$ will fail: ZooKeeper states that its assumption about the version number is incorrect. The best what C_1 could do is read n again to see if it still wants to update the node.

Clearly, each client may need to try several times before an update actually takes place. This may not always seem so efficient, yet this approach ensures that data maintained by ZooKeeper is at least consistent with what clients expect it to be. As mentioned, we will return to consistency in much more detail in Chapter 7.

A ZooKeeper locking protocol

Implementing a lock using ZooKeeper is now fairly straightforward. ZooKeeper uses the same path notation for nodes as in Unix file systems. That means that we can create a node /lock at the root of the tree. The existence of that node means that a client has successfully acquired the lock. Releasing the lock is simply done by deleting node /lock.

Any client wanting to create the same node will receive the message that the node already exists and thus that the operation failed. Capturing such exceptions is at the core of blocking a client until /lock is removed. When the node already exists, the client will request ZooKeeper to send a notification when the node is deleted. Until that moment, the client simply waits (i.e., locally blocks) until notified, after which it tries to create the node again.

There are many subtleties to deal with. For example, a decent locking mechanism should allow a client to bail out after several attempts. Likewise, if a client who has created /lock crashes before deleting it again, we need to make sure that ZooKeeper will delete the node. Furthermore, we will find ourselves in an unfortunate race when the following happens:

1. A client C_1 creates a node /lock.

2. A client C_2 wants to acquire the lock but is notified that the associated node already exists.

3. Before C_2 subscribes to a notification, C_1 releases the lock, i.e., deletes /lock.

4. Client C_2 subscribes to changes to /lock and blocks locally.

This is analogous to the situation we described before: C_2 should be able to subscribe to changes based on the *existence* of /lock. In other words, when performing the fourth step, C_2 should be immediately notified that the situation has already changed since it last visited the tree. These subtleties are handled by ZooKeeper.

5.4 Election algorithms

Many distributed algorithms require one process to act as coordinator, initiator, or otherwise perform some special role. In general, it does not matter which process takes on this special responsibility, but one of them has to do it. In this section, we will look at algorithms for **electing a coordinator**. We will often also speak of a leader election.

If all processes are the same, with no distinguishing characteristics, there is no way to select one of them to be special. Consequently, we will assume that each process P has a unique identifier $id(P)$. In general, election algorithms attempt to locate the process with the highest identifier and designate it as coordinator. The algorithms differ in the way they locate the coordinator.

Furthermore, we also assume that every process knows the identifier of every other process. In other words, each process has complete knowledge of the process group in which a coordinator must be elected. What the processes do not know is which ones are currently up and which ones are currently down. The goal of an election algorithm is to ensure that when an election starts, it concludes with all processes agreeing on whom the new coordinator is to be. There are many algorithms and variations, of which several important ones are discussed in the textbooks by Tel [2000] and Lynch [1996].

5.4.1 The bully algorithm

A well-known solution for electing a coordinator is the **bully algorithm** devised by Garcia-Molina [1982]. In the following, we consider N processes $\{P_0, \ldots, P_{N-1}\}$ and let $id(P_k) = k$. When any process notices that the coordinator is no longer responding to requests, it initiates an election. A process, P_k, holds an election as follows:

1. P_k sends an ELECTION message to all processes with higher identifiers: $P_{k+1}, P_{k+2}, \ldots, P_{N-1}$.

2. If no one responds, P_k wins the election and becomes coordinator.

3. If one of the higher-ups answers, it takes over and P_k's job is done.

At any moment, a process can get an ELECTION message from one of its lower-numbered colleagues. When such a message arrives, the receiver sends an OK message back to the sender to indicate that it is alive and will take

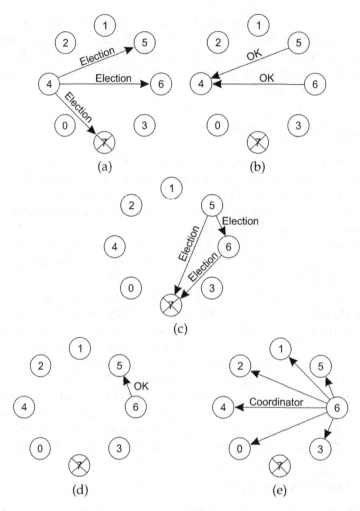

Figure 5.20: The bully election algorithm. (a) Process 4 holds an election. (b) Processes 5 and 6 respond, telling 4 to stop. (c) Now 5 and 6 each hold an election. (d) Process 6 tells 5 to stop. (e) Process 6 wins and tells everyone.

over. The receiver then holds an election, unless it is already holding one. Eventually, all processes give up but one, and that one is the new coordinator. It announces its victory by sending all processes a message telling them that starting immediately it is the new coordinator.

If a process that was previously down comes back up, it holds an election. If it happens to be the highest-numbered process currently running, it will win the election and take over the coordinator's job. Thus the biggest guy in town always wins, hence the name "bully algorithm."

In Figure 5.20 we see an example of how the bully algorithm works. The group consists of eight processes, with identifiers numbered from 0 to 7.

Previously, process P_7 was the coordinator, but it has just crashed. Process P_4 is the first one to notice this, so it sends ELECTION messages to all the processes higher than it, namely P_5, P_6, and P_7, as shown in Figure 5.20(a). Processes P_5 and P_6 both respond with OK, as shown in Figure 5.20(b). Upon getting the first of these responses, P_4 knows that its job is over, knowing that either one of P_5 or P_6 will take over and become coordinator. Process P_4 just sits back and waits to see who the winner will be (although at this point it can make a pretty good guess).

In Figure 5.20(c) both P_5 and P_6 hold elections, each one sending messages only to those processes with identifiers higher than itself. In Figure 5.20(d), P_6 tells P_5 that it will take over. At this point, P_6 knows that P_7 is dead and that it (P_6) is the winner. If there is state information to be collected from disk or elsewhere to pick up where the old coordinator left off, P_6 must now do what is needed. When it is ready to take over, it announces the takeover by sending a COORDINATOR message to all running processes. When P_4 gets this message, it can now continue with the operation it was trying to do when it discovered that P_7 was dead, but using P_6 as the coordinator this time. In this way, the failure of P_7 is handled, and the work can continue.

If process P_7 is ever restarted, it will send all the others a COORDINATOR message and bully them into submission.

5.4.2 A ring algorithm

Consider the following election algorithm that is based on the use of a **(logical) ring**. Unlike some ring algorithms, this one does not use a token. We assume that each process knows who its successor is. When any process notices that the coordinator is not functioning, it builds an ELECTION message containing its own process identifier and sends the message to its successor. If the successor is down, the sender skips over the successor and goes to the next member along the ring, or the one after that, until a running process is located. At each step along the way, the sender adds its own identifier to the list in the message, effectively making itself a candidate to be elected as coordinator.

Eventually, the message gets back to the process that started it all. That process recognizes this event when it receives an incoming message containing its own identifier. At that point, the message type is changed to COORDINATOR and circulated once again, this time to inform everyone else who the coordinator is (the list member with the highest identifier) and who the members of the new ring are. When this message has circulated once, it is removed and everyone goes back to work.

In Figure 5.21 we see what happens if two processes, P_3 and P_6, discover simultaneously that the previous coordinator, process P_7, has crashed. Each of these builds an ELECTION message and each of them starts circulating its message, independent of the other one. Eventually, both messages will go all the way around, and both P_3 and P_6 will convert them into COORDINATOR

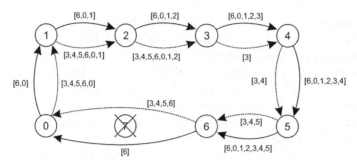

Figure 5.21: Election algorithm using a ring. The solid line shows the election messages initiated by P_6; the dashed one those by P_3.

messages, with exactly the same members and in the same order. When both have gone around again, both will be removed. It does no harm to have extra messages circulating; at worst it consumes a little bandwidth, but this is not considered wasteful.

5.4.3   Example: Leader election in ZooKeeper

Let us look at a practical example of how leader election takes place in a distributed system. As mentioned, ZooKeeper is logically centralized coordination service. In Section 5.3.6 we considered a simple setup with just a single ZooKeeper server. In practice, we see that ZooKeeper maintains a (relatively small) set of servers, forming what is called an **ensemble**. For a client, an ensemble appears as just a single server. For ZooKeeper, this ensemble is also coordinated by a single server, called the leader. The other servers are called followers and essentially act as up-to-date standbys for whenever the leader malfunctions. In that case, one of the followers will be elected as the new leader. From the client's perspective, a malfunctioning leader is mostly invisible: as soon as one of the standbys has taken over the role of leader, everything proceeds as if nothing happened. We return to many details of such fault-tolerant behavior in Chapter 8, but for now, let us dive a bit deeper into how the server in a ZooKeeper ensemble choose their leader.

It is important to note that a leader-election algorithm *within* a ZooKeeper ensemble is fundamentally different from devising a leader-election algorithm *by means of* ZooKeeper. The first deals with the *implementation of ZooKeeper* as a coordination service; the second with *using ZooKeeper* as a coordination service, perhaps as part of the implementation of a larger distributed system.

Which leader-election algorithm is used within a ZooKeeper ensemble is not that important, as long as, in the end, a single leader is chosen and enough followers are running as up-to-date standbys. Enough in this case means that a majority of the servers that form an ensemble are operating properly. For now, we will simply assume this to be the case.

The default election algorithm in an implementation of ZooKeeper is a simple version of bullying and works as follows [Junqueira and Reed, 2014]. Each server s in the ensemble has an identifier $id(s)$, as well as a monotonically increasing counter $tx(s)$ of the latest transaction it handled. Think of a transaction as a series of operations the server has executed, such as the combination of adding a node and registering that it should send a client a notification when anything changes. Typically, the leader of the ensemble will have performed the transaction on its own, locally stored, namespace and instructed its followers to do so as well on their respective local copy of that namespace.

When a follower s believes something is wrong with the leader (e.g., it suspects that the leader crashed), it sends out an ELECTION message to all other servers, along with the pair (voteID,voteTX). For this first message, it sets voteID to $id(s)$ and voteTX to $tx(s)$. During an election, each server s maintains two variables. The first, $leader(s)$, records the identifier of the server that s believes may turn out to be the final leader, and is initialized to $id(s)$. The second, $lastTX(s)$ is what s has learned to be the most recent transaction, initially being its own value, namely $id(s)$.

When a server s^* receives (voteID,voteTX), it proceeds as follows:

- If $lastTX(s^*) <$ voteTX, then s^* just received more up-to-date information on the most recent transaction. In that case, it sets

  - $leader(s^*) \leftarrow$ voteID
  - $lastTX(s^*) \leftarrow$ voteTX

- If $lastTX(s^*) =$ voteTX *and* $leader(s^*) <$ voteID, then s^* knows as much about the most recent transaction as what it was just sent, but its perspective on which server will be the next leader needs to be update:

  - $leader(s^*) \leftarrow$ voteID

Each time a server s^* receives a (voteID,voteTX) message, it may update its own information on whom it suspects to be the next leader. If s^* believes it should be the next leader, and has not sent out a message stating this, it will broadcast the pair $(id(s^*),tx(s^*))$. Under the assumption that communication is reliable, this broadcast alone should do the job. Typically, s^* will send out a message stating that it is the leader, when either initiating an election, or when receiving a message with a lower voteTX than its own $tx(s^*)$, or receiving a message with an up-to-date value for voteTX, but with a smaller voteID than $id(s^*)$. Once a leader has been elected, all servers will make sure that they synchronize on the latest transaction.

Note 5.6 (Advanced: ZooKeeper leader election in Python)

```python
1  class Process:
2    def __init__(self, chanID, procID, procIDSet, initTX):
3      self.txID      = initTX       # Your own most recent transaction
4      self.leader    = self.procID  # Who you believe may become leader
5      self.lastTX    = self.txID    # What is the most recent transaction
6      self.noleader  = False        # Are you still in the race for leader?
7
8    def receive(self):
9      while True:
10       msg             = self.chan.recvFrom(self.otherProcs)
11       sender, payload = msg[0], msg[1]
12       if payload[0] == ELECTION: # A process started an election
13         voteID, voteTX = payload[1], payload[2]
14
15         if self.lastTX < voteTX: # You're not up to date on most recent transaction
16           self.leader = voteID   # Record the suspected leader
17           self.lastTX = voteTX   # As well as the likely most recent transaction
18
19         elif (self.lastTX == voteTX) and (self.leader < voteID): # Wrong leader
20           self.leader = voteID   # Update your suspected leader
21
22         elif (self.procID > voteID) and (self.txID >= voteTX) and (not self.noleader):
23           # At this point, you may very well be the new leader (having a sufficiently
24           # high process identifier as well as perhaps the most recent transaction).
25           # No one has told you so far that you could not be leader. Tell the others.
26           self.chan.sendTo(self.otherProcs, (LEADER, self.procID, self.txID))
27
28       if payload[0] == LEADER:
29         # Check if the sender should indeed be leader
30         if ((self.lastTX < payload[2]) or
31             ((self.lastTX == payload[2]) and (self.leader <= payload[1]))):
32           # The sender is more up-to-date than you, or is equally up-to-date but
33           # has a higher process identifier. Declare yourself follower.
34           self.chan.sendTo(sender, (FOLLOWER, self.procID))
35         else:
36           # Sender is wrong: you have information that the sender based its decision
37           # on outdated information
38           self.chan.sendTo(sender, (NOLEADER))
```

Figure 5.22: A simplified version of ZooKeeper's leader election for an ensemble of servers.

Coming to the conclusion that one of the servers in a ZooKeeper ensemble is now indeed the new leader, can be a bit tricky. One way is to let a server come to the conclusion that it may never become a leader in the current round, in which case it tells the alleged leader that it will become a follower. This means that as soon as a server has collected enough followers, it can promote itself to leader. In ZooKeeper, this happens when a server has a majority of the other servers in the ensemble as followers. If we take an oversimplified approach by assuming that messages are never lost, nor do servers crash during an election, a leader is elected when all other servers are its followers. The code is shown in Figure 5.22 (again, omitting many details).

5.4.4 Example: Leader election in Raft

As another example of a leader-election algorithm that is in practical use, let us take a look at **Raft** [Ongaro and Ousterhout, 2014]. We will return to Raft in Chapter 8 when discussing consensus algorithms and focus here only on how it selects a leader.

Raft operates in a setting in which a handful of known replicated servers (typically five) collaborate by ensuring that each server executes the same set of operations, and all in the same order. To this end, one of the servers is elected as leader to tell the others what the exact order is of those operations. The protocol assumes that messages may be lost and that servers may crash.

Each server can be in one of three states: follower, candidate, or leader. Furthermore, the protocol operates in **terms**, where during each term there is exactly one leader, although it could have perhaps crashed. Each term is numbered, starting with 0. The leader is assumed to regularly send out a message, either containing information on an operation that should be carried out, or otherwise a heartbeat message to tell the other servers that their leader is still up and running.

Each server initially starts in the follower state (that is, there is initially no leader). Adopting the terminology from Howard et al. [2015], after a *follower timeout*, a following server concludes that the leader may have crashed (which, by the way, may be a false conclusion). As a result, it enters the candidate state and starts an election, volunteering to be the new leader. An election starts with a broadcast to all other servers, along with increasing the term number by 1. At that point, three situations may happen.

1. A candidate may receive a message from an alleged leader. If that server indicates it is operating in the same term as the candidate server, the latter will become follower again for the current term.

2. When a following server receives an election message for the first time (in a new term), it simply votes for the candidate and ignores any other election messages (for that new term). Therefore, a candidate server can also receive a vote. If it has a majority of votes (i.e., more than half of the servers, including itself), it promotes itself as leader for the new term.

3. As long as there is no alleged leader, or not enough votes have been received, the candidate server waits until a *candidate timeout* happens. At that point, the candidate server will simply start a new election (and again, for a next term).

Of course, if all servers enter the candidate state, we bear the risk of indefinitely not being able to cast enough votes for a single server. A simple solution is to slightly vary the *follower timeout* and *candidate timeout* on a per-server basis. The result is that, generally, there is only a single candidate for the new term, allowing each other server to vote for that candidate and become a follower. As soon as a server becomes leader, it will send out a heartbeat message to the rest.

5.4.5   Elections in large-scale systems

Many leader-election algorithms apply to only relatively small distributed systems. In such cases, the various nodes exchange information among each other, often through several rounds, to eventually collectively decide on the new leader. In Chapter 8, we shall see that this collective decision-making can take place even when a fraction of the participating nodes exhibits noncon-forming behavior, as in the case of security attacks or faults. The problem of electing a leader becomes rather nasty when there are potentially many processes to choose from. This is the case, for example, in **permissionless blockchains**.

Proof of work

A relatively simple, yet by now heavily criticized solution, is to have the candidates run a computational race, referred to as **proof of work**. Running such a race, which is done by solving a computational puzzle, should be known to be possible, yet difficult. The first process solving the puzzle, wins, and may proceed as leader to append a block of validated transactions to the existing blockchain.

The type of problem used for blockchains is based on what is known as **hashing**. As introduced in Section 1.2.5, a hash function takes as input a (possibly large) data set and produces a fixed-length string of bits, typically of length 1024 or 2048, called a *hash*. A cryptographically well-defined hash function has several important properties [Ferguson and Schneier, 2003]:

1. Computing the hash of a given data set is relatively easy, i.e., it does not require significant computational efforts.

2. However, given a specific hash, it is computationally very difficult to find a corresponding data set with the same associated hash.

3. With very high probability, any two different input data sets will lead to two seemingly unrelated, different hashes. Even if the two data sets are minimally different, their associated hashes will most likely be very different.

The third property is used to securely protect blocks of validated transactions against adversarial modifications: even the change of a single bit will not go unnoticed. Combined with the second property, it becomes virtually impossible to modify a block meaningfully, such that the modified block's hash is the same as the original block's hash.

To set up a race between validators, each validator computes the hash of its block of validated transactions. Note again that a hash is technically just a fixed-length string of bits. We denote the computed hash over a block a **digest**. The validator is then required to find an *additional* bit string, called a **nonce**, such that the hash computed over the digest and the nonce when taken together produces a bit string with a predetermined number of leading zeroes. Given property 2 of hash functions, we know that it is computationally very difficult to find a data set that matches a given hash. In our case, we have as input the hash of the block of validated transactions (i.e., the digest), and are now required to find a bit string (i.e., nonce) that, taken together with the digest, has an associated hash that starts with a given number of zeroes. This is computationally very difficult. In essence, each validator simply needs to go through a most likely lengthy trial-and-error process of generating a nonce and checking whether that nonce, combined with the digest, will lead to the required result.

By controlling how many leading zeroes that the outcome should have, we essentially control the difficulty of the computations. For example, with just 1 leading zero, there is a 50% chance that a generated nonce will lead to the desired result. Demanding 2 leading zeroes reduces this probability to 25%, 3 leading zeroes to 12.5%, and so forth. With 64 leading zeroes, which is common practice, the chance that an arbitrarily chosen nonce will do the trick is a mere 0.0000 0000 0000 0000 05% (that is, 17 zeroes after the decimal dot). Put differently, a validator will on average need to check about 18 billion billion nonces to find one that leads to the desired result. Using dedicated supercomputers, this takes about 10 minutes. It would take an average laptop about 100 years.

With increasing hardware capacity, the time it takes to find a nonce will drop. For this reason, the difficulty of finding a nonce is deliberately controlled in such a way that a race will have an expected duration. For Bitcoin systems, a popular application of blockchains, the duration is approximately 10 minutes. If races tend to become shorter, then the difficulty for finding a nonce is increased. If races turn out to be too lengthy, the difficulty is lowered. Adjusting the difficulty is done by regularly computing the average time it took to run the race over the last 2000 blocks of transactions, or so. The adjustment of the difficulty is done by all validators using the same globally known method, and is therefore done in a completely decentralized manner.

There is a reason for properly setting the expected duration of a race. Suppose we have very lengthy races. This means that validators would have to do a lot of work to find a proper nonce. The good part of the story is that the chance that two validators find a nonce at more or less the same time is relatively small (although this depends, of course, on how many validators participate in the race). As a consequence, the chance that there will be only one winner who will have enough time to successfully broadcast its victory to all others is relatively high.

The downside of the story, however, is that with lengthy races, the transaction processing capacity may be too low. Suppose that we have a race duration of 10 minutes and an average number of 2500 transactions per block (which are common values for Bitcoin). This means that, effectively, the system can handle about 4 transactions per second. Increasing the number of transactions per block is an obvious path to follow, yet even such improvements still lead to low rates in comparison to many centralized solutions with a fixed, trusted third party validating transactions.

On the other hand, assume we would have very short-lasting races. In that case, two validators may more easily concurrently find a proper nonce, both will declare victory, append their block to the blockchain (which was already massively replicated), and before other validators had the chance to stop their work, we would find ourselves with different copies of the same blockchain. There are different ways to correct for these concurrent versions of what is supposed to be a single blockchain, but obviously, it comes at the price of invalidating potentially many transactions, and rolling back to a valid state. Of course, the advantage of a smaller race duration is that, in principle, we can handle more transactions per time unit.

Proof of stake

As a reaction to the waste of computational resources found in proof-of-work systems, much effort has been spent on alternative leader-election algorithms for permissionless blockchains. An important class is formed by so-called **proof-of-stake** systems. Leaving out many details, as well as the many variants of such systems, the basic principle is as follows. An easy-to-read overview of the principles of proof-of-stake leader election is provided by Nguyen et al. [2019].

First, we need to make the assumption that each transaction as recorded in a blockchain has one or more associated tokens. Moreover, at each moment, each token has exactly one owner. This is typically the case with monetary transactions, where a token is associated with a digital coin. Because blockchains are fully readable by any participant, we may also assume that tokens may be *passed* between owners, and that, indeed, *copying* a token and associating it with multiple owners cannot go undetected. How this can be realized is discussed in Section 9.4.3. Each token will, therefore, have only a single owner. Second, we make also make the (realistic) assumption that for a given blockchain, there are a total of N tokens, which may vary over time depending on the application for which a blockchain is being used.

A simple leader-election process for blockchains then consists of a function that generates a random number k between 1 and N. That number is used as an index of the kth token, of which the owner becomes the next leader. The function used to generate a random number is public, meaning that any participant can execute it to determine k. Obviously, the more tokens a process P owns, the higher the probability that P will be elected as leader.

The simplicity of this algorithm and the fact that there are still so many race-based blockchains, indicates that there are many issues to deal with before proof-of-stake solutions can actually work. To understand, we need to realize that with proof of work, there is a price to pay to become leader, namely using considerable computational resources. If that price is compensated by a reward (namely a transaction fee), we have some sort of balance. In many proof-of-stake systems, there may also be a reward, but there is no price to be paid in advance for becoming a leader. As a result, these systems are generally more vulnerable to security attacks, for example, by letting participants generate invalid transactions that will disrupt the work of honest leaders.

Leader election in blockchains is part of reaching consensus on the status of a blockchain. We return to these matters in Section 8.2.6.

Note 5.7 (Advanced: Selecting superpeers)

Many leader-election algorithms often concentrate on the selection of only a single node. There are situations when several nodes should actually be selected, such as in the case of **super peers** in peer-to-peer networks, which we discussed in Section 2.4.3.

The following requirements need to be met for super-peer selection (see also [Lo et al., 2005]):

1. Normal nodes should have low-latency access to super peers.
2. Super peers should be evenly distributed across the overlay network.
3. There should be a predefined portion of super peers relative to the total number of nodes in the overlay network.
4. Each super peer should not need to serve more than a fixed number of normal nodes.

Fortunately, these requirements are relatively easy to meet in most peer-to-peer systems, given the fact that the overlay network is either structured (as in DHT-based systems), or randomly unstructured (as, for example, can be realized with gossip-based solutions). Let us take a look at solutions proposed by Lo et al. [2005].

In the case of DHT-based systems, the basic idea is to reserve a fraction of the identifier space for super peers. In a DHT-based system, each node receives a random and uniformly assigned m-bit identifier. Now suppose we reserve the first (i.e., leftmost) k bits to identify super peers. For example, if we need N superpeers, then the first $\lceil log_2(N) \rceil$ bits of any *key* can be used to identify these nodes.

To explain, assume we have a (small) Chord system with $m = 8$ and $k = 3$. When looking up the node responsible for a specific key K, we can first decide to route the lookup request to the node responsible for the pattern K $\wedge$ 11100000 which is then treated as the superpeer. (We use the binary operator "$\wedge$" to denote a bitwise and.) Note that each node with identifier ID can check whether it is a super peer by looking up ID $\wedge$ 11100000 to see if this request is routed to itself. Provided node identifiers are uniformly assigned to nodes, it can be seen that with a total of N nodes the number of super peers is, on average, equal to $2^{k-m}N$.

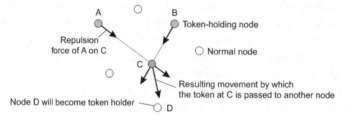

Figure 5.23: Moving tokens in a two-dimensional space using repulsion forces.

A different approach is based on positioning nodes in an m-dimensional geometric space. In this case, assume we need to place N super peers *evenly* throughout the overlay. The basic idea is simple: a total of N tokens are spread across N randomly chosen nodes. No node can hold more than one token. Each token represents a repelling force by which another token is inclined to move away. The net effect is that if all tokens exert the same repulsion force, they will move away from each other and spread themselves evenly in the geometric space.

This approach requires that nodes holding a token learn about other tokens. To this end, we can use a gossiping protocol, by which a token's force is disseminated throughout the network. If a node discovers that the total forces that are acting on it exceed a threshold, it will move the token in the direction of the combined forces, as shown in Figure 5.23. When a token is held by a node for a given amount of time, that node will promote itself to superpeer.

5.4.6   Elections in wireless environments

Traditional election algorithms are generally based on assumptions that are not realistic in wireless environments. For example, they assume that message passing is reliable and that the topology of the network does not change. These assumptions are false in most wireless environments, especially when dealing with mobile devices.

Only few protocols for elections have been developed that work in mobile environments. Vasudevan et al. [2004] propose a solution that can handle failing nodes and partitioning networks. An important property of their solution is that the *best* leader can be elected rather than just a random one as was more or less the case in the previously discussed solutions. Their protocol works as follows. To simplify our discussion, we concentrate only on ad hoc networks and ignore that nodes can actually move. This may be the case, for example, in sensor networks.

Consider such a wireless ad hoc network. To elect a leader, any node in the network, called the source, can initiate an election by sending an ELECTION message to its immediate neighbors (i.e., the nodes in its range). When a node receives an ELECTION for the first time, it designates the sender as its parent, and subsequently sends out an ELECTION message to all its immediate neighbors, except for the parent. When a node receives an ELECTION message from a node besides its parent, it merely acknowledges the receipt.

When node R has designated node Q as its parent, it forwards the ELECTION message to its immediate neighbors (excluding Q) and waits for acknowledgments to come in before acknowledging the ELECTION message from Q. This waiting has an important consequence. First, note that neighbors who have already selected a parent will immediately respond to R. More specifically, if all neighbors already have a parent, R is a leaf node and will be able to report back to Q quickly. In doing so, it will also report information such as its battery lifetime and other resource capacities.

This information will later allow Q to compare R's capacities to that of other downstream nodes, and select the best eligible node for leadership. Of course, Q had sent an ELECTION message only because its own parent P had done so as well. In turn, when Q eventually acknowledges the ELECTION message previously sent by P, it will pass the most eligible node to P as well. In this way, the source will eventually get to know which node is best to be selected as leader, after which it will broadcast this information to the rest.

This process is illustrated in Figure 5.24. Nodes have been labeled a to j, along with their capacity. Node a initiates an election by broadcasting an ELECTION message to nodes b and j, as shown in Figure 5.24(b) After that step, ELECTION messages are propagated to all nodes, ending with the situation shown in Figure 5.24(e), where we have omitted the last broadcast by nodes f and i. From there on, each node reports to its parent the node with the best capacity, as shown in Figure 5.24(f). For example, when node g receives the acknowledgments from its children e and h, it will notice that h is the best node, propagating $[h, 8]$ to its own parent, node b. In the end, the source will note that h is the best leader and will broadcast this information to all other nodes.

When multiple elections are initiated, each node will decide to join only one election. To this end, each source tags its ELECTION message with a unique identifier. Nodes will participate only in the election with the highest identifier, stopping any running participation in other elections.

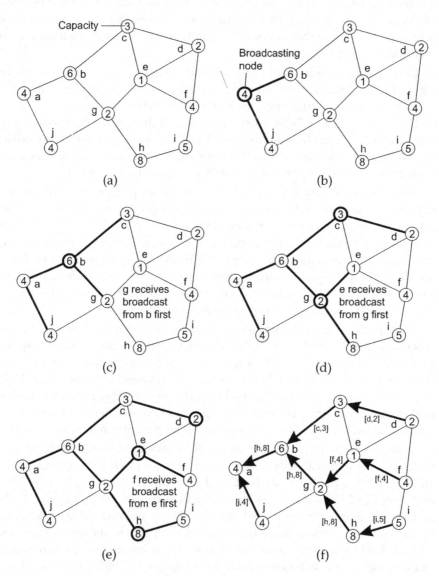

Figure 5.24: Election algorithm in a wireless network, with node a as the source. (a) Initial network. (b)–(e) The build-tree phase (last broadcast step by nodes f and i not shown). (f) Reporting of best node to source.

With some minor adjustments, the protocol can be shown to operate also when the network partitions, and when nodes join and leave. The details can be found in Vasudevan et al. [2004].

5.5 Gossip-based coordination

As a next topic in coordination, we take a look at a few important examples in which gossiping is deployed. In the following, we look at aggregation, large-scale peer sampling, and overlay construction, respectively.

5.5.1 Aggregation

Let us take a look at some interesting applications of **epidemic protocols**. We already mentioned spreading updates, which is perhaps the most widely deployed application. In the same light, gossiping can be used to discover nodes that have a few outgoing wide-area links, to subsequently apply directional gossiping.

Another interesting application area is simply collecting, or actually aggregating information [Jelasity et al., 2005]. Consider the following information exchange. Every node P_i initially chooses an arbitrary number, say v_i. When node P_i contacts node P_j, they each update their value as:

$$v_i, v_j \leftarrow (v_i + v_j)/2$$

Obviously, after this exchange, both P_i and P_j will have the same value. In fact, it is not difficult to see that eventually all nodes will have the same value, namely the average of all initial values. Propagation speed is again exponential.

What use does computing the average have? Consider the situation that all nodes P_i have set v_i to zero, except for P_1 who has set v_1 to 1:

$$v_i \leftarrow \begin{cases} 1 & \text{if } i = 1 \\ 0 & \text{otherwise} \end{cases}$$

If there are N nodes, then eventually each node will compute the average, which is $1/N$. As a consequence, every node P_i can estimate the size of the system as being $1/v_i$.

Computing the average may be difficult when nodes regularly join and leave the system. One practical solution to this problem is to introduce epochs. Assuming that node P_1 is stable, it simply starts a new epoch now and then. When node P_i sees a new epoch for the first time, it resets its own variable v_i to zero and starts computing the average again.

Of course, other results can also be computed. For example, instead of having a fixed node such as P_1 start the computation of the average, we can easily pick a random node as follows. Every node P_i initially sets v_i to a random number from the same interval, say $(0, 1]$, and also stores it permanently as m_i. Upon an exchange between nodes P_i and P_j, each change their value to:

$$v_i, v_j \leftarrow \max\{v_i, v_j\}$$

Each node P_i for which $m_i < v_i$ will lose the competition for being the initiator in starting the computation of the average. In the end, there will be a single winner. Of course, although it is easy to conclude that a node has lost, it is much more difficult to decide that it has won, as it remains uncertain whether all results have come in. The solution to this problem is to be optimistic: a node always assumes it is the winner until proven otherwise. At that point, it simply resets the variable it is using for computing the average to zero. Note that by now, several computations (in our example, computing a maximum and computing an average) may be executing simultaneously.

5.5.2   A peer-sampling service

An important aspect in epidemic protocols is the ability of a node P to choose another node Q *at random* from all available nodes in the network. When giving the matter some thought, we may actually have a serious problem: if the network consists of thousands of nodes, how can P ever pick one of these nodes at random without having a complete overview of the network? For smaller networks, one could often resort to a central service that had registered every participating node. Obviously, this approach can never scale to large networks.

A solution is to construct a fully decentralized **peer-sampling service**, or **PSS** for short. As it turns out, and somewhat counter-intuitive, a PSS can be built using an epidemic protocol. As explored by Jelasity et al. [2007], each node maintains a list of c neighbors, where, ideally, each of these neighbors represents a randomly chosen *live* node from the current set of nodes. This list of neighbors is also referred to as a **partial view**. There are many ways to construct such a partial view. In the solution of Jelasity et al., it is assumed that nodes regularly exchange entries from their partial view. Each entry identifies another node in the network, and has an associated age that indicates how old the reference to that node is. Two threads are used, as shown in Figure 5.25.

The different selection operations are specified as follows:

- selectPeer: Randomly select a neighbor from the local partial view

- selectToSend: Select some other entries from the partial view, and add to the list intended for the selected neighbor.

- selectToKeep: Add received entries to the partial view, remove repeated items, and shrink the view to c items.

```
1  selectPeer(&Q);                          1
2  selectToSend(&bufs);                      2
3  sendTo(Q, bufs);               ⟶          3  receiveFromAny(&P, &bufr);
4                                             4  selectToSend(&bufs);
5  receiveFrom(Q, &bufr);         ⟵          5  sendTo(P, bufs);
6  selectToKeep(p_view, bufr);               6  selectToKeep(p_view, bufr);
```

(a)   (b)

Figure 5.25: Communication between the (a) active and (b) passive thread in a peer-sampling service.

The active thread takes the initiative to communicate with another node. It selects that node from its current partial view. It continues by constructing a list containing $c/2 + 1$ entries, including an entry identifying itself. The other entries are taken from the current partial view. After sending the list to the selected neighbor, it waits for a response.

That neighbor, meanwhile, will also have constructed a list through the passive thread shown in Figure 5.25(b) whose activities strongly resemble that of the active thread.

The crucial point is the construction of a new partial view. This view, for contacting as well as for the contacted peer, will contain exactly c entries, part of which will come from the received list. In essence, there are two ways to construct the new view. First, the two nodes may decide to discard the entries that they had sent to each other. Effectively, this means that they will *swap* part of their original views. The second approach is to discard as many *old* entries as possible (meaning, in practice, that after every gossiping round, the age of each entry in every partial view is incremented by one).

As it turns out, as long as peers regularly run the exchange algorithm just described, selecting a random peer from a thus dynamically changing partial view, is statistically indistinguishable from randomly selecting a peer from the entire network. Of course, selecting a peer from a partial view should occur at approximately the same frequency as the refreshing of partial views. We have thus constructed a fully decentralized gossip-based peer-sampling service. A simple and often-used implementation of a peer-sampling service is Cyclon [Voulgaris et al., 2005].

5.5.3 Gossip-based overlay construction

Although it would seem that structured and unstructured peer-to-peer systems form strict independent classes, this need actually not be the case (see also Castro et al. [2005]). One key observation is that by carefully exchanging and selecting entries from partial views, it is possible to construct and maintain specific topologies of overlay networks. This topology management is achieved by adopting a two-layered approach, as shown in Figure 5.26.

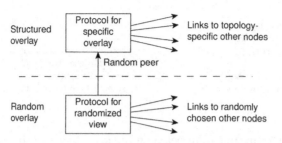

Figure 5.26: A two-layered approach for constructing and maintaining specific overlay topologies using techniques from unstructured peer-to-peer systems.

The lowest layer constitutes an unstructured peer-to-peer system in which nodes periodically exchange entries of their partial views with the aim to provide a peer-sampling service. Accuracy in this case refers to the fact that the partial view should be filled with entries referring to randomly selected *live* nodes.

The lowest layer passes its partial view to the higher layer, where an additional selection of entries takes place. This then leads to a second list of neighbors corresponding to the desired topology. Jelasity and Kermarrec [2006] propose to use a *ranking function* by which nodes are ordered according to some criterion relative to a given node. A simple ranking function is to order a set of nodes by increasing distance from a given node P. In that case, node P will gradually build up a list of its nearest neighbors, provided the lowest layer continues to pass randomly selected nodes.

As an illustration, consider a logical grid of size $N \times N$ with a node placed on each point of the grid. Every node is required to maintain a list of c nearest neighbors, where the distance between a node at (a_1, a_2) and (b_1, b_2) is defined as $d_1 + d_2$, with $d_i = \min(N - |a_i - b_i|, |a_i - b_i|)$. If the lowest layer periodically executes the protocol as outlined in Figure 5.25, the topology that will evolve is a two-dimensional torus, shown in Figure 5.27. In this example, $N = 50$ and we show the results after first initializing each list with random entries. Figure 5.27(b) shows the results after five rounds of exchanges, while the final result, shown in Figure 5.27(c) is achieved after 20 rounds.

Note 5.8 (Advanced:Gossip-based overlay construction in Python)
To better appreciate and understand the construction of overlay networks through gossiping, let us see what a concrete implementation in Python would look like. As we have mentioned, the principle is simple: we have two separate layers and each node is responsible for exchanging links with selected neighbors. A straightforward implementation would seem to be to use a separate thread per layer, as suggested in Figure 5.26. However, such a choice will instantly lead to potential deadlock problems. Suppose node A decides to exchange links with

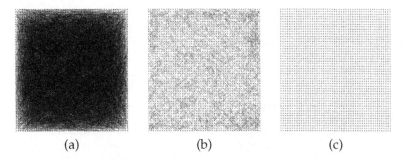

(a)   (b)   (c)

Figure 5.27: Generating a torus overlay network using a two-layered unstructured peer-to-peer system.

node B, but B has chosen another node, say C for exchanging links. If C chooses A for exchanging links, we may have a deadlock if these three nodes first collectively choose their respective neighbor for exchanging links, and then collectively wait for that neighbor to respond.

The general solution to this problem is to essentially avoid **synchronous request-response behavior**, but instead to use **asynchronous, persistent communication**. In other words, we let the middleware store a message before it is delivered, after which the sender can continue doing other things. This type of communication is precisely supported by the channel package used for many of our Python examples. The outline of the code is shown in Figure 5.28. (The complete code is readily available as accompanying online material for the book.)

Note that for each layer, the approach is essentially always the same: select a peer, decide on the links to exchange, and send that information asynchronously to the selected peer. Thereafter, a node that initiated an exchange will have to wait for a response. When that comes in, it merely needs to update its own view. (There are many subtleties that need to be considered, which we will discuss shortly.) In principle, there will be a regular call to maintainViews(), if only to ensure that a node will also react to incoming exchange requests. Note that in our solution, we simply let a node ignore an incoming exchange request when it has an outstanding initiated exchange itself. Ignoring a request is done by telling the initiating node to give up its own attempt. Although this approach will prevent deadlocks, it bears the risk that no exchange will take place at all.

As mentioned, the actual code for handling gossip-based overlay construction involves more than what we have shown in Figure 5.28. Crucial are the criteria for selecting a neighboring peer, as well as the selection of links to exchange. As explained by Voulgaris and van Steen [2013], there are several things that can be done to speed up convergence of the overlay in comparison to random choices. At the same time, including random choices is essential to achieve convergence to the requested overlay.

In the first place, at the top layer for constructing the overlay, links should be exchanged that make most sense for the receiving peer. In our example, this means that when a node A sends links to a node B, it should select the ones to neighbors that are closest to B. Furthermore, B should not return links that A had just sent: it is much better that A learns about new nodes first.

```
 1  def maintainViews():
 2    for viewType in [viewOverlay, viewPSS]: # For each view, do the same
 3      peer[viewType] = None
 4      if time to maintain viewType: # This viewType needs to be updated
 5        peer[viewType] = selectPeer(viewType)          # Select a peer
 6        links = selectLinks(viewType, peer[viewType])   # Select links
 7        sendTo(peer[viewType], Request[viewType], links) # Send links asynchronously
 8
 9    while True:
10      block = (peer[viewOverlay] != None) or (peer[viewPSS] != None)
11      sender, msgType, msgData = recvFromAny(block) # Block if expecting something
12
13      if msg == None: # All work has been done, simply return from the call
14        return
15
16      for viewType in [viewOverlay, viewPSS]: # For each view, do the same
17        if msgType == Response[viewType]:  # Response to previously sent links
18          updateOwnView(viewType, msgData) # Just update the own view
19
20        elif msgType == Request[viewType]: # Request for exchanging links
21          if peer[viewType] == None:       # No outstanding exchange request
22            links = selectLinks(viewType, sender)     # Select links
23            sendTo(sender, Response[viewType], links) # Send them asynchronously
24            updateOwnView(viewType,msgData)           # Update own view
25          else: # This node already has a pending exchange request, ignore this one
26            sendTo(sender, IgnoreRequest[viewType])
27
28        elif msgType == IgnoreRequest[viewType]: # Request has been denied, give up
29          peer[viewType] = None
```

Figure 5.28: Pseudocode in Python for implementing a gossip-based approach toward overlay construction.

Moreover, when A selects a peer, we should try to prevent selecting one with which a recent exchange has taken place. In other words, A should try to maximize diversity in selecting a peer. This diversity can be obtained by selecting peers in a round-robin fashion. This approach also has the benefit that in a dynamic network, nodes that have left are guaranteed to be discovered quickly and can thus be removed from a view.

If we were to use only the top layer, the greediness of exchanging only best links may lead to a situation that a collection of nodes will jointly form a closed set within the network: jointly, they are referring to each other and as such, may be missing out on better nodes. This is the reason introducing randomness is essential, and why we need to incorporate information from the lower random overlay in the selection process of the higher structured overlay.

This aspect is completely analogous to getting stuck in a local optimum when optimizing through hill-climbing procedures. What is needed is to introduce some randomness to ensure that indeed a global optimum will eventually be reached.

5.5.4   Secure gossiping

Gossiping is an attractive means for coordination. However, the speed by which a large collection of nodes manages to synchronize, is also an inherent vulnerability. The time it takes to exchange and disseminate proper information is also the time it takes to spread false information. This is perhaps best illustrated by means of an example. Consider a peer-sampling service for some large network. Assume that each node maintains a partial view of size c, and that, on average, $c/2$ references to neighboring nodes are exchanged. Let us also assume that there are c colluding attackers. Their behavior is simple: each attacker also maintains a partial view, but when returning $c/2$ references, only references to other colluding attackers are returned. The effect is that, gradually, the partial view of each benign node in the network is polluted by references to the attackers, to the extent that each partial view contains *only* references to attackers.

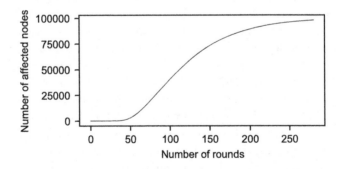

Figure 5.29: The speed by which a hub attack can take effect.

The effect can be dramatic. Figure 5.29 shows the speed by which partial views are fully polluted, that is, each contains references only to attackers. In this example, we consider a network of 100,000 nodes, a partial view size of 30, and only 30 attackers. After less than 300 rounds, all benign nodes have fully polluted partial views. Also note that, completely consistent with the push-pull behavior of epidemic protocols, it may take a while before any serious effect is seen. However, as soon as a few hundred nodes are completely polluted, they increasingly contribute to contaminating the rest of the nodes, and so on.

It can be argued that there is no standard security measure that can combat these kinds of attacks. For example, even with using secure channels by which both parties have genuinely authenticated each other, there is no reason to assume that both of them will also behave as they should. In other words, authentication provides no guarantees for trust. In the case of gossiping systems, security often comes in the form of trying to detect and prevent malicious behavior. For our example, the question is how can a benign node can detect that it is under attack, and which countermeasures can it take to mitigate the effects of an attack?

A solution in the case of peer sampling, and developed by Jesi et al. [2010], works as follows. The essence is to discover if there are nodes that behave badly. The attack we just described is characterized by the fact that, eventually, many nodes will be referencing a very small of set of nodes. In terms of graphs, this means that the *indegree* of some nodes is extraordinarily high, while for most nodes, their indegree will be low, and actually 0. An indegree of 0 means that a node is unknown to any other node in the network.

When using Cyclon [Voulgaris et al., 2005] as the peer-sampling service, we know that the indegrees follow a normal distribution, as shown in Figure 5.30(a). In this example, the y-axis shows the fraction of nodes with a specific indegree value. Even with a mere 30 colluding attackers, we already see that after 10 rounds, the indegree distribution has started to becoming wider and shifting to the left, as shown in Figure 5.30(b). This continues, and after 40 rounds (Figure 5.30(e)), we already have that about 15% of all nodes have an indegree of 0. (Note that for Figure 5.29, we were counting the number of nodes that were referencing *only* attacking nodes, which is different from measuring indegrees. An attacked node can still be referenced by others.) Finally, after less than 300 rounds, virtually all nodes have an indegree of 0; the attackers have now full control over the entire network.

Figure 5.30 also gives us a hint toward a solution. As explained by Jesi et al. [2010], each node can gather statistics on which nodes are being referenced. If certain nodes are gradually being referenced unusually more often than others, then something fishy may be going on. There are a few issues we need to deal with. First, spreading of "bad" links can be so efficient, that we need to consider that once a benign node has come to the conclusion that it has identified an attacker, it may already be too late. Second, we also want to prevent that every benign node has to build up complete knowledge of the entire network, partly also because attackers have to be identified quickly. Third, attackers do not want to be caught, i.e., be recognized as acting maliciously, as they collectively do need some time to be successful.

Notably the last aspect, not wanting to be caught, provides a solution to mitigating an attack. In essence, a benign node can force an attacker to behave

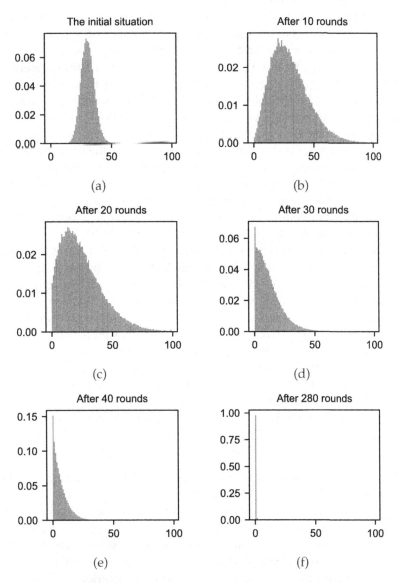

Figure 5.30: The development of the indegree distribution at several stages of a peer-sampling service under attack. Each x-axis shows the indegree, and the y-axis the fraction of nodes with that degree.

according to the rules. What happens is that when a benign node initiates an exchange of links with a selected node, it will process the returned links either for updating its own partial view, or for gathering statistics (it may do both, but this may not be on par with efficient resource usage). Moreover, to accelerate the process of discovering attackers, a node will initiate several link exchanges simultaneously (and, in the end, process only one of the replies). A malicious node is now faced with a dilemma: always returning references to its colluders will quickly reveal the attackers. The only thing that it can do, is occasionally play by the rules and return links to other, benign nodes. As it turns out, this dilemma is enough to force the attackers to behave decently enough, effectively rendering an attack useless. Note that this procedure will also be applied when an *attacker* initiates an exchange: the recipient can decide to use the links passed to it for updating its statistics on indegrees, as well as use it for running the exchange protocol. The attacker will, however, never know whether the recipient is going to collect statistics. To fly under the radar, it will have to behave according to the rules of the game enough in order not to be caught. The details can be found in [Jesi et al., 2010].

There are many other types of attacks possible. For example, attackers may decide to initiate information exchange at a much higher frequency than specified by the protocol. With a push-based approach, this may result in attackers rapidly polluting values of benign nodes, which are then further disseminated. Mousazadeh and Ladani [2015] come to the conclusion that for such attacks, in principle, only pulling should be allowed (as the benign nodes will then collectively dictate the pace at which information is disseminated).

Likewise, in the case of aggregation, attackers may deliberately return incorrect values. To illustrate, suppose that when collectively computing the average value as we described in Section 5.5.1, an attacker A always returns its own value v_A. Every node v_i communicating with A will therefore compute

$$v_i \leftarrow (v_i + v_A)/2$$

which gradually converges to the value v_A. In all these cases, attacks can be mitigated only by trying to detect if a node is not behaving according to the protocol. That detection mechanism, of course, should be known to the attacker, while at the same time will be effective if it forces an attacker to try to go ahead unnoticed. In turn, if well designed, the mechanism will force the attacker to actually behave well, or at least to the extent that any possible damage remains limited. More on how these **data-injection attacks** work and can be mitigated, are described by Gentz et al. [2016].

5.6   Distributed event matching

Let us now draw our attention to distributed event matching. Event matching, or more precisely, **notification filtering**, is at the heart of **publish-subscribe systems**. The problem boils down to the following:

- A process specifies through a subscription S in which events it is interested.

- When a process publishes a notification N on the occurrence of an event, the system needs to see if S *matches* N.

- In the case of a match, the system should send the notification N, possibly including the data associated with the event that took place, to the subscriber.

As a consequence, we need to facilitate at least two things: (1) matching subscriptions against events, and (2) notifying a subscriber in the case of a match. The two can be separated, but this need not always be the case. In the following, we assume the existence of a function $match(S, N)$ which returns true when subscription S matches the notification N, and false otherwise. As we argue below, publish-subscribe systems turn out to face difficult scalability problems when the matching function cannot be easily distributed across multiple servers. This is often the case when subscriptions can be expressive, as in content-based publish-subscribe systems. We discuss scalability of distributed event matching separately below.

Another, rather nasty problem, is combining security and privacy while keeping publishers and subscribers mutually unaware of each other, but also ensuring that servers have only enough information available to perform their matching function. In this sense, it may seem that the goals of publish-subscribe systems, and those of secure distributed systems conflict. We return to this issue below as well.

5.6.1 Centralized implementations

A simple, naive implementation of event matching is to have a fully centralized server that handles all subscriptions and notifications. In such a scheme, a subscriber simply submits a subscription, which is subsequently stored. When a publisher submits a notification, that notification is checked against each and every subscription, and when a match is found, the notification is copied and forwarded to the associated subscriber.

Obviously, this is not a very scalable solution. Nevertheless, provided the matching can be done efficiently and the server itself has enough processing power, the solution is feasible for many cases. For example, using a centralized server is the canonical solution for implementing **Linda tuple spaces**. Likewise, many publish-subscribe systems that run within a single department or organization can be implemented through a central server. Important, in these cases, is that the matching function can be implemented efficiently. In practice, this is often the case when dealing with topic-based filtering: matching then resorts to checking for equality of attribute values.

Note that a simple way to scale up a centralized implementation, is to deterministically divide the work across multiple servers. A standard approach is to make use of two functions, as explained by Baldoni et al. [2009]:

- a function *sub2node*(S), which takes a subscription S and maps it to a nonempty subset of servers

- a function *not2node*(N), which takes a notification N and maps it to a nonempty subset of servers.

The servers to which *sub2node*(S) is mapped are called the **rendezvous nodes** for S. Likewise, *sub2node*(N) are the rendezvous nodes for N. The only constraint that needs to be satisfied, is that for any subscription S and matching notification N, $sub2node(S) \cap not2node(N) \neq \varnothing$. In other words, there must be at least one server that can handle the subscription when there is a matching notification. In practice, this constraint is satisfied by topic-based publish-subscribe systems by using a hashing function on the names of the topics.

The idea of having a central server can be extended by distributing the matching across multiple servers and dividing the work. The servers, generally referred to as **brokers**, are organized into an overlay network. The issue then becomes how to route notifications to the appropriate set of subscribers. A straightforward way to make sure that notifications reach their subscribers, is to deploy flooding. There are essentially two approaches. First, we store each subscription at every broker, while publishing notifications only at a single broker. The latter will handle identifying the matching subscriptions and subsequently copy and forward the notification. The alternative is to store a subscription only at one broker, while broadcasting notifications to all brokers. In that case, matching is distributed across the brokers, which may lead to a more balanced workload among the brokers.

Note 5.9 (Example: TIB/Rendezvous)
Flooding notifications is used in **TIB/Rendezvous**, of which the basic architecture is shown in Figure 5.31 [TIBCO]. In this approach, a notification is a message tagged with a compound keyword describing its content, such as news.comp.os.books. A subscriber provides (parts of) a keyword, or indicating the messages it wants to receive, such as news.comp. $*$ .books. These keywords are said to indicate the **subject** of a message.

Fundamental to its implementation is the use of broadcasting common in local-area networks, although it also uses more efficient communication facilities when possible. For example, if it is known exactly where a subscriber resides, point-to-point messages will generally be used. Each host on such a network will run a **rendezvous daemon**, which takes care that messages are sent and delivered according to their subject. Whenever a message is published, it is multicasted to each host on the network running a rendezvous daemon. Typically, multicasting is implemented using the facilities offered by the underlying network, such as IP-multicasting or hardware broadcasting.

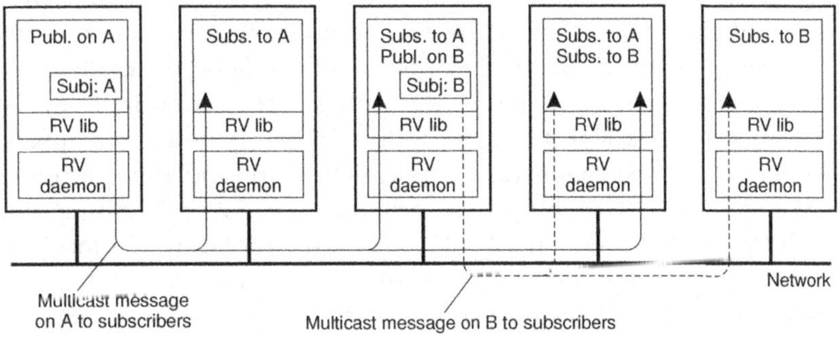

Figure 5.31: The principle of a publish/subscribe system as implemented in TIB/Rendezvous.

Processes that subscribe to a subject pass their subscription to their local daemon. The daemon constructs a table of (*process, subject*), entries and whenever a message on subject S arrives, the daemon simply checks in its table for local subscribers, and forwards the message to each one. If there are no subscribers for S, the message is discarded immediately.

When using multicasting as is done in TIB/Rendezvous, there is no reason why subscriptions cannot be elaborate and be more than string comparison, as is currently the case. The crucial observation here is that because messages are forwarded to every node anyway, the potentially complex matching of published data against subscriptions can be done entirely locally without further network communication needed.

When subscriptions are allowed to be more expressive, scalability may easily become a problem. In practice, expressive subscriptions take the form of (*attribute,value*) pairs in which a *value* returns as an expression on the possible values for the specified attribute. Examples include range values ("$1 \leq x < 10$"), containment ("$x \in \{red, blue\}$"), prefix and suffix expressions ("url.startswith("https")"), etc. More complicated expressions including combinations of conjunctions and disjunctions are, in theory, also possible, thus gradually resembling what one would find in SQL queries for databases. It is not hard to imagine that expressive subscriptions can be handled by centralized brokers, but when scalability is at stake, we may need to limit expressiveness altogether to the point that we find ourselves looking at topic-based event matching.

One way out that has been explored is combining peer-to-peer networks and publish-subscribe systems, as described in Kermarrec and Triantafillou [2013]. As the authors show, there is no simple general solution, and most solutions often have very specific limitations.

Selective routing

If we consider that publish-subscribe is all about routing messages between publishers and subscribers, one thought is to install specific filters in an overlay network that effectively ignore paths toward nodes that are not interested in what is being published. In other words, instead of flooding a network with either subscriptions or publications, we apply **selective routing**, as proposed by Carzaniga et al. [2004]. Consider a publish-subscribe system consisting of N brokers to which clients (i.e., applications) can send subscriptions and retrieve notifications. Carzaniga et al. propose a two-layered routing scheme, in which the lowest layer consists of a shared broadcast tree connecting the N brokers. There are various ways for setting up such a tree, ranging from network-level multicast support to application-level multicast trees, as we discussed in Chapter 4. Here, we also assume that such a tree has been set up with the N brokers as end nodes, along with a collection of intermediate nodes forming routers. Note that the distinction between a server and a router is only a logical one: a single machine may host both kinds of processes.

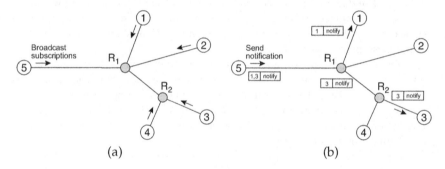

Figure 5.32: A first approach toward content-based routing in which brokers (a) first broadcast subscriptions to later (b) forward notifications only to relevant brokers.

Every broker broadcasts its subscriptions to all other brokers, as shown in Figure 5.32(a). As a result, every broker will be able to compile a list of (*subject, destination*) pairs. Then, whenever a process publishes a notification N, its associated broker prepends the destination brokers to that message and forwards the notification to the others, shown in Figure 5.32(b). When the message reaches a router, the latter can use the list to decide on the paths that the message should follow, as shown in Figure 5.32.

We can now refine the capabilities of routers for deciding where to forward notifications. To that end, each broker broadcasts its subscription across the network so that routers can compose **routing filters**. For example, assume that node 3 in Figure 5.32 subscribes to notifications for which an attribute a lies in the range $[0, 3]$, but that node 4 wants messages with a $\in [2, 5]$. In this case, router R_2 will create a routing filter as a table with an entry for each of its outgoing links (in this case three: one to node 3, one to node 4, and one toward router R_1), as shown in Figure 5.33.

Interface	Filter
To node 3	$a \in [0,3]$
To node 4	$a \in [2,5]$
Toward router R_1	(unspecified)

Figure 5.33: A partially filled routing table.

More interesting is what happens at router R_1. In this example, the subscriptions from nodes 3 and 4 dictate that any notification with a lying in the interval $[0,3] \cup [2,5] = [0,5]$ should be forwarded along the path to router R_2, and this is precisely the information that R_1 will store in its table. It is not difficult to imagine that more intricate subscription compositions can be supported.

This simple example also illustrates that whenever a node leaves the system, or when it is no longer interested in specific notifications, it should cancel its subscription and essentially broadcast this information to all routers. This cancellation, in turn, may lead to adjusting various routing filters. Late adjustments will at worst lead to unnecessary traffic, as notifications may be forwarded along paths for which there are no longer subscribers. Nevertheless, timely adjustments are needed to keep performance at an acceptable level.

Gossiping

Selective routing may help to avoid broadcasting notifications to all routers, but ultimately, it may still not be enough to reach acceptable scalable solutions. Another approach is based on gossiping. The basic idea is that subscribers interested in the same notifications form their own overlay network (which is constructed through gossiping as we describe further below), so that once a notification is published, it merely needs to be routed to the appropriate overlay. For the latter, a **random walk** can be deployed. This approach is following in TERA [Baldoni et al., 2007].

A more sophisticated approach toward combining gossiping and event matching is followed in Sub-2-Sub [Voulgaris et al., 2006]. It is still one of the very few content-based approaches that combines scalability with expressiveness of subscriptions. Consider a publish-subscribe system in which data items can be described by N attributes $a_1, \ldots, a_N$ whose value can be directly mapped to a floating-point number. Such values include, for example, floats, integers, enumerations, Booleans, and strings. A subscription S takes the form of a tuple of (*attribute, value/range*) pairs, such as

$$S = \langle a_1 \rightarrow 3.0, a_4 \rightarrow [0.0, \ 0.5) \rangle$$

In this example, S specifies that a_1 should be equal to 3.0, and a_4 should lie in the interval $[0.0, 0.5)$. Other attributes are allowed to take on any value. For clarity, assume that every node i enters only one subscription S_i.

Note that each subscription S_i actually specifies a subset $\mathbf{S_i}$ in the N-dimensional space of floating-point numbers. Such a subset is also called a **hyperspace**. For the system as a whole, notifications that fall in the union $\overline{\mathbf{S}} = \cup \mathbf{S_i}$ of these hyperspaces are the only ones of interest. The whole idea is to automatically partition $\overline{\mathbf{S}}$ into M disjoint hyperspaces $\overline{\mathbf{S}}_1, \ldots, \overline{\mathbf{S}}_M$ such that each falls completely in one of the subscription hyperspaces $\mathbf{S_i}$, and together they cover all subscriptions. More formally, we have that:

$$(\overline{\mathbf{S}}_\mathbf{m} \cap \mathbf{S_i} \neq \emptyset) \Rightarrow (\overline{\mathbf{S}}_\mathbf{m} \subseteq \mathbf{S_i})$$

Sub-2-Sub keeps M minimal in the sense that there is no partitioning with fewer parts $\overline{\mathbf{S}}_\mathbf{m}$. To this end, for each hyperspace $\overline{\mathbf{S}}_\mathbf{m}$, it registers exactly those nodes i for which $\overline{\mathbf{S}}_\mathbf{m} \subseteq \mathbf{S_i}$. In that case, when a notification is published, the system need merely find the $\overline{\mathbf{S}}_\mathbf{m}$ to which the associated event belongs, from which point it can forward the notification to the appropriate nodes.

To this end, nodes regularly exchange subscriptions through gossiping. If two nodes i and j notice that their respective subscriptions intersect, that is, $\mathbf{S_{ij}} \equiv \mathbf{S_i} \cap \mathbf{S_j} \neq \emptyset$ they will record this fact and keep references to each other. If they discover a third node k with $\mathbf{S_{ijk}} \equiv \mathbf{S_{ij}} \cap \mathbf{S_k} \neq \emptyset$, the three of them will connect to each other so that a notification N from $\mathbf{S_{ijk}}$ can be efficiently disseminated. Note that if $\mathbf{S_{ij}} - \mathbf{S_{ijk}} \neq \emptyset$, nodes i and j will maintain their mutual references, but now associate it strictly with $\mathbf{S_{ij}} - \mathbf{S_{ijk}}$.

In essence, what we are seeking is a means to cluster nodes into M different groups, such that nodes i and j belong to the same group if and only if their subscriptions S_i and S_j intersect. Moreover, nodes in the same group should be organized into an overlay network that allows efficient dissemination of a data item in the hyperspace associated with that group. This situation for a single attribute is sketched in Figure 5.34.

Here, we see a total of seven nodes, in which the horizontal line for node i indicates its range of interest for the value of the single attribute. Also shown is the grouping of nodes into disjoint ranges of interests in values of the attribute. For example, nodes 3, 4, 7, and 10 will be grouped together representing the interval $[16.5, 21.0]$. Any data item with a value in this range should be disseminated to only these four nodes.

To construct these groups, the nodes are organized into a gossip-based unstructured network. Each node maintains a list of references to other neighbors (i.e., a **partial view**), which it periodically exchanges with one of its neighbors. Such an exchange allows a node to learn about random other nodes in the system. Every node keeps track of the nodes it discovers with overlapping interests (i.e., with an intersecting subscription).

At a certain moment, every node i will generally have references to other nodes with overlapping interests. As part of exchanging information with a

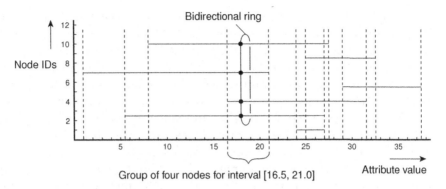

Figure 5.34: Grouping nodes for supporting range queries in a gossip-based publish-subscribe system.

node j, node i orders these nodes by their identifiers and selects the one with the lowest identifier $i_1 > j$, such that its subscription overlaps with that of node j, that is, $S_{j,i_1} \equiv S_{i_1} \cap S_j \neq \emptyset$.

The next one to be selected is $i_2 > i_1$ such that its subscription also overlaps with that of j, but only if it contains elements not yet covered by node i_1. In other words, we should have that $S_{j,i_1,i_2} \equiv (S_{i_2} - S_{j,i_1}) \cap S_j \neq \emptyset$. This process is repeated until all nodes that have an overlapping interest with node i have been inspected, leading to an ordered list $i_1 < i_2 < \cdots < i_n$. Note that a node i_k is in this list because it covers a region **R** of common interest to node i and j not yet jointly covered by nodes with a lower identifier than i_k. In effect, node i_k is the *first* node that node j should forward a notification to that falls in this unique region **R**. This procedure can be expanded to let node i construct a bidirectional ring. Such a ring is also shown in Figure 5.34.

Whenever a notification N is published, it is disseminated as quickly as possible to *any* node that is interested in it. As it turns out, with the information available at every node finding a node i interested in N is simple. From there on, node i need simply forward N along the ring of subscribers for the particular range that N falls into. To speed up dissemination, shortcuts are maintained for each ring as well.

5.6.2 Secure publish-subscribe solutions

A characteristic feature of publish-subscribe systems is that publishers and subscribers are **referentially decoupled**, and possibly also **temporally decoupled**. Notably, referential decoupling means that in a secure system messages should be able to flow from a publisher to subscribers while guaranteeing mutual anonymity. To guarantee confidentiality and integrity of messages, communicating parties usually set up a secure channel, but such an approach would break the party's anonymity.

A simple solution is to let a (possibly distributed) broker handle messages. The broker would handle all the matching and storage, if necessary. Obviously, such a broker would need to be trusted. Yet, it is not obvious at all that such trust is justified. For example, many publish-subscribe services are offered by third parties operating in a cloud setting. It is often unclear to which extent they can actually provide guarantees when it comes to protecting data. In addition, messages may often contain information that should definitely not, often even by law, be revealed to third parties, such as medical records.

We now seem to have several clashing requirements. First, for any publish-subscribe system, we need to ensure that the communicating parties remain referentially decoupled, that is, we need to guarantee mutual anonymity. Not knowing where messages come from imposes integrity issues: how can we be sure the messages have not been tampered with? Second, we cannot simply assume that brokers can be trusted. Facing confidentiality issues, we then cannot allow them to see (all of) the content of messages, yet this may impose serious routing problems. But there is more: if we cannot trust brokers, how can we ensure availability in the sense that subscribers, entitled to specific messages, actually receive those messages? Equally important is to ensure that messages are not delivered to unauthorized subscribers. Cui et al. [2021] also address an additional requirement: assuming there are colluders in place, brokers should not learn about the interests of innocent subscribers.

These problems are not unique to publish-subscribe systems, and have become more prevalent with the advent of cloud-based services. The key question is how to let a third party search through data to make decisions, yet without revealing that data. This is also known as **searchable encryption** [Bosch et al., 2014]. For publish-subscribe systems, an important technique is to conduct secure keyword search. Boneh et al. [2004] introduced **Public Key Encryption with Keyword Search**, generally known as **PEKS**. We will explain only the principle of PEKS without going into the cryptographic details.

In PEKS, a message is accompanied by a collection of keywords. To that end, using a public key PK, a message m and its n keywords $KW_1, \ldots, KW_n$ are stored at a server as the message m*:

$$m^* = [PK(m)|PEKS(PK, KW_1)|PEKS(PK, KW_2)| \cdots |PEKS(PK, KW_n)]$$

For each keyword KW_i a trapdoor T_{KW_i} is generated: $T_W(m^*)$ will return true if $W \in \{KW_1, \ldots, KW_n\}$ and false otherwise.

Using PEKS, we can now set up a cloud-based publish-subscribe system with (conceptually) a single broker that resides in the cloud. Such a scheme is described in [Yang et al., 2017] and sketched in Figure 5.35. We note we have deliberately simplified matters significantly to focus on the essentials.

An important role is played by the key authority: a trusted third party that generates keys for publishers and subscribers. In our example, it provides the

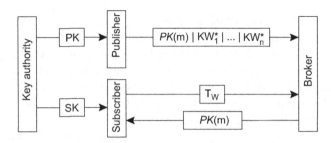

Figure 5.35: The principle of privacy-preserving publish-subscribe.

publisher with a key PK that can be used for encrypting the publication m. In addition, the key is used for constructing the encrypted tags $KW_i^* = PEKS(PK, KW_i)$. Likewise, each subscriber is given a secret key SK that it can use to generate a trapdoor T_W to be used by the broker to see whether the tag W is associated with the publication m. If there is a match, the broker returns $PK(m)$ which can then be decrypted using SK.

Our simplified scheme misses many important details, for which we refer the interested reader to Yang et al. [2017]. The authors assume that the broker is **honest-but-curious** and does not collude with publishers or subscribers. Honest-but-curious means that the server will behave according to the specifications, but may keep track of everything it does and use that information. Cui et al. [2021] describe a system that drops the assumption on collusion, and is one of the few known publish-subscribe systems that can handle colluding brokers. An overview of the security issues in publish-subscribe systems is given by Uzunov [2016]. For a good overview on preserving confidentiality, we refer to Onica et al. [2016]. The authors also come to the conclusion that security becomes easier if brokers can be trusted. Otherwise, good support for operating on encrypted data is needed.

5.7 Location systems

When looking at large distributed systems that are dispersed across a wide-area network, it is often necessary to take proximity into account. Just imagine a distributed system organized as an overlay network in which two processes are neighbors in the overlay network, but are actually placed far apart in the underlying network. If these two processes communicate a lot, it may have been better to ensure that they are also physically placed in each other's proximity. In this section, we take a look at location-based techniques to coordinate the placement of processes and their communication.

5.7.1 GPS: Global Positioning System

Let us start by considering how to determine your geographical position anywhere on Earth. This positioning problem is by itself solved through a highly specific, dedicated distributed system, namely **GPS**, which is an

acronym for **Global Positioning System**. GPS is a satellite-based distributed
system that was launched in 1978. Although it initially was used mainly for
military applications, it by now has found its way to many civilian applications,
notably for traffic navigation. However, many more application domains exist.
For example, modern smartphones now allow owners to track each other's
position. This principle can easily be applied to tracking other things as well,
including pets, children, cars, boats, and so on.

GPS uses up to 72 satellites, each circulating in an orbit at a height of
approximately 20,000 km. Each satellite has up to four atomic clocks, which
are regularly calibrated from special stations on Earth. A satellite continuously
broadcasts its position, and time stamps each message with its local time. This
broadcasting allows every receiver on Earth to accurately compute its own
position using, in principle, only four satellites. To explain, let us first assume
that all clocks, including the receiver's, are synchronized.

To compute a position, consider first the two-dimensional case, as shown
in Figure 5.36, in which three satellites are drawn, along with the circles
representing points at the same distance from each respective satellite. We see
that the intersection of the three circles is a unique point.

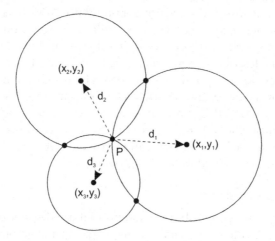

Figure 5.36: Computing a node's position in a two-dimensional space.

This principle of intersecting circles can be expanded to three dimensions,
meaning that we need to know the distance to four satellites to determine the
longitude, latitude, and altitude of a receiver on Earth. This positioning is
all fairly straightforward, but determining the distance to a satellite becomes
complicated when we move from theory to practice. There are at least two
important real-world facts that we need to take into account:

1. It takes a while before data on a satellite's position reaches the receiver.

2. The receiver's clock is generally not in sync with that of a satellite.

Assume that the timestamp from a satellite is completely accurate. Let Δ_r denote the deviation of the receiver's clock from the actual time. When a message is received from satellite S_i with timestamp T_i, then the measured delay Δ_i by the receiver consists of two components: the actual delay, along with its own deviation:

$$\Delta_i = (T_{now} - T_i) + \Delta_r$$

where T_{now} is the actual current time. As signals travel with the speed of light, c, the *measured* distance $\tilde{d}_i$ to satellite S_i is equal to $c \cdot \Delta_i$. With

$$d_i = c \cdot (T_{now} - T_i)$$

being the real distance between the receiver and satellite S_i, the measured distance can be rewritten to $\tilde{d}_i = d_i + c \cdot \Delta_r$. The real distance is now computed as:

$$\tilde{d}_i - c \cdot \Delta_r = \sqrt{(x_i - x_r)^2 + (y_i - y_r)^2 + (z_i - z_r)^2}$$

where x_i, y_i, and z_i denote the coordinates of satellite S_i. What we see now is a system of quadratic equations with four unknowns (x_r, y_r, z_r, and also Δ_r). We thus need four reference points (i.e., satellites) to find a unique solution that will also give us Δ_r. A GPS measurement will thus also give an account of the actual time.

So far, we have assumed that measurements are perfectly accurate. Of course, they are not. There are many sources of errors, starting with the fact that the atomic clocks in the satellites are not always in perfect sync, the position of a satellite is not known precisely, the receiver's clock has a finite accuracy, the signal propagation speed is not constant (as signals appear to slow down when entering, e.g., the ionosphere), and so on. On average, this leads to an error of some 5–10 meters. Special modulation techniques, as well as special receivers, are needed to improve accuracy. Using so-called **differential GPS**, by which corrective information is sent through wide-area links, accuracy can be further improved. More information can be found in [LaMarca and de Lara, 2008], as well as an excellent overview by Zogg [2002].

5.7.2 When GPS is not an option

A major drawback of GPS is that it generally cannot be used indoors. For that purpose, other techniques are necessary. An increasingly popular technique is to make use of the numerous WiFi access points available. The basic idea is simple: if we have a database of known access points along with their coordinates, and we can estimate our distance to an access point, then with only three detected access points, we should be able to compute our position. Of course, it really is not that simple at all.

A major problem is determining the coordinates of an access point. A popular approach is to do this through **war driving**: using a WiFi-enabled device along with a GPS receiver, someone drives or walks through an area and records observed access points. An access point can be identified through its SSID or its MAC-level network address. An access point AP should be detected at several locations before its coordinates can be estimated. A simple method is to compute the centroid: assume we have detected AP at N different locations $\{\vec{x_1}, \vec{x_2}, \ldots, \vec{x_N}\}$, where each location $\vec{x_i}$ consists of a (*latitude, longitude*)-pair as provided by the GPS receiver. We then simply estimate AP's location $\vec{x}_{AP}$ as

$$\vec{x}_{AP} = \frac{\sum_{i=1}^{N} \vec{x_i}}{N}.$$

Accuracy can be improved by taking the observed signal strength into account, and giving more weight to a location with relatively high observed signal strength than to a location where only a weak signal was detected. In the end, we obtain an estimation of the coordinates of the access point. The accuracy of this estimation is strongly influenced by:

- the accuracy of each GPS detection point $\vec{x_i}$
- the fact that an access point has a nonuniform transmission range
- the number of sampled detection points N.

Studies show that estimates of the coordinates of an access point may be tens of meters off from the actual location (see, e.g., Kim et al. [2006] or Tsui et al. [2010]). Moreover, access points come and go at a relatively high rate. Nevertheless, locating and positioning access points is widely popular, exemplified by the open-access Wigle database which is populated through crowdsourcing.[1]

5.7.3 Logical positioning of nodes

Instead of trying to find the absolute location of a node in a distributed system, an alternative is to use a logical, proximity-based location. In **geometric overlay networks** each node is given a position in an m-dimensional geometric space, such that the distance between two nodes in that space reflects a real-world performance metric. Computing such a position is the core business of a **Network Coordinates System**, or simply **NCS**, which are surveyed by Donnet et al. [2010]. The simplest, and most applied example, is where distance corresponds to internode latency. In other words, given two nodes P and Q, then the distance $\hat{d}(\mathsf{P}, \mathsf{Q})$ reflects how long it would take for a message to travel from P to Q and *vice versa*. We use the notation $\hat{d}$ to denote distance in a system where nodes have been assigned coordinates.

There are many applications of geometric overlay networks. Consider the situation where a Website at server O has been replicated to multiple servers

---

[1]See wigle.net.

$S_1, \ldots, S_N$ on the Internet, as typically happens with a **Content Delivery Network** (CDN). When a client C requests a page from O, the CDN may decide to redirect that request to the server closest to C, that is, the one that will give the best response time. If the geometric location of C is known, as well as those of each replica server, the CDN can then simply pick that server S_i for which $\hat{d}(C, S_i)$ is minimal.

Another example is optimal replica placement. Consider again a CDN that has gathered the positions of clients for one of its major customers. If the CDN were to replicate content to N servers, it can compute the N best positions where to place replicas such that the average client-to-replica response time is minimal. Performing such computations is almost trivially feasible if clients and servers have geometric positions that reflect internode latencies.

As a last example, consider **position-based routing** (see, e.g., [Popescu et al., 2012] or [Bilal et al., 2013]). In such schemes, a message is forwarded to its destination using only positioning information. For example, a naive routing algorithm to let each node forward a message to the neighbor closest to the destination. Although it can be easily shown that this specific algorithm need not converge, it illustrates that only local information is used to decide. There is no need to propagate link information or such to all nodes in the network, as is the case with conventional routing algorithms.

Centralized positioning

Positioning a node in an m-dimensional geometric space requires $m + 1$ distance measures to nodes with known positions. Assuming that node P wants to compute its own position, it contacts three other nodes with known positions and measures its distance to each of them. Contacting only one node would tell P about the circle it is located on; contacting only two nodes would tell it about the position of the intersection of two circles (which generally consists of two points); a third node would subsequently allow P to compute its actual location.

Node P can compute its own coordinates (x_P, y_P) by solving the three *quadratic* equations with the two unknowns x_P and y_P:

$$\tilde{d}_i = \sqrt{(x_i - x_P)^2 + (y_i - y_P)^2} \qquad (i = 1, 2, 3)$$

Here, we use $\tilde{d}$ to denote measured, or estimated distance. As said, $\tilde{d}_i$ generally corresponds to measuring the latency between P and the node at (x_i, y_i). This latency can be estimated as being half the round-trip delay, but it should be clear that its value will be different over time. The effect is a different positioning whenever P would want to recompute its position. Moreover, if other nodes would use P's current position to compute their own coordinates, then it should be clear that the error in positioning P will affect the accuracy of the positioning of other nodes.

It should also be clear that measured distances between a set of nodes will generally not even be consistent. For example, assume we are computing distances in a one-dimensional space, as shown in Figure 5.37. In this example, we see that although R measures its distance to Q as 2.0, and $\tilde{d}(P, Q)$ has been measured to be 1.0, when R measures $\tilde{d}(P, R)$ it finds 2.8, which is clearly inconsistent with the other two measurements.

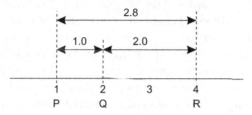

Figure 5.37: Inconsistent distance measurements in a one-dimensional space.

Figure 5.37 also suggests how this situation can be improved. In our simple example, we could solve the inconsistencies by merely computing positions in a two-dimensional space. This by itself, however, is not a general solution when dealing with many measurements. In fact, considering that Internet latency measurements may violate the **triangle inequality**, it is generally impossible to resolve inconsistencies completely. The triangle inequality states that in a geometric space, for any arbitrary three nodes P, Q, and R it must always be true that

$$d(P, R) \leq d(P, Q) + d(Q, R).$$

There are various ways to approach these issues. One common approach, proposed by Ng and Zhang [2002], is to use N special nodes $L_1, \ldots, L_N$, known as **landmarks**. Landmarks measure their pairwise latencies $\tilde{d}(L_i, L_j)$ and subsequently let a central node compute the coordinates for each landmark. To this end, the central node seeks to minimize the following aggregated error function:

$$\sum_{i=1}^{N} \sum_{j=i+1}^{N} \left(\frac{\tilde{d}(L_i, L_j) - \hat{d}(L_i, L_j)}{\tilde{d}(L_i, L_j)} \right)^2$$

where, again, $\hat{d}(L_i, L_j)$ corresponds to the distance after nodes L_i and L_j have been positioned.

The hidden parameter in minimizing the aggregated error function is the dimension m. Obviously, we have that $N > m$, but nothing prevents us from choosing a value for m that is much smaller than N. In that case, a node P measures its distance to each of the N landmarks and computes its coordinates by minimizing

$$\sum_{i=1}^{N} \left(\frac{\tilde{d}(L_i, P) - \hat{d}(L_i, P)}{\tilde{d}(L_i, P)} \right)^2$$

As it turns out, with well-chosen landmarks, m can be as small as 6 or 7, with $\hat{d}(P,Q)$ being no more than a factor 2 different from the actual latency $d(P,Q)$ for arbitrary nodes P and Q [Szymaniak et al., 2004; 2008].

Decentralized positioning

Another way to tackle this problem is to view the collection of nodes as a huge system in which nodes are attached to each other through springs. In this case, $|\tilde{d}(P,Q) - \hat{d}(P,Q)|$ indicates to what extent nodes P and Q are displaced relative to the situation in which the system of springs would be at rest. By letting each node (slightly) change its position, it can be shown that the system will eventually converge to an optimal organization in which the aggregated error is minimal. This approach is followed in Vivaldi, described in [Dabek et al., 2004a].

In a system with N nodes $P_1, \ldots, P_N$, Vivaldi aims at minimizing the following aggregated error:

$$\sum_{i=1}^{N} \sum_{j=1}^{N} |\tilde{d}(P_i, P_j) - \hat{d}(P_i, P_j)|^2$$

where $\tilde{d}(P_i, P_j)$ is the *measured* distance (i.e., latency) between nodes P_i and P_j, and $\hat{d}(P_i, P_j)$ the distance computed from the network coordinates of each node. Let $\vec{x}_i$ denote the coordinates of node P_i. In a situation that each node is placed in a geometric space, the *force* that node P_i exerts on node P_j is computed as:

$$\vec{F}_{ij} = (\tilde{d}(P_i, P_j) - \hat{d}(P_i, P_j)) \times u(\vec{x}_i - \vec{x}_j)$$

with $u(\vec{x}_i - \vec{x}_j)$ denoting the unit vector in the direction of $\vec{x}_i - \vec{x}_j$. In other words, if $F_{ij} > 0$, node P_i will push P_j away from itself, and will otherwise pull it toward itself. Node P_i now repeatedly executes the following steps:

1. Measure the latency $\tilde{d}_{ij}$ to node P_j, and also receive P_j's coordinates $\vec{x}_j$.

2. Compute the error $e = \tilde{d}(P_i, P_j) - \hat{d}(P_i, P_j)$

3. Compute the direction $\vec{u} = u(\vec{x}_i - \vec{x}_j)$.

4. Compute the force vector $F_{ij} = e \cdot \vec{u}$

5. Adjust own position by moving along the force vector: $\vec{x}_i \leftarrow \vec{x}_i + \delta \cdot \vec{u}$.

A crucial element is the choice of δ: too large and the system will oscillate; too small and convergence to a stable situation will take a long time. The trick is to have an adaptive value, which is large when the error is large as well, but small when only small adjustments are needed. Details can be found in [Dabek et al., 2004a].

5.8 Summary

Strongly related to communication between processes is the issue of how processes in distributed systems synchronize. Synchronization is all about doing the right thing at the right time. A problem in distributed systems, and computer networks in general, is that there is no notion of a globally shared clock. In other words, processes on different machines have their own idea of what time it is.

There are various ways to synchronize clocks in a distributed system, but all methods are essentially based on exchanging clock values, while considering the time it takes to send and receive messages. Variations in communication delays, and the way those variations are dealt with, largely determine the accuracy of clock synchronization algorithms.

Knowing the absolute time is often not necessary. What counts is that related events at different processes happen in the correct order. Lamport showed that by introducing a notion of logical clocks, it is possible for a collection of processes to reach global agreement on the correct ordering of events. In essence, each event e, such as sending or receiving a message, is assigned a globally unique logical timestamp $C(e)$ such that when event a happened before b, $C(a) < C(b)$. Lamport timestamps can be extended to vector timestamps: if $C(a) < C(b)$, we even know that event a causally preceded b.

An important class of synchronization algorithms is that of distributed mutual exclusion. These algorithms ensure that in a distributed collection of processes, at most one process at a time has access to a shared resource. Distributed mutual exclusion can easily be achieved if we make use of a coordinator that keeps track of whose turn it is. Fully distributed algorithms also exist, but have the drawback that they are generally more susceptible to communication and process failures.

Synchronization between processes often requires that one process acts as a coordinator. In those cases where the coordinator is not fixed, it is necessary that processes in a distributed computation decide on who is going to be that coordinator. Such a decision is taken by election algorithms. Election algorithms are primarily used in cases where the coordinator can crash. However, they can also be applied for the selection of superpeers in peer-to-peer systems.

The most important aspect in gossip-based coordination is being able to select another peer randomly from an entire overlay. As it turns out, we can implement such a peer-sampling service using gossiping, by ensuring that the partial view is refreshed regularly and randomly. Combining peer sampling with a selective replacement of entries in a partial view allows us to efficiently construct structured overlay networks.

Particularly challenging when it comes to coordination is distributed event matching, which sits at the core of publish-subscribe systems. Relatively simple is the case when we have a central implementation where matching subscriptions against notifications can be done by essentially doing one-to-one comparisons. However, as soon as we aim at distributing the load, we are faced with the problem of deciding beforehand which node is responsible for which part of the subscriptions, without knowing what kind of notifications to expect. This is particularly problematic for content-based matching, which, in the end, requires advanced filtering techniques to route notifications to the proper subscribers.

Related to these synchronization problems is positioning nodes in a geometric overlay. The basic idea is to assign each node coordinates from an m-dimensional space such that the geometric distance can be used as an accurate measure for the latency between two nodes. The method of assigning coordinates strongly resembles the one applied in determining the location and time in GPS.

NAMING

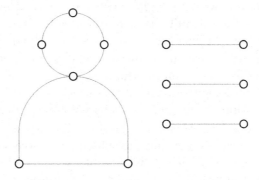

Names play an important role in all computer systems. They are used to sharing resources, to uniquely identify entities, to refer to locations, and more. An important issue with naming is that a name can be resolved to the entity it refers to. Name resolution thus allows a process to access the named entity. To resolve names, it is necessary to implement a naming system. The difference between naming in distributed systems and nondistributed systems lies in the way naming systems are implemented.

In a distributed system, the implementation of a naming system is itself often distributed across multiple machines. How this distribution is done plays a key role in the efficiency and scalability of the naming system. In this chapter, we concentrate on three different, important ways that names are used in distributed systems.

First, we consider so-called flat-naming systems. In such systems, entities are referred to by an identifier that, in principle, has no meaning at all. In addition, flat names bear no structure, implying that we need special mechanisms to trace the location of such entities. We discuss various approaches, ranging from distributed hash tables to hierarchical location services.

In practice, humans prefer to use readable names. Such names are often structured, as is well known from the way Web pages are referred to. Structured names allow for a highly systematic way of finding the server responsible for the named entity, as exemplified by the Domain Name System. We discuss the general principles, as well as scalability issues.

Finally, humans often prefer to describe entities through various characteristics, leading to a situation in which we need to resolve a description using the attributes assigned to an entity. As we shall see, this type of name resolution is notoriously difficult, especially with searching.

Name resolution and routing are closely related to each other. Normally, we look up an address given a name, to subsequently access the named entity through its address. As an alternative to looking up an address, researchers have been exploring how a name can be directly used to route toward the entity, to subsequently return a copy of its associated data. This so-called named-based routing is gradually maturing as an alternative for a future Internet. We discuss it briefly in this chapter.

6.1   Names, identifiers, and addresses

A name in a distributed system is a string of bits or characters that is used to refer to an entity. An entity in a distributed system, can be practically anything. Typical examples include resources such as hosts, printers, disks, and files. Other well-known examples of entities that are often explicitly named are processes, users, mailboxes, Web pages, graphical windows, messages, network connections, and so on.

Entities can be operated on. For example, a resource such as a printer offers an interface containing operations for printing a document, requesting the status of a print job, and the like. Furthermore, an entity such as a network connection may provide operations for sending and receiving data, setting quality-of-service parameters, requesting the status, and so forth.

To operate on an entity, it is necessary to access it, for which we need an **access point**. An access point is yet another, but special, kind of entity in a distributed system. The name of an access point is called an **address**. The address of an access point of an entity is also simply called an address of that entity.

An entity can offer more than one access point. As a comparison, a telephone can be viewed as an access point of a person, whereas the phone number corresponds to an address. Indeed, many people have several phone numbers, each number corresponding to a point where they can be reached. In a distributed system, a typical example of an access point is a host running a specific server, with its address formed by the combination of, for example, an IP address and port number (i.e., the server's transport-level address).

An entity may change its access points over time. For example, when a mobile computer moves to another location, it is often assigned a different IP address than the one it had before. Likewise, when a person changes jobs, there is likely a change in phone numbers as well. Similarly, changing your Internet Service Provider, often means changing an e-mail address.

An address is thus just a special kind of name: it refers to an access point of an entity. Because an access point is tightly associated with an entity, it would seem convenient to use the address of an access point as a regular name for the associated entity. Nevertheless, this is hardly ever done, as such naming is generally very inflexible and often human unfriendly.

For example, it is not uncommon to regularly reorganize a distributed system so that a specific server is now running on a different host than it did previously. The old machine on which the server used to be running may be reassigned to a different server. In other words, an entity may easily change an access point, or an access point may be reassigned to a different entity. If an address is used to refer to an entity, we will have an invalid reference the instant the access point changes or is reassigned to another entity. Therefore, it is much better to let a service be known by a separate name independent of the address of the associated server.

Likewise, if an entity offers more than one access point, it is not clear which address to use as a reference. For instance, many organizations distribute their Web service across several servers. If we would use the addresses of those servers as a reference for the Web service, it is not obvious which address should be chosen as the best one. Again, a much better solution is to have a single name for the Web service, independent of the addresses of the different Web servers.

These examples illustrate that a name for an entity that is independent of its addresses is often much easier and more flexible to use. Such a name is called **location independent**.

In addition to addresses, there are other types of names that deserve special treatment, such as names that are used to uniquely identify an entity. A true **identifier** is a name that has the following properties [Wieringa and de Jonge, 1995]:

1. An identifier refers to at most one entity.

2. Each entity is referred to by at most one identifier.

3. An identifier always refers to the same entity (i.e., it is never reused).

By using identifiers, it becomes much easier to unambiguously refer to an entity. For example, assume two processes each refer to an entity by an identifier. To check if the processes are referring to the same entity, it is sufficient to test if the two identifiers are equal. Such a test would not be sufficient if the two processes were using regular, nonunique, nonidentifying names. For example, the name "John Smith" cannot be taken as a unique reference to just a single person.

Likewise, if an address can be reassigned to a different entity, we cannot use an address as an identifier. Consider again the use of phone numbers, which are reasonably stable in the sense that a phone number will often for some time refer to the same person or organization. However, using a phone number as an identifier will not work, as it can be, and often is, reassigned over time. Consequently, Bob's new bakery may be receiving phone calls for Alice's old antique store for a long time. In this case, it would have been better to use a true identifier for Alice instead of her phone number.

Addresses and identifiers are two important types of names that are each used for very different purposes. In many computer systems, addresses and identifiers are represented in machine-readable form only, that is, in the form of bit strings. For example, an Ethernet address is essentially a random string of 48 bits. Likewise, memory addresses are typically represented as 32-bit or 64-bit strings.

Another important type of name is that which is tailored to be used by humans, also referred to as **human-friendly names**. In contrast to addresses and identifiers, a human-friendly name is generally represented as a character string. These names appear in many different forms. For example, files in Unix systems have character-string names that can generally be as long as 255 characters, and which are defined entirely by the user. Similarly, DNS names are represented as relatively simple case-insensitive character strings.

Having names, identifiers, and addresses brings us to the central theme of this chapter: how do we resolve names and identifiers to addresses? As we shall see, there are essentially two approaches. In the first one, we maintain

a (generally distributed) table of *(name, address)* pairs. This is the approach
followed by naming systems such as DNS, which we discuss extensively in
this chapter. In the second approach, a name is resolved by routing the request
gradually to the name's associated address, or even directly to an access point.
Typically, this is the approach followed in structured peer-to-peer systems,
but also in what is known as **information-centric networking** (which we
also discuss later in this chapter). It is interesting to note that in such cases
the boundaries between name resolution and message routing are starting
to blur, as was noted by Shoch [1978] already almost 50 years ago. In fact,
we will challenge the need for name-to-address resolution when discussing
named-data networking. To stay in historical perspective, it is then also
interesting to note how certain discussions become topical again: in a sense,
naming and resolving a name to an address is precisely what is referred to
as the **identifier-location split** (see also Ramirez et al. [2014] and Feng et al.
[2017]).

In the following sections, we will consider four different classes of naming
systems. First, we will take a look at how identifiers can be resolved to
addresses. In this case, we will also see an example where name resolution
is actually indistinguishable from message routing. After that, we consider
human-friendly names and then descriptive names (i.e., entities that are
described by a collection of names). Finally, we pay attention to named-based
networking.

6.2 Flat naming

Above, we explained that identifiers are convenient to uniquely represent entities. Often, identifiers are simply random bit strings, which we conveniently
refer to as unstructured, or **flat names**. An important property of such a name
is that it does not contain any information whatsoever on how to locate the
access point of its associated entity. In the following, we will take a look at
how flat names can be resolved, or, equivalently, how we can locate an entity
when given only its identifier.

6.2.1 Simple solutions

We first consider two simple solutions for locating an entity: broadcasting and
forwarding pointers. Both solutions are mainly applicable only to local-area
networks. Nevertheless, in that environment, they often do the job well,
making their simplicity particularly attractive.

Broadcasting

Consider a distributed system built on a computer network that offers efficient
broadcasting facilities. Typically, such facilities are offered by local-area

networks, in which all machines are connected to a single cable or the logical equivalent thereof. Also, local-area wireless networks fall into this category.

Locating an entity in such an environment is simple: a message containing the identifier of the entity is broadcasted to each machine, and each machine is requested to check whether it has that entity. Only the machines that can offer an access point for the entity send a reply message containing the address of that access point.

This principle is used in the Internet **Address Resolution Protocol (ARP)** to find the data-link address of a machine when given only an IP address [Plummer, 1982]. In essence, a machine broadcasts a packet on the local-network asking who is the owner of a given IP address. When the message arrives at a machine, the receiver checks whether it should listen to the requested IP address. If so, it sends a reply packet containing, for example, its Ethernet address.

Broadcasting becomes inefficient when the network grows. Not only is network bandwidth wasted by request messages, but, more seriously, too many hosts may be interrupted by requests they cannot answer. One possible solution is to switch to multicasting, by which only a restricted group of hosts receives the request. Ethernet networks support data-link level multicasting directly in hardware.

Multicasting can also be used to locate entities in point-to-point networks. For example, the Internet supports network-level multicasting by allowing hosts to join a specific multicast group. Such groups are identified by a multicast address. When a host sends a message to a multicast address, the network layer provides a best-effort service to deliver that message to all group members. Efficient implementations for multicasting on the Internet are discussed in Deering and Cheriton [1990] and Deering et al. [1996].

A multicast address can be used as a general location service for multiple entities. Consider an organization where each employee has his or her own mobile computer. When such a computer connects to the locally available network, it is dynamically assigned an IP address. In addition, it joins a specific multicast group. When a process wants to locate a computer A, it sends a "where is A?" request to the multicast group. If A is connected, it responds with its current IP address.

Another way to use a multicast address is to associate it with a replicated entity, and to use multicasting to locate the *nearest* replica. When sending a request to the multicast address, each replica responds with its current (normal) IP address. A crude way to select the nearest replica is to choose the one whose reply comes in first, but as it turns out, selecting a nearest replica is generally not that easy.

Forwarding pointers

Another approach to locating mobile entities is to make use of forwarding pointers [Fowler, 1985]. The principle is simple: when an entity moves from A to B, it leaves behind in A a reference to its new location at B. The main advantage of this approach is its simplicity: as soon as an entity has been located, for example by using a traditional naming service, a client can look up the current address by following the chain of forwarding pointers.

There are also drawbacks. First, if no special measures are taken, a chain for a highly mobile entity can become so long that locating that entity is prohibitively expensive. Second, all intermediate locations in a chain will have to maintain their part of the chain of forwarding pointers as long as needed. A third (and related) drawback is the vulnerability to broken links. As soon as any forwarding pointer is lost, the entity can no longer be reached. An important issue is, therefore, to keep chains relatively short, and to ensure that forwarding pointers are robust.

6.2.2 Home-based approaches

A popular approach to supporting mobile entities in large-scale networks is to introduce a **home location**, which keeps track of the current location of an entity. Special techniques may be applied to safeguard against network or process failures. In practice, the home location is often chosen to be the place where an entity was created.

The home-based approach is used as a fall-back mechanism for location services based on forwarding pointers. Another example where the home-based approach is followed is in Mobile IP [Perkins et al., 2011]. Each mobile host uses a fixed IP address. All communication to that IP address is initially directed to the mobile host's **home agent**. This home agent is located on the local-area network corresponding to the network address contained in the mobile host's IP address. In the case of IPv6, it is realized as a network-layer component. Whenever the mobile host moves to another network, it requests a temporary address that it can use for communication. This **care-of address** is registered at the home agent.

When the home agent receives a packet for the mobile host, it looks up the host's current location. If the host is on the current local network, the packet is simply forwarded. Otherwise, it is *tunneled* to the host's current location, that is, wrapped as data in an IP packet and sent to the care-of address. At the same time, the sender of the packet is informed of the host's current location. This principle is shown in Figure 6.1 Note that the IP address is effectively used as an identifier for the mobile host.

An important aspect is that this whole mechanism is largely hidden for applications. In other words, the original IP address associated with the mobile host can be used by an application without further ado. Client-side software that is part of the application-independent communication layer will handle the redirection to the target's current location. Likewise, at the target's location, a message that has been tunneled will be unpacked and handed to the application on the mobile host as if it were using its original address. Indeed, Mobile IP establishes a high degree of location transparency.

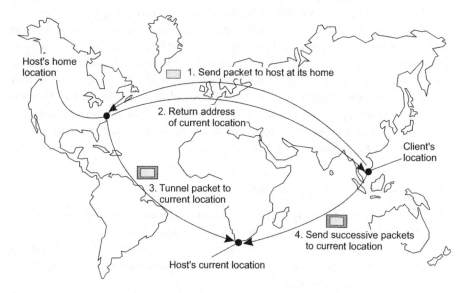

Figure 6.1: The principle of Mobile IP.

Figure 6.1 also illustrates a drawback of home-based approaches in large-scale networks. To communicate with a mobile entity, a client first has to contact the home, which may be at an entirely different location than the entity itself. The result is an increase in communication latency.

Another drawback of the home-based approach is the use of a fixed home location. For one thing, it must be ensured that the home location always exists. Otherwise, contacting the entity will become impossible. Problems are aggravated when a long-lived entity decides to move permanently to an entirely different part of the network than where its home is located. In that case, it would have been better if the home could have moved along with the host.

A solution to this problem is to register the home at a traditional naming service and to let a client first look up the location of the home. Because the home location can be assumed to be relatively stable, that location can be effectively cached after it has been looked up.

6.2.3 Distributed hash tables

Let us now take a closer look at how to resolve an identifier to the address of the associated entity. We have already mentioned distributed hash tables a number of times, but have deferred discussion on how they actually work. In this section, we correct this situation by first considering the Chord system as an easy-to-explain DHT-based system.

General mechanism

Many DHT-based systems have been developed in the past decade, with the Chord system [Stoica et al., 2003] being a typical representative. Chord uses an m-bit identifier space to assign randomly chosen identifiers to nodes as well as keys to specific entities. The latter can be virtually anything: files, processes, etc. The number m of bits is usually 128 or 160, depending on which hash function is used. An entity with key k falls under the jurisdiction of the node with the smallest identifier $id \geq k$. This node is referred to as the **successor** of k and denoted as $succ(k)$. To keep our notation simple and consistent, in the following, we refer to a node with identifier p as node p.

The main issue in DHT-based systems is to efficiently resolve a key k to the address of $succ(k)$. A naive approach is to let each node p keep track of the successor $succ(p+1)$. In that case, whenever a node p receives a request to resolve key k, it will simply forward the request to its successor, unless $pred(p) < k \leq p$, in which case node p should return its own address to the process that initiated the resolution of key k. A lookup request would, on average, need to travel half of the ring. Obviously, this approach is not scalable. Keeping track of the predecessor and forwarding a request in that direction will cut the expected number of hops by only 50%, which is not by far good enough.

Instead of this linear approach toward key lookup, each Chord node maintains a **finger table** containing $s \leq m$ entries. If FT_p denotes the finger table of node p, then

$$FT_p[i] = succ(p + 2^{i-1})$$

Put in other words, the ith entry points to the first node succeeding p by at least 2^{i-1} units. Note that these references are actually shortcuts to existing nodes in the identifier space, where the short-cutted distance from node p increases exponentially as the index in the finger table increases. To look up a key k, node p will then immediately forward the request to node q with index j in p's finger table where:

$$q = FT_p[j] \leq k < FT_p[j+1]$$

or $q = FT_p[1]$ when $p < k < FT_p[1]$. (For clarity, we ignore modulo arithmetic.) Note that when the finger-table size s is equal to 1, a Chord lookup corresponds to naively traversing the ring linearly, as we just discussed.

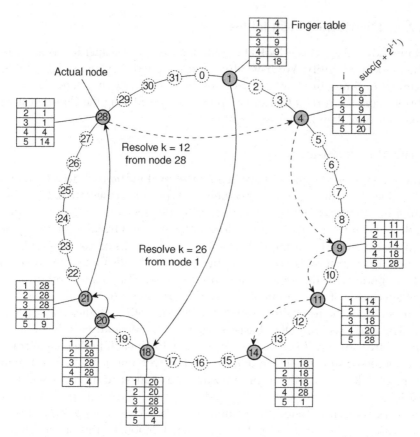

Figure 6.2: Resolving key 26 from node 1 and key 12 from node 28 in a Chord system.

To illustrate this lookup, consider resolving $k = 26$ from node 1 as shown in Figure 6.2. First, node 1 will look up $k = 26$ in its finger table to discover that this value is larger than $FT_1[5]$, meaning that the request will be forwarded to node $18 = FT_1[5]$. Node 18, in turn, will select node 20, as $FT_{18}[2] \leq k < FT_{18}[3]$. Finally, the request is forwarded from node 20 to node 21 and from there to node 28, which is responsible for $k = 26$. At that point, the address of node 28 is returned to node 1 and the key has been resolved. For similar reasons, when node 28 is requested to resolve the key $k = 12$, a request will be routed as shown by the dashed line in Figure 6.2.

It should come as no surprise that a lookup will generally require $\mathcal{O}(\log(N))$ steps, with N being the number of nodes in the system. The result of a simple experiment by which we look up $k = p - 1$ starting at node p, yet initially ignore p's predecessor, is shown in Figure 6.3. Note that, by ignoring p's predecessor at the first lookup step, we need to effectively go to a node at distance roughly 2^{i-1} for decreasing values of i.

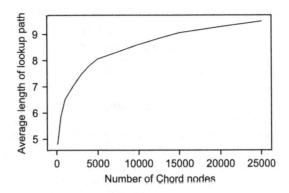

Figure 6.3: The length of a lookup path as function of the size of a Chord ring.

In large distributed systems, the collection of participating nodes can be expected to change all the time. Not only will nodes join and leave voluntarily, we also need to consider the case of nodes failing (and thus effectively leaving the system), to later recover again (at which point they rejoin).

Joining a DHT-based system such as Chord is relatively simple. Suppose node p wants to join. It simply contacts an arbitrary node in the existing system and requests a lookup for $succ(p + 1)$. Once this node has been identified, p can insert itself into the ring. Likewise, leaving can be just as simple. Note that nodes also keep track of their predecessor.

Obviously, the complexity comes from keeping the finger tables up-to-date. Most important is that for every node q, $FT_q[1]$ is correct as this entry refers to the next node in the ring, that is, the successor of $q + 1$. To achieve this goal, each node q regularly runs a simple procedure that contacts $succ(q + 1)$ and requests to return $pred(succ(q + 1))$. If $q = pred(succ(q + 1))$ then q knows its information is consistent with that of its successor. Otherwise, if q's successor has updated its predecessor, then apparently a new node p had entered the system, with $q < p \leq succ(q + 1)$, so that q will adjust $FT_q[1]$ to p. At that point, it will also check whether p has recorded q as its predecessor. If not, another adjustment of $FT_q[1]$ is needed.

Similarly, to update a finger table, node q simply needs to find the successor for $k = q + 2^{i-1}$ for each entry i. Again, this can be done by issuing a request to resolve $succ(k)$. In Chord, such requests are issued regularly using a background process.

Likewise, each node q will regularly check whether its predecessor is alive. If the predecessor has failed, the only thing that q can do is record the fact by setting $pred(q)$ to "unknown." On the other hand, when node q is updating its link to the next known node in the ring, and finds that the predecessor of $succ(q + 1)$ has been set to "unknown," it will simply notify $succ(q + 1)$ that it suspects it to be the predecessor. By and large, these simple procedures ensure that a Chord system is generally consistent, only perhaps except for a few nodes. The details can be found in [Stoica et al., 2003].

Note 6.1 (Advanced: Chord in Python)

Coding Chord in Python is relatively simple. Again, omitting many of the nonessential coding details, the core of the behavior of a Chord node can be described as shown in Figure 6.4. The function finger(i) with succNode(i) computes $succ(i)$ for the given node. All nodes known to a specific Chord node are collected in a local set nodeSet, which is sorted by node identifier. The node first looks up its own position in this set, and that of its right-hand neighbor. The operation inbetween(k,l,u) computes if $k \in [l, u)$, taking modulo arithmetic into account. Computing inbetween(k,l+1,u+1) is therefore the same as testing whether $k \in (l, u]$. We thus see that finger(i) returns the largest existing node identifier, less or equal to i.

```
1   class ChordNode:
2
3     def __succNode(self, key):
4       if (key <= self.nodeSet[0] or
5           key > self.nodeSet[len(self.nodeSet)-1]): # key is in segment for which
6         return self.nodeSet[0]                       # this node is responsible
7       for i in range(1,len(self.nodeSet)):
8         if (key <= self.nodeSet[i]):                 # key is in segment for which
9           return self.nodeSet[i]                     # node (i+1) may be responsible
10
11    def __finger(self, i):
12      return self.__succNode((self.nodeID + pow(2,i-1)) % self.MAXPROC) # succ(p+2^(i-1))
13
14    def __recomputeFingerTable(self):
15      self.FT[0]  = self.nodeSet[(self.nodeInd - 1)%len(self.nodeSet)] # Predecessor
16      self.FT[1:] = [self.__finger(i) for i in range(1,self.nBits+1)]  # Successors
17      self.FT.append(self.nodeID)                                      # This node
18
19    def __localSuccNode(self, key):
20      if self.__inbetween(key, self.FT[0]+1, self.nodeID+1):   # key in (pred,self]
21        return self.nodeID                                     # this node is responsible
22      elif self.__inbetween(key, self.nodeID+1, self.FT[1]):   # key in (self,FT[1]]
23        return self.FT[1]                                      # successor responsible
24      for i in range(1, self.nBits+2):                         # go through rest of FT
25        if self.__inbetween(key, self.FT[i], self.FT[(i+1)]):  # key in [FT[i],FT[i+1])
26          return self.FT[i]                                    # FT[i] is responsible
```

Figure 6.4: The essence of a Chord node expressed in Python.

Every time a node learns about a new node in the system (or discovers that one has left), it simply adjusts the local nodeSet and recomputes its finger table by calling recomputeFingerTable. The finger table itself is implemented as a local table FT, with FT[0] pointing to the node's predecessor and FT[nBits+1] to the node itself, where nBits is the number of bits used for node identifiers and keys.

The core of what a node does during a lookup is encoded in localSuccNode(k). When handed a key k, it will either return itself, its immediate successor FT[1], or go through the finger table to search the entry satisfying FT[i] $\leq k <$ FT[i+1]. The code does not show what is done with the returned value (which is a node identifier), but typically in an *iterative scheme*, the referenced node will be contacted to continue looking up k, unless the node had returned itself as the one being responsible for k. When deploying a *recursive scheme*, the node itself contacts the referenced node.

Exploiting network proximity

One of the potential problems with systems such as Chord is that requests may be routed erratically across the Internet. For example, assume that node 1 in Figure 6.2 is placed in Amsterdam, The Netherlands; node 18 in San Diego, California; node 20 in Amsterdam again; and node 21 in San Diego. The result of resolving key 26 will then incur three wide-area message transfers, which arguably could have been reduced to at most one. To minimize these pathological cases, designing a DHT-based system requires taking the underlying network into account.

Castro et al. [2002a] distinguish three different ways for making a DHT-based system aware of the underlying network. In the case of **topology-based assignment of node identifiers** the idea is to assign identifiers such that two nearby nodes will have identifiers that are also close to each other. It is not difficult to imagine that this approach may impose severe problems in the case of relatively simple systems such as Chord. In the case where node identifiers are sampled from a one-dimensional space, mapping a logical ring to the Internet is far from trivial. Moreover, such a mapping can easily expose correlated failures: nodes on the same enterprise network will have identifiers from a relatively small interval. When that network becomes unreachable, we suddenly have a gap in the otherwise uniform distribution of identifiers.

With **proximity routing**, nodes maintain a list of alternatives to forward a request to. For example, instead of having only a single successor, each node in Chord could equally well keep track of r successors. In fact, this redundancy can be applied for every entry in a finger table. For node p, $FT_p[i]$ normally points to the first node in the range $[p + 2^{i-1}, p + 2^i - 1]$. Whenever it needs to look up a key k, it tries to prevent "overshooting" by passing the request to a node q with $k < q$ without knowing for sure if there is a node q' with $k \leq q' < q$. For this reason, p passes k to the node known to p with the *largest* identifier smaller or equal to k.

However, there is no reason why p cannot keep track of r nodes in range $[p + 2^{i-1}, p + 2^i - 1]$: each node q in this range can be used to route a lookup request for a key k as long as $q \leq k$. In that case, when choosing to forward a lookup request, a node can pick one of the r successors that is closest to itself while making sure not to "overshoot." An additional advantage of having multiple successors for every table entry is that node failures need not immediately lead to failures of lookups, as multiple routes can be explored.

Finally, in **proximity neighbor selection** the idea is to optimize routing tables such that the nearest node is selected as neighbor. This selection works only when there are more nodes to choose from. In Chord, this is normally not the case. However, in other protocols such as Pastry [Rowstron and Druschel, 2001], when a node joins, it receives information about the current overlay from multiple other nodes. This information is used by the new node to construct a routing table. Obviously, when there are alternative nodes to choose from, proximity neighbor selection will allow the joining node to choose the best one.

Note that it may not be that easy to draw a line between proximity routing and proximity neighbor selection. In fact, when Chord is modified to include r successors for each finger table entry, proximity neighbor selection resorts to identifying the closest r neighbors, which comes very close to proximity routing, as we just explained [Dabek et al., 2004b].

6.2.4 Hierarchical approaches

We now discuss a general approach to a hierarchical location scheme, including a number of optimizations. The approach we present is based on the Globe location service [van Steen et al., 1998]. A detailed description can be found in [Ballintijn, 2003]. This is a general-purpose location service that is representative of many hierarchical location services proposed for what are called Personal Communication Systems, of which a general overview can be found in Pitoura and Samaras [2001].

In a hierarchical scheme, a network is divided into a collection of **domains**. There is a single top-level domain that spans the entire network. Each domain can be subdivided into multiple, smaller subdomains. A lowest-level domain, called a **leaf domain**, typically corresponds to a local-area network in a computer network or a cell in a mobile telephone network. The general assumption is that within a smaller domain, the average time it takes to transfer a message from one node to another is less than in a large domain.

Each domain D has an associated directory node dir(D) that keeps track of the entities in that domain. This leads to a tree of directory nodes. The directory node of the top-level domain, called the **root (directory) node**, knows about all entities. This general organization of a network into domains and directory nodes is illustrated in Figure 6.5

To keep track of the whereabouts of an entity, each entity currently located in a domain D is represented by a **location record** in the directory node dir(D). A location record for entity E in the directory node N for a leaf domain D contains the entity's current address in that domain. In contrast,

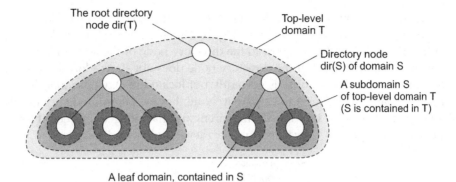

Figure 6.5: Hierarchical organization of a location service into domains, each having an associated directory node.

the directory node N′ for the next higher-level domain D′ that contains D, will have a location record for E containing only a pointer to N. Likewise, the parent node of N′ will store a location record for E containing only a pointer to N′. Consequently, the root node will have a location record for each entity, where each location record stores a pointer to the directory node of the next lower-level subdomain where that record's associated entity is currently located.

An entity may have multiple addresses, for example if it is replicated. If an entity has an address in leaf domain D_1 and D_2 respectively, then the directory node of the smallest domain containing both D_1 and D_2, will have two pointers, one for each subdomain containing an address. This leads to the general organization of the tree as shown in Figure 6.6.

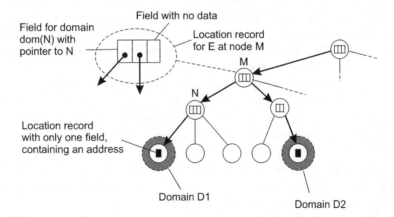

Figure 6.6: An example of storing information of an entity having two addresses in different leaf domains.

Let us now consider how a lookup operation proceeds in such a hierarchical location service. As is shown in Figure 6.7, client,nt wishing to locate an entity E, issues a lookup request to the directory node of the leaf domain D in which the client resides. If the directory node does not store a location record for the entity, then the entity is currently not located in D. Consequently, the node forwards the request to its parent. Note that the parent node represents a larger domain than its child. If the parent also has no location record for E, the lookup request is forwarded to a next level higher, and so on.

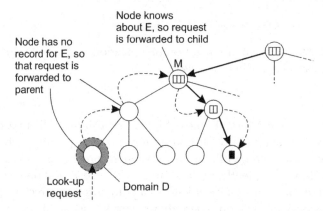

Figure 6.7: Looking up a location in a hierarchically organized location service.

As soon as the request reaches a directory node M that stores a location record for entity E, we know that E is somewhere in the domain $dom(M)$ represented by node M. In Figure 6.7, M is shown to store a location record containing a pointer to one of its subdomains. The lookup request is then forwarded to the directory node of that subdomain, which in turn forwards it further down the tree, until the request finally reaches a leaf node. The location record stored in the leaf node will contain the address of E in that leaf domain. This address can then be returned to the client that initially requested the lookup to take place.

An important observation regarding hierarchical location services is that the lookup operation exploits locality. In principle, the entity is searched in a gradually increasing ring centered around the requesting client. The search area is expanded each time the lookup request is forwarded to a next higher-level directory node. In the worst case, the search continues until the request reaches the root node. Because the root node has a location record for each entity, the request can then simply be forwarded along a downward path of pointers to one of the leaf nodes.

Update operations exploit locality similarly, as shown in Figure 6.8. Consider an entity E that has created a replica in a leaf domain D for which it needs to insert its address. The insertion is initiated at the leaf node $dir(D)$

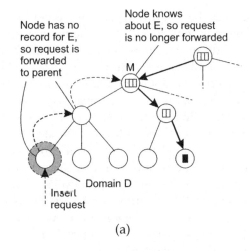

(a)

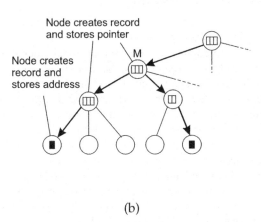

(b)

Figure 6.8: (a) An insert request is forwarded to the first node that knows about entity E. (b) A chain of forwarding pointers to the leaf node is created.

of D which immediately forwards the insert request to its parent. The parent will forward the insert request as well, until it reaches a directory node M that already stores a location record for E.

Node M will then store a pointer in the location record for E, referring to the child node from where the insert request was forwarded. At that point, the child node creates a location record for E, containing a pointer to the next lower-level node from where the request came. This process continues until we reach the leaf node from which the insert was initiated. The leaf node, finally, creates a record with the entity's address in the associated leaf domain.

Inserting an address as just described leads to installing the chain of pointers in a top-down fashion, starting at the lowest-level directory node that has a location record for entity E. An alternative is to create a location record before passing the insert request to the parent node. In other words, the chain of pointers is constructed from the bottom up. The advantage of the latter is that an address becomes available for lookups as soon as possible. Consequently, if a parent node is temporarily unreachable, the address can still be looked up within the domain represented by the current node.

A delete operation is analogous to an insert operation. When an address for an entity E in a leaf domain D needs to be removed, the directory node $dir(D)$ is requested to remove that address from its location record for E. If that location record becomes empty, that is, it contains no other addresses for E in D, the record can be removed. In that case, the parent node of $dir(D)$ wants to remove its pointer to $dir(D)$. If the location record for E at the parent now also becomes empty, that record should be removed as well and the next higher-level directory node should be informed. Again, this process continues until a pointer is removed from a location record that remains nonempty afterward or until the root is reached.

Note 6.2 (Advanced: Scalability issues)

One question that immediately comes to mind is whether the hierarchical approach just described can actually scale. A seemingly obvious design flaw, is that the root node needs to keep track of *all* identifiers. However, it is important to make a distinction between a logical design and its physical implementation. Let us make this distinction here and see how we can actually come to a highly scalable implementation of a hierarchical location service.

To this end, we assume that each entity is assigned a unique identifier uniform at random from a large space of m-bit identifiers, just as in Chord. Furthermore, let us assume that there are a total of N physical hosts $\{H_1, H_2, \ldots, H_N\}$ that can accommodate the lookup service, spread across the Internet. Each host is capable of running one or more location servers. Typically, two servers running on the same host will represent two nodes at different levels of the logical tree. Let $D_k(A)$ denote the domain at level k that contains address A, with $k = 0$ denoting the root domain. Likewise, let $LS_k(E, A)$ denote the unique location server in $D_k(A)$ responsible for keeping track of the whereabouts of the entity E.

We can now make a distinction between a logical root and its implementation. Let $\mathbf{D}_k = \{D_{k,1}, D_{k,2}, \ldots, D_{k,N_k}\}$ denote the N_k domains at level k, with, obviously, $N_0 = |\mathbf{D}_0| = 1$. For each level k, the set of hosts is partitioned into N_k subsets, with each host running a location server representing exactly one of the domains $D_{k,i}$ from $\mathbf{D}_k$. This principle is shown in Figure 6.9.

In this example, we consider a simple tree with four levels and nine hosts. There are two level-1 domains, four level-2 domains, and eight leaf domains. We also show a tree for one specific entity E: any contact address associated with E will be stored in one of the eight level-3 location servers, depending, of course, on the domain to which that address belongs. The root location server for E is running on host H_3. Note that this host also runs a leaf-level location server for E.

As explained by van Steen and Ballintijn [2002], by judiciously choosing which host should run a location server for E, we can combine the principle of local operations (which is good for geographical scalability) and full distribution of higher level servers (which is good for size scalability).

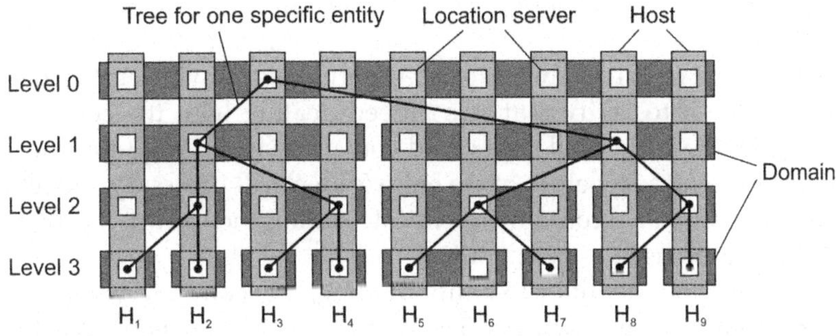

Figure 6.9: The principle of distributing logical location servers over physical hosts.

6.2.5 Secure flat naming

Flat names do not contain any information on how to resolve a name to the entity it is referring to. As a consequence, one needs to, in principle, entirely rely on the name-resolution process to eventually access the associated entity. If the name-resolution process cannot be trusted, there is no reason to believe that any response can be trusted as well. There are then, essentially, two approaches to follow: (1) secure the name-resolution process, or (2) secure the identifier-to-entity association. Let us first take a look at this last option.

Securing the identifier-to-entity association is what happens in a so-called **self-certifying name**. As a general principle, we can compute an identifier from an entity by simply using a hash function:

$$id(entity) = hash(data\ associated\ with\ the\ entity).$$

The crux is, of course, which associated data is used. In the case of nonmodifiable entities, such as read-only files, a client can simply check that it received the correct file by separately computing the hash over the file and comparing it to the identifier it used for looking up that file. Of course, to make this work, the client would need to know which hash function to use along with perhaps other information.

In practice, entities are modified, such as when dealing with mobile objects. In that case, the entity is the current address of the object. What we need to know, for sure, is that the returned address is indeed the one that can be used for accessing the object. Likewise, when dealing with modifiable files, the returned information should allow the client to check that it is indeed accessing the correct file. Omitting various details, a scheme proposed in [Dannewitz et al., 2010] is to have

$$id(entity) = public\ key(entity).$$

A client will be returned the associated entity, along with additional data that will allow it to verify that it is indeed dealing with the correct entity. For example, the additional data could contain a signed digest of the entity, effectively forming a signature of the entity's owner. If necessary, the returned information could also contain a certificate stating the validity of the public key that has been used as an identifier.

By securing the identifier-to-entity binding, it becomes less important to trust the name-resolution process. The worse that can now happen is that the process returns false or no entities. However, whatever it returns, the client will be able to verify its correctness. Trust is now degraded to providing a decent service.

Securing the name-resolution process is more involved, yet equally important, if only to guarantee proper reliability (we will return to the relationship between security and reliability in Chapter 8). For lookup services such as those for mobile IP or hierarchical location services, we need to ensure that returned (intermediate) answers make sense. We will discuss this in the next section when zooming into Secure DNS. As mentioned before, securing DHT-based systems has proved to be rather problematic. There are several problems to deal with, yet the most important ones deal with addressing **Sybil** and **eclipse attacks**, as also discussed in Section 9.4.2. The bottom line is that robustness for DHT-based systems comes largely from ensuring that a node identifier is genuine: it belongs to exactly one owner, and this fact can be verified. In practice, this means that a centralized authority should be used for handing out identifiers [Urdaneta et al., 2011].

6.3   Structured naming

Flat names are good for machines, but are generally not very convenient for humans to use. As an alternative, naming systems generally support structured names that are composed from simple, human-readable names. Not only file naming, but also host naming on the Internet, follows this approach. In this section, we concentrate on structured names and the way that these names are resolved to addresses.

6.3.1   Name spaces

Names are commonly organized into what is called a **name space**. Name spaces for structured names can be represented as a labeled, directed graph with two types of nodes. A **leaf node** represents a named entity and has the property that it has no outgoing edges. A leaf node generally stores information on the entity it is representing–for example, its address–so that a client can access it. Alternatively, it can store the state of that entity, such as in the case of file systems in which a leaf node actually contains the complete file it is representing. We return to the contents of nodes below.

In contrast to a leaf node, a **directory node** has a number of outgoing edges, each labeled with a name, as shown in Figure 6.10 Each node in a naming graph is considered as yet another entity in a distributed system, and, in particular, has an associated identifier. A directory node stores a table in which an outgoing edge is represented as a pair *(node identifier, edge label)*. Such a table is called a **directory table**.

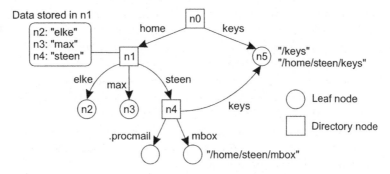

Figure 6.10: A general naming graph with a single root node.

The naming graph shown in Figure 6.10 has one node, namely n0, which has only outgoing and no incoming edges. Such a node is called the **root (node)** of the naming graph. Although it is possible for a naming graph to have several root nodes, for simplicity, many naming systems have only one. Each path in a naming graph can be referred to by the sequence of labels corresponding to the edges in that path, such as $N:[label_1, label_2, ..., label_n]$, where N refers to the first node in the path. Such a sequence is called a **path name**. If the first node in a path name is the root of the naming graph, it is called an **absolute path name**. Otherwise, it is called a **relative path name**.

It is important to realize that names are always organized in a name space. As a consequence, a name is always defined relative only to a directory node. In this sense, the term "absolute name" is somewhat misleading. Likewise, the difference between global and local names can often be confusing. A **global name** is a name that denotes the same entity, no matter where that name is used in a system. In other words, a global name is always interpreted regarding the same directory node. In contrast, a **local name** is a name whose interpretation depends on where that name is being used. Put differently, a local name is essentially a relative name whose directory in which it is contained is (implicitly) known.

This description of a naming graph comes close to what is implemented in many file systems. However, instead of writing the sequence of edge labels to represent a path name, path names in file systems are generally represented as a single string in which the labels are separated by a special separator character, such as a slash ("/"). This character is also used to indicate whether a path name is absolute. For example, in Figure 6.10 instead of using n0:[home, steen, mbox], that is, the actual path name, it is common practice to use its string representation "/home/steen/mbox." Note also that when there are several paths that lead to the same node, that node can be represented by different path names. For example, node n5 in Figure 6.10 can be referred to by "/home/steen/keys" as well as "/keys." The string representation of path names can be equally well applied to naming graphs other than those used for only file systems. In Plan 9 [Pike et al., 1995], all resources, such as processes, hosts, I/O devices, and network interfaces, are named in the same fashion as traditional files. This approach is analogous to implementing a single naming graph for all resources in a distributed system.

There are many ways to organize a name space. As we mentioned, most name spaces have only a single root node. Often, a name space is also strictly hierarchical, in the sense that the naming graph is organized as a tree. This means that each node, except the root, has exactly one incoming edge; the root has no incoming edges. As a consequence, each node also has exactly one associated (absolute) path name.

The naming graph shown in Figure 6.10 is an example of **directed acyclic graph**. In such an organization, a node can have more than one incoming edge, but the graph is not permitted to have a cycle. There are also name spaces that do not have this restriction.

Note 6.3 (More information: Implementing the Unix naming graph)

To make matters more concrete, consider the way that files in a traditional Unix file system are named. In a naming graph for Unix a directory node represents a file directory, whereas a leaf node represents a file. There is a single root directory, represented in the naming graph by the root node. The implementation of the naming graph is an integral part of the complete implementation of the file system. That implementation consists of a contiguous series of blocks from a logical disk, generally divided into a boot block, a superblock, a series of index nodes (called inodes), and file data blocks. See also [Silberschatz et al., 2019] or [Tanenbaum and Bos, 2022]. This organization is shown in Figure 6.11.

The boot block is a special block of data and instructions that are automatically loaded into main memory when the system is booted. The boot block is used to load the operating system into main memory.

The superblock contains information on the entire file system, such as its size, which blocks on disk are not yet allocated, which inodes are not yet used, and so on. Inodes are referred to by an index number, starting at number zero, which is reserved for the inode representing the root directory.

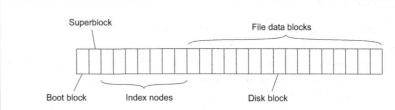

Figure 6.11: The general organization of the Unix file system implementation on a logical disk of contiguous disk blocks.

Each inode contains information on where the data of its associated file can be found on disk. In addition, an inode contains information on its owner, time of creation and last modification, protection, and the like. Consequently, when given the index number of an inode, it is possible to access its associated file. Each directory is implemented as a file as well. This is also the case for the root directory, which contains a mapping between file names and index numbers of inodes. It is thus seen that the index number of an inode corresponds to a node identifier in the naming graph.

6.3.2 Name resolution

Name spaces offer a convenient mechanism for storing and retrieving information about entities through names. More generally, given a path name, it should be possible to look up any information stored in the node referred to by that name. The process of looking up a name is called **name resolution**.

To explain how name resolution works, let us consider a path name such as $N:[label_1, label_2, ..., label_n]$. Resolution of this name starts at node N of the naming graph, where the name $label_1$ is looked up in the directory table, and which returns the identifier of the node to which $label_1$ refers. Resolution then continues at the identified node by looking up the name $label_2$ in its directory table, and so on. Assuming that the named path actually exists, resolution stops at the last node referred to by $label_n$, by returning that node's content.

Note 6.4 (More information: The Unix naming graph again)
A name lookup returns the identifier of a node, from where the name resolution process continues. In particular, it is necessary to access the directory table of the identified node. Consider again a naming graph for a Unix file system. As mentioned, a node identifier is implemented as the index number of an inode. Accessing a directory table means that first the inode has to be read to find out where the actual data are stored on disk, and then subsequently to read the data blocks containing the directory table.

Closure mechanism

Name resolution can take place only if we know how and where to start. In our example, the starting node was given, and we assumed we had access to its directory table. Knowing how and where to start name resolution is generally referred to as a **closure mechanism**. Essentially, a closure mechanism deals with selecting the initial node in a name space, from which name resolution is to start [Radia, 1989]. What makes closure mechanisms sometimes hard to understand is that they are necessarily partly implicit and may be very different when comparing them to each other.

Consider, for example, the string "00312059837784". Many people will not know what to do with these numbers, unless they are told that the sequence is a telephone number. That information is enough to start the resolution process, in particular, by entering the number at a device for making phone calls. The telephone system subsequently does the rest.

As another example, consider the use of global and local names in distributed systems. A typical example of a local name is an environment variable. For example, in Unix systems, the variable named HOME is used to refer to the home directory of a user. Each user has their own copy of this variable, which is initialized to the global, systemwide name corresponding to the user's home directory. The closure mechanism associated with environment variables ensure that the name of the variable is properly resolved by looking it up in a user-specific table.

Note 6.5 (More information: The Unix naming graph and its closure mechanism)
Name resolution in the naming graph for a Unix file system makes use of the fact that the inode of the root directory is the first inode in the logical disk representing the file system. Its actual byte offset is calculated from the values in other fields of the superblock, together with hard-coded information in the operating system itself on the internal organization of the superblock.

To make this point clear, consider the string representation of a file name, such as /home/steen/mbox. To resolve this name, it is necessary to already have access to the directory table of the root node of the appropriate naming graph. Being a root node, the node itself cannot have been looked up unless it is implemented as a different node in another naming graph, say G. But in that case, it would have been necessary to already have access to the root node of G. Consequently, resolving a file name requires that some mechanism has already been implemented by which the resolution process can start.

In this respect, observe how the closure mechanism works in the case of containers: the chroot command is used to make applications within a specific container see a different root than those in another container. In other words, each container offers its own naming graph to the contained applications, whereas the operating system hosting the containers provides a closure to properly start name resolution independent of each other.

Linking and mounting

Strongly related to name resolution is the use of **aliases**. An alias is another name for the same entity. An environment variable is an example of an alias. In terms of naming graphs, there are basically two different ways to implement an alias. The first approach is to simply allow multiple absolute paths names to refer to the same node in a naming graph. This approach is illustrated in Figure 6.10, in which the node n5 can be referred to by two different path names. In Unix terminology, both path names /keys and /home/steen/keys in Figure 6.12 are called **hard links** to node n5.

The second approach is to represent an entity by a leaf node, say N, but instead of storing the address or state of that entity, the node stores an absolute path name. When first resolving an absolute path name that leads to N, name resolution will return the path name stored in N, at which point it can continue with resolving that new path name. This principle corresponds to the use of **symbolic links** in Unix file systems, and is illustrated in Figure 6.12 In this example, the path name /home/steen/keys, which refers to a node containing the absolute path name /keys, is a symbolic link to node n5.

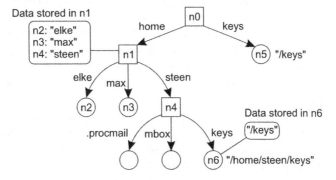

Figure 6.12: The concept of a symbolic link explained in a naming graph.

Name resolution as described so far takes place completely within a single name space. However, name resolution can also be used to merge different name spaces transparently. Let us first consider a **mounted file system**. In terms of our naming model, a mounted file system corresponds to letting a directory node store the identifier of a directory node from a *different* name space, which we refer to as a **foreign name space**. The directory node storing the node identifier is called a **mount point**. Accordingly, the directory node in the foreign name space is called a **mounting point**. Normally, the mounting point is the root of a name space. During name resolution, the mounting point is looked up and resolution proceeds by accessing its directory table.

The principle of mounting can be generalized to other name spaces as well. In particular, what is needed is a directory node that acts as a mount point and stores all the necessary information for identifying and accessing the mounting point in the foreign name space. This approach is followed in many distributed file systems.

Consider a collection of name spaces that is distributed across different machines. In particular, each name space is implemented by a different server, each possibly running on a separate machine. Consequently, if we want to mount a foreign name space NS_2 into a name space NS_1, it may be necessary to communicate over a network with the server of NS_2, as that server may be running on a different machine than the server for NS_1. To mount a foreign name space in a distributed system requires at least the following information:

1. The name of an access protocol.

2. The name of the server.

3. The name of the mounting point in the foreign name space.

Note that each of these names needs to be resolved. The name of an access protocol needs to be resolved to the implementation of a protocol by which communication with the server of the foreign name space can take place. The name of the server needs to be resolved to an address where that server can be reached. As the last part in name resolution, the name of the mounting point needs to be resolved to a node identifier in the foreign name space.

In nondistributed systems, none of the three points may actually be needed. For example, in Unix there is no access protocol and no server. Also, the name of the mounting point is not necessary, as it is simply the root directory of the foreign name space.

The name of the mounting point is to be resolved by the server of the foreign name space. However, we also need name spaces and implementations for the access protocol and the server name. One possibility is to represent the three names listed above as a URL.

To make matters concrete, consider a situation in which a user with a laptop computer wants to access files that are stored on a remote file server. The client machine and the file server are both configured with the **Network File System (NFS)**. In particular, to allow NFS to work across the Internet, a client can specify exactly which file it wants to access by means of an NFS URL, for example, nfs: //flits.cs.vu.nl/home/steen. This URL names a file (which happens to be a directory) called /home/steen on an NFS file server flits.cs.vu.nl, which can be accessed by a client through the NFS protocol [Haynes, 2015; Noveck and Lever, 2020].

The name nfs is a well-known name, in the sense that worldwide agreement exists on how to interpret that name. Given that we are dealing with a URL, the name nfs will be resolved to an implementation of the NFS protocol. The server name is resolved to its address using DNS, which is discussed in a later section. As we said, /home/steen is resolved by the server of the foreign name space.

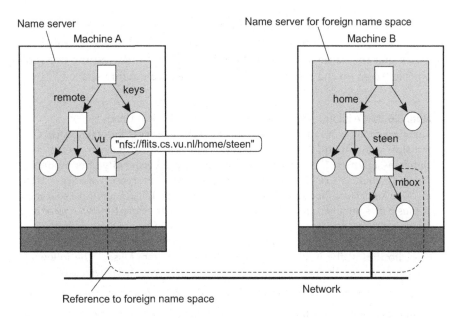

Figure 6.13: Mounting remote name spaces through a specific protocol.

The organization of a file system on the client machine is partly shown in Figure 6.13 The root directory has a number of user-defined entries, including a subdirectory called /remote. This subdirectory is intended to include mount points for foreign name spaces, such as the user's home directory at VU University. To this end, a directory node named /remote/vu is used to store the URL nfs://flits.cs.vu.nl/home/steen.

Now consider the name /remote/vu/mbox. This name is resolved by starting in the root directory on the client's machine and continues until the node /remote/vu is reached. The process of name resolution then continues by returning the URL nfs://flits.cs.vu.nl/home/steen, in turn leading the client machine to contact the file server flits.cs.vu.nl through the NFS protocol, and to subsequently access directory /home/steen. Name resolution can then be continued by reading the file named mbox in that directory, after which the resolution process stops.

Distributed systems that allow mounting a remote file system as just described allow a client machine to, for example, execute the following commands (assume the client machine is named horton):

```
horton$ cd /remote/vu
horton$ ls -l
```

which subsequently lists the files in the directory /home/steen on the remote file server. The beauty of all this is that the user is spared the details of the actual access to the remote server. Ideally, only some loss in performance is noticed compared to accessing locally available files. In effect, to the client it appears that the name space rooted on the local machine, and the one rooted at /home/steen on the remote machine, form a single name space.

Note 6.6 (More information: Mounting across a network in Unix)

There are many ways in which mounting across a network can take place. One practical solution and adopted by many small-scale distributed systems, is to simply assign fixed IP addresses to machines and subsequently offer mounting points to clients. Consider the following example. Suppose we have a Unix machine named coltrane using the private address 192.168.2.3, storing a collection of music files under the local directory /audio. This directory can be *exported* as a mounting point, and as a consequence can be *imported* by another machine.

Let quandar be such a machine, and suppose it wants to mount the collection of audio files at the local mount point /home/maarten/Music. The following command will do the job (assuming the correct privileges have been set):

```
quandar$ mount -t nfs 192.168.2.3:/audio /home/maarten/Music
```

From that moment on, all files available on coltrane in its directory /audio can be accessed by quandar in the directory /home/maarten/Music. The beauty of this scheme is that once mounted, there is no need to think of remote access anymore (until something fails, of course).

6.3.3   The implementation of a name space

A name space forms the heart of a naming service, that is, a service that allows users and processes to add, remove, and look up names. A naming service is implemented by name servers. If a distributed system is restricted to a local-area network, it is often feasible to implement a naming service by only a single name server. However, in large-scale distributed systems with many entities, possibly spread across a large geographical area, it is necessary to distribute the implementation of a name space over multiple name servers.

Name space distribution

Name spaces for a large-scale, possibly worldwide distributed system, are usually organized hierarchically. As before, assume such a name space has only a single root node. To effectively implement such a name space, it is convenient to partition it into logical layers. Cheriton and Mann [1989] distinguish the following three layers.

The **global layer** is formed by highest-level nodes, that is, the root node and other directory nodes logically close to the root, namely its children. Nodes in the global layer are often characterized by their stability, in the sense that directory tables are rarely changed. Such nodes may represent organizations, or groups of organizations, for which names are stored in the name space.

The **administrational layer** is formed by directory nodes that, together, are managed within a single organization. A characteristic feature of the directory nodes in the administrational layer is that they represent groups of entities that belong to the same organization or administrational unit. For example, there may be a directory node for each department in an organization, or a directory node from which all hosts can be found. Another directory node may be used as the starting point for naming all users, and so forth. The nodes in the administrational layer are relatively stable, although changes generally occur more frequently than to nodes in the global layer.

Finally, the **managerial layer** consists of nodes that may typically change regularly. For example, nodes representing hosts in the local network belong to this layer. For the same reason, the layer includes nodes representing shared files, such as those for libraries or binaries. Another important class of nodes includes those that represent user-defined directories and files. In contrast to the global and administrational layer, the nodes in the managerial layer are maintained not only by system administrators, but also by individual end users of a distributed system.

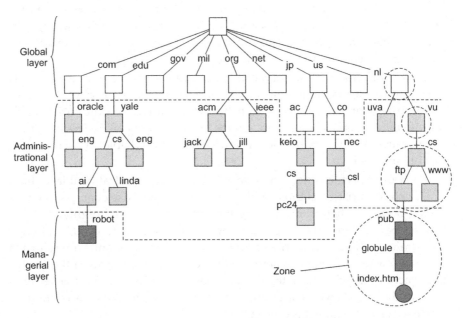

Figure 6.14: An example partitioning of the DNS name space, including Internet-accessible files, into three layers.

To make matters more concrete, Figure 6.14 shows an example of the partitioning of part of the DNS name space, including the names of files within an organization that can be accessed through the Internet, for example, Web pages and transferable files. The name space is divided into nonoverlapping parts, called **zones** in DNS [Mockapetris, 1987a;b]. A zone is a part of the name space that is implemented by a separate name server. Some of these zones are illustrated in Figure 6.14.

If we take a look at availability and performance, name servers in each layer have to meet different requirements. High availability is especially critical for name servers in the global layer. If a name server fails, a large part of the name space will be unreachable because name resolution cannot proceed beyond the failing server.

Performance is somewhat subtle. Due to the low rate of change of nodes in the global layer, the results of lookup operations generally remain valid for a long time. Consequently, those results can be effectively cached (i.e., stored locally) by the clients. The next time the same lookup operation is performed, the results can be retrieved from the client's cache instead of letting the name server return the results. As a result, name servers in the global layer do not have to respond quickly to a single lookup request. On the other hand, throughput may be important, especially in large-scale systems with millions of users.

The availability and performance requirements for name servers in the global layer can be met by replicating servers, with client-side caching. Updates in this layer generally do not have to come into effect immediately, making it much easier to keep replicas consistent.

Availability for a name server in the administrational layer is primarily important for clients in the same organization as the name server. If the name server fails, many resources within the organization become unreachable because they cannot be looked up. On the other hand, it may be less important that resources in an organization are temporarily unreachable for users outside that organization.

Regarding performance, name servers in the administrational layer have similar characteristics as those in the global layer. Because changes to nodes do not occur all that often, caching lookup results can be highly effective, making performance less critical. However, in contrast to the global layer, the administrational layer should take care that lookup results are returned within a few milliseconds, either directly from the server or from the client's local cache. Likewise, updates should generally be processed quicker than those of the global layer. For example, it is unacceptable that an account for a new user takes hours to become effective.

These requirements can often be met by using relatively powerful machines to run name servers. In addition, client-side caching should be applied, combined with replication, for increased overall availability.

Availability requirements for name servers at the managerial level are generally less demanding. In particular, it often suffices to use a single machine to run name servers at the risk of temporary unavailability. However, performance is crucial: operations must take place immediately. Because updates occur regularly, client-side caching is often less effective.

Issue	Global	Administrational	Managerial
Geographical scale	Worldwide	Organization	Department
Number of nodes	Few	Many	Vast numbers
Responsiveness to lookups	Seconds	Milliseconds	Immediate
Update propagation	Lazy	Immediate	Immediate
Number of replicas	Many	None or few	None
Client-side caching	Yes	Yes	Sometimes

Figure 6.15: A comparison between name servers for implementing nodes from a large-scale name space partitioned into a global layer, an administrational layer, and a managerial layer.

A comparison between name servers at different layers is shown in Figure 6.15. In distributed systems, name servers in the global and administrational layer are the most difficult to implement. Difficulties are caused by replication and caching, which are needed for availability and performance, but which also introduce consistency problems. Some of the problems are aggravated by the fact that caches and replicas are spread across a wide-area network, which may introduce long communication delays during lookups.

Implementation of name resolution

The distribution of a name space across multiple name servers affects the implementation of name resolution. To explain the implementation of name resolution in large-scale name services, we assume for the moment that name servers are not replicated and that no client-side caches are used. Each client has access to a local **name resolver**, which is responsible for ensuring that the name resolution process is carried out. Referring to Figure 6.14, assume the (absolute) path name root:[nl, vu, cs, ftp, pub, globe, index.html] is to be resolved. Using a URL notation, this path name would correspond to ftp://ftp.cs.vu.nl/pub/globe/index.html. There are now two ways to implement name resolution.

In **iterative name resolution**, a name resolver hands over the complete name to the root name server. It is assumed that the address where the root server can be contacted is well known. The root server will resolve the path name as far as it can, and return the result to the client. In our example, the root server can resolve only the label nl, for which it will return the address of the associated name server.

At that point, the client passes the remaining path name (i.e., nl:[vu, cs, ftp, pub, globe, index.html]) to that name server. This server can resolve only the label vu, and returns the address of the associated name server, along with the remaining path name vu:[cs, ftp, pub, globe, index.html].

The client's name resolver will then contact this next name server, which responds by resolving the label cs, and subsequently also ftp, returning the address of the FTP server along with the path name ftp:[pub, globe, index.html]. The client then contacts the FTP server, requesting it to resolve the last part of the original path name. The FTP server will subsequently resolve the labels pub, globe, and index.html, and transfer the requested file (in this case using FTP). This process of iterative name resolution is shown in Figure 6.16. (The notation #[cs] is used to indicate the address of the server responsible for handling the node referred to by [cs].)

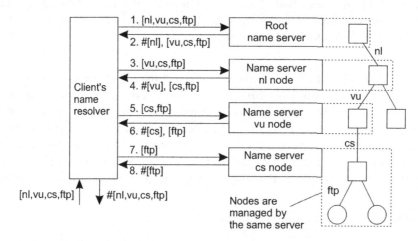

Figure 6.16: The principle of iterative name resolution.

In practice, the last step, namely contacting the FTP server and requesting it to transfer the file with path name ftp:[pub, globe, index.html], is carried out separately by the client process. In other words, the client would normally hand only the path name root:[nl, vu, cs, ftp] to the name resolver, from which it would expect the address where it can contact the FTP server, as is also shown in Figure 6.16

An alternative to iterative name resolution is to use recursion during name resolution. Instead of returning each intermediate result to the client's name resolver, with **recursive name resolution**, a name server passes the result to the next name server it finds. So, for example, when the root name server finds the address of the name server implementing the node named nl, it requests that name server to resolve the path name nl:[vu, cs, ftp, pub, globe, index.html]. Using recursive name resolution as well, this next server will resolve the complete path and eventually return the file index.html to the root server, which, in turn, will pass that file to the client's name resolver.

Recursive name resolution is shown in Figure 6.17. As in iterative name resolution, the last step (contacting the FTP server and asking it to transfer the indicated file) is generally carried out as a separate process by the client.

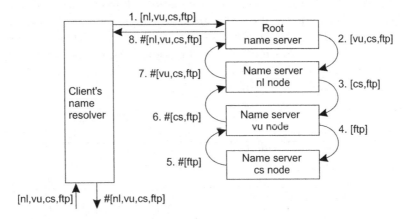

Figure 6.17: The principle of recursive name resolution.

The main drawback of recursive name resolution is that it puts a higher performance demand on each name server. Basically, a name server is required to handle the complete resolution of a path name, although it may do so in cooperation with other name servers. This additional burden is generally so high that name servers in the global layer of a name space support only iterative name resolution.

There are two important advantages to recursive name resolution. The first advantage is that caching results is more effective compared to iterative name resolution. The second advantage is that communication costs may be reduced. To explain these advantages, assume that a client's name resolver will accept path names referring only to nodes in the global or administrational layer of the name space. To resolve that part of a path name that corresponds to nodes in the managerial layer, a client will separately contact the name server returned by its name resolver, as we discussed above.

Recursive name resolution allows each name server to gradually learn the address of each name server responsible for implementing lower-level nodes. As a result, caching can be effectively used to enhance performance. For example, when the root server is requested to resolve the path name root:[nl, vu, cs, ftp], it will eventually get the address of the name server implementing the node referred to by that path name. To come to that point, the name server for the nl node has to look up the address of the name server for the vu node, whereas the latter has to look up the address of the name server handling the cs node.

Because changes to nodes in the global and administrational layer do not occur often, the root name server can effectively cache the returned address.

Moreover, because the address is also returned, by recursion, to the name server responsible for implementing the vu node and to the one implementing the nl node, it might as well be cached at those servers too.

Likewise, the results of intermediate name lookups can also be returned and cached. For example, the server for the nl node will have to look up the address of the vu node server. That address can be returned to the root server when the nl server returns the result of the original name lookup. A complete overview of the resolution process, and the results that can be cached by each name server, is shown in Figure 6.18.

Server for node	Should resolve	Looks up	Passes to child	Receives and caches	Returns to requester
cs	[ftp]	#[ftp]	—	—	#[ftp]
vu	[cs, ftp]	#[cs]	[ftp]	#[ftp]	#[cs] #[cs, ftp]
nl	[vu, cs, ftp]	#[vu]	[cs, ftp]	#[cs] #[cs, ftp]	#[vu] #[vu, cs] #[vu, cs, ftp]
root	[nl, vu, cs, ftp]	#[nl]	[vu, cs, ftp]	#[vu] #[vu, cs] #[vu, cs, ftp]	#[nl] #[nl, vu] #[nl, vu, cs] #[nl, vu, cs, ftp]

Figure 6.18: Recursive name resolution of [nl, vu, cs, ftp]. Name servers cache intermediate results for subsequent lookups.

The main benefit of this approach is that, eventually, lookup operations can be handled quite efficiently. For example, suppose that another client later requests resolution of the path name root:[nl, vu, cs, flits]. This name is passed to the root, which can immediately forward it to the name server for the cs node, and request it to resolve the remaining path name cs:[flits].

With iterative name resolution, caching is necessarily restricted to the client's name resolver. Consequently, if a client A requests the resolution of a name, and another client B later requests that same name to be resolved, name resolution will have to pass through the same name servers as was done for client A. As a compromise, many organizations use a local, intermediate name server that is shared by all clients. This local name server handles all naming requests and caches results. Such an intermediate server is also convenient from a management point of view. For example, only that server needs to know where the root name server is located; other machines do not require this information.

The second advantage of recursive name resolution is that it is often cheaper regarding communication. Again, consider the resolution of the path name root:[nl, vu, cs, ftp] and assume the client is located in San Francisco. Assuming that the client knows the address of the server for the nl node, with recursive name resolution, communication follows the route from the client's host in San Francisco to the nl server in The Netherlands, shown as R1 in Figure 6.19 From there on, communication is subsequently needed between the nl server and the name server of VU University on the campus in Amsterdam, The Netherlands. This communication is shown as R2. Finally, communication is needed between the vu server and the name server in the Computer Science Department, shown as R3. The route for the reply is the same, but in the opposite direction. Clearly, communication costs are dictated by the message exchange between the client's host and the nl server.

In contrast, with iterative name resolution, the client's host has to communicate separately with the nl server, the vu server, and the cs server, of which the total costs may be roughly three times that of recursive name resolution. The arrows in Figure 6.19 labeled I1, I2, and I3 show the communication path for iterative name resolution.

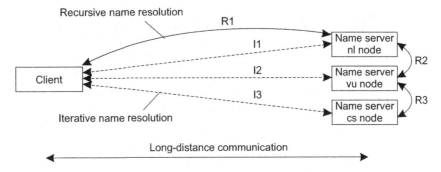

Figure 6.19: The comparison between recursive and iterative name resolution regarding communication costs.

6.3.4 Example: The Domain Name System

One of the largest distributed naming services in use today is the Internet **Domain Name System (DNS)**. DNS is primarily used for looking up IP addresses of hosts and mail servers. In the following pages, we concentrate on the organization of the DNS name space and the information stored in its nodes. Also, we take a closer look at the actual implementation of DNS. More information can be found in [Mockapetris, 1987a;b] and [Liu and Albitz, 2006]. An excellent tutorial on DNS is provided by van der Toorn et al. [2022].

The DNS name space

The DNS name space is hierarchically organized as a rooted tree. A label is a case-insensitive string made up of alphanumeric characters. A label has a maximum length of 63 characters; the length of a complete path name is restricted to 255 characters. The string representation of a path name consists of listing its labels, starting with the rightmost one, and separating the labels by a dot ("."). The root is represented by a dot. So, for example, the path name root:[nl, vu, cs, flits], is represented by the string "flits.cs.vu.nl.", which includes the rightmost dot to indicate the root node. We generally omit this dot for readability.

Because each node in the DNS name space has exactly one incoming edge (except for the root node, which has no incoming edges), the label attached to a node's incoming edge is also used as the name for that node. A subtree is called a **domain**; a path name to its root node is called a **domain name**. Note that, just like a path name, a domain name can be either absolute or relative.

The contents of a node is formed by a collection of **resource records**. There are different types of resource records. The major ones are shown in Figure 6.20.

Type	Refers to	Description
SOA	Zone	Holds info on the represented zone
A	Host	IP addr. of host this node represents
MX	Domain	Mail server to handle mail for this node
SRV	Domain	Server handling a specific service
NS	Zone	Name server for the represented zone
CNAME	Node	Symbolic link
PTR	Host	Canonical name of a host
HINFO	Host	Info on this host
TXT	Any kind	Any info considered useful

Figure 6.20: The most important types of resource records forming the contents of nodes in the DNS name space.

A node in the DNS name space will often represent several entities at the same time. For example, a domain name such as vu.nl is used to represent a domain and a zone. In this case, the domain is implemented by means of several (nonoverlapping) zones.

An SOA (start of authority) resource record contains information such as an e-mail address of the system administrator responsible for the represented zone, the name of the host where data on the zone can be fetched, and so on.

An A (address) record, represents a particular host on the Internet. The A record contains an IP address for that host to allow communication. If a host has several IP addresses, as is the case with multi-homed machines, the node will contain an A record for each address.

Another type of record is the MX (mail exchange) record, which is like a symbolic link to a node representing a mail server. For example, the node representing the domain cs.vu.nl has an MX record that used to contain the name zephyr.cs.vu.nl which refers to a mail server. That server would handle all incoming mail addressed to users in the cs.vu.nl domain. There may be several MX records stored in a node.

Related to MX records are SRV records, which contain the name of a server for a specific service. The service itself is identified through a name along with the name of a protocol. For example, the Web server in the cs.vu.nl domain could be named using an SRV record, such as website.cs.vu.nl. This record would then refer to the actual name of the server (which is soling.cs.vu.nl). An important advantage of SRV records is that clients need no longer know the DNS name of the host providing a specific service. Instead, only service names need to be standardized, after which the providing host can be looked up.

Nodes that represent a zone, contain one or more NS (name server) records. Like MX records, an NS record contains the name of a name server that implements the zone represented by the node. In principle, each node in the name space can store an NS record referring to the name server that implements it. However, as we discuss below, the implementation of the DNS name space is such that only nodes representing zones need to store NS records.

DNS distinguishes aliases from what are called **canonical names**. Each host is assumed to have a canonical, or primary name. An alias is implemented using a node storing a CNAME record containing the canonical name of a host. The name of the node storing such a record is thus the same as a symbolic link, as was shown in Figure 6.12.

DNS maintains an inverse mapping of IP addresses to host names using PTR (pointer) records. To accommodate the lookups of host names when given only an IP address, DNS maintains a domain named in-addr.arpa, which contains nodes that represent Internet hosts and which are named by the IP address of the represented host. For example, host www.cs.vu.nl once had IP address 130.37.20.20. DNS creates a node named 20.20.37.130.in-addr.arpa, which is used to store the canonical name of that host (which happens to be soling.cs.vu.nl in a PTR record).

Finally, an HINFO (host info) record is used to store additional information on a host, such as its machine type and operating system. Similarly, TXT records are used for any other kind of data that a user finds useful to store about the entity represented by the node.

DNS implementation

In essence, the DNS name space can be divided into a global layer and an administrational layer, as shown in Figure 6.14. The managerial layer, which is generally formed by local file systems, is formally not part of DNS, and is therefore also not managed by it.

Each zone is implemented by a name server, which is virtually always replicated for availability. Updates for a zone are normally handled by the primary name server. Updates take place by modifying the DNS database local to the primary server. Secondary name servers do not access the database directly, but, instead, request the primary server to transfer its content. The latter is called a **zone transfer** in DNS terminology.

A DNS database is implemented as a (small) collection of files, of which the most important one contains all the resource records for *all* the nodes in a particular zone. This approach allows nodes to be simply identified through their domain name, by which the notion of a node identifier reduces to an (implicit) index into a file.

Note 6.7 (More information: An example DNS database)

To better understand these implementation issues, Figure 6.21 shows a small part of the file that contains most of the information for a previous organization of the cs.vu.nl domain. Note that we have deliberately chosen an outdated version for security reasons. The file has been edited for readability. It shows the content of several nodes that used to be part of the cs.vu.nl domain, where each node is identified through its domain name.

In this example, the node cs.vu.nl represents the domain as well as the zone. Its SOA resource record contains specific information on the validity of this file, which will not concern us further. There are four name servers for this zone, referred to by their canonical host names in the NS records. The TXT record is used to give some additional information on this zone, but cannot be automatically processed by any name server. Furthermore, there is a single mail server that can handle incoming mail addressed to users in this domain. The number preceding the name of a mail server specifies a selection priority. A sending mail server should always first attempt to contact the mail server with the lowest number.

The host star.cs.vu.nl operates as a name server for this zone. Name servers are critical to any naming service. What can be seen about this name server is that additional robustness has been created by giving two separate network interfaces, each represented by a separate A resource record. In this way, the effects of a broken network link can be somewhat alleviated, as the server will remain accessible.

The next four lines (for zephyr.cs.vu.nl) give the necessary information about one of the department's mail servers. Note that this mail server is also backed up by another mail server, whose path is tornado.cs.vu.nl.

The next six lines show a typical configuration in which the department's Web server, as well as the department's FTP server, are implemented by a single machine, called soling.cs.vu.nl. By executing both servers on the same machine (and essentially using that machine only for Internet services and not anything else), system management becomes easier. For example, both servers will have the same view of the file system, and for efficiency, part of the file system may be implemented on soling.cs.vu.nl. This approach is often applied in the case of Web and FTP services.

The following two lines show information on one of the department's server clusters at that time. In this case, it tells us that the address 130.37.198.0 is associated with the host name vucs-das1.cs.vu.nl.

Name	Record type	Record value
cs.vu.nl.	SOA	star.cs.vu.nl. hostmaster.cs.vu.nl. 2005092900 7200 3600 2419200 3600
cs.vu.nl.	TXT	"VU University - Computer Science"
cs.vu.nl.	MX	1 mail.few.vu.nl.
cs.vu.nl.	NS	ns.vu.nl.
cs.vu.nl.	NS	top.cs.vu.nl.
cs.vu.nl.	NS	solo.cs.vu.nl.
cs.vu.nl.	NS	star.cs.vu.nl.
star.cs.vu.nl.	A	130.37.24.6
star.cs.vu.nl.	A	192.31.231.42
star.cs.vu.nl.	MX	1 star.cs.vu.nl.
star.cs.vu.nl.	MX	666 zephyr.cs.vu.nl.
star.cs.vu.nl.	HINFO	"Sun" "Unix"
zephyr.cs.vu.nl.	A	130.37.20.10
zephyr.cs.vu.nl.	MX	1 zephyr.cs.vu.nl.
zephyr.cs.vu.nl.	MX	2 tornado.cs.vu.nl.
zephyr.cs.vu.nl.	HINFO	"Sun" "Unix"
ftp.cs.vu.nl.	CNAME	soling.cs.vu.nl.
www.cs.vu.nl.	CNAME	soling.cs.vu.nl.
soling.cs.vu.nl.	A	130.37.20.20
soling.cs.vu.nl.	MX	1 soling.cs.vu.nl.
soling.cs.vu.nl.	MX	666 zephyr.cs.vu.nl.
soling.cs.vu.nl.	HINFO	"Sun" "Unix"
vucs-das1.cs.vu.nl.	PTR	0.198.37.130.in-addr.arpa.
vucs-das1.cs.vu.nl.	A	130.37.198.0
inkt.cs.vu.nl.	HINFO	"OCE" "Proprietary"
inkt.cs.vu.nl.	A	192.168.4.3
pen.cs.vu.nl.	HINFO	"OCE" "Proprietary"
pen.cs.vu.nl.	A	192.168.4.2
localhost.cs.vu.nl.	A	127.0.0.1

Figure 6.21: An excerpt from an (old) DNS database for the zone cs.vu.nl.

The next four lines show information on two major printers connected to the local network. Note that addresses in the range 192.168.0.0 to 192.168.255.255 are private: they can be accessed only from inside the local network and are inaccessible from an arbitrary Internet host.

Because the cs.vu.nl domain was implemented as a single zone, Figure 6.21 does not include references to other zones. The way to refer to nodes in a subdomain that are implemented in a different zone is shown in Figure 6.22. What needs to be done is to specify a name server for the subdomain by simply giving its domain name and IP address. When resolving a name for a node that lies in the cs.vu.nl domain, name resolution will continue at a certain point by reading the DNS database stored by the name server for the cs.vu.nl domain.

Name	Record type	Record value
cs.vu.nl.	NS	solo.cs.vu.nl.
cs.vu.nl.	NS	star.cs.vu.nl.
cs.vu.nl.	NS	ns.vu.nl.
cs.vu.nl.	NS	top.cs.vu.nl.
ns.vu.nl.	A	130.37.129.4
top.cs.vu.nl.	A	130.37.20.4
solo.cs.vu.nl.	A	130.37.20.5
star.cs.vu.nl.	A	130.37.24.6
star.cs.vu.nl.	A	192.31.231.42

Figure 6.22: Part of the description for the vu.nl domain which contains the cs.vu.nl domain.

Modern DNS

Following the terminology from van der Toorn et al. [2022], we speak of the *modern DNS* to refer to the current-day implementation of DNS. There are a number of changes to the DNS implementation that are important for understanding its behavior. The presentation so far, roughly assumes that that applications contact a local DNS resolver, and that this resolver subsequently contacts various name servers, as shown in Figure 6.23(a). The bounding boxes with dashed lines represent the borders of the organization where the clients, resolver, and name servers belong to, respectively. In the traditional setup, the clients contact the local DNS resolver, which can be thought of as connected to the same local network, or the one from the local ISP. The name servers each belong to a different organization.

In the modern DNS, we see three phenomena. First, many organizations will make use of an external DNS resolver. We explained in Section 3.4.4 that services like CDNs use the client's address to select a nearby server when resolving a URL. However, the address that the CDN service gets is not that of the client, but of the DNS resolver that the client uses. Clearly, if the DNS resolver is not close to the client, then a CDN may make a poor decision on selecting a nearby server. This problem can be mitigated if the local DNS resolver allows the client (or the requesting host) to also specify its own IP address. In that case, a CDN DNS name server can use that address to select the best server to eventually redirect the client to [Contavalli et al., 2016].

Second, is that many clients, and notably browsers, may actually bypass any configuration of their local organization and directly contact the DNS

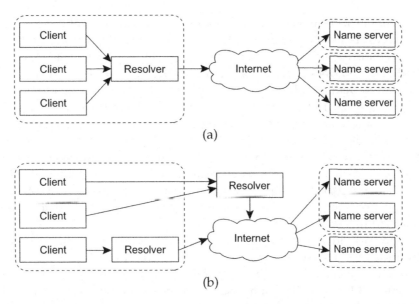

Figure 6.23: (a) The traditional organization of the implementation of DNS and (b) the modern organization that has already been partly realized (adapted from [van der Toorn et al., 2022]).

resolver of their own choice. Of course, there is nothing wrong with this, yet it makes it much harder to measure what is happening with DNS requests from an organization's perspective, especially if the client-to-resolver communication is also encrypted. In addition, the drawback of using an external resolver for redirecting requests to a nearby server also holds in this case.

The third phenomenon is that increasingly fewer organizations are running their own DNS servers. Instead, the name-resolution process is outsourced to third parties. In a sense, this means that the DNS is becoming increasingly less decentralized [Moura et al., 2020]. It is yet unclear what the consequences are of this centralization, but considering the many discussions on the role of the Big Tech companies, striving for spreading the DNS across multiple organizations may not be a bad idea.

As with so many (public) naming and lookup services, we need to provide the means for checking the validity of an answer. DNS is in the sense no exception. Moreover, being one of the most used and even necessary services on the Internet, securing the DNS is crucial. At the same time, when we realize that the DNS is becoming more centralized *and* end users are actually submitting a lot of information on how they make use of the Internet using their DNS queries, we also need to consider protecting the privacy of end users. Let us look briefly into these two subjects. A systematic overview of security and privacy issues in DNS is provided by Khormali et al. [2021].

Securing DNS responses   Discussions on facilitating the validation of DNS responses started already in the 1990s. At present, we see that in a vast majority of countries worldwide, all top-level domains support what is known as **DNSSEC**, i.e., **DNS Security extensions**. DNSSEC is, in principle, a straightforward system by which resource records are signed by the organization owning a zone. To this end, DNS needed to be extended in two ways. The first, obvious one, is that new fields needed to be added to the set of records for containing signatures and keys. Second, and quite important, is that larger queries and responses had to be supported than what traditional UDP messages would allow. The original DNS completely relied on fitting everything into 512-byte packets. Using so-called extension mechanisms for DNS allows for the acceptance of DNS queries and responses beyond 512 bytes [Damas et al., 2013].

The basic idea is simple. First, resource records of the same type are grouped into a separate set, which is then subsequently signed. So, for example, a zone will contain a separate set with all its IPv4 addresses, a separate set for all its IPv6 addresses, its name servers, and so on. The public key associated with the secret key used for signing a set of resource records is also added to a zone. At that point, any client receiving a set of resource records can check that set against the provided signature. To recall, this means that the set of resource records is hashed, and the hashed value is encrypted with the secret key of the zone owner. When receiving the set, the client hashes it as well, and decrypts the version that was also in the response. When the two match, the client will believe the returned records are valid.

Of course, the client will need to trust that the provided public key, known as a **zone-signing key** is valid. To this end, all the provided zone-signing keys are grouped again into a separate set, which is subsequently signed using yet another secret key. The associated public key is known as the **key-signing key**. What happens is that a hash of the key-signing key is stored, and signed by the parent domain. The parent domain, of course, signs this hash with the secret key associated with its zone-signing key, which, in turn, is signed with the secret key associated with the parent's key-signing key. In this way, we establish a **trust chain** all the way to the root. This scheme of signing in DNSSEC is shown in Figure 6.24.

We show part of the zone information available at three different levels, including the root level (level 0). For the lowest level, we show only one specific set of resource records RR. The zone at each level k includes information concerning which hash function HZ_k is used for signing records, or HK_k for signing a zone-signing key. We use the notation SKZ_k to denote the secret key associated with the (public) key ZSK_k and, likewise, SKK_k for the secret key associated with the key-signing key KSK_k. Knowing HZ_2 and ZSK_2 will allow a client to verify the signature $SKZ_2(HZ_2(\text{RR}))$ by checking

$$ZSK_2(SKZ_2(HZ_2(\text{RR}))) \overset{?}{=} HZ_2(\text{RR})$$

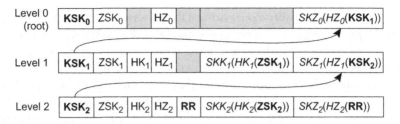

Figure 6.24: The relation between various resource records and keys in DNSSEC across three levels.

If the client wants to be sure that the public zone-signing key ZSK_2 is in order, it needs to get information from the parent zone, i.e., the zone at level 1. At that level, the zone owner has stored a signed hash value $SKZ_1(HZ_1(KSK_2))$, effectively allowing anyone to validate the key-signing key KSK_2 and the use of its associated secret key SKK_2 that was used for signing ZSK_2. Obviously, the parent zone would never store such information without having going through a process of ensuring that its child zone is indeed properly owned and operating as it should.

Protecting DNS users In general, one can state that information stored in DNS is public: it can be viewed as a huge open database that allows us to resolve human-friendly names to addresses and other data. However, *what* a client is asking from the DNS is, in principle, no one else's business. That means that queries should be kept confidential. There are roughly two increasingly often supported protection mechanisms deployed in the modern DNS.

First, systems today allow applications to set up a secure channel to a remote DNS resolver through TLS, mostly by that application's local resolver, which runs on the local operating system. We discuss TLS in Section 9.3.2. In effect, having DNS over TLS prevents a third party from discovering to which Websites an application is actually referring. Obviously, both the local DNS resolver and the remote resolver need to be trusted not to leak information, and are sufficiently protected against attacks. Note that facilitating DNS over TLS requires that a resolver uses a specific port (in this case, port 853).

Second, many modern browsers support issuing DNS queries over **HTTPS**. In this case, the browser is configured to directly access a remote DNS resolver that supports DNS over HTTPS. As HTTPS runs over TLS, this mechanism essentially offers the same protection as DNS over TLS. A major difference, of course, is that DNS queries are now completely handled out of the control of local administrators. This also means that local policies concerning allowing or denying access to certain sites are bypassed, for better or for worse.

Using DNS over either TLS or HTTPS is already an improvement over

having no confidentiality concerning DNS queries, yet it may not be sufficient. Name resolution as explained so far, and illustrated in Figure 6.16 and
Figure 6.17, shows that the entire path is sent to a name server. Of course,
the queries between name servers can also be protected, yet a more efficient
and generally sufficient protection mechanism is to let a name server ask for
resolving *only* the relevant part of a path. So, for example, instead of asking
to return an answer for ftp.cs.vu.nl (and get the address for the name server
handling the nl domain), a resolver asks the root server to resolve .nl. We omit
a few important details (such as how does the resolver know whether multiple
components in a path are handled by the same name server), yet it can be
seen that simply limiting a query can indeed help in attaining confidentiality.

Note 6.8 (Advanced: Decentralized versus hierarchical DNS implementations)
The implementation of DNS we described so far is the standard one. It follows
a hierarchy of servers with 13 well-known root nodes and ending in millions of
servers at the leaves (but read on). An important observation is that higher-level
nodes receive many more requests than lower-level nodes. Only by caching the
name-to-address bindings of these higher levels, it becomes possible to avoid
sending requests to them and thus swamping them.

These scalability problems can, in principle, be avoided altogether with fully
decentralized solutions. In particular, we can compute the hash of a DNS name,
and subsequently take that hash as a key value to be looked up in a distributed
hash table or a hierarchical location service with a fully partitioned root node.
The obvious drawback of this approach is that we lose the structure of the original
name. This loss may prevent efficient implementations of, for example, finding all
children in a specific domain.

As argued by Walfish et al. [2004], when there is a need for many names,
using identifiers as a semantic-free way of accessing data will allow different
systems to make use of a single naming system. The reason is simple: by now,
it is well understood how a huge collection of (flat) names can be efficiently
supported. What needs to be done is to maintain the mapping of identifier-to-
name information, where in this case a name may come from the DNS space,
be a URL, and so on. Using identifiers can be made easier by letting users or
organizations use a strict local name space. The latter is completely analogous to
maintaining a private setting of environment variables on a computer.

Nevertheless, stating that a decentralized implementation of DNS will circumvent many of its scalability problems is too simple. In a comparative study,
Pappas et al. [2006] showed that there are many trade-offs to consider and that
the current, hierarchical design of DNS is not so bad for at least two reasons:

- In a hierarchical design, not all nodes are equal and in the case of DNS,
  notably the higher-level nodes are *engineered* differently. For example,
  despite that there are officially 13 root nodes, each of these nodes is highly
  distributed and replicated for performance and availability. To illustrate,
  the root node provided by RIPE NCC is implemented at some 25 different

sites (all using the same IP address), each implemented as a highly robust and replicated server cluster.

Again, we see the important difference between a logical and physical design. Exploiting this difference is crucial for the operation of a distributed system such as DNS. However, in virtually all DHT-based systems, making this distinction can be much more difficult when dealing with a logical naming hierarchy, as all names are necessarily treated to be equal. In such cases, it becomes much more difficult to engineer the system so that, for example, top-level domains are separated out by special (physical) nodes.

Of course, the obvious drawback of not having all nodes being equal, is that special measures need to be taken to protect the more important parts of a system against abuse. We have already mentioned that top-level nodes in DNS are implemented as distributed and replicated servers (clusters), but also that an associated server will not provide recursive name resolution. Such implementation decisions are necessary also from a perspective of robustness.

- DNS caches are highly effective and driven almost entirely by the local distribution of queries: if a domain D is queried often at a server S, then the references for name servers of D will be cached at S. The behavior at another server S′ is determined by what is queried at S′. This important feature has been confirmed in a more recent study that also shows how difficult it can be to understand the effectiveness of caching and the locality principles of DNS resolvers. In particular, an ISP's DNS resolver may be very effective in redirecting traffic to content that is localized in that ISP [Ager et al., 2010].

  In contrast, caching and replication in DHT-based systems generally does not show such principles of locality: results are simply cached at nodes on the return path of a lookup and have very little to do with the fact that a lookup was locally initiated at a specific node in the DHT, or a resolver for which the local ISP can assist in looking up content.

The fact remains that replacing DNS by a decentralized implementation is not necessarily a good idea. DNS as it stands today, is a well-engineered system that is difficult to beat when it comes to performance and robustness (see Vixie [2009], Vixie [2014], but also Allman [2020]).

6.3.5 Example: The Network File System

As another, and very different example, consider naming in NFS. The fundamental idea underlying the NFS naming model is to provide clients complete transparent access to a remote file system as maintained by a server. This transparency is achieved by letting a client be able to mount a remote file system into its own local file system, as shown in Figure 6.25.

Instead of mounting an entire file system, NFS allows clients to mount only part of a file system, as also shown in Figure 6.25. A server is said to

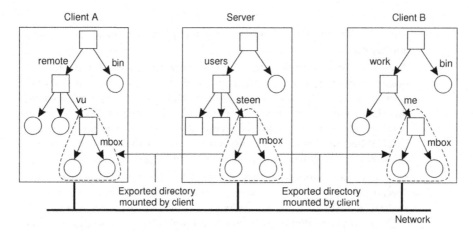

Figure 6.25: Mounting (part of) a remote file system in NFS.

export a directory when it makes that directory and its entries available to clients. An exported directory can be mounted into a client's local name space.

This design approach has a serious implication: in principle, users do not share name spaces. As shown in Figure 6.25 the file named /remote/vu/mbox at client A is named /work/me/mbox at client B. A file's name therefore depends on how clients organize their own local name space, and where exported directories are mounted. The drawback of this approach in a distributed file system is that sharing files becomes much harder. For example, Alice cannot tell Bob about a file using the name she assigned to that file, for that name may have an entirely different meaning in Bob's name space of files.

There are several ways to solve this problem, but the most common one is to provide each client with a name space that is partly standardized. For example, each client may be using the local directory /usr/bin to mount a file system containing a standard collection of programs that are available to everyone. Likewise, the directory /local may be used as a standard to mount a local file system that is located on the client's host.

An NFS server can itself mount directories that are exported by other servers. However, it is not allowed to export those directories to its own clients. Instead, a client will have to explicitly mount such a directory from the server that maintains it, as shown in Figure 6.26. This restriction comes partly from simplicity. If a server could export a directory that it mounted from another server, it would have to return special file handles that include an identifier for a server. NFS does not support such file handles.

To explain this point in more detail, assume that the server A hosts a file system FS_A from which it exports the directory /packages. This directory contains a subdirectory /draw that acts as a mount point for a file system

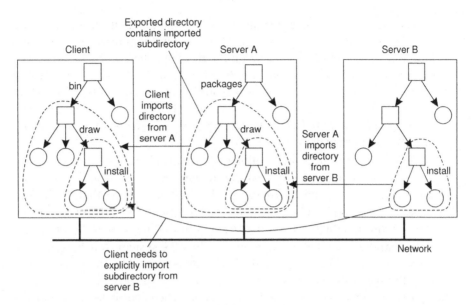

Figure 6.26: Mounting nested directories from multiple servers in NFS.

FS$_B$ that is exported by the server B and mounted by A. Let A also export /packages/draw to its own clients, and assume that a client has mounted /packages into its local directory /bin as shown in Figure 6.26.

If name resolution is iterative, then to resolve the name /bin/draw/install, the client contacts server A when it has locally resolved /bin and requests A to return a **file handle** for directory /draw. In that case, server A should return a file handle that includes an identifier for server B, as only B can resolve the rest of the path name, in this case /install. As we have said, this kind of name resolution is not supported by NFS.

Name resolution in earlier versions of NFS is strictly iterative, in the sense that only a single file name at a time can be looked up. In other words, resolving a name such as /bin/draw/install requires three separate calls to the NFS server. Moreover, the client is fully responsible for implementing the resolution of a path name. NFSv4 also supports recursive name lookups. In this case, a client can pass a complete path name to a server and request that server to resolve it.

There is another peculiarity with NFS name lookups that has been solved with the most recent version (NFSv4). Consider a file server hosting several file systems. With the strict iterative name resolution, whenever a lookup is done for a directory on which another file system was mounted, the lookup would return the file handle of the directory. Subsequently, reading that directory would return its *original* content, not that of the root directory of the mounted file system.

To explain, assume that in our previous example that both file systems FS_A and FS_B are hosted by a single server. If the client has mounted /packages into its local directory /bin, then looking up the file name draw at the server would return the file handle for draw. A subsequent call to the server for listing the directory entries of draw by readdir would then return the list of directory entries that were *originally* stored in FS_A in subdirectory /packages/draw. Only if the client had also mounted file system FS_B, would it be possible to properly resolve the path name draw/install relative to /bin.

NFSv4 solves this problem by allowing lookups to cross mount points at a server. In particular, lookup returns the file handle of the *mounted* directory instead of that of the original directory. The client can detect that the lookup has crossed a mount point by inspecting the file system identifier of the looked up file. If required, the client can locally mount that file system as well.

A **file handle** is a reference to a file within a file system. It is independent of the name of the file it refers to. A file handle is created by the server that is hosting the file system and is unique regarding all file systems exported by the server. It is created when the file is created. The client is kept ignorant of the actual content of a file handle; it is completely opaque. File handles were 32 bytes in NFS version 2, but were variable up to 64 bytes in version 3 and 128 bytes in version 4. Of course, the length of a file handle is not opaque.

Ideally, a file handle is implemented as a true identifier for a file relative to a file system. For one thing, this means that as long as the file exists, it should have one and the same file handle. This persistence requirement allows a client to store a file handle locally once the associated file has been looked up through its name. One benefit is performance: as most file operations require a file handle instead of a name, the client can avoid having to look up a name repeatedly before every file operation. Another benefit of this approach is that the client can now access the file regardless which (current) name it has.

Because a file handle can be locally stored by a client, it is also important that a server does not reuse a file handle after deleting a file. Otherwise, a client may mistakenly access the wrong file when it uses its locally stored file handle.

Note that the combination of iterative name lookups and not letting a lookup operation allow crossing a mount point introduces a problem with getting an initial file handle. To access files in a remote file system, a client will need to provide the server with a file handle of the directory where the lookup should take place, along with the name of the file or directory that is to be resolved. NFSv3 solves this problem through a separate mount protocol, by which a client actually mounts a remote file system. After mounting, the client is passed back the **root file handle** of the mounted file system, which it can subsequently use as a starting point for looking up names.

In NFSv4, this problem is solved by providing a separate operation putrootfh that tells the server to solve all file names relative to the root file handle of the file system it manages. The root file handle can be used to look up any other file handle in the server's file system. This approach has the additional benefit that there is no need for a separate mount protocol. Instead, mounting can be integrated into the regular protocol for looking up files. A client can simply mount a remote file system by requesting the server to resolve names relative to the file system's root file handle using putrootfh.

Note 6.9 (Advanced: Automounting)

As we mentioned, the NFS naming model essentially provides users with their own name space. Sharing in this model may become difficult if users name the same file differently. One solution to this problem is to provide each user with a local name space that is partly standardized, and subsequently mounting remote file systems the same for each user.

Another problem with the NFS naming model has to do with deciding *when* a remote file system should be mounted. Consider a large system with thousands of users. Assume that each user has a local directory /home that is used to mount the home directories of other users. For example, Alice's home directory may be locally available to her as /home/alice, although the actual files are stored on a remote server. This directory can be automatically mounted when Alice logs into her workstation. In addition, she may have access to Bob's public files by accessing Bob's directory through /home/bob.

The question, however, is whether Bob's home directory should also be mounted automatically when Alice logs in. The benefit of this approach would be that the whole business of mounting file systems would be transparent to Alice. However, if this policy were followed for every user, logging in could incur a lot of communication and administrative overhead. In addition, it would require that all users are known in advance. A much better approach is to transparently mount another user's home directory on demand, that is, when it is first needed.

On-demand mounting of a remote file system (or actually an exported directory) is handled in NFS by an **automounter**, which runs as a separate process on the client's machine. The principle underlying an automounter is relatively simple. Consider a simple automounter implemented as a user-level NFS server on a Unix operating system. (For other implementations, see [Callaghan, 2000]).

Assume that for each user, the home directories of all users are available through the local directory /home, as described above. When a client machine boots, the automounter starts with mounting this directory. The effect of this local mount is that whenever a program attempts to access /home, the Unix kernel will forward a lookup operation to the NFS client, which, in this case, will forward the request to the automounter in its role as NFS server, as shown in Figure 6.27.

For example, suppose that Alice logs in. The login program will attempt to read the directory /home/alice to find information such as login scripts. The automounter will thus receive the request to look up subdirectory /home/alice, for which reason it first creates a subdirectory /alice in /home. It then looks up the NFS server that exports Alice's home directory to subsequently mount that directory in /home/alice. At that point, the login program can proceed.

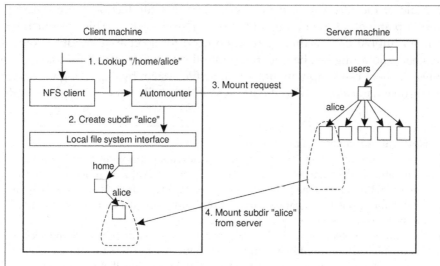

Figure 6.27: A simple automounter for NFS.

The problem with this approach is that the automounter will have to be involved in all file operations to guarantee transparency. If a referenced file is not locally available because the corresponding file system has not yet been mounted, the automounter will have to know. In particular, it will need to handle all read and write requests, even for file systems that have already been mounted. This approach may incur a large performance problem. It would be better to have the automounter only mount and unmount directories, and otherwise, stay out of the loop. A simple solution is to let the automounter mount directories in a special subdirectory, and install a symbolic link to each mounted directory. This approach is shown in Figure 6.28.

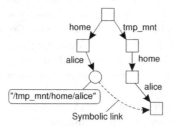

Figure 6.28: Using symbolic links with automounting.

In our example, the user home directories are mounted as subdirectories of /tmp_mnt. When Alice logs in, the automounter mounts her home directory in /tmp_mnt/home/alice and creates a symbolic link /home/alice that refers to that subdirectory. In this case, whenever Alice executes a command such as ls -l /home/alice the NFS server that exports Alice's home directory is contacted directly without further involvement of the automounter.

6.4 Attribute-based naming

Flat and structured names generally provide a unique and location-independent way of referring to entities. Moreover, structured names have been partly designed to provide a human-friendly way to name entities so that they can be conveniently accessed. In most cases, it is assumed that the name refers to only a single entity. However, location independence and human friendliness are not the only criterion for naming entities. In particular, as more information is being made available, it becomes important to effectively search for entities. This approach requires that a user can provide merely a description of what she is looking for.

There are many ways in which descriptions can be provided, but a popular one in distributed systems is to describe an entity in terms of (*attribute, value*) pairs, generally referred to as **attribute-based naming**. In this approach, an entity is assumed to have an associated collection of attributes. Each attribute says something about that entity. By specifying which values a specific attribute should have, a user essentially constrains the set of entities that she is interested in. It is up to the naming system to return one or more entities that meet the user's description. In this section, we take a closer look at attribute-based naming systems.

6.4.1 Directory services

Attribute-based naming systems are also known as **directory services**, whereas systems that support structured naming are generally called **naming systems**. With directory services, entities have a set of associated attributes that can be used for searching. In some cases, the choice of attributes can be relatively simple. For example, in an e-mail system, messages can be tagged with attributes for the sender, recipient, subject, and so on. However, even in the case of e-mail, matters become difficult when other types of descriptors are needed, as is illustrated by the difficulty of developing filters that will allow only certain messages (based on their descriptors) to be passed through.

What it all boils down to is that designing an appropriate set of attributes is not trivial. In most cases, attribute design has to be done manually. Even if there is consensus on the set of attributes to use, practice shows that setting the values consistently by a diverse group of people is a problem by itself, as many will have experienced when accessing music and video databases on the Internet.

To alleviate some of these problems, research has been conducted on unifying the ways that resources can be described. In the context of distributed systems, one particularly relevant development is the **Resource Description Framework (RDF)**. Fundamental to the RDF model is that resources are described as triplets consisting of a subject, a predicate, and an object. For example, (Person, name, Alice) describes a resource referred to as Person whose name is Alice. In RDF, each subject, predicate, or object can be a resource itself. This means that Alice may be implemented as a reference to a file that can be subsequently retrieved. In the case of a predicate, such a resource could contain a textual description of that predicate. Resources associated with subjects and objects can be anything. References in RDF are essentially URLs.

If resource descriptions are stored, it becomes possible to query that storage in a way that is common for many attribute-based naming systems. For example, an application could ask for the information associated with a person named Alice. Such a query would return a reference to the person resource associated with Alice. This resource can then subsequently be fetched by the application.

In this example, the resource descriptions are stored at a central location. There is no reason why the resources should reside at the same location as well. However, not having the descriptions in the same place may incur a serious performance problem. Unlike structured naming systems, looking up values in an attribute-based naming system essentially requires an exhaustive search through all descriptors. (Various techniques can be applied to avoid such exhaustive searches, an obvious one being indexing.) When considering performance, an exhaustive search may be less of a problem within a single, nondistributed data store, but simply sending a search query to hundreds of servers that jointly implement a distributed data store is generally not such a good idea. In the following, we will take a look at different approaches to solving this problem in distributed systems.

6.4.2   Hierarchical implementations: LDAP

A common approach to tackling distributed directory services is to combine structured naming with attribute-based naming. This approach has been widely adopted, for example, in Microsoft's Active Directory service and other systems. Many of these systems use, or rely on the **Lightweight Directory Access Protocol** commonly referred simply as **LDAP**. The LDAP directory service has been derived from OSI's X.500 directory service. As with many OSI services, the quality of their associated implementations hindered widespread use, and simplifications were needed to make it useful. Detailed information on LDAP can be found in [Arkills, 2003].

Conceptually, an LDAP directory service consists of a number of records, usually referred to as directory entries. A directory entry is comparable to a resource record in DNS. Each record is made up of a collection of (*attribute, value*) pairs, where each attribute has an associated type. A distinction is made between single-valued attributes and multiple-valued attributes. The latter typically represent arrays and lists. As an example, a simple directory entry identifying the network addresses of some general servers from Figure 6.22 is shown in Figure 6.28.

Attribute	Abbr.	Value
Country	C	NL
Locality	L	Amsterdam
Organization	O	VU University
OrganizationalUnit	OU	Computer Science
CommonName	CN	Main server
Mail_Servers	–	137.37.20.3, 130.37.24.6, 137.37.20.10
FTP_Server	–	130.37.20.20
WWW_Server	–	130.37.20.20

Figure 6.29: A simple example of an LDAP directory entry using LDAP naming conventions.

In our example, we have used a naming convention described in the LDAP standards, which applies to the first five attributes. The attributes Organization and OrganizationUnit describe, respectively, the organization and the department associated with the data that are stored in the record. Likewise, the attributes Locality and Country provide additional information on where the entry is stored. The CommonName attribute is often used as an (ambiguous) name to identify an entry within a limited part of the directory. For example, the name "Main server" may be enough to find our example entry given the specific values for the other four attributes Country, Locality, Organization, and OrganizationalUnit. In our example, only attribute Mail_Servers has multiple values associated with it. All other attributes have only a single value.

The collection of all directory entries in an LDAP directory service is called a **directory information base (DIB)**. An important aspect of a DIB is that each record is uniquely named so that it can be looked up. Such a globally unique name appears as a sequence of naming attributes in each record. Each naming attribute is called a **relative distinguished name**, or **RDN** for short. In our example in Figure 6.29 the first five attributes are all naming attributes. Using the conventional abbreviations for representing naming attributes in LDAP, as shown in Figure 6.29, the attributes Country, Organization, and OrganizationalUnit could be used to form the name

/C = NL/O = VU University/OU = Computer Science

which is globally unique, analogous to the DNS name nl.vu.cs.

As in DNS, the use of globally unique names by listing RDNs in sequence, leads to a hierarchy of the collection of directory entries, which is referred to as a **directory information tree (DIT)**. A DIT essentially forms the naming graph of an LDAP directory service, in which each node represents a directory entry. In addition, a node may also act as a directory in the traditional sense, in that there may be several children for which the node acts as parent. To explain, consider the naming graph, as partly shown in Figure 6.30. (Recall that labels are associated with edges.)

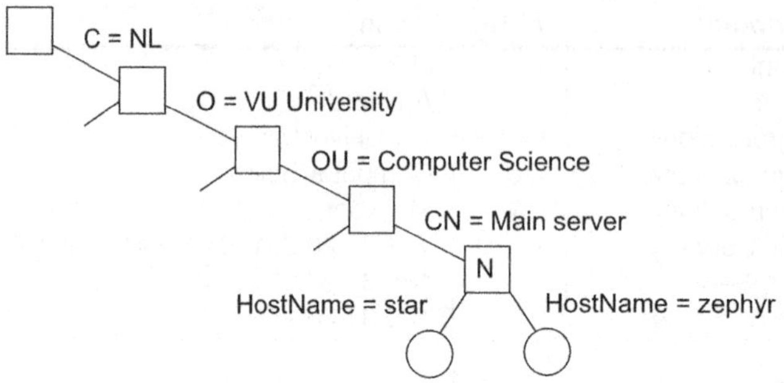

(a)

Attribute	Value	Attribute	Value
Locality	Amsterdam	Locality	Amsterdam
Organization	VUUniversity	Organization	VUUniversity
OrganizationalUnit	ComputerScience	OrganizationalUnit	ComputerScience
CommonName	Mainserver	CommonName	Mainserver
HostName	star	HostName	zephyr
HostAddress	192.31.231.42	HostAddress	137.37.20.10

(b)

Figure 6.30: (a) Part of a directory information tree. (b) Two directory entries having HostName as RDN.

The node N corresponds to the directory entry shown in Figure 6.29. At the same time, this node acts as a parent to a number of other directory entries that have an additional naming attribute HostName that is used as an RDN. For example, such entries may be used to represent hosts as shown in Figure 6.30.

A node in an LDAP naming graph can thus simultaneously represent a directory in the traditional sense, as we discussed previously, as well as an LDAP record. This distinction is supported by two different lookup operations. The read operation is used to read a single record given its path name in the DIT. In contrast, the list operation is used to list the names of all outgoing edges of a given node in the DIT. Each name corresponds to a child node of the given node. Note that the list operation does not return any records; it merely returns names. In other words, calling read with as input the name

$$/C = NL/O = VU \text{ University}/OU = \text{Computer Science}/CN = \text{Main server}$$

will return the record shown in Figure 6.30, whereas calling list will return the names star and zephyr from the entries shown in Figure 6.30 as well as the names of other hosts that have been registered in a similar way.

Implementing an LDAP directory service proceeds in much the same way as implementing a naming service, such as DNS, except that LDAP supports more lookup operations, as we will discuss shortly. When dealing with a large-scale directory, the DIT is usually partitioned and distributed across several servers, known as **directory service agents (DSA)**. Each part of a partitioned DIT thus corresponds to a zone in DNS. Likewise, each DSA behaves very much the same as a normal name server, except that it implements a number of typical directory services, such as advanced search operations.

Clients are represented by what are called **directory user agents**, or simply **DUA**. A DUA is similar to a name resolver in structured-naming services. A DUA exchanges information with a DSA according to a standardized access protocol.

What makes an LDAP implementation different from a DNS implementation are the facilities for searching through a DIB. In particular, facilities are provided to search for a directory entry given a set of criteria that attributes of the searched entries should meet. For example, suppose that we want a list of all main servers at VU University. Using the notation defined in Smith and Howes [2006], such a list can be returned using a search operation like

```
search("(C=NL)(O=VU University)(OU=*)(CN=Main server)")
```

In this example, we have specified that the place to look for main servers is the organization named VU_University in country NL, but that we are not interested in a particular organizational unit. However, each returned result should have the CN attribute equal to Main_server.

As we already mentioned, searching in a directory service is generally an expensive operation. For example, to find all main servers at VU University requires searching all entries at each department and combining the results in a single answer. In other words, we will generally need to access several leaf nodes of a DIT in order to get an answer. In practice, this also means that several DSAs need to be accessed. In contrast, naming services can often be implemented in such a way that a lookup operation requires accessing only a single leaf node.

This whole setup of LDAP can be taken one step further by allowing several trees to co-exist, while also being linked to each other. This approach is followed in Microsoft's Active Directory leading to a *forest* of LDAP domains [Allen and Lowe-Norris, 2003]. Obviously, searching in such an organization can be overwhelmingly complex. To circumvent some of the scalability problems, Active Directory usually assumes there is a global index server (called a global catalog) that can be searched first. The index will indicate which LDAP domains need to be searched further.

Although LDAP by itself already exploits hierarchy for scalability, it is common to combine LDAP with DNS. For example, every tree in LDAP needs to be accessible at the root (known in Active Directory as a domain controller).

The root is often known under a DNS name, which, in turn, can be found through an appropriate SRV record, as we explained above.

6.4.3   Decentralized implementations

Notably with the advent of peer-to-peer systems, researchers have also been looking for solutions for decentralized attribute-based naming systems. In particular, peer-to-peer systems are often used to store files. Initially, files could not be searched—they could only be looked up by their key. However, having the possibility to search for a file based on descriptors can be extremely convenient, where each descriptor is nothing but an *(attribute, value)* pair. Obviously, querying every node in a peer-to-peer system to see if it contains a file matching one or more of such pairs, is infeasible. What we need is a mapping of *(attribute, value)* pairs to **index servers**, which, in turn, point to files matching those pairs.

Using a distributed index

Let us first look at the situation of building a (distributed) index. The basic idea is that a search query is formulated as a list of *(attribute, value)* pairs, just as in the case of our LDAP examples. The result should be a list of (references to) entities that match *all* pairs. In the case of a peer-to-peer system storing files, a list of keys to relevant files may be returned, after which the client can look up each of those files using the returned keys.

A straightforward approach toward a distributed index is the following. Assume there are d different attributes. In that case, we can use a server for each of the d attributes, where a server for attribute A maintains a set of (E,val) pairs for each entity E that has the value val for attribute A. A search query such as

```
search("(Country=NL)(Organization=VU University)
       (OrganizationalUnit=*)(CommonName=Main server)")
```

would be sent to the servers for Country, Organization, and CommonName, respectively, after which the client would need to see which entities occur in *all* three sets as returned by the servers. To prevent that a server needs to maintain a large set of entities, the set for each server can be further partitioned and distributed across several subservers, each subserver associated with the same attribute.

More precisely, if we have a set of attributes $\{a^1, \ldots, a^N\}$, then for each attribute a^k we associate a set $\mathbf{S^k} = \{S_1^k, \ldots, S_{n_k}^k\}$ of n_k servers. Assuming that an attribute a^k takes values from a set R^k, we construct a global mapping F such that

$$F(a^k, v) = S_j^k \text{ with } S_j^k \in \mathbf{S^k} \text{ and } v \in R^k$$

In this example, the server S_j^k would keep track of each key associated with a file having $a^k = v$. The beauty of this scheme is its simplicity. If $L(a^k, v)$ is the set of keys returned by the server $F(a^k, v)$, then a query can be formulated as a logical expression such as

$$\left(F(a^1, v^1) \wedge F(a^2, v^2) \right) \vee F(a^3, v^3)$$

which can then be processed on the client side by constructing the set

$$\left(L(a^1, v^1) \cap L(a^2, v^2) \right) \cup L(a^3, v^3)$$

Unfortunately, there are important drawbacks to this scheme. First, any query involving k attributes requires contacting k index servers, which may incur significant communication costs. Furthermore, and related, is that the client is required to process the sets returned by the index servers. Just imagine that each file has two attributes firstName and lastName, respectively, and that a client is looking for the file owned by Pheriby Smith. Now, although Pheriby may be quite unique for a first name, Smith definitely is not. However, our poor client will have to receive perhaps millions of keys of files for which lastName = Smith, while there may actually be only a handful of files for which firstName = Pheriby. Thirdly, although this scheme does allow leaving certain attributes unspecified (by simply not mentioning them in the query), it does not easily support range queries, such as, price = $[1000 - -2500]$.

Space-filling curves

A common approach to implementing decentralized attribute-based naming systems is to use what are known as **space-filling curves**. The basic idea is to map the N-dimensional space covered by the N attributes $\{a^1, \ldots, a^N\}$ into a single dimension, and then use, for example, a simple hashing technique to distribute the resultant space among index servers. One of the key issues is to have *(attribute, value)* pairs that are "close" to each other be handled by the same index server.

Let us make matters concrete and look into one popular case, namely Hilbert space-filling curves (see, for example, [Lawder and King, 2000]). These are easiest to explain by looking at only two dimensions, that is, considering only two distinct attributes. The possible values that each attribute can have corresponds to one axis in a two-dimensional space. Without loss of generality, we assume that each attribute takes on values in the interval $[0, 1)$. As a first approximation of the square, we divide it into four quadrants, as shown in Figure 6.31(a). All data values (x, y) with $0 \leq x, y < 0.5$ are associated with index 0. Values (x, y) with $0.5 \leq x, y < 1.0$ are associated with index 2.

We can repeat this procedure recursively for each subsquare: divide it into four smaller squares and connect the smaller squares through a single line. Using rotation and reflection, we make sure that this line can be nicely

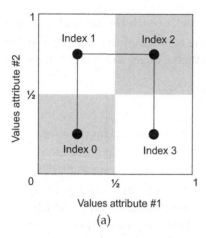 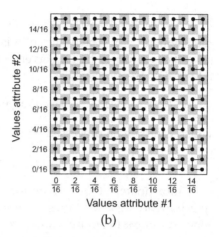

Figure 6.31: Reducing a two-dimensional space to a single dimension through a Hilbert space-filling curve of (a) order 1, and (b) order 4.

connected to the one in the previously neighboring larger subsquare (which has also been divided into smaller squares). To illustrate, where Figure 6.31(a) shows a Hilbert curve of order 1, Figure 6.31(b) shows a curve of order 4 with 256 indices. In general, a Hilbert curve of order k connects 2^{2k} subsquares, and thus has also 2^{2k} indices. There are various ways in which we can systematically draw a curve through a two-dimensional space that has been partitioned into equally sized squares. Furthermore, the process can be easily expanded to higher dimensions, as explained by Sagan [1994] and Bader [2013].

An important property of space-filling curves is that they preserve locality: two indices that are close to each other on the curve correspond to two points that are also close to each other in the multidimensional space. (Note that the reverse is not always true: two points close to each other in the multidimensional space need not necessarily lie close to each other on the curve.)

To complete the story, several things need to be done. First, attribute values need to be indexed. Assume that we are dealing with a total of N possible attributes $\{a^1, \ldots, a^N\}$, and that each entity assigns a value to each of these N attributes (possibly including the equivalent of a "don't care" value). To keep matters simple, we assume that each attribute value is normalized to a value in the interval $[0, 1)$. Then clearly, an entity E having the tuple of values $(v^1, \ldots, v^N)$ is associated with a real-valued coordinate in an N-dimensional space, in turn uniquely associated with an N-dimensional subsquare as we discussed for the two-dimensional case. The center of such a subsquare corresponds to an index on the associated Hilbert space-filling curve, and is now the index associated with the entity E. Of course, multiple entities whose associated coordinates fall in the same subsquare will all have the same index. If we want to avoid such collisions as much as possible, we need to use high-ordered space-filling curves. Orders of 32 or 64 are not uncommon.

Second, we also need to be able to search for entities. The principle of searching for entities based on their attribute values should now be clear. Suppose we were looking for files whose two attribute values a^1 and a^2 lie in intervals $[v_l^1, v_u^1)$ and $[v_l^2, v_u^2)$, respectively (with $v_l^i < v_u^i$). Clearly, this delineates a rectangular region through which the curve passes, and all files indexed by those segments of the curve that intersect with that region match the search criterion. We therefore need an operation that returns a series of curve-related indices given a region (expressed in terms of subsquares) in the associated N-dimensional space. Such an operation is clearly dependent on which space-filling curve has been used, but interestingly, need not be dependent on actual entities.

Finally, we need to maintain (references to) the entities associated with indices. One approach, used in the Squid system [Schmidt and Parashar, 2008], is to use a Chord ring. In Squid, the index space is chosen to be the same as that of the Chord ring, that is, both use m-bit identifiers. Then clearly, the Chord node responsible for index i will store (references to) the entities indexed by i.

Note 6.10 (Example: The SWORD system)
Decentralized implementations of attribute-based naming systems have received a lot of attention. The ones based on space-filling curves are relatively popular, but several alternatives have been proposed as well. As an example, we discuss a solution adopted in the SWORD resource discovery system [Albrecht et al., 2008].

In SWORD, (*attribute, value*) pairs are first transformed into a key for a DHT. These pairs always contain a single value; only queries may contain value ranges for attributes. When computing the key (by means of a hash) the name of the attribute and its value are kept separate. Specific bits in the key will identify the attribute name, while others identify its value. In addition, the key will contain a number of random bits to guarantee uniqueness among all keys that need to be generated. In this way, the space of attributes is conveniently partitioned: if n bits are reserved to code attribute names, 2^n different server groups can be used, one group for each attribute name. Likewise, by using m bits to encode values, a further partitioning per server group can be applied to store specific (*attribute, value*) pairs. DHTs are used only for distributing attribute names.

For each attribute name, the possible range of its value is partitioned into subranges and a single server is assigned to each subrange. To explain, consider a resource description with two attributes: a^1 taking values in the range [1..10] and a^2 taking values in the range [101...200]. Assume there are two servers for a^1: S^{11} takes care of recording values of a^1 in [1..5], and S^{12} for values in [6..10]. Likewise, server S^{21} records values for a^2 in range [101..150] and server S^{22} for values in [151..200]. Then, when an entity E has associated attribute values

$(a^1 = 7, a^2 = 175)$, server S^{12} *and* server S^{22} will maintain a copy of, or a reference to E.

The advantage of this scheme is that range queries can be easily supported. When a query is issued to return resources that have a^2 lying between 165 and 189, the query can be forwarded to the server S^{22} who can then return the resources that match the query range. The drawback, however, is that updates need to be sent to multiple servers. Moreover, it is not immediately clear how well the load is balanced between the various servers. In particular, if certain range queries turn out to be very popular, specific servers will receive a high fraction of all queries.

Summarizing remarks   There are indeed many ways of supporting attribute-based naming systems in a decentralized fashion. The essence in all cases is to assign attributes to servers so that clients know where to direct their queries, yet at the same time make sure that there is a balance in the load for the set of servers. In this light, supporting range queries requires special attention, if only to decide which server will be responsible for which subrange.

In practice, we see that when dealing with N attributes, many systems model the collection of *(attribute, value)* pairs as an N-dimensional space in which each entity is represented by a unique point in that space. Conceptually, a search addresses a subspace and leads to identifying the servers responsible for that subspace. In the simplest case, we assign each attribute to one server, leading to $\mathcal{O}(N)$ servers. In this scheme, a query addressing k attributes needs to be sent to k servers, while the querying client needs to combine the results. We have discussed this case previously. The problem is to divide the ranges per attribute among subservers such that we have a reasonable balance of the workload. A solution to this problem is discussed in [Bharambe et al., 2004].

Instead of letting a client combine results, we can let servers collaborate. To this end, the N-dimensional space is divided into subspaces by splitting each dimension d into n_d intervals. This splitting leads to a total of $n_1 \times \cdots \times n_N$ subspaces, where each subspace is assigned to a separate server. Even with $n_d = 2$ for each dimension, we will face a total of $\mathcal{O}(2^N)$ servers. Using space-filling curves, we can reduce the number of dimensions to one, and use a separate technique for deciding which N-dimensional subspace is served by which server. Practice indicates that load balancing may become an issue. An alternative solution in which the number of dimensions is still reduced, but larger than one, while also maintaining load balancing, has been built into HyperDex [Escriva et al., 2012]. The authors also address the problem of replication and consistency in case the naming system at the same time stores the entities which it indexes. In that case, whenever a server indexes an entity E, it will have to be copied to the respective server.

Attribute-based naming is particularly relevant for distributed systems when it comes to resource discovery and selection. An interesting case is

described by Stratan et al. [2012]. Again, the attribute space is modeled by an
N-dimensional space in which each resource is associated with a coordinate.
In this situation, each resource maintains a link to another resource, but one
that is responsible for a subspace of exponentially increasing size. The net
effect is that each resource needs to have only a fixed number of neighbors,
while routing a query to the relevant subspace, takes only a linear number
of steps. The organization is akin to the use of finger tables in Chord. An
extensive overview of resource discovery in distributed systems is discussed
by Zarrin et al. [2018].

6.5 Named-data networking

In our discussion so far, we have made a distinction between names, identifiers,
and addresses. In particular, we have argued that a name needs to be resolved
to an address, to access the named entity (recall that we referred to an address
as the name of an entity's access point). At least on one occasion, we dropped
this name-resolution process, namely when discussing how an identifier as
used in Chord, or other DHTs, could be directly used to route a lookup
request to a specific node. Let us now challenge the need for name-to-address
resolution by taking a closer look into **Information-centric networking**, or
simply **ICN** [Ahlgren et al., 2012]. In particular, we concentrate on its perhaps
most popular form, namely **named-data networking (NDN)**.

6.5.1 Basics

Named-data networking revolves around the principle that applications are
not really interested to know *where* an entity is stored, but rather that they can
get a copy to access it locally when needed. To this end, much research has
been spent since approximately 2007 on designing an alternative to the host-
based addressing schemes that are common in today's Internet. In particular,
the main idea is that an application can retrieve an entity from the network
by using that entity's name. The network takes that name as input, and
subsequently routes a request to an appropriate location where the entity is
stored, to return a copy to the requester. In effect, NDN takes over the role of
IP in a future architecture of the Internet, as illustrated in Figure 6.32.

An important consequence of this organization is that instead of first
resolving a name to an address, and then routing a request toward that
address, the name of an entity is directly used to fetch the associated data.
We already came across this scheme when discussing how a lookup request
in DHTs, based on a unique key associated with an entity, is routed toward a
node responsible for that key.

In NDN, names are assumed to be structured. For example, this chapter
may be referred to as

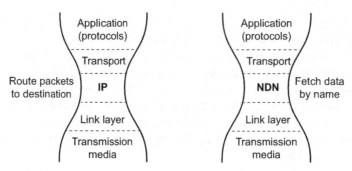

Figure 6.32: The role of NDN in comparison to IP when viewing the Internet protocol stack as an hourglass (slightly adapted from [Afanasyev et al., 2018]).

/distributed-systems.net/books/Distributed Systems/4/01/Naming

indicating the book at distributed-systems.net entitled Distributed Systems, its 4th edition, version 01, and, in particular, the chapter called Naming. This immediately raises the question how users and applications can and should name entities. One way or the other, the name, or naming scheme, of an entity should be globally known, and otherwise it becomes impossible to fetch the data associated with a name. Likewise, globally available entities should have globally unique names. How this naming is realized is outside the scope of NDN. A general overview and introduction to NDN can be found in [Afanasyev et al., 2018] and [Saxena et al., 2016].

Note that named-data networking assumes that data cannot be modified without generating a new name. Without this assumption, efficiency may be at stake, as caching by routers becomes by far less effective (as we describe shortly). This may seem to be a drawback, yet as long as a user knows that updates may be available, she can always ask for the latest version. There are various ways to achieve this. For example, when sending out a request for named data, a source may respond with the required data, but also with additional information that an update is available (and may even send that update along with the originally requested data). An example of how such schemes can be deployed for keeping up-to-date in a chat conversation is described in [Zhu and Afanasyev, 2013].

To better facilitate updates, named-data networking provides separate synchronization protocols, which are surveyed in [Moll et al., 2021]. In essence, all these protocols allow the owner of named data to announce updates to interested parties, thus essentially sending a multicast message within an NDN network. Depending on what is actually announced, a recipient may subsequently decide to fetch the update through an explicit request (which, again, is a name for the updated data).

6.5.2 Routing

For our discussion, perhaps the most interesting part of NDN is how to realize routing and forwarding of requests for named data. Initially, one might think that with seemingly arbitrary structured names routing may be inherently subject to serious scalability problems, for how to find content on the Internet by using just its name? When giving the matter some thought, the problem is fundamentally not very different when deploying IP addresses, for how would one find the access point associated with the IPv4 address 145.100.190.243, or the IPv6 address 2001:610:508:108:192:87:108:15 (both belong to surf.nl)? As argued by Zhang et al. [2019], there is really no difference and a decision needs to be made on which part of a name or address (i.e., a prefix) should be announced within a global routing substrate, just as is currently done with IPv4 addresses with BGP routers. Once a named packet has found its way into an organization's network, specific techniques can be used to forward it to places where the associated content can be found.

Returning to our example name, for

distributed-systems.net/books/Distributed Systems/4/01/Naming

we could decide to use /distributed-systems.net as a global prefix that should be used at the level of BGP routers for globally routing requests to an organization's network responsible for that prefix. Within that network, we can use the rest of the name to search for the associated content. Special NDN routers will be needed for this purpose, which we explain next.

An NDN router, shown in Figure 6.33, consists of three elements:

1. A **content store** is essentially a cache for keeping data associated with a (previously looked up) name. If a named request enters a router, and the named data is in this cache, the router immediately returns that data to the requester, as shown in Figure 6.33(a).

2. A **pending interest table** is nothing but a table that keeps track of a *(name,interface)* pair: if a request for data named N arrived through interface I of the router, then (N,I) is stored. This will allow a router to return a response whenever the associated data arrives at the router. As shown in Figure 6.33(b), if data enters the router but there is no (longer any) interest, the router can decide to drop the data.

3. A **forwarding information base** tells the router what to do when it cannot serve a request, as shown in Figure 6.33(a). For example, the request may be flooded to all neighboring routers, a random walk may be initiated, or, perhaps for whatever reason, the request may be dropped. Again, note that these decisions are fundamentally not different from routing using IPv4 or IPv6 address.

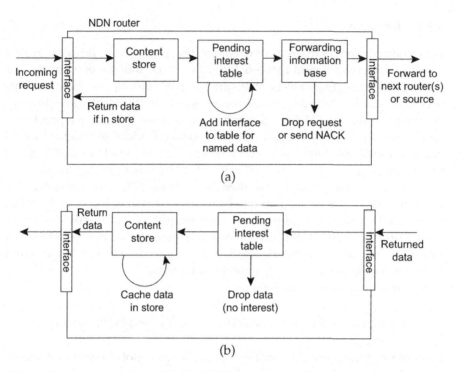

Figure 6.33: The proposed general organization of an NDN router when (a) a request flows in to the router and (b) the data is returned from another router or the source.

When a request forwarded by a router eventually returns a response, the router will look up whether there was a pending request, send it through the associated interface, and clear the entry in the pending interest table. Also, the router may decide to store the returned content in its content store for future requests, as also shown in Figure 6.33(b).

This design opens many opportunities for routing optimizations, including decisions on what to cache, when to evict data from the content store, how and to whom to forward requests, and so on. Practice will have to show whether named-data networking can indeed form a (partial) replacement of the current IP-based Internet.

6.5.3 Security in named-data networking

There are various aspects related to security in named-data networking. Besides secure naming, a weak aspect of any naming system is that the name servers and routers need to be protected as well. There are numerous threats to the NDN routers, which in the end all boil down to effectively attempting to disrupt the service. A complete overview of the various threats and possible solutions is provided by Tourani et al. [2018] to which we refer the interested reader. Here, analogous to our discussion on secure DNS, we briefly discuss secure naming.

Secure naming is all about ensuring that the provided name is unforgeably linked to the content it refers to. The simplest way of doing this, is by including a signed digest of that content into the name, similar to self-certifying names, as we discussed in Section 6.2.5. Assuming additional information is available to the recipient of the named data, such as information on which hash function has been used, as well as the public key (perhaps including its certificate), the recipient can verify that the returned content is indeed associated with the name.

6.6 Summary

Names are used to refer to entities. Essentially, there are three types of names. An address is the name of an access point associated with an entity, also simply called the address of an entity. An identifier is another type of name. It has three properties: each entity is referred to by exactly one identifier, an identifier refers to only one entity, and is never assigned to another entity. Finally, human-friendly names are targeted to be used by humans, and as such are represented as character strings. Given these types, we make a distinction between flat naming, structured naming, and attribute-based naming.

Systems for flat naming essentially need to resolve an identifier to the address of its associated entity. This locating of an entity can be done in different ways. The first approach is to use broadcasting or multicasting. The identifier of the entity is broadcast to every process in the distributed system. The process offering an access point for the entity responds by providing an address for that access point. Obviously, this approach has limited scalability.

A second approach is to use forwarding pointers. Each time an entity moves to a next location, it leaves behind a pointer telling where it will be next. Locating the entity requires traversing the path of forwarding pointers. To avoid large chains of pointers, it is important to reduce chains periodically

A third approach is to allocate a home to an entity. Each time an entity moves to another location, it informs its home where it is. Locating an entity proceeds by first asking its home for the current location.

A fourth approach is to organize all nodes into a structured peer-to-peer system, and systematically assign nodes to entities, taking their respective identifiers into account. By subsequently devising a routing algorithm by which lookup requests are moved toward the node responsible for a given entity, efficient and robust name resolution is possible.

A fifth approach is to build a hierarchical search tree. The network is divided into nonoverlapping domains. Domains can be grouped into higher-level (nonoverlapping) domains, and so on. There is a single top-level domain that covers the entire network. Each domain at every level has an associated directory node. If an entity is located in a domain D, the directory node of the next higher-level domain will have a pointer to D. A lowest-level directory node stores the address of the entity. The top-level directory node knows about all entities.

Structured names are easily organized in a name space. A name space can be represented by a naming graph in which a node represents a named entity and the label on an edge represents the name under which that entity is known. A node having multiple outgoing edges represents a collection of entities and is also known as a context node or directory. Large-scale naming graphs are often organized as rooted acyclic directed graphs.

Naming graphs are convenient to organize human-friendly names in a structured way. An entity can be referred to by a path name. Name resolution is the process of traversing the naming graph by looking up the components of a path name, one at a time. A large-scale naming graph is implemented by distributing its nodes across multiple name servers. When resolving a path name by traversing the naming graph, name resolution continues at the next name server as soon as a node is reached, implemented by that server.

More problematic are attribute-based naming schemes in which entities are described by a collection of (*attribute, value*) pairs. Queries are also formulated as such pairs, essentially requiring an exhaustive search through all descriptors. Such a search is feasible only when the descriptors are stored in a single database. However, alternative solutions have been devised by which the pairs are mapped onto DHT-based systems, essentially leading to a distribution of the collection of entity descriptors. Using space-filling curves, we can then make different nodes responsible for different values of an attribute, which helps in effectively distributing the load among the nodes in the case of search operations.

Instead of making the distinction between the name and an address of an entity, researchers have been exploring the possibility of routing requests directly based on an entity's name, similar to using an identifier when looking up information in a peer-to-peer system. In so-called named-data networks, an application systematically fetches (read only) data by providing a name. In the end, the network returns the associated data instead of an address of the access point.

07

CONSISTENCY
AND
REPLICATION

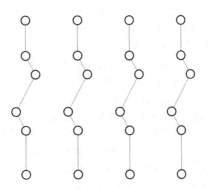

An important issue in distributed systems is the replication of data. Data are generally replicated to enhance reliability or improve performance. One of the major problems is keeping replicas consistent. Informally, this means that when one copy is updated, we need to ensure that the other copies are updated as well; otherwise the replicas will no longer be the same. In this chapter, we take a detailed look at what consistency of replicated data actually means, and the various ways that consistency can be achieved.

We start with a general introduction discussing why replication is useful and how it relates to scalability. We then continue by focusing on what consistency actually means. An important class of what are known as consistency models assumes that multiple processes simultaneously access shared data. Consistency for these situations can be formulated regarding what processes can expect when reading and updating the shared data, knowing that others are accessing that data as well.

Consistency models for shared data are often hard to implement efficiently in large-scale distributed systems. Moreover, often simpler models can be used, which are also often easier to implement. One specific class is formed by client-centric consistency models, which concentrate on consistency from the perspective of a single (possibly mobile) client. Client-centric consistency models are discussed in a separate section.

Consistency is only half of the story. We also need to consider how consistency is actually implemented. There are essentially two, more or less independent, issues we need to consider. First, we start with concentrating on managing replicas, which considers not only the placement of replica servers, but also how content is distributed to these servers.

The second issue is how replicas are kept consistent. In most cases, applications require a strong form of consistency. Informally, this means that updates are to be propagated more or less immediately between replicas. There are various alternatives for implementing strong consistency, which are discussed in a separate section. Also, attention is paid to caching protocols, which form a special case of consistency protocols.

Being arguably the largest distributed system, we pay separate attention to caching and replication in Web-based systems, notably looking at content delivery networks as well as edge-server caching techniques.

7.1 Introduction

In this section, we start with discussing the important reasons for wanting to replicate data in the first place. We concentrate on replication as a technique for achieving scalability, and motivate why reasoning about consistency is so important.

7.1.1 Reasons for replication

There are two primary reasons for replicating data. First, data are replicated to increase the reliability of a system. If a file system has been replicated, it may be possible to continue working after one replica crashes by simply switching to one of the other replicas. Also, by maintaining multiple copies, it becomes possible to provide better protection against corrupted data. For example, imagine there are three copies of a file, and every read and write operation is performed on each copy. We can safeguard ourselves against a single, failing write operation, by considering the value that is returned by at least two copies as being the correct one.

The other reason for replicating data is performance. Replication for performance is important when a distributed system needs to scale in terms of size or in terms of the geographical area it covers. Scaling regarding size occurs, for example, when an increasing number of processes needs to access data that are managed by a single server. In that case, performance can be improved by replicating the server and subsequently dividing the workload among the processes accessing the data.

Scaling regarding a geographical area may also require replication. The basic idea is that by placing a copy of data in proximity of the process using them, the time to access the data decreases. As a consequence, the performance as perceived by that process increases. This example also illustrates that the benefits of replication for performance may be hard to evaluate. Although a client process may perceive better performance, it may also be the case that more network bandwidth is now consumed keeping all replicas up to date.

If replication helps to improve reliability and performance, who could be against it? Unfortunately, there is a price to be paid when data are replicated. The problem with replication is that having multiple copies may lead to consistency problems. Whenever a copy is modified, that copy becomes different from the rest. Consequently, modifications have to be carried out on all copies to ensure consistency. Exactly when and how those modifications need to be carried out determines the price of replication.

To understand the problem, consider improving access times to Web pages. If no special measures are taken, fetching a page from a remote Web server may sometimes even take seconds to complete. To improve performance, Web browsers often locally store a copy of a previously fetched Web page (i.e., they **cache** a Web page). If a user requires that page again, the browser automatically returns the local copy. The access time as perceived by the user, is excellent. However, if the user always wants to have the latest version of a page, she may be in for bad luck. The problem is that if the page has been modified in the meantime, modifications will not have been propagated to cached copies, making those copies out-of-date.

One solution to the problem of returning a stale copy to the user is to forbid the browser to keep local copies in the first place, effectively letting the server be fully in charge of replication. However, this solution may still lead to poor access times if no replica is placed near the user. Another solution is to let the Web server invalidate or update each cached copy, but this requires that the server keeps track of all caches and sending them messages. This, in turn, may degrade the overall performance of the server. We return to performance versus scalability issues below.

In the following, we will mainly concentrate on replication for performance. Replication for reliability is discussed in Chapter 8.

7.1.2   Replication as scaling technique

Replication and caching for performance are widely applied as scaling techniques. Scalability issues generally appear in the form of performance problems. Placing copies of data close to the processes using them can improve performance through reduction of access time, and thus solve scalability problems.

A possible trade-off that needs to be made is that keeping copies up to date may require more network bandwidth. Consider a process P that accesses a local replica N times per second, whereas the replica itself is updated M times per second. Assume that an update completely refreshes the previous version of the local replica. If $N \ll M$, that is, the access-to-update ratio is very low, we have the situation where many updated versions of the local replica will never be accessed by P, rendering the network communication for those versions useless. In this case, it may have been better not to install a local replica close to P, or to apply a different strategy for updating the replica.

A more serious problem, however, is that keeping multiple copies consistent may itself be subject to serious scalability problems. Intuitively, a collection of copies is consistent when the copies are always the same. This means that a read operation performed at any copy will always return the same result. Consequently, when an update operation is performed on one copy, the update should be propagated to all copies before a subsequent operation takes place, no matter at which copy that operation is initiated or performed.

This type of consistency is sometimes informally (and imprecisely) referred to as tight consistency, as provided by what is also called synchronous replication. (In Section 7.2, we will provide precise definitions of consistency and introduce a range of consistency models.) The key idea is that an update is performed at all copies as a single atomic operation, or transaction. Unfortunately, implementing atomicity involving many replicas that may be widely dispersed across a large-scale network is inherently difficult when operations are also required to complete quickly.

Difficulties come from the fact that we need to synchronize all replicas. In essence, this means that all replicas first need to reach agreement on when exactly an update is to be performed locally. For example, replicas may need to decide on a global ordering of operations using Lamport timestamps, or let a coordinator assign such an order. Global synchronization simply takes a lot of communication time, especially when replicas are spread across a wide-area network.

We are now faced with a dilemma. On the one hand, scalability problems can be alleviated by applying replication and caching, leading to improved performance. On the other hand, to keep all copies consistent generally requires global synchronization, which is inherently costly in terms of performance. The cure may be worse than the disease.

Often, the only real solution is to relax the consistency constraints. In other words, if we can relax the requirement that updates need to be executed as atomic operations, we may be able to avoid (instantaneous) global synchronizations, and may thus gain performance. The price paid is that copies may not always be the same everywhere. As it turns out, to what extent consistency can be relaxed depends highly on the access and update patterns of the replicated data, as well as on the purpose for which those data are used.

There is a range of consistency models and many ways to implement models through what are called distribution and consistency protocols. Approaches to classifying consistency and replication can be found in [Gray et al., 1996; Wiesmann et al., 2000; Aguilera and Terry, 2016], and [Viotti and Vukolic, 2016].

7.2 Data-centric consistency models

Traditionally, consistency has been discussed in the context of read and write operations on shared data, available through (distributed) shared memory, a (distributed) shared database, or a (distributed) file system. Here, we use the broader term **data store**. A data store may be physically distributed across multiple machines. In particular, each process that can access data from the store is assumed to have a local (or nearby) copy available of the entire store. Write operations are propagated to the other copies, as shown in Figure 7.1. A data operation is classified as a write operation when it changes the data, and is otherwise classified as a read operation.

A **(date centric) consistency model** is essentially a contract between processes and the data store. It says that if processes agree to obey certain rules, the store promises to work correctly. Normally, a process that performs a read operation on a data item, expects the operation to return a value that shows the results of the last write operation on that data.

Lacking a global clock, it is difficult to define precisely which write operation is the last one. As an alternative, we need to provide other definitions, leading to a range of consistency models. Each model effectively restricts the values that a read operation on a data item can return. As is to be expected,

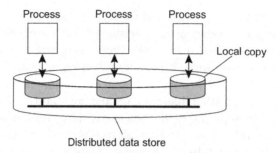

Figure 7.1: The general organization of a logical data store, physically distributed and replicated across multiple processes.

the ones with major restrictions are easy to use, for example when developing applications, whereas those with minor restrictions are generally considered to be difficult to use in practice. The trade-off is, of course, that the easy-to-use models do not perform nearly as well as the difficult ones. Such is life.

7.2.1   Consistent ordering of operations

There is a huge body of work on data-centric consistency models from the past decades. An important class of models comes from the field of parallel programming. Confronted with the fact that in parallel and distributed computing multiple processes will need to share resources and access these resources simultaneously, researchers have sought to express the semantics of concurrent accesses when shared resources are replicated. The models that we discuss here all deal with consistently ordering operations on shared, replicated data.

Sequential consistency

In the following, we will use a special notation in which we draw the operations of a process along a time axis. The time axis is always drawn horizontally, with time increasing from left to right. We use the notation $W_i(x)a$ to denote that process P_i writes value a to data item x. Similarly, $R_i(x)b$ represents the fact that process P_i reads x and is returned the value b. We assume that each data item has an initial value NIL. When there is no confusion about which process is accessing data, we omit the index from the symbols W and R.

As an example, in Figure 7.2 P_1 does a write to a data item x, modifying its value to a. Note that, according to our system model the operation $W_1(x)a$ is first performed on a copy of the data store that is local to P_1, and only then is it propagated to the other local copies. In our example, P_2 later reads the value NIL, and some time after that a (from its local copy of the store). What

Figure 7.2: Behavior of two processes operating on the same data item. The horizontal axis is time.

we are seeing here is that it took some time to propagate the update of x to P_2, which is perfectly acceptable.

Sequential consistency is an important data-centric consistency model, which was first defined by Lamport [1979] in the context of shared memory for multiprocessor systems. A data store is said to be sequentially consistent when it satisfies the following condition:

> *The result of any execution is the same as if the (read and write) operations by all processes on the data store were executed in some sequential order and the operations of each individual process appear in this sequence in the order specified by its program.*

What this definition means is that when processes run concurrently on (possibly) different machines, any valid interleaving of read and write operations is acceptable behavior, but *all processes see the same interleaving of operations*. Note that nothing is said about time; that is, there is no reference to the "most recent" write operation on a data item. Also, a process "sees" the writes from all process, but only through its own reads.

That time does not play a role can be seen from Figure 7.3. Consider four processes operating on the same data item x. In Figure 7.3(a) process P_1 first performs $W_1(x)a$ on x. Later (in absolute time), process P_2 also performs a write operation $W_2(x)b$, by setting the value of x to b. However, both processes P_3 and P_4 *first* read value b, and *later* value a. In other words, the write operation $W_2(x)b$ of process P_2 appears to have taken place before $W_1(x)a$ of P_1.

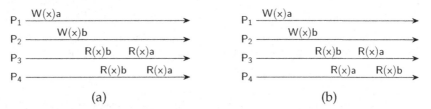

Figure 7.3: (a) A sequentially consistent data store. (b) A data store that is not sequentially consistent.

In contrast, Figure 7.3(b) violates sequential consistency because not all processes see the same interleaving of write operations. In particular, to process P$_3$, it appears as if the data item has first been changed to b, and later to a. On the other hand, P$_4$ will conclude that the final value is b.

Process P$_1$	Process P$_2$	Process P$_3$
x ← 1;	y ← 1;	z ← 1;
print(y,z);	print(x,z);	print(x,y);

Figure 7.4: Three concurrently executing processes.

To make the notion of sequential consistency more concrete, consider three concurrently executing processes P$_1$, P$_2$, and P$_3$, shown in Figure 7.4 (taken from [Dubois et al., 1988]). The data items in this example are formed by the three integer variables x, y, and z, which are stored in a (possibly distributed) shared sequentially consistent data store. We assume that each variable is initialized to 0. In this example, an assignment corresponds to a write operation, whereas a print statement corresponds to a simultaneous read operation of its two arguments. All statements are assumed to be indivisible.

Various interleaved execution sequences are possible. With six independent statements, there are potentially 720 (6!) possible execution sequences, although some of these violate program order. Consider the 120 (5!) sequences that begin with x ← 1. Half of these have print(x,z) before y ← 1 and thus violate program order. Half also have print(x,y) before z ← 1 and also violate program order. Only 1/4 of the 120 sequences, or 30, are valid. Another 30 valid sequences are possible starting with y ← 1 and another 30 can begin with z ← 1, for a total of 90 valid execution sequences. Four of these are shown in Figure 7.5.

Execution 1		Execution 2		Execution 3		Execution 4	
P$_1$:	x ← 1;	P$_1$:	x ← 1;	P$_2$:	y ← 1;	P$_2$:	y ← 1;
P$_1$:	print(y,z);	P$_2$:	y ← 1;	P$_3$:	z ← 1;	P$_1$:	x ← 1;
P$_2$:	y ← 1;	P$_2$:	print(x,z);	P$_3$:	print(x,y);	P$_3$:	z ← 1;
P$_2$:	print(x,z);	P$_1$:	print(y,z);	P$_2$:	print(x,z);	P$_2$:	print(x,z);
P$_3$:	z ← 1;	P$_3$:	z ← 1;	P$_1$:	x ← 1;	P$_1$:	print(y,z);
P$_3$:	print(x,y);	P$_3$:	print(x,y);	P$_1$:	print(y,z);	P$_3$:	print(x,y);
Prints: 001011		*Prints:* 101011		*Prints:* 010111		*Prints:* 111111	
Signature: 00 10 11		*Signature:* 10 10 11		*Signature:* 11 01 01		*Signature:* 11 11 11	
(a)		(b)		(c)		(d)	

Figure 7.5: Four valid execution sequences for the processes of Figure 7.4. The vertical axis is time.

In Figure 7.5(a) the three processes are run in order, first P$_1$, then P$_2$, then P$_3$. The other three examples demonstrate different, but equally valid, interleaving of the statements in time. Each of the three processes prints two variables. Since the only values each variable can take on are the initial value (0), or the assigned value (1), each process produces a 2-bit string. The numbers after *Prints* are the actual outputs that appear on the output device.

If we concatenate the output of P_1, P_2, and P_3 in that order, we get a 6-bit string that characterizes a particular interleaving of statements. This is the string listed as the *Signature* in Figure 7.5. Below, we will characterize each ordering by its time-independent signature rather than by its printout.

Not all 64 signature patterns are allowed. As a trivial example, 00 00 00 is not permitted because that would imply that the print statements ran before the assignment statements, violating the requirement that statements are executed in program order. A more subtle example is 00 10 01. The first two bits, 00, mean that y and z were both 0 when P_1 did its printing. This situation occurs only when P_1 executes both statements before P_2 or P_3 starts. The next two bits, 10, mean that P_2 must run after P_1 has started but before P_3 has started. The last two bits, 01, mean that P_3 must complete before P_1 starts, but we have already seen that P_1 must go first. Therefore, 00 10 01 is not allowed.

In short, the 90 different valid statement orderings produce a variety of different program results (less than 64, though) that are allowed under the assumption of sequential consistency. The contract between the processes and the distributed shared data store is that the processes must accept all of these as valid results. In other words, the processes must accept the four results shown in Figure 7.5 and all the other valid results as proper answers, and must work correctly if any of them occurs. A program that works for some of these results and not for others violates the contract with the data store and is incorrect.

This example also shows that sequential consistency is not easy to understand at first sight. In the following note, we zoom more into the intricacies.

Note 7.1 (Advanced: The importance and intricacies of sequential consistency)
There is no doubt that sequential consistency is an important model. In essence, of all consistency models that exist and have been developed, it is the easiest one to understand when developing concurrent and parallel applications. This is because the model matches our expectations best when we let several programs operate on shared data simultaneously. At the same time, implementing sequential consistency is far from trivial [Adve and Boehm, 2010]. To illustrate, consider the example involving two variables x and y, shown in Figure 7.6.

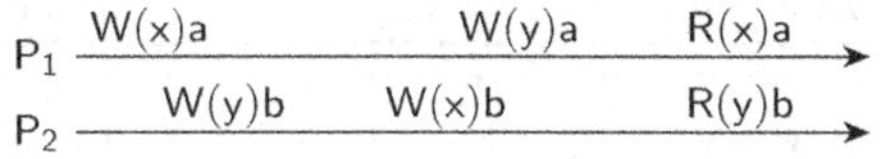

Figure 7.6: Both x and y are each handled in a sequentially consistent manner, but taken together, sequential consistency is violated.

If we just consider the write and read operations on x, the fact that P_1 reads the value a is perfectly consistent. The same holds for the operation $R_2(y)b$ by process P_2. However, when taken together, there is no way that we can order the write operations on x and y such that we can have $R_1(x)a$ and $R_2(y)b$ (note that we need to keep the ordering as executed by each process):

Ordering of operations	Result	
$W_1(x)a; W_1(y)a; W_2(y)b; W_2(x)b$	$R_1(x)b$	$R_2(y)b$
$W_1(x)a; W_2(y)b; W_1(y)a; W_2(x)b$	$R_1(x)b$	$R_2(y)a$
$W_1(x)a; W_2(y)b; W_2(x)b; W_1(y)a$	$R_1(x)b$	$R_2(y)a$
$W_2(y)b; W_1(x)a; W_1(y)a; W_2(x)b$	$R_1(x)b$	$R_2(y)a$
$W_2(y)b; W_1(x)a; W_2(x)b; W_1(y)a$	$R_1(x)b$	$R_2(y)a$
$W_2(y)b; W_2(x)b; W_1(x)a; W_1(y)a$	$R_1(x)a$	$R_2(y)a$

In terms of transactions, the operations carried out by P_1 and P_2 are not **serializable**. Our example shows that sequential consistency is not **compositional**: when having data items that are each kept sequentially consistent, their composition as a set need not be so [Herlihy et al., 2021]. The problem of noncompositional consistency can be solved by assuming **linearizability**. This is best explained by making a distinction between the start and completion of an operation, and assuming that it may take some time. Linearizability [Herlihy and Wing, 1991] states that:

> *Each operation should appear to take effect instantaneously at some moment between its start and completion.*

Returning to our example, Figure 7.7 shows the same set of write operations, but we have now also indicated when they take place: the shaded area designates the time the operation is being executed. Linearizability states that the effect of an operation should take place somewhere during the interval indicated by the shaded area. In principle, this means that at the time of completion of a write operation, the results should be propagated to the other data stores.

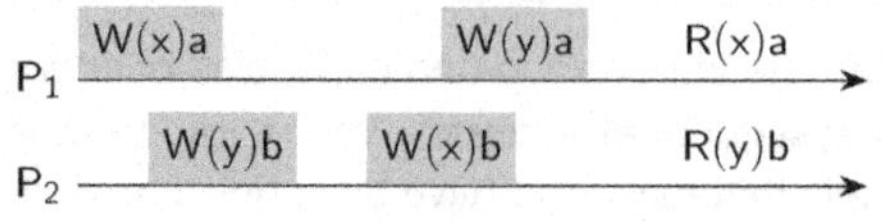

Figure 7.7: An example of taking linearizable sequential consistency into account, with only one possible outcome for x and y.

With that in mind, the possibilities for properly ordering become limited:

Ordering of operations	Result	
$W_1(x)a; W_2(y)b; W_1(y)a; W_2(x)b$	$R_1(x)b$	$R_2(y)a$
$W_1(x)a; W_2(y)b; W_2(x)b; W_1(y)a$	$R_1(x)b$	$R_2(y)a$
$W_2(y)b; W_1(x)a; W_1(y)a; W_2(x)b$	$R_1(x)b$	$R_2(y)a$
$W_2(y)b; W_1(x)a; W_2(x)b; W_1(y)a$	$R_1(x)b$	$R_2(y)a$

In particular, $W_2(y)b$ is completed before $W_1(y)a$ starts, so that y will have the value a. Likewise, $W_1(x)a$ completes before $W_2(x)b$ starts, so that x will have value b. It should not come as a surprise that implementing linearizability on a many-core architecture may impose serious performance problems. Yet at the same time, it eases programmability considerably, so a trade-off needs to be made.

Causal consistency

The **causal consistency** model [Hutto and Ahamad, 1990] represents a weakening of sequential consistency in that it makes a distinction between events that are potentially causally related and those that are not. We already came across causality when discussing vector timestamps in the previous chapter. If event b is caused or influenced by an earlier event a, causality requires that everyone else first see a, then see b.

Consider a simple interaction using a distributed shared database. Suppose that process P_1 writes a data item x. Then P_2 reads x and writes y. Here, the reading of x and the writing of y are potentially causally related because the computation of y may have depended on the value of x as read by P_2 (i.e., the value written by P_1).

On the other hand, if two processes spontaneously and simultaneously write two different data items, these are not causally related. Operations that are not causally related are said to be **concurrent**.

For a data store to be considered causally consistent, it is necessary that the store obeys the following condition:

> *Writes that are potentially causally related must be seen by all processes in the same order. Concurrent writes may be seen in a different order on different machines.*

As an example of causal consistency, consider Figure 7.8. Here we have an event sequence that is allowed with a causally consistent store, but which is forbidden with a sequentially consistent store or a strictly consistent store. The thing to note is that the writes $W_2(x)b$ and $W_1(x)c$ are concurrent, so it is not required that all processes see them in the same order.

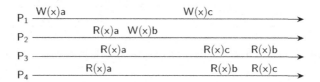

Figure 7.8: This sequence is allowed with a causally consistent store, but not with a sequentially consistent store.

Now consider a second example. In Figure 7.9(a) we have $W_2(x)b$ potentially depending on $W_1(x)a$ because writing the value b into x may be a result of a computation involving the previously read value by $R_2(x)a$. The two writes are causally related, so all processes must see them in the same order. Therefore, Figure 7.9(a) is incorrect. On the other hand, in Figure 7.9(b) the read has been removed, so $W_1(x)a$ and $W_2(x)b$ are now concurrent writes. A causally consistent store does not require concurrent writes to be globally ordered, so Figure 7.9(b) is correct. Note that Figure 7.9(b) reflects a situation that would not be acceptable for a sequentially consistent store.

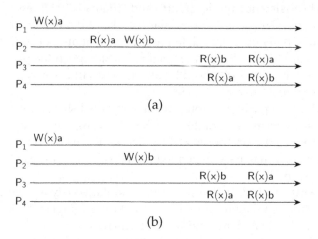

Figure 7.9: (a) A violation of a causally consistent store. (b) A correct sequence of events in a causally consistent store.

Implementing causal consistency requires keeping track of which processes have seen which writes. There are many subtle issues to consider. To illustrate, assume we replace $W_2(x)b$ in Figure 7.9(a) with $W_2(y)b$, and likewise $R_3(x)b$ with $R_3(y)b$, respectively. This situation is shown in Figure 7.10.

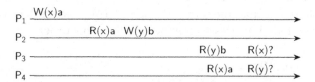

Figure 7.10: A slight modification of Figure 7.9(a). What should $R_3(x)$ or $R_4(y)$ return?

Let us first look at operation $R_3(x)$. Process P_3 executes this operation after $R_3(y)b$. We know at this point for sure that $W(x)a$ *happened before* $W(y)b$. In particular, $W(x)a \rightarrow R(x)a \rightarrow W(y)b$, meaning that if we are to preserve causality, reading x after reading b from y can return only a. If the system returned NIL to P_3 it would violate the preservation of causal relationships.

What about $R_4(y)$? Could it return the initial value of y, namely NIL? The answer is affirmative: although we have the formal *happened-before* relationship $W(x)a \rightarrow W(y)b$, without having read b from y, process P_4 can still justifiably observe that $W(x)a$ took place independently of the initialization of y.

Implementation wise, preserving causality introduces some interesting questions. Consider, for example, the middleware underlying process P_3 from Figure 7.10. At the point that this middleware returns the value b from reading y, it must know about the relationship $W(x)a \rightarrow W(y)b$. In other words, when the most recent value of y was propagated to P_3's middleware, at the very least, metadata on y's dependency should have been propagated as well. Alternatively, the propagation may have also been done together with updating x at P_3's node. By-and-large, the bottom line is that we need a dependency graph of which operation is dependent on which other operations. Such a graph may be pruned at the moment that dependent data is also locally stored.

Grouping operations

Many consistency models are defined at the level of elementary read and write operations. This level of granularity is for historical reasons: these models have initially been developed for shared-memory multiprocessor systems and were actually implemented at the hardware level.

The fine granularity of these consistency models often does not match the granularity as provided by applications. What we see there is that concurrency between programs sharing data is generally kept under control through synchronization mechanisms for mutual exclusion and transactions. Effectively, what happens is that at the program level, read and write operations are bracketed by the pair of operations ENTER_CS and LEAVE_CS. A process that has successfully executed ENTER_CS will be ensured that all the data in its local store is up-to-date. At that point, it can safely execute a series of read and write operations on that store, and subsequently wrap things up by calling LEAVE_CS. Data and instructions between ENTER_CS and LEAVE_CS is denoted as a **critical region**.

In essence, what happens is that within a program, the data that are operated on by a series of read and write operations are protected against concurrent accesses that would lead to seeing something else than the result of executing the series as a whole. Put differently, the bracketing turns the series of read and write operations into an atomically executed unit, thus raising the level of granularity.

To reach this point, we do need to have precise semantics concerning the operations ENTER_CS and LEAVE_CS. These semantics can be formulated in terms of shared **synchronization variables**, or simply **locks**. A lock has shared data items associated with it, and each shared data item is associated with at most one lock. In the case of coarse-grained synchronization, all shared data items would be associated to just a single lock. Fine-grained synchronization is achieved when each shared data item has its own unique lock. Of course, these are just two extremes of associating shared data to a lock. When a process enters a critical region, it should *acquire* the relevant locks, and likewise when it leaves the critical region, it *releases* these locks.

Each lock has a current owner, namely, the process that last acquired it. A process not currently owning a lock but wanting to acquire it has to send a message to the current owner asking for ownership and the current values of the data associated with that lock. While having *exclusive access* to a lock, a process is allowed to perform read and write operations. It is also possible for several processes to simultaneously have *nonexclusive access* to a lock, meaning that they can read, but not write, the associated data. Of course, nonexclusive access can be granted if and only if there is no other process having exclusive access.

We now demand that the following criteria are met [Bershad et al., 1993]:

- Acquiring a lock can succeed only when all updates to its associated shared data have completed.

- Exclusive access to a lock can succeed only if no other process has exclusive or nonexclusive access to that lock.

- Nonexclusive access to a lock is allowed only if any previous exclusive access has been completed, including updates to the lock's associated data.

Note that we are effectively demanding that the usage of locks is linearized, adhering to sequential consistency. Figure 7.11 shows an example of what is known as **entry consistency**. We associate a lock with each data item separately. We use the notation $L(x)$ as an abbreviation for acquiring the lock for x, that is, *locking* x. Likewise, $U(x)$ stands for releasing the lock on x, or *unlocking* it. In this case, P_1 locks x, changes x once, after which it locks y. Process P_2 also acquires the lock for x but not for y so that it will read value a for x, but may read NIL for y. However, because process P_3 first acquires the lock for y, it will read the value b when y was unlocked by P_1. It is important to note here that each process has a *copy* of a variable, but that this copy need not be instantly or automatically updated. When locking or unlocking a variable, a process is explicitly telling the underlying distributed system that the copies of that variable need to be synchronized. A simple read operation without locking may thus result in reading a local value that is effectively stale.

One of the programming problems with entry consistency is properly associating data with locks. One straightforward approach is to explicitly tell the middleware which data will be accessed, as is generally done by declaring which database tables will be affected by a transaction. In an object-

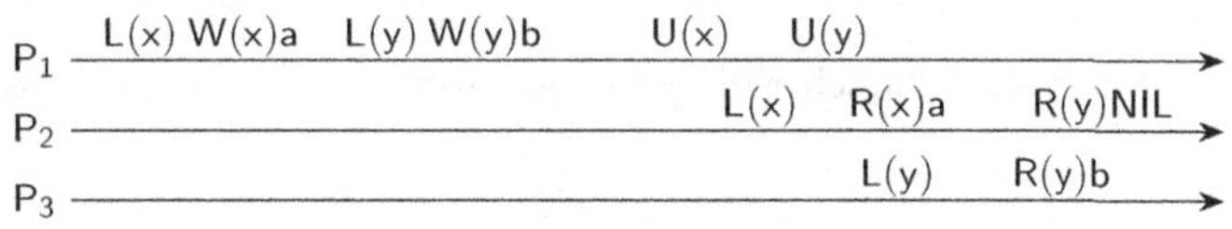

$$P_1 \quad \underline{L(x) \; W(x)a \quad L(y) \; W(y)b \qquad\qquad U(x) \quad U(y)}$$

$$P_2 \quad \underline{\qquad\qquad\qquad\qquad\qquad\qquad L(x) \quad R(x)a \qquad R(y)NIL}$$

$$P_3 \quad \underline{\qquad\qquad\qquad\qquad\qquad\qquad\qquad\quad L(y) \qquad R(y)b}$$

Figure 7.11: A valid event sequence for entry consistency.

based approach, we could associate a unique lock with each declared object, effectively serializing all invocations to such objects.

Note 7.2 (More information: Consistency models, serializability, transactions)
Coming to this point, the consistency models may at first sight appear to be overwhelming. Yet, despite their seemingly complexity, there are strong analogies with models that many of us are used to. In particular, let us consider transactions. As discussed in Section 1.3.2, transactions effectively group a series of read and write operations such that it is guaranteed that these operations are executed in the order of their appearance in the transaction. Moreover, when considering a collection of transactions that simultaneously operate on a data set, then the final values of that data set can be explained by one specific ordering of those transactions.

The keyword here is **serializability**: can we order the execution of operations that comprise the transactions in such a way that the final result matches a serial execution of the transactions? Consider the example shown in Figure 7.12. It is important to note that it is not necessary to know what is exactly being computed, but instead, only that we are dealing with read and write operations. In this sense, each transaction T_i can be represented as the series $\langle W_i(x); R_i(x); W_i(x) \rangle$.

```
BEGIN_TRANSACTION    BEGIN_TRANSACTION    BEGIN_TRANSACTION
     x = 0                x = 0                x = 0
     x = x + 1            x = x + 2            x = x + 3
END_TRANSACTION      END_TRANSACTION      END_TRANSACTION
```
$$\text{Transaction } T_1 \qquad\qquad \text{Transaction } T_2 \qquad\qquad \text{Transaction } T_3$$

Figure 7.12: Three transactions.

To ensure consistency, the underlying transaction system will have to devise legal **schedules**: orderings of the read and write operations from the three transactions such that the final result corresponds to a serial execution of those transactions. Consider the four schedules shown in Figure 7.13.

Both schedules S1 and S2 produce the result $x == 3$. This result can be explained by assuming that the scheduler executed the transactions in the order $T_1 \rightarrow T_2 \rightarrow T_3$. This ordering happens to match S1, but not S2, yet that is not relevant. Likewise, S3 is an illegal schedule, having the final result $x == 5$. Schedule S4 is interesting: the final result is $x == 3$, but that is only because of a coincidence. As the scheduler sees only (read and) write operations, and not the effects of write operations, scheduling the operations $x = x + 1$ and then $x = x + 2$ is illegal.

	Time $\longrightarrow$						
S1	x = 0	x = x + 1	x = 0	x = x + 2	x = 0	x = x + 3	Legal
S2	x = 0	x = 0	x = x + 1	x = x + 2	x = 0	x = x + 3	Legal
S3	x = 0	x = 0	x = x + 1	x = 0	x = x + 2	x = x + 3	Illegal
S4	x = 0	x = 0	x = x + 3	x = 0	x = x + 1	x = x + 2	Illegal

Figure 7.13: Various schedules from the transactions shown in Figure 7.12.

Note that what we have just described corresponds to entry consistency. Transactions consisting of only a single operation are, from a consistency point of view, analogous to sequential consistency.

Consistency versus coherence

At this point, it is useful to clarify the difference between two closely related concepts. The models we have discussed so far, all deal with the fact that a number of processes execute read and write operations on a set of data items. A **consistency model** describes what can be expected regarding that set when multiple processes concurrently operate on that data. The set is then said to be consistent if it adheres to the rules described by the model.

Where data consistency is concerned with a set of data items, **coherence models** describe what can be expected to hold for only a single data item [Cantin et al., 2005]. In this case, we assume that a data item is replicated; it is said to be coherent when the various copies abide to the rules as defined by its associated consistency model. A popular model is that of sequential consistency, but now applied to only a single data item. In effect, it means that in the case of concurrent writes, all processes will eventually see the same order of updates taking place.

7.2.2 Eventual consistency

To what extent processes actually operate in a concurrent fashion, and to what extent consistency needs to be guaranteed, may vary. There are many examples in which concurrency appears only in a restricted form. For example, in many database systems, most processes hardly ever perform update operations; they mostly read data from the database. Only one, or very few, processes perform update operations. The question then is how fast updates should be made available to only-reading processes. In the advent of globally operating content delivery networks, developers often choose to propagate updates slowly, implicitly assuming that most clients are always redirected to the same replica and will therefore never experience inconsistencies.

Another example is the Web. In virtually all cases, Web pages are updated by a single authority, such as a webmaster or the actual owner of the page. There are normally no write-write conflicts to resolve. On the other hand, to improve efficiency, browsers and Web proxies are often configured to keep a fetched page in a local cache and to return that page upon the next request. An important aspect of both types of Web caches is that they may return out-of-date Web pages. In other words, the cached page that is returned to the requesting client is an older version compared to the one available at the actual Web server. As it turns out, many users find this inconsistency acceptable (to a certain degree), as long as they have access only to the same cache. In effect, they remain unaware of the fact that an update had taken place, just as in the previous case of content delivery networks.

Yet another example, is a worldwide naming system such as DNS. The DNS name space is partitioned into domains, where each domain is assigned to a naming authority, which acts as owner of that domain. Only that authority is allowed to update its part of the name space. Consequently, conflicts resulting from two operations that both want to perform an update on the same data (i.e., **write-write conflicts**), never occur. The only situation that needs to be handled are **read-write conflicts**, in which one process intends to update a data item while another is concurrently attempting to read that item. As it turns out, also in this case it is often acceptable to propagate an update in a lazy fashion, meaning that a reading process will see an update only after some time has passed since the update took place.

These examples can be viewed as cases of (large scale) distributed and replicated databases that tolerate a relatively high degree of inconsistency. They have in common that if no updates take place for a long time, all replicas will gradually become consistent, that is, have the same data stored. This form of consistency is called **eventual consistency** [Vogels, 2009].

Data stores that are eventually consistent thus have the property that lacking write-write conflicts, all replicas will converge toward identical copies of each other. Eventual consistency essentially requires only that updates are guaranteed to propagate to all replicas. Write-write conflicts are often relatively easy to solve when assuming that only a small group of processes can perform updates. In practice, we often also see that in the case of conflicts, one specific write operation is (globally) declared as "winner," overwriting the effects of any other conflicting write operation. Eventual consistency is therefore often cheap to implement.

Note 7.3 (Advanced: Making eventual consistency stronger)
Eventual consistency is a relatively easy model to understand, but equally important is the fact that it is also relatively easy to implement. Nevertheless, it is a weak-consistency model with its own peculiarities. Consider a calendar shared between Alice, Bob, and Chuck. A meeting M has two attributes: a pro-

posed starting time and a set of people who have confirmed their attendance. When Alice proposes to start meeting M at time T, and assuming no one else has confirmed attendance, she executes the operation $W_A(M)[T, \{A\}]$. When Bob confirms his attendance, he will have read the tuple $[T, \{A\}]$ and update M accordingly: $W_B(M)[T, \{A, B\}]$. In our example two meetings M_1 and M_2 need to be planned.

Assume the sequence of events

$$W_A(M_1)[T_1, \{A\}] \rightarrow R_B(M_1)[T_1, \{A\}] \rightarrow$$

$$W_B(M_1)[T_1, \{A, B\}] \rightarrow W_B(M_2)[T_2, \{B\}].$$

In other words, Bob confirms his attendance at M_1 and then immediately proposes to schedule M_2 at T_2. Unfortunately, Chuck *concurrently* proposes to schedule M_1 at T_3 when Bob confirms he can attend M_1 at T_1. Formally, using the symbol "$\|$" to denote concurrent operations, we have,

$$W_B(M_1)[T_1, \{A, B\}] \parallel W_C(M_1)[T_3, \{C\}].$$

Using our usual notation, these operations can be illustrated as shown in Figure 7.14.

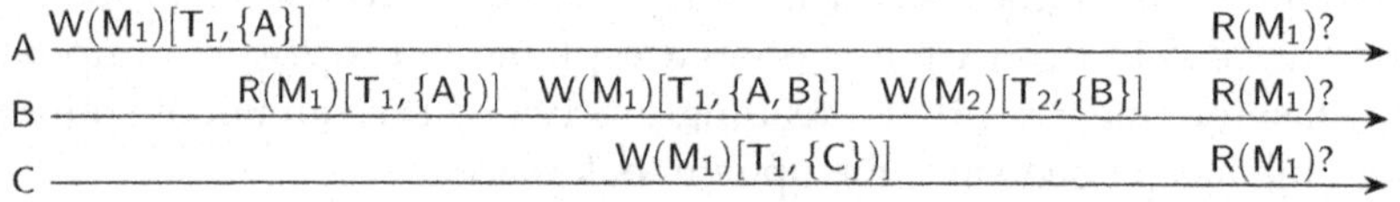

Figure 7.14: The situation of updating two meetings M_1 and M_2.

Eventual consistency may lead to very different scenarios. There are a number of write-write conflicts, but in any case, eventually $[T_2, \{B\}]$ will be stored for meeting M_2, as the result of the associated write operation by Bob. For the value of meeting M_1 there are different options. In principle, we have *three* possible outcomes: $[T_1, \{A\}]$, $[T_1, \{A, B\}]$, and $[T_3, \{C\}]$. Assuming we can maintain some notion of a global clock, it is not very likely that $W_A(M_1)[T_1, \{A\}]$ will prevail. However, the two write operations $W_B(M_1)[T_1, \{A, B\}]$ and $W_C(M_1)[T_3, \{C\}]$ are truly in conflict. In practice, one of them will win, presumably through a decision by a central coordinator.

Researchers have been seeking to combine eventual consistency with stricter guarantees on ordering. Bailis et al. [2013] propose to use a separate layer that operates on top of an eventually consistent, distributed store. This layer implements **causal consistency**, of which it has been formerly proven that it is the best attainable consistency in the presence of network partitioning [Mahajan et al., 2011]. In our example, we have only one chain of dependencies:

$$W_A(M_1)[T_1, \{A\}] \rightarrow R_B(M_1)[T_1, \{A\}] \rightarrow$$

$$W_B(M_1)[T_1, \{A, B\}] \rightarrow W_B(M_2)[T_2, \{B\}].$$

An important observation is that with causal consistency in place, once a process reads $[T_2, \{B\}]$ for meeting M_2, obtaining the value for M_1 returns either $[T_1, \{A, B\}]$ or $[T_3, \{C\}]$, but certainly not $[T_1, \{A\}]$. The reason is that $W_B(M_1)[T_1, \{A, B\}]$ immediately precedes $W_B(M_2)[T_2, \{B\}]$, and at worse may have been overwritten by $W_C(M_1)[T_3, \{C\}]$. Causal consistency rules out that the system could return $[T_1, \{A\}]$.

However, eventual consistency may overwrite previously stored data items. In doing so, dependencies may be lost. To make this point clear, it is important to realize that in practice, an operation at best keeps track of the immediate preceding operation it depends on. As soon as $W_c(M_1)[T_3, \{C\}]$ *overwrites* $W_B(M_1)[T_1, \{A, B\}]$ (and propagates to all replicas), we also break the chain of dependencies

$$W_A(M_1)[T_1, \{A\}] \rightarrow R_B(M_1)[T_1, \{A\}] \rightarrow \cdots \rightarrow W_B(M_2)[T_2, \{B\}]$$

which would normally prevent $W_A(M_1)[T_1, \{A\}]$ ever overtaking $W_B(M_1)[T_1, \{A, B\}]$ and any operation depending on it. As a consequence, maintaining causal consistency requires that we do maintain a history of dependencies, instead of just keeping track of immediately preceding operations.

Assuming that write-write conflicts hardly occur is generally not realistic. As mentioned, improvements can be made by grouping operations and using locks. What this entails, is that processes need to *coordinate* their actions by making use of mutual-exclusion mechanisms. For many large-scale systems, coordination among processes has turned out to form a real performance bottleneck. Note that we are dealing here with coordination for consistency. Alleviating potential bottleneck problems then boils down to bringing down coordination, or weakening consistency requirements. At least two approaches have been, by now, reasonably well explored, and are gradually finding their way into practical solutions.

The first one, referred to as **strong eventual consistency**, ensures that if there are conflicting updates, that nevertheless the replicas where those updates have taken place, are in the same state. Note that this is indeed stronger than (weak) eventual consistency, as in that case, nothing is specified what to do when the same replicated data item is updated by two different processes, except that the conflict may be reported. The seminal paper by Shapiro et al. [2011] introduced the **Conflict-Free Replicated Data Type**, or simply **CRDT**. A CRDT is a data type that can be replicated at many different sites, yet most importantly, can be updated in a concurrent fashion without further coordination. Of course, the meaning of concurrent updates may be different per type. For example, in the case of a variable for which the last update wins, its implementation will need to keep track of dependencies. A crude, but perhaps acceptable semantics, is that a good approximation of the actual time when an update is initiated is considered (e.g., using NTP), along with some random number to come to a deterministic choice when several updates happen within the same small time span. An alternative is to keep all updates so that a final decision can be made at application level. Many of such examples are discussed by Preguica [2018]. Kleppmann and Beresford [2017] describe how CRDTs can be implemented to support data structures in which no update is lost. In effect, it boils down to keeping all updates while at the same time avoiding clear duplicates, and maintaining clear dependencies.

The second approach is to move away from data-centric consistency and to look at **program consistency**. Again motivated by the observation that coordination for consistency may be extremely costly, the question arises if and where coordination is truly necessary. Program consistency is all about the question whether a program produces the expected outcome, despite various kinds of anomalies that may occur (like race conditions). A key observation is that of **problem monotonicity**:

A problem P is monotonic if for any input sets S and T, $P(S) \subseteq P(T)$.

The basic idea behind a monotonic problem is that it can come to a (partial) solution even if certain input information is missing. In other words, a program solving a monotonic problem can start with incomplete information, but is guaranteed not to have to roll back when missing information becomes available. A typical example of such a problem is filling a (digital) shopping cart: operations can be performed in any order by any server. Indeed, there is no write-write conflict. However, if we also need to support the removal of items, we bump into a problem. In this case, monotonicity can help if we split the add and delete operations into two different sets, and let each of them simply grow to a final state. In this case, we need to coordinate *only* when each set has converged to a final state. The difference between what has been added and what has been deleted is what needs to be coordinated to reach consistency. Further details on program consistency can be found in [Hellerstein and Alvaro, 2020].

7.2.3 Continuous consistency

There is no such thing as the best solution to replicating data. Replicating data poses consistency problems that cannot be solved efficiently in a general way. Only if we loosen consistency can there be hope for attaining efficient solutions. Unfortunately, there are also no general rules for loosening consistency: exactly what can be tolerated is highly dependent on applications.

There are different ways for applications to specify what inconsistencies they can tolerate. Yu and Vahdat [2002] take a general approach by distinguishing three independent axes for defining inconsistencies: deviation in numerical values between replicas, deviation in staleness between replicas, and deviation with respect to the ordering of update operations. They refer to these deviations as forming **continuous consistency** ranges.

Measuring inconsistency in terms of numerical deviations can be used by applications for which the data have numerical semantics. One obvious example is the replication of records containing stock market prices. In this case, an application may specify that two copies should not deviate more than $0.02, which would be an *absolute numerical deviation*. Alternatively, a *relative numerical deviation* could be specified, stating that two copies should differ by no more than, for example, 0.5%. In both cases, we would see that if a stock goes up (and one of the replicas is immediately updated) without violating the specified numerical deviations, the replicas would still be considered to be mutually consistent.

Numerical deviation can also be understood in terms of the number of updates that have been applied to a given replica, but have not yet been seen by others. For example, a Web cache may not have seen a batch of operations carried out by a Web server. In this case, the associated deviation in the *value* is also referred to as its *weight*.

Staleness deviations relate to the last time a replica was updated. For some applications, it can be tolerated that a replica provides old data as long as it is not *too* old. For example, weather reports typically stay reasonably accurate over some time, say a few hours. In such cases, a main server may receive timely updates, but may decide to propagate updates to the replicas only once in a while.

Finally, there are classes of applications in which the ordering of updates is allowed to be different at the various replicas, as long as the differences remain bounded. One way of looking at these updates is that they are applied tentatively to a local copy, awaiting global agreement from all replicas. As a consequence, some updates may need to be rolled back and applied in a different order before becoming permanent. Intuitively, ordering deviations are much harder to grasp than the other two consistency metrics.

The notion of a conit

To define inconsistencies, Yu and Vahdat introduce a **consistency unit**, abbreviated to **conit**. A conit specifies the unit over which consistency is to be measured. For example, in our stock-exchange example, a conit could be defined as a record representing a single stock. Another example is an individual weather report.

To give an example of a conit, and at the same time illustrate numerical and ordering deviations, consider the situation of keeping track of a fleet of cars. In particular, the fleet owner is interested in knowing how much she pays on average for gas. To this end, whenever a driver tanks gasoline, she reports the amount of gasoline that has been tanked (recorded as g), the price paid (recorded as p), and the total distance since the last time she tanked (recorded by the variable d). Technically, the three variables g, p, and d form a conit. This conit is replicated across two servers, as shown in Figure 7.15, and a driver regularly reports her gas usage to one of the servers by separately updating each variable (without further considering the car in question).

The task of the servers is to keep the conit "consistently" replicated. To this end, each replica server maintains a two-dimensional vector clock. We use the notation $\langle T, R \rangle$ to express an operation that was carried out by replica R at (its) logical time T.

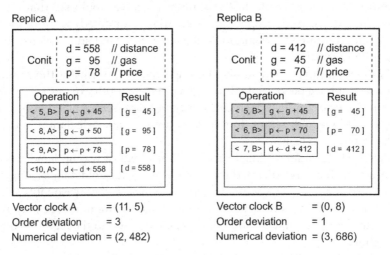

Figure 7.15: An example of keeping track of consistency deviations.

In this example, we see two replicas that operate on a conit containing the data items g, p, and d from our example. All variables are assumed to have been initialized to 0. Replica A received the operation

$$\langle 5, B \rangle : g \leftarrow g + 45$$

from replica B. We have shaded this operation gray to indicate that A has *committed* this operation to its local store. In other words, it has been made permanent and cannot be rolled back. Replica A also has three *tentative* update operations listed: $\langle 8, A \rangle$, $\langle 9, A \rangle$, and $\langle 10, A \rangle$, respectively. In terms of continuous consistency, the fact that A has three tentative operations pending to be committed is referred to as an **order deviation** of, in this case, value 3. Analogously, with in total three operations of which two have been committed, B has an order deviation of 1.

From this example, we see that A's logical clock value is now 11. Because the last operation from B that A had received had timestamp 5, the vector clock at A will be $(11, 5)$, where we assume the first component of the vector is used for A and the second for B. Along the same lines, the logical clock at B is $(0, 8)$.

The *numerical deviation* at a replica R consists of two components: the number of operations at all *other* replicas that have not yet been seen by

R, along with the sum of corresponding missed values (more sophisticated schemes are, of course, also possible). In our example, A has not yet seen operations $\langle 6, B \rangle$ and $\langle 7, B \rangle$ with a total value of $70 + 412$ units, leading to a numerical deviation of $(2, 482)$. Likewise, B is still missing the three tentative operations at A, with a total summed value of 686, bringing B's numerical deviation to $(3, 686)$.

Using these notions, it becomes possible to specify specific consistency schemes. For example, we may restrict order deviation by specifying an acceptable maximal value. Likewise, we may want two replicas to never numerically deviate by more than 1000 units. Having such consistency schemes does require that a replica knows how much it is deviating from other replicas, implying that we need separate communication to keep replicas informed. The underlying assumption is that such communication is much less expensive than communication to keep replicas synchronized. Admittedly, it is questionable if this assumption also holds for our example.

Note 7.4 (Advanced: On the granularity of conits)
There is a trade-off between maintaining fine-grained and coarse-grained conits. If a conit represents a lot of data, such as a complete database, then updates are aggregated for all the data in the conit. As a consequence, this may bring replicas sooner in an inconsistent state. For example, assume that in Figure 7.16 two replicas may differ in no more than one outstanding update. In that case, when the data items in Figure 7.16 have each been updated once at the first replica, the second one will need to be updated as well. This is not the case when choosing a smaller conit, as shown in Figure 7.16 There, the replicas are still considered to be up-to-date. This problem is particularly important when the data items contained in a conit are used completely independently, in which case they are said to **falsely share** the conit.

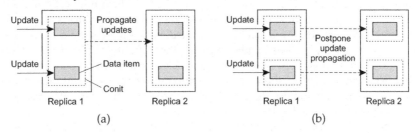

Figure 7.16: Choosing the appropriate granularity for a conit. (a) Two updates lead to update propagation. (b) No update propagation is needed.

Unfortunately, making conits small is not a good idea, for the simple reason that the total number of conits that need to be managed grows as well. In other words, there is an overhead related to managing the conits that needs to be considered. This overhead, in turn, may adversely affect overall performance, which also has to be considered.

Although, from a conceptual point of view, conits form an attractive means for capturing consistency requirements, there are two important issues that need to be dealt with before they can be put to practical use. First, to enforce consistency, we need to have protocols. Protocols for continuous consistency are discussed later in this chapter.

A second issue is that program developers must specify the consistency requirements for their applications. Practice indicates that obtaining such requirements may be extremely difficult. Programmers are generally not used to handling replication, let alone understanding what it means to provide detailed information on consistency. Therefore, it is mandatory that there are simple and easy-to-understand programming interfaces.

Note 7.5 (Advanced: Programming conits)

Continuous consistency can be implemented as a toolkit which appears to programmers as just another library that they link with their applications. A conit is simply declared alongside an update of a data item. For example, the fragment of pseudocode

```
AffectsConit(ConitQ, 1, 1);
append message m to queue Q;
```

states that appending a message to queue Q belongs to a conit named ConitQ. Likewise, operations may now also be declared as being dependent on conits:

```
DependsOnConit(ConitQ, 4, 0, 60);
read message m from head of queue Q;
```

In this case, the call to DependsOnConit() specifies that the numerical deviation, ordering deviation, and staleness should be limited to the values 4, 0, and 60 (seconds), respectively. This can be interpreted as that there should be at most 4 unseen update operations at other replicas, there should be no tentative local updates, and the local copy of Q should have been checked for staleness no more than 60 seconds ago. If these requirements are not fulfilled, the underlying middleware will attempt to bring the local copy of Q to a state such that the read operation can be carried out.

The question, of course, is how does the system know that Q is associated with ConitQ? For practical reasons, we can avoid explicit declarations of conits and concentrate only on the grouping of operations. The data to be replicated is collectively considered belonging together. By subsequently associating a write operation with a named conit, and likewise for a read operation, we tell the middleware layer when to start synchronizing the *entire* replica. Indeed, there may be a considerable amount of false sharing in such a case. If false sharing needs to be avoided, we would have to introduce a separate programming construct to explicitly declare conits.

7.3 Client-centric consistency models

Data-centric consistency models aim at providing a systemwide consistent view on a data store. An important assumption is that concurrent processes may be simultaneously updating the data store, and that it is necessary to provide consistency in the face of such concurrency. For example, in the case of object-based entry consistency, the data store guarantees that when an object is called, the calling process is provided with a copy of the object that reflects all changes to the object that have been made so far, possibly by other processes. During the call, it is also guaranteed that no other process can interfere, that is, mutual exclusive access is provided to the calling process.

Being able to handle concurrent operations on shared data while maintaining strong consistency is fundamental to distributed systems. For performance reasons, strong consistency may be guaranteed only when processes use mechanisms such as transactions or synchronization variables. Along the same lines, it may be impossible to guarantee strong consistency, and weaker forms need to be accepted, such as causal consistency with eventual consistency.

In this section, we take a look at a special class of distributed data stores. The data stores we consider are characterized by the lack of simultaneous updates, or when such updates happen, it is assumed that they can be relatively easily resolved. Most operations involve reading data. These data stores offer a weak consistency model, such as eventual consistency. By introducing special **client-centric consistency models**, it turns out that many inconsistencies can be hidden in a relatively cheap way.

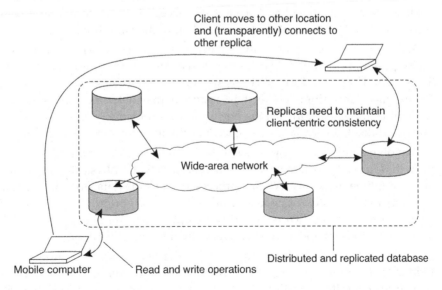

Figure 7.17: The principle of a mobile user accessing different replicas of a distributed database.

Eventually, consistent data stores generally work fine as long as clients always access the same replica. However, problems arise when different replicas are accessed over a short period of time. This is best illustrated by considering a mobile user accessing a distributed database, as shown in Figure 7.17.

The mobile user, say, Alice, accesses the database by connecting to one of the replicas in a transparent way. In other words, the application running on Alice's mobile device is unaware on which replica it is actually operating. Assume Alice performs several update operations and then disconnects again. Later, she accesses the database again, possibly after moving to a different location or by using a different access device. At that point, she may be connected to a different replica than before, as shown in Figure 7.17. However, if the updates performed previously have not yet been propagated, Alice will notice inconsistent behavior. In particular, she would expect to see all previously made changes, but instead, it appears as if nothing at all has happened.

This example is typical for eventually consistent data stores and is caused by the fact that users may sometimes operate on different replicas, while updates have not been fully propagated. The problem can be alleviated by introducing **client-centric consistency**. In essence, client-centric consistency provides guarantees *for a single client* concerning the consistency of accesses to a data store by that client. No guarantees are given concerning concurrent accesses by different clients. If Bob modifies data that is shared with Alice but which is stored at a different location, we may easily create write-write conflicts. Moreover, if neither Alice nor Bob access the same location for some time, such conflicts may take a long time before they are discovered.

Client-centric consistency models originate from the work on Bayou and, more general, from mobile-data systems (see, for example, Terry et al. [1994], Terry et al. [1998], or Terry [2008]). Bayou is a database system developed for mobile computing, where it is assumed that network connectivity is unreliable and subject to various performance problems. Wireless networks and networks that span large areas, such as the Internet, fall into this category.

Bayou essentially distinguishes four different consistency models. To explain these models, we again consider a data store that is physically distributed across multiple machines. When a process accesses the data store, it generally connects to the locally (or nearest) available copy, although, in principle, any copy will do just fine. All read and write operations are performed on that local copy. Updates are eventually propagated to the other copies.

Client-centric consistency models are described using the following notations. Let x_i denote the *version* of data item x. The version x_i is the result of a series of write operations that took place since initialization, its **write set** $WS(x_i)$. By appending write operations to thatseries, series we obtain another version x_j and say that x_j *follows from* x_i. We use the notation $W(x_i; x_j)$

to indicate that x_j follows from x_i. If we do not know if x_j follows from x_i, we use the notation $W(x_i|x_j)$.

7.3.1 Monotonic reads

The first client-centric consistency model is that of monotonic reads. A (distributed) data store is said to provide **monotonic-read consistency** if the following condition holds:

> *If a process reads the value of a data item x, any successive read operation on x by that process will always return that same value or a more recent value.*

In other words, monotonic-read consistency guarantees that once a process has seen a value of x, it will never see an older version of x.

As an example where monotonic reads are useful, consider a distributed e-mail database. In such a database, each user's mailbox may be distributed and replicated across multiple machines. Mail can be inserted in a mailbox at any location. However, updates are propagated in a lazy (i.e., on demand) fashion. Only when a copy needs certain data for consistency are those data propagated to that copy. Suppose a user reads her mail in San Francisco. Assume that only reading mail does not affect the mailbox, that is, messages are not removed, stored in subdirectories, or even tagged as having already been read, and so on. When the user later flies to New York and opens her mailbox again, monotonic-read consistency guarantees that the messages that were in the mailbox in San Francisco will also be in the mailbox when it is opened in New York.

Using a notation similar to that for data-centric consistency models, monotonic-read consistency can be graphically represented as shown in Figure 7.18. Rather than showing *processes* along the vertical axis, we now show *local data stores*, in our example L_1 and L_2. A write or read operation is indexed by the process that executed the operation, that is, $W_1(x)a$ denotes that process P_1 wrote value a to x. As we are not interested in specific values of shared data items, but rather their versions, we use the notation $W_1(x_2)$ to indicate that process P_1 produces version x_2 without knowing anything about other versions. $W_2(x_1;x_2)$ indicates that process P_2 is responsible for producing version x_2 that follows from x_1. Likewise, $W_2(x_1|x_2)$ denotes that process P_2 producing version x_2 *concurrently* to version x_1 (and thus potentially introducing a write-write conflict). $R_1(x_2)$ simply means that P_1 reads version x_2.

In Figure 7.18(a) process P_1 first performs a write operation on x at L_1, producing version x_1 and later reads this version. At L_2 process P_2 first produces version x_2, following from x_1. When process P_1 moves to L_2 and reads x again, it finds a more recent value, but one that at least took its previous write into account.

L₁ $\xrightarrow{\quad W_1(x_1) \qquad\qquad R_1(x_1)\quad}$

L₂ $\xrightarrow{\qquad W_2(x_1;x_2) \qquad R_1(x_2)\quad}$

(a)

L₁ $\xrightarrow{\quad W_1(x_1) \qquad\qquad R_1(x_1)\quad}$

L₂ $\xrightarrow{\qquad W_2(x_1|x_2) \qquad R_1(x_2)\quad}$

(b)

Figure 7.18: The read operations performed by a single process P at two different local copies of the same data store. (a) A monotonic-read consistent data store. (b) A data store that does not provide monotonic reads.

Figure 7.18(b) shows a situation in which monotonic-read consistency is violated. After process P_1 has read x_1 at L_1, it later performs the operation $R_1(x_2)$ at L_2. However, the preceding write operation $W_2(x_1|x_2)$ by process P_2 at L_2 is known to produce a version that does not follow from x_1. As a consequence, P_1's read operation at L_2 is known not to include the effect of the write operations when it performed $R_1(x_1)$ at location L_1.

7.3.2 Monotonic writes

In many situations, it is important that write operations are propagated in the correct order to all copies of the data store. This property is expressed in monotonic-write consistency. In a **monotonic-write consistent** store, the following condition holds:

> *A write operation by a process on a data item x is completed before any successive write operation on x by the same process.*

More formally, if we have two successive operations $W_k(x_i)$ and $W_k(x_j)$ by process P_k, then, regardless where $W_k(x_j)$ takes place, we also have $W_k(x_i; x_j)$. Thus, completing a write operation means that the copy on which a successive operation is performed reflects the effect of a previous write operation by the same process, no matter where that operation was initiated. In other words, a write operation on a copy of item x is performed only if that copy has been brought up to date through any preceding write operation by that same process, which may have taken place on other copies of x. If need be, the new write must wait for old ones to finish.

Note that monotonic-write consistency resembles data-centric FIFO consistency. The essence of FIFO consistency is that write operations by the same process are performed in the correct order everywhere. This ordering constraint also applies to monotonic writes, except that we are now considering consistency only for a single process, instead of for a collection of processes.

Bringing a copy of x up to date need not be necessary when each write operation completely overwrites the present value of x. However, write operations are often performed on only part of the state of a data item. Consider, for example, a software library. Often, updating such a library is done by replacing one or more functions, leading to a next version. With monotonic-write consistency, guarantees are given that if an update is performed on a copy of the library, all preceding updates will be performed first. The resulting library will then indeed become the most recent version and will include all updates that have led to previous versions of the library.

Monotonic-write consistency is shown in Figure 7.19. In Figure 7.19(a) process P_1 performs a write operation on x at L_1, presented as the operation $W_1(x_1)$. Later, P_1 performs another write operation on x, but this time at L_2, shown as $W_1(x_2; x_3)$. The version produced by P_1 at L_2 follows from an update by process P_2, in turn based on version x_1. The latter is expressed by the operation $W_2(x_1; x_2)$. To ensure monotonic-write consistency, it is necessary that the previous write operation at L_1 has already been propagated to L_2, and possibly updated.

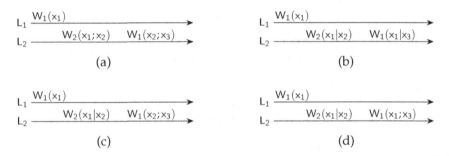

Figure 7.19: The write operations performed at two different local copies of the same data store. (a) A monotonic-write consistent data store. (b) A data store that does not provide monotonic-write consistency. (c) Again, no consistency as $W_2(x_1|x2)$ and thus also $W_1(x_1|x3)$. (d) Consistent as $W_1(x_1; x_3)$ although x_1 has apparently overwritten x_2.

In contrast, Figure 7.19(b) shows a situation in which monotonic-write consistency is not guaranteed. Compared to Figure 7.19(a), what is missing is the propagation of x_1 to L_2 before another version of x is produced, expressed by the operation $W_2(x_1|x_2)$. In this case, process P_2 produced a concurrent version to x_1, after which process P_1 simply produces version x_3, but again concurrently to x_1. Only slightly more subtle, but still violating monotonic-write consistency, is the situation sketched in Figure 7.19(c). Process P_1 now produces version x_3 which follows from x_2. However, because x_2 does not incorporate the write operations that led to x_1, that is, $W_2(x_1|x_2)$, we also have $W_1(x_1|x_3)$.

An interesting case is shown in Figure 7.19(d). The operation $W_2(x_1|x_2)$ produces version x_2 concurrently to x_1. However, later, process P_1 produces version x_3, but apparently based on the fact that version x_1 had become available at L_2. How and when x_1 was transferred to L_2 is left unspecified, but in any case a write-write conflict was created with version x_2 and resolved in favor of x_1. A consequence is that the situation shown in Figure 7.19(d) follows the rules for monotonic-write consistency. Note, however, that any subsequent write by process P_2 at L_2 (without having read version x_1) will immediately violate consistency again. How such a violation can be prevented is left as an exercise to the reader.

Note that, by the definition of monotonic-write consistency, write operations by the same process are performed in the same order as they are initiated. A somewhat weaker form of monotonic writes is one in which the effects of a write operation are seen only if all preceding writes have been carried out as well, but perhaps not in the order in which they have been originally initiated. This consistency is applicable in those cases in which write operations are commutative, so that ordering is really not necessary. Details are found in [Terry et al., 1994].

7.3.3 Read your writes

A data store is said to provide **read-your-writes consistency**, if the following condition holds:

> *The effect of a write operation by a process on data item x will always be seen by a successive read operation on x by the same process.*

In other words, a write operation is always completed before a successive read operation by the same process, no matter the location where that read operation takes place.

The absence of read-your-writes consistency is sometimes experienced when updating Web documents and subsequently viewing the effects. Update operations frequently take place through a standard editor or word processor, perhaps embedded as part of a content management system, which then saves the new version on a file system that is shared by the Web server. The user's Web browser accesses that same file, possibly after requesting it from the local Web server. However, once the file has been fetched, either the server or the browser often caches a local copy for subsequent accesses. Consequently, when the Web page is updated, the user will not see the effects if the browser or the server returns the cached copy instead of the original file. Read-your-writes consistency can guarantee that if the editor and browser are integrated into a single program, the cache is invalidated when the page is updated, so that the updated file is fetched and displayed.

Similar effects occur when updating passwords. For example, to enter a digital library on the Web, it is often necessary to have an account with an accompanying password. However, changing a password may take some time to come into effect, with the result that the library may be inaccessible to the user for a few minutes. The delay can be caused because a separate server is used to manage passwords, and it may take some time to subsequently propagate (encrypted) passwords to the various servers that constitute the library.

Figure 7.20(a) shows a data store that provides read-your-writes consistency. Note that Figure 7.20(a) is very similar to Figure 7.18(a), except that consistency is now determined by the last write operation by process P_1, instead of its last read.

$$L_1 \quad \underline{W_1(x_1)} \longrightarrow \qquad\qquad L_1 \quad \underline{W_1(x_1)} \longrightarrow$$

$$L_2 \quad \underline{\qquad W_2(x_1;x_2) \qquad R_1(x_2)} \longrightarrow \qquad L_2 \quad \underline{\qquad W_2(x_1|x_2) \qquad R_1(x_2)} \longrightarrow$$

$$\text{(a)} \qquad\qquad\qquad\qquad\qquad \text{(b)}$$

Figure 7.20: (a) A data store that provides read-your-writes consistency. (b) A data store that does not.

In Figure 7.20(a) process P_1 performed a write operation $W_1(x_1)$ and later a read operation at a different local copy. Read-your-writes consistency guarantees that the effects of the write operation can be seen by the succeeding read operation. This is expressed by $W_2(x_1;x_2)$, which states that a process P_2 produced a new version of x, yet one based on x_1. In contrast, in Figure 7.20(b) process P_2 produces a version concurrently to x_1, expressed as $W_2(x_1|x_2)$. This means that the effects of the previous write operation by process P_1 have not been propagated to L_2 at the time x_2 was produced. When P_1 reads x_2, it will not see the effects of its own write operation at L_1.

7.3.4 Writes follow reads

The last client-centric consistency model is one in which updates are propagated as the result of previous read operations. A data store is said to provide **writes-follow-reads** consistency, if the following holds.

> *A write operation by a process on a data item x following a previous read operation on x by the same process is guaranteed to take place on the same or a more recent value of x that was read.*

In other words, any successive write operation by a process on a data item x will be performed on a copy of x that is up to date with the value most recently read by that process.

Writes-follow-reads consistency can be used to guarantee that users of a network newsgroup see a posting of a reaction to an article only after they have seen the original article [Terry et al., 1994]. To understand the problem, assume that a user first reads an article A. Then, she reacts by posting a response B. By requiring writes-follow-reads consistency, B will be written to any copy of the newsgroup only after A has been written as well. Note that users who only read articles need not require any specific client-centric consistency model. The writes-follows-reads consistency assures that reactions to articles are stored at a local copy only if the original is stored there as well.

$$
\begin{array}{ll}
L_1 \; \xrightarrow{\quad W_1(x_1) \qquad\quad R_2(x_1) \quad\quad} & \qquad L_1 \; \xrightarrow{\quad W_1(x_1) \qquad\quad R_2(x_1) \quad\quad} \\
L_2 \; \xrightarrow{\quad W_3(x_1;x_2) \quad\; W_2(x_2;x_3) \;\;} & \qquad L_2 \; \xrightarrow{\quad W_3(x_1|x_2) \quad\; W_2(x_2|x_3) \;\;} \\
\qquad\qquad\quad (a) & \qquad\qquad\qquad\quad (b)
\end{array}
$$

Figure 7.21: (a) A writes-follow-reads consistent data store. (b) A data store that does not provide writes-follow-reads consistency.

This consistency model is shown in Figure 7.21. In Figure 7.21(a), process P_2 reads version x_1 at local copy L_1. This version of x was previously produced at L_1 by process P_1 through the operation $W_1(x_1)$. That version was subsequently propagated to L_2, and used by another process P_3 to produce a new version x_2, expressed as $W_3(x_1;x_2)$. When process P_2 later updates its version of x after moving to L_2, it is known that it will operate on a version that follows from x_1, expressed as $W_2(x_2;x_3)$. Because we also have $W_3(x_1;x_2)$, we known that $W_1(x_1;x_3)$.

The situation shown in Figure 7.21(b) is different. Process P_3 produces a version x_2 concurrently to that of x_1. As a consequence, when P_2 updates x after reading x_1, it will be updating a version it had not read before. Writes-follow-reads consistency is then violated.

7.3.5   Example: client-centric consistency in ZooKeeper

An interesting example in which we see elements of data-centric and client-centric consistency combined, is the model provided by ZooKeeper [Hunt et al., 2010]. First, ZooKeeper guarantees that update operations are **serializable** and keep precedence. What this means, is that the state of ZooKeeper can always be explained by some linear ordering in the execution of *all* submitted update operations, while preserving monotonic writes. In other words, while multiple clients can concurrently update ZooKeeper's state, the final result can be understood by some interleaving of those updates while the ordering of operations as submitted per client is preserved. In addition, ZooKeeper guarantees monotonic reads. It does not, however, guarantee read-your-writes or writes-follow-read consistency.

A simple perspective is to consider ZooKeeper as a collection of servers, while each client is connected to its own specific server. There is one, fixed primary server to which all write operations are forwarded, and processed in the order as submitted by their respective clients. Read operations are executed by the server to which the client is connected (and in the order as submitted by that client). Nothing, however, is said about when the primary

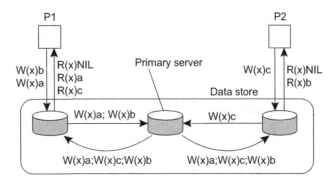

Figure 7.22: The consistency model of ZooKeeper explained through a naive implementation.

server brings the other servers up to date. In other words, a client is left in the dark concerning when it will see its own updates, or concurrent updates from other clients. This model is sketched in Figure 7.22.

Assume that P_1 first submits the operation $W(x)a$ and then $W(x)b$. Process P_2 submits the operation $W(x)c$. What is important is that monotonic writes are supported. In our example, the primary server receives the three write operations and decides to forward the operations $W(x)a$, $W(x)c$, and $W(x)b$ in that order to the other stores. We have not specified *when* these operations are submitted or actually performed. Important is that this order needs to be obeyed.

If P_1 submits read requests $R(x)$, it may first read the initial value NIL, and then subsequently $R(x)a$ and later $R(x)c$ (and eventually, it will be able to read only $R(x)b$). Likewise, P_2 may initially read NIL and later the final value $R(x)b$. Note that both P_1 and P_2 may read NIL even after having submitted their respective write operations. This demonstrates that ZooKeeper does not provide read-your-writes consistency. Also, even if P_1 had first read NIL and then submitted $W(x)a; W(x)b$, it may still read $R(x)c$ if its latest write operation ($R(x)b$) had not yet been processed. This demonstrates that ZooKeeper also does not provide writes-follow-reads consistency.

7.4 Replica management

A key issue for any distributed system that supports replication is to decide where and when replicas should be placed, and subsequently which mechanisms to use for keeping the replicas consistent. The placement problem itself should be split into two subproblems: that of placing *replica servers*, and that of placing *content*. The difference is subtle and the two issues are often not clearly separated. Replica-server placement is concerned with finding the best locations to place a server that can host (part of) a data store. Content placement deals with finding the best servers for placing content. Note that this often means that we are looking for the optimal placement of only a single data item. Obviously, before content placement can take place, replica servers will have to be placed first.

7.4.1 Finding the best server location

Where perhaps over a decade ago one could be concerned about where to place an individual server, matters have changed considerably with the advent of the many large-scale data centers located across the Internet. Likewise, connectivity continues to improve, making *precisely* locating servers less critical.

There are various ways to compute the best placement of replica servers, but virtually all boil down to an optimization problem in which the best K out of N locations need to be selected ($K < N$). These problems are known to be computationally complex and can be solved only through heuristics. Important in this respect is to decide on the criteria to even judge on a "best" solution. In an extensive overview, Sahoo et al. [2017] distinguish cost-related criteria and network-related criteria. Typical network-related criteria are latencies between a server and its clients, the available bandwidth, the (logical) distance as discussed in Section 5.7.3, and hop count. Of course, combinations are possible as well.

By now, there are many (often theoretical) models for deciding on the placement of replica servers. Sahoo et al. [2017] classify these models as shown in Figure 7.23.

Main class	Subclass
QoS Aware	Optimized QoS
	Bounded QoS
Consistency Aware	Periodic update
	Aperiodic update
	Expiration-based update
	Cache-based update
Energy	
Others	

Figure 7.23: Taxonomy of replica-placement algorithms (adapted from [Sahoo et al., 2017]).

Let us take a closer look at these different classes. When considering **Quality of Service**, that is **QoS**, server placement is decided by optimizing for some or more QoS parameters. QoS is generally expressed in terms of one or more of the network-related parameters. In the case of bounded QoS, solutions are sought that guarantee a value of a certain QoS parameter, for example, guaranteed bandwidth.

As mentioned, QoS awareness requires solving a computationally difficult problem, meaning in practice that we need to resort to heuristics, and thus approximations of optimal values. This is generally not a problem, considering that the QoS parameters itself may be rather imprecise. Consider, for example, accurately measuring latency between a client (end user) and a replica server. As discussed in Section 5.7.3, this is by itself not an easy problem to solve when we cannot simply access that client. The best one can hope for, is that an *existing* server is often enough connected to a client to get some idea of latencies. The same problem occurs for other parameters, in particular, bandwidth. As a consequence, we can try to accurately optimize on QoS, but when the basic input values are already very difficult to measure accurately, optimizations can quickly become quite theoretical. Quick-and-dirty heuristics may be enough, yet we will need to take their results with a grain of salt.

Consistency-aware algorithms take an entirely different approach. The basic assumption is that there is an existing network for which we can decide where to place replica servers. Placement of servers will then involve costs for keeping replicated content up to date. Those costs can be expressed in terms of when updates take place, as well as how. We return to these matters later in Section 7.4.3 where we discuss replica management. The four different subclasses deal with deciding on *when* updates are propagated to the replica server (periodically, instantly, or only after some time), or from *where* (is a replica server going to check the main server, or is it going to see whether a nearby server has an update). Again, we see that many theoretical models have been developed to optimize consistency-aware algorithms, yet in this case, such optimizations rely heavily on knowledge concerning read and update patterns. In practice, such knowledge is not readily available and may even be hard to get, let alone when it comes to predicting future patterns.

Energy-aware algorithms also assume an existing network to which clients connect. Placement of a replica server is then decided based on energy consumption. To keep it simple, placing a server at a specific node and keeping it up and running when there are only few clients, may be costly in terms of energy. The server in that case does not have enough work to do, while its idle time does consume energy. Another criterion is to decide on placement at nodes that support energy efficiency, for example, by switching between different power modes. Finally, placement may also be influenced by optimizing the distribution of work (measured in terms of energy consumption) among more or less replica servers, given that we know the various access patterns of a set of clients. As before, we see that much needs to be known about those patterns, as well as the capacities and facilities of the network, to make practically sensible decisions.

Finally, there are other classes for deciding on replica-server placement. Sahoo et al. have concentrated on server placement for CDNs. Such distributed systems are spread across many organizations (formally known as

Autonomous Systems, that is, an organization in charge of a separate network within the Internet). Replica-server placement then also involves monetary costs that need to be negotiated with those organizations. Likewise, placement decisions can be based on the connectivity of clients to a specific autonomous system, along with the costs in terms of QoS parameters or monetary costs. Further details can be found in [Sahoo et al., 2017].

7.4.2 Content replication and placement

When it comes to content replication and placement, three different types of replicas can be distinguished, logically organized as shown in Figure 7.24.

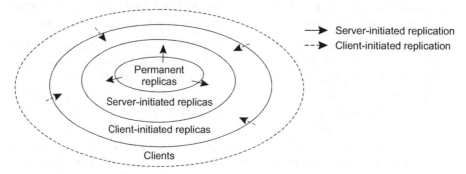

Figure 7.24: The logical organization of different kinds of copies of a data store into three concentric rings.

Permanent replicas

Permanent replicas can be considered as the initial set of replicas that constitute a distributed data store. Often, the number of permanent replicas is small. Consider, for example, a Website. Distribution of a Website generally comes in one of two forms. The first kind of distribution is one in which the files that constitute a site are replicated across a limited number of servers at a single location. Whenever a request comes in, it is forwarded to one of the servers, for instance, using a round-robin strategy.

The second form of distributed Websites is what is called **mirroring**. In this case, a Website is copied to a limited number of servers, called **mirror sites**, which are geographically spread across the Internet. Often, clients simply choose one of the various mirror sites from a list offered to them, or are transparently forwarded to one of the mirrors. Mirrored Websites have in common with cluster-based Websites that there are only a few replicas, which are more or less statically configured.

Similar static organizations also appear with distributed databases [Kemme et al., 2010; Özsu and Valduriez, 2020]. Again, the database can be distributed and replicated across a number of servers that together form a cluster of servers, often referred to as a **shared-nothing architecture**, emphasizing that neither disks nor main memory are shared by processors. Alternatively, a database is distributed and possibly replicated across a number of geographically dispersed sites. This architecture is generally deployed in federated databases [Sheth and Larson, 1990; Azevedo et al., 2020].

Server-initiated replicas

In contrast to permanent replicas, **server-initiated replicas** are copies of a data store that exist to enhance performance, and created at the initiative of the (owner of the) data store. Consider, for example, a Web server placed in New York. Normally, this server can handle incoming requests effortlessly, but it may happen that over a couple of days a sudden burst of requests come in from an unexpected location far from the server. In that case, it may be worthwhile to install a number of temporary replicas in regions where requests are coming from.

Web hosting has often been taken over by Content Delivery Networks, and for good reasons. Most important is that Web pages are no longer just a simple collection of static pages, but combine databases with static and dynamic content. As a result, replication needs to be much more sophisticated than just pushing pages to specific locations. We outlined the principal operation of a CDN in Section 3.4.4. Important is that, in general, replication is on demand. The CDN notices that requests are coming from a client, the client is directed to a nearest replica server, and that server checks to see whether it has the requested content cached locally. Obviously, there are many options concerning decisions on where to redirect the client to, and also when and which content to actually store. For our discussion here, despite that content is replicated to a server because of a client request, because the CDN is in control when it comes to the aforementioned decisions, it is still appropriate to speak of server-initiated replication. That the initiative has been delegated to a CDN is less important.

Note 7.6 (More information: An example of dynamic Web-content placement)
The problem of dynamically placing replicas has since long been addressed in Web hosting services (and by now in content delivery networks). Historically, these services offered an often relatively static collection of servers spread across the Internet that maintained and provided access to Web files belonging to third parties. To provide optimal facilities, such hosting services dynamically replicated files to servers where those files are needed to enhance performance, that is, close to demanding (groups of) clients.

Given that the replica servers are already in place, deciding where to place content is not that difficult. An early case toward dynamic replication of files in the case of a Web hosting service is described by Rabinovich et al. [1999]. The algorithm is designed to support Web pages, for which reason it assumes that updates are relatively rare compared to read requests. Using files as the unit of data, the algorithm works as follows.

The algorithm for dynamic replication takes two issues into account. First, replication can take place to reduce the load on a server. Second, specific files on a server can be migrated or replicated to servers placed in the proximity of clients that issue many requests for those files. In the following, we concentrate only on this second issue. We also omit a number of details, which can be found in [Rabinovich et al., 1999].

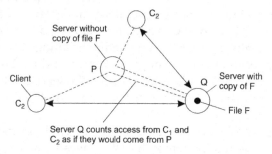

Figure 7.25: Counting access requests from different clients.

Each server keeps track of access counts per file, and where access requests come from. In particular, when a client C enters the service, it does so through a server close to it. If client C_1 and client C_2 share the same closest server P, all access requests for file F at server Q from C_1 and C_2 are jointly registered at Q as a single access count $cnt_Q(P, F)$. This situation is shown in Figure 7.25.

When the number of requests for a specific file F at server S drops below a deletion threshold $del(S, F)$, that file can be removed from S. As a consequence, the number of replicas of that file is reduced, possibly leading to higher work loads at other servers. Special measures are taken to ensure that at least one copy of each file continues to exist.

A replication threshold $rep(S, F)$, which is always chosen higher than the deletion threshold, indicates that the number of requests for a specific file is so high that it may be worthwhile replicating it on another server. If the number of requests lies somewhere between the deletion and replication threshold, the file is allowed to be only migrated. In other words, in that case, it is important to at least keep the number of replicas for that file the same.

When a server Q decides to reevaluate the placement of the files it stores, it checks the access count for each file. If the total number of access requests for F at Q drops below the deletion threshold $del(Q, F)$, it will delete F unless it is the last copy. Furthermore, if for some server P, $cnt_Q(P, F)$ exceeds more than half of the total requests for F at Q, server P is requested to take over the copy of F. In other words, server Q will attempt to migrate F to P.

Migration of file F to server P may not always succeed, for example because P is already heavily loaded or is out of disk space. In that case, Q will attempt to replicate F on other servers. Of course, replication can take place only if the total number of access requests for F at Q exceeds the replication threshold $rep(Q, F)$. Server Q checks all other servers in the Web hosting service, starting with the one farthest away. If, for some server R, $cnt_Q(R, F)$ exceeds a certain fraction of all requests for F at Q, an attempt is made to replicate F to R.

What we have just described is an alternative to simply caching content at a replica server when a client request comes in, as we described for content delivery networks. There is no fundamental reason why the algorithm for copying and migration of content cannot be applied in CDNs as well.

Client-initiated replicas

An important kind of replica is the one initiated by a client. **Client-initiated replicas** are more commonly known as **client caches**. In essence, a cache is a local storage facility that is used by a client to temporarily store a copy of the data it has just requested. In principle, managing the cache is left entirely to the client. The data store from where the data had been fetched has nothing to do with keeping cached data consistent. However, there are many occasions in which the client can rely on participation from the data store to inform it when cached data has become stale.

Client caches are used only to improve access times to data. Normally, when a client wants access to some data, it connects to the nearest copy of the data store from where it fetches the data it wants to read, or to where it stores the data it had just modified. When most operations involve only reading data, performance can be improved by letting the client store requested data in a nearby cache. Such a cache could be located on the client's machine, or on a separate machine in the same local-area network as the client. The next time that same data needs to be read, the client can simply fetch it from this local cache. This scheme works fine as long as the fetched data have not been meanwhile modified.

Data are generally kept in a cache for a limited amount of time, for example, to prevent extremely stale data from being used, or simply to make room for other data. Whenever requested data can be fetched from the local cache, a **cache hit** is said to have occurred. To improve the number of cache hits, caches can be shared between clients. The underlying assumption is that a data request from client C_1 may also be useful for a request from another nearby client C_2.

Whether this assumption is correct depends very much on the type of data store. For example, in traditional file systems, data files are rarely shared at all (see, e.g., Muntz and Honeyman [1992] and Blaze [1993]) rendering a shared cache useless. Likewise, it turns out that using Web caches to share data has been losing ground, partly also because of the improvement in network and server performance. Instead, server-initiated replication schemes are becoming more effective.

Placement of client caches is relatively simple: a cache is normally placed on the same machine as its client, or otherwise on a machine shared by clients on the same local-area network. However, in some cases, extra levels of caching are introduced by system administrators by placing a shared cache between a number of departments or organizations, or even placing a shared cache for an entire region such as a province or country.

Yet another approach is to place (cache) servers at specific points in a wide-area network and let a client locate the nearest server. When the server is located, it can be requested to hold copies of the data the client was previously fetching from somewhere else [Noble et al., 1999].

7.4.3   Content distribution

Replica management also deals with propagation of (updated) content to the relevant replica servers. There are various trade-offs to make.

State versus operations

An important design issue concerns what is actually to be propagated. Basically, there are three possibilities:

- Propagate only a notification of an update.
- Transfer data from one copy to another.
- Propagate the update operation to other copies.

Propagating a notification is what **invalidation protocols** do. In an invalidation protocol, other copies are informed that an update has taken place and that the data they contain are no longer valid. The invalidation may specify which part of the data store has been updated, so that only part of a copy is actually invalidated. The important issue is that no more than a notification is propagated. Whenever an operation on an invalidated copy is requested, that copy generally needs to be updated first, depending on the specific consistency model that is to be supported.

The main advantage of invalidation protocols is that they use little network bandwidth. The only information that needs to be transferred is a specification of which data are no longer valid. Such protocols generally work best when there are many update operations compared to read operations, that is, the read-to-write ratio is relatively small.

Consider, for example, a data store in which updates are propagated by sending the modified data to all replicas. If the size of the modified data is large, and updates occur frequently compared to read operations, we may have the situation that two updates occur after one another without any read operation being performed between them. Consequently, propagation of the first update to all replicas is effectively useless, as it will be overwritten by the second update. Instead, sending a notification that the data have been modified would have been more efficient.

Transferring the modified data among replicas is the second alternative, and is useful when the read-to-write ratio is relatively high. In that case, the probability that an update will be effective in the sense that the modified data will be read before the next update takes place is high. Instead of propagating modified data, it is also possible to log the changes and transfer only those logs to save bandwidth. In addition, transfers are often aggregated in the sense that multiple modifications are packed into a single message, thus saving communication overhead.

The third approach is not to transfer any data modifications at all, but to tell each replica which update operation it should perform (and sending only the parameter values that those operations need). This approach, also referred to as **active replication**, assumes that each replica is represented by a process capable of "actively" keeping its associated data up to date by performing operations [Schneider, 1990]. The main benefit of active replication is that updates can often be propagated at minimal bandwidth costs, provided the size of the parameters associated with an operation are relatively small. Moreover, the operations can be of arbitrary complexity, which may allow further improvements in keeping replicas consistent. On the other hand, more processing power may be required by each replica, especially in those cases when operations are relatively complex.

Pull versus push protocols

Another design issue is whether updates are pulled or pushed. In a **push-based approach**, also referred to as **server-based protocols**, updates are propagated to other replicas without those replicas even asking for the updates. Push-based approaches are often used between permanent and server-initiated replicas, but can also be used to push updates to client caches. Server-based protocols are generally applied when strong consistency is required.

This need for strong consistency is related to the fact that permanent and server-initiated replicas, as well as large shared caches, are often shared by many clients, which, in turn, mainly perform read operations. Consequently, the read-to-update ratio at each replica is relatively high. In these cases, push-based protocols are efficient in the sense that every pushed update can be expected to be of use for at least one, but perhaps more readers. In addition, push-based protocols make consistent data immediately available when asked for.

In contrast, in a **pull-based approach**, a server or client requests another server to send it any updates it has at that moment. Pull-based protocols, also called **client-based protocols**, are often used by client caches. For example, a common strategy applied to Web caches is first to check whether cached data items are still up-to-date. When a cache receives a request for items that are still locally available, the cache checks with the original Web server, whether those data items have been modified since they were cached. In the case of a modification, the modified data are first transferred to the cache, and then returned to the requesting client. If no modifications took place, the cached data are returned. In other words, the client polls the server to see whether an update is needed. A similar approach is followed in content delivery networks where a replica server caches content, yet checks with the origin server whether updates are available before delivering its (cached) content to the actual client (i.e., end user). Note that in this respect, the replica server acts as a client to the origin server.

A pull-based approach is efficient when the read-to-update ratio is relatively low. This is often the case with (nonshared) client caches, which have only one client. However, even when a cache is shared by many clients, a pull-based approach may also be efficient when the cached data items are rarely shared. The main drawback of a pull-based strategy in comparison to a push-based approach is that the response time increases in the case of a cache miss.

When comparing push-based and pull-based solutions, there are a number of trade-offs to be made, as shown in Figure 7.26. For simplicity, consider a client-server system consisting of a single, nondistributed server, and a number of client processes, each having their own cache. We make no distinction between clients at end users (such as Web browsers), or clients within, for example, a content delivery network (such as replica servers).

Issue	Push-based	Pull-based
State at server	List of client replicas and caches	None
Messages sent	Update (and possibly fetch update later)	Poll and update
Response time at client	Immediate (or fetch-update time)	Fetch-update time

Figure 7.26: A comparison between push-based and pull-based protocols in the case of multiple-client, single-server systems.

An important issue is that in push-based protocols, the server needs to keep track of all client caches, be they at end users or replica servers. Apart from the fact that stateful servers are often less fault tolerant, keeping track of all such caches may introduce a considerable overhead at the server. For example, in a push-based approach, a Web server may easily need to keep track of tens of thousands of client caches. Each time a Web page is updated, the server will have to go through its list of client caches holding a copy of that page and subsequently propagate the update. Worse yet, if a client purges a page due to lack of space, it has to inform the server, leading to even more communication.

The messages that need to be sent between a client and the server also differ. In a push-based approach, the only communication is that the server sends updates to each client. When updates are only invalidations, additional communication is needed by a client to fetch the modified data. In a pull-based approach, a client will have to poll the server, and, if necessary, fetch the modified data.

Finally, the response time at the client is also different. When a server pushes modified data to the client caches, it is clear that the response time at the client side is zero. When invalidations are pushed, the response time is the same as in the pull-based approach, and is determined by the time it takes to fetch the modified data from the server.

These trade-offs have lead to a hybrid form of update propagation based on leases. In the case of replica management, a **lease** is a promise by the server that it will push updates to the client for a specified time. When a lease expires, the client is forced to poll the server for updates and pull in the modified data if necessary. An alternative is that a client requests a new lease for pushing updates when the previous lease expires.

Leases, originally introduced by Gray and Cheriton [1989], provide a convenient mechanism for dynamically switching between a push-based and pull-based strategy. Consider the following lease system that allows the expiration time to be dynamically adapted depending on different lease criteria, described in [Duvvuri et al., 2003]. We distinguish the following three types of leases. (Note that in all cases, updates are pushed by the server as long as the lease has not expired.)

First, **age-based leases** are given out on data items depending on the last time the item was modified. The underlying assumption is that data that have not been modified for a long time can be expected to remain unmodified for some time yet to come. This assumption has shown to be reasonable in the case of, for example, Web-based data and regular files. By granting long-lasting leases to data items that are expected to remain unmodified, the number of update messages can be strongly reduced compared to the case where all leases have the same expiration time.

Another lease criterion is how often a specific client requests its cached copy to be updated. With **renewal-frequency-based leases**, a server will hand out a long-lasting lease to a client whose cache often needs to be refreshed. On the other hand, a client that asks only occasionally for a specific data item will be handed a short-term lease for that item. The effect of this strategy is that the server essentially keeps track only of those clients where its data are popular; moreover, those clients are offered a high degree of consistency.

The last criterion is that of state-space overhead at the server. When the server realizes that it is gradually becoming overloaded, it lowers the expiration time of new leases it hands out to clients. The effect of this **state-based lease** strategy is that the server needs to keep track of fewer clients as leases expire more quickly. In other words, the server dynamically switches to a more stateless mode of operation, thereby expecting to offload itself so that it can handle requests more efficiently. The obvious drawback is that it may need to do more work when the read-to-update ratio is high.

Unicasting versus multicasting

Related to pushing or pulling updates is deciding whether unicasting or multicasting should be used. In unicast communication, when a server that is part of the data store sends its update to N other servers, it does so by sending N separate messages, one to each server. With multicasting, the underlying network takes care of sending a message efficiently to multiple receivers.

Often, it is cheaper to use available multicasting facilities. An extreme situation is when all replicas are located in the same local-area network and that hardware broadcasting is available. In that case, broadcasting or multicasting a message is no more expensive than a single point-to-point message. Unicasting updates would then be less efficient.

Multicasting can often be efficiently combined with a push-based approach to propagating updates. When the two are carefully integrated, a server that decides to push its updates to a number of other servers simply uses a single multicast group to send its updates. In contrast, with a pull-based approach, it is generally only a single client or server that requests its copy to be updated. In that case, unicasting may be the most efficient solution.

7.4.4   Managing replicated objects

As we mentioned, data-centric consistency for distributed objects comes naturally in the form of entry consistency. Recall that in this case, the goal is to group operations on shared data using synchronization variables (e.g., in the form of locks). As objects naturally combine data and the operations on that data, locking objects during an invocation serializes access and keeps them consistent.

Although conceptually associating a lock with an object is simple, it does not necessarily provide a proper solution when an object is replicated. There are two issues that need to be solved for implementing entry consistency. The first one is that we need a means to prevent concurrent execution of multiple invocations on the same object. In other words, when any method of an object is being executed, no other methods may be executed. This requirement ensures that access to the internal data of an object is indeed serialized. Simply using local locking mechanisms will ensure this serialization.

The second issue is that in the case of a replicated object, we need to ensure that all changes to the replicated state of the object are the same. In other words, we need to make sure that no two independent method invocations take place on different replicas at the same time. This requirement implies that we need to order invocations such that each replica sees all invocations in the same order. We describe a few general solutions in Section 7.5.

Often, designing replicated objects is done by first designing a single object, possibly protecting it against concurrent access through local locking, and subsequently replicating it. The role of middleware is to ensure that if a client invokes a replicated object, the invocation is passed to the replicas and handed to the their respective object servers in the same order everywhere. However, we also need to ensure that all threads in those servers process those requests in the correct order as well. The problem is sketched in Figure 7.27.

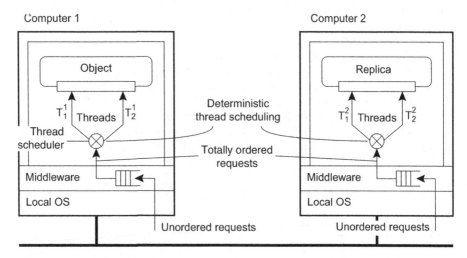

Figure 7.27: Deterministic thread scheduling for replicated object servers.

Multithreaded (object) servers simply pick up an incoming request, pass it on to an available thread, and wait for the next request to come in. The server's thread scheduler subsequently allocates the CPU to runnable threads. Of course, if the middleware has done its best to provide a total ordering for request delivery, the thread schedulers should operate in a deterministic fashion in order not to mix the ordering of method invocations on the same object. In other words, If threads T_1^1 and T_1^2 from Figure 7.27 handle the same incoming (replicated) invocation request, they should both be scheduled before T_2^1 and T_2^2, respectively.

Simply scheduling *all* threads deterministically is not necessary. In principle, if we already have totally ordered request delivery, we need only to ensure that all requests for the same replicated object are handled in the order they were delivered. Such an approach would allow invocations for different objects to be processed concurrently, and without further restrictions from the thread scheduler. Only few systems exist that support such concurrency.

One approach, described by Basile et al. [2002], ensures that threads
sharing the same (local) lock are scheduled in the same order on every replica.
At the basics lies a primary-based scheme in which one of the replica servers
takes the lead in determining, for a specific lock, which thread goes first.
An improvement that avoids frequent communication between servers is
described in [Basile et al., 2003]. Note that threads that do not share a lock
can thus operate concurrently on each server.

One drawback of this scheme is that it operates at the level of the underlying operating system, meaning that every lock needs to be managed. By
providing application-level information, a huge improvement in performance
can be made by identifying only those locks that are required for serializing
access to replicated objects (see Taiani et al. [2005]).

Note 7.7 (Advanced: Replicated invocations)
Another problem that needs to be solved is that of **replicated invocations**. Consider an object A calling another object B as shown in Figure 7.28. Object B is
assumed to call yet another object C. If B is replicated, each replica of B will,
in principle, call C independently. The problem is that C is now called multiple
times instead of only once. If the called method on C results in the transfer of
$100,000, then clearly, someone is, sooner or later, going to complain.

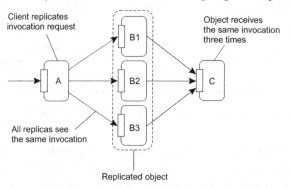

Figure 7.28: The problem of replicated object invocations.

There are not many general-purpose solutions to solve the problem of replicated invocations. One solution is to simply forbid it [Maassen et al., 2001],
which makes sense when performance is at stake. However, when replicating for
fault tolerance, the following solution proposed by Mazouni et al. [1995] may be
deployed. Their solution is independent of the replication policy, that is, the exact
details of how replicas are kept consistent. The essence is to provide a replication-
aware communication layer on top of which (replicated) objects execute. When
a replicated object B invokes another replicated object C, the invocation request
is first assigned the same, unique identifier by each replica of B. At that point, a
coordinator of the replicas of B forwards its request to all the replicas of object C,

while the other replicas of B hold back their copy of the invocation request, as shown in Figure 7.29. The result is that only a single request is forwarded to each replica of C.

The same mechanism is used to ensure that only a single reply message is returned to the replicas of B. This situation is shown in Figure 7.29. A coordinator of the replicas of C notices it is dealing with a replicated reply message that has been generated by each replica of C. However, only the coordinator forwards that reply to the replicas of object B, while the other replicas of C hold back their copy of the reply message.

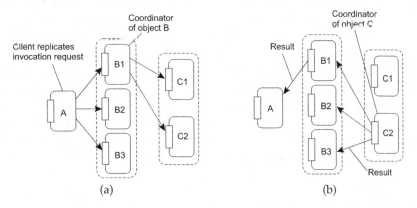

(a) (b)

Figure 7.29: (a) Forwarding an invocation request from a replicated object to another replicated object. (b) Returning a reply from one replicated object to another.

When a replica of B receives a reply message for an invocation request it had either forwarded to C or held back because it was not the coordinator, the reply is then handed to the actual object.

In essence, the scheme just described is based on using multicast communication, but preventing that the same message is multicast by different replicas. As such, it is essentially a sender-based scheme. An alternative solution is to let a receiving replica detect multiple copies of incoming messages belonging to the same invocation, and to pass only one copy to its associated object. Details of this scheme are left as an exercise.

7.5 Consistency protocols

We now concentrate on the actual implementation of consistency models by taking a look at several consistency protocols. A **consistency protocol** describes an implementation of a specific consistency model. We follow the organization of our discussion on consistency models by first taking a look at data-centric models, followed by protocols for client-centric models.

7.5.1 Sequential consistency: Primary-based protocols

In practice, we see that distributed applications generally follow consistency models that are relatively easy to understand. These models include those for bounding staleness deviations, and to a lesser extent also those for bounding numerical deviations. When it comes to models that handle consistent ordering of operations, sequential consistency, notably those in which operations can be grouped through locking or transactions, are popular.

As soon as consistency models become slightly difficult to understand for application developers, we see that they are ignored even if performance could be improved. The bottom line is that if the semantics of a consistency model are not intuitively clear, application developers will have a hard time building correct applications. Simplicity is appreciated (and perhaps justifiably so).

In the case of sequential consistency, it turns out that **primary-based protocols** prevail. In these protocols, each data item x in the data store has an associated primary, which is responsible for coordinating write operations on x. A distinction can be made whether the primary is fixed at a remote server or if write operations can be carried out locally after moving the primary to the process where the write operation is initiated.

Remote-write protocols

The simplest primary-based protocol that supports replication is the one in which all write operations need to be forwarded to a fixed single server. Read operations can be carried out locally. Such schemes are also known as **primary-backup protocols** [Budhijara et al., 1993]. A primary-backup protocol works as shown in Figure 7.30. A process wanting to perform a write operation on data item x, forwards that operation to the primary server for x. The primary performs the update on its local copy of x, and subsequently forwards the update to the backup servers. Each backup server performs the update as well, and sends an acknowledgment to the primary. When all backups have updated their local copy, the primary sends an acknowledgment to the initial process, which, in turn, informs the client.

A potential performance problem with this scheme is that it may take a relatively long time before the process that initiated the update is allowed to continue. In effect, an update is implemented as a blocking operation. An alternative is to use a nonblocking approach. As soon as the primary has updated its local copy of x, it returns an acknowledgment. After that, it tells the backup servers to perform the update as well. Nonblocking primary-backup protocols are discussed in [Budhiraja and Marzullo, 1992].

The main problem with nonblocking primary-backup protocols has to do with fault tolerance. In a blocking scheme, the client process knows for sure that the update operation is backed up by several other servers. This is not

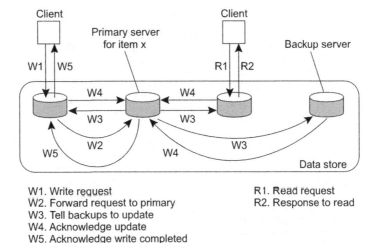

W1. Write request
W2. Forward request to primary
W3. Tell backups to update
W4. Acknowledge update
W5. Acknowledge write completed

R1. Read request
R2. Response to read

Figure 7.30: The principle of a primary-backup protocol.

the case with a nonblocking solution. The advantage, of course, is that write operations may speed up considerably.

Primary-backup protocols provide a straightforward implementation of sequential consistency, as the primary can order all incoming writes in a globally unique order. Evidently, all processes see all write operations in the same order, no matter which backup server they use to perform read operations. Also, with blocking protocols, processes will always see the effects of their most recent write operation (note that this cannot be guaranteed with a nonblocking protocol without taking special measures).

Local-write protocols

A variant of primary-backup protocols is one in which the primary copy migrates between processes that wish to perform a write operation. As before, whenever a process wants to update a data item x, it locates the primary copy of x, and subsequently moves it to its own location, as shown in Figure 7.31. The main advantage of this approach is that multiple, successive write operations can be carried out locally, while reading processes can still access their local copy. However, such an improvement can be achieved only if a nonblocking protocol is followed by which updates are propagated to the replicas after the primary has finished with locally performing the updates.

This primary-backup local-write protocol can also be applied to mobile computers that can operate in disconnected mode. Before disconnecting, the mobile computer becomes the primary server for each data item it expects to update. While being disconnected, all update operations are carried out locally, while other processes can still perform read operations (but no updates).

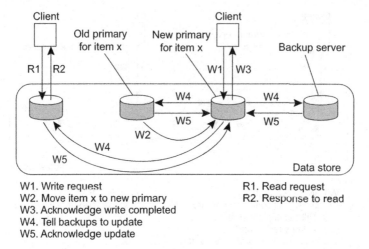

Figure 7.31: Primary-backup protocol in which the primary migrates to the process wanting to perform an update.

Later, when connecting again, updates are propagated from the primary to the backups, bringing the data store in a consistent state again.

As a last variant of this scheme, nonblocking local-write primary-based protocols are also used for distributed file systems in general. In this case, there may be a fixed central server through which normally all write operations take place, as in the case of remote-write primary backup. However, the server temporarily allows one of the replicas to perform a series of local updates, as this may considerably speed up performance. When the replica server is done, the updates are propagated to the central server, from where they are then distributed to the other replica servers.

7.5.2 Sequential consistency: Replicated-write protocols

In **replicated-write protocols**, write operations can be carried out at multiple replicas instead of only one, as in the case of primary-based replicas. A distinction can be made between active replication, in which an operation is forwarded to all replicas, and consistency protocols based on majority voting.

Active replication

In **active replication**, each replica has an associated process that carries out update operations. In contrast to other protocols, updates are generally propagated through the write operation that causes the update. In other words, the operation is sent to each replica. However, it is also possible to send the update.

One problem with active replication is that operations need to be carried out in the same order everywhere. Consequently, what is needed is a totally ordered multicast mechanism. A practical approach to accomplish total ordering is by a central coordinator, also called a **sequencer**. One approach is to first forward each operation to the sequencer, which assigns it a unique sequence number and subsequently forwards the operation to all replicas. Operations are carried out in the order of their sequence number.

Note 7.8 (Advanced: Achieving scalability)

Note that using a sequencer may easily introduce scalability problems. In fact, if totally ordered multicasting is needed, a combination of symmetric multicasting using Lamport timestamps [Lamport, 1978] and sequencers may be necessary. Such a solution is described by Rodrigues et al. [1996]. The essence of that solution is to have multiple sequencers multicast update operations to each other and order the updates using Lamport's total-ordering mechanism, as described in Chapter 5. Nonsequencing processes are grouped such that each group uses a single sequencer. Any nonsequencing process sends update requests to its sequencer and waits until it receives an acknowledgment that its request has been processed (i.e., multicast to the other sequencers in a totally ordered fashion). Obviously, there is a trade-off between the number of processes that act as sequencer and those that do not, as well as the choice of processes to act as sequencer. As it turns out, this trade-off depends very much on the application and, in particular, the relative update rate at each process.

Quorum-based protocols

A different approach to supporting replicated writes is to use voting, as originally proposed by Thomas [1979] and generalized by Gifford [1979]. The basic idea is to require clients to request and acquire the permission of multiple servers before either reading or writing a replicated data item.

As a simple example of how the algorithm works, consider a distributed file system and suppose that a file is replicated on N servers. We could make a rule stating that to update a file, a client must first contact at least half the servers plus one (a majority) and get them to agree to do the update. Once they have agreed, the file is changed and a new version number is associated with the new file. The version number is used to identify the version of the file and is the same for all the newly updated files.

To read a replicated file, a client must also contact at least half the servers plus one and ask them to send the version numbers associated with the file. If all the version numbers are the same, this must be the most recent version because an attempt to update only the remaining servers would fail because there are not enough of them.

For example, if there are five servers and a client determines that three of them have version 8, it is impossible that the other two have version 9. After all, any successful update from version 8 to version 9 requires getting three servers to agree to it, not just two.

When quorum-based replication was originally introduced, a somewhat more general scheme was proposed. In it, to read a file of which N replicas exist, a client needs to assemble a **read quorum**, an arbitrary collection of any N_R servers, or more. Similarly, to modify a file, a **write quorum** of at least N_W servers is required. The values of N_R and N_W are subject to the following two constraints:

1. $N_R + N_W > N$
2. $N_W > N/2$

The first constraint is used to prevent read-write conflicts, whereas the second prevents write-write conflicts. Only after the appropriate number of servers has agreed to participate can a file be read or written.

To see how this algorithm works, consider Figure 7.32(a) which has $N_R = 3$ and $N_W = 10$. Imagine that the most recent write quorum consisted of the 10 servers C through L. All of these get the new version and the new version number. Any subsequent read quorum of three servers will have to contain at least one member of this set. When the client looks at the version numbers, it will know which is most recent and take that one.

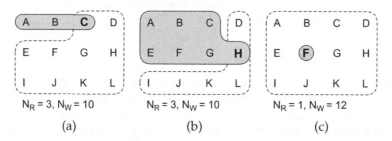

Figure 7.32: Three examples of the voting algorithm. The gray areas denote a read quorum; the white ones a write quorum. Servers in the intersection are denoted in boldface. (a) A correct choice of read and write set. (b) A choice that may lead to write-write conflicts. (c) A correct choice, known as ROWA (read one, write all).

In Figure 7.32 we see two more examples. In Figure 7.32(b) a write-write conflict may occur because $N_W \leq N/2$. In particular, if one client chooses $\{A, B, C, E, F, G\}$ as its write set and another client chooses $\{D, H, I, J, K, L\}$ as its write set, then clearly we will run into trouble, as the two updates will both be accepted without detecting that they actually conflict.

The situation shown in Figure 7.32(c) is especially interesting because it sets N_R to one, making it possible to read a replicated file by finding any copy and using it. The price paid for this good read performance, however, is that write updates need to acquire all copies. This scheme is generally referred to as **Read-One, Write-All, (ROWA)**.

Quorum-based replication has been an active field of research and an inspiration for various protocols. However, in practice, we often see primary-based protocols at work (to which we return in Chapter 8). Jalote [1994] provides a good overview of various quorum-based protocols. A more formal introduction is given by Merideth and Reiter [2010], whereas many formal details and analyses of different protocols are described in [Vukolić, 2012].

7.5.3 Cache-coherence protocols

Caches form a special case of replication, in the sense that they are generally controlled by clients instead of servers. However, **cache-coherence protocols**, which ensure that a cache is consistent with the server-initiated replicas are, in principle, not very different from the consistency protocols discussed so far.

There has been much research in the design and implementation of caches, especially in the context of shared-memory multiprocessor systems. Many solutions are based on support from the underlying hardware, for example, by assuming that snooping or efficient broadcasting can be done. In the context of middleware-based distributed systems that are built on top of general-purpose operating systems, software-based solutions to caches are more interesting. In this case, two separate criteria are often maintained to classify caching protocols (see also Min and Baer [1992], Lilja [1993], or Tartalja and Milutinovic [1997]).

First, caching solutions may differ in their **coherence detection strategy**, that is, *when* inconsistencies are actually detected. In static solutions, a compiler is assumed to perform the necessary analysis before execution, and to determine which data may actually lead to inconsistencies because they may be cached. The compiler simply inserts instructions that avoid inconsistencies. Dynamic solutions are typically applied in the distributed systems studied in this book. In these solutions, inconsistencies are detected at runtime. For example, a check is made with the server to see whether the cached data have been modified since they were cached.

In the case of distributed databases, dynamic detection-based protocols can be further classified by considering exactly when, during a transaction, the detection is done. Franklin et al. [1997] distinguish the following three cases. First, when during a transaction a cached data item is accessed, the client needs to verify whether that data item is still consistent with the version stored at the (possibly replicated) server. The transaction cannot proceed to use the cached version until its consistency has been definitively validated.

A second, optimistic, approach is to let the transaction proceed while verification is taking place. In this case, it is assumed that the cached data were up-to-date when the transaction started. If that assumption later proves to be false, the transaction will have to abort.

The third approach is to verify whether the cached data are up-to-date only when the transaction commits. In effect, the transaction just starts operating on the cached data and hopes for the best. After all the work has been done, accessed data are verified for consistency. When stale data were used, the transaction is aborted.

Another design issue for cache-coherence protocols is the **coherence enforcement strategy**, which determines *how* caches are kept consistent with the copies stored at servers. The simplest solution is to disallow shared data to be cached at all. Instead, shared data are kept only at the servers, which maintain consistency using one of the primary-based or replication-write protocols discussed above. Clients are allowed to cache only private data. Obviously, this solution can offer only limited performance improvements.

When shared data can be cached, there are two approaches to enforce cache coherence. The first is to let a server send an invalidation to all caches whenever a data item is modified. The second is to simply propagate the update. Most caching systems use one of these two schemes. Dynamically choosing between sending invalidations or updates is sometimes supported in client-server databases.

Finally, we also need to consider what happens when a process modifies cached data. When read-only caches are used, update operations can be performed only by servers, which subsequently follow some distribution protocol to ensure that updates are propagated to caches. Often, a pull-based approach is followed. In this case, a client detects that its cache is stale, and requests a server for an update.

An alternative approach is to allow clients to directly modify the cached data, and forward the update to the servers. This approach is followed in **write-through caches**, which are often used in distributed file systems. In effect, write-through caching is similar to a primary-based local-write protocol in which the client's cache has become a temporary primary. To guarantee (sequential) consistency, it is necessary that the client has been granted exclusive write permissions, or otherwise write-write conflicts may occur.

Write-through caches potentially offer improved performance over other schemes, as all operations can be carried out locally. Further enhancements can be made if we delay the propagation of updates by allowing multiple writes to take place before informing the servers. This leads to what is known as a **write-back cache**, which is, again, mainly applied in distributed file systems.

Note 7.9 (Example: Client-side caching in NFS)
As a practical example, consider the general caching model in NFS as shown in Figure 7.33. Each client can have a memory cache that contains data previously

read from the server. In addition, there may also be a disk cache that is added as an extension to the memory cache, using the same consistency parameters.

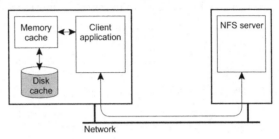

Figure 7.33: Client-side caching in NFS.

Typically, clients cache file data, attributes, file handles, and directories. Different strategies exist to handle consistency of the cached data, cached attributes, and so on. Let us first take a look at caching file data.

NFSv4 supports two different approaches for caching file data. The simplest approach is when a client opens a file and caches the data it obtains from the server as the result of various read operations. In addition, write operations can be carried out in the cache as well. When the client closes the file, NFS requires that if modifications have taken place, the cached data must be flushed back to the server. This approach corresponds to implementing session semantics as discussed earlier.

Once (part of) a file has been cached, a client can keep its data in the cache even after closing the file. Also, several clients on the same machine can share a single cache. NFS requires that whenever a client opens a previously closed file that has been (partly) cached, the client must immediately revalidate the cached data. Revalidation takes place by checking when the file was last modified and invalidating the cache in case it contains stale data.

In NFSv4 a server may delegate some of its rights to a client when a file is opened. **Open delegation** takes place when the client machine is allowed to locally handle open and close operations from other clients on the same machine. Normally, the server is in charge of checking whether opening a file should succeed, for example because share reservations need to be considered. With open delegation, the client machine is sometimes allowed to make such decisions, avoiding the need to contact the server.

For example, if a server has delegated the opening of a file to a client that requested write permissions, file locking requests from other clients on the same machine can also be handled locally. The server will still handle locking requests from clients on other machines, by simply denying those clients access to the file. Note that this scheme does not work in the case of delegating a file to a client that requested only read permissions. In that case, whenever another local client wants to have write permissions, it will have to contact the server; it is not possible to handle the request locally.

An important consequence of delegating a file to a client is that the server needs to be able to recall the delegation, for example, when another client on a different machine needs to obtain access rights to the file. Recalling a delegation requires that the server can do a callback to the client, as illustrated in Figure 7.34.

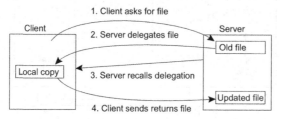

Figure 7.34: Using the NFSv4 callback mechanism to recall file delegation.

A callback is implemented in NFS using its underlying RPC mechanisms. Note, however, that callbacks require that the server keeps track of clients to which it has delegated a file. Here, we see another example where an NFS server cannot be implemented in a stateless manner. Note, however, that the combination of delegation and stateful servers may lead to various problems in the presence of client and server failures. For example, what should a server do when it had delegated a file to a now unresponsive client?

Clients can also cache attribute values, but are largely left on their own when it comes to keeping cached values consistent. In particular, attribute values of the same file cached by two different clients may be different unless the clients keep these attributes mutually consistent. Modifications to an attribute value should be immediately forwarded to the server, thus following a write-through cache coherence policy.

A similar approach is followed for caching file handles (or rather, the name-to-file handle mapping) and directories. To mitigate the effects of inconsistencies, NFS uses leases on cached attributes, file handles, and directories. After some time has elapsed, cache entries are thus automatically invalidated and revalidation is needed before they are used again.

7.5.4   Implementing continuous consistency

As part of their work on continuous consistency, Yu and Vahdat [2000] have developed a number of protocols to tackle the three forms of continuous consistency. In the following, we briefly consider a number of solutions, omitting details for clarity.

Bounding numerical deviation

We first concentrate on one solution for keeping the numerical deviation within bounds. Again, our purpose is not to go into all the details for each protocol, but rather to give the general idea. Details for bounding numerical deviation can be found in [Yu and Vahdat, 2000].

We concentrate on writes to a single data item x. Each write W(x) has an associated *value* that represents the numerical value by which x is updated, denoted as $val(W(x))$, or simply $val(W)$. For simplicity, we assume that $val(W) > 0$. Each write W is initially submitted to one out of the N available replica servers, in which case that server becomes the write's *origin*, denoted as $origin(W)$. If we consider the system at a specific moment we will see several submitted writes that still need to be propagated to all servers. To this end, each server S_i will keep track of a *log* L_i of writes that it has performed on its own local copy of x.

Let $TW[i, j]$ be the effect of performing the writes executed by server S_i that originated from server S_j:

$$TW[i,j] = \sum \{val(W) | origin(W) = S_j \text{ and } W \in L_i\}$$

Note that $TW[i, i]$ represents the aggregated writes submitted to S_i. Our goal is for any time t, to let the current value v_i of x at server S_i deviate within bounds from the actual value v of x. This actual value is completely determined by all submitted writes. That is, if v_0 is the initial value of x, then

$$v = v_0 + \sum_{k=1}^{N} TW[k, k]$$

and

$$v_i = v_0 + \sum_{k=1}^{N} TW[i, k]$$

Note that $v_i \leq v$. Let us concentrate only on absolute deviations. In particular, for every server S_i, we associate an upper bound δ_i such that we need to enforce:

$$v - v_i \leq \delta_i$$

Writes submitted to a server S_i will need to be propagated to all other servers. There are different ways in which this can be done, but typically an epidemic protocol will allow rapid dissemination of updates. In any case, when a server S_i propagates a write originating from S_j to S_k, the latter will be able to learn about the value $TW[i, j]$ at the time the write was sent. In other words, S_k can maintain a *view* $TW_k[i, j]$ of what it believes S_i will have as value for $TW[i, j]$. Obviously,

$$0 \leq TW_k[i, j] \leq TW[i, j] \leq TW[j, j]$$

The whole idea is that when a server S_k notices that S_i has not been staying in the right pace with the updates that have been submitted to S_k, it forwards writes from its log to S_i. This forwarding effectively advances the view $TW_k[i, k]$ that S_k has of $TW[i, k]$, making the deviation $TW[i, k] - TW_k[i, k]$ smaller. In particular, S_k advances its view on $TW[i, k]$ when an application submits a new write that would increase $TW[k, k] - TW_k[i, k]$ beyond $\delta_i / (N - 1)$. We leave it as an exercise to the reader to show that advancement always ensures that $v - v_i \leq \delta_i$.

Bounding staleness deviations

There are many ways to keep the staleness of replicas within specified bounds. One simple approach is to let the server S_k keep a real-time vector clock RVC_k where $RVC_k[i] = t_i$ means that S_k has seen all writes that have been submitted to S_i up to time t_i. In this case, we assume that each submitted write is timestamped by its origin server, with t_i denoting the time *local to S_i*.

If the clocks between the replica servers are loosely synchronized, then an acceptable protocol for bounding staleness would be the following. Whenever the server S_k notes that $t_k - RVC_k[i]$ is about to exceed a specified limit, it simply starts pulling in writes that originated from S_i with a timestamp later than $RVC_k[i]$.

Note that in this case, a replica server is responsible for keeping its copy of x up to date regarding writes that have been issued elsewhere. In contrast, when maintaining numerical bounds, we followed a push approach by letting an origin server keep replicas up to date by forwarding writes. The problem with pushing writes in the case of staleness is that no guarantees can be given for consistency when it is unknown in advance what the maximal propagation time will be. This situation is somewhat improved by pulling in updates, as multiple servers can help to keep a server's copy of x up to date.

Bounding ordering deviations

Recall that ordering deviations in continuous consistency are caused by the fact that a replica server tentatively applies updates that have been submitted to it. As a result, each server will have a local queue of tentative writes for which the actual order in which they are to be applied to the local copy of x still needs to be determined. The deviation is bounded by specifying the maximal length of the queue of tentative writes.

As a consequence, detecting when ordering consistency needs to be enforced is simple: when the length of this local queue exceeds a specified maximal length. At that point, a server will no longer accept any newly submitted writes, but will instead attempt to commit tentative writes by negotiating with other servers in which order its writes should be executed. We thus have to enforce a globally consistent ordering of tentative writes.

7.5.5 Implementing client-centric consistency

For our last topic on consistency protocols, let us draw our attention to implementing client-centric consistency. Implementing client-centric consistency is relatively straightforward if performance issues are ignored.

In a naive implementation of client-centric consistency, each write operation W is assigned a globally unique identifier. Such an identifier is assigned by the server to which the write had been submitted. We refer to this server as the *origin* of W. Then, for each client, we keep track of two sets of writes.

The read set for a client consists of the writes relevant for the read operations performed by a client. Likewise, the write set consists of the (identifiers of the) writes performed by the client.

Monotonic-read consistency is implemented as follows. When a client wants to perform a read operation at a server, that server is handed the client's read set to check whether all the identified writes have taken place locally. If not, it contacts the other servers to ensure that it is brought up to date before carrying out the read operation. Alternatively, the read operation is forwarded to a server where the write operations have already taken place. After the read operation is performed, the write operations that have taken place at the selected server and which are relevant for the read operation are added to the client's read set.

Note that it should be possible to determine exactly where the write operations identified in the read set have taken place. For example, the write identifier could include the identifier of the server to which the operation was submitted. That server is required to, for example, log the write operation so that it can be replayed at another server. In addition, write operations should be performed in the order they were submitted. Ordering can be achieved by letting the client generate a globally unique sequence number that is included in the write identifier. If each data item can be modified only by its owner, the latter can supply the sequence number.

Monotonic-write consistency is implemented analogous to monotonic reads. Whenever a client initiates a new write operation at a server, the server is handed over the client's write set. (Again, the size of the set may be prohibitively large in the face of performance requirements. An alternative solution is discussed below.) It then ensures that the identified write operations are performed first and in the correct order. After performing the new operation, that operation's write identifier is added to the write set. Note that bringing the current server up to date with the client's write set may introduce a considerable increase in the client's response time, since the client then waits for the operation to fully complete.

Likewise, read-your-writes consistency requires that the server where the read operation is to be performed has seen all the write operations in the client's write set. The writes can simply be fetched from other servers before the read operation is actually executed, although this may lead to a poor response time. Alternatively, the client-side software can search for a server where the identified write operations in the client's write set have already been performed.

Finally, writes-follow-reads consistency can be implemented by first bringing the selected server up to date with the write operations in the client's read set, and then later adding the identifier of the write operation to the write set, along with the identifiers in the read set (which have now become relevant for the write operation just performed).

Note 7.10 (Advanced: Improving efficiency)

It is easy to see that the read set and write set associated with each client can become very large. To keep these sets manageable, a client's read and write operations are grouped into sessions. A *session* is typically associated with an application: it is opened when the application starts and is closed when it exits. However, sessions may also be associated with applications that are temporarily exited, such as user agents for e-mail. Whenever a client closes a session, the sets are simply cleared. Of course, if a client opens a session that it never closes, the associated read and write sets can still become very large.

The main problem with a naive implementation lies in the representation of the read and write sets. Each set consists of a number of identifiers for write operations. Whenever a client forwards a read or write request to a server, a set of identifiers is handed to the server as well to see whether all write operations relevant to the request have been carried out by that server.

This information can be more efficiently represented by vector timestamps as follows. First, whenever a server accepts a new write operation W, it assigns that operation a globally unique identifier along with a timestamp $ts(W)$. A subsequent write operation submitted to that server is assigned a higher-valued timestamp. Each server S_i maintains a vector timestamp WVC_i, where $WVC_i[j]$ is equal to the timestamp of the most recent write operation originating from S_j that has been processed by S_i.

For clarity, assume that for each server, writes from S_j are processed in the order that they were submitted. Whenever a client issues a request to perform a read or write operation O at a specific server, that server returns its current timestamp along with the results of O. Read and write sets are subsequently represented by vector timestamps. More specifically, for each session A, we construct a vector timestamp SVC_A with $SVC_A[i]$ set equal to the maximum timestamp of all write operations in A that originate from server S_i:

$$SVC_A[j] = \max\{ts(W)|W \in A \text{ and } origin(W) = S_j\}$$

In other words, the timestamp of a session always represents the latest write operations that have been seen by the applications that are being executed as part of that session. The compactness is obtained by representing all observed write operations originating from the same server through a single timestamp.

As an example, suppose a client, as part of session A, logs in at server S_i. To that end, it passes SVC_A to S_i. Assume that $SVC_A[j] > WVC_i[j]$. What this means is that S_i has not yet seen all the writes originating from S_j that the client has seen. Depending on the required consistency, server S_i may now have to fetch these writes before being able to consistently report back to the client. Once the operation has been performed, server S_i will return its current timestamp WVC_i. At that point, SVC_A is adjusted to:

$$SVC_A[j] \leftarrow \max\{SVC_A[j], WVC_i[j]\}$$

Again, we see how vector timestamps can provide an elegant and compact way of representing history in a distributed system.

7.6 Example: Caching and replication in the Web

The Web is arguably the largest distributed system ever built. Originating from a relatively simple client-server architecture, it is now a sophisticated system consisting of many techniques to ensure stringent performance and availability requirements. These requirements have led to numerous proposals for caching and replicating Web content. Where the original schemes (which are still largely deployed) have been targeted toward supporting static content, much effort has also been put into supporting dynamic content, that is, supporting documents that are generated on-the-spot as the result of a request, as well as those containing scripts and such. An overview of traditional Web caching and replication is provided by Rabinovich and Spastscheck [2002].

Client-side caching in the Web generally occurs at two places. In the first place, most browsers are equipped with a relatively simple caching facility. Whenever a document is fetched, it is stored in the browser's cache, from where it is loaded the next time. In the second place, a client's site often runs a Web proxy. A Web proxy accepts requests from local clients and passes these to Web servers. When a response comes in, the result is passed to the client. The advantage of this approach is that the proxy can cache the result and return that result to another client, if necessary. In other words, a Web proxy can implement a shared cache. With so many documents being generated on the fly, the server generally provides the document in pieces, instructing the client to cache only those parts that are not likely to change when the document is requested a next time.

In addition to caching at browsers and proxies, ISPs generally also place caches in their networks. Such schemes are mainly used to reduce network traffic (which is good for the ISP) and to improve performance (which is good for end users). However, with multiple caches along the request path from client to server, there is a risk of increased latencies when caches do not contain the requested information.

Note 7.11 (Advanced: Cooperative caching)

As an alternative to building hierarchical caches, one can also organize caches for cooperative deployment, as shown in Figure 7.35. In **cooperative caching** or **distributed caching**, whenever a cache miss occurs at a Web proxy, the proxy first checks a number of neighboring proxies to see if one of them contains the requested document. If such a check fails, the proxy forwards the request to the Web server responsible for the document. In more traditional settings, this scheme is primarily deployed with Web caches belonging to the same organization or institution.

A study by Wolman et al. [1999] shows that cooperative caching may be effective for only relatively small groups of clients (in the order of tens of thousands of users). However, such groups can also be serviced by using a single proxy cache, which is much cheaper in terms of communication and resource usage.

However, in a study from a decade later, Wendell and Freedman [2011] show that in a highly decentralized system, cooperative caching actually turned out to be highly effective. These studies do not necessarily contradict each other: in both cases, the conclusion is that the effect of cooperative caching depends highly on the demands from clients.

A comparison between hierarchical and cooperative caching by Rodriguez et al. [2001] makes clear that there are various trade-offs to make. For example, because cooperative caches are generally connected through high-speed links, the transmission time needed to fetch a document is much lower than for a hierarchical cache. Also, as is to be expected, storage requirements are less strict for cooperative caches than hierarchical ones.

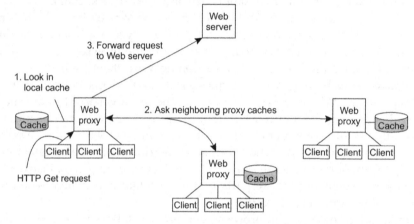

Figure 7.35: The principle of cooperative caching.

Different cache-consistency protocols have been deployed in the Web. To guarantee that a document returned from the cache is consistent, some Web proxies first send a conditional HTTP get request to the server with an additional If-Modified-Since request header, specifying the last modification time associated with the cached document. Only if the document has been changed since that time, will the server return the entire document. Otherwise, the Web proxy can simply return its cached version to the requesting local client, which corresponds to a pull-based protocol.

Unfortunately, this strategy requires that the proxy contacts a server for each request. To improve performance at the cost of weaker consistency, the widely used Squid Web proxy [Wessels, 2004] assigns an expiration time T_{expire} that depends on how long ago the document was last modified when it is cached. In particular, if $T_{last\_modified}$ is the last modification time of a document (as recorded by its owner), and T_{cached} is the time it was cached, then

$$T_{expire} = \alpha \left(T_{cached} - T_{last\_modified} \right) + T_{cached}$$

with $\alpha = 0.2$ (this value has been derived from practical experience). Until T_{expire}, the document is considered valid, and the proxy will not contact the server. After the expiration time, the proxy requests the server to send a fresh copy, unless it had not been modified. We note that Squid also allows the expiration time to be bounded by a minimum and a maximum time.

As an alternative to a pull-based protocol is that the server notifies proxies that a document has been modified by sending an invalidation. The problem with this approach for Web proxies is that the server may need to keep track of many proxies, inevitably leading to a scalability problem. However, by combining leases and invalidations, the state to be maintained at the server can be kept within acceptable bounds. Note that this state is largely dictated by the expiration times set for leases: the lower, the less caches a server needs to keep track of. Nevertheless, invalidation protocols for Web proxy caches are hardly ever applied. A comparison of Web caching consistency policies can be found in [Cao and Ozsu, 2002]. Their conclusion is that letting the server send invalidations can outperform any other method in terms of bandwidth and perceived client latency, while maintaining cached documents consistent with those at the origin server.

Finally, we should also mention that much research has been conducted to find out what the best cache replacement strategies are. Numerous proposals exist, but by-and-large, simple replacement strategies such as evicting the least recently used object work well enough. An in-depth survey of replacement strategies is presented by Podling and Boszormenyi [2003]; Ali et al. [2011] provide a more recent overview, which also includes Web prefetching techniques.

As the importance of the Web continues to increase as a vehicle for organizations to present themselves and to directly interact with end users, we see a shift between maintaining the content of a Web site and making sure that the site is easily and continuously accessible. This distinction has paved the way for **Content Delivery Networks** (CDN). The main idea underlying these CDNs is that they act as a Web hosting service, providing an infrastructure for distributing and replicating the Web documents of multiple sites across the Internet. The size of the infrastructure can be impressive. As mentioned before, as of 2022, Akamai is reported to have over 400,000 servers worldwide.

The sheer size of a CDN requires that hosted documents are automatically distributed and replicated. In most cases, a large-scale CDN is organized similar to a feedback-control loop, as shown in Figure 7.36 and which is described extensively in [Sivasubramanian et al., 2004b].

There are essentially three different kinds of aspects related to replication in Web hosting systems: metric estimation, adaptation triggering, and taking appropriate measures. The latter can be subdivided into replica placement decisions, consistency enforcement, and client-request routing. In the following, we briefly pay attention to each of these.

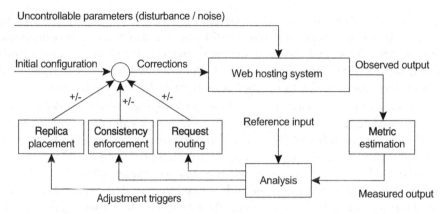

Figure 7.36: The general organization of a CDN as a feedback-control system.

An interesting aspect of CDNs is that they need to make a trade-off between many aspects when it comes to hosting replicated content. For example, access times for a document may be optimal if a document is massively replicated, but at the same time this incurs a financial cost, as well as a cost in terms of bandwidth usage for disseminating updates. By and large, there are many proposals for estimating how well a CDN is performing. These proposals can be grouped into several classes.

First, there are *latency metrics*, by which the time is measured for an action, for example, fetching a document, to take place. Trivial as this may seem, estimating latencies becomes difficult when, for example, a process deciding on the placement of replicas needs to know the delay between a client and some remote server. Typically, an algorithm for globally positioning nodes as discussed in Section 5.7.3 will need to be deployed.

Instead of estimating latency, it may be more important to measure the available bandwidth between two nodes. This information is particularly important when large documents have to be transferred, as in that case, the responsiveness of the system is largely dictated by the time that a document can be transferred. There are various tools for measuring available bandwidth, but in all cases it turns out that accurate measurements can be difficult to attain (see also Strauss et al. [2003], Shriram and Kaur [2007], Chaudhari and Biradar [2015], and Atxutegi et al. [2016]).

Another class consists of *spatial metrics*, which mainly consist of measuring the distance between nodes in terms of the number of network-level routing hops, or hops between autonomous systems. Again, determining the number of hops between two arbitrary nodes can be very difficult, and may also not even correlate with latency [Huffaker et al., 2002]. Moreover, simply looking at routing tables is not going to work when low-level techniques such as **Multi-Protocol Label Switching (MPLS)** are deployed. MPLS circumvents network-level routing by using virtual-circuit techniques to immediately and efficiently forward packets to their destination (see also Guichard et al. [2005]). Packets may thus follow entirely different routes than advertised in the tables of network-level routers.

A third class is formed by *network usage metrics*, which most often entails consumed bandwidth. Computing consumed bandwidth in terms of the number of bytes to transfer is generally easy. However, to do this correctly, we need to consider how often the document is read, how often it is updated, and how often it is replicated.

Consistency metrics tell us to what extent a replica is deviating from its master copy. We already discussed extensively how consistency can be measured in the context of continuous consistency [Yu and Vahdat, 2002].

Finally, *financial metrics* form another class for measuring how well a CDN is doing. Although not technical at all, considering that most CDN operate on a commercial basis, it is clear that often financial metrics will be decisive. Moreover, the financial metrics are closely related to the actual infrastructure of the Internet. For example, most commercial CDNs place servers at the edge of the Internet, meaning that they hire capacity from ISPs directly servicing end users. At this point, business models become intertwined with technological issues, an area that is not at all well understood. There is only few material available on the relation between financial performance and technological issues [Janiga et al., 2001].

From these examples, it should become clear that simply measuring the performance of a CDN, or even estimating its performance, may by itself be an extremely complex task. In practice, for commercial CDNs the issue that really counts is whether they can meet the service-level agreements that have been made with customers. These agreements are often formulated simply in terms of how quickly customers are to be serviced. It is then up to the CDN to make sure that these agreements are met.

Another question that needs to be addressed is when and how adaptations are to be triggered. A simple model is to periodically estimate metrics and subsequently take measures as needed. This approach is often seen in practice. Special processes located at the servers collect information and periodically check for changes.

An interesting aspect of this scheme is the simplicity by which consistency of documents can be enforced. Clearly, whenever a main document is changed, a client will always be able to fetch it from the origin server. In the case of embedded documents, a different approach needs to be followed as these documents are, in principle, fetched from a nearby replica server. To this end, a URL for an embedded document not only refers to a special host name that eventually leads to a CDN DNS server, but also contains a unique identifier that is changed every time the embedded document changes. In effect, this identifier changes the name of the embedded document. As a consequence,

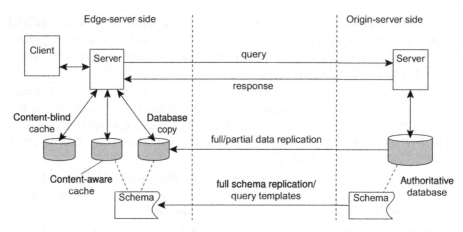

Figure 7.37: Alternatives for caching and replication with Web applications.

when the client is redirected to a specific CDN server, that server will not find the named document in its cache and will thus fetch it from the origin server. The old document will eventually be evicted from the server's cache as it is no longer referenced.

Up to this point, we have mainly concentrated on caching and replicating static Web content. In practice, we see that the Web is increasingly offering more dynamically generated content, but that it is also expanding toward offering services that can be called by remote applications. Also in these situations we see that caching and replication can help considerably in improving the overall performance, although the methods to reach such improvements are more subtle than what we discussed so far (see also Conti et al. [2005]).

When considering improving performance of Web applications through caching and replication, matters are complicated by the fact that several solutions can be deployed, with no single one standing out as the best. Let us consider the edge-server situation as sketched in Figure 7.37 (see also Sivasubramanian et al. [2007]). In this case, we assume a CDN in which each hosted site has an origin server that acts as the authoritative site for all read and update operations. An edge server is used to handle client requests, and has the ability to store (partial) information as also kept at an origin server.

Recall that in an edge-server architecture, Web clients request data through an edge server, which, in turn, gets its information from the origin server associated with the specific Website referred to by the client. As also shown in Figure 7.37 we assume that the origin server consists of a database from which responses are dynamically created. Although we have shown only a single Web server, it is common to organize each server according to a multitiered architecture, as we discussed before. An edge server can now be roughly organized along the following lines.

First, to improve performance, we can decide to apply full replication of the data stored at the origin server. This scheme works well whenever the update ratio is low and when queries require an extensive database search. As mentioned above, we assume that all updates are carried out at the origin server, which takes responsibility for keeping the replicas and the edge servers in a consistent state. Read operations can thus take place at the edge servers. Here, we see that replicating for performance will fail when the update ratio is high, as each update will incur communication over a wide-area network to bring the replicas into a consistent state. As shown by Sivasubramanian et al. [2004a], the read-to-update ratio is the determining factor to what extent the origin database in a wide-area setting should be replicated

Another case for full replication is when queries are generally complex. In the case of a relational database, this means that a query requires that multiple tables need to be searched and processed, as is generally the case with a join operation. Opposed to complex queries are simple ones that generally require access to only a single table to produce a response. In the latter case, **partial replication** by which only a subset of the data is stored at the edge server may suffice.

An alternative to partial replication is to make use of **content-aware caches**. The basic idea in this case is that an edge server maintains a local database that is now tailored to the type of queries that can be handled at the origin server. To explain, in a full-fledged database system a query will operate on a database in which the data has been organized into tables such that, for example, redundancy is minimized. Such databases are also said to be *normalized*.

In such databases, any query that adheres to the data schema can, in principle, be processed, although perhaps at considerable costs. With content-aware caches, an edge server maintains a database that is organized according to the structure of queries. What this means is that queries are assumed to adhere to a limited number of templates, effectively meaning that the different kinds of queries that can be processed is restricted. In these cases, whenever a query is received, the edge server matches the query against the available templates, and subsequently looks in its local database to compose a response, if possible. If the requested data is not available, the query is forwarded to the origin server, after which the response is cached before returning it to the client.

In effect, what the edge server is doing is checking whether a query can be answered with the data that is stored locally. This is also referred to as a **query containment check**. Note that such data was stored locally as responses to previously issued queries. This approach works best when queries tend to be repeated.

Part of the complexity of content-aware caching comes from the fact that the data at the edge server needs to be kept consistent. To this end, the origin server needs to know which records are associated with which templates, so that any update of a record, or any update of a table, can be properly addressed by, for example, sending an invalidation message to the appropriate edge servers. Another source of complexity comes from the fact that queries still need to be processed at edge servers. In other words, there is nonnegligible computational power needed to handle queries. Considering that databases often form a performance bottleneck in Web servers, alternative solutions may be needed. Finally, caching results from queries that span multiple tables (i.e., when queries are complex) such that a query containment check can be carried out effectively is not trivial. The reason is that the organization of the results may be very different from the organization of the tables on which the query operated.

These observations lead us to a third solution, namely **content-blind caching**. The idea of content-blind caching is simple: when a client submits a query to an edge server, the server first computes a unique hash value for that query. Using this hash value, it subsequently looks in its cache whether it has processed this query before. If not, the query is forwarded to the origin and the result is cached before returning it to the client. If the query had been processed before, the previously cached result is returned to the client.

The main advantage of this scheme is the reduced computational effort that is required from an edge server in comparison to the database approaches described above. However, content-blind caching can be wasteful in terms of storage, as the caches may contain much more redundant data in comparison to content-aware caching or database replication. Note that such redundancy also complicates the process of keeping the cache up-to-date, as the origin server may need to keep an accurate account of which updates can potentially affect cached query results. These problems can be alleviated when assuming that queries can match only a limited set of predefined templates, as we discussed above.

7.7 Summary

There are primarily two reasons for replicating data: improving the reliability of a distributed system and improving performance. Replication introduces a consistency problem: whenever a replica is updated, that replica becomes different from the others. To keep replicas consistent, we need to propagate updates in such a way that temporary inconsistencies are not noticed. Unfortunately, doing so may severely degrade performance, especially in large-scale distributed systems.

The only solution to this problem is to relax consistency somewhat. Different consistency models exist. For continuous consistency, the goal is to set bounds to numerical deviation between replicas, staleness deviation, and deviations in the ordering of operations.

Numerical deviation refers to the value by which replicas may be different. This type of deviation is highly application dependent, but can, for example, be used in replication of stocks. Staleness deviation refers to the time by which a replica is still considered to be consistent, despite that updates may have taken place some time ago. Staleness deviation is often used for Web caches. Finally, ordering deviation refers to the maximum number of tentative writes that may be outstanding at any server without having synchronized with the other replica servers.

Consistent ordering of operations has since long formed the basis for many consistency models. Many variations exist, but only a few seem to prevail among application developers. Sequential consistency essentially provides the semantics that programmers expect in concurrent programming: all write operations are seen by everyone in the same order. Less used, but still relevant, is causal consistency, which reflects that operations that are potentially dependent on each other are carried out in the order of that dependency.

Weaker consistency models consider series of read and write operations. In particular, they assume that each series is appropriately "bracketed" by accompanying operations on synchronization variables, such as locks. Although this requires explicit effort from programmers, these models are generally easier to implement efficiently than, for example, pure sequential consistency.

As opposed to these data-centric models, researchers in the field of distributed databases for mobile users have defined a number of client-centric consistency models. Such models do not consider the fact that data may be shared by several users, but instead, concentrate on the consistency that an individual client should be offered. The underlying assumption is that a client connects to different replicas in the course of time, but that such differences should be made transparent. In essence, client-centric consistency models ensure that whenever a client connects to a new replica, that replica is brought up to date with the data that had been manipulated by that client before, and which may reside at other replica sites.

To propagate updates, different techniques can be applied. A distinction needs to be made concerning *what* is exactly propagated, to *where* updates are propagated, and *by whom* propagation is initiated. We can decide to propagate notifications, operations, or state. Likewise, not every replica always needs to be updated immediately. Which replica is updated at which time depends on the distribution protocol. Finally, a choice can be made whether updates are pushed to other replicas, or that a replica pulls in updates from another replica.

Consistency protocols describe specific implementations of consistency models. Regarding sequential consistency and its variants, a distinction can be made between primary-based protocols and replicated-write protocols. In primary-based protocols, all update operations are forwarded to a primary copy that subsequently ensures the update is properly ordered and forwarded. In replicated-write protocols, an update is forwarded to several replicas at the same time. In that case, correctly ordering operations often becomes more difficult.

We pay separate attention to caching and replication in the Web and, related, content delivery networks. As it turns out, using existing servers and services, much of the techniques discussed before can be readily implemented using appropriate redirection techniques. Particularly challenging is caching content when databases are involved, as in those cases, much of what a Web server returns is dynamically generated. However, even in those cases, by carefully administrating what has already been cached at the edge, it is possible to invent highly efficient and effective caching schemes.

08

FAULT
TOLERANCE

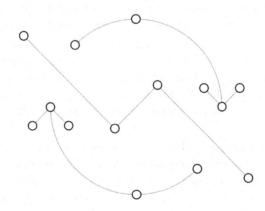

A characteristic feature of distributed systems that distinguishes them from single-machine systems is the notion of partial failure: part of the system is failing while the remaining part continues to operate, and seemingly correctly. An important goal in distributed-systems design is to construct the system in such a way that it can automatically recover from partial failures without seriously affecting the overall performance. In particular, whenever a failure occurs, the system should continue to operate in an acceptable way while repairs are being made. In other words, a distributed system is expected to be fault tolerant.

In this chapter, we take a closer look at techniques to achieve fault tolerance. After providing some general background, we will first look at process resilience through process groups. In this case, multiple identical processes cooperate, providing the appearance of a single logical process, to ensure that one or more of them can fail without a client noticing. A specifically difficult point in process groups is reaching consensus among the group members on which a client-requested operation is to perform. By now, Paxos is a commonly adopted, yet relatively intricate algorithm. We take two approaches in explaining Paxos. One that builds on how the protocol can be logically viewed as it is now, and one that gradually builds it up from scratch. The latter may help to understand many of its design decisions. We also pay extensive attention to the case in which servers may not just crash, but actually produce faulty results that cannot be immediately recognized as being faulty.

Achieving fault tolerance and reliable communication are strongly related. Next to reliable client-server communication, we pay attention to reliable group communication and notably atomic multicasting. In the latter case, a message is delivered to all nonfaulty processes in a group, or to none. Having atomic multicasting makes development of fault-tolerant solutions much easier.

Atomicity is a property that is important in many applications. In this chapter, we look into what are known as distributed commit protocols by which a group of processes is conducted to either jointly commit their local work, or collectively abort and return to a previous system state.

Finally, we will examine how to recover from a failure. In particular, we consider when and how the state of a distributed system should be saved to allow recovery to that state later on.

8.1   Introduction to fault tolerance

Fault tolerance has been subject to much research in computer science. In this section, we start with presenting the basic concepts related to processing failures, followed by a discussion of failure models. The key technique for handling failures is redundancy, which is also discussed. For more general information on fault tolerance in distributed systems, see, for example Jalote [1994]; Shooman [2002] or Koren and Krishna [2007].

8.1.1 Basic concepts

To understand the role of fault tolerance in distributed systems, we first need to take a closer look at what it actually means for a distributed system to tolerate faults. Being fault tolerant is strongly related to what are called **dependable systems**. Dependability is a term that covers a number of useful requirements for distributed systems, including the following [Kopetz and Verissimo, 1993]:

- Availability
- Reliability
- Safety
- Maintainability

Availability is defined as the property that a system is ready to be used *immediately*. In general, it refers to the probability that the system is operating correctly at any given moment, and is available to perform its functions on behalf of its users. In other words, a highly available system is one that will most likely be working at a given instant in time.

Reliability refers to the property that a system can run *continuously* without failure. In contrast to availability, reliability is defined in terms of a time interval, instead of an instant in time. A highly reliable system is one that will most likely continue to work without interruption during a relatively long period of time. This is a subtle but important difference when compared to availability. If a system goes down on average for one, seemingly random millisecond every hour, it has an availability of more than 99.9999 percent, but is still unreliable. Similarly, a system that never crashes but is shut down for two specific weeks every August, has high reliability but only 96 percent availability. The two are not the same.

Safety refers to the situation that when a system temporarily fails to operate correctly, no catastrophic event happens. For example, many process-control systems, such as those used for controlling nuclear power plants or sending people into space, are required to provide a high degree of safety. If such control systems temporarily fail for only a very brief moment, the effects could be disastrous. Many examples from the past (and probably many more yet to come) show how hard it is to build safe systems.

Finally, **maintainability** refers to how easily a failed system can be repaired. A highly maintainable system may also show a high degree of availability, especially if failures can be detected and repaired automatically. However, as we shall see later in this chapter, automatically recovering from failures is easier said than done.

Note 8.1 (More information: Traditional metrics)
We can be a bit more precise when it comes to describing availability and reliability. Formally, the **availability** $A(t)$ of a component in the time interval $[0, t)$ is defined as the average fraction of time that the component has been functioning correctly during that interval. The **long-term availability** A of a component is defined as $A(\infty)$.

Likewise, the **reliability** $R(t)$ of a component in the time interval $[0, t)$ is formally defined as the conditional probability that it has been functioning correctly during that interval, given that it was functioning correctly at time $T = 0$. Following Pradhan [1996], to establish $R(t)$ we consider a system of N identical components. Let $N_0(t)$ denote the number of correctly operating components at time t and $N_1(t)$ the number of failed components. Then, clearly,

$$R(t) = \frac{N_0(t)}{N} = 1 - \frac{N_1(t)}{N} = \frac{N_0(t)}{N_0(t) + N_1(t)}$$

The rate at which components are failing can be expressed as the derivative $dN_1(t)/dt$. Dividing this by the number of correctly operating components at time t gives us the **failure rate function** $z(t)$:

$$z(t) = \frac{1}{N_0(t)} \frac{dN_1(t)}{dt}$$

From

$$\frac{dR(t)}{dt} = -\frac{1}{N} \frac{dN_1(t)}{dt}$$

it follows that

$$z(t) = \frac{1}{N_0(t)} \frac{dN_1(t)}{dt} = -\frac{N}{N_0(t)} \frac{dR(t)}{dt} = -\frac{1}{R(t)} \frac{dR(t)}{dt}$$

If we make the simplifying assumption that a component does not age (and thus essentially has no wear-out phase), its failure rate will be constant, i.e., $z(t) = z$, implying that

$$\frac{dR(t)}{dt} = -zR(t)$$

Because $R(0) = 1$, we obtain

$$R(t) = e^{-zt}$$

In other words, if we ignore aging of a component, we see that a constant failure rate leads to a reliability following an exponential distribution, having the form shown in Figure 8.1.

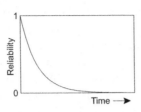

Figure 8.1: The reliability of a component having a constant failure rate.

Traditionally, fault-tolerance has been related to the following three metrics:

- **Mean Time To Failure** (*MTTF*): The average time until a component fails.
- **Mean Time To Repair** (*MTTR*): The average time needed to repair a component.
- **Mean Time Between Failures** (*MTBF*): Simply *MTTF + MTTR*.

Note that

$$A = \frac{MTTF}{MTBF} = \frac{MTTF}{MTTF + MTTR}$$

Also, these metrics make sense only if we have an accurate notion of what a failure actually is. As we will encounter later, identifying the occurrence of a failure may actually not be so obvious.

Often, dependable systems are also required to provide a high degree of security, especially when it comes to issues such as integrity. We will discuss security extensively in the next chapter.

A system is said to **fail** when it does not meet its promises. In particular, if a distributed system is designed to provide its users with a number of services, the system has failed when one or more of those services cannot be (completely) provided. An **error** is a part of a system's state that may lead to a failure. For example, when transmitting packets across a network, it is to be expected that some packets have been damaged when they arrive at the receiver. Damaged in this context means that the receiver may incorrectly sense a bit value (e.g., reading a 1 instead of a 0), or may even be unable to detect that something has arrived.

The cause of an error is called a **fault**. Clearly, finding out what caused an error is important. For example, a wrong or bad transmission medium may easily cause packets to be damaged. In this case, it is relatively easy to remove the fault. However, transmission errors may also be caused by bad weather conditions, such as in wireless networks. Changing the weather to reduce or prevent errors is a bit trickier.

As another example, a crashed program is clearly a failure, which may have happened because the program entered a branch of code containing a programming bug (i.e., a programming error). The cause of that bug is typically a programmer. In other words, the programmer is the cause of the error (programming bug), in turn leading to a failure (a crashed program).

Building dependable systems closely relates to controlling faults. As explained by Avizienis et al. [2004], a distinction can be made between preventing, tolerating, removing, and forecasting faults. For our purposes, the most important issue is **fault tolerance**, meaning that a system can provide its services even in the presence of faults. For example, by applying error-correcting codes for transmitting packets, it is possible to tolerate, to a certain extent, relatively poor transmission lines and reducing the probability that an error (a damaged packet) may lead to a failure.

Faults are generally classified as transient, intermittent, or permanent. **Transient faults** occur once and then disappear. If the operation is repeated, the fault goes away. A bird flying through the beam of a microwave transmitter may cause lost bits on some network. If the transmission times out and is retried, it will probably work the second time.

An **intermittent fault** occurs, then vanishes of its own accord, then reappears, and so on. A loose contact on a connector will often cause an intermittent fault. Intermittent faults cause a great deal of aggravation because they are difficult to diagnose. Typically, when the fault doctor shows up, the system works fine.

A **permanent fault** is one that continues to exist until the faulty component is replaced. Burnt-out chips, software bugs, and disk-head crashes are examples of permanent faults.

8.1.2 Failure models

A system that fails is not adequately providing the services it was designed for. If we consider a distributed system as a collection of servers that communicate with one another and with their clients, not adequately providing services means that servers, communication channels, or possibly both, are not doing what they are supposed to do. However, a malfunctioning server itself may not always be the fault we are looking for. If such a server depends on other servers to adequately provide its services, the cause of an error may need to be searched for somewhere else.

Such dependency relations appear in abundance in distributed systems. A failing disk may make life difficult for a file server that is designed to provide a highly available file system. If such a file server is part of a distributed database, the proper working of the entire database may be at stake, as only part of its data may be accessible.

To get a better grasp on how serious a failure actually is, several classification schemes have been developed. One such scheme is shown in Figure 8.2, and is based on schemes described by Cristian [1991] and Hadzilacos and Toueg [1993].

Type of failure	Description of server's behavior
Crash failure	Halts, but is working correctly until it halts
Omission failure	Fails to respond to incoming requests
Receive omission	Fails to receive incoming messages
Send omission	Fails to send messages
Timing failure	Response lies outside a specified time interval
Response failure	Response is incorrect
Value failure	The value of the response is wrong
State-transition failure	Deviates from the correct flow of control
Arbitrary failure	May produce arbitrary responses at arbitrary times

Figure 8.2: Different types of failures.

A **crash failure** occurs when a server prematurely halts, but was working correctly until it stopped. An important aspect of crash failures is that once the server has halted, nothing is heard from it anymore. A typical example of a crash failure is an operating system that comes to a grinding halt, and for which there is only one solution: reboot it. Many personal computer systems (be they desktop computers or laptops) suffer from crash failures so often that people have come to expect them to be normal. Consequently, moving the reset button, for example, from the back of a cabinet to the front was done for good reason. Perhaps one day it can be moved to the back again, or even removed altogether.

An **omission failure** occurs when a server fails to respond to a request. Several things might go wrong. In the case of a **receive-omission failure**, possibly the server never got the request in the first place. Note that it may well be the case that the connection between a client and a server has been correctly established, but that there was no thread listening for incoming requests. Also, a receive-omission failure will generally not affect the current state of the server, as the server is unaware of any message sent to it.

Likewise, a **send-omission failure** happens when the server has done its work, but somehow fails in sending a response. Such a failure may happen, for example, when a send buffer overflows while the server was not prepared for such a situation. Note that, in contrast to a receive-omission failure, the server may now be in a state reflecting that it has just completed a service for the client. As a consequence, if the sending of its response fails, the server has to be prepared for the client to reissue its previous request.

Other types of omission failures not related to communication may be caused by software errors such as infinite loops or improper memory management, by which the server is said to "hang."

Another class of failures is related to timing. **Timing failures** occur when the response lies outside a specified real-time interval. For example, in the case of streaming videos, providing data too soon may easily cause trouble for a recipient if there is not enough buffer space to hold all the incoming data.

More common, however, is that a server responds too late, in which case a **performance** failure is said to occur.

A serious type of failure is a **response failure**, by which the server's response is simply incorrect. Two kinds of response failures may happen. In the case of a value failure, a server simply provides the wrong reply to a request. For example, a search engine that systematically returns Web pages not related to any of the search terms used, has failed.

The other type of response failure is known as a state-transition failure. This kind of failure happens when the server reacts unexpectedly to an incoming request. For example, if a server receives a message it cannot recognize, a state-transition failure happens if no measures have been taken to handle such messages. In particular, a faulty server may incorrectly take default actions it should never have initiated.

The most serious are **arbitrary failures**, also known as **Byzantine failures**. In effect, when arbitrary failures occur, clients should be prepared for the worst. In particular, a server may be producing output it should never have produced, but which cannot be detected as being incorrect. Byzantine failures were first analyzed by Pease et al. [1980] and Lamport et al. [1982]. We return to such failures below.

Note 8.2 (More information: Omission and commission failures)
It has become somewhat of a habit to associate the occurrence of Byzantine failures with maliciously operating processes. The term "Byzantine" refers to the Byzantine Empire, a time (330–1453) and place (the Balkans and modern Turkey) in which endless conspiracies, intrigue, and untruthfulness were alleged to be common in ruling circles.

However, it may not be possible to detect whether an act was actually benign or malicious. Is a networked computer running a poorly engineered operating system that adversely affects the performance of other computers acting maliciously? In this sense, it is better to make the following distinction, which effectively excludes judgment:

- An **omission failure** occurs when a component fails to take an action that it should have taken.
- A **commission failure** occurs when a component takes an action that it should not have taken.

This difference, introduced by Mohan et al. [1983], also illustrates that a separation between dependability and security may at times be pretty difficult to make.

Many of the aforementioned cases deal with the situation that a process P no longer perceives any actions from another process Q. However, can P conclude that Q has indeed come to a halt? To answer this question, we need to make a distinction between two types of distributed systems:

- In an **asynchronous system**, no assumptions about process execution speeds or message delivery times are made. The consequence is that when process P no longer perceives any actions from Q, it cannot conclude that Q crashed. Instead, it may just be slow, or its messages may have been lost.

- In a **synchronous system**, process execution speeds and message-delivery times are bounded. This also means that when Q shows no more activity when it is expected to do so, process P can rightfully conclude that Q has crashed.

Unfortunately, pure synchronous systems exist only in theory. On the other hand, simply stating that every distributed system is asynchronous also does not do justice to what we see in practice, and we would be overly pessimistic in designing distributed systems under the assumption that they are necessarily asynchronous. Instead, it is more realistic to assume that a distributed system is **partially synchronous**: most of the time it behaves as a synchronous system, yet there is no bound on the time that it behaves in an asynchronous fashion. In other words, asynchronous behavior is an exception, meaning that we can normally use timeouts to conclude that a process has indeed crashed, but that occasionally such a conclusion is false. In practice, this means that we will have to design fault-tolerant solutions that can withstand incorrectly detecting that a process halted.

In this context, halting failures can be classified as follows, from the least to the most severe (see also Cachin et al. [2011]). We let process P attempt to detect that process Q has failed.

- **Fail-stop failures** refer to crash failures that can be reliably detected. This may occur when assuming nonfaulty communication links and when the failure-detecting process P can place a worst-case delay on responses from Q.

- **Fail-noisy failures** are like fail-stop failures, except that P will only *eventually* come to the correct conclusion that Q has crashed. This means that there may be some a priori unknown time in which P's detections of the behavior of Q are unreliable.

- When dealing with **fail-silent failures**, we assume that communication links are nonfaulty, but that process P cannot distinguish crash failures from omission failures.

- **Fail-safe failures** cover the case of dealing with arbitrary failures by process Q, yet these failures are benign: they cannot do any harm.

- Finally, when dealing with **fail-arbitrary failures**, Q may fail in any possible way; failures may be unobservable in addition to being harmful to the otherwise correct behavior of other processes.

Clearly, having to deal with fail-arbitrary failures is the worst that can happen. As we shall discuss shortly, we can design distributed systems in such a way that they can even tolerate these types of failures.

8.1.3   Failure masking by redundancy

If a system is to be fault tolerant, the best it can do is to try to hide the occurrence of failures from other processes. The key technique for masking faults is to use redundancy. Three kinds are possible: information redundancy, time redundancy, and physical redundancy (see also Johnson [1995]). With **information redundancy**, extra bits are added to allow recovery from garbled bits. For example, a Hamming code can be added to transmitted data to recover from noise on the transmission line.

With **time redundancy**, an action is performed, and then, if need be, it is performed again. Transactions use this approach. If a transaction aborts, it can be redone with no harm because nothing has yet been finalized. Another well-known example is retransmitting a request to a server when lacking an expected response. Time redundancy is especially helpful when the faults are transient or intermittent.

With **physical redundancy**, extra equipment or processes are added to make it possible for the system as a whole to tolerate the loss or malfunctioning of some components. Physical redundancy can thus be done either in hardware or in software. For example, extra processes can be added to the system, so that if a few of them crash, the system can still function correctly. In other words, by replicating processes, a high degree of fault tolerance may be achieved. We return to this type of software redundancy later in this chapter.

Note 8.3 (More information: Triple modular redundancy)
It is illustrative to see how redundancy has been applied in the design of electronic devices. Consider, for example, the circuit of Figure 8.3(a). Here signals pass through devices A, B, and C, in sequence. If one of them is faulty, the final result will probably be incorrect.

In Figure 8.3(b), each device is replicated three times. Following each stage in the circuit is a triplicated voter. Each voter is a circuit that has three inputs and one output. If two or three of the inputs are the same, the output is equal to that input. If all three inputs are different, the output is undefined. This kind of design is known as **triple modular redundancy** (TMR).

Suppose that element A2 fails. Each of the voters, V1, V2, and V3 gets two good (identical) inputs and one rogue input, and each of them outputs the correct value to the second stage. In essence, the effect of A2 failing is completely masked so that the inputs to B1, B2, and B3 are the same as they would have been had no fault occurred.

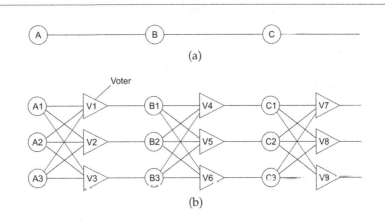

Figure 8.3: Triple modular redundancy.

Now consider what happens if B3 and C1 are also faulty, in addition to A2. These effects are also masked, so the three final outputs are still correct.

At first, it may not be obvious why three voters are needed at each stage. After all, one voter could also detect and pass the majority view. However, a voter is also a component and can be faulty. Suppose, for example, that voter V1 malfunctions. The input to B1 will then be wrong, but as long as everything else works, B2 and B3 will produce the same output and V4, V5, and V6 will all produce the correct result into stage three. A fault in V1 is effectively no different from a fault in B1. In both cases B1 produces incorrect output, but in both cases, it is voted down later, and the final result is still correct.

Although not all fault-tolerant distributed systems use TMR, the technique is very general, and should give a clear feeling for what a fault-tolerant system is, as opposed to a system whose individual components are highly reliable but whose organization cannot tolerate faults (i.e., operate correctly even in the presence of faulty components). Of course, TMR can be applied recursively, for example, to make a chip highly reliable by using TMR inside it, unknown to the designers who use the chip, possibly in their own circuit containing multiple copies of the chips along with voters.

8.2 Process resilience

Now that the basic issues of fault tolerance have been discussed, let us concentrate on how fault tolerance can actually be achieved in distributed systems. The first topic we discuss is protection against process failures, which is achieved by replicating processes into groups. In the following pages, we consider the general design issues of process groups and discuss what a fault-tolerant group actually is. Also, we look at how to reach consensus within a process group when one or more of its members cannot be trusted to give correct answers.

8.2.1   Resilience by process groups

The key approach to tolerating a faulty process is to organize several identical processes into a **group**. The key property that all groups have is that when a message is sent to the group itself, all members of the group receive it. In this way, if one process in a group fails, hopefully some other process can take over for it [Guerraoui and Schiper, 1997].

Process groups may be dynamic. New groups can be created, and old groups can be destroyed. A process can join a group or leave one during system operation. A process can be a member of several groups at the same time. Consequently, mechanisms are required for managing groups and group membership.

The purpose of introducing groups is to allow a process to deal with collections of other processes as a single abstraction. Thus, a process P can send a message to a group $Q = \{Q_1, \ldots, Q_N\}$ of servers without having to know who they are, how many there are, or where they are, which may change from one call to the next. To P, the group Q appears to be a single, logical process.

Group organization

An important distinction between different groups has to do with their internal structure. In some groups, all processes are equal, i.e., we have a **flat group**. There is no distinctive leader and all decisions are made collectively. Typically, many peer-to-peer systems operate in this way. An alternative organization is that of a **hierarchical group**. For example, one process is the coordinator and all the others are workers. In this model, when a request for work is generated, either by an external client or by one of the workers, it is sent to the coordinator. The coordinator then decides which worker is best suited to carry it out, and forwards it there. More complex hierarchies are also possible, of course. The Domain Name System can be argued to operate as a (indeed, quite complex) hierarchical group. Simpler organizations include primary-based backup schemes, as we discussed in Section 7.5.1. These communication patterns within groups are illustrated in Figure 8.4.

Each of these organizations has its own advantages and disadvantages. The flat group is symmetrical and has no single point of failure. If one of the processes crashes, the group simply becomes smaller, but can otherwise continue. A disadvantage is that decision-making may be more complicated. For example, to decide anything, a vote often has to be taken, incurring some delay and overhead.

The hierarchical group has the opposite properties. Loss of the coordinator brings the entire group to a grinding halt, but as long as it is running, it can make decisions without bothering everyone else. In practice, when the coordinator in a hierarchical group fails, its role will need to be taken over and

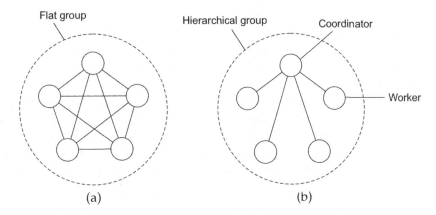

Figure 8.4: Communication in a (a) flat group and in a (b) hierarchical group.

one of the workers is elected as new coordinator. We discussed leader-election algorithms in Section 5.4.

Membership management

When group communication is present, some method is required for creating and deleting groups, as well as for allowing processes to join and leave groups. One possible approach is to have a **group server** to which all these requests can be sent. The group server can then maintain a complete database of all the groups and their exact membership. This method is straightforward, efficient, and fairly easy to implement. Unfortunately, it shares a major disadvantage with many (physically) centralized solutions: a single point of failure. If the group server crashes, group management ceases to exist. Probably most or all groups will have to be reconstructed from scratch, possibly terminating whatever work was going on.

The opposite approach is to manage group membership in a distributed way. For example, if (reliable) multicasting is available, an outsider can send a message to all group members announcing its wish to join the group.

Ideally, to leave a group, a member just sends a goodbye message to everyone. In the context of fault tolerance, assuming fail-stop failure semantics, is generally not appropriate. The trouble is, there is no polite announcement that a process crashes, as there is when a process leaves voluntarily. The other members have to discover this experimentally by noticing that the crashed member no longer responds to anything. Once it is certain that the crashed member is really down (and not just slow), it can be removed from the group.

Another knotty issue is that leaving and joining have to be synchronous with data messages being sent. In other words, starting at the instant that a process has joined a group, it must receive all messages sent to that group.

Similarly, as soon as a process has left a group, it must not receive any more messages from the group, and the other members must not receive any more messages from it. One way of making sure that a join or leave is integrated into the message stream at the right place is to convert this operation into a sequence of messages sent to the whole group.

One final issue relating to group membership is what to do if so many processes go down that the group can no longer function at all. Some protocol is needed to rebuild the group. Invariably, some process will have to take the initiative to start the ball rolling, but what happens if two or three try at the same time? The protocol must be able to withstand this. Again, coordination through, for example, a leader-election algorithm may be needed.

8.2.2 Failure masking and replication

Process groups are part of the solution for building fault-tolerant systems. In particular, having a group of identical processes allows us to mask one or more faulty processes in that group. In other words, we can replicate processes and organize them into a group to replace a single (vulnerable) process with a (fault tolerant) group. As discussed in the previous chapter, there are two ways to approach such replication: by means of primary-based protocols, or through replicated-write protocols.

Primary-based replication in the case of fault tolerance generally appears in the form of a **primary-backup protocol**. In this case, a group of processes is organized in a hierarchical fashion, in which a primary coordinates all write operations. In practice, the primary is fixed, although its role can be taken over by one of the backups if need be. In effect, when the primary crashes, the backups execute some election algorithm to choose a new primary.

Replicated-write protocols are used in the form of **active replication**, as well as by **quorum-based protocols**. These solutions correspond to organizing a collection of identical processes into a flat group. The main advantage is that such groups have no single point of failure, at the cost of distributed coordination.

An important issue with using process groups to tolerate faults is how much replication is needed. To simplify our discussion, let us consider only replicated-write systems. A system is said to be **k-fault tolerant** if it can survive faults in k components and still meet its specifications. If the components, say processes, fail silently, then having $k + 1$ of them is enough to provide k-fault tolerance. If k of them simply stop, then the answer from the other one can be used.

On the other hand, if processes exhibit arbitrary failures, continuing to run when faulty and sending out erroneous or random replies, a minimum of $2k + 1$ processes is needed to achieve k-fault tolerance. In the worst case, the k failing processes could accidentally (or even intentionally) generate the same reply. However, the remaining $k + 1$ will also produce the same answer, so the client or voter can just believe the majority.

Now suppose that in a k-fault tolerant group, a single process fails. The group as a whole is still living up to its specifications, namely that it can tolerate the failure of up to k of its members (of which one has just failed). But what happens if more than k members fail? In that case, all bets are off and whatever the group does, its results, if any, cannot be trusted. Another way of looking at this is that the process group, in its appearance of mimicking the behavior of a single, robust process, has failed.

8.2.3 Consensus in faulty systems with crash failures

As mentioned, in terms of clients and servers, we have adopted a model in which a potentially considerable collection of clients now send commands to a *group of processes* that jointly behave as a *single, highly robust process*. To make this work, we need to make an important assumption:

> *In a fault-tolerant process group, each nonfaulty process executes the same commands, in the same order, as every other nonfaulty process.*

Formally, this means that the group members need to reach **consensus** on which command to execute. If failures cannot happen, reaching consensus is easy. For example, we can use Lamport's totally ordered multicasting, as described in Section 5.2.1. Or, to keep it simple, using a centralized sequencer that hands out a sequence number to each command that needs to be executed will do the job as well. Unfortunately, life is not without failures, and reaching consensus among a group of processes under more realistic assumptions turns out to be tricky.

Flooding-based consensus

To illustrate the problem at hand, let us assume we have a group of processes $\mathbf{P} = \{P_1, \ldots, P_n\}$ operating under fail-stop failure semantics. In other words, we assume that crash failures can be reliably detected among the group members. Typically, a client contacts a group member requesting it to execute a command. Every group member maintains a list of proposed commands: some which it received directly from clients; others which it received from its fellow group members. We can reach consensus using the following approach, adopted from Cachin et al. [2011], and referred to as **flooding consensus**.

Conceptually, the algorithm operates in rounds. In each round, a process P_i sends its list of proposed commands it has seen so far to every other process in $\mathbf{P}$. At the end of a round, each process merges all received proposed commands into a new list, from which it then will deterministically select the command to execute, if possible. It is important to realize that the selection algorithm is the same for all processes. In other words, if all process have the same list, they will all select the same command to execute (and remove that command from their list).

It is not difficult to see that this approach works as long as processes do not fail. Problems start when a process P_i detects, during round r, that, say, process P_k has crashed. To make this concrete, assume we have a process group of four processes $\{P_1, \ldots, P_4\}$ and that P_1 crashes during round r. Also, assume that P_2 receives the list of proposed commands from P_1 before it crashes, but that P_3 and P_4 do not (in other words, P_1 crashes before it got a chance to send its list to P_3 and P_4). This situation is sketched in Figure 8.5.

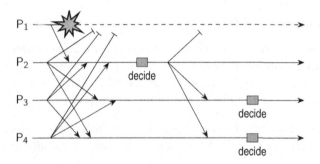

Figure 8.5: Reaching consensus through flooding in the presence of crash failures. Adopted from Cachin et al. [2011].

Assuming that all processes knew who was a group member at the beginning of round r, P_2 is ready to decide on which command to execute when it receives the respective lists of the other members: it has all commands proposed so far. Not so for P_3 and P_4. For example, P_3 may detect that P_1 crashed, but it does not know if either P_2 or P_4 had already received P_1's list. From P_3's perspective, if there is another process that did receive P_1's proposed commands, that process may then make a different decision than itself. As a consequence, the best that P_3 can do is postpone its decision until the next round. The same holds for P_4 in this example. A process will decide to move to a next round when it has received a message from every nonfaulty process. This assumes that each process can reliably detect the crashing of another process, for otherwise it would not be able to decide who the nonfaulty processes are.

Because process P_2 received all commands, it can indeed decide and can subsequently broadcast that decision to the others. Then, during the next round $r + 1$, processes P_3 and P_4 will also be able to decide: they will decide to execute the same command selected by P_2.

To understand why this algorithm is correct, it is important to realize that a process will move to a next round without having made a decision, only when it detects that another process has failed. In the end, this means that in the worst case at most one nonfaulty process remains, and this process can simply decide whatever proposed command to execute. Again, note that we are assuming reliable failure detection.

But then, what happens when the decision by process P_2 that it sent to P_3 was lost? In that case, P_3 can still not make a decision. Worse, we need to make sure that it makes the same decision as P_2 and P_4. If P_2 did not crash, we can assume that a retransmission of its decision will save the day. If P_2 did crash, this will also be detected by P_4 who will then subsequently rebroadcast its decision. Meanwhile, P_3 has moved to a next round, and after receiving the decision by P_4, will terminate its execution of the algorithm.

A more realistic approach: Raft

Let us now take a look at a consensus protocol that operates under crash-failure semantics, or actually, a fail-noisy failure model: a process will *eventually* correctly conclude that another process has crashed. **Raft**, described by Ongaro and Ousterhout [2014] was developed in reaction to the inherent intricacies of a famous consensus protocol, Paxos (which we discuss further below). In this section, we will stick to the essence of Raft, thereby even simplifying a few matters to focus entirely on understanding how and why it works.

In Raft, we typically have a group of some five replicated servers. We assume the set of servers is fixed (although Raft allows servers to join and leave the group). Each server maintains a **log** of operations, some of which have already been executed (i.e., committed), as well as pending operations. Consensus is expressed in terms of these logs: committed operations have the same position in each of the respective server's logs. One of the servers operates as a **leader** and decides on the order in which pending operations are to be committed. In essence, Raft is a primary-backup protocol, with the primary acting as leader and the backups as **followers**. We discussed Raft's leader-election algorithm in Section 5.4.4.

A client always sends an operation request to the leader (possibly after having been redirected by one of the followers). That means that the leader is fully aware of all pending requests. Each client request for executing an operation o is appended to the leader's log, in the form of a tuple $\langle o, t, k \rangle$ in which t is the **term** under which the current leader serves, and k the index of o in the leader's log. To recall, after electing a *next* leader, the term for new operations will be $t + 1$. Let c be the index of the most recently committed operation. Raft guarantees that operations that have been registered as committed, have been performed by a majority of the servers, and that the result has been returned to the original client.

Assume the leader has a log of length n, is operating in term t, and receives a request for executing operation o. In that case, it appends $\langle o, t, n + 1 \rangle$ and *conceptually* sends its entire log to all the other servers, along with the current value of c. Again conceptually, each following server copies the entire log, and returns an acknowledgement to the leader, while ensuring that all operations up to and including index c have been executed. Note that operation o cannot yet be committed by a follower.

As soon as the leader receives a majority of acknowledgements, it executes o, returns the result (if any, but at least an acknowledgement) to the client, and sets c to $n + 1$. The next time it communicates with the other servers, it also sends c so that each of them can commit operations, in particular, o. It is important to note that in this scheme, the leader is indeed in full control: its state (as expressed by its log), is to be seen as the collective state of the server group. Of course, in reality, the leader will send only the tuple $\langle o, t, n + 1 \rangle$, where it will be appended to the local log of the respective followers. In this sense, the protocol essentially follows the one described in Section 7.5.1 (except that clients always send a request to the primary, and not through a follower). More important, however, is that by stating that the leader, conceptually speaking, sends the entire log, it overwrites the log of its followers. If the leader receives no acknowledgement from one of its followers, it will simply repeat sending the log until acknowledged.

Suppose the leader crashes. In that case, a new one is elected as described in Section 5.4.4, and this new leader's log is the collective state of the server group. There is only one problem: if that log misses committed operations, then it is not representative for what the majority of servers has decided on. For this reason, during an election, a server S will *not* vote for a candidate server S' if it turns out that S's log is more up to date, than that of S'. Oversimplifying matters somewhat, a log is more up to date when it contains more committed operations (meaning that S' has missed several commits already done by a majority of other servers), or when it contains operations from more recent terms (meaning that S' has missed elections). Assuming that the new leader will have executed all the committed operations, its state will therefore be the same as that of the previous leader before it crashed. However, do note that the new leader may not necessarily have received all pending requests. From a consensus point of view, this is not a problem. To avoid missing any client requests, Raft does assume that when a client does not receive a response from the server, it will resubmit its original request.

What if the leader crashed after executing o^1 (because there was a majority of servers), yet did not have a chance to inform (all of) the other servers? First, note that the new leader will have a log that is at least a subset of the logs of a majority of the remaining servers, in terms of committed operations (otherwise it would have never been elected as new leader). When handling a new operation o^2, broadcasting its log to the other servers, and receiving an acknowledgement from a majority, it can not only commit o^2, but now also o^1. This situation is shown in Figure 8.6. First, note that server S_5 will be brought up to date about operation o^1 as soon as the new leader tells about o^2. After receiving enough acknowledgements, the leader can go ahead and commit o^1

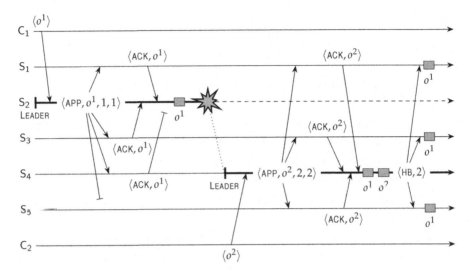

Figure 8.6: The situation when a leader crashes after executing an operation but before being able to tell other servers that the operation has been committed.

(as well as o^2). All other servers can commit o^1 as soon as they know that the leader did so as well.

We have skipped a number of details, notably details related to the fact that the leader does not send entire logs, but only operation requests. For one, this means that after an election, servers may be missing operations, or could have extraneous operations, or both. Bringing the logs of followers into a consistent state with the new leader requires some attention, which can be ignored by assuming that entire logs are sent. These, and other details, are found in Ongaro and Ousterhout [2014] and Ongaro [2014].

8.2.4 Example: Paxos

Discussing consensus in the presence of crash failures cannot be decently done without discussing **Paxos**. It was originally published in 1989 as a technical report by Leslie Lamport, but it took about a decade before someone decided that it may not be such a bad idea to disseminate it through a regular scientific channel [Lamport, 1998]. The original publication is not easy to understand, exemplified by other publications that aim at explaining it [Lampson, 1996; Prisco et al., 1997; Lamport, 2001; van Renesse and Altinbuken, 2015]. In fact, it is generally agreed that Paxos is not only quite difficult to explain and understand, but that these intricacies have led to implementations that actually differ from the original protocol. These intricacies formed an important motivation for developing Raft, which we explained above.

Essential Paxos

The assumptions under which Paxos operates are rather weak:

- The distributed system is partially synchronous (in fact, it may even be asynchronous).

- Communication between processes may be unreliable, meaning that messages may be lost, duplicated, or reordered.

- Messages that are corrupted can be detected as such (and thus subsequently ignored).

- All operations are deterministic: once an execution is started, it is known exactly what it will do.

- Processes may exhibit crash failures, but not arbitrary failures, nor do processes collude.

By-and-large, these are realistic assumptions for many practical distributed systems.

We first roughly follow the explanation given by Lamport [2001] and Kirsch and Amir [2008]. The algorithm operates as a network of *logical* processes, of which there are different types. First, there are **clients** that request a specific operation to be executed. At the server side, each client is represented by a single **proposer**, which attempts to have a client's request accepted. Normally, a single proposer has been designated as being the **leader**, and drives the protocol toward reaching consensus.

What we need to establish is that a proposed operation is accepted by an **acceptor**. If a majority of acceptors accepts the same proposal, the proposal is said to be *chosen*. However, what is chosen still needs to be *learned*. To this end, we will have a number of **learner** processes, each of which will execute a chosen proposal once it has been informed by a majority of acceptors.

It is important to note that a single proposer, acceptor, and learner form a single *physical* process, running on a single machine that the client communicates with, as shown in Figure 8.7. We thus assume that if, for example, a proposer crashes, then the physical process that it is part of will have crashed. By replicating this server, we aim at obtaining fault tolerance in the presence of crash failures.

The basic model is that the leading proposer receives requests from clients, one at a time. A nonleading proposer forwards any client request to the leader. The leading proposer sends its proposal to all acceptors, telling each to accept the requested operation. Each acceptor will subsequently broadcast a learn message. If a learner receives the same learn message from a majority of acceptors, it knows that consensus has been reached on which operation to execute, and will execute it.

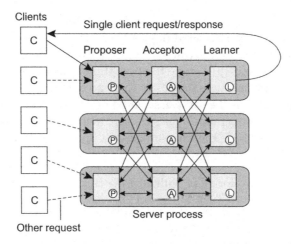

Figure 8.7: The organization of Paxos into different logical processes.

There are at least two specific issues that need further attention. First, not only do the servers need to reach consensus on which operation to execute, we also need to make sure that each of them actually executes it. In other words, how do we know for sure that a majority of the nonfaulty servers will carry out the operation? There is essentially only one way out: have learn messages be retransmitted. However, to make this work, an acceptor will have to log its decisions (in turn requiring a mechanism for purging logs). Because we are assuming globally ordered proposal timestamps (as explained shortly), missing messages can be easily detected, and also accepted operations will always be executed in the same order by all learners.

As a general rule, the server hosting the leading proposer will also inform the client when its requested operation has been executed. If another process had taken over the lead, then it will also handle the response to the client.

This brings us to the second important issue: a failing leader. Life would be easy if the failure of a leader would be reliably detected, after which a new leader would be elected, and later, the recovering leader would instantly notice that the world around it had changed. Unfortunately, life is not so easy. Paxos has been designed to tolerate proposers who still believe they are in the lead. The effect is that proposals may be sent out concurrently by different proposers (each believing to be the leader). We therefore need to make sure that these proposals can be distinguished from one another to ensure that the acceptors handle only the proposals from the current leader.

Note that relying on a leading proposer implies that any practical implementation of Paxos will need to be accompanied by a leader-election algorithm. In principle, that algorithm can operate independently of Paxos, but is normally part of it.

To distinguish concurrent proposals from different proposers, each proposal p has a uniquely associated (logical) timestamp $ts(p)$. How uniqueness is achieved is left to an implementation, but we will describe some of the details shortly. Let $oper(p)$ denote the operation associated with proposal p. The trick is to allow multiple proposals to be accepted, but that each of these accepted proposals has the same associated operation. This can be achieved by guaranteeing that if a proposal p is chosen, then any proposal with a higher timestamp will also have the same associated operation. In other words, we require that

$$p \text{ is chosen } \Rightarrow \text{ for all } p' \text{ with } ts(p') > ts(p) : oper(p') = oper(p)$$

Of course, for p to be chosen, it needs to be accepted. That means that we can guarantee our requirement when guaranteeing that if p is chosen, then any higher-timestamped proposal accepted by any acceptor, has the same associated operation as p. However, this is not sufficient, for suppose that at a certain moment, a proposer simply sends a new proposal p', with the highest timestamp so far, to an acceptor A that had not received any proposal before. Note that this may indeed happen according to our assumptions concerning message loss and multiple proposers, each believing to be in the lead. In absence of any other proposals, A will simply accept p'. To prevent this situation from happening, we thus need to guarantee that

> *If proposal p is chosen, then any higher-timestamped proposal issued by a proposer, has the same associated operation as p.*

When explaining the Paxos algorithm below, we will indeed see that a proposer may need to adopt an operation coming from acceptors in favor of its own. This will happen after a leading proposer had failed, but its proposed operation had already made it to a majority of the acceptors.

The processes collectively formally ensure *safety*, in the sense that only proposed operations will be learned, and that at most one operation will be learned at a time. In general, a **safety property** asserts that nothing bad will happen. Furthermore, Paxos ensures *conditional liveness* in the sense that if enough processes remain up-and-running, then a proposed operation will eventually be learned (and thus executed). **Liveness**, which tells us that eventually something good will happen, is not guaranteed in Paxos, unless some adaptations are made. We return to liveness in Note 8.4.

There are now two phases, each, in turn, consisting of two subphases. During the first phase, the leading proposer interacts with acceptors to get a requested operation accepted for execution. The first phase is needed to rule out any trouble caused by different proposers, each believing they are the leader. The best that can happen is that an individual acceptor promises to consider the proposer's operation and ignore other requests. The worst is that the proposer was too late and that it will be asked to adopt some other proposer's request instead. Apparently, a leadership change had taken place and there may be former requests that need to be handled first.

In the second phase, the acceptors will have informed proposers about the promises they have made. The leading proposer essentially takes up a slightly different role by promoting a single operation to the one to be executed, and subsequently telling the acceptors.

Phase 1a (prepare): The goal of this phase is that a proposer P who believes it is the leader and is proposing operation o, tries to get its proposal timestamp *anchored*, in the sense that any lower timestamp failed, or that o had also been previously proposed (i.e., with some lower proposal timestamp). To this end, P broadcasts its proposal to the acceptors. For the operation o, the proposer selects a proposal number m higher than any of its previously selected numbers. This leads to a **proposal timestamp** $t = (m, i)$ where i is the (numerical) process identifier of P. Note that

$$(m, i) < (n, j) \Leftrightarrow (m < n) \text{ or } (m = n \text{ and } i < j)$$

This timestamp for a proposal p is an implementation of the previously mentioned timestamp $ts(p)$. Proposer P sends PREPARE(t) to all acceptors (but note that messages may be lost). In doing so, it is (1) asking the acceptors to promise not to accept any proposals with a lower proposal timestamp, and (2) to inform it about an accepted proposal, if any, with the highest timestamp less than t. If such a proposal exists, the proposer will adopt it.

Phase 1b (promise): An acceptor A may receive multiple proposals. Assume it receives PREPARE(t) from P. There are three cases to consider:

(1) t is the highest proposal timestamp received from any proposer so far. In that case, A will return PROMISE(t) to P stating that A will ignore any future proposals with a lower timestamp.

(2) If t is the highest timestamp so far, but another proposal (t', o') had already been accepted, A also returns (t', o') to P. This will allow P to decide on the final operation that needs to be accepted.

(3) In all other cases, do nothing: there is apparently another proposal with a higher timestamp that is being processed.

Once the first phase has been completed, the leading proposer P knows what the acceptors have promised. Essentially, the leading proposer knows that all acceptors have agreed on the same operation. This will put P into a position to tell the acceptors that they can go ahead. This is needed because although the leading proposer knows on which operation consensus has been reached, this consensus is not known to the others. Again, we assume that P received a response from a majority of acceptors (whose respective responses may be different).

Phase 2a (accept): There are two cases to consider:

(1) If P does not receive any accepted operation from any of the acceptors, it will forward its own proposal for acceptance by sending ACCEPT(t, o) to all acceptors.

(2) Otherwise, it was informed about another operation o', which it will adopt and forward for acceptance. It does so by sending ACCEPT(t, o'), where t is P's proposal timestamp and o' is the operation with proposal timestamp highest among all accepted operations that were returned by the acceptors in Phase 1b.

Phase 2b (learn): Finally, if an acceptor receives ACCEPT(t, o'), but did not previously send a promise with a higher proposal timestamp, it will accept operation o', and tell all learners to execute o' by sending LEARN(o'). At that point, the acceptor can forget about o'. A learner L receiving LEARN(o') from a majority of acceptors, will execute the operation o'. We now also know that a majority of learners share the same idea on which operation to execute.

It is important to realize that this description of Paxos indeed captures only its essence: using a leading proposer to drive the acceptors toward the execution of the same operation. When it comes to practical implementations, much more needs to be done (and more than we are willing to describe here). An excellent description of what it means to realize Paxos has been written by Kirsch and Amir [2008]. Another write-up on its practical implications can be found in [Chandra et al., 2007].

Understanding Paxos

To properly understand Paxos, but also many other consensus algorithms, it is useful to see how its design could have evolved. We say "could have," as the evolution of the algorithm has never been documented. The following description is largely based on work described by Meling and Jehl [2013][1]. As our starting point, we consider a server that we wish to make more robust. By now, we know that this can be achieved through replication and making sure that all commands submitted by clients are executed by all servers in the same order. The simplest situation is to add one server, thus creating a group of two processes, say S_1 and S_2. Also, to make sure that all commands are executed in the same order, we appoint one process to be a sequencer, which increments and associates a unique timestamp with every submitted command. Servers

---

[1]Special credits go to Hein Meling for helping us better understand what Paxos is all about.

are required to execute commands according to their timestamp. In Paxos, such a server is referred to as the **leader**. We can also consider it to be a **primary server**, with the other acting as a **backup server**.

We assume that a client broadcasts its requested command to all servers. If a server notices it is missing a command, it can rely on the other server to forward it when necessary. We will not describe how this happens, but silently assume that all commands are stored at the servers and that we merely need to make sure that the servers agree on which command to execute next. As a consequence, all remaining communication between servers consists of control messages. To make this point clear, consider the situation sketched in Figure 8.8. (In what follows, we use subscripts to designate processes, and superscripts to designate operations and states.)

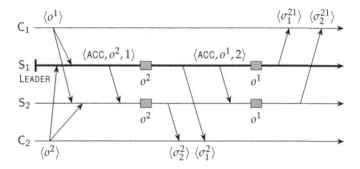

Figure 8.8: Two clients communicating with a 2-server process group.

In this example, server S_1 is the leader and as such will hand out timestamps to submitted requests. Client C_1 has submitted command o^1 while C_2 submitted o^2. S_1 instructs S_2 to execute operation o^2 with timestamp 1, and later operation o^1 with timestamp 2. After processing a command, a server will return the result to the associated client. We designate this using the notation $\langle \sigma_i^j \rangle$, where i is the index of the reporting server, and j the state it was in, expressed as the sequence of operations it has carried out. In our example, client C_1 will thus see the results $\langle \sigma_1^{21} \rangle$ and $\langle \sigma_2^{21} \rangle$, meaning that each server has executed o^1 after executing o^2.

In Paxos, when a leader associates a timestamp with an operation, it does so by sending an **accept message** to the other server(s). As we assume that messages may be lost, a server accepting an operation o does so by telling the leader it has **learned** the operation by returning a LEARN(o) message. When the leader does not notice that operation o has been learned, it simply retransmits an ACCEPT(o, t) message, with t being the original timestamp. Note that in our description, we are skipping the phase of coming to agreement on the operation to be carried out: we assume the leader has decided and now needs to reach consensus on executing that operation.

Compensating for a lost message is relatively easy, but what happens when also a server crashes? Let us first assume that a crash can be reliably detected. Consider the situation sketched in Figure 8.9(a). The issue, of course, is that server S_2 will never have learned (about) operation o^1. This situation can be prevented by demanding that a server may execute an operation only if it knows that the other server has learned the operation as well, as illustrated in Figure 8.9(b).

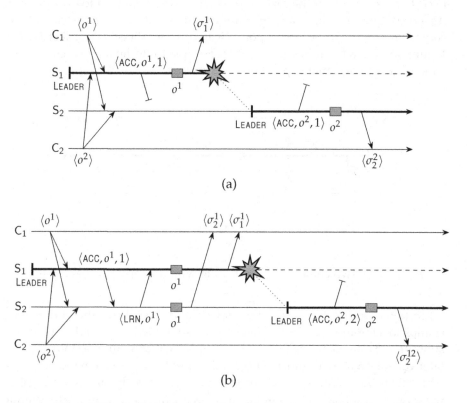

(a)

(b)

Figure 8.9: (a) What may happen when the leader crashes in combination with a lost accept, and (b) the solution, namely demanding that the other server has learned the operation as well before executing it.

It is not difficult to see that with a larger process group, we can get into the same situation as in Figure 8.9(a). Simply consider a group of three servers $\{S_1, S_2, S_3\}$ with S_1 being the leader. If its ACCEPT(o^1, t) message to S_3 is lost, yet it knows that S_2 has learned o^1, then it should still not execute o^1 until it has also received a LEARN(o^1) message from S_3. This situation is shown in Figure 8.10.

Let us consider the three-server case and imagine what would happen if LEARN(o^1) returned by S_2 would not make it to S_1. Of course, S_1 would

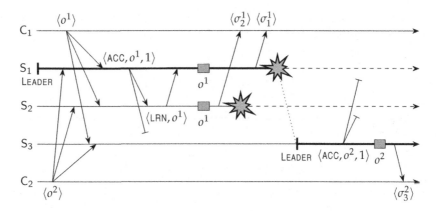

Figure 8.10: The situation when dealing with three servers, of which two crash. In this case, S_1 should have waited with executing operation o^1 until it had received LEARN(o^1) from S_3, but also S_2 should wait until it knows that S_3 has learned about o^1.

not execute o^1, but otherwise we would still be in trouble: S_2 will execute o^1 while S_3 would take over leadership and execute o^2 without ever knowing that o^1 had already been processed. In other words, also S_2 must wait with the execution of o^1 until it knows that S_3 has learned that operation. This brings us to the following:

> *In Paxos, a server S cannot execute an operation o until it has received a* LEARN(o) *from all other nonfaulty servers.*

Up to this point, we have assumed that a process can reliably detect that another process has crashed. In practice, this is not the case. As we will discuss more extensively shortly, a standard approach toward failure detection is to set a timeout on expected messages. For example, each server is required to send a message declaring it is still alive, and at the same time the other servers set timeouts on the expected receipt of such messages. If a timeout expires, the sender is suspected to have failed. In a partially synchronous or fully asynchronous system, there is essentially no other solution. However, the consequence is that a failure may be falsely detected, as the delivery of such "I'm alive" messages may have simply been delayed or lost.

Let us assume that Paxos has realized a failure detection mechanism, but that the two servers falsely conclude that the other has failed, as shown in Figure 8.11. The problem is clear: each may now independently decide to execute their operation of choice, leading to divergent behavior. It is at this point that we need to introduce an extra server, and demand that a server can execute an operation only if it is certain that a *majority* will execute that operation. Note, that in the three-server case, execution of operation o by server S can take place as soon as S has received at least one (other) LEARN(o) message. Together with the sender of that message, S will form a majority.

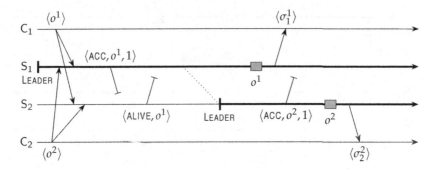

Figure 8.11: The situation in the case of false failure detections.

We have now come to a point where it should be clear that Paxos requires at least three replicated servers $\{S_1, S_2, S_3\}$ to operate correctly. Let us concentrate on the situation that one of these servers crashes. We make the following assumptions.

- Initially, S_1 is the leader.

- A server can reliably detect it has missed a message. The latter can be realized, for example, through timestamps in the form of strictly increasing sequence numbers. Whenever a server notices it has missed a message, it can then simply request a retransmission and catch up before continuing.

- When a new leader needs to be elected, the remaining servers follow a strictly deterministic algorithm. For example, we can safely assume that if S_1 crashes, then S_2 will become leader. Likewise, if S_2 crashes, S_3 will take over, and so on.

- Clients may receive duplicate responses, but besides being required to recognize duplicates, form no further part of the Paxos protocol. In other words, a client cannot be asked to help the servers to resolve a situation.

Under these circumstances, no matter when one of S_2 or S_3 crashes, Paxos will behave correctly. Of course, we are still demanding that execution of an operation can take place only if a server knows that a majority will execute that operation.

Suppose now that S_1 in its role as leader, crashes after the execution of operation o^1. The worst that can happen in this case is that S_3 is completely ignorant of the situation until the new leader, S_2 tells it to accept operation o^2. Note that this is announced through an ACCEPT($o^2, 2$) message such that the timestamp $t = 2$ will alert S_3 that it missed a previous accept message. S_3 will tell so to S_2, who can then retransmit $\textsc{accept}(o^1, 1)$, allowing S_3 to catch up.

Likewise, if S_2 missed $\textsc{accept}(o^1, 1)$, but did detect that S_1 crashed, it will eventually either send $\textsc{accept}(o^1, 1)$ or $\textsc{accept}(o^2, 1)$ to S_3 (i.e., in both cases using timestamp $t = 1$, which was previously used by S_1). Again, S_3 has enough information to get S_2 on the right track again. If S_2 had sent $\textsc{accept}(o^1, 1)$, S_3 can simply tell S_2 that it already learned o^1. In the other case, when S_2 sends $\textsc{accept}(o^2, 1)$, S_3 will inform S_2 that it apparently missed operation o^1. We conclude that when S_1 crashes after executing an operation, Paxos behaves correctly.

So, what can happen if S_1 crashes immediately after having sent $\textsc{accept}(o^1, 1)$ to the other two servers? Suppose again that S_3 is completely ignorant of the situation because messages are lost, until S_2 has taken over leadership and announces that o^2 should be accepted. Like before, S_3 can tell S_2 that it (i.e., S_3) missed operation o^1, so that S_2 can help S_3 to catch up. If S_2 misses messages, but does detect that S_1 crashed, then as soon as it takes over leadership and proposes an operation, it will be using a stale timestamp. This will trigger S_3 to inform S_2 that it missed operation o^1, which saves the day. Again, Paxos is seen to behave correctly.

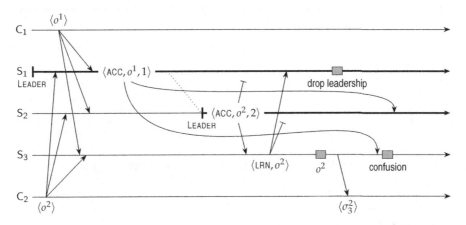

Figure 8.12: Why incorporating the ID of the current leader is needed: S_2 falsely concludes that S_1 has crashed.

Problems may arise with false detections of crashes. Consider the situation sketched in Figure 8.12. We see that the accept messages from S_1 are considerably delayed and that S_2 falsely detects S_1 having crashed. S_2 takes over leadership and sends $\textsc{accept}(o^2, 1)$, i.e., with a timestamp $t = 1$. However, when finally $\textsc{accept}(o^1, 1)$ arrives, S_3 cannot do anything: this is not a message it is expecting. Note that, in principle, S_3 does not check who is the current leader. The only thing it knows is that it is itself *not* the leader.

Precisely for this reason, it does not expect an ACCEPT message with the same timestamp as before. Things change, however, if it does know who the current leader is, in combination with a deterministic leader election. In that case, it could safely reject $\text{ACCEPT}(o^1, 1)$, knowing that by now S_2 has taken over, and even perhaps retransmit $\text{LEARN}(o^2)$ to S_1. A (perhaps previously sent) $\text{LEARN}(o^2)$ message received by S_1 will allow S_1 to conclude that leadership had been taken over. We conclude that the leader should include its ID in an accept message.

We have covered almost all cases and have thus far shown that Paxos behaves correctly. Unfortunately, although being correct, the algorithm can still come to a grinding halt. Consider the situation illustrated in Figure 8.13. What we are seeing here is that because the LEARN messages returned by S_3 are lost, neither S_1 nor S_2 will ever be able to know what S_3 actually executed: did it learn (and execute) $\text{ACCEPT}(o^1, 1)$ before or after learning $\text{ACCEPT}(o^2, 1)$, or perhaps it learned neither operation? A solution to this problem is discussed in Note 8.4.

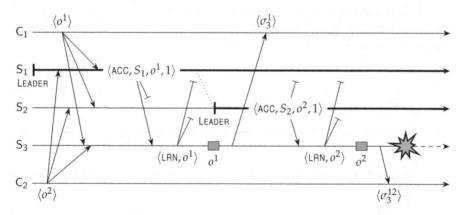

Figure 8.13: When Paxos can make no further progress.

Note 8.4 (Advanced: Making progress in Paxos)
Up to this point, we have discussed the development of Paxos such that **safety** is ensured. Safety essentially means that nothing bad will happen, or, put differently, that the behavior of the algorithm is correct. To also ensure that eventually something good will happen, generally referred to as **liveness** of an algorithm, we need to do a bit more. In particular, we need to get out of the situation sketched in Figure 8.13.

The real problem with this situation is that the servers have no consensus on whom the leader is. Once S_2 decides it should take over leadership, it needs to ensure that any outstanding operations initiated by S_1 have been properly dealt with. In other words, it has to ensure that its own leadership is not hindered by operations that have not yet been completed by all nonfaulty processes. If leadership is taken over too quickly and a new operation is proposed, a previous operation that has been executed by at least one server may not get a chance to be executed by all servers first.

To this end, Paxos enforces an explicit leadership takeover, and this is where the role of **proposers** come from. When a server crashes, the next one in line will need to take over (recall that Paxos assumes a deterministic leader-election algorithm), but also ensure that any outstanding operations are dealt with. This explicit takeover is implemented by broadcasting a **proposal message**: PROPOSE(S_i), where S_i is the next server to be leader. When server S_j receives this message, it replies with a PROMISE(o^j, t_j) message, containing the most recently *executed* operation o^j and its corresponding timestamp t_j. Note that S_i is particularly interested in the most recent operation o^* executed by a majority of servers. By "adopting" this operation from the (apparently crashed) server S^* that had originally proposed its acceptance, S_i can effectively complete what S^* could not due to its failure.

There are two obvious optimizations to this procedure. The first one is not that servers return the most recently executed operation, but the most recently *learned* operation that is still waiting to be executed, if any. Furthermore, because it may be that the collection of servers has no more pending operations, S_i can also suggest a next operation o^i when initially proposing to take over leadership, giving rise to a PROPOSE(S_i, o^i) message. In essence, this is the situation we described earlier, yet now it should be clear where the idea of proposals actually comes from.

When S_i receives a majority of promises for operation o^*, and the highest returned timestamp is t^*, it broadcasts ACCEPT(S_i, o^*, t^*), which is essentially a retransmission of the last operation proposed before S_i took over leadership. If no such o^* exists, S_i will propose to accept its own operation o^i.

8.2.5 Consensus in faulty systems with arbitrary failures

So far, we assumed that replicas were subject to only crash failures, in which case a process group needs to consist of $2k + 1$ servers to survive k crashed members. An important assumption in these cases, is that a process does not collude with another process, or, more specifically, is consistent in its messages to others. The situations shown in Figure 8.14 should not happen. In the first case, we see that process P_2 is forwarding a different value or operation than it is supposed to. Referring to Paxos, this could mean that a primary tells the backups that not operation o had been accepted, but instead propagates a different operation o'. In the second case, P_1 is telling different things to different processes, such as having a leader sending operation o to some backups, and at the same time operation o' to others. Again, we note that this need not be malicious actions, but simply omission or commission failures.

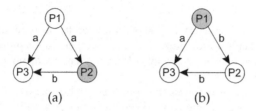

Figure 8.14: A process in a replicated group acting inconsistently: (a) not forwarding properly, and (b) telling different things to different processes.

In this section, we take a look at reaching consensus in a fault-tolerant process group in which k members can fail, assuming arbitrary failures. In particular, we will show that we need at least $3k + 1$ members to reach consensus under these failure assumptions.

Consider a process group consisting of n members, of which one has been designated to be the *primary*, P, and the remaining $n - 1$ to be the *backups* $B_1, \ldots, B_{n-1}$. We make the following assumptions:

- A client sends a value $v \in \{T, F\}$ to the primary, where v stands for either *true* or *false*.
- Messages may be lost, but this can be detected.
- Messages cannot be corrupted without that being detected (and thus subsequently ignored).
- A receiver of a message can reliably detect its sender.

To achieve what is known as **Byzantine agreement**, we need to satisfy the following two requirements:

BA1: Every nonfaulty backup process stores the same value.

BA2: If the primary is nonfaulty, then every nonfaulty backup process stores exactly what the primary had sent.

Note that if the primary is faulty, BA1 tells us that the backups may store the same, but different (and thus wrong) value than the one initially sent by the client. Furthermore, it should be clear that if the primary is not faulty, satisfying BA2 implies that BA1 is also satisfied.

Why having 3k processes is not enough

To see why having only $3k$ processes is not enough to reach consensus, let us consider the situation in which we want to tolerate the failure of a single process, that is, $k = 1$. Consider Figure 8.15, which is essentially an extension of Figure 8.14.

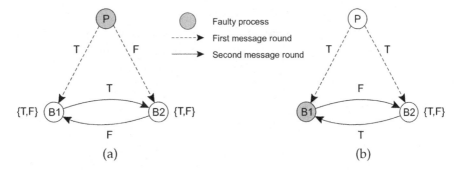

Figure 8.15: Impossibility to reach consensus with 3 processes and trying to tolerate a single arbitrarily failing process.

In Figure 8.15(a), we see that the faulty primary P is sending two different values to the backups B_1 and B_2, respectively. To reach consensus, both backup processes forward the received value to the other, leading to a second round of message exchanges. At that point, B_1 and B_2 each have received the set of values $\{T, F\}$, from which it is impossible to draw a conclusion.

Likewise, we cannot reach consensus when wrong values are forwarded. In Figure 8.15(b), the primary P and backup B_2 operate correctly, but B_1 is not. Instead of forwarding the value T to process B_2, it sends the incorrect value F. The result is that B_2 will now have seen the set of values $\{T, F\}$ from which it cannot draw any conclusions. In other words, P and B_2 cannot reach consensus. More specifically, B_2 can not decide what to store so that we cannot satisfy requirement BA2.

Note 8.5 (Advanced: The case where $k > 1$ and $n \leq 3k$)
Generalizing this situation to other values of k is not that difficult. As explained by Kshemkalyani and Singhal [2008], we can use a simple reduction scheme. Assume that there is a solution for the case where $k \geq 1$ and $n \leq 3k$. Partition the n processes $Q_1, \ldots, Q_n$ into three disjoint sets S_1, S_2, and S_3, together containing all processes. Moreover, let each set S_k have less or equal than $n/3$ members. Formally, this means that

- $S_1 \cap S_2 = S_1 \cap S_3 = S_2 \cap S_3 = \varnothing$
- $S_1 \cup S_2 \cup S_3 = \{Q_1, \ldots, Q_n\}$
- for each S_i, $|S_i| \leq n/3$

Now consider a situation in which three processes Q_1^*, Q_2^*, and Q_3^* *simulate* the actions that take place in and between the processes of S_1, S_2, and S_3, respectively. In other words, if a process in S_1 sends a message to another process in S_2, then Q_1^* will send a same message to Q_2. The same holds for process communication within a group. Assume that Q_1^* is faulty, yet Q_2^* and Q_3^* are not. All processes simulated by Q_1^* are now assumed to be faulty, and will thus lead to incorrect

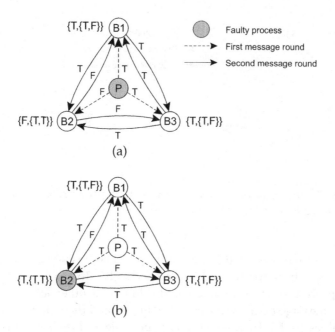

Figure 8.16: Reaching consensus with four processes, of which one may fail arbitrarily.

messages being sent to Q_2^* and Q_3^*, respectively. Not so for Q_2^* (and Q_3^*): all messages coming from processes in S_2 (and S_3, respectively) are assumed to be correct. Because $n \leq 3k$ and for each set S_i we have that $|S_i| \leq n/3$, at most $n/3$ of the simulated processes $Q_1, \ldots, Q_n$ are faulty. In other words, we are satisfying the condition for which we assumed that there would be a general solution.

We can now come to a contradiction, for if there would exist a solution for the general case, then the processes Q_1^*, Q_2^*, and Q_3^* could simulate this solution, which would then also be a solution for the special case that $n = 3$ and $k = 1$. Yet, we just proved that this cannot be so, leading to a contradiction. We conclude that our assumption that there is a general solution for $k \geq 1$ and $n \leq 3k$ is false.

Why having 3k + 1 processes is enough

Let us now focus on the case in which we have a group of $3k + 1$ processes. Our goal is to show that we can establish a solution in which k group members may suffer from fail-arbitrary failures, yet the remaining nonfaulty processes will still reach consensus. Again, we first concentrate on the case $n = 4$, $k = 1$. Consider Figure 8.16, which shows a situation with one primary P and three backup processes B_1, B_2, and B_3.

In Figure 8.16(a) we have sketched the situation in which the primary P is faulty and is providing inconsistent information to its backups. In our solution, the processes will forward what they receive to the others. During the first round, P sends T to B_1, F to B_2, and T to B_3, respectively. Each of the backups then sends what they have to the others. With only the primary failing, this means that after two rounds, each of the backups will have received the set of values $\{T, T, F\}$, meaning that they can reach consensus on the value T.

When we consider the case that one of the backups fails, we get the situation sketched in Figure 8.16(b). Assume that the (nonfaulty) primary sends T to all the backups, yet B_2 is faulty. Where B_1 and B_3 will send out T to the other backups in a second round, the worst that B_2 may do is send out F, as shown in the figure. Despite this failure, B_1 and B_3 will come to the same conclusion, namely that P had sent out T, thereby meeting our requirement BA2 as stated before.

Note 8.6 (Advanced: The case where $k > 1$ and $n = 3k + 1$)

As a sketch toward a general solution, consider the more intricate case in which $n = 7$ and $k = 2$. We let the primary P send out a value v_0. Using a similar notation as found in [Kshemkalyani and Singhal, 2008], we proceed as follows. Note that we effectively use the index 0 to denote the primary P (think of P being equal to a special backup process B_0).

1. We let P send v_0 to the six backups. Backup B_i stores the received value as $v_{i,0}\langle \rangle$. This notation indicates that the value was received by process B_i, that it was sent by $P = B_0$, and that the value of v_0 was directly sent to B_i and not through another process (using the notation $\langle \rangle$). So, for example, B_4 will store v_0 in $v_{4,0}\langle \rangle$.

2. Each backup B_i, in turn, will send $v_{i,0}\langle \rangle$ to every one of the other five backups, which is stored by B_j as $v_{j,i}\langle 0 \rangle$. This notation indicates that the value is stored at B_j, was sent by B_i, but that it originated from $P = B_0$ (through the notation $\langle 0 \rangle$). Looking at B_4 again, it will receive values from B_1, B_2, B_3, B_5, and B_6. For example, B_2 will send $v_{2,0}\langle \rangle$, which is then stored as $v_{4,2}\langle 0 \rangle$ by B_4. Likewise, B_4 will also store $v_{4,1}\langle 0 \rangle$, $v_{4,3}\langle 0 \rangle$, $v_{4,5}\langle 0 \rangle$, and $v_{4,6}\langle 0 \rangle$.

3. Suppose that B_i now has the value $v_{i,j}\langle 0 \rangle$. Again, it will send out this value to all processes except $P = B_0$, B_j, and B_i (i.e., itself). If B_k receives $v_{i,j}\langle 0 \rangle$ from B_i, it stores this received value in $v_{k,i}\langle j, 0 \rangle$. Indeed, by then v_0 will have traveled the path $P \rightarrow B_j \rightarrow B_i \rightarrow B_k$. For example, in the previous round, B_2 will have stored $v_{2,1}\langle 0 \rangle$, which it eventually sends to B_4, who, in turn, will store it as $v_{4,2}\langle 1, 0 \rangle$. Note at this point, that B_4 can send out *this* value only to processes B_3, B_5, and B_6. There is no use in sending it out to other processes.

4. Continuing this line of thought, assume that B_i has value $v_{i,j}\langle k, 0 \rangle$, which it sends out to the three remaining processes not equal to $P = B_0$, B_k, B_j, and B_i (itself). Returning to B_4, eventually, B_4 will also receive a similar message from, say, B_3, such as $v_{3,2}\langle 5, 0 \rangle$: the value v_0 initially sent to B_5,

which then forwarded it to B_2, who, in turn, sent it to B_3. B_4 will store that value as $v_{4,3}\langle 2,5,0 \rangle$. That value can be sent only to B_1 and B_6, after which only a single round is left.

Once all these messages have been sent, each backup can start moving out of the recursion again. Note that in the above scheme we have effectively constructed a tree, rooted at value v_0 with six child nodes (representing the six backups). Each of these nodes, in turn, will have five children of its own, and so on. In total, there will be $6! = 720$ leaf nodes. Each path from the root to a leaf node is encoded by the value stored at that leaf node, such as $v_{4,1}\langle 6,5,3,2,0 \rangle$. This leaf node will have a single parent (namely B_1 storing $v_{1,6}\langle 5,3,2,0 \rangle$), in turn with a single sibling (B_4 storing $v_{4,6}\langle 5,3,2,0 \rangle$).

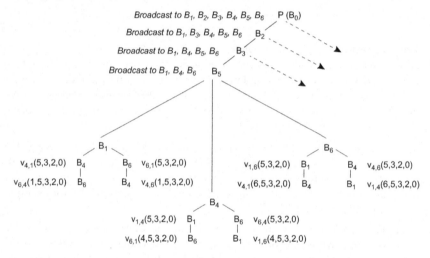

Figure 8.17: Rounds of broadcasting v_0 to the backups, by P and the backups $B_1, \ldots, B_6$.

We can now let each backup start computing *estimates* of v_0, that is, a value that it believes v_0 should be. To this end, we assume that each (nonfaulty) process executes the same procedure *majority()* that selects a unique value from a given set of inputs. In practice, this will be the majority among the input set. If there is no majority, a default value is chosen. To give a few examples, also shown in Figure 8.17:

$$
\begin{aligned}
w_{4,1}\langle 5,3,2,0 \rangle &\leftarrow majority(v_{4,1}\langle 5,3,2,0 \rangle, v_{6,4}\langle 1,5,3,2,0 \rangle) \\
w_{6,1}\langle 5,3,2,0 \rangle &\leftarrow majority(v_{6,1}\langle 5,3,2,0 \rangle, v_{4,6}\langle 1,5,3,2,0 \rangle) \\
w_{1,4}\langle 5,3,2,0 \rangle &\leftarrow majority(v_{1,4}\langle 5,3,2,0 \rangle, v_{6,1}\langle 4,5,3,2,0 \rangle) \\
w_{6,4}\langle 5,3,2,0 \rangle &\leftarrow majority(v_{6,4}\langle 5,3,2,0 \rangle, v_{1,6}\langle 4,5,3,2,0 \rangle) \\
w_{1,6}\langle 5,3,2,0 \rangle &\leftarrow majority(v_{1,6}\langle 5,3,2,0 \rangle, v_{4,1}\langle 6,5,3,2,0 \rangle) \\
w_{4,6}\langle 5,3,2,0 \rangle &\leftarrow majority(v_{4,6}\langle 5,3,2,0 \rangle, v_{1,4}\langle 6,5,3,2,0 \rangle)
\end{aligned}
$$

In turn, B_1, B_4, and B_6 can compute estimates like:

$$w_{1,5}\langle 3,2,0 \rangle \quad \leftarrow \quad majority(v_{1,5}\langle 3,2,0 \rangle, w_{4,1}\langle 5,3,2,0 \rangle, w_{6,1}\langle 5,3,2,0 \rangle)$$
$$w_{4,5}\langle 3,2,0 \rangle \quad \leftarrow \quad majority(v_{4,5}\langle 3,2,0 \rangle, w_{1,4}\langle 5,3,2,0 \rangle, w_{6,4}\langle 5,3,2,0 \rangle)$$
$$w_{6,5}\langle 3,2,0 \rangle \quad \leftarrow \quad majority(v_{6,5}\langle 3,2,0 \rangle, w_{1,6}\langle 5,3,2,0 \rangle, w_{4,6}\langle 5,3,2,0 \rangle)$$

And from there, B_5 can continue, for example, with:

$$w_{5,3}\langle 2,0 \rangle \quad \leftarrow \quad majority(v_{5,3}\langle 2,0 \rangle, w_{1,5}\langle 3,2,0 \rangle, w_{4,5}\langle 3,2,0 \rangle, w_{6,5}\langle 3,2,0 \rangle)$$

This process continues until, eventually, B_2 from Figure 8.17 will be able to execute

$$w_{2,0}\langle \rangle \leftarrow majority(v_{2,0}\langle \rangle, w_{1,2}\langle 0 \rangle, w_{3,2}\langle 0 \rangle, w_{4,2}\langle 0 \rangle, w_{5,2}\langle 0 \rangle, w_{6,2}\langle 0 \rangle)$$

and reach the final outcome.

Let us now see why this scheme actually works. We denote by **BAP(n,k)** the above sketched protocol to reach consensus. **BAP(n,k)** starts by having the primary send out its value v_0 to the $n-1$ backups. In the case the primary operates correctly, each of the backups will indeed receive v_0. If the primary is faulty, some backups receive v_0 while others receive $\overline{v_0}$ (i.e., the opposite of v_0).

Because we assume a backup B_i cannot know whether the primary is working correctly, it will have to check with the other backups. We therefore let B_i run the protocol again, but in this case, with value $v_{i,0}\langle \rangle$ and with a smaller process group, namely $\{B_1, \ldots, B_{i-1}, B_{i+1}, \ldots, B_n\}$. In other words, B_i executes **BAP(n-1,k-1)** with a total of $n-2$ other processes. Note that at this point there are $n-1$ instances of **BAP(n-1,k-1)** being executed in parallel.

In the end, we see that these executions result in each backup B_i taking the majority of $n-1$ values:

- One value comes from the primary: $v_{i,0}\langle \rangle$
- $n-2$ values come from the other backups, in particular, B_i is dealing with the values $v_{i,1}\langle \rangle, \ldots, v_{i,i-1}\langle \rangle, v_{i,i+1}\langle \rangle, \ldots, v_{i,n-1}\langle \rangle$.

However, because B_i cannot trust a received value $v_{i,j}\langle \rangle$, it will have to check that value with the other $n-2$ backups: $B_1, \ldots, B_{i-1}, B_{i+1}, \ldots, B_{j-1}, B_{j+1}, \ldots, B_{n-1}$. This leads to the execution of **BAP(n-2,k-2)**, of which a total of $n-2$ instances will be running in parallel. This story continues, and eventually, a backup process will need to run **BAP(n-k,0)**, which simply returns the value sent by the primary, after which we can move up the recursion as described above.

With this general scheme, we can now see why the protocol is correct. Following Koren and Krishna [2007], we use induction on k to prove that **BAP(n,k)** meets the requirements BA1 and BA2 for $n \geq 3k+1$ and for all $k \geq 0$.

First, consider the case $k = 0$. In other words, we assume that there are no faulty processes. In that case, whatever the primary sends to the backups, that value will be consistently propagated throughout the system, and no other value will ever pop up. In other words, for any n, **BAP(n,0)** is correct. Now consider the case $k > 0$.

First, consider the case that the primary is operating correctly. Without loss of generality, we can assume the primary sends out T. All the backups receive the same value, namely T. Each backup will then run **BAP(n-1,k-1)**. By induction, we know that each of these instances will be executed correctly. This means that for any nonfaulty backup B, all the other nonfaulty backups will store the value that was sent by B, namely T. Each nonfaulty backup receives, in total, $n - 1$ values, of which $n - 2$ come from other backups. Of those $n - 2$, at most k values may be wrong (i.e., F). With $k \leq (n-1)/3$, this means that every nonfaulty backup receives at least $1 + (n-2) - (n-1)/3 = (2n-2)/3$ values T. Because $(2n-2)/3 > n/3$ for all $n > 2$, this means that every nonfaulty backup can take a correct majority vote on the total number of received values, thus satisfying requirement BA2.

Let us now consider the case that the primary is faulty, meaning that at most $k - 1$ backups may operate incorrectly as well. The primary is assumed to send out any value it likes. There are a total of $n - 1$ backups, of which at most $k - 1$ are faulty. Each backup runs **BAP(n-1,k-1)** and by, induction, each one of these instances is executed correctly. In particular, for every nonfaulty backup B, all the other nonfaulty backups will vote for the value sent by B. This means that all nonfaulty backups will have the same vector of $n - 2$ results from their fellow backups. Any difference between two nonfaulty backups can be caused only by the fact that the primary sent something else to each of them. As a result, when applying *majority*() to those complete vectors, the result for each backup will be the same, so that requirement BA1 is met.

Example: Practical Byzantine Fault Tolerance

Byzantine fault tolerance was for long more or less an exotic topic, partly because it turned out that combining safety, liveness, *and* practical performance was difficult to achieve. It was around 2000 that Barbara Liskov and Miguel Castro managed to come up with a practical implementation of a protocol for replicating servers that could handle arbitrary failures. Let us briefly take a look at their solution, which has been coined **Practical Byzantine Fault Tolerance**, or simply **PBFT** [Castro and Liskov, 2002]. To better understand how the protocol works, it may help to also consult Liskov [2010].

Like Paxos, PBFT makes only a few assumptions about its environment. It makes no assumptions about the behavior of replica servers: a faulty server is assumed to exhibit arbitrary behavior. Likewise, messages may be lost, delayed, and received out of order. However, a message's sender is assumed to be identifiable (which is achieved by having messages signed, as we discuss in Section 9.2.3). Under these assumptions, and as long as no more than k servers fail, it can be proven that PBFT is *safe*, meaning that a client will always receive a correct answer. If we can additionally assume synchrony, meaning that message delays and response times are bounded, it also provides *liveness*. In practice, this means that PBFT assumes a partially synchronous model, in which unbounded delays are an exception, for example, caused by an attack.

To understand the algorithm, let us take a step back and partly review what we have discussed so far on establishing a k-fault-tolerant process group. An essential issue is that such a group behaves as a single, central server. As a consequence, under the assumption of having only crash failures, when a client sends a request, it should expect $k + 1$ identical answers. If a server had crashed, fewer responses would be returned, but they would be the same.

The first problem that we need to solve is that concurrent requests are all handled in the same order. To this end, PBFT adopts a primary-backup model with a total of $3k + 1$ replica servers. To keep matters simple, let us assume for now that the primary is nonfaulty. In that case, a client C sends a request to execute operation o to the primary (denoted as P in Figure 8.18). The primary has a notion of the current collection of nonfaulty replica servers, expressed in terms of a **view** v, which is simply a number. The primary assigns a timestamp t to o, which is then incremented to be used for a subsequent request. The primary subsequently sends a (signed) *pre-prepare* message PRE-PREPARE$(t, v,$ o) to the backups (denoted as B_i in Figure 8.18). We assume that backup B_2 is faulty, indicated by the dashed line used for its messages.

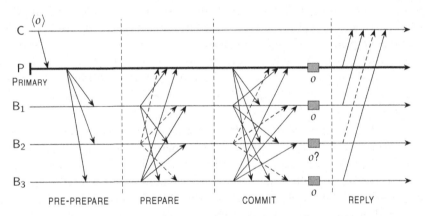

Figure 8.18: The different phases in PBFT. C is the client, P is the primary, and B_1, B_2, B_3 are the backups. We assume that B_2 is faulty.

A (nonfaulty) backup will accept to *pre-prepare* if it is in v and has never accepted an operation with timestamp t in v before. Each backup that accepts to *pre-prepare* sends an (again signed) message PREPARE(t, v, o) to the others, including the primary. A key observation is that when a nonfaulty replica server S has logged $2k$ messages PREPARE(t, v, o) (including its own) that all match the *pre-prepare* message S itself received by the primary (i.e., all have the same value for t, v, and o, respectively), there is consensus among the nonfaulty servers on the order of which operation goes first. To see why, let a **prepare certificate** PC(t, v, o) denote a certificate that is based on such a set of $2k + 1$ messages. Let PC(t, v, o') be another prepare certificate with the same values for t and v respectively, but with a different operation o'. Because each prepare certificate is based on $2k + 1$ values from a total of $3k + 1$ replica servers, the intersection of two certificates will necessarily be based on messages from a subset of at least $k + 1$ servers. Of this subset, we know that there is at least one nonfaulty server, which will have sent the same *prepare* message. Hence, $o = o'$.

In Figure 8.18, notice that, regardless what B_2 sends (or does not send), the two other nonfaulty backups, namely B_1 and B_2, will each have logged three ($2k + 1$, with $k = 1$) messages for the tuple $\langle t, v, o \rangle$: the original message from P, their own message, and the same message from the other backup. At that point, there is consensus to execute o, and not some other operation. We can then move on to the next phase.

The next phase for a replica server starts when it has a prepare certificate: it *commits* to the operation by broadcasting COMMIT(t, v, o) to the other members in v. Each server S, in turn, collects $2k$ of such commit messages from other servers, leading to a **commit certificate** to execute operation o. At that point, it executes o and sends a response to the client. Again, with its own message and the $2k$ other messages, S knows that there is consensus among the nonfaulty servers on which operation to actually execute *now*. In Figure 8.18, we see that for the primary, as well as the backups B_1 and B_3, there are indeed again three messages that state the same: we can execute o. Each server knows that there are at least two other servers besides itself that will indeed execute o, and it is therefore good to go. What B_2 had sent is not relevant: it will not affect the decision of the others.

The client collects all the results and takes as the answer the response that is returned by at least $k + 1$ replicas, of which it knows that there is at least one nonfaulty replica server contributing to that answer. Again notice that in Figure 8.18, regardless what B_2 tells the client about which operation B_2 had executed, the client can safely assume that its requested operation was executed by a majority of the servers.

So far, so good. However, we also need to deal with the situation that the primary fails. If a backup detects that the primary fails, it broadcasts a *view-change* message for view $v + 1$. What we wish to establish is that a request that was still being processed at the time the primary failed, will eventually get executed *once and only once* by all nonfaulty servers. To this end, we first need to ensure that there are no two commit certificates with the same timestamp that have different associated operations, regardless the view that each of them is associated with. This situation can be prevented by having a quorum of $2k + 1$ commit certificates just as before, but this time based on prepare certificates. In other words, we want to regenerate commit certificates, but now for the new view, and only to make sure that a nonfaulty server is not missing any operation. In this respect, note that we may be generating a certificate for an operation that a server S had already executed (which can be observed by looking at timestamps), but that certificate will be ignored by S as long as it keeps an account of its execution history.

A backup server will broadcast a (signed) message VIEW-CHANGE$(v + 1, \mathbf{P})$, with $\mathbf{P}$ being the set of its prepare certificates. (Note that we ignore garbage collecting issues.) PBFT includes a deterministic function primary(w) known to all backups that returns who the next primary will be given a view w. This new primary will wait until it has a total of $2k + 1$ *view-change* messages, leading to a **view-change certificate X** of prepare certificates. The new primary then broadcasts NEW-VIEW$(v + 1, \mathbf{X}, \mathbf{O})$, where $\mathbf{O}$ consists of *new* pre-prepare messages constructed according to one of the following situations:

- PRE-PREPARE$(t, v + 1, \mathrm{o}) \in \mathbf{O}$ if the prepare certificate $PC(t, v', \mathrm{o}) \in \mathbf{X}$ such that there is no prepare certificate $PC(t, v'', \mathrm{o}')$ with $v'' > v'$,
- PRE-PREPARE$(t, v + 1, none) \in \mathbf{O}$ if there is no prepare certificate $PC(t, v', \mathrm{o}') \in \mathbf{X}$.

What happens is that any outstanding, pre-prepared operation from a previous view is moved to the new view, but considering only the most recent view that led to the installment of the current new view. In this sense, the new primary effectively sends out appropriate new pre-prepare messages, based on what the other backups had already committed to in their prepare phase. Simplifying matters a bit, each backup will check $\mathbf{O}$ and $\mathbf{X}$ to make sure that all operations are indeed authentic and broadcast *prepare* messages for all *pre-prepare* messages in $\mathbf{O}$. We are then back into the situation shown in Figure 8.18, but now with one of the backups operating as primary, all the other original backups operating as nonfaulty servers, and the old primary operating as a faulty backup.

We have skipped many elements of PBFT that deal with its correctness and above all its efficiency. For example, we did not touch upon garbage collecting logs or efficient ways of authenticating messages. Such details can be found in [Castro and Liskov, 2002]. A description of a wrapper that will allow the incorporation of Byzantine fault tolerance with legacy applications is described in [Castro et al., 2003]. Notably the performance of Byzantine fault tolerance has been subject to much research, leading to many new protocols (see, for example, Zyzzyva [Kotla et al., 2009] and Abstract [Guerraoui et al., 2010]), yet even these new proposals often rely on the original PBFT implementation. That there is still room for improvement when actually using PBFT for developing robust applications is discussed by Chondros et al. [2012]. For example, PBFT assumes static membership (i.e., clients and servers are known to each other in advance), but also assumes that a replica server's memory acts as a stable, persistent storage.

These and other shortcomings along with the inherent complexity of Byzantine fault tolerance have formed a hurdle for widespread use of PBFT. Interestingly, attention for PBFT returned in the advent of **permissioned**

blockhains, being one of the few alternatives that could offer a consenus protocol in a public network. New research was initiated to address shortcomings, notably the relatively small number of participants that PBFT can maximally handle. An important development has been HotStuff [Yin et al., 2019], which effectively provides a much more efficient view change than in PBFT, significantly contributing to the scalability of the protocol.

8.2.6   Consensus in blockchain systems

Coming to this point, let us return to the much debated blockchain systems. In particular, let us zoom in a bit into what consensus entails in these systems. Following the approach presented by Xiao et al. [2020], we can distinguish four requirements for blockchain consensus:

1. **Agreement**: All nonfaulty nodes agree on the acceptance of a block of transactions and its position in the blockchain, or agree that it should be discarded.

2. **Integrity**: Each nonfaulty node sees the same blocks of accepted transactions, and the same positions of these blocks in the blockchain.

3. **Termination**: Every nonfaulty node either discards or accepts a transaction, as contained within a block, to be part of the blockchain.

4. **Validity**: If every node receives the same validated block, it should be accepted for the blockchain.

The first two requirements are at the core of **safety**: the blockchain does what it is supposed to do (i.e., nothing bad happens). The last two can be argued to deal with **liveness**: eventually everything turns out to be good. For our present discussion, reaching agreement is crucial.

For permissionless blockchains, we see that leader election is important: once a leader has been elected, we can essentially ensure agreement by letting the leader decide on the block that is to be appended to the blockchain. As we discuss in Section 9.4.3, guaranteeing the integrity of a blockchain can be established using well-known cryptographic techniques. The only problem with leader elections happens if two or more leaders are elected, which may happen when the declaration of a winner does not reach its competitor in time. In such a case, two processes will start to append blocks to a chain, effectively leading to two branches. A common solution is that once a participant discovers it is reading from the smallest branch, it ignores that branch completely and makes sure that it gets the blocks from the longer branch.

For permissioned blockchains, a common solution is to adopt PBFT. In other words, the decision to append blocks to an existing chain is handled by a relatively small fault-tolerant group of processes (who need not trust each other). Because PBFT is a relatively costly and nonscalable solution, alternatives have been designed, with HotStuff [Yin et al., 2019] playing a prominent role as experiments showed that the number of replica servers could go up beyond 100.

Xiao et al. [2020] provides an excellent overview of the various consensus protocols for blockchains, along with a discussion on the many trade-offs to be made.

8.2.7 Some limitations on realizing fault tolerance

Organizing replicated processes into a group helps to increase fault tolerance. However, what should have become clear by now is that there is a price to pay, namely a potential loss of performance. In the solutions discussed so far, processes in a fault-tolerant group may need to exchange numerous messages before reaching a decision. The Byzantine agreement protocol is an excellent illustration of how tightly coupled processes may be. The question that comes to mind is whether realizing specific forms of fault tolerance, like being able to withstand arbitrary failures, is always possible.

On reaching consensus

As we mentioned, if a client can base its decisions through a voting mechanism, we can tolerate that k out of $2k + 1$ processes are lying about their result. The assumption we are making, however, is that processes do not team up to produce a wrong result. In general, matters become more intricate if we demand that a process group reaches consensus, which is needed in many cases. There are three requirements for reaching consensus [Fischer et al., 1985]:

- Processes produce the same output value
- Every output value must be valid
- Every process must eventually provide output

Some examples where reaching consensus is necessary include electing a coordinator, deciding whether to commit a transaction, and dividing up tasks among workers. When the communication and processes are all perfect, reaching consensus is often straightforward, but when they are not, problems arise.

The general goal of distributed consensus algorithms is to have all the nonfaulty processes reach consensus on some issue, and to establish that consensus within a finite number of steps. The problem is complicated by the fact that different assumptions about the underlying system require different solutions, assuming solutions even exist. Turek and Shasha [1992] distinguish the following cases:

1. Synchronous versus asynchronous systems. Rephrasing our description somewhat, a system is **synchronous** if and only if the processes are known to operate in a lock-step mode. Formally, this means that there should be some constant $c \geq 1$, such that if any process has taken $c + 1$ steps, every other process has taken at least 1 step.

2. Communication delay is bounded or not. Delay is bounded if and only if we know that every message is delivered with a globally and predetermined maximum time.

3. Message delivery is ordered (in real time) or not. In other words, we distinguish the situation where messages from the different senders are delivered in the order that they were sent in real global time, from the situation in which we do not have such guarantees.

4. Message transmission is done through unicasting or multicasting.

As it turns out, reaching consensus is possible only for the situations shown in Figure 8.19. In all other cases, it can be shown that no solution exists. Note that most distributed systems in practice assume that processes behave asynchronously, message transmission is unicast, and communication delays are unbounded. As a consequence, we need to make use of ordered (reliable) message delivery, such as provided by TCP. And again, in practical situations we assume synchronous behavior to be the default, but take into account that there may be unbounded delays as well. Figure 8.19 illustrates the nontrivial nature of distributed consensus when processes may fail.

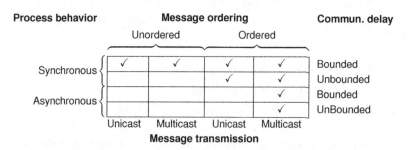

Figure 8.19: Circumstances under which distributed consensus can be reached.

Reaching consensus may not be possible. Fischer et al. [1985] proved that if messages cannot be guaranteed to be delivered within a known, finite time, no consensus is possible if even one process is faulty (albeit if that one process fails silently). The problem with such systems is that arbitrarily slow processes are indistinguishable from crashed ones (i.e., you cannot tell the dead from the living). These and other theoretical results are surveyed by Barborak et al. [1993] and Turek and Shasha [1992].

It should also be noted that the schemes described so far assume that nodes are either Byzantine, or collaborative. The latter cannot always be simply assumed when processes are from different administrative domains. In that case, they will more likely exhibit *rational* behavior, for example, by reporting timeouts when doing so is cheaper than executing an update operation. How to deal with these cases is not trivial. A first step toward a solution is captured in the form of **BAR fault tolerance**, which stands for Byzantine, Altruism, and Rationality. BAR fault tolerance is described in Aiyer et al. [2005] and Clement et al. [2008].

Consistency, availability, and partitioning

Strongly related to the conditions under which consensus can (not) be reached, is when consistency can be reached. Consistency in this case means that when we have a process group to which a client is sending requests, that the responses returned to that client are correct. We are dealing with a **safety property**: a property that asserts that nothing bad will happen. For our purposes, the types of operations we consider are those that seem to be executed in a clearly defined order by a single, centralized server. By now, we know better: these operations are executed by a process group to withstand the failures of k group members.

We introduced process groups to improve fault tolerance, and, more specifically, to improve availability. Availability is typically a **liveness property**: eventually, something good will happen. In terms of our process groups, we aim to eventually get a (correct) response to every request issued by a client. Being consistent in responses while also being highly available is not an unreasonable requirement for services that are part of a distributed system. Unfortunately, we may be asking too much.

In practical situations, our underlying assumption that the processes in a group can indeed communicate with each other may be false. Messages may be lost; a group may be partitioned due to a faulty network. In 2000, Eric Brewer posed an important theorem which was later proven to be correct by Gilbert and Lynch [2002]:

> **CAP Theorem**: *Any networked system providing shared data can provide only two of the following three properties:*
> - **C**: *consistency, by which a shared and replicated data item appears as a single, up-to-date copy*
> - **A**: *availability, by which updates will always be eventually executed*
> - **P**: *Tolerant to the partitioning of process group (e.g., because of a failing network).*

In other words, in a network subject to communication failures, it is impossible to realize an atomic read/write shared memory that guarantees a response to every request [Gilbert and Lynch, 2012].

This has now become known as the **CAP theorem**, first published as [Fox and Brewer, 1999]. As explained by Brewer [2012], one way of understanding the theorem is to think of two processes unable to communicate because of a failing network. Allowing one process to accept updates leads to inconsistency, so that we can only have properties $\{A, P\}$. If the illusion of consistency is to be provided while the two processes cannot communicate, then one of the two processes will have to pretend to be unavailable, implying having only $\{C, P\}$. However, only if the two processes can communicate, is it possible to maintain both consistency and high availability, meaning that we have only $\{C, A\}$, but no longer property P.

Note also the relationship with reaching consensus; in fact, where consensus requires proving that processes produce the same output, providing consistency is weaker. This also means that if achieving CAP is impossible, then so is consensus.

For some time, many people thought that the CAP theorem actually told us we were dealing with a practical horrendous situation. However, the CAP theorem is all about reaching a trade-off between safety and liveness, based on the observation that obtaining both in an inherently unreliable system cannot be achieved. Practical distributed systems *are* inherently unreliable. What Brewer and his colleagues observed is that in practical distributed systems, one simply has to make a choice to proceed, although another process cannot be reached. In other words, we need to do something when a partition manifests itself through high latency. What this means, is that we need to look at the distributed application at hand to see how we can salvage the seemingly impossibility implications of the CAP theorem.

The bottom line when it seems that partitioning is taking place, is to proceed (tolerating partitions in favor of either consistency or availability), while simultaneously starting a recovery procedure that can mitigate the effects of potential inconsistencies. Exactly deciding on how to proceed is application-dependent: in many cases having duplicate keys in a database can easily be fixed (implying that we should tolerate an inconsistency), while duplicate transfers of large sums of money may not (meaning that we should decide to tolerate lower availability). One can argue that the CAP theorem essentially moves designers of distributed systems from theoretical solutions to engineering solutions. The interested reader is referred to [Brewer, 2012] to see how such a move can be made.

8.2.8 Failure detection

It may have become clear from our discussions so far that to properly mask failures, we generally need to detect them as well. **Failure detection** is one of the cornerstones of fault tolerance in distributed systems. What it all boils down to is that for a group of processes, nonfaulty members should be able to decide who is still a member, and who is not. In other words, we need to be able to detect when a member has failed.

When it comes to detecting process failures, there are essentially only two mechanisms. Either processes actively send "are you alive?" messages to each other (for which they obviously expect an answer), or passively wait until messages come in from different processes. The latter approach makes sense only when it can be guaranteed that there is enough communication.

There is a huge body of theoretical work on failure detectors. What it, in the end, all boils down to is that a timeout mechanism is used to check whether a process has failed. If a process P probes another process Q to see if it has failed, P is said to **suspect** Q to have crashed if Q has not responded within some time.

Note 8.7 (More information: On perfect failure detectors)
It should be clear that in a synchronous distributed system, a suspected crash corresponds to a known crash. In practice, however, we will be dealing with partially synchronous systems. In that case, it makes more sense to assume **eventually perfect failure detectors**. In this case, a process P will suspect another process Q to have crashed after t time units have elapsed and still Q did not respond to P's probe. However, if Q later does send a message that is (also) received by P, P will (1) stop suspecting Q, and (2) increase the timeout value t. Note that if Q does crash (and does not recover), P will continue to suspect Q.

In real settings, there are problems with using probes and timeouts. For example, due to unreliable networks, simply stating that a process has failed because it does not return an answer to a probe message may be wrong. In other words, it is easy to generate false positives. If a false positive has the effect that a perfectly healthy process is removed from a membership list, then clearly we are doing something wrong. Another serious problem is that timeouts are just plain crude. As noticed by Birman [2012], there is hardly any work on building proper failure detection subsystems that take more into account than only the lack of a reply to a single message. This statement is even more evident when looking at industry-deployed distributed systems.

There are various issues that need to be considered when designing a failure-detection subsystem (see also Zhuang et al. [2005]). For example, failure detection can take place through gossiping in which each node regularly announces to its neighbors that it is still up and running. As we mentioned, an alternative is to let nodes actively probe each other.

Failure detection can also be done as a side effect of regularly exchanging information with neighbors, as is the case with gossip-based information dissemination (which we discussed in Chapter 4). This approach was essentially also adopted in Obduro [Vogels, 2003]: processes periodically gossip their service availability. This information is gradually disseminated through the network. Eventually, every process will know about every other process, but more importantly, will have enough information locally available to decide whether a process has failed or not. A member for which the availability information is old, will presumably have failed.

Another important issue is that a failure detection subsystem should ideally be able to distinguish network failures from node failures. One way of dealing with this problem is not to let a single node decide whether one of its neighbors has crashed. Instead, when noticing a timeout on a probe message, a node requests other neighbors to see whether they can reach the presumed failing node. Of course, positive information can also be shared: if a node is still alive, that information can be forwarded to other interested parties (who may be detecting a link failure to the suspected node).

This brings us to another key issue: when a member failure is detected, how should other nonfaulty processes be informed? One simple, and somewhat radical approach is the following. In FUSE [Dunagan et al., 2004], processes can be joined in a group that spans a wide-area network. The group members create a spanning tree that is used for monitoring member failures. Members send ping messages to their neighbors. When a neighbor does not respond, the pinging node immediately switches to a state in which it will also no longer respond to pings from other nodes. By recursion, it is seen that a single node failure is rapidly promoted to a group failure notification.

8.3   Reliable client-server communication

Often, fault tolerance in distributed systems concentrates on faulty processes. However, we also need to consider **communication failures**. Most of the failure models discussed previously apply equally well to communication channels. In particular, a communication channel may exhibit crash, omission, timing, and arbitrary failures. In practice, when building reliable communication channels, the focus is on masking crash and omission failures. Arbitrary failures may occur in the form of duplicate messages, resulting from the fact that in a computer network messages may be buffered for a relatively long time, and are reinjected into the network after the original sender has already issued a retransmission (see, for example, Tanenbaum et al. [2021]).

8.3.1   Point-to-point communication

In many distributed systems, reliable point-to-point communication is established by making use of a reliable transport protocol, such as TCP. TCP masks omission failures, which occur in the form of lost messages, by using acknowledgments and retransmissions. Such failures are completely hidden from a TCP client.

However, crash failures of connections are not masked. A crash failure may occur when (for whatever reason) a TCP connection is abruptly broken so that no more messages can be transmitted through the channel. In most cases, the client is informed that the channel has crashed by raising an exception. The only way to mask such failures is to let the distributed system attempt to automatically set up a new connection, by simply resending a connection request. The underlying assumption is that the other side is still, or again, responsive to such requests.

8.3.2 RPC semantics in the presence of failures

Let us now take a closer look at client-server communication when using high-level communication facilities such as remote procedure calls (RPCs). The goal of RPC is to hide communication by making remote procedure calls look just like local ones. With a few exceptions, so far we have come fairly close. Indeed, as long as both client and server are functioning perfectly, RPC does its job well. The problem comes about when errors occur. It is then that the differences between local and remote calls are not always easy to mask.

To structure our discussion, let us distinguish between five different classes of failures that can occur in RPC systems, as follows:

1. The client is unable to locate the server.
2. The request message from the client to the server is lost.
3. The server crashes after receiving a request.
4. The reply message from the server to the client is lost.
5. The client crashes after sending a request.

Each of these categories poses different problems and requires different solutions.

Client cannot locate the server

To start with, it can happen that the client cannot locate a suitable server. All servers might be down, for example. Alternatively, suppose that the client is compiled using a particular version of the client stub, and the binary is not used for a considerable period of time. Meanwhile, the server evolves and a new version of the interface is installed; new stubs are generated and put into use. When the client is eventually run, the binder will be unable to match it up with a server and will report failure. While this mechanism is used to protect the client from accidentally trying to talk to a server that may not agree with it in terms of what parameters are required or what it is supposed to do, the problem remains of how should this failure be dealt with.

One possible solution is to have the error raise an **exception**. In some languages, (e.g., Java), programmers can write special procedures that are invoked upon specific errors, such as division by zero. In C, signal handlers can be used for this purpose. In other words, we could define a new signal type SIGNOSERVER, and allow it to be handled in the same way as other signals.

This approach, too, has drawbacks. To start with, not every language has exceptions or signals. Another point is that having to write an exception or signal handler destroys the transparency we have been trying to achieve. Suppose that you are a programmer, and you are requested to write the append procedure. You smile and tell her it will be written, tested, and documented in five minutes. Then she mentions that you also have to write an exception handler as well, just in case the procedure is not there today. At this point, it is pretty hard to maintain the illusion that remote procedures are no different from local ones, since writing an exception handler for "Cannot locate server" would be a rather unusual request in a nondistributed system.

Lost request messages

The second item on the list is dealing with lost request messages. This is the easiest one to deal with: just have the operating system or client stub start a timer when sending the request. If the timer expires before a reply or an acknowledgment comes back, the message is sent again. If the message was truly lost, the server will not be able to tell the difference between the retransmission and the original, and everything will work fine. Unless, of course, so many request messages are lost that the client gives up and falsely concludes that the server is down, in which case we are back to "Cannot locate server." If the request was not lost, the only thing we need to do is let the server be able to detect it is dealing with a retransmission. Unfortunately, doing so is not so simple, as we explain when discussing lost replies.

Server crashes

The next failure on the list is a server crash. The normal sequence of events at a server is shown in Figure 8.20(a). A request arrives, is carried out, and a reply is sent. Now consider Figure 8.20(b). A request arrives and is carried out, just as before, but the server crashes before it can send the reply. Finally, look at Figure 8.20(c). Again a request arrives, but this time the server crashes before it can even be carried out. And, of course, no reply is sent back.

The annoying part of Figure 8.20 is that the correct treatment differs for (b) and (c). In (b) the system has to report failure back to the client (e.g., raise an exception), whereas in (c) it can just retransmit the request. The problem is that the client's operating system cannot tell which is which. All it knows is that its timer has expired.

Three schools of thought exist on what to do here [Spector, 1982]. One philosophy is to wait until the server reboots (or let the client's middleware transparently rebind to a new server) and try the operation again. The idea is

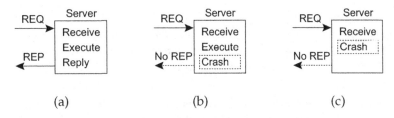

Figure 8.20: A server in client-server communication. (a) The normal case. (b) Crash after execution. (c) Crash before execution.

to keep trying until a reply has been received, then give it to the client. This technique is called **at-least-once semantics** and guarantees that the RPC has been carried out at least one time, but possibly more.

The second philosophy gives up immediately and reports back failure. This approach is called **at-most-once semantics** and guarantees that the RPC has been carried out at most one time, but possibly not at all.

The third philosophy is to guarantee nothing. When a server crashes, the client gets no help and no promises about what happened. The RPC may have been carried out anywhere from zero to many times. The main virtue of this scheme is that it is easy to implement.

None of these are terribly attractive. What one would like is **exactly-once semantics**, but in general, there is no way to arrange this. Imagine that the remote operation consists of processing a document, such as producing a number of PDF files from LaTeX and other sources. The server sends a completion message to the client when the document has been completely processed. Also assume that when a client issues a request, it receives an acknowledgment that the request has been delivered to the server. There are two strategies the server can follow. It can either send a completion message just before it actually tells the document processor to do its work, or after the document has been processed.

Assume that the server crashes and subsequently recovers. It announces to all clients that it has just crashed but is now up and running again. The problem is that the client does not know whether its request to process a document will actually have been carried out.

There are four strategies the client can follow. First, the client can decide to *never* reissue a request, at the risk that the document will not be processed. Second, it can decide to *always* reissue a request, but this may lead to the document being processed twice (which may easily incur a significant amount of work when dealing with intricate documents). Third, it can decide to reissue a request only if it did not yet receive an acknowledgment that its request had been delivered to the server. In that case, the client is counting on the fact that the server crashed before the request could be delivered. The fourth and last strategy is to reissue a request only if it has received an acknowledgment for the request. With two strategies for the server, and four for the client, there are a total of eight combinations to consider. Unfortunately, as it turns out, no combination is satisfactory: it can be shown that for any combination either the request is lost forever, or carried out twice.

Note 8.8 (Advanced: Why fully transparent server recovery is impossible)

To explain about server recovery, note that there are three events that can happen at the server: send the completion message (M), complete the processing of the document (P), and crash (C). Note that crashing *during* the processing of a document is considered the same as crashing before its completion. These events can occur in six different orderings:

1. $M \rightarrow P \rightarrow C$: A crash occurs after sending the completion message and processing the document.
2. $M \rightarrow C(\rightarrow P)$: A crash happens after sending the completion message, but before the document could be (completely) processed.
3. $P \rightarrow M \rightarrow C$: A crash occurs after sending the completion message and processing the document.
4. $P \rightarrow C(\rightarrow M)$: The document was processed, after which a crash occurs before the completion message could be sent.
5. $C(\rightarrow P \rightarrow M)$: A crash happens before the server could complete the processing of the document.
6. $C(\rightarrow M \rightarrow P)$: A crash happens before the server could even do anything.

The parentheses indicate an event that can no longer happen because the server already crashed. Figure 8.21 shows all possible combinations. As can be readily verified, there is no combination of client strategy and server strategy that will work correctly under all possible event sequences. The bottom line is that the client can never know whether the server crashed just before or after having the text printed.

Reissue strategy	Strategy M → P			Strategy P → M		
	MPC	MC(P)	C(MP)	PMC	PC(M)	C(PM)
Always	DUP	OK	OK	DUP	DUP	OK
Never	OK	ZERO	ZERO	OK	OK	ZERO
Only when ACKed	DUP	OK	ZERO	DUP	OK	ZERO
Only when not ACKed	OK	ZERO	OK	OK	DUP	OK
Client	**Server**			**Server**		

OK	=	Document processed once
DUP	=	Document processed twice
ZERO	=	Document not processed at all

Figure 8.21: Different combinations of client and server strategies in the presence of server crashes. Events between brackets never take place because of a previous crash.

In short, the possibility of server crashes radically changes the nature of RPC and clearly distinguishes single-processor systems from distributed ones. In the former case, a server crash also implies a client crash, so recovery is neither possible nor necessary. In the latter we can and should take action.

Lost reply messages

Lost replies can also be difficult to deal with. The obvious solution is just to rely on a timer again that has been set by the client's operating system. If no reply is forthcoming within a reasonable period, just send the request once more. The trouble with this solution is that the client is not really sure why there was no answer. Did the request or reply get lost, or is the server merely slow? It may make a difference.

In particular, some operations can safely be repeated as often as necessary with no damage being done. A request such as asking for the first 1024 bytes of a file has no side effects and can be executed as often as necessary without any harm being done. A request that has this property is said to be **idempotent**.

Now consider a request to a banking server asking to transfer money from one account to another. If the request arrives and is carried out, but the reply is lost, the client will not know this and will retransmit the message. The bank server will interpret this request as a new one, and will carry it out too. Twice the amount of money will be transferred. Transferring money is not idempotent.

One way of solving this problem is to try to structure all the requests in an idempotent way. In practice, however, many requests (e.g., transferring money) are inherently nonidempotent, so something else is needed. Another method is to have the client assign each request a sequence number. By having the server keep track of the most recently received sequence number from each client that is using it, the server can tell the difference between an original request and a retransmission and can refuse to carry out any request a second time. However, the server will still have to send a response to the client. Note that this approach does require that the server maintains administration on each client. Furthermore, it is not clear how long to maintain this administration. An additional safeguard is to have a bit in the message header that is used to distinguish initial requests from retransmissions (the idea being that it is always safe to perform an original request; retransmissions may require more care).

Client crashes

The final item on the list of failures is the client crash. What happens if a client sends a request to a server to do some work and crashes before the server replies? At this point a computation is active and no parent is waiting for the result. Such a computation is called an **orphan (computation)**.

Orphan computations can cause a variety of problems that can interfere with normal operation of the system. As a bare minimum, they waste processing power. They can also lock files or otherwise tie up valuable resources. Finally, if the client reboots and does the RPC again, but the reply from the orphan comes back immediately afterward, confusion can result. Note that, in this case, we are essentially dealing with the problem of guaranteeing at-most-once semantics and bringing the client back into a state just before it crashed. As we will explain later, checkpointing just before sending a request, and restoring the client to the checkpointed state will solve many problems with orphan computations. In essence, it boils down to let the orphan do its work, and properly restoring the client.

Yet, what can be done about orphans? Four solutions have been proposed [Nelson, 1981]. First, before a client stub sends an RPC message, it makes a log entry telling what it is about to do. The log is kept on disk or some other medium that survives crashes. After a reboot, the log is checked and the orphan is explicitly killed off. This solution is called **orphan extermination**, an admittedly not very empathically sounding name.

The disadvantage of this scheme is the expense of writing a disk record for every RPC. Furthermore, it may not even work, since orphans themselves may do RPCs, thus creating **grandorphans** or further descendants that are difficult or impossible to locate. Finally, the network may be partitioned, for example because of a failed gateway, making it impossible to kill them, even if they can be located. All in all, this is not a promising approach, and, in general, will need to be avoided due to its complexity.

With the second solution, called **reincarnation**, all these problems can be solved without the need to write disk records. The way it works is to divide time up into sequentially numbered epochs. When a client recovers, it broadcasts a message to all machines declaring the start of a new epoch. When such a broadcast comes in, all remote computations are killed. Of course, if the network is partitioned, some orphans may survive. Fortunately, however, when they report back, their replies will contain an obsolete epoch number, making them easy to detect.

The third solution is a variant on this idea, but somewhat less Draconian. It is called **gentle reincarnation**. When an epoch broadcast comes in, each machine checks to see if it has any remote computations running locally, and if so, tries its best to locate their owners. Only if the owners cannot be located anywhere is the computation killed.

In the fourth solution, called **expiration**, each RPC is given a standard amount of time, T, to do the job. If it cannot finish, it must explicitly ask for another quantum. Of course, this is quite a nuisance. On the other hand, if after a crash the client waits a time T before rebooting, all orphans are sure to be gone. The problem to be solved here is choosing a reasonable value of T in the face of RPCs with wildly differing requirements.

In practice, all of these methods are crude and undesirable. Worse yet, killing an orphan may have unforeseen consequences. For example, suppose that an orphan has obtained locks on one or more files or database records. If the orphan is suddenly killed, these locks may remain forever. Also, an orphan may have already made entries in various remote queues to start up other processes at some future time, so even killing the orphan may not remove all traces of it. Conceivably, it may even have started again, with unforeseen consequences. Orphan elimination is discussed in more detail by Panzieri and Shrivastava [1988].

As mentioned, the best solution is often not to do anything special, but attempt to restore the client to a state in which it can handle any response from its previously orphaned computation. This brings us to checkpointing and message logging, which we discuss in Section 8.6.

8.4 Reliable group communication

Considering how important process resilience by replication is, it is not surprising that reliable multicast services are important as well. Such services guarantee that messages are delivered to all members in a process group. Unfortunately, reliable multicasting turns out to be surprisingly tricky. In this section, we take a closer look at the issues involved in reliably delivering messages to a process group.

8.4.1 Introduction

Let us first define what reliable group communication actually is. Intuitively, it means that a message that is sent to a process group should be delivered to each member of that group. If we separate the logic of handling messages from the core functionality of a group member, we can conveniently make the distinction between *receiving* messages and *delivering* messages, as illustrated in Figure 8.22. A message is received by a message-handling component, which, in turn, delivers a message to the component containing the core functionality of a group member. Informally, a message that is received by process P will also be delivered by P.

As an example, ensuring that messages from the same sender are delivered in the same order as they were sent, is typically taken care of by a message-handling component. Likewise, providing reliable message-passing is a feature that can and should be separated from the core functionality of a group member, and is typically implemented by a message-handling component (if not by the underlying operating system).

With this separation between receiving and delivering messages, we can be more precise about what reliable group communication means. Let us make a distinction between reliable communication in the presence of faulty processes, and reliable communication when processes are assumed to operate

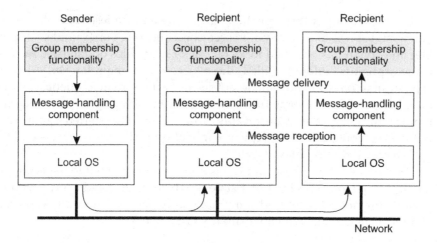

Figure 8.22: The distinction between receiving and delivering messages.

correctly. In the first case, group communication is considered to be reliable when it can be guaranteed that a message is received by and subsequently delivered to all nonfaulty group members.

The tricky part here is that agreement should be reached on what the group actually looks like before a message can be delivered. If a sender intended to have a message delivered by each member of a group **G**, but that, for whatever reason, at the time of delivery we actually have another group $\mathbf{G}' \neq \mathbf{G}$, we should ask ourselves whether the message can be delivered.

The situation becomes simpler if we can ignore consensus on group membership. In particular, let us first assume that a sending process has a list of intended recipients. In that case, it can simply deploy reliable transport-level protocols such as TCP and, one by one, sends its message to each recipient. If a receiving process fails, the message may be resent later when the process recovers, or ignored altogether (for example, because the sender had left the group). In case a group member is expected to send a response, even if it is just an acknowledgement, communication can be speeded up by separating the sending of a request from receiving a response, as illustrated by the message sequence charts in Figure 8.23.

Most transport layers offer reliable point-to-point channels; they rarely offer reliable communication to a group of processes. The best they offer is to let a process set up a point-to-point connection to each other process it wants to communicate with. When process groups are relatively small, this approach to establishing reliability is a straightforward and practical solution. On the other hand, we can often assume that the underlying communication system does offer unreliable multicasting, meaning that a multicast message may be lost part way and delivered by some, but not all, of the intended receivers.

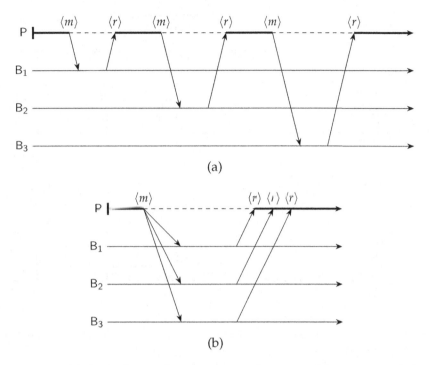

Figure 8.23: (a) A sender sends out requests, but waits for a response before sending out the next one. (b) Requests are sent out in parallel, after which the sender waits for incoming responses.

A simple solution to reach reliable group communication is shown in Figure 8.24. The sending process assigns a sequence number to each message it multicasts and stores the message locally in a history buffer. Assuming the receivers are known to the sender, the sender simply keeps the message in its history buffer until each receiver has returned an acknowledgement. A receiver can suspect it is missing a message m with sequence number s when it has received messages with sequence numbers higher than s. In that case, it returns a negative acknowledgement to the sender, requesting for a retransmission of m.

There are various design trade-offs to be made. For example, to reduce the number of messages returned to the sender, acknowledgements could possibly be piggybacked with other messages. Also, retransmitting a message can be done using point-to-point communication to each requesting process, or using a single multicast message sent to all processes. General issues on reliable multicasting are discussed by Popescu et al. [2007]. A survey and overview of reliable multicasting in the context of publish/subscribe systems, which is also relevant here, is provided by Esposito et al. [2013].

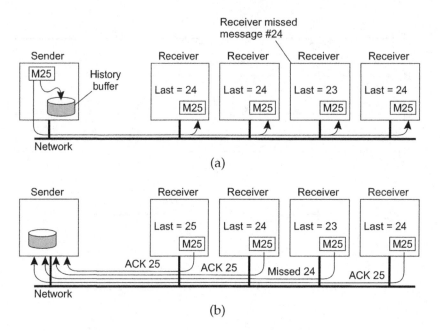

Figure 8.24: A solution for reliable multicasting. (a) Message transmission. (b) Reporting feedback.

8.4.2   Scalability in reliable multicasting

The main problem with the reliable multicast scheme just described is that it cannot support large numbers of receivers. If there are N receivers, the sender must be prepared to accept at least N acknowledgements. With many receivers, the sender may be swamped with such feedback messages, which is also referred to as a **feedback implosion**. When replicating processes for fault tolerance, this situation is not likely to occur as process groups are relatively small. When replicating for performance, we have a different case. Moreover, we may then also need to take into account that the receivers are spread across a wide-area network.

One solution to the problem of a feedback implosion is not to have receivers acknowledge the receipt of a message. Instead, a receiver returns a feedback message only to inform the sender it is missing a message. Returning only such negative acknowledgements can be shown to generally scale better [Towsley et al., 1997], but no hard guarantees can be given that feedback implosions will never happen.

Another problem with returning only negative acknowledgements is that the sender will, in theory, be forced to keep a message in its history buffer forever. Because the sender can never know if a message has been correctly delivered to all receivers, it should always be prepared for a receiver requesting the retransmission of an old message. In practice, the sender will remove a message from its history buffer after some time has elapsed to prevent the buffer from overflowing. However, removing a message is done at the risk of a request for a retransmission not being honored.

Several proposals for scalable, reliable multicasting exist. A comparison between different schemes can be found in [Levine and Garcia-Luna-Aceves, 1998]. We now briefly discuss two very different approaches that are representative of many existing solutions.

The key issue to scalable solutions for reliable multicasting is to reduce the number of feedback messages that are returned to the sender. A popular model that has been applied to several wide-area applications is **feedback suppression**. This scheme underlies the **Scalable Reliable Multicasting (SRM)** protocol developed by Floyd et al. [1997] and works as follows.

First, in SRM, receivers never acknowledge the successful delivery of a multicast message, but instead, report only when they are missing a message. How message loss is detected is left to the application. Only negative acknowledgements are returned as feedback. Whenever a receiver notices that it missed a message, it *multicasts* its feedback to the rest of the group.

Multicasting feedback allows another group member to suppress its own feedback. Suppose several receivers missed message m. Each of them will need to return a negative acknowledgement to the sender, S, so that m can be retransmitted. However, if we assume that retransmissions are always multicast to the entire group, it is sufficient that only a single request for retransmission reaches S.

For this reason, a receiver R that did not receive message m schedules a feedback message with some random delay. That is, the request for retransmission is not sent until some random time has elapsed. If, in the meantime, another request for retransmission for m reaches R, R will suppress its own feedback, knowing that m will be retransmitted shortly. In this way, ideally, only a single feedback message will reach S, which in turn subsequently retransmits m. This scheme is shown in Figure 8.25.

Feedback suppression has shown to scale reasonably well, and has been used as the underlying mechanism for a number of collaborative Internet applications, such as a shared whiteboard. However, the approach also introduces a number of serious problems. First, ensuring that only one request for retransmission is returned to the sender requires a reasonably accurate scheduling of feedback messages at each receiver. Otherwise, many receivers will still return their feedback at the same time. Setting timers accordingly in a group of processes that is dispersed across a wide-area network is not that easy.

Another problem is that multicasting feedback also interrupts those processes to which the message has been successfully delivered. In other words, other receivers are forced to receive and process messages that are useless

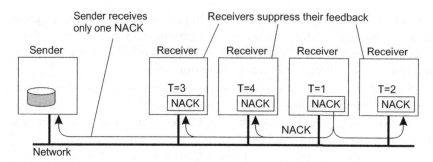

Figure 8.25: Several receivers have scheduled a request for retransmission, but the first retransmission request leads to the suppression of others.

to them. The only solution to this problem is to let receivers that have not received message m join a separate multicast group for m, as explained by Kasera et al. [1997]. Unfortunately, this solution requires that groups can be managed in a highly efficient manner, which is hard to accomplish in a wide-area system. A better approach is therefore to let receivers that tend to miss the same messages team up and share the same multicast channel for feedback messages and retransmissions. Details on this approach are found in [Liu et al., 1998].

To enhance the scalability of SRM, it is useful to let receivers assist in local recovery. In particular, if a receiver to which message m has been successfully delivered, receives a request for retransmission, it can decide to multicast m even before the retransmission request reaches the original sender. Further details can be found in [Floyd et al., 1997] and [Liu et al., 1998].

Feedback suppression as just described is basically a nonhierarchical solution. However, achieving scalability for large groups of receivers requires that hierarchical approaches are adopted. A solution is shown in Figure 8.26. The group of receivers is partitioned into a number of subgroups, which are subsequently organized into a tree. Within each subgroup, any reliable multicasting scheme that works for small groups can be used. Each subgroup appoints a local coordinator, which represents that group in the multicast tree. A link in the tree between two nodes corresponds to a reliable connection between the coordinators of the respective subgroups.

When a process S in group **G** wants to send a message, it simply uses the reliable multicast scheme for **G** to reach all its members, including the group's coordinator, say C. C, in turn, will forward the message to its neighboring coordinators. As a general rule, a coordinator will forward an incoming message m to all its neighboring coordinators, except the one from which it received m. In addition, a coordinator will reliably multicast the incoming message to all members of the subgroup it represents, and notably also handle retransmissions for that group.

In an ACK-based scheme, if coordinator C of group **G** sends a message m to coordinator C′ of another, neighboring group **G**′, it will keep m in its history buffer at least until C′ has sent an acknowledgement. In a NACK-based scheme, only if **G**′ detects it has missed m (and thus also all members of **G**′, and all coordinators to which **G**′ would have forwarded m), it will send a NACK message to C. It is thus seen that a single ACK or NACK message from a coordinator, aggregates many feedback control messages from other processes, leading to a much more scalable, reliable multicasting scheme. Scalability is further improved by letting a coordinator handle the retransmissions to neighboring coordinators, to which it had forwarded a message.

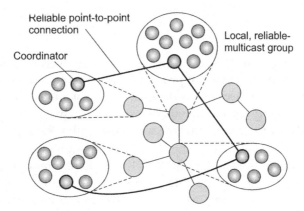

Figure 8.26: The essence of hierarchical reliable multicasting. Each local coordinator forwards the message to its neighboring coordinators in the tree and later handles retransmission requests.

Note that the nonhierarchical feedback control which we discussed before can be used to improve the scalability of a single multicast group. Together with hierarchical feedback control, we would combine relatively large reliable-multicast subgroups into potentially large trees, thus being able to support reliable multicasting for large groups of processes.

The main problem with hierarchical solutions is the construction and management of the tree: how are subgroups formed, which processes are appointed to be coordinator, and how are the subgroups organized in a tree. In many cases, a tree needs to be constructed dynamically. Unfortunately, traditional network-level solutions provide almost no adequate services for tree management. For this reason, application-level multicasting solutions as we discussed in Section 4.4.1 have gained popularity.

Finally, let us briefly consider gossip-based multicasting schemes, in particular the following push-pull **anti-entropy** scheme that we discussed extensively in Section 4.4.3.

In this scheme, a node P picks another node Q at random, and subsequently exchanges updates with Q. In other words, P pushes updates that Q has not seen before to Q, and pulls in any updates that Q has, but which were missed by P. After the exchange, both processes have the same data. Clearly, this scheme is already inherently robust, for if the communication between P and Q fails for whatever reason, P will simply pick some other node to exchange updates. The net effect is that the speed by which an update propagates through the system slows down, but the reliability is affected only in extreme cases. Nevertheless, this slowdown is considered important for some applications. In this light, the comparison between traditional tree-based multicasting and gossip-based multicasting for the purpose of aggregation as discussed by Nyers and Jelasity [2015] may be of interest.

8.4.3 Atomic multicast

Let us now return to the situation in which we need to achieve reliable multicasting in the presence of process failures. In particular, what is often needed in a distributed system is the guarantee that a message is delivered to either all (nonfaulty) group members or to none. This is also known as the **atomic multicast problem**, to which we return with greater precision below.

To see why atomicity is so important, consider a replicated database constructed as an application on top of a distributed system. The distributed system offers reliable multicasting facilities. In particular, it allows the construction of process groups to which messages can be reliably sent. The replicated database is therefore constructed as a group of processes, one process for each replica. Update operations are always multicasted to all replicas and subsequently performed locally. We are thus assuming that an active-replication protocol is being used.

To keep matters simple, assume a client contacts a replica P and requests it to perform an update. The replica does so by multicasting the update to the other group members. Unfortunately, before the multicast completes, P crashes, leaving the rest of the group in a difficult position: some group members will have received the update request; others will not. If the members who have received the request, deliver it to the database, then obviously we will have an inconsistent replicated database. Some replicas will have processed the update, others will not. This situation needs to be avoided, and we should either have that the update is delivered to all nonfaulty members, or to none. The former case reflects that P crashed *after* completing the multicast, while the latter represents P crashing before it even got a chance to request the update.

Both these situations are fine, and correspond to the case in which a client communicates with a single server that is allowed to crash. If a number of the group members would execute the update, while others would not, distribution transparency is at stake, but even worse, the client would not know what to make of the situation.

Virtual synchrony

Reliable multicast in the presence of process failures can be accurately defined in terms of process groups and changes to group membership. As we did earlier, we make a distinction between *receiving* and *delivering* a message. In particular, we again adopt a model in which the distributed system consists of message-handling components, as was shown in Figure 8.22. A received message is locally buffered in this component until it can be delivered to the application, which is logically placed as a group member at a higher layer.

The whole idea of atomic multicasting is that a multicast message m is uniquely associated with a list of processes that should deliver it. This delivery list corresponds to a **group view**, namely, the view on the set of processes contained in the group, which the sender had at the time message m was multicasted. An important observation is that each process on that list has the same view. In other words, they should all agree that m should be delivered by each one of them and by no other process.

Now suppose that message m is multicasted at the time its sender, say P, has group view **G**. Furthermore, assume that while the multicast is taking place, another process Q joins or leaves the group. This change in group membership is naturally announced to all processes in **G**. Stated somewhat differently, a **view change** takes place by multicasting a message vc announcing the joining or leaving of Q. We now have two multicast messages simultaneously in transit: m and vc. What we need to guarantee is that m is either delivered by all processes in **G** before any one executes the view change as specified by vc, or m is not delivered at all. Note that this requirement is comparable to totally ordered multicasting, which we discussed in Section 5.2.1.

A question that quickly comes to mind is that if m is not delivered by any process, how can we speak of a *reliable* multicast protocol? In principle, there is only one case in which delivery of m is allowed to fail: when the group membership change is the result of the sender P of m crashing. In that case, either all remaining (nonfaulty) members of **G** should deliver m before agreeing P is no longer member of the group, or none should deliver m. As mentioned before, the latter corresponds to the situation that P is considered to have crashed before it had a chance to send m.

This stronger form of reliable multicast guarantees that a message multicast to group view **G** is delivered by each nonfaulty process in **G**. If the sender of the message crashes during the multicast, the message is either delivered to all remaining processes, or ignored by each of them. Such a reliable multicast is said to be **virtually synchronous** [Birman and Joseph, 1987].

To illustrate these matters, consider the four processes shown in Figure 8.27. At a certain moment, we have a group consisting of S_1, S_2, S_3, and S_4. After some messages have been multicast, S_3 crashes. However, before crashing, it succeeded in multicasting a message to processes S_2 and S_4, but not to S_1.

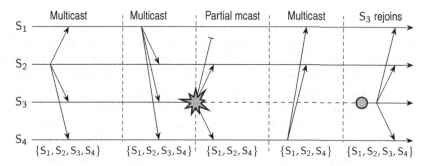

Figure 8.27: The principle of virtual synchronous multicast.

Virtual synchrony in this case guarantees that the message is not delivered at all, effectively establishing the situation that the message was never sent before S_3 crashed.

After S_3 has been removed from the group, communication proceeds between the remaining group members. Later, when S_3 recovers, it can join the group again, after its state has been brought up to date.

The principle of virtual synchrony comes from the fact that all multicasts take place between view changes. Put somewhat differently, a view change acts as a barrier across which no multicast can pass. In a sense, it is comparable to the use of a synchronization variable in distributed data stores, as discussed in the Chapter 7. All multicasts that are in transit while a view change takes place are completed before the view change comes into effect. The implementation of virtual synchrony is not trivial, as we discuss below.

Message Ordering

Virtual synchrony allows an application developer to think about multicasts as taking place in epochs that are separated by group membership changes. However, nothing has yet been said concerning the ordering of multicasts. In general, four different orderings are distinguished:

1. Unordered multicasts

2. FIFO-ordered multicasts

3. Causally ordered multicasts

4. Totally ordered multicasts

A **reliable, unordered multicast** is a virtually synchronous multicast in which no guarantees are given concerning the order in which received messages are delivered by different processes. (Note that reliable multicasting is still about realizing the all-or-nothing property when it comes to delivering messages to group members.) To explain, assume that reliable multicasting is supported by a library providing a send and a receive primitive. The receive operation blocks the caller until a message can be delivered.

Event order	Process P_1	Process P_2	Process P_3
1	sends m_1	receives m_1	receives m_2
2	sends m_2	receives m_2	receives m_1

Figure 8.28: Three communicating processes in the same group. The ordering of events per process is shown along the vertical axis.

Now suppose a sender P_1 multicasts two messages to a group, while two other processes in that group are waiting for messages to arrive, as shown in Figure 8.28. Assuming that processes do not crash or leave the group during these multicasts, it is possible that the message-handling component at P_2 first receives message m_1 and then m_2. Because there are no message-ordering constraints, the messages may be delivered in the order that they are received. In contrast, the message-handling component at P_3 may first receive message m_2 followed by m_1, and delivers these two in this same order to the higher-level application of P_3.

In the case of **reliable FIFO-ordered multicasts**, the message-handling component layer is forced to deliver incoming messages from the same process in the same order as they have been sent. Consider the communication within a group of four processes, as shown in Figure 8.29. With FIFO ordering, the only thing that matters is that message m_1 is always delivered before m_2, and, likewise, that message m_3 is always delivered before m_4. This rule has to be obeyed by all processes in the group. In other words, when the communication layer at P_3 receives m_2 first, it will wait with delivery to P_3 until it has received and delivered m_1.

Event order	Process P_1	Process P_2	Process P_3	Process P_4
1	sends m_1	receives m_1	receives m_3	sends m_3
2	sends m_2	receives m_3	receives m_1	sends m_4
3		receives m_2	receives m_2	
4		receives m_4	receives m_4	

Figure 8.29: Four processes in the same group with two different senders, and a possible delivery order of messages under FIFO-ordered multicasting.

However, there is no constraint regarding the delivery of messages sent by different processes. In other words, if process P_2 receives m_1 before m_3, it may deliver the two messages in that order. Meanwhile, process P_3 may have received m_3 before receiving m_1. FIFO ordering states that P_3 may deliver m_3 before m_1, although this delivery order is different from that of P_2.

Finally, **reliable causally ordered multicast** delivers messages so that potential causality between different messages is preserved. In other words, if a message m_1 causally precedes another message m_2, regardless of whether they were multicasted by the same sender, then the communication layer at each receiver will always deliver m_2 after it has received and delivered m_1. Note that causally ordered multicasts can be implemented using vector timestamps, as discussed in Chapter 5.

Besides these three orderings, there may be the additional constraint that message delivery is to be totally ordered as well. **Totally ordered delivery** means that regardless of whether message delivery is unordered, FIFO ordered, or causally ordered, it is required additionally that when messages are delivered, they are delivered in the same order to all group members.

For example, with the combination of FIFO and totally ordered multicast, processes P_2 and P_3 in Figure 8.29 may both first deliver message m_3 and then message m_1. However, if P_2 delivers m_1 before m_3, while P_3 delivers m_3 before delivering m_1, they would violate the total-ordering constraint. Note that FIFO ordering should still be respected. In other words, m_2 should be delivered after m_1 and, accordingly, m_4 should be delivered after m_3.

Virtually synchronous reliable multicasting offering totally ordered delivery of messages is called **atomic multicasting**. It encompasses the all-or-nothing property discussed before (i.e., all members have the message delivered to, or none of them do), yet atomic multicasting also requires a totally ordered delivery of messages. With the three different message ordering constraints discussed above, this leads to six forms of reliable multicasting, as shown in Figure 8.30 [Hadzilacos and Toueg, 1993].

Multicast	Basic message ordering	TO delivery?
Reliable multicast	None	No
FIFO multicast	FIFO-ordered delivery	No
Causal multicast	Causal-ordered delivery	No
Atomic multicast	None	Yes
FIFO atomic multicast	FIFO-ordered delivery	Yes
Causal atomic multicast	Causal-ordered delivery	Yes

Figure 8.30: Six different versions of virtually synchronous reliable multicasting and considering totally ordered delivery.

Note 8.9 (Advanced: Implementing virtual synchrony)
Let us now consider a possible implementation of a virtually synchronous reliable multicast. An example of such an implementation appears in Isis, a fault-tolerant distributed system that has been in practical use in industry for several years. We will focus on some of the implementation issues of this technique as described in Birman et al. [1991].

Reliable multicasting in Isis makes use of available reliable point-to-point communication facilities of the underlying network, in particular, TCP. Multicasting a message m to a group of processes is implemented by reliably sending m to each group member. As a consequence, although each transmission is guaranteed to succeed, there are no guarantees that *all* group members receive m. In particular, the sender may fail before having transmitted m to each member.

Besides reliable point-to-point communication, Isis also assumes that messages from the same source are received by a communication layer in the order they were sent by that source. In practice, this requirement is solved by using TCP connections for point-to-point communication.

The main problem that needs to be solved is to guarantee that all messages sent to view G are delivered to all nonfaulty processes in G before the next group membership change takes place. The first issue that needs to be taken care of is making sure that each process in G has received all messages that were sent to G. Note that because the sender of a message m to G may have failed before completing its multicast, there may indeed be processes in G that will never receive m. Because the sender has crashed, these processes should get m from somewhere else.

The solution to this problem is to let every process in G keep m until it knows for sure that all members in G have received it. If m has been received by all members in G, m is said to be **stable**. Only stable messages are allowed to be delivered. To ensure stability, it is sufficient to select an arbitrary live process in G and request it to send m to all other processes in G.

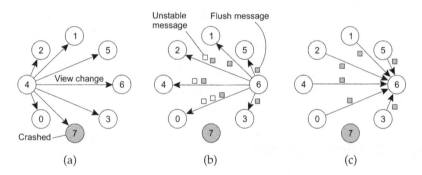

Figure 8.31: (a) Process 4 notices that process 7 has crashed and sends a view change. (b) Process 6 sends out all its unstable messages, followed by a flush message. (c) Process 6 installs the new view when it has received a flush message from everyone else.

To be more specific, assume the current view is G_i, but that it is necessary to install the next view G_{i+1}. Without loss of generality, we assume that G_i and G_{i+1} differ by at most one process. A process P notices the view change when it receives a view-change message. Such a message may come from the process wanting to join or leave the group, or from a process that had detected the failure of a process in G_i that is now to be removed, as shown in Figure 8.31(a).

When a process P receives the view-change message for G_{i+1}, it first forwards a copy of any unstable message from G_i it still has to every process in G_{i+1}, and subsequently marks it as being stable. Recall that Isis assumes point-to-point communication is reliable, so that forwarded messages are never lost. Such forwarding guarantees that all messages in G_i that have been received by at least one process are received by all nonfaulty processes in G_i. Note that it would also have been sufficient to elect a single coordinator to forward unstable messages.

To indicate that P no longer has any unstable messages and that it is prepared to install G_{i+1} as soon as the other processes can do that as well, it multicasts a **flush message** for G_{i+1}, as shown in Figure 8.31(b). After P has received a flush message for G_{i+1} from each other process, it can safely install the new view, as shown in Figure 8.31(c).

When a process Q receives a message m while Q still believes the current view is G_i, it delivers m taking any additional message-ordering constraints into account. If it had already received m, it considers the message to be a duplicate and discards it.

Because process Q will eventually receive the view-change message for G_{i+1}, it will also first forward any of its unstable messages and subsequently wrap things up by sending a flush message for G_{i+1}. Note that due to the assumed FIFO-message ordering as provided by the underlying communication layer, a flush message from a process is always received after the receipt of an unstable message from that same process.

The major flaw in the protocol described so far is that it cannot deal with process failures while a new view change is being announced. In particular, it assumes that until the new view G_{i+1} has been installed by each member in G_{i+1}, no process in G_{i+1} will fail (which would lead to a next view G_{i+2}). This problem is solved by announcing view changes for any view G_{i+k} even while previous changes have not yet been installed by all processes. The details are rather intricate, yet the principle should be clear.

8.5   Distributed commit

The atomic multicasting problem discussed in the previous section is an example of a more general problem, known as **distributed commit**. The distributed commit problem involves having an operation being performed by each member of a process group, or none at all. In the case of reliable multicasting, the operation is the delivery of a message. With distributed transactions, the operation may be the commit of a transaction at a single site that takes part in the transaction. Other examples of distributed commit, and how it can be solved, are discussed by Tanisch [2000].

Distributed commit is often established by a coordinator. In a simple scheme, this coordinator tells all other processes that are also involved, called participants, whether to (locally) perform the operation in question. This scheme is referred to as a **one-phase commit protocol**. It has the obvious drawback that if one of the participants cannot actually perform the operation, there is no way to tell the coordinator. For example, in the case of distributed transactions, a local commit may not be possible because this would violate concurrency control constraints.

In practice, more sophisticated schemes are needed, the most common one being the **two-phase commit protocol**, which we discuss in detail below. The main drawback of this protocol is that it cannot generally efficiently handle the failure of the coordinator. To that end, a three-phase protocol has been developed, which we discuss separately in Note 8.11.

The original two-phase commit protocol (**2PC**) is due to Gray [1978]. Without loss of generality, consider a distributed transaction involving the participation of a number of processes, each running on a different machine. Assuming that no failures occur, the protocol consists of the following two phases, each consisting of two steps (see also Bernstein and Newcomer [2009]):

1. The coordinator sends a VOTE-REQUEST message to all participants.

2. When a participant receives a VOTE-REQUEST message, it returns either a VOTE-COMMIT message to the coordinator, telling the coordinator that it is prepared to locally commit its part of the transaction, or otherwise, a VOTE-ABORT message.

3. The coordinator collects all votes from the participants. If all participants have voted to commit the transaction, then so will the coordinator. In that case, it sends a GLOBAL-COMMIT message to all participants. However, if one participant had voted to abort the transaction, the coordinator will also decide to abort the transaction and multicasts a GLOBAL-ABORT message.

4. Each participant that voted for a commit waits for the final reaction by the coordinator. If a participant receives a GLOBAL-COMMIT message, it locally commits the transaction. Otherwise, when receiving a GLOBAL-ABORT message, the transaction is locally aborted as well.

The first phase is the voting phase, and consists of steps 1 and 2. The second phase is the decision phase, and consists of steps 3 and 4. These four steps are shown as finite state diagrams in Figure 8.32.

Several problems arise when this basic 2PC protocol is used in a system where failures occur. First, note that the coordinator as well as the participants have states in which they block waiting for incoming messages. Consequently, the protocol can easily fail when a process crashes, as other processes may be indefinitely waiting for a message from that process. For this reason, timeout mechanisms are used. These mechanisms are explained next.

When taking a look at the finite state machines in Figure 8.32, it can be seen that there are a total of three states in which either a coordinator or participant

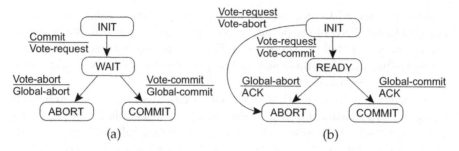

Figure 8.32: (a) The finite state machine for the coordinator in 2PC. (b) The finite state machine for a participant.

is blocked waiting for an incoming message. First, a participant may be waiting in its INIT state for a VOTE-REQUEST message from the coordinator. If that message is not received after some time, the participant will simply decide to locally abort the transaction, and thus send a VOTE-ABORT message to the coordinator.

Likewise, the coordinator can be blocked in state WAIT, waiting for the votes of each participant. If not all votes have been collected after a certain period of time, the coordinator should vote for an abort as well, and subsequently send GLOBAL-ABORT to all participants.

Finally, a participant can be blocked in state READY, waiting for the global vote as sent by the coordinator. If that message is not received within a given time, the participant cannot simply decide to abort the transaction. Instead, it must find out which message the coordinator actually sent. The simplest solution to this problem is to let each participant block until the coordinator recovers again.

A better solution is to let a participant P contact another participant Q to see if it can decide from Q's current state what it should do. For example, suppose that Q had reached state COMMIT. This is possible only if the coordinator had sent a GLOBAL-COMMIT message to Q just before crashing. Apparently, this message had not yet been sent to P. Consequently, P may now also decide to locally commit. Likewise, if Q is in state ABORT, P can safely abort as well.

Now suppose that Q is still in state INIT. This situation can occur when the coordinator has sent VOTE-REQUEST to all participants, but this message has reached P (which subsequently responded with a VOTE-COMMIT message), but has not reached Q. In other words, the coordinator had crashed while multicasting VOTE-REQUEST. In this case, it is safe to abort the transaction: both P and Q can make a transition to state ABORT.

The most difficult situation occurs when Q is also in state READY, waiting for a response from the coordinator. In particular, if it turns out that all participants are in state READY, no decision can be taken. The problem is that although all participants are willing to commit, they still need the coordinator's vote to reach the final decision. Consequently, the protocol blocks until the coordinator recovers. The various options are summarized in Figure 8.33.

State of Q	Action by P
COMMIT	Make transition to COMMIT
ABORT	Make transition to ABORT
INIT	Make transition to ABORT
READY	Contact another participant

Figure 8.33: Actions taken by a participant P when residing in state READY and having contacted another participant Q.

To ensure that a process can actually recover, it is necessary that it saves its state to persistent storage. For example, if a participant was in state INIT, it can safely decide to locally abort the transaction when it recovers, and then inform the coordinator. Likewise, when it had already taken a decision such as when it crashed while being in either state COMMIT or ABORT, it is to recover to that state again, and retransmit its decision to the coordinator.

Problems arise when a participant crashed while residing in state READY. In that case, when recovering, it cannot decide on its own what it should do next, that is, commit or abort the transaction. Consequently, it is forced to contact other participants to find what it should do, analogous to the situation when it times out while residing in state READY as described above.

The coordinator has only two critical states it needs to keep track of. When it starts the 2PC protocol, it should record that it is entering state WAIT so that it can possibly retransmit the VOTE-REQUEST message to all participants after recovering. Likewise, if it had come to a decision in the second phase, it is sufficient if that decision has been recorded so that it can be retransmitted when recovering.

It may thus be possible that a participant will need to block until the coordinator recovers. This situation occurs when all participants have received and processed the VOTE-REQUEST message from the coordinator, while meanwhile, the coordinator crashed. In that case, participants cannot cooperatively decide on the final action to take. For this reason, 2PC is also referred to as a **blocking commit protocol**.

There are several solutions to avoid blocking. One solution is to use a multicast primitive, by which a receiver immediately multicasts a received message to all other processes [Babaoglu and Toueg, 1993]. It can be shown that this approach allows a participant to reach a final decision, even if the coordinator has not yet recovered. Another solution is to use three instead of two phases, as we discuss in Note 8.11.

Note 8.10 (Advanced: 2PC outlined in Python)
An outline of the actions that are executed by the coordinator is given in Figure 8.34. The coordinator starts by multicasting a VOTE-REQUEST to all participants to collect their votes. It subsequently records that it is entering the WAIT state, after which it waits for incoming votes from participants.

If not all votes have been collected, but no more votes are received within a given time interval prescribed in advance, the coordinator assumes that one or more participants have failed. Consequently, it should abort the transaction and multicasts a GLOBAL-ABORT to the (remaining) participants. Likewise, if only a single participant decides to abort the transaction, the coordinator will have to call off the transaction. If all participants vote to commit, GLOBAL-COMMIT is first logged and subsequently sent to all processes. Otherwise, the coordinator multicasts a GLOBAL-ABORT (after recording it in the local log).

```
 1  class Coordinator:
 2    def run(self):
 3      yetToReceive = list(self.participants)
 4      self.log.info('WAIT')
 5      self.chan.sendTo(self.participants, VOTE_REQUEST)
 6      while len(yetToReceive) > 0:
 7        msg = self.chan.recvFrom(self.participants, BLOCK, TIMEOUT)
 8        if msg == -1 or (msg[1] == VOTE_ABORT):
 9          self.log.info('ABORT')
10          self.chan.sendTo(self.participants, GLOBAL_ABORT)
11          return
12        else: # msg[1] == VOTE_COMMIT
13          yetToReceive.remove(msg[0])
14      self.log.info('COMMIT')
15      self.chan.sendTo(self.participants, GLOBAL_COMMIT)
```

Figure 8.34: The steps taken by the coordinator in a 2PC protocol.

After receiving a vote request, the participant does its work. All bets are off if its work failed, but otherwise, it will vote for committing the transaction. It records its decision in a local log and informs the coordinator by sending a VOTE-COMMIT message. The participant must then wait for the global decision. Assuming this decision (which again should come from the coordinator) comes in on time, it is simply written to the local log, after which it can be carried out (the latter is not shown in the code).

Figure 8.35 shows the steps taken by a participant. First, the process waits for a vote request from the coordinator. If no message comes in, the transaction is simply aborted. Apparently, the coordinator had failed.

However, if the participant times out while waiting for the coordinator's decision to come in, it executes a termination protocol by first multicasting a DECISION-REQUEST message to the other processes, after which it subsequently blocks while waiting for a response. When a decisive response comes in (possibly from the coordinator, which is assumed to eventually recover), the participant writes the decision to its local log and handles accordingly. Any request from another participant for the final decision is left unanswered as long as that decision is not known.

```
1  class Participant:
2    def run(self):
3      self.log.info('INIT')
4      msg = self.chan.recvFrom(self.coordinator, BLOCK, TIMEOUT)
5      if msg == -1:  # Crashed coordinator - give up entirely
6        decision = LOCAL_ABORT
7      else: # Coordinator will have sent VOTE_REQUEST
8        decision = self.do_work()
9        if decision == LOCAL_ABORT:
10         self.chan.sendTo(self.coordinator, VOTE_ABORT)
11         self.log.info('LOCAL_ABORT')
12       else: # Ready to commit, enter READY state
13         self.log.info('READY')
14         self.chan.sendTo(self.coordinator, VOTE_COMMIT)
15         msg = self.chan.recvFrom(self.coordinator, BLOCK, TIMEOUT)
16         if msg == -1: # Crashed coordinator - check the others
17           self.log.info('NEED_DECISION')
18           self.chan.sendTo(self.participants, NEED_DECISION)
19           while True:
20             msg = self.chan.recvFromAny()
21             if msg[1] in [GLOBAL_COMMIT, GLOBAL_ABORT, LOCAL_ABORT]:
22               decision = msg[1]
23               break
24         else: # Coordinator came to a decision
25           decision = msg[1]
26   if decision == GLOBAL_COMMIT:
27     self.log.info('COMMIT')
28   else: # decision in [GLOBAL_ABORT, LOCAL_ABORT]:
29     self.log.info('ABORT')
30   while True: # Help any other participant when coordinator crashed
31     msg = self.chan.recvFrom(self.participants)
32     if msg[1] == NEED_DECISION:
33       self.chan.sendTo([msg[0]], decision)
```

Figure 8.35: The steps taken by a participant process in 2PC.

We keep every participant up-and-running after it decided to either commit or abort. It can then assist other participants in need of a decision after detecting that the coordinator had crashed. To this end, a participant blocks on incoming messages and returns its own decision when asked for. Note that we are actually providing an implementation that supports partially synchronous behavior: we assume that timeouts can be applied as a mechanism to detect failures, but take into account that we may have mistakenly concluded that a server crashed.

Of course, the final, now endless loop should eventually terminate. To that end, we need a mechanism to detect that all processes have indeed come to a decision. We leave it as an exercise to the reader for designing such a detector.

Note 8.11 (Advanced: Three-phase commit)

A problem with the two-phase commit protocol is that when the coordinator has crashed, participants may not be able to reach a final decision. Consequently, participants may need to remain blocked until the coordinator recovers. Skeen [1981] developed a variant of 2PC, called the **three-phase commit protocol** (**3PC**), that avoids blocking processes in the presence of fail-stop crashes. Although 3PC is widely referred to in the literature, it is not applied often in practice, as the conditions under which 2PC blocks rarely occur. We discuss the protocol, as it provides further insight into solving fault-tolerance problems in distributed systems.

Like 2PC, 3PC is also formulated in terms of a coordinator and a number of participants. Their respective finite state machines are shown in Figure 8.36. The essence of the protocol is that the states of the coordinator and each participant satisfy the following two conditions:

1. There is no single state from which it is possible to make a transition directly to either a COMMIT or an ABORT state.

2. There is no state in which it is not possible to make a final decision, and from which a transition to a COMMIT state can be made.

It can be shown that these two conditions are necessary and sufficient for a commit protocol to be nonblocking [Skeen and Stonebraker, 1983].

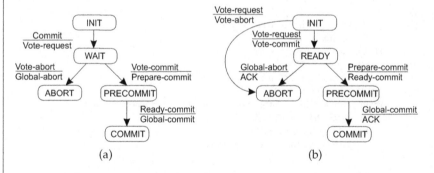

(a)   (b)

Figure 8.36: (a) The finite state machine for the coordinator in 3PC. (b) The finite state machine for a participant.

The coordinator in 3PC starts with sending a VOTE-REQUEST message to all participants, after which it waits for incoming responses. If any participant votes to abort the transaction, the final decision will be to abort as well, so the coordinator sends GLOBAL-ABORT. However, when the transaction can be committed, a PREPARE-COMMIT message is sent. Only after each participant has acknowledged it is now prepared to commit, will the coordinator send the final GLOBAL-COMMIT message by which the transaction is actually committed.

Again, there are only a few situations in which a process is blocked while waiting for incoming messages. First, if a participant is waiting for a vote request from the coordinator while residing in state INIT, it will eventually make a transition to state ABORT, thereby assuming that the coordinator has crashed. This situation is identical to that in 2PC. Analogously, the coordinator may be in state WAIT, waiting for the votes from participants. On a timeout, the coordinator will conclude that a participant crashed, and will thus abort the transaction by multicasting a GLOBAL-ABORT message.

Now suppose the coordinator is blocked in state PRECOMMIT. On a timeout, it will conclude that one of the participants had crashed, but that participant is known to have voted for committing the transaction. Consequently, the coordinator can instruct the operational participants to commit by multicasting a GLOBAL-COMMIT message. In addition, it relies on a recovery protocol for the crashed participant to commit its part of the transaction when it comes up again.

A participant P may block in the READY state or in the PRECOMMIT state. On a timeout, P can conclude only that the coordinator has failed so that it now needs to find out what to do next. As in 2PC, if P contacts any other participant that is in state COMMIT (or ABORT), P should move to that state as well. In addition, if all participants are in state PRECOMMIT, the transaction can be committed.

Again analogous to 2PC, if another participant Q is still in the INIT state, the transaction can safely be aborted. It is important to note that Q can be in state INIT only if no other participant is in state PRECOMMIT. A participant can reach PRECOMMIT only if the coordinator had reached state PRECOMMIT before crashing, and has thus received a vote to commit from each participant. In other words, no participant can reside in state INIT while another participant is in state PRECOMMIT.

If each of the participants that P can contact is in state READY (and they together form a majority), the transaction should be aborted. The point to note is that another participant may have crashed and will later recover. However, neither P, nor any other of the operational participants knows what the state of the crashed participant will be when it recovers. If the process recovers to state INIT, then deciding to abort the transaction is the only correct decision. At worst, the process may recover to state PRECOMMIT, but in that case, it cannot do any harm to still abort the transaction.

This situation is the major difference with 2PC, where a crashed participant could recover to a COMMIT state while all the others were still in state READY. In that case, the remaining operational processes could not reach a final decision and would have to wait until the crashed process recovered. With 3PC, if any operational process is in its READY state, no crashed process will recover to a state other than INIT, ABORT, or PRECOMMIT. For this reason, surviving processes can always come to a final decision.

Finally, if the processes that P can reach are in state PRECOMMIT (and they form a majority), then it is safe to commit the transaction. Again, it can be shown that in this case, all other processes will either be in state READY or at least, will recover to state READY, PRECOMMIT, or COMMIT when they had crashed. More on 3PC can be found in [Bernstein et al., 1987].

8.6 Recovery

So far, we have mainly concentrated on algorithms that allow us to tolerate faults. However, once a failure has occurred, it is essential that the process where the failure happened can recover to a correct state. In what follows, we first concentrate on what it actually means to recover to a correct state, and subsequently when and how the state of a distributed system can be recorded and recovered to, through checkpointing and message logging.

8.6.1 Introduction

Fundamental to fault tolerance is the recovery from an error. Recall that an error is that part of a system that may lead to a failure. The whole idea of error recovery is to replace an erroneous state with an error-free state. There are essentially two forms of error recovery.

In **backward recovery**, the main issue is to bring the system from its present erroneous state back into a previously correct state. To do so, it will be necessary to record the system's state from time to time, and to restore such a recorded state when things go wrong. Each time (part of) the system's present state is recorded, a **checkpoint** is said to be made.

Another form of error recovery is **forward recovery**. In this case, when the system has entered an erroneous state, instead of moving back to a previous, checkpointed state, an attempt is made to bring the system to a correct new state from which it can continue to execute. The main problem with forward error recovery mechanisms is that it has to be known in advance which errors may occur. Only in that case, it is possible to correct those errors and move to a new state.

The distinction between backward and forward error recovery is easily explained when considering the implementation of reliable communication. The common approach to recover from a lost packet is to let the sender retransmit that packet. In effect, packet retransmission establishes that we attempt to go back to a previous, correct state, namely the one in which the packet that was lost is being sent. Reliable communication through packet retransmission is therefore an example of applying backward error recovery techniques.

An alternative approach is to use a method known as **erasure correction**. In this approach, a missing packet is constructed from other, successfully delivered packets. For example, in an (n, k)-block erasure code, a set of k *source packets* is encoded into a set of n *encoded packets*, such that *any* set of k encoded packets is enough to reconstruct the original k source packets. Typical values are $k = 16$ or $k = 32$, and $k < n \leq 2k$ (see, for example, Rizzo [1997]). If not enough packets have yet been delivered, the sender will have to continue transmitting packets until a previously lost packet can be constructed. Erasure correction is a typical example of a forward error recovery approach.

By and large, backward error recovery techniques are widely applied as a general mechanism for recovering from failures in distributed systems. The major benefit of backward error recovery is that it is a generally applicable method independent of any specific system or process. In other words, it can be integrated into (the middleware layer) of a distributed system as a general-purpose service.

However, backward error recovery also introduces some problems [Singhal and Shivaratri, 1994]. First, restoring a system or process to a previous state is generally a relatively costly operation in terms of performance. As will be discussed in succeeding sections, much work generally needs to be done to recover from, for example, a process crash or site failure. A potential way out of this problem is to devise very cheap mechanisms by which components are simply rebooted.

Second, because backward error recovery mechanisms are independent of the distributed application for which they are actually used, no guarantees can be given that once recovery has taken place, the same or similar failure will not happen again. If such guarantees are needed, handling errors often requires that the application gets into the loop of recovery. In other words, full-fledged failure transparency can generally not be provided by backward error recovery mechanisms.

Finally, although backward error recovery requires checkpointing, some states can simply never be rolled back to. For example, once a (possibly malicious) person has taken the $1,000 that suddenly came rolling out of the incorrectly functioning automated teller machine, there is only a small chance that money will be stuffed back in the machine. Likewise, recovering to a previous state in most Unix systems after having enthusiastically typed

```
/bin/rm -fr *
```

but from the wrong working directory, may turn a few people pale. Some things are simply irreversible.

Checkpointing allows the recovery to a previous, correct state. However, taking a checkpoint is often a costly operation and may have a severe performance penalty. As a consequence, many fault-tolerant distributed systems combine checkpointing with **message logging**. In this case, after a checkpoint has been taken, a process logs its messages before sending them off (called **sender-based logging**). An alternative solution is to let the receiving process first log an incoming message before delivering it to the application it is executing. This scheme is also referred to as **receiver-based logging**. When a receiving process crashes, it is necessary to restore the most recently checkpointed state, and from there on *replay* the messages that have been sent. Consequently, combining checkpoints with message logging makes it possible to restore a state that lies beyond the most recent checkpoint without the cost of checkpointing.

In a system where only checkpointing is used, processes will be restored to a checkpointed state. From there on, their behavior may be different from it was before the failure occurred. For example, because communication times are not deterministic, messages may now be delivered in a different order, in turn leading to different reactions by the receivers. However, if message logging takes place, an actual replay of the events that happened since the last checkpoint takes place. Such a replay makes it easier to interact with the outside world.

For example, consider the case that a failure occurred because a user provided erroneous input. If only checkpointing is used, the system would have to take a checkpoint before accepting the user's input in order to recover to the same state. With message logging, an older checkpoint can be used, after which a replay of events can take place up to the point that the user should provide input. In practice, the combination of having fewer checkpoints and message logging is more efficient than having to take many checkpoints.

Elnozahy et al. [2002] provide a survey of checkpointing and logging in distributed systems. Various algorithmic details can be found in Chow and Johnson [1997].

8.6.2 Checkpointing

In a fault-tolerant distributed system, backward error recovery requires that the system regularly saves its state[2]. In particular, we need to record a consistent global state, also called a **distributed snapshot**. In a distributed snapshot, if a process P has recorded the receipt of a message, then there should also be a process Q that has recorded the sending of that message. After all, it must have come from somewhere.

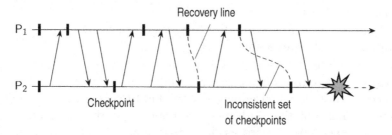

Figure 8.37: A recovery line.

To recover after a process or system failure requires that we construct a consistent global state from local states as saved by each process. In particular, it is best to recover to the *most recent* distributed snapshot, also referred to as a **recovery line**. In other words, a recovery line corresponds to the most recent consistent collection of checkpoints, as shown in Figure 8.37.

---

[2]We assume that each process has access to a local, reliable storage.

Coordinated checkpointing

In **coordinated checkpointing** all processes synchronize to jointly write their state to local storage. The main advantage of coordinated checkpointing is that the saved state is automatically globally consistent. A simple solution is to use a two-phase blocking protocol. A coordinator first multicasts a CHECKPOINT-REQUEST message to all processes. When a process receives such a message, it takes a local checkpoint, queues any subsequent message handed to it by the application it is executing, and acknowledges to the coordinator that it has taken a checkpoint. When the coordinator has received an acknowledgment from all processes, it multicasts a CHECKPOINT-DONE message to allow the (blocked) processes to continue.

It is easy to see that this approach will indeed lead to a globally consistent state because no incoming message will ever be registered as part of a checkpoint. This is because any message that follows a request for taking a checkpoint is not considered to be part of the local checkpoint. At the same time, outgoing messages (as handed to the checkpointing process by the application it is running), are queued locally until the CHECKPOINT-DONE message is received.

An improvement to this algorithm is to send a checkpoint request only to those processes that depend on the recovery of the coordinator, and ignore the other processes. A process is dependent on the coordinator if it has received a message that is directly or indirectly causally related to a message that the coordinator had sent since the last checkpoint. This leads to the notion of an **incremental snapshot**.

To take an incremental snapshot, the coordinator sends a checkpoint request only to those processes it had sent a message to since it last took a checkpoint. When a process P receives such a request, it forwards the request to all those processes to which P itself had sent a message since the last checkpoint, and so on. A process forwards the request only once. When all processes have been identified, a second multicast is used to actually trigger checkpointing and to let the processes continue where they had left off.

Independent checkpointing

Now consider the case in which each process simply records its local state from time to time in an uncoordinated fashion. To discover a recovery line, requires that each process is rolled back to its most recently saved state. If these local states jointly do not form a distributed snapshot, further rolling back is necessary. This process of a cascaded rollback may lead to what is called the **domino effect** and is shown in Figure 8.38.

When process P_2 crashes, we need to restore its state to the most recently saved checkpoint. As a consequence, process P_1 will also need to be rolled back. Unfortunately, the two most recently saved local states do not form a

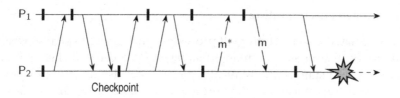

Figure 8.38: The domino effect.

consistent global state: the state saved by P_2 indicates the receipt of a message m, but no other process can be identified as its sender. Consequently, P_2 needs to be rolled back to an earlier state.

However, the next state to which P_2 is rolled back also cannot be used as part of a distributed snapshot. In this case, P_1 will have recorded the receipt of message m*, but there is no recorded event of this message being sent. It is therefore necessary to also roll P_1 back to a previous state. In this example, it turns out that the recovery line is actually the initial state of the system.

As processes take local checkpoints independent of each other, this method is also referred to as **independent checkpointing**. Its implementation requires that dependencies are recorded in such a way that processes can jointly roll back to a consistent global state. To that end, let $CP_i(m)$ denote the mth checkpoint taken by process P_i. Also, let $INT_i(m)$ denote the interval between checkpoints $CP_i(m-1)$ and $CP_i(m)$.

When process P_i sends a message in interval $INT_i(m)$, it piggybacks the pair (i, m) to the receiving process. When process P_j receives a message in interval $INT_j(n)$, along with the pair of indices (i, m), it records the dependency $INT_i(m) \rightarrow INT_j(n)$. Whenever P_j takes checkpoint $CP_j(n)$, it additionally saves this dependency to its local storage, along with the rest of the recovery information that is part of $CP_j(n)$.

Now suppose that at a certain moment, process P_i is required to roll back to checkpoint $CP_i(m-1)$. To ensure global consistency, we need to ensure that all processes that have received messages from P_i and that were sent in interval $INT_i(m)$, are rolled back to a checkpointed state preceding the receipt of such messages. In particular, process P_j in our example, will need to be rolled back at least to checkpoint $CP_j(n-1)$. If $CP_j(n-1)$ does not lead to a globally consistent state, further rolling back may be necessary.

Calculating the recovery line requires an analysis of the interval dependencies recorded by each process when a checkpoint was taken. It turns out that such calculations are fairly complex. In addition, as it turns out, it is often not the coordination between processes that is the dominating performance factor, but the overhead as the result of having to save the state to local stable storage. Therefore, coordinated checkpointing, which is much simpler than independent checkpointing, is often more popular, and will presumably stay so even when systems grow to much larger sizes [Elnozahy and Plank, 2004]

8.6.3 Message logging

Considering that checkpointing can be an expensive operation, techniques have been sought to reduce the number of checkpoints, but still enable recovery. One such technique is logging messages. The basic idea underlying message logging is that if the transmission of messages can be *replayed*, we can still reach a globally consistent state, but without having to restore that state from local storage. Instead, a checkpointed state is taken as a starting point, and all messages that have been sent since are simply retransmitted and handled accordingly.

This approach works fine under the assumption of what is called a **piece-wise deterministic execution model**. In such a model, the execution of each process is assumed to take place as a series of intervals in which events take place. These events are the same as those discussed in the context of Lamport's happened-before relationship in Section 5.2.1. For example, an event may be the execution of an instruction, the sending of a message, and so on. Each interval in the piecewise deterministic model is assumed to start with a nondeterministic event, such as the receipt of a message. However, from that moment on, the execution of the process is completely deterministic. An interval ends with the last event before a nondeterministic event occurs.

In effect, an interval can be replayed with a known result, that is, in a completely deterministic way, provided it is replayed, starting with the same nondeterministic event as before. Consequently, if we record all nondeterministic events in such a model, it becomes possible to completely replay the entire execution of a process in a deterministic way.

Considering that message logs are necessary to recover from a process crash so that a globally consistent state is restored, it becomes important to know precisely when messages are to be logged. Following the approach described by Alvisi and Marzullo [1998], it turns out that many existing message-logging schemes can be easily characterized if we concentrate on how they deal with orphan processes.

An **orphan process** is a process that survives the crash of another process, but whose state is inconsistent with the crashed process after its recovery. As an example, consider the situation shown in Figure 8.39. Process Q receives messages m_1 and m_2 from process P and R, respectively, and subsequently sends a message m_3 to R. However, in contrast to all other messages, message m_2 is not logged. If process Q crashes and later recovers again, only the logged messages required for the recovery of Q are replayed, in our example, m_1. Because m_2 was not logged, its transmission will not be replayed, meaning that the transmission of m_3 may also not take place.

However, the situation after the recovery of Q is inconsistent with that before its recovery. In particular, R holds a message (m_3) that was sent before the crash, but whose receipt and delivery do not take place when replaying what had happened before the crash. This should obviously be avoided.

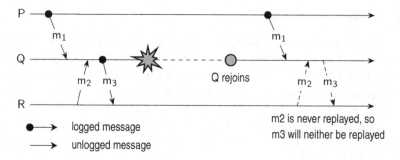

Figure 8.39: Incorrect replay of messages after recovery, leading to an orphan process R.

Note 8.12 (Advanced: Characterizing message-logging schemes)
To characterize different message-logging schemes, we follow the approach described by Alvisi and Marzullo [1998]. Each message m is considered to have a header that contains all information necessary to retransmit m, and to properly handle it. For example, each header will identify the sender and the receiver, but also a sequence number to recognize it as a duplicate. In addition, a delivery number may be added to decide when exactly it should be handed over to the receiving application.

A message is said to be *stable* if it can no longer be lost, for example because it has been written to reliable, local storage. Stable messages can thus be used for recovery by replaying their transmission.

Each message m leads to a set **DEP**(m) of processes that depend on the delivery of m. In particular, **DEP**(m) consists of those processes to which m has been delivered. In addition, if another message m^* is causally dependent on the delivery of m, and m^* has been delivered to a process Q, then Q will also be contained in **DEP**(m). Note that m^* is causally dependent on the delivery of m, if it was sent by the same process that previously delivered m, or which had delivered another message that was causally dependent on the delivery of m.

The set **COPY**(m) consists of those processes that have a copy of m, but have not (yet) reliably stored it. When a process Q delivers message m, it also becomes a member of **COPY**(m). Note that **COPY**(m) consists of those processes that could hand over a copy of m that can be used to replay the transmission of m. If all these processes crash, replaying the transmission of m is clearly not feasible.

Using these notations, it is now easy to define precisely what an orphan process is. Let **FAIL** denote the collection of crashed processes, and assume Q is one of the survivors. Q is an orphan process if there is a message m, such that Q is contained in **DEP**(m), while at the same time every process in **COPY**(m) has crashed. More formally:

$$Q \text{ is orphaned} \Leftrightarrow \exists m : Q \in \textbf{DEP}(m) \text{ and } \textbf{COPY}(m) \subseteq \textbf{FAIL}$$

In other words, an orphan process appears when it is dependent on m, but there is no way to replay m's transmission.

To avoid orphan processes, we thus need to ensure that if each process in **COPY**(m) crashed, then no surviving process is left in **DEP**(m). In other words, all processes in **DEP**(m) should have crashed as well. This condition can be enforced if we can guarantee that whenever a process becomes a member of **DEP**(m), it also becomes a member of **COPY**(m). In other words, whenever a process becomes dependent on the delivery of m, it will keep a copy of m.

There are essentially two approaches that can now be followed. The first approach is represented by what are called **pessimistic logging protocols**. These protocols take care that for each *nonstable* message m, there is at most one process dependent on m. In other words, pessimistic logging protocols ensure that each nonstable message m is delivered to at most one process. Note that as soon as m is delivered to, say, process P, P becomes a member of **COPY**(m).

The worst that can happen is that process P crashes without m ever having been logged. With pessimistic logging, P is not allowed to send any messages after the delivery of m without first having ensured that m has been written to reliable storage. Consequently, no other processes will ever become dependent on the delivery of m to P, without having the possibility of replaying the transmission of m. In this way, orphan processes are always avoided.

In contrast, in an **optimistic logging protocol**, the actual work is done *after* a crash occurs. In particular, assume that for some message m, each process in **COPY**(m) has crashed. In an optimistic approach, any orphan process in **DEP**(m) is rolled back to a state in which it no longer belongs to **DEP**(m). Clearly, optimistic logging protocols need to keep track of dependencies, which complicates their implementation.

As pointed out by Elnozahy et al. [2002], pessimistic logging is so much simpler than optimistic approaches, that it is the preferred way of message logging in practical distributed systems design.

8.7 Summary

Fault tolerance is an important subject in distributed systems design. Fault tolerance is defined as the characteristic by which a system can mask the occurrence and recovery from failures. In other words, a system is fault tolerant if it can continue to operate in the presence of failures.

Several types of failures exist. A crash failure occurs when a process simply halts. An omission failure occurs when a process does not respond to incoming requests. When a process responds too soon or too late to a request, it is said to exhibit a timing failure. Responding to an incoming request, but in the wrong way, is an example of a response failure. The most difficult failures to handle are those by which a process exhibits any kind of failure, called arbitrary or Byzantine failures.

Redundancy is the key technique needed to achieve fault tolerance. When applied to processes, the notion of process groups becomes important. A process group consists of a number of processes that closely cooperate to provide a service. In fault-tolerant process groups, one or more processes can fail without affecting the availability of the service the group implements. Often, it is necessary that communication within the group be highly reliable, and adheres to stringent ordering and atomicity properties to achieve fault tolerance.

The real problem is that members of a process group need to reach consensus in the presence of various failures. Paxos is by now a well-established and highly robust consensus algorithm. By using $2k + 1$ servers, it can establish k-fault tolerance. However, we need a total of $3k + 1$ servers if it is needed to deal with arbitrary failures.

Reliable group communication, also called reliable multicasting, comes in different forms. As long as groups are relatively small, it turns out that implementing reliability is feasible. However, as soon as large groups have to be supported, scalability of reliable multicasting becomes problematic. The key issue in achieving scalability is to reduce the number of feedback messages by which receivers report the (un)successful receipt of a multicasted message.

Matters become worse when atomicity is to be provided. In atomic multicast protocols, it is essential that each group member has the same view concerning to which members a multicasted message has been delivered. Atomic multicasting can be precisely formulated in terms of a virtual synchronous execution model. In essence, this model introduces boundaries between which group membership does not change and which messages are reliably transmitted. A message can never cross a boundary.

Group membership changes are an example where each process needs to agree on the same list of members. Such agreement can be reached through a commit protocol, of which the two-phase commit protocol is the most widely applied. In a two-phase commit protocol, a coordinator first checks whether all processes agree to perform the same operation (i.e., whether they all agree to commit), and in a second round, multicasts the outcome of that poll. A three-phase commit protocol is used to handle the crash of the coordinator without having to block all processes to reach agreement until the coordinator recovers.

Recovery in fault-tolerant systems is invariably achieved by checkpointing the state of the system on a regular basis. Checkpointing is completely distributed. Unfortunately, taking a checkpoint is an expensive operation. To improve performance, many distributed systems combine checkpointing with message logging. By logging the communication between processes, it becomes possible to replay the execution of the system after a crash has occurred.

SECURITY

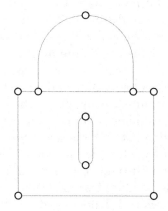

What makes a distributed system secure? Answering this question can easily fill entire books, and can certainly not be fully addressed in a single chapter. One of the challenges in making systems secure is that we need to address a negative goal [Saltzer and Kaashoek, 2009]: we need to protect a system against all unauthorized actions. Proving or demonstrating that this goal has been reached is generally (close to) impossible. Much easier is to show that a positive goal has been accomplished, for example, showing that Alice can log in to a system.

In this chapter, we aim to provide a brief introduction into secure distributed systems. We do so by mainly concentrating on two important mechanisms: authentication and authorization. Authentication is all about ensuring that you are dealing with people and devices that have been properly identified before providing access to a system. Authorization is all about ensuring that identified entities, having access to the system, can perform only those operations they are allowed to execute.

Yet, authentication and authorization are not enough. It is equally important to ensure that operations are carried out correctly: have they affected data in a way that may leave the system in an inconsistent state, has the request to execute an operation not been tampered with, etc.? This aspect of ensuring integrity, or at the very least identifying that integrity has been affected, is essential for any secure system and will be discussed as well.

This brings us to perhaps one of the most discussed topics in the last decade: confidentiality, or, to keep it simple, ensuring that information is kept private. Achieving confidentiality time and again turns out to be a difficult subject, not in the least because keeping information private depends so much on the context of that information. For example, in the European's General Data Protection Regulation (GDPR) it is stated that without explicit consent, no data set should allow for the identification of an individual. However, realizing this otherwise indisputable reasonable requirement turns out to be technically a very demanding task in general, yet solutions for specific situations have been developed. Understanding the context turns out to be important, and as we shall see in this chapter, this actually holds for many situations when trying to secure a distributed system.

Realizing security mechanisms and establishing confidentiality and integrity relies heavily on cryptography, which is a huge field in itself. Nevertheless, explaining the basic principles of cryptographic protocols necessary for distributed systems is actually not too difficult and are also discussed in this chapter.

9.1   Introduction to security

We start our description of security in distributed systems by taking a look at some general security issues. First, it is necessary to define what a secure system is. We distinguish security *policies* from security *mechanisms*. Our second concern is to consider some general design issues for secure systems. Finally, we briefly discuss some cryptographic algorithms, which play a key role in the design of security protocols.

9.1.1 Security threats, policies, and mechanisms

Security in a computer system is strongly related to the notion of dependability. Informally, a dependable computer system is one that we justifiably trust to deliver its services [Laprie, 1995]. Dependability includes availability, reliability, safety, and maintainability. However, if we are to put our trust in a computer system, then confidentiality and integrity should also be considered. **Confidentiality** refers to the property that information is disclosed only to authorized parties. **Integrity** is the characteristic that alterations to a system's assets can be made only in an authorized way, ensuring accuracy and completeness during the lifetime of assets. In other words, improper alterations in a secure computer system should be detectable and recoverable. Major assets of any computer system are its hardware, software, and data (see also Beckers et al. [2015]).

Another way of looking at security in computer systems is that we attempt to protect the services and data it offers against **security threats**. Following Saltzer and Kaashoek [2009] we distinguish the following three broad classes of threats:

1. Unauthorized information disclosure

2. Unauthorized information modification

3. Unauthorized denial of use

In all these cases, we explicitly mention unauthorized actions: actions taken by people, software, or devices (and generally as a combination) that are, simply put, not allowed, or have not been intended to be allowed. To what extent allowing or disallowing actions has been sufficiently expressed or enforced is less important for qualifying a security threat as such: the intent is sufficient for now.

Each of these three classes of threats relate directly to confidentiality, integrity, and availability, respectively.

Simply stating that a system should be able to protect itself against all possible security threats is not the way to actually build a secure system. What is first needed is a description of security requirements, that is, a security policy. A **security policy** describes precisely which actions the entities in a system are allowed to take and which ones are prohibited. Entities include users, services, data, machines, and so on. We will not go into the many aspects of formulating security policies. A good introduction is given by Bishop [2019]. Once a security policy has been laid down, it becomes possible to concentrate on the **security mechanisms** by which a policy can be enforced. We distinguish the following four important security mechanisms:

1. Encryption

2. Authentication

3. Authorization

4. Monitoring and auditing

Encryption is fundamental to computer security. **Encryption** allows us to transform data into something an attacker cannot understand. In other words, encryption provides a means to implement data confidentiality. In addition, encryption allows us to check whether data have been modified. It thus also provides support for integrity checks.

   Authentication is used to verify the claimed identity of a user, client, server, host, device, and so on. In the case of clients, the basic premise is that before a service starts to perform any work on behalf of a client, the service must learn the client's identity (unless the service is available to all). Typically, users are still authenticated through passwords, but there are many other ways to authenticate clients.

   After a client has been authenticated, it is necessary to check whether that client is **authorized** to perform the action requested. Access to records in a medical database is a typical example. Depending on who accesses the database, permission may be granted to read records, to modify certain fields in a record, or to add or remove a record.

   Monitoring and auditing tools are used to trace accesses to assets, such as which clients are accessing or have accessed what, and in which way. It has become increasingly important to not just record what has happened, but to continuously monitor what is going on in a system with the aim to detect any unauthorized intrusions. With the rise of advanced machine-learning techniques, we are witnessing increasingly sophisticated intrusion detection systems, which we shall discuss further in Section 9.6. Although auditing does not really provide any protection against security threats, audit logs can be extremely useful for the analysis of a security breach, and subsequently taking measures against intruders. For this reason, attackers are generally keen not to leave any traces that could eventually lead to exposing their identity. In this sense, logging accesses makes attacking sometimes a riskier business.

9.1.2 Design issues

Security principles

A distributed system, or any computer system for that matter, must provide security services by which a wide range of security policies can be implemented. There are a number of important design issues that need to be considered when implementing general-purpose security services. Various **design principles** have been devised over the years, starting with the influential list of eight such principles by Saltzer and Schroeder [1975]. Almost 40 years later, Smith [2012] concluded that many still thrive:

- Fail-safe defaults
- Open design
- Separation of privilege
- Least privilege
- Least common mechanism

Fail-safe defaults are assuming that any set of defaults will generally not be changed. Perhaps the most infamous example is the initial *(user,password)* combination "(admin, admin)" or something similar, for edge devices. In many cases, the password is never changed, making edge devices the source of countless security breaches. This principle states that defaults should already guarantee a good degree of protection. In particular, access decisions should be based on permissions, not exclusions. For edge devices, it could mean that each should be shipped with a default, unique strong password (which has become common practice by now when purchasing and installing a new modem, for example).

The principle of **open design** is all about *not* applying security by obscurity: it is essential that every aspect of a distributed system is open for review. Everyone should be able to see which mechanisms are being used, how they are being used, how they have been implemented, etc. An obvious problem with this principle for modern distributed systems, is that many of them have become so immense complex that a mere inspection of design and implementation is no longer a guarantee for openness. Good documentation next to the continuous focus on keeping systems and their components as simple as possible are key. Unfortunately, simplicity is increasingly becoming more of an ideal state than something that most engineers can realize.

Separation of privilege is about ensuring that truly critical aspects of a system can never be fully controlled by just a single entity. A top-secret file may need to be double encrypted, with keys in the hands of two different people. Likewise, shutting down critical services may need to be controlled by two authorized administrators, each having their own keys to push the (digital) button.

The principle of **least privilege** states that a process should operate with the fewest possible privileges. As a practical example, in Unix systems, most processes (and thus users) cannot execute operations that are intended to be executed by the root. It is therefore needed to explicitly execute the sudo operation, after which one would normally need to provide a password in order to gain administrative rights.

Finally, the **least common mechanism** refers to designing systems in such a way that if multiple components require the same mechanism, then they should all be offered the same implementation of that mechanism. An important motivation for this principle is that maintenance and simplicity is much easier to achieve with a single implementation than having a mechanism spread across the system, possibly with different implementations. A typical example of this approach is that all users have access to the same library (implementation).

Saltzer and Schroeder [1975] also mentioned three other principles, including economy of mechanism, complete mediation, and psychological acceptability. Economy of mechanism means making systems as simple as possible. Although this is still an excellent goal, achieving it is often close to impossible considering how modern distributed systems are, literally, composed. Nevertheless, it also sometimes seems that designers have let go of this principle entirely. Accepting that systems can become complex in an almost uncontrolled fashion does not mean, however, that striving for simplicity should be abandoned.

Complete mediation means that every access to every object must be checked when it comes to whether it is allowed. With the complex, distributed nature of modern systems, it has become extremely difficult to even figure out how and where an adversary has entered a system.

Finally, psychological acceptance often translates to building the appropriate user interfaces so that people can do only the right thing. It has a lot to do with building a mental model of how a system is operating, and subsequently operate according to that model. Smith [2012] may be correct in stating that this aspect is receiving more attention than before, but that further advancements are simply hindered by costs. This may change, however, as organizations are increasingly becoming aware of how vulnerable they are, only because their employees find it so difficult to work with modern information systems.

Layering of security mechanisms

An important issue in designing secure systems is to decide at which level security mechanisms should be placed. A level in this context is related to the logical organization of a system into a number of layers. For example, computer networks are often organized into layers following some reference model, as we discussed in Section 4.1.1. In Section 2.2, we introduced the organization of distributed systems consisting of separate layers for applications, middleware, operating system services, and the operating system kernel. Combining the two organizations leads roughly to what is shown in Figure 9.1.

Typically, what we have shown as low-level protocols encompass general network-security solutions. An often-used solution is to set up a **virtual**

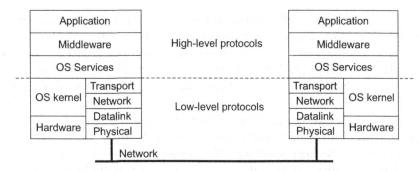

Figure 9.1: The logical organization of a distributed system into several layers.

private network, generally abbreviated to **VPN**. In essence, a VPN sets up a **tunnel** between two remote local networks, or between a host and a remote network. The effect is that a computer on one network seems to be directly connected to the remote network. Although not strictly necessary, a VPN normally encrypts all traffic between its end points and operates at the level of the data link layer or the network layer, as we discussed in Section 4.1.1.

Going higher up the network stack, a well-known example is the **transport-layer security** (**TLS**) service, which can be used to securely send messages across a TCP connection. TLS forms the standard approach for secure communication with Websites employing HTTPS. HTTPS establishes an authenticated connection to a Website through which all data exchanged between a client and the server is encrypted.

Where VPNs and secure Website communication can be considered as operating at the level of networking protocols, this is less obvious for protocols such as SSH. The **Secure Shell Protocol** (**SSH**) is used to establish a secure remote login. As such, one can argue that it operates as an operating-system service. Unlike HTTPS (which formally operates at the application level in terms of networking stacks), SSH comes with its own security protocol and does not rely on a transport-layer security service.

One of the main reasons for introducing middleware was to offer services that are useful for a wide range of distributed applications, while at the same being independent of specific operating systems. One example that we will discuss in detail later is that of an authentication service such as **Kerberos**. The service is indeed independent of a specific operating system (Kerberos has been implemented for a wide range of operating systems, including Windows, many Unix versions, and other non-Unix systems). Other examples of secure middleware services include secure RPC, secure Web servers (think of WordPress), as well as a range of secure databases.

Finally, an approach that is increasingly being adopted is developing **end-to-end application-level security**. In these cases, all secure communication within the distributed application is handled by the application itself. There is no reliance on middleware security services. A well-known example is formed by modern user-messaging services like WhatsApp, Signal, and Telegram. Likewise, distributed applications that, for example, make use of cloud storage services, may be configured to first encrypt any data before sending it off to the cloud, as is done with BoxCryptor.

What these examples illustrate is that there are choices to be made concerning where and which security mechanisms will be deployed. Obviously, application-level security need generally not rely on lower-level security guarantees, yet the price to pay is that all mechanisms need to be deployed and maintained by the application itself. This is not always the best choice, as it does make sense to separate application functionality from what is needed regarding security. Just imagine automating your own backup services for a collection of remote computers. Making use of available operating-system level services for secure execution of remote commands and file transfers makes life a lot easier.

Trusted Computing Base

Dependencies between services regarding trust lead to the notion of a **trusted computing base (TCB)**. A TCB is the set of all security mechanisms in a (distributed) computer system that are necessary and sufficient to enforce a security policy, and that thus need to be trusted [Committee on National Security Systems, 2015]. The TCB encompasses firmware, hardware, software, as well as humans. The smaller the TCB, the better. The idea is that if the TCB can be clearly identified, we at least know what to concentrate on when scrutinizing a computer system to state that it is secure.

Identifying the TCB means identifying the modules that need to be trusted, and those that do not. Unfortunately, identifying the trusted modules is not that simple, nor is it even that simple to design a system such that there is always a clear distinction between trusted and untrusted modules.

For example, it is clear that a program needing administrative privileges to be executed will be part of the TCB, for the simple reason that if that program is compromised, an attacker may be able to do much more than what that program was designed for. But what about a Web-based service that facilitates storage on a local server, such as ownCloud? Such a service is typically implemented as a collection of scripts that are executed by a process spawned by the Apache server. The spawned process runs entirely without any special privileges, yet the collection of scripts also include code for adding and removing users (separate from the users known to the underlying operating system). Are the set of scripts that make up this service to be trusted or not? Or more specifically, which scripts from this set are to be trusted? Clearly, the answer to this question depends on the security specifications for, in this case, the ownCloud service. If the policy states that users should be fully separated, then the scripts for user management and access control will need to be inspected, but also the dependency of those scripts (and perhaps others) on other modules that ownCloud depends on (such as a mysql database and the Apache server).

The ownCloud example illustrates that it may not be that easy to separate trusted from untrusted modules, especially when no security policy has been explicitly specified, or is perhaps otherwise incomplete. The same may hold when designing for security. For example, often we assume a so-called **honest-but-curious** server: a server that behaves according to some protocol, but in the worst case keeps track of all the things it does [Goldreich, 2009]. Making such an assumption may be fine, but what measures have been taken that justify such an assumption? Equally important, are those measures sufficient? When components or modules are complex, it may be very difficult to establish whether a module actually satisfies its specifications and to what extent we may need to classify it as trusted or not.

Privacy

If there is one thing clear when it comes to designing for secure distributed systems, then it is the role of data. In this era of data and notably the effect it has on the personal lives of many, protecting privacy has become a major issue for distributed systems. Privacy and confidentiality are closely related, yet are different. Following Francis [2008], one could state that privacy is *invaded*, whereas confidentiality is *breached*. Important is to recognize that just ensuring confidentiality, that is, data and information is not disclosed in any unauthorized manner, is not enough to guarantee privacy. In this light, one can understand why Nissenbaum [2010] states that the right to privacy is about "a right to *appropriate* flow of personal information." In other words, controlling who gets to see what, when, and how. This also implies, for example, that a person should be able to stop and revoke a flow of personal information.

Discussions on how to design distributed systems that meet such privacy requirements have only recently started to mature. One approach is to concentrate on ownership, such as done in Solid [Sambra et al., 2016], which essentially puts control on personal information at a single person. To what extent this will be sufficient remains to be seen. A point of debate is whether ownership by itself is sufficient to provide the necessary privacy guarantees.

Another approach is to look at what regulations state and to what extent it is possible to design systems that comply to those regulations. Important in this respect is the **General Data Protection Regulation**, or simply **GDPR** [Voigt and Von dem Bussche, 2017], which was installed in 2016. The GDPR is a comprehensive set of regulations aiming to protect personal data. As with many regulations, it is yet unclear to what extent one can develop a truly GDPR-compliant distributed system, but it can be argued that making a system GDPR-compliant after the fact may be much more difficult, if not impossible.

Like Solid, Schwarzkopf et al. [2019] follow an approach in which a user has a separate, privately owned and controlled database with personal information, denoted as a **shard**. Acknowledging that the real challenge lies in keeping track of how personal information flows into other systems, the authors argue for designing a distributed system by considering it to consist of as being a large dataflow computation. A user can contribute her shard to the system, but equally remove it and along with that removal, revoke participation in all related data flows.

As an example, consider a collection of users, each maintaining their own shard. A shard represents a user's contributions to an online social network with three elements:

- Some personal information, such as name, organization, etc.

- A set of connections, each connection referring to another shard.

- A set of posts, as is common in many social networks, often as a reaction to another post.

An application can be developed that builds a tree consisting of posts and reactions to posts. The development of that tree starts with a single, new post P and implements the function react taking the original post P and a (dynamic) list of reactions $R_1, R_2, \ldots, R_n$ as input. Each reaction is, of course, also a post and can be reacted to. When Alice at a certain point decides she wants to completely withdraw from the discussion, she can simply withdraw her post(s), leading to a new tree. All reactions to her posts may necessarily be removed as well, as each of her posts operates as the root of a branch. This can be done automatically, assuming that the function react is continuously updated on its inputs, and we assume that removal of the post that led to reactions, recursively leads to the removal of the entire branch.

More intricate examples are described by Agarwal et al. [2022], yet the essence is that removal of an element as part of a dataflow leads to an update of that flow but without the personal information represented by that element. The example above also illustrates that we may not be out of the woods yet, for what happens if Alice is explicitly mentioned in one of the reactions? In other words, more needs to be done to ensure that all references to Alice and her posts are indeed removed.

This example already illustrates that taking a database perspective may help in designing GDPR-compliant systems. Shastri et al. [2020] show that such a perspective may indeed be fruitful, yet the real challenge is maintaining a large amount of metadata, as shown in Figure 9.2. The authors come to the conclusion that extending databases so that a system can meet GDPR requirements is doable from a functional point of view, but has serious adverse effect on performance and, in turn, on the scalability of solutions.

GDPR regulation	Impact on database systems	
	Attributes	**Actions**
Collect data for explicit purposes	Purpose	Metadata indexing
Do not store data indefinitely	TTL	Timely deletion
Inform customers about GDPR metadata associated with their data	Purpose, TTL, Origin, Sharing	Metadata indexing
Allow customers to access their data	Person id	Metadata indexing
Allow customers to erase their data	TTL	Timely deletion
Do not use data for objected reasons	Objections	Metadata indexing
Allow customers to withdraw from algorithmic decision-making	Automated decisions	Metadata indexing
Safeguard and restrict access to data		Access control
Do not grant unlimited access to data		Access control
Audit operations on personal data	Audit trail	Monitor and log
Implement appropriate data security		Encryption
Share audit trails from affected systems	Audit trail	Monitor and log

Figure 9.2: The effects on (distributed) databases when designing for GDPR compliance (adapted from [Shastri et al., 2020]).

9.2 Cryptography

Let us now draw attention to an essential mechanism in developing secure distributed systems, namely the application of cryptographic solutions. In the following, we first pay attention to some basic cryptographic functions, including symmetric and asymmetric cryptosystems, and secure hashing, to then continue with managing security.

9.2.1 Basics

Fundamental to security in distributed systems is the use of cryptographic techniques. The basic idea of applying these techniques is simple. Consider a sender S wanting to transmit message m to a receiver R. To protect the message against security threats, the sender first **encrypts** it into an unintelligible message m′, and subsequently sends m′ to R. R, in turn, must **decrypt** the received message into its original form m.

Encryption and decryption are accomplished by using cryptographic methods parameterized by keys, as shown in Figure 9.3. The original form of the message that is sent is called the **plaintext**, shown as P in Figure 9.3. The encrypted form is referred to as the **ciphertext**, illustrated as C.

To describe the various security protocols that are used in building security services for distributed systems, it is useful to have a notation to relate

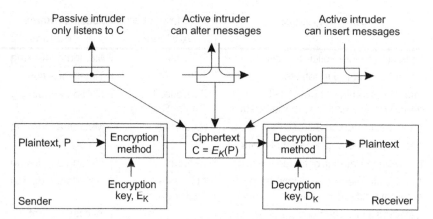

Figure 9.3: Intruders and eavesdroppers in communication.

plaintext, ciphertext, and keys. Following common notational conventions, we will use $C = E_K(P)$ to denote that the ciphertext C is obtained by encrypting the plaintext P using key E_K. Likewise, $P = D_K(C)$ is used to express the decryption of the ciphertext C using key D_K, resulting in the plaintext P.

Returning to our example shown in Figure 9.3, while transferring a message as ciphertext C, there are three different attacks that we need to protect against, and for which encryption helps. First, an **intruder** may intercept the message without either the sender or receiver being aware that eavesdropping is happening. Of course, if the transmitted message has been encrypted in such a way that it cannot be easily decrypted without having the proper key, interception is useless: the intruder will see only unintelligible data. (By the way, the fact alone that a message is being transmitted may sometimes be enough for an intruder to draw conclusions. For example, if during a world crisis, the amount of traffic into the White House suddenly drops dramatically while the amount of traffic going into a certain mountain in Colorado increases, there may be useful information in knowing that.)

The second type of attack that needs to be dealt with is that of modifying the message. Modifying plaintext is easy; modifying ciphertext that has been properly encrypted is much more difficult because the intruder will first have to decrypt the message before it can be meaningfully modified. In addition, the intruder will also have to properly encrypt it again, or otherwise the receiver may notice that the message has been tampered with.

The third type of attack is when an intruder inserts encrypted messages into the communication system, attempting to make R believe these messages came from S. Again, encryption can help protect against such attacks. Note that if an intruder can modify messages, she can also insert messages.

The art and science of devising algorithms for cryptographic systems has a long and fascinating history [Kahn, 1967], and building secure systems is often surprisingly difficult. It is beyond the scope of this book to discuss any of these algorithms in detail. Information on cryptographic algorithms can be found in [Ferguson et al., 2010] and [Smart, 2016].

9.2.2 Symmetric and asymmetric cryptosystems

There is a fundamental distinction between different cryptographic systems, based on whether the encryption and decryption key are the same. In a **symmetric cryptosystem**, the same key is used to encrypt and decrypt a message:

$$if\ P = D_K(E_K(P))\ then\ D_K = E_K.$$

Symmetric cryptosystems are also referred to as **secret-key** or **shared-key systems** because the sender and receiver are required to share the same key, and to ensure that protection works, this shared key must be kept secret; no one else is allowed to see the key. We will use the notation $K_{A,B}$ to denote a key shared by A and B.

In an **asymmetric cryptosystem**, the keys for encryption and decryption are different, but together form a unique pair. In other words, there is a separate key E_K for encryption and one for decryption, D_K, such that

$$if\ P = D_K(E_K(P))\ then\ D_K \neq E_K.$$

One of the keys in an asymmetric cryptosystem is kept private; the other is made public. For this reason, asymmetric cryptosystems are also referred to as **public-key systems**. In what follows, we use the notation PK_A to denote a public key belonging to A, and SK_A as its corresponding private (i.e., secret) key.

Which one of the encryption or decryption keys that is actually made public depends on how the keys are used. For example, if Alice wants to send a confidential message m to Bob, she should use Bob's public key to encrypt the message. Because Bob is the only one holding the associated and private decryption key, he is also the only person who can decrypt the message:

$$if\ \textsf{m}\ is\ to\ be\ kept\ private:\ \textsf{C} = PK_B(\textsf{m}).$$

On the other hand, suppose that Bob wants to know for sure that the message he just received actually came from Alice. In that case, Alice can keep her encryption key private to encrypt the messages she sends. If Bob can successfully decrypt a message using Alice's public key (and the plaintext in the message has enough information to make it meaningful to Bob), he knows that message must have come from Alice because the decryption key is uniquely tied to the encryption key:

$$if\ \textsf{m}\ is\ to\ be\ authenticated:\ \textsf{C} = SK_A(\textsf{m}).$$

We return to digitally signing messages shortly.

An aspect of asymmetric cryptosystems that is becoming increasingly important is that of **homomorphic encryption**. What it boils down to is that when using homomorphic encryption, mathematical operations on plaintext can also be performed on the corresponding ciphertext. In particular, if x and y are two numbers, then

$$E_K(x) \star E_K(y) = E_K(x \star y)$$

where "$\star$" is some mathematical operation, typically an addition or multiplication. The importance of homomorphic encryption cannot be underestimated. By now, we understand what it takes to store data safely on a remote, untrusted server: simply encrypt it with a public key before sending it to the server. This is what tools such as BoxCryptor do. However, whenever stored data needs to be operated on, servers generally require that the data is available as plaintext. Homomorphic encryption changes that: a server can apply operations on encrypted data and the result (also automatically encrypted with the same key) can be safely stored as well, or used in other computations.

There is only one problem with homomorphic encryption: its general form (known as **full homomorphic encryption** or simply **FHE**) is performance-wise slow. FHE supports addition and multiplication, which is enough to implement any mathematical operation. Currently, FHE implementations are often too slow to be generally applicable. In contrast, there are also **partial homomorphic encryption (PHE)** schemes, which support either addition or multiplication, for which efficient implementations exist. However, PHE schemes do require often very specific applications. For a good overview of homomorphic encryption, see Acar et al. [2018].

Note 9.1 (Example: Counting pedestrians over time and space)

As a practical and advanced example of how homomorphic encryption can be applied, consider the following. In many cities, it has become common practice to monitor pedestrian behavior by simply picking up Wi-Fi signals from carry-on devices, notably Wi-Fi–enabled smartphones. Most of these signals are network packets carrying the unique MAC address of the device. By extracting the MAC address as a device identifier, it becomes possible to track movements. That by itself need not necessarily be a problem, but without having explicit consent from a device owner, it is simply a serious infringement of privacy.

Interestingly, many cities are not interested in actually tracking individuals. They are interested in simple questions such as how many people moved from one location to another, or what is the average time that people stayed at a specific location. Such questions are easy to answer when you know the identifier of a device, yet become much more difficult when keeping those identifiers long enough to come to an answer, is simply forbidden.

Stanciu et al. [2020] propose a solution that allows to count devices over time and space without the need to keep device identifiers. A setup consists of a collection of sensors, each sensor essentially being a Wi-Fi–packet sniffer.

During a short epoch (typically a few minutes), a sensor picks up Wi-Fi packets, extracts MAC addresses, and subsequently stores (a pseudonymized version) of each MAC address in a so-called Bloom filter. A Bloom filter is a vector of m bits, initially all set to 0 [Bloom, 1970]. Using a collection of k hash functions, an element x is added to a Bloom filter by setting the position $h_i(x)$ to 1 for each of the k hash functions. Each element is thus represented as an m-bit vector consisting of exactly k bits set to 1. More elements are added by performing a bitwise OR operation each time an element is added.

A Bloom filter has the important property that one cannot retrieve the elements of the set it represents other than by exhaustively testing for all possible elements. In other words, a Bloom filter supports only membership tests. To check if x is in a set **A** represented by the Bloom filter BF, one needs to check if every position $h_i(x)$ has been set to 1:

$$x \in \mathbf{A} \text{ only if } \prod_{i=i}^{k} BF[h_i(x)] = 1$$

Counting is possible by a simple estimation n^* of the number of elements in a Bloom filter [Swamidass and Baldi, 2007]:

$$n^* = -\frac{m}{k} \ln(1 - \frac{X}{m})$$

where X is the number of nonzero elements in the Bloom filter.

Counting the number of devices that were at one location and later at another, then resorts to taking the intersection of two Bloom filters and estimating the size of the intersection. Likewise, checking how many people stayed at a location for a specific, long time, amounts to constructing intersections of Bloom filters and estimating the size. In all cases, there is, strictly speaking, no need to test for membership.

However, using Bloom filters in the clear is not safe: a simple brute-force attack can easily give a very good impression of detected devices, and thus also the ability to track devices. Of course, when the Bloom filters are encrypted, detecting actual devices becomes more difficult. Moreover, computing intersections should preferably be done on encrypted Bloom filters. Fortunately, computing an intersection is nothing else but constructing a Bloom filter through a bitwise AND operation, which is equivalent to a multiplication of 0's and 1's. Specifically, if we need to compute the intersection of two Bloom filters A and B, we do so using their homomorphically encrypted versions and compute:

$$\forall i : PK(A \odot B)[i] = PK(A[i]) \cdot PK(B[i])$$

where "$\odot$" represents an elementwise multiplication of two vectors. The basic idea is that a third party, say Alice, who needs the value of a count provides a public key PK by which each sensor homomorphically encrypts the entries of its Bloom filters. Note that if a value p is encrypted, leading to $p_1 = PK(p)$, and that same value is encrypted a next time, leading to $p_2 = PK(p)$, the two encrypted values will be different: $p_1 \neq p_2$ and an observer will not be able to distinguish the two underlying values to be the same.

An encrypted filter can be handed out to a separate server without disclosing any detections. That server also computes intersections, but completely ignorant of the results, for the simple reason that it cannot decrypt any of the filters. The only thing the server does is shuffle the elements of any (computed) Bloom filter before handing it to Alice, who owns the private key SK associated with PK. This shuffling is important: when Alice decrypts the result, she will have a Bloom filter that has nothing to do with the original, unshuffled Bloom filter. One might say that it represents a completely random set of detections. The only thing in common with the original filter is the number of nonzero elements, from which she can then estimate the size and thus the number of detections. This number is the only information that Alice can get from the server's response.

9.2.3   Hash functions

One final application of cryptography in distributed systems, is the use of **hash functions**. A hash function H takes a message m of arbitrary length as input and produces a bit string h having a fixed length as output:

$$h = H(m) \text{ with length of h fixed.}$$

A hash h is somewhat comparable to the extra bits that are appended to a message in communication systems to allow for error detection, such as a cyclic-redundancy check (CRC). A well-known application is securely storing passwords: instead of storing a password pw, we keep only $H(pw)$. Then, when Alice logs in with a password pw', we need merely check if $H(pw) = H(pw')$.

Hash functions that are used in cryptographic systems, also known as **trapdoors**, have a number of essential properties. First, they are **one-way functions**, meaning that it is computationally infeasible to find the input m that corresponds to a known output h. On the other hand, computing h from m is easy. Second, they have the **weak collision resistance** property, meaning that given an input m and its associated output $h = H(m)$, it is computationally infeasible to find another, different input $m' \neq m$, such that $H(m) = H(m')$. Finally, cryptographic hash functions also have the **strong collision resistance** property, which means that, when given only H, it is computationally infeasible to find any two different input values m and m', such that $H(m) = H(m')$. In this way, an attacker will need to guess passwords instead of simply stealing or trying to derive them what is already known.

Similar properties must apply to any encryption function E and the keys that are used. For any encryption function E_K, it should be computationally infeasible to find the key E_K when given the plaintext P and associated ciphertext $C = E_K(P)$. Likewise, analogous to collision resistance, when given a plaintext P and a key E_K, it should be effectively impossible to find another key $E_{K'}$ such that $E_K(P) = E_{K'}(P)$.

Digital signatures

Let us now take a look at an often-used application of hash functions, namely placing **digital signatures** as part of sending messages. Consider the situation in which Bob has just sold Alice a collector's item of some vinyl record for $500. The whole deal was done through e-mail. In the end, Alice sends Bob a message confirming that she will buy the record for $500. There are at least two issues that need to be taken care of regarding the integrity of the message.

1. Alice needs to be assured that Bob will not maliciously change the $500 mentioned in her message into something higher, and claim she promised more than $500.

2. Bob needs to be assured that Alice cannot deny ever having sent the message, for example because she had second thoughts.

These two issues can be dealt with if Alice digitally signs the message in such a way that her signature is uniquely tied to its content. The unique association between a message and its signature prevents that modifications to the message will go unnoticed. In addition, if Alice's signature can be verified to be genuine, she cannot later repudiate the fact that she signed the message.

There are several ways to place digital signatures. One popular form is to use a public-key cryptosystem. When Alice sends a message m to Bob, she encrypts it with her *private* key SK_A, and sends it off to Bob. If she also wants to keep the message content a secret, she can use Bob's *public* key and send $PK_B(m, SK_A(m))$, which combines m and the version signed by Alice:

$$\text{Alice: } send\ C = PK_B([m, sig])\ with\ sig = SK_A(m).$$

When Bob receives the ciphertext C, he decrypts it with his private key SK_B and uses Alice's public key to verify the signature:

$$\text{Bob: } receive\ and\ decrypt\ [m, sig] = SK_B(C)\ and\ verify\ m = PK_A(sig).$$

If Bob can be assured that the public key is indeed owned by Alice, then decrypting the signed version of m and successfully comparing it to m can mean only that it came from Alice. Alice is protected against any malicious modifications to m by Bob because Bob will always have to prove that the modified version of m was also signed by Alice. In other words, the decrypted message alone essentially never counts as proof. It is also in Bob's own interest to keep the signed version of m to protect himself against repudiation by Alice.

An issue with the scheme just described is that Alice encrypts the entire message with her private key. Such an encryption may be costly in terms of processing requirements and is actually unnecessary. Recall that we need to uniquely associate a signature with only a specific message. A cheaper and arguably more elegant scheme is to use a **message digest**.

A message digest is a fixed-length bit string h that has been computed from an arbitrary-length message m through a cryptographic hash function H. If m is changed to m', its hash $H(m')$ will be different from h = $H(m)$ so that it can easily be detected that a modification has taken place.

To digitally sign a message, Alice can first compute a message digest and subsequently encrypt the digest with her private key. The encrypted digest is sent along with the message to Bob:

$$\text{Alice: } send \text{ } [m, \text{sig}] \text{ } with \text{ } \text{sig} = SK_A(H(m)).$$

When Bob receives the message and its encrypted digest, he need merely decrypt the digest with Alice's public key, and separately calculate the message digest. If the digest calculated from the received message and the decrypted digest match, Bob knows the message has been signed by Alice:

$$\text{Bob: } receive \text{ } [m, \text{sig}], compute \text{ } h' = H(m) \text{ } and \text{ } verify \text{ } h' = PK_A(\text{sig}).$$

Note that the message itself is sent as plaintext: everyone is allowed to read it. If confidentiality is required, then the message should also be encrypted with Bob's public key.

There are still a number of problems with both schemes, although the protocols are correct. First, the validity of Alice's signature holds only as long as Alice's private key remains a secret. If Alice wants to bail out of the deal even after sending Bob her confirmation, she could claim that her private key was stolen before the message was sent. We will later describe how blockchains may help in keeping a decentralized account of transactions, such as those between Alice and Bob.

Another problem occurs when Alice decides to change her private key. Doing so may in itself be not such a bad idea, as changing keys from time to time generally helps against intrusion. However, once Alice has changed her key, her statement sent to Bob, becomes worthless. What may be needed in such cases is a central authority that keeps track of when keys are changed, in addition to using timestamps when signing messages. We look at this issue next; Figure 9.4 summarizes the notations and abbreviations we use in the mathematical expressions throughout this book.

9.2.4   Key management

So far, we have described cryptographic protocols in which we (implicitly) assumed that various keys are readily available. For example, in the case of public-key cryptosystems, we assumed that a sender of a message had the public key of the receiver at its disposal so that it could encrypt the message

Notation	Description
$K_{A,B}$	Secret key shared by A and B
PK_A	Public key of A
SK_A	Private (secret) key of A
$E_K(P)$	Encryption of plaintext P using key E_K (or key K)
$D_K(C)$	Decryption of ciphertext C using key D_K (or key K)
$H(m)$	The hash of m computed using function H
$[m]_A$	The message m digitally signed by A

Figure 9.4: Notations used in this chapter.

to ensure confidentiality. Likewise, when verifying the signature of a message, the receiver will need to have the public key of the sender. In both these examples, we also need to be sure that the public key being used actually belongs to the presumed owner.

However, establishing and distributing keys is not a trivial matter. For example, digitally distributing secret keys without using encryption is out of the question and there are cases where we even have to resort to out-of-band methods. Also, mechanisms are needed to revoke keys, that is, prevent a key from being used after it has been compromised or invalidated.

Key establishment

How are keys actually established? Let us take a look at a simple and widely deployed approach for automatically establishing remote secure connections through SSH. As we mentioned, SSH allows a person to securely log in to a remote computer. We can also use SSH to let a user alice at computer A log in as user bob at computer B using a (*public, private*)-key pair. An actual authentication protocol will be described later; here we are interested in establishing and distributing keys in the SSH system using the openSSL framework.

First, Alice needs to generate a (*public, private*)-key pair, which can be done as follows:[1]

```
ssh-keygen -f a
```

This will generate two keys: a private key contained in the file a and a corresponding public key in the file a.pub. The file a will be stored in a special directory (namely in .ssh in Alice's home directory). The file a.pub will have to be transferred to computer B, which can be done as follows:

---

[1]We are deliberately taking an extremely simple example that works in practice yet is not very sophisticated.

```
ssh-copy-id -i a bob@B
```

We assume that B is the actual computer name that can be used when Alice would normally log in to B as user bob. It is important to note that Alice is assumed to know the password of Bob at B. The ssh-copy-id command will ask for Bob's password at B before completing the transfer. If successful, the file a.pub will be appended to a special file in the .ssh directory in the home directory of user bob at B. From that moment on, Alice can simply log in to B through the command

```
ssh bob@B
```

where she will no longer be asked for a password.

   This simple example illustrates two important issues. First, security keys are simply generated through programs such as ssh-keygen and stored in files that can be distributed as any other file (or should be kept secret and properly protected against unauthorized access). Second, we can easily distribute keys *provided we have the authorization to do so*. That authorization can come from knowing a password, but there are other means as well, as we discuss shortly. Interestingly, in lack of authorization (and thus authentication), we would need to rely on the receiving party to *trust* the claimed ownership of the keys. We return to trust below.

   Let us move on to a more sophisticated example and consider how session keys can be established. As it name suggests, a **session key** is a *temporary* shared secret key that is used during a single communication session between two parties. A session typically consists of a series of message exchanges. When the session ends, the session key is discarded and never used again. As we shall also explain later, an important reason for using session keys is that one should use long-lasting keys, be they shared, public, or private as little as possible: the more data that is used for encrypting or decrypting data, the easier it becomes to discover the keys used. Two ways immediately come to mind, by which Alice and Bob can agree on establishing a session key. In a symmetric cryptosystem and assuming that Alice and Bob already have a long-lasting shared secret key $K_{A,B}$, Alice could decide to generate a session key sk and send it to Bob as the message

$$\text{Alice: } send \text{ m} = K_{A,B}(\text{sk}).$$

Likewise, in an asymmetric cryptosystem, Alice could encrypt the key with Bob's public key:

$$\text{Alice: } send \text{ m} = PK_B(\text{sk}).$$

After that, sk can be used for encrypting and decrypting messages for as long as the session lasts.

   Both methods require that the communicating parties already have the means available to send and receive encrypted messages. In other words, some form of key establishment and distribution must have taken place before.

An elegant scheme that is widely applied for establishing a shared key across an insecure channel is the **Diffie-Hellman key exchange** [Diffie and Hellman, 1976]. The protocol works as follows. Suppose that Alice and Bob want to establish a shared secret key. The first requirement is that they agree on two large numbers, p and g that are subject to a number of mathematical properties (which we do not discuss here). Both p and g can be made public; there is no need to hide them from outsiders. Alice picks a large random number, say x, which she keeps secret. Likewise, Bob picks his own secret large number, say y. At this point, there is enough information to construct a shared secret key, as shown in Figure 9.5.

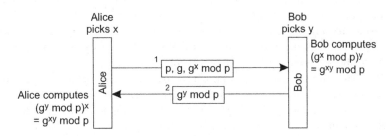

Figure 9.5: The principle of Diffie-Hellman key exchange.

Alice starts by sending g^x mod p to Bob, along with p and g. It is important to note that this information can be sent as plaintext, as it is virtually impossible to compute x given g^x mod p. When Bob receives the message, he subsequently calculates $(g^x$ mod $p)^y$ which is mathematically equal to g^{xy} mod p. In addition, he sends g^y mod p to Alice, who can then compute $(g^y$ mod $p)^x = g^{xy}$ mod p. Consequently, both Alice and Bob, and only those two, will now have the shared secret key g^{xy} mod p. Note that neither of them needed to make their private number (x and y, respectively), known to the other. Diffie-Hellman can also be viewed as a public-key cryptosystem. In the case of Alice, x is her private key, whereas g^x mod p is her public key.

In practice, Alice will not send p and g to Bob, but first negotiate which so-called **Diffie-Hellman group** they will use. In essence, the choice of group defines p and g, but also exactly which cryptographic algorithm to use. In our example, we have used g^x mod p, yet an alternative is to use a so-called elliptic curve.

It is also relevant to note that in practice, Alice and Bob will regularly change their respective private keys. In particular, new values for x and y may be chosen for each new communication session between Alice and Bob, in which case we speak of **ephemeral Diffie-Hellman key exchange**. As we shall see, the Diffie-Hellman key exchange has shown to be a powerful security mechanism throughout many practical situations. In the following note, we discuss another example of its application.

Note 9.2 (Advanced: Computing while keeping data private)
In many distributed systems, we see that security comes almost as an afterthought: designers focus on providing functionality to later adjust the system to meet specific security requirements. For long, it has been thought that functionality may actually suffer from imposing security (or privacy) demands, yet it is unclear to what extent there is actually a tradeoff to consider [Rowe et al., 2012]. Let us look at an increasingly popular technique that makes use of Diffie-Hellman key exchange.

As also mentioned in our discussion on privacy, an important challenge that many distributed systems will need to face is to deal with enormous amounts of data while preserving privacy. A particular case is when private data is essential to compute important statistics. A simple example is computing who has the highest salary among a number of people without anyone having to reveal their salary. Along the same lines, we may wish to compute the number of votes cast for a specific candidate without revealing who voted for whom.

What we are dealing with is known as **(secure) multiparty computations** (**MPC**). For a long time, it has been a field of cryptography that was difficult to put into practice for its low performance, but the last decade has shown impressively better implementations that make MPC a practical tool for secure distributed computations. At the same time, one may need to devise application-specific solutions for the simple reason that there are too many parties to make general tools practically feasible. We will discuss an example in which resource constraints demand an alternative solution.

It is beyond the scope of this chapter to go into any significant depth concerning MPC; the interested reader is referred to Evans et al. [2018] for a good introduction. Let us first consider an important building block for MPC, namely **oblivious transfer**. In this case, we assume Alice has n secret messages $m_1, \ldots, m_n$, while Bob is interested (and allowed) to know only one of those messages. Which specific message he wants to know should be kept secret to Alice, while at the same time all other messages should be kept secret to Bob. Assume Bob wishes to know the ith message. In that case, he generates a number Q that Alice, in turn, uses to generate a total of n different keys $PK_1, \ldots, PK_n$ to encrypt each message:

$$m_i^* = PK_i(m_i)$$

Bob, meanwhile, uses Q to generate a decryption key SK_i that matches *only* PK_i. Clearly, when Bob receives the set of encrypted messages $m_1^*, \ldots, m_n^*$ there will be only a single message that he can decrypt, namely m_i^*. Using SK_i any attempt to decrypt m_j^* (with $i \neq j$) will fail.

An important assumption for this scheme to work, is that having only Q, Bob cannot successfully generate any decryption key SK_j for PK_j. For the case that $n = 2$, there is an elegant, simple protocol that achieves this, based on a Diffie-Hellman key exchange [Chou and Orlandi, 2015]. The protocol is shown in Figure 9.6 (note that all computations are assumed to take place in $\mathbb{Z}_p$, that is, modulo p).

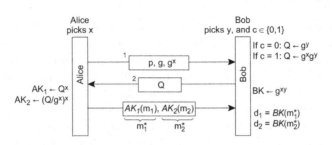

Figure 9.6: A simple 1-out-of-2 oblivious transfer.

In the protocol, besides having his own private key y, Bob also has a choice for an additional binary parameter, denoted here as c. The value of c determines what Bob will do in response to the initial message from Alice. Assume first that $c = 0$, in which case Bob will choose $Q = g^y$. This is, actually, the regular Diffie-Hellman key exchange: Bob computes $BK = g^{xy}$, while Alice also computes $AK_1 = g^{xy}$, after which she encrypts m_1 using the now shared secret key $g^{xy} = BK$. Alice also computes $AK_2 = g^{xy-x^2}$, yet using BK is useless. Moreover, because Bob does not have x, computing g^{xy-x^2} is computationally infeasible.

Now assume that $c = 1$, so that Bob sets $Q = g^{x+y}$. Alice computes $AK_1 = g^{x^2+xy}$ and $AK_2 = (g^x g^y / g^x)^x = g^{xy}$. In other words, we now see that $BK = AK_2$ allowing Bob to successfully decrypt *only* message m_2^*. He will never get to know m_1^*, while Alice in this setup will also never know which message Bob was able to decrypt.

To illustrate how oblivious transfer is used in MPC, suppose we have two parties P_1 and P_2 who need to compute a function $F(a, b)$ on two input values: a secret a known only to P_1 and a secret b known only to P_2. For simplicity, let us also assume that $a \in \mathbf{X}$ and $b \in \mathbf{Y}$ and that both $\mathbf{X}$ and $\mathbf{Y}$ are finite, i.e., each contains only a finite number of elements. In that case, we can construct a matrix F of size $|\mathbf{X}| \cdot |\mathbf{Y}|$ with $\mathbf{F}[i, j] = F(x_i, y_j)$ for each pair $(x_i, y_j) \in \mathbf{X} \times \mathbf{Y}$. The problem we want to solve is to let both P_1 and P_2 compute $F(a, b)$ yet the other should not be able to discover b or a, respectively.

To this end, P_1 generates $|\mathbf{X}| \cdot |\mathbf{Y}|$ unique key pairs (K_i, K_j) and encrypts each entry of the table $\mathbf{F}$, leading to a table $\mathbf{F}^*[i, j] = K_i(K_j(F(x_i, x_j)))$. Assume that a corresponds to the ith element of $\mathbf{X}$ (i.e., $a = x_i$). P_1 then sends $\mathbf{F}^*$ and K_i to P_2, but not before having permuted all its elements. In addition, it sends Q using a 1-out-of-$|Y|$ oblivious transfer. Assume that $b = y_j$. Using Q, P_2 can construct the key K_j, and only the key K_j that allows it to decrypt $\mathbf{F}^*[i, j]$, corresponding to $F(a, b)$. All other entries will remain a secret to P_2, while at the same time, P_1 will not know about $b = y_j$.

Note that permuting the table before sending it to P_2 is essential, for otherwise a and b could be looked up. Also, we assume that P_2 can recognize that it decrypted the correct entry, for how would it otherwise know that the decrypted value makes sense? This recognition can be done by adding some extra information, such as a specific bit string that pops up after successful decryption.

Key distribution

One of the more difficult parts in key management is the actual distribution of initial keys. In a symmetric cryptosystem, the initial shared secret key must be communicated along a **secure channel**: a communication channel that, in principle, provides mutual authentication of the two communicating parties, as well as confidentiality for the messages that are exchanged, as shown in Figure 9.7. We will return to secure channels later in this chapter. If there are no keys available to Alice and Bob to set up such a secure channel, it is necessary to distribute the key out-of-band. In other words, Alice and Bob will have to get in touch with each other using some other communication channel.

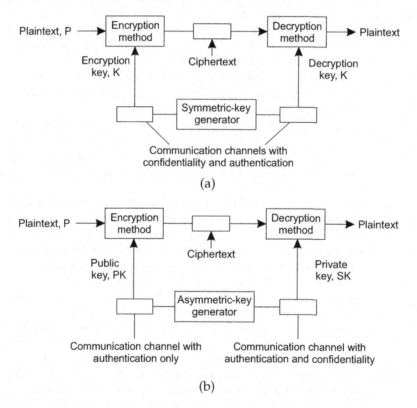

Figure 9.7: (a) Secret-key distribution. (b) Public-key distribution (see also [Menezes et al., 1996]).

In the case of a public-key cryptosystem, we need to distribute the public key in such a way that the receivers can be sure that the key is indeed paired to a claimed private key. In other words, as shown in Figure 9.7, although the public key itself may be sent as plaintext, it is necessary that the channel through which it is sent can provide authentication. The private key, of course, needs to be sent across a secure channel, providing authentication as well as confidentiality.

When it comes to key distribution, the authenticated distribution of public keys is perhaps the most interesting. In practice, public-key distribution takes place by **public-key certificates**. Such a certificate consists of a public key together with a string identifying the entity to which that key is associated. The entity could be a user, but also a host or some special device. The public key and identifier have together been signed by a **certification authority**, and this signature has been placed on the certificate as well. (The identity of the certification authority is naturally part of the certificate.) Signing takes place by a private key SK_{CA} that belongs to the certification authority. The corresponding public key PK_{CA} is assumed to be well known. For example, the public keys of various certification authorities are built into most Web browsers and shipped with the binaries.

Using a public-key certificate works as follows. Assume that a client wishes to ascertain that the public key found in the certificate, indeed belongs to the identified entity. It then uses the public key of the associated certification authority to verify the certificate's signature. If the signature on the certificate matches the *(public key, identifier)*-pair, the client accepts that the public key indeed belongs to the identified entity.

It is important to note that by accepting the certificate as being in order, the client actually trusts that the certificate has not been forged. In particular, the client must assume that the public key PK_{CA} indeed belongs to the associated certification authority. If in doubt, it should be possible to verify the validity of PK_{CA} through another certificate coming from a different, possibly more trusted certification authority.

Note 9.3 (More information: Lifetime of certificates)

An important issue concerning certificates is their longevity. First, let us consider the situation in which a certification authority hands out lifelong certificates. Essentially, what the certificate then states is that the public key will always be valid for the entity identified by the certificate. Clearly, such a statement is not what we want. If the private key of the identified entity is ever compromised, no unsuspecting client should ever be able to use the public key (let alone malicious clients). In that case, we need a mechanism to **revoke** the certificate by making it publicly known that the certificate is no longer valid.

There are several ways to revoke a certificate. One common approach is with a **certificate revocation list (CRL)** published regularly by the certification authority. Whenever a client checks a certificate, it will have to check the CRL to see whether the certificate has been revoked or not. This means that the client will at least have to contact the certification authority each time a new CRL is published. Note that if a CRL is published daily, it also takes a day to revoke a certificate. Meanwhile, a compromised certificate can be falsely used until it is published on the next CRL. Consequently, the time between publishing CRLs cannot be too long.

An alternative approach is to restrict the lifetime of each certificate. The validity of a certificate automatically expires after some time. If, for whatever reason, the certificate should be revoked before it expires, the certification authority can still publish it on a CRL. However, this approach will still force clients to check the latest CRL whenever verifying a certificate.

A final extreme case is to reduce the lifetime of a certificate to nearly zero. In effect, this means that certificates are no longer used; instead, a client will always have to contact the certification authority to check the validity of a public key. As a consequence, the certification authority must be continuously online and capable of handling potentially continuous streams of validity checks.

In practice, certificates are handed out with restricted lifetimes, after which they need to be renewed. Depending on the application, renewal may require manual intervention, akin to renewing automatically expired passwords. In other cases, such as identifying Web servers, renewal can also be done completely automatically as essentially a check of the existence of a specific file at a specific location suffices. The latter happens with the Let's Encrypt system for TLS certificates.

Using certification authorities is one way of ensuring that a public key is valid in the sense of claimed ownership. However, it can easily come with administrative hassle. Also, making use of certification authorities is no guarantee that certificates are correct: there have been cases in which the ownership of a public key was systematically not properly established, and also certification authorities are known to have been subject to successful attacks.

As an alternative, systems have been developed relying on developing a **web of trust**. A well-known example comes from its initiator, Phil Zimmerman, the developer of the **Pretty Good Privacy (PGP)** system, which has been around ever since the 1990s [Garfinkel, 1995]. The key idea, when developing a web of trust, is that groups of people get to together and exchange their public keys. At that point, one establishes the true ownership of a public key. In particular, Alice may digitally sign Bob's public key PK_{bob}, effectively endorsing that the public key belongs to Bob. Other people will also endorse Bob's public key (and that of many others during the meeting). The result is that anyone who trusts the ownership of Alice's public key, that is, trusts the signature attached to Bob's public key, has no reason not to believe that PK_{bob} is indeed owned by Bob.

In a more sophisticated setup, one can also attach a weight to Alice's signature. For example, if Chuck believes Alice to be somewhat sloppy when it comes to signing other people's public key, he may decide to wait until he has seen at least $k > 1$ people in his web of trust who have signed Bob's public key as well before deciding that PK_{bob} is genuinely owned by Bob. An important question is whether Chuck, in turn, could ever endorse Bob's key without ever having truly established his identity. With automatic endorsements, we open the floor to digital attacks of all sorts, including ones in which an attacker behaves well for a long time to strike hard only after considerable trust has been established. For this reason, the big question with a web of trust is how quickly, and with which confidence, can we actually disseminate trustworthy certificates? It has been a topic of much research, yet after all these years there is no consensus to what extent webs of trust can operate on a large scale. In this sense, Ulrich et al. [2011] draw interesting conclusions from a practical analysis of that web: its core is formed by mutually connected (and endorsed) relationships, yet is relatively small. In particular, many users are connected to each other and that core through relatively few and often long paths. Such paths make it much harder to establish trust in a robust way.

9.3 Authentication

We continue our discussion by looking at authentication. After discussing some of the basics, we concentrate on various authentication protocols, the use of an authentication service, and how various aspects come together when setting up a secure communication channel.

9.3.1 Introduction to authentication

As we mentioned before, **authentication** is all about verifying the claimed identity of a person, a software component, a device, and so on. In the following, we shall use the generic term "client" for any of these types of entities. Following Stallings [2017], we distinguish four means of authentication:

1. Authentication based on what a client **knows**, such as a password or a personal identification number.

2. Authentication based on what a client **has**, such as an ID card, cell phone, or software token.

3. Authentication based on what a client **is**, i.e., static biometrics such as a fingerprint or facial characteristics.

4. Authentication based on what a client **does**, i.e., dynamic biometrics such as voice patterns or typing patterns.

In the case of **single-factor authentication**, only one of the four means of authentication is used. In practice, this means that clients are asked to enter something they know, such as a password. However, we have also come across single-factor authentication based on what a client has, namely a software token in the case of automatically logging in within the SSH framework using a *(private,public)*-key pair. With modern cell phones, it is by now also common to make use of what a client is, typically, face recognition or fingerprints. Single-factor authentication based on dynamic biometrics is less common.

It is safe to say that humans are generally not good at all when it comes to managing passwords (see, for example, a study by Ur et al. [2016] that shows that users are generally not even aware of how bad their passwords are). In this light, we have been seeing increasingly more **multi-factor authentication** schemes being used. A common one is to use a cell phone that a user has registered with a service. When logging into a system using a password or PIN, the user is asked to acknowledge the login through that cell phone, or even provide additional information like a number sent by the service to that phone, a PIN code, or have a fingerprint scanned and verified (in which case we sometimes speak of additional **electronic authentication**).

An important observation is that, in general, authentication takes place only once: when a client wants access to a service. However, this one-time authentication for the duration of a session is often not good enough to guarantee that the service is dealing with the client it originally authenticated. The simplest example is when someone is helping out, but for a different account. Alice logs in, and grants Bob access from the same computer. Of course, this may be fine if Alice trusts Bob (and the service trusts Alice enough to allow for these type of take-overs to happen), but the situation becomes different if Alice is forced by Bob to let him into the system. In such cases, **continuous authentication** is needed: the client is not only authenticated when requesting access at the beginning of a session, but also during the entire session.

Continuous authentication is not new, yet with the availability of powerful internet-of-things devices, new scenarios have been considered [Ayeswarya and Norman, 2019; Gonzalez-Manzano et al., 2019]. For example, if a user can be continuously authenticated, it becomes possible to monitor different situations, such as safely driving a vehicle, or ensuring that a room is optimized for a specific person. When ensuring that logins are not handed off to unauthorized people, as just described, it may help to see if a personalized device is still close to the computer accessing the service. Jakubeit et al. [2022] describe a situation in which the location of a user is fingerprinted based on Wi-Fi signals to see whether the client is at a known location from which it was previously authenticated. If not, a second authentication factor may be explicitly required from the client.

9.3.2 Authentication protocols

Before going into the details of various authentication protocols, it is worthwhile noting that authentication and message integrity cannot do without each other. Consider, for example, a distributed system that supports authentication of two communicating parties, but does not provide mechanisms to ensure message integrity. In such a system, Bob may know for sure that Alice is the sender of a message m. However, if Bob cannot be given guarantees that m has not been modified during transmission, what use is it to him to know that Alice sent (the original version of) m?

Likewise, suppose that only message integrity is supported, but no mechanisms exist for authentication. When Bob receives a message stating that he has just won $1,000,000 in the lottery, how happy can he be if he cannot verify that the message was sent by the organizers of that lottery?

Consequently, authentication and message integrity should go together. In many protocols, the combination works roughly as follows. Again, assume that Alice and Bob want to communicate, and that Alice takes the initiative in setting up a channel. Alice starts by sending a message to Bob, or otherwise to a trusted third party, who will help set up the channel. Once the channel has been set up, Alice knows for sure that she is talking to Bob, and Bob knows for sure he is talking to Alice, they can exchange messages.

To subsequently ensure integrity of the data messages that are exchanged after authentication has taken place, it is common practice to use secret-key cryptography through session keys. As we explained, a **session key** is a shared (secret) key that is used to encrypt messages for integrity and possibly also confidentiality. Such a key is generally used only for as long as the channel exists. When the channel is closed, its associated session key is destroyed. We return to session keys below.

Authentication based on a shared secret key

Let us start by taking a look at an authentication protocol based on a secret key that is already shared between Alice and Bob. How the two actually managed to obtain a shared key securely is not essential for now. In the description of the protocol, Alice and Bob are abbreviated by A and B, respectively, and their shared key is denoted as $K_{A,B}$. The protocol takes a common approach whereby one party challenges the other to a response that can be correct only if the other knows the shared secret key. Such solutions are also known as **challenge-response protocols**.

In the case of authentication based on a shared secret key, the protocol proceeds as shown in Figure 9.8. First, Alice sends her identity to Bob (message 1), indicating that she wants to set up a communication channel between the two. Bob subsequently sends a **challenge** R_B to Alice, shown as message 2. Such a challenge could take the form of a random number. Alice is required to encrypt the challenge with the secret key $K_{A,B}$ that she shares with Bob, and return the encrypted challenge to Bob. This response is shown as message 3 in Figure 9.8 containing $K_{A,B}(R_B)$.

When Bob receives the response $K_{A,B}(R_B)$ to his challenge R_B, he can decrypt the message using the shared key again to see if it contains R_B. If so, he then knows that Alice is on the other side, for who else could have encrypted R_B with $K_{A,B}$ in the first place? In other words, Bob has now

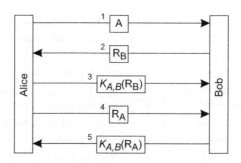

Figure 9.8: Authentication based on a shared secret key.

verified that he is indeed talking to Alice. However, note that Alice has not yet verified that it is indeed Bob on the other side of the channel. Therefore, she sends a challenge R_A (message 4), which Bob responds to by returning $K_{A,B}(R_A)$, shown as message 5. When Alice decrypts it with $K_{A,B}$ and sees her R_A, she knows she is talking to Bob.

Note 9.4 (Advanced: On the design of security protocols)

One of the difficult issues in security is designing protocols that actually work. To illustrate how easily things can go wrong, consider an "optimization" of the authentication protocol in which the number of messages has been reduced from five to three, as shown in Figure 9.9. The basic idea is that if Alice eventually wants to challenge Bob anyway, she might as well send a challenge along with her identity when setting up the channel. Likewise, Bob returns his response to that challenge, along with his own challenge, in a single message.

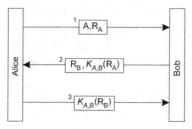

Figure 9.9: Authentication based on a shared secret key, but using three instead of five messages.

Unfortunately, this protocol no longer works. It can easily be defeated by what is known as a **reflection attack**. To explain how such an attack works, consider an intruder called Chuck, whom we denote as C in our protocols. Chuck's goal is to set up a channel with Bob so that Bob believes he is talking to Alice. Chuck can establish this if he responds correctly to a challenge sent by Bob, for instance, by returning the encrypted version of a number that Bob sent. Without knowledge

---

of $K_{A,B}$, only Bob can do such an encryption, and this is precisely what Chuck tricks Bob into doing.

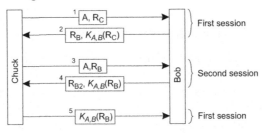

Figure 9.10: The reflection attack.

The attack is illustrated in Figure 9.10 Chuck starts out by sending a message containing Alice's identity A, along with a challenge R_C. Bob returns his challenge R_B and the response $K_{A,B}(R_C)$ in a single message. At that point, Chuck would need to prove he knows the secret key by returning $K_{A,B}(R_B)$ to Bob. Unfortunately, he does not have $K_{A,B}$. Instead, what he does is attempt to set up a second channel to let Bob do the encryption for him.

Therefore, Chuck sends A and R_B in a single message as before, but now pretends that he wants a second channel. This is shown as message 3 in Figure 9.10 Bob, not recognizing that he, himself, had used R_B before as a challenge, responds with $K_{A,B}(R_B)$ and another challenge R_{B2}, shown as message 4. At that point, Chuck has $K_{A,B}(R_B)$ and finishes setting up the first session by returning message 5 containing the response $K_{A,B}(R_B)$, which was originally requested from the challenge sent in message 2.

As explained by Kaufman et al. [2003], one of the mistakes made during the adaptation of the original protocol was that the two parties in the new version of the protocol were using the same challenge in two different runs of the protocol. A better design is to always use different challenges for the initiator and for the responder. For example, if Alice always uses an odd number and Bob an even number, Bob would have recognized that something fishy was going on when receiving R_B in message 3 in Figure 9.10. (Unfortunately, this solution is subject to other attacks, notably the one known as the "man-in-the-middle-attack," which is explained in [Ferguson et al., 2010].) In general, letting the two parties setting up a secure channel doing a number of things identically is not a good idea.

Another principle that is violated in the adapted protocol is that Bob gave away valuable information in the form of the response $K_{A,B}(R_C)$ without knowing for sure to whom he was giving it. This principle was not violated in the original protocol, in which Alice first needed to prove her identity, after which Bob was willing to pass her encrypted information.

There are many principles that developers of cryptographic protocols have gradually come to learn over the years. One important lesson is that designing security protocols that do what they are supposed to do is often much harder than it looks. Also, tweaking an existing protocol to improve its performance, can easily affect its correctness. More on design principles for protocols can be found in [Abadi and Needham, 1996] with a more recent analysis in [Fiebig et al., 2018].

Authentication using a key distribution center

One of the problems with using a shared secret key for authentication is scalability. If a distributed system contains N hosts, and each host is required to share a secret key with each of the other $N - 1$ hosts, the system as a whole needs to manage $N(N - 1)/2$ keys, and each host has to manage $N - 1$ keys. For large N, this will lead to problems. An alternative is to use a centralized approach by a **key distribution center** (**KDC**). This KDC shares a secret key with each of the hosts, but no pair of hosts is required to have a shared secret key as well. In other words, using a KDC requires that we manage N keys instead of $N(N - 1)/2$, which is clearly an improvement.

   If Alice wants to set up a secure channel with Bob, she can do so through a (trusted) KDC. The whole idea is that the KDC hands out a key to both Alice and Bob that they can use for communication, shown in Figure 9.11.

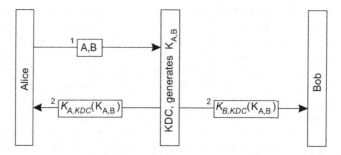

Figure 9.11: The principle of using a Key Distribution Center (KDC).

   Alice first sends a message to the KDC, telling it that she wants to talk to Bob. The KDC returns a message containing a shared secret key $K_{A,B}$ that she can use. The message is encrypted with the secret key $K_{A,KDC}$ that Alice shares with the KDC. In addition, the KDC sends $K_{A,B}$ also to Bob, but now encrypted with the secret key $K_{B,KDC}$ it shares with Bob.

   The main drawback of this approach is that Alice may want to start setting up a secure channel with Bob even before Bob had received the shared key from the KDC. In addition, the KDC is required to get Bob into the loop by passing him the key. These problems can be circumvented if the KDC just passes $K_{B,KDC}(K_{A,B})$ back to Alice, and lets her take care of connecting to Bob. This leads to the protocol shown in Figure 9.12. The message $K_{B,KDC}(K_{A,B})$ is also known as a **ticket**. It is Alice's job to pass this ticket to Bob. Note that Bob is still the only one who can make sensible use of the ticket, as he is the only one besides the KDC who knows how to decrypt the information it contains.

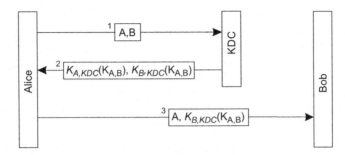

Figure 9.12: Using a ticket and letting Alice set up a connection to Bob.

Note 9.5 (Advanced: The Needham-Schroeder protocol)
The protocol shown in Figure 9.12 is actually a variant of a well-known example of an authentication protocol using a KDC, known as the **Needham-Schroeder authentication protocol**, named after its inventors [Needham and Schroeder, 1978]. The Needham-Schroeder protocol, shown in Figure 9.13 is a so-called **multiway challenge-response protocol** and works as follows.

When Alice wants to set up a secure channel with Bob, she sends a request to the KDC containing a challenge R_A, along with her identity A and, of course, that of Bob. The KDC responds by giving her the ticket $K_{B,KDC}(K_{A,B})$, along with the secret key $K_{A,B}$ that she can subsequently share with Bob.

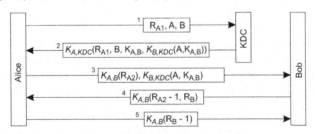

Figure 9.13: The Needham-Schroeder authentication protocol.

The challenge R_{A1} that Alice sends to the KDC along with her request to set up a channel to Bob is also known as a nonce. A **nonce** is a random number that is used only once, such as one chosen from a very large set. The main purpose of a nonce is to uniquely relate two messages to each other, in this case message 1 and message 2. In particular, by including R_{A1} again in message 2, Alice will know for sure that message 2 is sent as a response to message 1, and that it is not, for example, a replay of an older message.

To understand the problem at hand, assume that we did not use nonces, and that Chuck has stolen one of Bob's old keys, say $K_{B,KDC}^{old}$. In addition, Chuck has intercepted an old response $K_{A,KDC}(B, K_{A,B}, K_{B,KDC}^{old}(A, K_{A,B}))$ that the KDC had returned to a previous request from Alice to talk to Bob. Meanwhile, Bob will have negotiated a new shared secret key with the KDC. However, Chuck patiently waits until Alice again requests to set up a secure channel with Bob. At that point, he replays the old response, and fools Alice into making her believe she is talking to Bob because he can decrypt the ticket and prove he knows the shared secret key $K_{A,B}$. Clearly this is unacceptable and must be defended against. By including a nonce, such an attack is impossible because replaying an older message (having a different nonce) will immediately be discovered.

Message 2 also contains B, the identity of Bob. By including B, the KDC protects Alice against the following attack. Suppose that B was left out of message 2. In that case, Chuck could modify message 1 by replacing the identity of Bob with his own identity, say C. The KDC would then think Alice wants to set up a secure channel to Chuck, and responds accordingly. As soon as Alice intends to contact Bob, Chuck intercepts the message and fools Alice into believing she is talking to Bob. By copying the identity of the other party from message 1 to message 2, Alice will immediately detect that her request had been modified.

After the KDC has passed the ticket to Alice, the secure channel between Alice and Bob can be set up. Alice starts with sending message 3, which contains the ticket to Bob, and a challenge R_{A2} encrypted with the shared key $K_{A,B}$ that the KDC had just generated. Bob then decrypts the ticket to find the shared key, and returns a response $R_{A2} - 1$ along with a challenge R_B for Alice.

The following remark regarding message 4 is in order. In general, by returning $R_{A2} - 1$ and not just R_{A2}, Bob not only proves he knows the shared secret key, but also that he has actually decrypted the challenge. Again, this ties message 4 to message 3 in the same way that the nonce R_A tied message 2 to message 1. The protocol is thus more protected against replays. However, in this special case, it would have been sufficient to just return $K_{A,B}(R_{A2}, R_B)$, for the simple reason that this message has not yet been used anywhere in the protocol before. $K_{A,B}(R_{A2}, R_B)$ already proves that Bob has been capable of decrypting the challenge sent in message 3. Message 4 as shown in Figure 9.13 is due to historical reasons.

The Needham-Schroeder protocol as presented here still has the weak point that if Chuck ever got a hold of an old key $K_{A,B}^{old}$, he could replay message 3 and get Bob to set up a channel. Bob will then believe he is talking to Alice, while, in fact, Chuck is at the other end. In this case, we need to relate message 3 to message 1, that is, make the key dependent on the initial request from Alice to set up a channel with Bob. The solution is shown in Figure 9.14.

The trick is to incorporate a nonce in the request sent by Alice to the KDC. However, the nonce has to come from Bob: this assures Bob that whoever wants to set up a secure channel with him, will have gotten the appropriate information from the KDC. Therefore, Alice first requests Bob to send her a nonce R_{B1}, encrypted with the key shared between Bob and the KDC. Alice incorporates this nonce in her request to the KDC, which will then subsequently decrypt it and put the result in the generated ticket. In this way, Bob will know for sure that the session key is tied to the original request from Alice to talk to Bob.

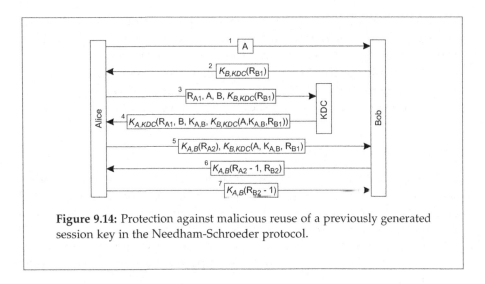

Figure 9.14: Protection against malicious reuse of a previously generated session key in the Needham-Schroeder protocol.

Authentication using public-key cryptography

Let us now look at authentication with a public-key cryptosystem that does not require a KDC. Again, consider the situation that Alice wants to set up a secure channel to Bob, and that both are in the possession of each other's public key. A typical authentication protocol based on public-key cryptography is shown in Figure 9.15 which we explain next.

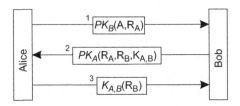

Figure 9.15: Mutual authentication in a public-key cryptosystem.

Alice starts with sending a **challenge** R_A to Bob encrypted with his public key PK_B. It is Bob's job to decrypt the message and return the challenge to Alice. Because Bob is the only person that can decrypt the message (using the private key that is associated with the public key Alice used), Alice will know that she is talking to Bob. Note again that it is important that Alice is guaranteed to be using Bob's public key, and not the public key of someone impersonating Bob.

When Bob receives Alice's request to set up a channel, he returns the decrypted challenge, along with his own challenge R_B to authenticate Alice. In addition, he generates a **session key** $K_{A,B}$ that can be used for further communication. Bob's response to Alice's challenge, his own challenge, and the session key are put into a message encrypted with the public key PK_A belonging to Alice, shown as message 2 in Figure 9.15. Only Alice will be capable of decrypting this message using her private key SK_A.

Alice, finally, returns her response to Bob's challenge using the session key $K_{A,B}$ generated by Bob. In that way, she will have proven that she could decrypt message 2, and thus that she is actually Alice to whom Bob is talking.

The need for session keys

During the establishment of a secure channel, after the authentication phase has completed, the communicating parties generally use a unique shared session key for confidentiality. The session key is safely discarded when the channel is no longer used. An alternative would have been to use the same keys for confidentiality as those that are used for setting up the secure channel. However, there are a number of important benefits to using session keys [Kaufman et al., 2003].

First, when a key is used often, it becomes easier to reveal it. In a sense, cryptographic keys are subject to "wear and tear" just like ordinary keys. The basic idea is that if an intruder can intercept a lot of data that has been encrypted using the same key, it becomes possible to mount attacks to find certain characteristics of the keys used, and possibly reveal the plaintext or the key itself. For this reason, it is much safer to use the authentication keys as little as possible. In addition, such keys are often exchanged using some relatively time-expensive out-of-band mechanism, such as regular mail or telephone. Exchanging keys that way should be kept to a minimum.

Another important reason for generating a unique key for each secure channel is to ensure protection against replay attacks, as we have come across previously a number of times. By using a unique session key each time a secure channel is set up, the communicating parties are at least protected against replaying an entire session. To protect replaying individual messages from a previous session, additional measures are generally needed, such as including timestamps or sequence numbers as part of the message content.

Suppose that message integrity and confidentiality were achieved by using the same key used for session establishment. In that case, whenever the key is compromised, an intruder may be able to decrypt messages transferred during an old conversation, clearly not a desirable feature. Instead, it is much safer to use per-session keys because if such a key is compromised, at worst, only a single session is affected. Messages sent during other sessions stay confidential.

Related to this last point is that Alice may want to exchange some confidential data with Bob, but she does not trust him so much that she would provide him information in the form of data that have been encrypted with long-lasting keys. She may want to reserve such keys for highly confidential messages that she exchanges with parties she really trusts. In such cases, using a relatively cheap session key to talk to Bob is sufficient.

By and large, authentication keys are often established in such a way that replacing them is relatively expensive. Therefore, the combination of such long-lasting keys with the much cheaper and more temporary session keys is often a good choice for implementing secure channels for exchanging data.

Example of an authentication service: Kerberos

It should be clear by now that incorporating security into distributed systems is not trivial. Problems are caused by the fact that the entire system must be secure; if some part is insecure, the whole system may be compromised. To assist the construction of distributed systems that can enforce a myriad of security policies, a number of supporting systems have been developed that can be used as a basis for further development. An important system that is widely used is **Kerberos** [Steiner et al., 1988; Kohl et al., 1994]

Kerberos was developed at M.I.T. and is based on the **Needham-Schroeder authentication protocol**. A detailed description of the Kerberos system can be found in [Neuman et al., 2005] whereas practical information on running Kerberos is described by Garman [2003]. A publicly available implementation of Kerberos, known as Shishi, is described in [Josefsson, 2015].

Kerberos can be viewed as a security system that assists clients in setting up a secure channel with any server that is part of a distributed system. Security is based on shared secret keys. There are two different components. The **authentication server** (**AS**) is responsible for handling a login request from a user. The AS authenticates a user and provides a key that can be used to set up secure channels with servers. Setting up secure channels is handled by a **ticket-granting service** (**TGS**). The TGS hands out special messages, known as **tickets**, that are used to convince a server that the client is really who it claims to be.

Let us take a look at how Alice logs onto a distributed system that uses Kerberos and how she can set up a secure channel with server Bob. We assume that Alice has previously been registered at the distributed system, so that there already exists a shared secret key $K_{A,AS}$ between her and the authentication server. That key is assumed to be derived from Alice's password. For example, assuming a character-string password, we can take a cryptographic hash of that password as the secret key. Of course, we do need to ensure that the secret key is protected against unauthorized access. For Alice to log onto the system, she can use any workstation available. The workstation sends her name in plaintext to the AS, which returns a session key $K_{A,TGS}$ and a ticket that she will need to hand over to the TGS.

The ticket that is returned by the AS contains the identity of Alice, along with a generated secret key that Alice and the TGS can use to communicate with each other. The ticket itself will be handed over to the TGS by Alice.

Therefore, it is important that no one but the TGS can read it. For this reason, the ticket is encrypted with the secret key $K_{AS,TGS}$ shared between the AS and the TGS.

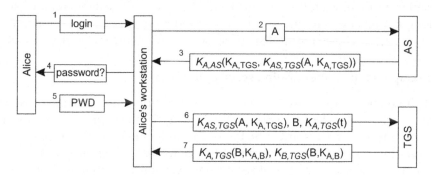

Figure 9.16: Authentication in Kerberos.

This part of the login procedure is shown as messages 1, 2, and 3 in Figure 9.16, respectively. Message 1 is not really a message, but corresponds to Alice typing in her login name at a workstation. Message 2 contains that name and is sent to the AS. Message 3 contains the session key $K_{A,TGS}$ and the ticket $K_{AS,TGS}(A, K_{A,TGS})$. To ensure privacy, message 3 is encrypted with the secret key $K_{A,AS}$ shared between Alice and the AS.

When the workstation receives the response from the AS, it prompts Alice for her password (shown as message 4), which it uses subsequently to generate the shared key $K_{A,AS}$. Note that this approach not only has the advantage that Alice's password is never sent as plaintext across the network, but also that the workstation does not even have to temporarily store it. Moreover, as soon as it has derived the shared key $K_{A,AS}$ from that password, the workstation will find the session key $K_{A,TGS}$, and can forget about Alice's password altogether (as well as the shared secret $K_{A,AS}$).

After this part of the authentication has taken place, Alice can consider herself logged into the system through the current workstation. The ticket received from the AS is stored temporarily (typically for 8–24 hours), and will be used for accessing remote services. Of course, if Alice leaves her workstation, she should destroy any cached tickets. If she wants to talk to Bob, she requests the TGS to generate a session key for Bob, shown as message 6 in Figure 9.16. The fact that Alice has the ticket $K_{AS,TGS}(A, K_{A,TGS})$ proves that she is Alice. The TGS responds with a session key $K_{A,B}$, again encapsulated in a ticket that Alice will later have to pass to Bob.

Message 6 also contains a timestamp, t, encrypted with the secret key shared between Alice and the TGS. This timestamp is used to prevent Chuck from maliciously replaying message 6 again, and trying to set up a channel to Bob. The TGS will verify the timestamp before returning a ticket to Alice. If it differs more than a few minutes from the current time, the request for a ticket is rejected.

This scheme establishes what is known as **single sign-on**. As long as Alice does not change workstations, there is no need for her to authenticate herself to any other server that is part of the distributed system. This feature is important when having to deal with many services that are spread across multiple machines. In principle, servers in a way have delegated client authentication to the AS and TGS, and will accept requests from any client that has a valid ticket. Of course, services such as remote login will require that the associated user has an account, but this is independent of authentication through Kerberos.

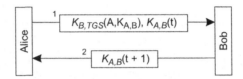

Figure 9.17: Setting up a secure channel in Kerberos.

Setting up a secure channel with Bob is now straightforward, and is shown in Figure 9.17. First, Alice sends to Bob a message containing the ticket she got from the TGS, along with an encrypted timestamp. When Bob decrypts the ticket, he notices that Alice is talking to him because only the TGS could have constructed the ticket. He also finds the secret key $K_{A,B}$, allowing him to verify the timestamp. At that point, Bob knows he is talking to Alice and not someone maliciously replaying message 1. By responding with $K_{A,B}(t+1)$, Bob proves to Alice that he is indeed Bob.

Example of a secure channel: HTTP over TLS

Let us now look at an often-used protocol suite for setting up a secure channel: the **Transport Layer Security** protocol, or simply **TLS**. The protocol suite comes in a number of flavors, originating from the **Secure Socket Layer** protocol that was designed in 1994. The most recent version is TLS 1.3, specified in [Rescorla et al., 2018]. TLS is generally best known for its use in securing the connection to a Web server when using HTTP, also known as **HTTPS**. In this case, HTTP is secured by setting up a secure channel between a client and the Web server using TLS in combination with TCP.

Understanding TLS can be quite difficult, mainly for two reasons. First, TLS 1.3 needs to be backward compatible with previous versions (at least the ones that have not been deprecated). Second, the two communicating parties need to go through a negotiation phase to decide precisely how they are actually going to use TLS. The latter starts with agreeing on the version, but also includes agreements on which cryptosystems (called cipher suites) to use. TLS 1.3 simplifies matters in comparison to its predecessors in that it limits the options. We are going to ignore all kinds of extra information that is sent during the negotiation phase and stick to the core of the protocol.

As mentioned, TLS 1.3 limits the choices for client and server when it comes to using cipher suites. Let us assume that a client wants to set up a secure channel based on ephemeral Diffie-Hellman key exchange, using one of the possible Diffie-Hellman groups, say G. For example, G could be ffdhe2048 which corresponds to $g = 2$ and p equal to

$$p = 2^{2048} - 2^{1984} + (\lfloor 2^{1918} * e \rfloor + 560316) * 2^{64} - 1$$

where e denotes the base of the natural logarithm (i.e., $e \approx 2.718281$).

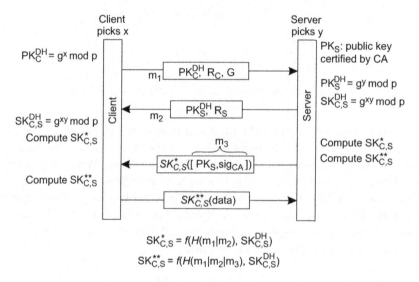

$$SK^{*}_{C,S} = f(H(m_1|m_2), SK^{DH}_{C,S})$$

$$SK^{**}_{C,S} = f(H(m_1|m_2|m_3), SK^{DH}_{C,S})$$

Figure 9.18: The principle of setting up a secure channel using TLS 1.3.

The client starts with choosing a private key x as explained when introducing Diffie-Hellman key exchange. By choice of G, the client computes a corresponding public key $PK^{DH}_C = g^x \bmod p$. The client continues by sending a client-hello message to the server. This message contains at least the public key PK^{DH}_C, a nonce R_C and G:

Client: sends client-hello $= [PK^{DH}_C, R_C, G]$

The server, assuming it accepts G, also chooses a private key y and generates its associated public key $PK^{DH}_S = g^y \bmod p$. It subsequently returns a server-hello message:

Server: responds server-hello $= [PK^{DH}_S, R_S]$

Note that at this point, the client has no guarantees that it is actually communicating with the intended server. The only thing the two have essentially communicated are generated public keys. These keys can be used to compute a shared secret key $SK_{C,S}^{DH} = g^{xy} \bmod p$. As a next step, the client and the server first each compute the following hash:

$$MAC = H([PK_C^{DH}, R_C, G, PK_S^{DH}, R_S])$$

where H is the SHA256 hashing function [Eastlake and Hansen, 2011]. In other words, MAC is the 256-bit hash obtained by concatenating the client-hello and server-hello messages. MAC and SK^{DH} are then used to generate the final shared secret session key $SK_{C,S}^* = f(MAC, SK_{C,S}^{DH})$ where f is a so-called **key-derivation function**. From this moment on, the communication between the client and the server is kept private, i.e., encrypted with the shared secret key $SK_{C,S}^*$. The server then continues with authenticating itself. To that end, we assume it can provide a certificate containing a public key PK_S signed by the certification authority CA. The server encrypts all its communication with the client using $SK_{C,S}^*$:

$$\text{Server } sends \text{ } SK_{C,S}^*([PK_S, sig_{CA}]) \text{ with } sig_{CA} = SK_{CA}(PK_S)$$

At this point, the client can authenticate the server. Applications running on top of TLS could, in principle, rely entirely on the use of the shared secret key $SK_{C,S}^*$ while keeping the communication private. Better is to generate keys that the application-level protocol can use, independent of what is being used by the TLS connection. To that end, both client and server each compute a shared secret key from the information exchanged so far:

$$AMAC = H([PK_C^{DH}, R_C, G, PK_S^{DH}, R_S, PK_S, sig_{CA}])$$

that is, essentially the concatenation of the messages client-hello and server-hello, along with the certificate and again hashed using $H = $ SHA256. The final application-level shared secret key is computed as $SK_{C,S}^{**} = f(AMAC, SK_{C,S}^*)$. A summary of what we have just discussed is shown in Figure 9.18.

9.4 Trust in distributed systems

Fundamental to authentication is that a process can prove to be who it claims to be. Once that proof has been given, the question arises how good that proof actually is. One can argue that this is where trust starts to play: does the receiver of the proof accept that proof to be sufficient to provide the process access to the system? Yet trust as facilitated or implemented in distributed systems extends beyond just authentication, as witnessed by the vast interest in distributed ledger systems such as those implemented by blockchains. The issue of trust has also become more prominent with the increase of

(semi-)automated decision-making procedures that have been installed in
numerous information systems and that directly affect the lives of many
human beings. Making unjustified decisions does not help in building trust,
and many such decisions have been made, and are presumably still being
made. Perhaps most problematic are the situations in which one needs to
trust decision-making without understanding the underlying process, as is
generally inherently the case when applying machine-learning techniques.

In this section, we will zoom into matters of trust, yet will stay close to
technical issues relevant for the design and implementation of distributed
systems. Wierzbicki [2010] discusses trust in a broader context while still
linking it strongly to information systems. A recent survey on trust and
reputation models for information systems is provided by Braga et al. [2018].

9.4.1   Trust in the face of Byzantine failures

Before we take a more explicit look at trust, it is worthwhile considering its
relation to failure models. Trust becomes an issue when there is a dependency
of one process P on another process Q and a possibility that the latter no
longer behaves according to what P expects. More specifically:

> *Trust is the assurance that one entity holds that another will perform
> particular actions according to a specific expectation.*

This definition, by Bursell [2022], can be refined in many ways, yet will do
for now. The point is that when expectations have been made explicit, i.e.,
specified, there may be no need to talk about trust anymore. If we take a look
at Byzantine failures within process groups, the underlying assumption is that
there may be processes from which we cannot expect anything anymore: they
may be behaving correctly or incorrectly, but we have no means of always
correctly detecting whether they are living up to their specifications.

The interesting aspect of Byzantine failure models is that we can let go of
trust and develop solutions in which there is no need to trust the individual
processes. The only thing that matters is that the process group lives up to its
specifications, that is, with a group size of n processes, at most $k \leq (n-1)/3$
will go rogue. Such a group can still reach a correct agreement among the
nonfaulty processes. If the group cannot meet its specifications, for example,
because of too many faulty processes, all bets are off.

9.4.2   Trusting an identity

Let us start by looking at a rather nasty issue when accepting incoming
requests from a source without bothering about further authentication. This
situation is not unusual: it constantly happens in many decentralized peer-
to-peer systems. The problem we need to face is that of a so-called **Sybil
attack** [Douceur, 2002]. The essence of this attack is that in distributed systems,

we generally rely on the fact that when presented with a logical identity, there is just a single associated physical entity. In other words, we rely on the following three properties, as also discussed in Section 6.1:

1. An identifier refers to at most one entity

2. Each entity is referred to by at most one identifier.

3. An identifier always refers to the same entity (i.e., it is never reused).

In the case of a Sybil attack, these assumptions are violated: an attacker simply creates multiple identities and joins the system separately with each of these identities to subsequently stage a specific attack. The general principle of a Sybil attack can be elegantly summarized as shown in Figure 9.19.

```
1  H = set of honest nodes
2  S = set of Sybil nodes
3  A = Attacker node
4  d = minimal fraction of Sybil nodes needed for an attack
5
6  while True:
7      s = A.createNode()        # create a Sybil node
8      S.add(s)                  # add it to the set S
9
10     h = random.choice(H)      # pick an arbitrary honets node
11     s.connectTo(h)            # connect the new sybil node to h
12
13     if len(S) / len(H) > d:   # enough sybil nodes for...
14         A.attack()            # ...an attack
```

Figure 9.19: The principle of a Sybil attack (adopted from [Iqbal and Matulevičius, 2021].

A typical example of a Sybil attack is when operating a decentralized peer-to-peer network such as Chord or Kademlia. An attacker simply creates multiple logical nodes that join the network. As the attacker has full control over these nodes, from a security perspective, they are viewed as a collection of colluders. In particular, there is no reason to assume that they behave as expected. For example, together, they can easily launch a denial-of-service attack by not forwarding lookup requests. If the attacker has control over a sufficient number of nodes, it is with high probability that any lookup request will need to go through a malicious node. Likewise, the colluding nodes can join in attacking the content stored in a network, if only to delete files they are collectively responsible for. Even in the face of using file replication, such a behavior may easily lead to permanent loss of data.

As another example of a Sybil attack, consider the aforementioned web of trust. If we allowed automatic endorsement of public keys, i.e., having Chuck endorse the public key of Bob without an out-of-band checking that the key is really owned by Bob, we may find ourselves in the following situation. Note that the web of trust is essentially based on reputation: assuming Chuck does not entirely trust Alice when it comes to validating the public key of Bob, he may decide to also consider the validations from $k > 1$ others before accepting the validity of Bob's public key. Yet, with automatic endorsement, Alice could launch a Sybil attack by simply cloning her efforts by installing many nodes claiming they have validated Bob's public key. If k of these nodes are consulted by Chuck, then Chuck will believe the key indeed belongs to Bob. There is no harm in this, unless Alice had stolen Bob's private key and is now trying to act as Bob. Without automatic endorsement, such an attack would be much more difficult to realize.

Closely related to a Sybil attack is the so-called **eclipse attack**. In this case, a collection of colluding nodes will try to isolate a node from the network. We showed in Section 5.5.4, how with almost minimal effort a gossip-based service can be brought to a grinding halt before benevolent nodes may even suspect that something fishy is going on. That service is based on continuously exchanging randomly chosen links with neighbors in an attempt to maintain an overlay network that resembles a random graph. The links are chosen from a relatively small list that is local to each node in the network. An exchanged link replaces the link in this local list. In an eclipse attack, a number of colluding nodes never return randomly chosen links, but only links to their fellow colluders. The effect is devastating: within only relatively few exchanges by all nodes in the network, the malicious links will have contaminated the local lists to the extent that each local list contains only links to the colluding nodes. At that point, the colluders have full control over the network (see also Jesi et al. [2007]).

The simple way out in both cases is to use a centralized certification authority: whenever Alice connects to Bob, she will have to prove to be the holder of the digital identity associated with her. A certificate signed by a trusted authority should, in principle, do the job. Suppose the certification authority is not (sufficiently) trusted. This may happen, for example because the certification authority is not known enough. In that case, we may rely on a **trust chain**, by which the public key PK_{CA} that is used to sign the certificate is accompanied by its own certificate, signed by another certification authority, say CA*. If the public key PK_{CA^*} is not trusted, then we can repeat the procedure by having that key be accompanied by another certificate signed by yet another certification authority CA**, and so on. However, in the end, the recipient will have to trust the certification authority at the end of this chain.

Preventing Sybil attacks: blockchain solutions

Levine et al. [2006] and later Urdaneta et al. [2011] have looked at Sybil attacks in decentralized networks. Both come to the conclusion, as also already stated by Douceur [2002] that these attacks are almost impossible to prevent without making use of a trusted authority. All other decentralized solutions up to that point could at best discourage Sybil attacks, but not prevent them. However, accepting a centralized, trusted party in an otherwise decentralized system is something that many find difficult to accept. Yet, if we could devise a system that would make having multiple identities unattractive, then maybe a trusted party may not be necessary. This is where **permissionless blockchains** come into play.

Launching multiple identities is attractive if the attacker knows that there is substantial gain in doing so compared to the price to pay for maintaining multiple identities. But the price is high when, for example, an identity is assumed to throw in considerable resources to be able to act. This is precisely what is expected in **proof-of-work (PoW)** blockchain systems. In PoW systems, validators of a block of transactions are engaged in a race, requiring considerable computational resources. There is no incentive for an attacker to launch another identity for the same physical node, as that identity will need to compete as well.

Having to run computational races is arguably a bad design choice for any distributed system. In an attempt to still prevent Sybil attacks but avoiding computational races, designers of blockchain systems have been investigating **proof-of-stake (PoS)** solutions [Nguyen et al., 2019]. In this case, those nodes for making decisions on validating transactions are selected according to how much stake they have in the system. Assuming stakes are expressed as certain tokens (such as digital coins), each token is indexed, after which a search is made for the owner of that indexed token. Obviously, the more tokens a node has, the higher the chance of being selected for decision-making. Again, we see that simply creating multiple identities is not rewarding, as each of these identities will need to obtain tokens before being able to act.

None of these blockchain solutions are without security problems (see Saad et al. [2020] and Li et al. [2020] for extensive overviews). Yet from the perspective of preventing Sybil attacks, one can argue that they do their job well.

Sybil-resistant accounting mechanisms

When trust in central authorities within a distributed system drops, we need to resort to decentralized solutions. The fundamental problem is that Alice has no reason whatsoever to trust Bob *a priori* whenever the two get in touch and one needs the other to engage in a transaction of some sort. A common solution is to build a reputation system by which Bob can prove to Alice that he is trustworthy. At the same time, such a system should be resistant to a Sybil attack, as we illustrated in the web-of-trust model.

As part of their work on building robust blockchain systems, Otte et al. [2020] introduced an accounting mechanism by which a node Q can show that it has already done considerable work to convince node P to let it do some work for P. The benefit for Q, of course, is that its own performed work further increases so that it may later use that to ask others to work for it. The **NetFlow** accounting mechanism introduced by Otte et al. is based on earlier work by Seuken and Parkes [2014]. Interesting for our current discussion is that this decentralized accounting mechanism is resistant to Sybil attacks.

The basic idea is that each node P in the network maintains a list of nodes that are interested in doing work for P, called the **choice set** of P, denoted as choice(P). Which node is selected from choice(P) depends on that node's reputation, expressed in terms of work done for others.

To this end, P maintains a view of what nodes in the network have done so far for each other. The view is necessarily *subjective*: it may be incomplete (because P has no knowledge of all the participating nodes) and it may be inaccurate. In any case, P does know what it has done for others, and also what others have done for P. This information is enough for P to compute a *capacity* cap(Q) for any node $Q \in$ choice(P):

$$cap(Q) = \max\{MF(Q,P) - MF(P,Q), 0\}$$

where $MF(P,Q)$ is the value of the maximum flow from P to Q, i.e., the amount of work that P has, or could have contributed to work done for Q, including the work done by others. For example, if node R directly contributed 3 units of work for Q, and R had processed 7 units for P, then P indirectly may have contributed 3 units of work for Q, yet through R. The reasoning is that R may never have been able to work for Q if not for the work it did for P. The capacity of node Q from P's perspective, is thus the result of the work Q has directly and indirectly done for P, minus the work P has done for Q. When positive, one could say that P "owes" Q some work to do. These capacities are then used in maximum-flow computations that result in reputation scores for each node.

Now let us consider a Sybil attack by a node $Q \in$ choice(P). To that end, Q creates n Sybil nodes $Q_1^*, \ldots, Q_n^*$. We denote $Q = Q_0^*$ as just another Sybil. First, note that for any work contributed by a Sybil Q_i^* to another Sybil Q_j^* to cause an increase in cap(Q_i^*), at least two conditions need to hold: (1) Q_j^* needs to have contributed work to some honest node R and (2) that node R needs to have contributed (indirectly) to P. What this means, is that Q can successfully launch an attack only if it had already performed work for honest nodes. Furthermore, the attack makes sense only if Q expects that other, honest nodes will contribute work to Q, and that this work is more than Q's total contributions to its Sybils. This can happen if the total capacity Tcap(Q) of the Sybils can grow, with

$$\text{Tcap}(Q) = \sum_{k=0}^{n} \text{cap}(Q_k^*)$$

Now assume that a unit of work is contributed by P to one of the Sybils, say Q_i^*. In that case, $MF(P, Q_i^*)$ increases by 1 unit, so that cap(Q_i^*) drops by 1 unit, and so does $\mathsf{Tcap}(Q)$. This may continue until $\mathsf{Tcap}(Q) = 0$, at which point P will direct its attention to other nodes and ignore any of the Sybils until their joint capacity has grown, notably because other honest nodes have contributed work to those Sybils.

Having the Sybils perform work for each other does not help: if Q_i^* performs a unit of work for Q_j^*, then $\mathsf{cap}(Q_i^*)$ goes up by 1 unit, yet $\mathsf{cap}(Q_j^*)$ goes down by 1, leaving $\mathsf{Tcap}(Q)$ unaffected. The only way that $\mathsf{Tcap}(Q)$ can go up without P contributing work to one of the Sybils, is if some other honest node R contributes work. If P is unaware of R, then P will not know about this work and keep $\mathsf{Tcap}(Q)$ the same. In other words, Q cannot benefit from work it does for R to trick P into contributing work to one of its Sybils, including itself. However, if P does know about R, we can expect that both will have the same perspective on the value of $\mathsf{Tcap}(Q)$. As a consequence, R will act the same as P: it will contribute work to one of the Sybils until $\mathsf{Tcap}(Q)$ drops to 0. At that point, Q is where it stood before the attack: empty-handed and in need of a node willing to let it do some work.

This rather intuitive reasoning shows that a proper accounting mechanism (in the case of NetFlow based on maximum flows in a network) is actually Sybil resistant. A precise and formal reasoning can be found in [Stannat et al., 2021]. Also, [Otte, 2016] will be useful in understanding some underlying details of NetFlow that we have purposefully omitted here.

9.4.3 Trusting a system

An important claimed feature of many blockchain systems is that they can operate without the need for a trusted third party (i.e., they are completely decentralized), in addition to the fact that there is also no need to trust any of the individual participants. To understand this reasoning, we need to separate the blockchain from the way it is maintained. The latter is strongly determined by the consensus protocol that is executed to figure out which block of validated transactions can be appended to the current blockchain. The former has everything to do with the transparency and protection of essentially a read-only distributed ledger. This is where ensuring data integrity is crucial.

Recall that a blockchain is literally a chain of blocks, with each block consisting of a number of validated transactions. When it comes to ensuring data integrity, we need a means to be able to detect that the current blockchain has not been tampered with, i.e., ensuring that any change to the current chain cannot go unnoticed and thus be flagged as an attack.

The principle of a blockchain is shown in Figure 9.20. The first block, called the **genesis block**, contains the number 0x00000000 which is effectively a null pointer. Important is that each block contains a number of transactions and a hash value over the data contained in the block. That hash value is copied to the successor in the chain, and also serves as input to the hash value of the succeeding block. This cryptographic linking between two blocks is

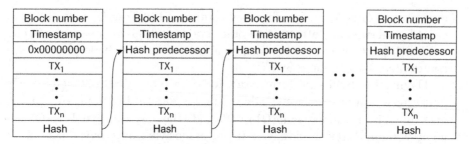

Figure 9.20: The principle of a blockchain.

important. Suppose that block B_i has hash value h_i and its successor, B_{i+1} has hash value h_{i+1}. Obviously, any change of block B_i will invalidate h_i. An attacker may compute a new hash value, say h_i^*, but this value will have to be propagated to block B_{i+1}, in turn invalidating h_{i+1}. In other words, an attack can be successful only if all blocks succeeding B_i are modified as well. Considering that a blockchain is assumed to be a read-only data structure, it will most likely have been massively replicated. Changing the chain while going unnoticed is deemed to be too difficult, to say the least.

A transaction can, in principle, take any form. Important is that a transaction has been validated, for example because signatures of the parties involved in the transaction have been verified as well as the content of the transaction. What this validation entails is thus specific to the application of a blockchain.

As a simple example, consider an e-voting system that is implemented using a blockchain. In such a system, voters are assumed to have been registered (and verified that they are entitled to vote). Registration entails that a voter receives a single token that is to be used for voting. When Alice wants to cast her vote, she can essentially engage in a transaction with her favorite candidate, say Bob, and transfer the token to Bob. The latter is the actual transaction. Validating that transaction means, for example, that the entire chain needs to be checked to see whether that token had not been used before. Of course, e-voting through blockchains violates some of its claimed advantages, such as being fully decentralized.

E-voting by making use of blockchains is also illustrative in the face of trust. Although one can set up a system with a tamper-proof and verifiable distributed ledger, may not be enough to warrant trust. In the case of e-voting, Park et al. [2021] are clear: blockchains suffer from the same problems as any electronic voting system. What it then boils down to is that one needs to trust that the distributed system has been properly implemented and secured against attacks.

As also argued by Werbach [2018], it is not just that one needs to trust the correctness of the implementation of a system, but also that it functions as intended. In the case of blockchains, an upcoming phenomenon is the use of **smart contracts**: programs that are automatically executed when certain conditions are met within a block. This can be as simple as sending a notification to Alice and Bob when their transaction made it to the chain, but could also entail automatically engaging new transactions. Even if such contracts can be proven to be correct given a specification, the question is whether the specification meets intentions. Practice in law shows that humans are not always that good at transforming intentions into specifications (or regulations).

Finally, the claim that (permissionless) blockchains do not require trust in each participating entity, but that only the ledger needs to be trusted, may not stand so firm. In practice, there are intermediaries who offer services to end users for making use of blockchain applications, if only to make it easy for people to participate. Those intermediaries, and the systems they use, will need to be trusted. In many ways, blockchain systems and any other distributed system share a lot when it comes to trusting a system.

For an extensive and in-depth discussion on trust in computer systems, we refer the interested reader to Bursell [2022].

9.5 Authorization

We now concentrate on providing an entity proper access to a system's resources after that entity has been authenticated.

9.5.1 General issues in access control

To understand the various issues involved in access control, the simple model shown in Figure 9.21 is generally adopted. It consists of *subjects* that issue a request to access an *object*. An object is very much like the objects we have been discussing so far. It can be thought of as encapsulating its own state and implementing the operations on that state. The operations of an object that subjects can request to be carried out are made available through interfaces. Subjects can best be thought of as being processes acting on behalf of users, but can also be objects that need the services of other objects in order to carry out their work.

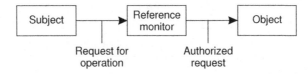

Figure 9.21: General model of controlling access to objects.

Controlling the access to an object is all about protecting the object against invocations by subjects that are not allowed to have specific (or even any) of the methods carried out. Also, protection may include object management issues, such as creating, renaming, or deleting objects. Protection is often enforced by a program called a **reference monitor**. A reference monitor records which subject may do what, and decides whether a subject is allowed to have a specific operation carried out. This monitor is called (e.g., by the underlying trusted operating system) each time an object is invoked. Consequently, it is critical that the reference monitor is itself tamperproof: an attacker must not be able to fool around with it.

Access control policies

When considering the protection of an application, there are essentially three approaches that can be followed, as shown in Figure 9.22. The first approach is to concentrate directly on the protection of the data that is associated with the application. By direct, we mean that irrespective of the various operations that can possibly be performed, the primary concern is to ensure data integrity. Typically, this type of protection occurs in database systems in which various integrity constraints can be formulated that are automatically checked each time a data item is modified (see, for example, Doorn and Rivero [2002]).

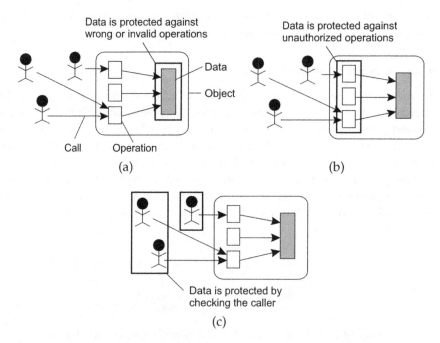

Figure 9.22: Three approaches for protection against security threats. (a) Protection against invalid operations, (b) Protection against unauthorized operations. (c) Protection against unauthorized callers.

The second approach is to concentrate on protection by specifying exactly which operations may be performed, and by whom, when certain data or resources are to be accessed. In this case, the focus of control is strongly related to **access control mechanisms**, which we discuss extensively later in this chapter. For example, in an object-based system, it may be decided to specify for each method that is made available which specific clients are permitted to invoke that method. Alternatively, access control methods can be applied to an entire interface offered by an object, or to the entire object itself. This approach thus allows for various granularities of access control.

A third approach is to focus directly on users by taking measures by which only specific people, or their proxies in the case of, for example, delegation, have access to the application, irrespective of the operations they want to carry out. For example, Alice may have been given read access to a specific file, but no write access. On the other hand, Bob may be allowed to change the file, or even delete it. Again, combinations of these three approaches are possible and occur in practice.

In general, we can distinguish several **access control policies**. A common distinction is often made into the following four types:

1. Mandatory access control

2. Discretionary access control

3. Role-based access control

4. Attribute-based access control

Perhaps conceptually the simplest access control policy is that of **Mandatory Access Control (MAC)**. In this case, access control policies are decided beyond the control of an individual: a central administration defines who gets access to what. In the context of military security, data is typically labeled according to some level of secrecy, ranging from "public access" to "top secret." Only if Alice has been assigned the appropriate confidentiality level, will she get access to data up to that level. Although conceptually simple, mandatory access control can be quite difficult from a security-management perspective.

Easier and generally more common in many distributed systems is to make use of **Discretionary Access Control (DAC)**. In this case, the owner of an object (such as a file) is entitled to change access rights (such as read, write, or execute), but also who may have access to that object. Typically, in Unix systems a distinction is made between the owner, a group, and the world. MAC and DAC are often seen to be combined.

As a next step, we can make objects in a distributed system less dependent on owners, but instead concentrate on how they are supposed to be used by looking at the roles of people. This leads to what is known as **Role-based Access Control (RBAC)** [Ferraiolo et al., 2007]. The essence of RBAC is that users are not authorized based on their identity, but based on the role they have within an organization. For example, within a university, we can distinguish roles such as teacher, student, project controller, data steward, group leader, dean, etc. When Alice is authenticated, she will also be linked to a role, which may need to be indicated at the time she logs into the system. Then, in the associated role, she will have been granted various access rights to specific objects.

More recently, attention is being paid to **Attribute-based Access Control (ABAC)** [Hu et al., 2014; 2015]. In ABAC, attributes of users *and* of objects they want to access are considered for deciding on the specific access rule. ABAC allows for much finer-grained access control in comparison to RBAC. For example, not all teachers at a university may be allowed access to the exam results of all students. Instead, one may want to formulate the constraint that only teachers of the Distributed Systems course have read access to grades from students enrolled in that course. Likewise, only the formal leader of the group on Pervasive Systems may be entitled to read the yearly review reports from members in that group, except the ones of the full professors. We will return to ABAC later in this chapter.

Access control matrix

A common approach to modeling the access rights of subjects with respect to objects is to construct an **access control matrix**. Each subject is represented by a row in this matrix; each object is represented by a column. If the matrix is denoted M, then an entry $M[s, o]$ lists precisely which operations subject s can request to be carried out on object o. In other words, whenever a subject s requests to perform the operation m on object o, the reference monitor should check if m is listed in $M[s, o]$. If m is not listed in $M[s, o]$, the execution of the operation fails.

Considering that a system may easily need to support thousands of users and millions of objects that require protection, implementing an access control matrix as a true matrix, is not the way to go. Many entries in the matrix will be empty: a single subject will generally have access to relatively few objects. Therefore, other, more efficient ways are followed to implement an access control matrix.

One widely applied approach is to have each object maintain a list of the access rights of subjects that want to access the object. In essence, this means that the matrix is distributed column-wise across all objects, and that empty entries are left out. This type of implementation leads to what is called an **access control list (ACL)**. Each object is assumed to have its own associated ACL.

Another approach is to distribute the matrix row-wise by giving each subject a list of **capabilities** it has for each object. A capability thus corresponds to an entry in the access control matrix. Not having a capability for a specific object means that the subject has no access rights for that object.

A capability can be compared to a ticket: its holder is given certain rights that are associated with that ticket. It is also clear that a ticket should be protected against modifications by its holder. One approach that is particularly suited in distributed systems, is to protect (a list of) capabilities with a signature.

The difference between how ACLs and capabilities are used to protect the access to an object is shown in Figure 9.23. Using ACLs, when a client sends a request to a server, the server's reference monitor will check whether it knows the client and if that client is known and allowed to have the requested operation carried out, as shown in Figure 9.23(a).

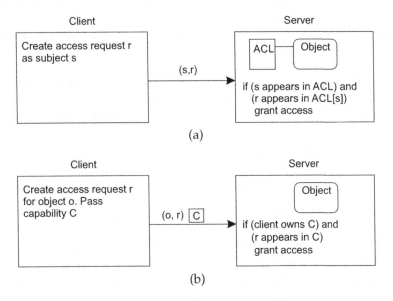

Figure 9.23: Comparison between ACLs and capabilities for protecting objects. (a) Using an ACL. (b) Using capabilities.

When using capabilities, a client simply sends its request to the server. The server is not necessarily interested in whether it knows the client; the capability may say enough. However, such an approach does not prevent a client to pass its capability to another program. This is precisely the problem of delegation that we discussed before. Therefore, in practice, the client will one way or the other have been registered at the server, while the capability is simply bound to that specific client. At that point, the server need only check whether the capability is valid (i.e., belongs to the client) and whether the requested operation is listed in the capability. This approach to protecting objects using capabilities is shown in Figure 9.23(b).

9.5.2 Attribute-based access control

Let us concentrate a bit more on an emerging type of access control, namely the one based on attributes. **Attribute-based access control (ABAC)** is a powerful access control policy that can viewed as superseding other policies. Yet, ABAC still has a long way to go when it comes to its adoption in distributed systems, as also explained by Servos and Osborn [2017] who investigated the various issues and challenges that ABAC is facing.

Basic model

In essence, ABAC assumes that access policies are described in terms of attributes and their values. Attributes can belong to many things, including users, objects, and also the current state of a distributed system. To make things concrete, let us consider ABAC for a university setting. We could then have the following:

- **User attributes** may include name, data of birth, current roles, home address, department, qualifiers obtained, contract status, etc. Depending on the role (e.g., teacher or student), a different set of attributes may be relevant.

- **Object attributes** can be anything, such as creator, last-modified time, version number, file type, file size, but also information related to its content, such as the student or course associated with the object.

- **Environmental attributes** describe the current state of the system in which access is requested, including date and time, current workload, maintenance status, storage properties, available services, and such.

- **Connection attributes** provide information on the current session, for example an IP address, session duration, available bandwidth and latency estimates, type and strength of security used, and so on.

- Finally, **administrative attributes** may reflect global policies, including minimal security settings, general access regulations, and maximum session durations, to name a few.

Example: The Policy Machine

To make matters concrete, let us look at an example system for attribute-based access control, namely the **Policy Machine**, described in [Ferraiolo et al., 2011; 2015]. The architecture of the Policy Machine is a simple client-server model, where a centralized server maintains a database of *(attribute,value)* pairs associated with users, applications, operations, and objects. At the client side, a small support program is used to communicate with the server, notably for handling the access privileges of client-side applications. Obviously, the server and the client-side support program need to be trusted to work as specified. Essential to the Policy Machine is the expression of access control rules. To that end, a distinction is made between assignments, prohibitions, and obligations.

An **assignment** is simply telling the system that a user u has an associated attribute ua: u is said to be assigned to ua, denoted as u → ua. Likewise, an object o can be assigned to an object attribute oa. In the same fashion, an attribute can be assigned to another attribute. For example, if ua_1 → ua_2, then all users associated with ua_1 will also be associated with ua_2. Assignments thus essentially yield sets: if u → ua, then u ∈ ua.

In a similar vein, user attributes can be assigned to operation sets, and operation sets can be assigned to object attributes. This leads to triplets of the form *allowed*(ua, ops, oa) which expresses that a user u can perform operation op on object o only if u ∈ ua, op ∈ ops, o ∈ oa.

A **prohibition** expresses what users or applications are *not* allowed to do. In particular, a user can be denied certain operations of certain objects, expressed as *denied*(u, ops, os) with ops a set of operations and os a set of objects. To ensure that operations are truly restricted to a given set of objects, that is, denied to all other objects, the Policy Machine supports expressions *denied*(u, ops, ¬os). In other words, if u requests to perform operation op ∈ ops on an object o ∉ os, the Policy Machine will deny that request.

Finally, an **obligation** is used to automatically take actions when certain events happen. A simple example is denying a user to copy information from one set of files to another:

$$\text{when u reads f} \in \text{fs then } \textit{denied}(u, \{write\}, \neg fs).$$

This is an interesting example in the sense that it forms the basis for preventing information leakage. We have mentioned only a part of what can be expressed by the Policy Machine, yet it should be clear that attribute-based access control is by itself a powerful approach for expressing many kinds of access control policies. Interestingly, the Policy Machine can also be used for MAC, DAC, and RBAC.

The simplest case is perhaps RBAC. By simple assignments such as Alice → Teachers we effectively assign the role of teacher to Alice. Alice can be assigned other roles as well, but the important aspect is that the system will take those roles as its starting point for access control. We do note that advanced RBAC schemes require more sophisticated assignments in terms of the Policy Machine, yet the principle should be clear.

When it comes to mandatory access control (MAC), the basic idea is that one can introduce a notion of security levels $L_1, \ldots, L_n$ where L_1 denotes the lowest and L_n the highest level of security. More concrete, if Alice has access to "top secret" documents, she should also have access to "secret" documents. The idea is straightforward: each object is assigned to an appropriate object security-level attribute, such as OL_i. Likewise, each user is assigned to a user security-level attribute, such as UL_j. Moreover, each user security-level attribute UL_i is assigned to UL_{i-1} indicating that all users assigned to UL_i have the same rights as users at a less secure level, represented by the user attribute UL_{i-1}.

The real issue with MAC is that we need to prevent information leaking from higher levels to lower levels. As before, this can be prevented by the obligation

$$\text{when } u \text{ reads } f \in OL_i \text{ then } denied(u, \{write\}, \neg\{\cup_{k=i}^n OL_k\}).$$

So, for example, if we have five security levels, then anyone who reads a document from level OL_3, cannot write to documents at level $\{OL_1, OL_2\}$ or equivalently cannot write to documents not in $\{OL_3, OL_4, OL_5\}$.

Finally, let us have a look at discretionary access (DAC). The essence of DAC is that each object has an owner, and that this owner can actually set access rights for others. For example, in Unix systems, a user alice belonging to a group teachers can set read, write and execute access rights for herself, members of the group teachers, and anyone else. A user with administrative privileges (typically, the root user) can additionally assign objects to users and groups. Some simple examples illustrate these principles.

```
alice$ chmod u=rw,g=r,o= document
```

expresses that user alice changes the rights for herself to read (r) and write (w) document, yet allows members of the group to which document has been assigned to only read the file, while anyone else has no access rights whatsoever. Likewise,

```
root# chown alice:teachers document
```

tells us that the user root assigns ownership of document to user alice and group teachers.

Following Ferraiolo et al. [2011], one can create a unique user attribute per user. So, Alice would be known to the system by assigning her to the user attribute alice. Likewise, each group is represented by a user attribute, and we could, for example, perform the assignment alice $\rightarrow$ teachers. Following Unix conventions, we create an object attribute alice home which represents the home directory of user alice. The trick is to make sure that Alice is entitled to execute an appropriate set of administrative commands, but also to ensure that the results match the DAC model. For example, we would need Alice to allow to create objects within the home directory. This can be done by assigning a create operation to the object attribute alice home and installing the obligation

when alice performs create(o) at alice home then o $\rightarrow$ alice home.

When considering the Unix DAC model, in which (almost) everything is a file, we also need to consider creating objects that represent a subdirectory. Again, being a directory can be expressed in terms of an object attribute, and typically each directory object will need to be associated with a parent directory. In general, we may thus have:

when alice performs create(o) at directory then o → directory.

These examples also illustrate that expressing a DAC model in an ABAC model requires careful consideration of all the operations and elements of the specific DAC model at hand. In fact, being able to accurately and completely expressing other models in terms of attribute-based access control is considered to be one of the open challenges [Servos and Osborn, 2017].

9.5.3 Delegation

Now consider the following problem. A user Alice makes use of an e-mail service provider who stores her mailbox somewhere within that provider's organization. Typically, she is required to log in to the provider through her Web browser, after which she gets to see an appropriate interface for handling her mail. However, Alice would prefer to use her own favorite mail client, which is installed on her laptop. The core question is how to allow that mail client to act on behalf of Alice? In other words, the mail client would need to get access to Alice's mailbox, and allow her to then retrieve new mail, read mail, send mail, and so on. In essence, Alice would like to **delegate** her access rights to the mail client, and in such a way that the mail client can also automatically log in and do its work.

Delegation of access rights is an important technique for implementing protection in computer systems and distributed systems, in particular. The basic idea is simple: by passing certain access rights from one process to another, it becomes easier to distribute work between several processes without adversely affecting the protection of resources. In the case of distributed systems, processes may run on different machines and even within different administrative domains. Delegation can avoid much overhead, as protection can often be handled locally.

There are several ways to implement delegation. The least favorable one is to hand over the user credentials directly to an application. In fact, doing so would be a bad idea: there is, in general, no reason to trust an application or the machine it is running on. A much better and general approach, as described by Neuman [1993] and implemented in the Kerberos system, is to make use of a proxy. A **proxy** in the context of security in computer systems is a token that allows its owner to operate with the same or restricted rights and privileges as the subject that granted the token. A process (or user for that matter) can create a proxy with at best the same rights and privileges it has itself. If a process creates a new proxy based on one it currently has, the derived proxy will have at least the same restrictions as the original one, and possibly more.

Before considering a general scheme for delegation, consider the following two approaches. First, delegation is relatively simple if Alice knows everyone. If she wants to delegate rights to Bob, she merely needs to construct a certificate saying "Alice says Bob has rights R," such as $[A, B, R]_A$ (i.e., the message containing the identifiers A of Alice and B of Bob, along with the specified access right R, and subsequently signed by Alice). If Bob wants to pass some of these rights to Chuck, he will ask Chuck to contact Alice and ask her for an appropriate certificate.

In a second case, Alice can simply construct a certificate saying, "The bearer of this certificate has rights R." However, in this case, we need to protect the certificate against illegal copying. Neuman's scheme handles this case, as well as avoiding the issue that Alice needs to know everyone to whom rights have to be delegated. Note that in this case, she does trust Bob in delegating rights to Chuck. In practice, this means that the user Alice trusts the application to which she delegated some rights, to correctly and justifiably delegate some of those rights to another application (she may not even be aware of). One obvious way to prevent further delegation is to ensure that it is not specified as part of Bob's rights. The service that hands out a delegation certificate for Bob, will check whether he actually is authorized to do so.

A proxy in Neuman's scheme has two parts, as illustrated in Figure 9.24. Let A be the process that created the proxy. The first part of the proxy is a set $C = \{R, PK_{proxy}\}$, consisting of a set R of access rights that have been delegated by A, along with a publicly known part of a secret that is used to authenticate the holder of the certificate. We will explain the use of PK_{proxy} below. The certificate carries the signature $sig(A, C)$ of A, to protect it against modifications. The second part contains the other part of the secret, denoted as SK_{proxy}. It is essential that SK_{proxy} is protected against disclosure when delegating rights to another process.

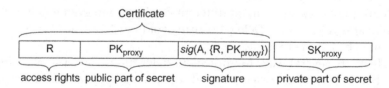

Figure 9.24: The general structure of a proxy as used for delegation.

Another way of looking at the proxy is as follows. If Alice wants to delegate some of her rights to Bob, she makes a list of rights (R) that Bob can exercise. By signing the list, she prevents Bob from tampering with it. However, having only a signed list of rights is often not enough. If Bob would like to exercise his rights, he may have to prove that he actually got the list from Alice and did not, for example, steal it from someone else. Therefore, Alice comes up with a very nasty question (PK_{proxy}) that only she knows the answer to (SK_{proxy}). Anyone can easily verify the correctness of the answer when given the question. The question is appended to the list before Alice adds her signature.

When delegating some of her rights, Alice gives the signed list of rights, along with the nasty question, to Bob. She also gives Bob the answer, ensuring that no one can intercept it. Bob now has a list of rights, signed by Alice, which he can hand over to, say, Chuck, when necessary. Chuck will ask him the nasty question at the bottom of the list. If Bob knows the answer to it, Chuck will know that Alice had indeed delegated the listed rights to Bob.

An important property of this scheme is that Alice need not be consulted. In fact, Bob may decide to pass on (some of) the rights on the list to Dave. In doing so, he will also tell Dave the answer to the question, so that Dave can prove the list was handed over to him by someone entitled to it. Alice never needs to know about Dave at all.

A protocol for delegating and exercising rights is shown in Figure 9.25. Assume that Alice and Bob share a secret key $K_{A,B}$ that can be used for encrypting messages they send to each other. Then, Alice first sends Bob the certificate $[R, PK_{proxy}]_A$, signed by Alice. There is no need to encrypt this message: it can be sent as plaintext. Only the private part of the secret needs to be encrypted, shown as $K_{A,B}(SK_{proxy})$ in message 1.

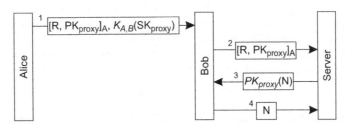

Figure 9.25: Using a proxy to delegate and prove ownership of access rights.

Now suppose that Bob wants to carry out an operation at a specific server. Also, assume that Alice is authorized to have that operation carried out, and that she has delegated those rights to Bob. Therefore, Bob hands over his credentials to the server in the form of the signed certificate $[R, PK_{proxy}]_A$.

At that point, the server will be able to verify that C has not been tampered with: any modification to the list of rights, or the nasty question will be noticed because both have been jointly signed by Alice. However, the server does not know yet whether Bob is the rightful owner of the certificate. To verify this, the server must use the secret that came with $[R, PK_{proxy}]_A$. To that end, the server sends Bob a **nonce** (which is just an arbitrarily chosen string) N, encrypted with PK_{proxy}. By decrypting $PK_{proxy}(N)$ and returning N, Bob proves he knows the secret and is thus the rightful holder of the certificate.

Note 9.6 (More information: OAuth (Open Authorization))

Delegation is, in principle, fairly straightforward. Yet, it has already taken many years to come to a practical scheme that was acceptable by many players. Also, solutions that are designed by multiple parties coming from different organizations tend not to be examples of simplicity, to say the least. This is certainly true for **Open Authorization**, generally known as **OAuth**. Nevertheless, OAuth is by now an important delegation protocol used by many organizations including Amazon, Google, Facebook, Microsoft, and Twitter. Its main purpose is to grant an application access to resources that are normally accessible to a user only through a Web interface. A typical example is that of using a local mail client, which acts on behalf of its owner, as described previously.

Let us take a closer look at the OAuth 2.1 framework, which distinguishes four different roles:

- A **resource owner**, which is typically an end user, such as Alice who normally accesses her mail through her provider's Web service.
- A **client**, which is an application that one would like to act on behalf of the resource owner, such as an e-mail client.
- A **resource server**, in practice forming some kind of Web interface through which a person like Alice would normally first authenticate herself after which she can access and manage her mail.
- An **authorization server**, forming the core entity when it comes to handing out certificates to a client on behalf of a resource owner.

The client application will have to be known at the authorization server through some separately executed registration process (which can also take place as part of the delegation process). The result is that the client receives its own, unique identifier, say cid. When Alice wants her application to operate on her behalf when it comes to a list R of rights, the application sends

$$\text{Client: } send\ [\text{cid}, \text{R}, H(\text{S})]$$

in which the hash of a temporary secret S is sent, computed with the hash function H. As its name suggests, the secret S is (for now) known only to the client application. In the message above, we omit some additional information, such as details of the hash function, as well as some other options.

If Alice is not yet logged in to the authorization server, she will be required to do so and confirm that the client application is entitled to the rights as expressed by R. At that point, the client receives a temporary **authorization code** AC from the server, which it should use to get the final **access token**. The client then sends a request for that token:

$$\text{Client: } sends\ [\text{cid}, \text{AC}, \text{S}].$$

By sending the secret S to the authorization server, the latter can check that it is dealing with the same client application as before, as it simply needs to compute $H(\text{S})$ that was sent with the previous message from that application. Note that by now, the authorization server has verified that Alice indeed wants to delegate access rights to the client. The client simply needs to prove that it is the same one that initiated the delegation request. If all is verified, the authorization server returns an access token AT to the client.

It should be clear that an access token is precious data: it gives the client application the same rights as Alice would have when going directly to the resource server. Therefore, the access token is communicated through a secure channel, and is also stored securely on the machine hosting the client (such as Alice's laptop). Likewise, one way or the other the client will have to authenticate itself, which is determined at registration time. There are different ways OAuth 2.1 supports authentication, a simple one being the scheme by which the client has a private key and the server keeps the associated public key, as we explained previously, when discussing SSH.

OAuth 2.1 distinguishes two types of access tokens. The first one is essentially just an identifier that the resource server can use to check the access rights of the client application. It does so by passing the token to the authorization server and retrieving those rights. This scheme requires that the resource server contacts the authorization server every time the client wants to perform an operation.

The second type takes the form of a (signed) certificate: it contains all the access rights of the client as granted by Alice. Those rights will hold until the certificate expires (and indeed, with this type of access token, there is an associated expiration time).

We have given a very concise description of OAuth 2.1, omitting many details and many of its options. The specification of OAuth 2.0 is found in [Hardt et al., 2012]. There are also several books that explain how to set up clients and servers so that they adhere to the framework (see, e.g., Parecki [2020] and Boyd [2012]).

9.5.4 Decentralized authorization: an example

So far, we have been discussing various authentication and authorization solutions, of which many have in common that there is a centralized component where permissions are checked and granted (or denied). For example, Kerberos deploys a centralized authentication server and a centralized ticket-granting service. Likewise, when dealing with delegation, a client application generally needs to be registered at an authorization server to receive a capability to perform certain operations at a service, or that the service can check the permissions at the authorization server. Each of these types of centralized services will have been made robust through replication using protocols such as Paxos or Byzantine Fault Tolerance. Also, using straightforward workload-balancing schemes, we can relatively easily scale out servers. For example, we may decide that all requests coming from applications with an ID less than some value K go to server #1, while the requests from other applications go to server #2.

The situation becomes more difficult when we decentralize a service across multiple administrative units, such as across different departments or organizations. We then bump into the problem of administrative scalability [Neuman, 1994]. In this section, we take a look at a scalable decentralized authorization service, called **WAVE**, specifically developed to operate across multiple organizations. WAVE is a good example of some of the things we need to deal with when scaling out across administrative domains. Detailed information on WAVE can be found in [Andersen, 2019; Andersen et al., 2019].

Graph-based authorization

Fundamental to the WAVE framework is the application of **graph-based authorization**. In this scheme, a global, possibly worldwide directed graph is maintained. Each vertex represents an entity that is capable of granting or receiving permissions. For example, a vertex may represent Alice's home directory (where she has the right to, for example, create and delete files, and set various permissions, including giving Bob access to some files). A vertex could also represent a department in charge of a collection of applications, an online cloud service that offers various resources, and so on. Each entity has a collection of public keys, from which a hash is derived that serves as a means to look up those keys. The collection of associated private keys is, of course, kept secret by the party represented by the entity. The key pairs are used for various protections and signatures that we describe below.

Each directed edge represents a delegation of permissions from one entity (the **issuer**) to another (the **subject**). For example, Alice can, as an issuer, delegate specific file permissions to Bob, the subject. In WAVE, an edge represents an **attestation**. Permissions are always granted on **resources**, such as files, database (records), devices, and so on. An entity B gathers proof of its right to operate on a resource owned by A by showing that there is a directed path in the graph from A to B.

To this end, WAVE uses a policy mechanism called an **RTree**, which stands for *resource tree*. Keeping it simple, a resource is denoted by a URI such as user-entity/music/albums/popular/band/. The first element in the URI is particularly important: it identifies the entity responsible for the resource and the one which is responsible for all permissions. Each resource has an associated collection of permissions, which is part of an RTree. The identification of a resource, a specification of granted permissions on that resource, a duration for which the grant is valid, and possible restrictions on further delegation add up to an **RTree statement**. An attestation will then roughly consist of:

- The hash of the issuer and that of the subject.

- Identifiers of where information on issuer and subject can be found.

- A set of RTree statements.

- A signature of the issuer.

There is more related to an attestation, which we describe below. Andersen [2019] shows that with these basic ingredients, graph-based authorization can be used to emulate DAC and RBAC models.

There are two important issues that need to be dealt with. First, the graph needs to be stored and maintained in a scalable and fully decentralized fashion. Second, delegating permissions is one thing, but letting the whole world know that Alice delegated specific permissions to Bob is maybe not such a good idea. In other words, there is data that needs to be protected. Let us next look into these issues.

Decentralized storage

It is important to realize that the authorization service need, essentially, store information only on resources and attestations. Moreover, there should preferably be no reason at all to trust the storage: the less, the better. As we stated before, there is increasingly more interest in using distributed systems in which the individual participating parties need not be trusted. Instead, one relies on the fact that the system ensures that the provided information can be trusted. This is precisely what happens in distributed ledgers implemented as blockchains. A similar reasoning is applied in WAVE: assuming that each entity is responsible for its own resources, then the party represented by that entity need not be trusted, as long as the information it provides is reliable. In essence, only availability of relevant information is required. With this in mind, Andersen [2019] formulated the following minimal requirements for storage:

1. **Proof of monotonicity**: A storage operates as an unforgeable append-only log.

2. **Proof of inclusion**: When an object is added or retrieved, it must exist in storage.

3. **Proof of nonexistence**: When an object does not exist, the storage should state so.

4. **Proof of nonequivocation**: The storage offers the same view to every client.

Together, these requirements ensure the integrity of the global authorization graph. Note that these requirements come very close to what blockchain-based distributed ledgers offer.

Assuming that these requirements can be met, we may also assume that each entity offers its own local storage. In this way, scalability should, in principle, be easy to realize as long as an application can indeed identify the location where that entity's information is stored. Including global identifiers along with proper name resolution as provided through DNS should do the trick. Of course, bundling multiple entities so that they make use of the same physical storage may be required for reaching certain efficiency goals, yet it should be clear that size scalability is not fundamentally hindered by letting each entity have its own storage. We will subsequently speak of an **entity store**.

Again, keeping things simple, every entity store essentially maintains an append-only **operation log**. Every time an object is appended to the log, it is cryptographically bound to its predecessor, very much like the secure linking in blockchains. In addition, the hash value of the appended object is securely appended to a separate **map log**, which is subsequently returned to the client performing the operation on the entity store.

When a client wants to retrieve on object (such as an attestation), it provides the entity store with the appropriate object identifier (namely its hash value) and its most recent version of the map log. Suppose the object has indeed been logged. The store will return (1) the object, (2) a proof that the object existed in the operation log (by returning a chain of hashes), (3) that the hash associated with the object is part of the map log, and (4) that the current map log is consistent with the one the client provided. Along the same lines, if the object does not exist, the store simply returns nil and proves that the object was not in the operation log by demonstrating that the hash value can never be part of the map log.

Meanwhile, separate processes regularly audit an entity store by reconstructing the operation log and checking its consistency with what is in the store. The scheme we just described is incomplete. More information can be found in [Andersen, 2019].

Data protection

Finally, let us see how data, and in particular attestations, can be protected. Again, we concentrate on only the simplest case of WAVE, called **structural security**. Assume A creates and attestation att for B. It appends the decryption key SK_A^{att} to the message, but not after encrypting it with an appropriate public key PK_B^{att} (as we shall see shortly, adding the decryption key by A, and only A, is strictly speaking not necessary):

$$\text{A sends: } PK_B^{att}(\underbrace{[att|SK_A^{att}]}_{m_1})$$

Let us now also assume that B creates an attestation att' for C that is derived from att. For example, if att allowed B to write to a specific file and to pass on read permissions to others, B may allow C to read the file. No one but A, B, and C should know about this: it is simply no one else's business. However, in order for C to read the file, it will have to prove it may do so.

When B creates att$'$, it sends the following to C:

$$\text{B sends: } PK_C^{att'}(\underbrace{[att'|m_1|SK_B^{att}]}_{m_2})$$

Being able to decrypt this message, C will find att$'$, m_1, and SK_B^{att}. Having SK_B^{att}, it can decrypt m_1 revealing att. Note that there is no reason for either A or B to be online: C has all the information it needs to prove it is allowed to read the file. It should now also be clear that having A also send SK_A^{att} is not necessary. We include it to show the systematic approach of chaining attestations such that a node on a path can reveal all necessary attestations in a reverse order. Note, by the way, that this scheme strongly resembles the way that delegation is handled in Kerberos.

9.6 Monitoring

An important security aspect of any system is to check that policies are sufficient, correctly implemented, and enforced. It would be naive to assume that this is always the case. For this reason alone, it is important to keep track of what is going on in a distributed system so that proper measures can be taken when needed. A passive way of keeping track is to simply log special events: when do users sign in to a system, when and which applications access specific resources, and so on. Logging is important to understand what to do *after the fact*, yet will not help when the damage has been done. In this section, we take a closer look at an increasingly more important aspect of monitoring for security, namely **intrusion detection**, which is all about detecting unauthorized activities. As intrusion detection is often tied to a single computer, we only briefly discuss the basics to subsequently concentrate on distributed monitoring. We start our discussion by having a look at an almost ubiquitous intrusion-detection system, namely firewalls.

9.6.1 Firewalls

Before we take a look at the basics of intrusion detection, consider a common approach to ensuring that intruders stay out: using a **firewall** [Cheswick and Bellovin, 2000; Zwicky et al., 2000]. Firewalls form one of the most often used protection mechanisms in networked systems. Essentially, a firewall disconnects any part of a distributed system from the outside world, as shown in Figure 9.26. All outgoing, but especially all incoming packets are routed through a special computer and inspected before they are passed through. Unauthorized traffic is discarded and not allowed to continue. An important issue is that the firewall itself should be heavily protected against any kind of security threat: it should never fail. Equally important is that the rules that prescribe what can pass through are consistent and establish what is intended.

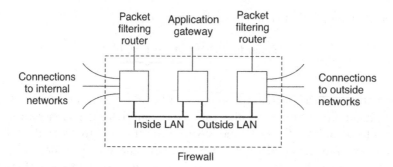

Figure 9.26: A common implementation of a firewall.

As reported by Wool [2010] and Voronkov et al. [2017], properly configuring a firewall is a considerable challenge.

Firewalls essentially come in two different flavors that are often combined. An important type of firewall is a **packet-filtering gateway**. This type of firewall operates as a router and makes decisions whether to pass a network packet based on the source and destination address as contained in the packet's header. Typically, the packet-filtering gateway shown on the outside LAN in Figure 9.26 would protect against incoming packets, whereas the one on the inside LAN would filter outgoing packets. For example, to protect an internal Web server against requests from hosts that are not on the internal network, a packet-filtering gateway could decide to drop all incoming packets addressed to the Web server.

More subtle is the situation in which a company's network consists of multiple local-area networks. Each LAN can be protected using a packet-filtering gateway, which is configured to pass incoming traffic only if it originated from a host on one of the other LANs. In this way, a private virtual network can be set up.

The other type of firewall is an **application-level gateway**. In contrast to a packet-filtering gateway, which inspects only the header of network packets, this type of firewall actually inspects the content of an incoming or outgoing message. A typical example is a mail gateway that discards incoming or outgoing mail exceeding a certain size. More sophisticated mail gateways exist that are, for example, capable of filtering spam e-mail.

Another example of an application-level gateway is one that allows external access to a digital library server, but will supply only abstracts of documents. If an external user wants more, an electronic payment protocol is started. Users inside the firewall have direct access to the library service.

A special kind of application-level gateway is what is known as a **proxy gateway**. This type of firewall works as a front end to a specific kind of application, and ensures that only those messages are passed that meet certain criteria. Consider, for example, surfing the Web. Many Web pages contain scripts or applets that are to be executed in a user's browser. To prevent such code to be downloaded to the inside LAN, all Web traffic could be directed through a Web proxy gateway. This gateway accepts regular HTTP requests, either from inside or outside the firewall. In other words, it appears to its users as a normal Web server. However, it filters all incoming and outgoing traffic, either by discarding certain requests and pages, or modifying pages when they contain executable code.

It should be clear that firewalls have important limitations when considered as a general-purpose security mechanism. As they operate on network traffic, they generally cannot handle authentication and authorization for specific resources. That also means that once an intruder has found a way to bypass the rules of a firewall, all bets are off that the firewall can protect the internal network. For example, if an attacker manages to take over an account, all unauthorized accesses will go unnoticed by the firewall. Instead, other detection mechanisms need to be in place to discover unusual or even unauthorized behavior.

9.6.2 Intrusion detection: basics

Intrusion detection systems generally come in two flavors. In **signature-based intrusion detection systems (SIDS)** patterns of known network-level intrusions have been collected against which a new pattern is matched. If there is a match, security operators are warned that an intrusion may be taking place. Patterns typically consist of a (collection of) specific network packets. What can easily complicate discovering patterns is when a pattern spans a series of network packets, intertwined with regular traffic. Most problematic with a SIDS is when no pattern is yet available, which typically happens with new, unknown attacks, such as zero-day attacks: attacks based on vulnerabilities that have not yet been made public [Bilge and Dumitraş, 2012]. The increase of zero-day attacks has rendered SIDS less useful.

More important are the **anomaly-based intrusion detection systems (AIDS)**. As it name suggests, an AIDS assumes that we can model or extract typical behavior to subsequently detect nontypical, or anomalous behavior. Anomaly-based detection relies heavily on modern artificial-intelligence technologies, and notably machine learning. To this end, an AIDS will first have to go through a *training phase* and collect data that reflects typical, nonmalicious behavior. Once appropriate data sets have been collected and a detection model has been constructed based on that data (such as decision trees, specific neural networks, or classifiers), a *test phase* starts by taking new data and letting the model decide on anomalies.

An important problem with an AIDS is minimizing so-called *false negatives*: flagging an anomaly as typical behavior. Doing so means that the model is missing events that should have been reported to a security operator. To minimize false negatives, many systems follow a pessimistic approach and flag behavior as being anomalous, in turn leading to many *false positives*. The result of many false positives is that security operators become weary of all the alerts [Hassan et al., 2019]. Combatting the number of false positives while still ensuring a very low number of false negatives has proven to be a difficult challenge requiring advanced techniques (see, for example, van Ede et al. [2022]).

There is much more to say about intrusion detection systems. Khraisat et al. [2019] provide a recent overview; a good introduction is provided by Bhuyan et al. [2014].

9.6.3   Collaborative intrusion detection

When considering large-scale distributed systems, it is clear that there cannot be a single point where monitoring can take place that allows to build a complete picture of all events that may indicate that the system is under attack. This is where a **collaborative intrusion detection system (CIDS)** becomes relevant. In essence, a CIDS is a collection of intrusion detection systems that share detections and analyses. Each of the IDS is considered to be positioned somewhere in the system. How a CIDS can be organized is discussed in [Vasilomanolakis et al., 2015], along with examples of existing systems. Here, we concentrate on the effects of such organizations when it comes to successfully detecting intrusions.

To this end, and inspired by Cordero et al. [2015], consider a collection of *sensors* that may be spread across a distributed system, each sensor measuring data potentially related to intrusions. For example, a sensor may be one that logs events related to a specific Web application, or one that captures network traffic at a specific node in the system. We assume that sensors can, in principle, not only collect data, but perform analyses and detect intrusions. Sensors are grouped into **communities**. Each community has a *community head*, which is responsible for collecting the data from the other members in its community, as well as conducting analyses on that data and detecting any intrusions. Communities may overlap: a sensor may be a member of multiple communities, in which case it will also report to multiple community heads. In a way, each community can be viewed as a single IDS.

The basic idea is that community heads exchange information with each other. If this does not happen, nor do any two communities have a sensor in common, then we are simply dealing with a collection of isolated IDSs. A common configuration is to let communities be disjunct, yet all community heads report to the same, single entity, leading to what is known as a *centralized CIDS*. More interesting is the configuration in which the community heads are organized into some kind of peer-to-peer network, i.e., a *distributed CIDS*.

Why is this setup interesting? As mentioned, from the perspective of intrusion detection, it is important to minimize false negatives, while not missing out on actual intrusions, that is, *true positives*. To be more specific, the performance of an IDS is generally measured along the following metrics. We denote by TP the **true positives**: detections that have been correctly flagged as belonging to an intrusion. TN are **true negatives**: detections that have been correctly flagged as belonging to authorized behavior. **False positives** (FP) are detections that are incorrectly labeled as belonging to an intrusion, while **false negatives** (FN) denote missed intrusion detections. The whole idea is then to configure the sensors into communities such that **accuracy** and **precision** are maximized, with:

$$\textbf{Accuracy:}\quad ACC \;=\; \frac{TP + TN}{TP + TN + FP + FN}$$

$$\textbf{Precision:}\quad PRE \;=\; \frac{TP}{TP + FP}$$

An aspect that was further investigated in [Cordero et al., 2015] is to have sensors be member of multiple communities. As a result, some sensors may report their findings to multiple community heads. The question then becomes how to configure the CIDS as a whole in terms of the number of communities, their sizes, and the sensors reporting to multiple community heads. One can expect that in a centralized setup (in particular, with just a single community and all sensors reporting to a single, centralized entity), accuracy and precision are best. This is indeed the case, but obviously, we may have a serious scalability problem when dealing with a large system.

In the experiments reported by Cordero et al. [2015], having large communities tends to lead to higher accuracy and precision, whereas it is also important to keep the total number of communities as low as scalability permits. Accuracy and precision also benefit from having overlapping communities, effectively meaning that sensor findings are considered by multiple community heads, to be later combined into the final detections.

To what extent the reported experiments are conclusive for other settings remains to be seen. However, the approach does give a means to think about how to organize a CIDS while taking scalability and performance into account. Typically, running various experiments with different datasets will be needed to find a satisfactory configuration.

9.7 Summary

Security plays an essential role in distributed systems. A distributed system should provide the mechanisms that allow a variety of different security policies to be enforced. Developing and properly applying those mechanisms generally makes security a difficult engineering exercise.

Secure distributed systems are built around at least five design principles: (1) having fail-safe defaults, (2) offering designs and implementations that are open, (3) providing a separation of privileges, (4) providing only those privileges that are needed, and (5) minimizing redundancy of mechanisms and their implementations. Furthermore, we see that it is important to provide mechanisms at different layers in a distributed system, ranging from the lower levels of operating systems to layers in which applications are running. In this sense, understanding what exactly the trusted computing base entails of a system is important, as this base that needs to meet all security requirements.

Finally, and increasingly important, is that distributed systems provide privacy where needed. Guaranteeing that privacy is protected is easier said than done, but the fact that regulations are more firmly installed, such as the GDPR, contributes to the awareness that systems should be designed and developed with security and privacy built in from the start.

Essential to realizing secure distributed systems is the understanding and application of cryptography. Next to symmetric and asymmetric cryptosystems, we see increasingly more cryptographic mechanisms come into practical use due to efficient implementations. Notably homomorphic encryption schemes and multiparty computations are gradually seeing their way into distributed systems, mainly because they allow for untrusted third parties, such as operating in the cloud, to do computations without having to reveal sensitive data.

One could argue that security in distributed systems largely boils down to realizing authentication and authorization. Authentication deals with verifying claim identities. Authorization deals with protecting resources in such a way that only processes that have the proper access rights can actually access and use those resources. Access control always take place after a process has been authenticated. It is important to realize that having being able to verify an identity is not enough for establishing trust.

As distributed systems scale out to multiple organizations, we see a demand for solutions that need to rely less on trusting the individual parties involved in an application. This is one of the reasons why blockchain-based systems have grown in popularity, yet whether blockchain-based solutions can be taken as a general solution for handling lack of trust remains to be seen. Often, simpler and more efficient application-specific solutions may do the job, and perhaps even better.

Besides cryptography, authentication, and authorization, it is important to continuously monitor what is going on in a distributed system. Advances in intrusion detection systems have led to using often advanced machine-learning techniques for detecting anomalous behavior. An open question is how such systems can be effectively scaled out to distributed settings.

Many existing designs of distributed systems have incorporated security and privacy as an afterthought, often also because one may easily think that security and functionality demand a tradeoff to be made. However, there is ample evidence that such a tradeoff is not necessary, provided security is considered from the start of a design.

INDEX

2PC, *see* Distributed commit, two-phase protocol

3PC, *see* Distributed commit, three phase protocol

ABAC, *see* Access control, attribute based

Abstract regions, 49

Acces control
  list, 596

Access control, 595
  attribute-based, 596, 598
  discretionary, 595, 599,600
  mandatory, 595, 599
  matrix, 596
  policy, 595
  role based, 595, 599

Access point, 9

Access transparency, *see* Distribution transparency

Accuracy, 613

ACL, *see* Access control, list

Activation policies, 155

Active Directory, 376, 379

Actuator, 43, 51

Adapter, 75

Adaptive redirection policy, 166

Address Resolution Protocol, 330

Advanced Message-Queuing Protocol, 227
  channel, 228
  connection, 228
  exchange, 231
  link, 228,229
  node, 229
  session, 228

AIDS, *see* Intrusion Detection System, anomaly based

Akamai, 6, 165, 453
  origin server, 165

Amazon
  Elastic Block Store, 141
  Elastic Compute Cloud, 140
  Machine Image, 140
  Simple Storage Service, 66,67, 75

Amazon AMI, *see* Amazon, Machine Image

Amazon S3, *see* Amazon, Simple Storage Service, 99
  bucket, 99

AMQP, *see* Advanced Message-Queuing Protocol

Apache, 122, 159, 552
  hook, 160
  module, 160
  Portable Runtime, 159

Apache APR, *see* Apache, Portable Runtime

API, *see* Application programming interface

Application layer, 188

Application programming interface, 129

Application-layer switch, 163

Architectural perspective, 8

Architectural style, 56

ARP, *see* Address resolution protocol

Asynchronous system, 469

Atomicity, 189

Authentication, 10, 21, 189
Authorization, 21, 189
    graph-based, 606
Autonomous System, 426
Availability, *see* Dependability, avail-
    ability

Backup server, 485
Big endian, 198
Bitcoin, 291
Bits-per-second, 2
BitTorrent, 10, 96
    magnet link, 98
    torrent file, 97
    tracker, 97
Blockchain, 5, 22, 104
    genesis block, 591
    permissioned, 106, 501,502
    permissionless, 106, 290, 502,
        589
    Proof of Stake, 292, 589
    Proof of Work, 290, 589
    smart contract, 593
Broadcasting, 236
Browser, 86
Byzantine agreement, 492
Byzantine failure, 468

Cache, 393, 407, 429
    cache hit, 429
    coherence detection, 443
    coherence enforcement, 444
    coherence protocol, 443
    content aware, 457
    content blind, 458
    cooperative cache, 451
    distributed cache, 451
    Network File System, 444
    Web, 451
    write back, 444
    write through, 444
Callback, 205
CAP theorem, 506
Capability, 596

Causal history, 267
Causality, 267
CDN, *see* Content Delivery Network
CGI, *see* Common Gateway Inter-
    face
Cgroups, 135
Challenge-response protocol, 573
    challenge, 573, 579
    multiway, 577
    nonce, 577
Checkpointing
    coordinated, 539
    distributed snapshot, 538
    domino effect, 539
    independent, 539,540
    recovery line, 538
Checksum, 186
Chord, 91, 233, 294, 333
    finger table, 333
    flooding, 239
    forwarder, 233
    successor, 91
Chrome OS, 145
CIDS, *see* Intrusion Detection Sys-
    tem, collaborative
Client, 27, 37, 60, 79
    fat, 82
    thin, 82, 142
Client stub, 148, 194
Client-server computing, 27, 172
Clock
    accuracy, 254
    clock drift rate, 254
    drift, 254
    external synchronization, 254
    internal synchronization, 254
    precision, 254
    skew, 251
    synchronization, 254
    tick, 250
Closure mechanism, 348
    container, 348
Cloud computing, 12, 98

Cluster computing, 32, 34
Code segment, 171
Code-on-demand, 172
Coherence model, 406
Collaborative Intrusion Detection System, *see* Intrusion Detection System, collaborative
Common Gateway Interface, 87
Communication
    asynchronous, 191, 214, 301
    asysnchronous, 219
    persistent, 191, 231, 301
    synchronous, 27, 191
    transient, 191, 219
Communication pattern, 214
    pipeline, 217
    publish-subscribe, 216
    request-reply, 214
Communication perspective, 9
Communication protocol, 59, 183
    stack, 58
Communication service, 58, 183
Computational grid, 27
Computer timer, 250
    counter, 250
    holding register, 250
Concurrency transparency, *see* Distribution transparency
Concurrent operations, 260, 401
Confidentiality, 20, 313
Conflict-Free Replicated Data Type, 409
Conit, *see* Consistency unit
Connection-oriented service, 60, 183
Connectionless service, 184
Consensus, 475
    flooding, 475
    Paxos, 477, 479
    Paxos, accept message, 485
    Paxos, acceptor, 480
    Paxos, client, 480
    Paxos, leader, 480, 485

    Paxos, learned message, 485
    Paxos, learner, 480
    Paxos, proposal message, 491
    Paxos, proposal timestamp, 483
    Paxos, proposer, 480, 491
    Raft, 289, 477
    Raft, follower, 477
    Raft, leader, 477
    Raft, leader election, 289
    Raft, log, 477
    Raft, term, 289, 477
Consistency, 31
Consistency and replication perspective, 9
Consistency model, 406
    causal consistency, 401, 408
    client centric, 415,416, 448
    compositional, 400
    continuous consistency, 410, 446
    data centric, 395
    entry consistency, 404, 415, 434
    eventual consistency, 407
    linearizable, 400
    monotonic read, 417
    monotonic write, 418
    program consistency, 410
    read your writes, 420
    schedule, 405
    sequential consistency, 397
    serializable, 400, 405, 422
    strong eventual consistency, 409
    writes-follow-reads, 421
Consistency protocol, 437
    primary based, 438,439, 474
    primary-backup, 438
    quorum based, 441
    read quorum, 442
    replicated-write, 440
    write quorum, 442
Consistency unit, 411
    declaration, 414
    false share, 413
Contact address, 223

Container, 133, 348
Content Delivery Network, 6, 95, 165, 319, 425, 427, 453
Context awareness, 45
Cookie, 153
Coordinated Universal Time, 252, 253
Coordination, 68, 248
    direct, 68
    event-based, 69
    mailbox, 69, 221
    referentially coupled, 68, 313
    temporally coupled, 68, 221, 313
Coordination perspective, 9
Copy-before-use, 15
CRDT, *see* Conflict-Free Replicated Data Type
Critical region, 264, 266, 275, 403
CRL, *see* Cryptosystem, certificate revocation list
Cryptosystem
    assymmetric, 21
    asymmetric, 557
    certificate revocation, 569
    certification authority, 569
    certification revocation list, 569
    public-key certificate, 569
    public-key system, 21, 557, 568
    secret-key system, 557
    session key, 564, 579, 580
    shared-key system, 557
    symmetric, 21, 557
Cyclon, 304

DAC, *see* Access control, discretionary
Data link layer, 186
    frame, 186
Data store, 395
Data synchronization, 248
Deadlock, 272
Decentralization, 3, 7
Decentralized system, 4
Decryption, 555
Delegation, 601

Dependability, 18, 463
    availability, 19, 463, 464
    availability, long-term, 464
    confidentiality, 547
    integrity, 547
    maintainability, 19, 463
    reliability, 19, 463, 464
    safety, 19, 272, 463
Detection
    false negative, 613
    false positive, 613
    true negative, 613
    true positive, 613
DHCP, *see* Dynamic Host Configuration Protocol
DHT, *see* Distributed hash table
Differential GPS, 317
Diffie-Hellman group, 565
Diffie-Hellman key exchange, 565, 566
    ephemeral, 565
Digital signature, 22, 561
Directed acyclic graph, 346
Directory node, 345
    location record, 338
    root, 338
Directory table, 345
Dispatcher, 125
Distribtion
    horizontal, 89
Distributed commit, 40, 189, 528
    blocking protocol, 531
    one-phase protocol, 529
    three-phase protocl, 534
    two-phase protocol, 529
Distributed consensus, 106
Distributed hash table, 90
Distributed ledger, 5, 104
Distributed object, 63
Distributed shared memory, 33
Distributed system, 4
Distributed transaction, 37
Distribution, 3
    vertical, 89

Distribution transparency, 6, 11, 148
    access transparency, 11, 15, 67,
        148
    concurrency transparency, 13,
        149
    failure transparency, 13, 149
    location transparency, 12, 148,
        332
    migration transparency, 12, 148
    relocation transparency, 12, 148
    replication transparency, 13, 149
DNS, *see* Domain Name System,
        359
    domain name, 189
DNSSEC, *see* Domain Name Sys-
        tem, security extension
Document Object Model, 145
DOM, *see* Document Object Model
Domain, 338
Domain name, 165
Domain Name System, 6, 165, 189,
        359,360, 472
    canonical name, 361
    domain, 30
    key-signing key, 366
    resource record, 360
    security extension, 366
    zone, 30, 354
    zone transfer, 362
    zone-signing key, 366
Downcall, 57
DSM, *see* Distributed shared mem-
        ory
Dynamic Host Configuration Pro-
        tocol, 46

EAI, *see* Enterprise application in-
        tegration
EBS, *see* Amazon, Elastic Block Store
Eclipse attack, 344, 588
Edge computing, 100, 456
    infrastructure, 100
    orchestration, 103
Encapsulation, 63,64

End point, 150
End-to-end principle, 271, 551
Enterprise application integration,
        38, 75, 226
Epidemic behavior, 240
    anti-entropy, 241, 521
    infected, 241
    removed, 241
    round, 241
    rumor spreading, 243
    susceptible, 241
Epidemic protocol, 240, 297
    death certificate, 245
    dormant death certificate, 245
Erdös-Rényi graph, 237
Error, 19, 465
Event bus, 70
Event counter, 261
Execution segment, 171
Extended markup language, 42, 224
Extensible, 16

FaaS, *see* Function-as-a-Service
Fail, 19
Failure, 465
    arbitrary, 468
    commission, 468
    communication, 508
    crash, 467
    exception handling, 509
    fail arbitrary, 469
    fail noisy, 469
    fail safe, 469
    fail silent, 469
    fail stop, 469
    omission, 467,468
    performance, 468
    receive omission, 467
    response, 468
    send omission, 467
    timing, 467
Failure detection, 506
    eventually perfect, 507
    suspect, 507

Failure rate function, 464
Failure transparency, *see* Distribution transparency
Farmer task, 217
Fault, 20, 465
    intermittent, 20, 466
    permanent, 20, 466
    transient, 20, 466
Fault tolerance, 5, 18, 20, 466
    Byzantine, Altruism, Rationality (BAR), 505
Fault-tolerance perspective, 9
Federated learning, 4, 168
FHE, *see* Security mechanism, full homomorphic encryption
File Transfer Protocol, 188
Firewall, 609
    application-level gateway, 610
    packet-filtering gateway, 610
    proxy gateway, 610
Fog computing, 101
Free riding, 96
Front end, 162
FTP, *see* File Transfer Protocol
Function-as-a-Service, 100

GDPR, *see* General Data Protection Regulation
General Data Protection Regulation, 553
Gentle reincarnation, 514
Global Positioning System, 316
Google Mail, 5
Gossiping, 240, 297, 311
    Data-injection attack, 306
    directional, 244, 297
    partial view, 298, 312
GPS, *see* Global Positioning System
Grid computer, 4
Grid computing, 32, 35
    application layer, 37
    collective layer, 37
    connectivity layer, 36
    fabric layer, 36

    resource layer, 36
Groupware, 10

Happens-before relation, 260
Hash function, 22, 290, 560
    digest, 291
    nonce, 291
    strong collision resistance, 560
    trapdoor, 560
    weak collision resistance, 560
Honest-but-curious, 315, 553
HTML, *see* HyperText Markup Language
HTTP, *see* HyperText Transfer Protocol
HTTPS, *see* HyperText Transfer Protocol, secure, 583
Hypercube, 90
Hyperspace, 312
HyperText Markup Language, 86
HyperText Transfer Protocol, 86, 188
    secure, 367, 551

IaaS, *see* Infrastructure-as-a-Service, 139
IANA, *see* Internet Assigned Numbers Authority
ICN, *see* Information-centric networking
Idempotent operation, 80, 513
Identifier-location split, 329
IDL, *see* Interface Definition Language
Implicit action, 45
In-network data processing, 50
Incremental snapshot, 539
Information-centric networking, *see* Named-data networking, 385
Infrastructure-as-a-Service, 99, 139
Instruction
    behavior-sensitive, 132
    control-sensitive, 132
    nonprivileged, 131

privileged, 131
Instruction set architecture, 129
Integrity, 20, 313
Interceptor, 76
    message-level, 77
    request-level, 77
Interface, 15, 184
Interface Definition Language, 15, 203
International Atomic Time, 252
Internet Assigned Numbers Authority, 150
Internet of Things, 44
Internet Protocol, 187
Internet Service Provider, 28, 100
Internet-of-Things, 100
Interoperability, 16
Interprocess communication, 115
Interrupt
    direct overhead, 116
    indirect overhead, 116
Intruder, 556
Intrusion detection, 609
Intrusion Detection System
    anomaly-based, 611
    collaborative, 612
    community, 612
    signature-based, 611
IoT, *see* Internet-of-Things
IP, *see* Internet Protocol
IPC, *see* Interprocess communication
ISA, *see* Instruction set architecture
ISP, *see* Internet Service Provider, *see* Internet Service Provider

JavaScript, 87, 146

KDC, *see* Key distribution center
Kerberos, 551, 581, 605
    authentication service, 581
    ticket-granting service, 581
Key distribution center, 576
    single sign-on, 583

ticket, 576, 581
Key-derivation function, 585

LAMP, 140
LAN, *see* Local-area network
Landmark, 320
LDAP, *see* Lightweight Directory Access Protocol
Leader election, 96, 106, 283
    bully algorithm, 283
    ring algorithm, 285
Leaf domain, 338
Lease, 72, 433
    age-based, 433
    renewal-frequency based, 433
    state-based, 434
Lightweight Directory Access Protocol, 376
    directory information base, 377
    directory information tree, 377
    directory service agent, 379
    directory user agent, 379
    relative distinguished name, 377
Linda, 70, 307
Little endian, 198
Liveness property, 482, 490, 502, 505
Local-area network, 2
Location transparency, *see* Distribution transparency
Lock, 403, 434
Logical clock, 260, 263

MAC, *see* Access control, mandatory
Maintainability, *see* Dependability, maintainability
MANET, *see* Mobile ad hoc network
MCC, *see* Mobile Cloud Computing
Mean Time Between Failures, 19, 465
Mean Time To Failure, 19, 465
Mean Time To Repair, 19, 465

MEC, *see* Mobile Edge Computing

Mechanism, 17

Memory Management Unit, 113

Mesh network, 233

Message broker, 75, 95, 225, 308

Message digest, 562

Message logging, 537, 542
    optimistic, 543
    pessimistic, 543
    receiver based, 537
    sender based, 537

Message transfer time unit, 279

Message-oriented middleware, 41, 220
    router, 224

Message-Passing Interface, 218

Message-queuing system, 220

Microservice, 65

Middleware, 11, 74
    modifiable, 78

Migration
    receiver initiated, 172
    sender initiated, 172

Migration transparency, *see* Distribution transparency

MMU, *see* Memory Management Unit

Mobile ad hoc network, 47

Mobile agent, 168, 172

Mobile Cloud Computing, 48

Mobile computing, 47

Mobile Edge Computing, 48

Mobile host
    care-of-address, 331
    home agent, 331

MOM, *see* Message-oriented middleware

MPC, *see* Multiparty computation

MPI, *see* Message-Passing Interface

MPLS, *see* Multi-Protocol Label Switching

MTBF, *see* Mean Time Between Failures

MTTF, *see* Mean Time To Failure

MTTR, *see* Mean Time To Repair

MTTU, *see* Message transfer time unit

Multi-Protocol Label Switching, 454

Multicasting, 232, 236
    application-level, 232
    atomic, 522, 526
    causally ordered, 270, 526
    feedback implosion, 518
    feedback suppression, 519
    FIFO-ordered, 525
    flooding, 237
    group view, 523
    link stress, 234
    probabilistic flooding, 237
    relative delay penalty, 234
    stretch, 234
    totally ordered, 264, 523, 526
    tree cost, 235
    unordered, 524
    view change, 523

Multicomputer, 33

Multiparty computation, 23, 566
    oblivious transfer, 566

Multiprocessor, 33

Mutual exclusion, 189
    permission-based, 272
    token based, 272

Name
    alias, 349
    global, 345
    local, 345

Name resolution, 347
    automounting, 373
    file handle, 371,372
    iterative, 355
    recursive, 356

Name resolver, 355

Name space, 344
    absolute path name, 345
    administrational layer, 353
    directory node, 345

foreign, 349
global layer, 352
hard link, 349
leaf node, 344
managerial layer, 353
mount point, 349
mounting, 349, 369
mounting point, 349
path name, 345
relative path name, 345
root node, 345
Unix, 346, 348
Named-data networking, 329, 385
content store, 387
forwarding information base, 387
pending interest table, 387
Naming
access point, 327
address, 327
attribute-based, 375
directory service, 375
flat name, 329
home location, 331
human-friendly name, 328
identifier, 328
index server, 380
location independent, 328
naming system, 375
Naming graph
symbolic link, 349
Naming perspective, 9
Naming service, 30
Nano computers, 2
NAS, *see* Network-Attached Storage
NAT, *see* Network-address translation
NCS, *see* Network Coordinates System
NDN, *see* Named-data networking
Needham-Schroeder authentication protocol, 577, 581

NetFlow, 590
choice set, 590
Network Coordinates System, 318
Network File System, 83, 350, 369, 445
export directory, 370
NFS client, 84
NFS server, 85
open delegation, 445
Network layer, 186
packet, 187
Network Time Protocol, 256
reference clock, 256
startum server, 256
Network-address translation, 140, 163
Network-Attached Storage, 6
Networked computer system, 2
expansive view, 4
integrative view, 4
NFS, *see* Network File System
Node, 89
Nonce, 603
Notification, 69
Notification filtering, 306
NTP, *see* Network Time Protocol

OAuth, *see* Open Authorization
Object
interface, 63
method, 63
persistent, 204
state, 63
transient, 204
Object adapter, 75, 155
Object wrapper, 155
OGSA, *see* Open Grid Services Architecture
One-way function, 560
Open Authorization, 604
access token, 604
authorization code, 604
Open Grid Services Architecture, 37

Open Systems Interconnection Reference Model, 183
Openness, 15
Orchestration, 65
Order deviation, 412
Orphan computation, 513, 541
    expiration, 514
    extermination, 514
    grandorphan, 514
    reincarnation, 514
OSI, *see* Open Systems Interconnection Reference Model
Out-of-band data, 151
Overlay network, 89, 224, 231, 299, 308, 310,311, 315
    geometric, 318

PaaS, *see* Platform-as-a-Service, 139
Parallel processing, 33
Parameter marshaling, 197
Parameter passing
    call-by-copy/restore, 194
    call-by-reference, 193
    call-by-value, 193
    object reference, 200
Paravirtualization, 133
Partial failure, 7, 18
Partially synchronous, 469
Paxos, *see* Consensus, Paxos
PBFT, *see* Practical Byzantine Fault Tolerance
Peer-sampling service, 244, 298, 300, 303
Peer-to-peer search
    flooding, 93
    policy-based, 94
    random walk, 93,94, 311
Peer-to-peer system, 89
    structured, 90
    unstructured, 92
PEKS, *see* Public Key Encryption with Keyword Search
Pervasive system, 43
PGP, *see* Pretty Good Privacy

PHE, *see* Security mechanism, partial homomorphic encryption
Physical layer, 186
Piecewise deterministic execution model, 541
PlanetLab, 136
Platform-as-a-Service, 99, 139
Plugin, 225
Policy, 17
Policy Machine, 598
    assignment, 599
    obligation, 599
    prohibition, 599
Port, 150
Portability, 16
PoS, *see* Blockchain, proof of stake
Position-based routing, 319
PoW, *see* Blockchain, proof of work
Practical Byzantine Fault Tolerance, 498
    commit certificate, 500
    prepare certificate, 499
    view, 499
    view-change certificate, 501
Precision, 613
Presentation layer, 188
Pretty Good Privacy, 570
Primary server, 485
Problem monotonicity, 410
Process, 113
    context, 113
    process table, 113
Process group, 472
    flat, 472
    group server, 473
    hierarchical, 472
    k-fault tolerant, 474
Process migration, 167
Process perspective, 9
Process synchronization, 248
Processor context, 113
Progressive Web app, 148

Protocol stack, 185
Protocol suite, 185
Proximity neighbor selection, 338
Proximity routing, 337
PSS, *see* Peer-sampling service
Public key, 21
Public Key Encryption with Keyword Search, 314
Publish, 69, 71
Publish-subscribe, 41, 226, 306
 content-based, 72
 matching, 72
 message subject, 308
 routing filter, 310
 topic-based, 72
PWA, *see* Progressive Web app

QoS, *see* Quality of Service
Quality of Service, 424
Query containment check, 457
Queue manager, 222

RabbitMQ, 231
Raft, *see* Consensus, Raft
Random graph, 92, 237
RBAC, *see* Access control, role based
RBS, *see* Reference Broadcast Synchronization
RDF, *see* Resource Description Framework
RDP, *see* Relative delay penalty
Read-One, Write-All, 443
Read-write conflict, 407
Real-time Transport Protocol, 187
Recovery
 backward, 536
 checkpointing, 536
 erasure correction, 536
 forward, 536
Redundancy
 information, 470
 physical, 470
 time, 470
 triple modular, 470

Reference Broadcast Synchronization, 257
Reference monitor, 594
Reflection attack, 574
Reliability, *see* Dependability, reliability
Relocation transparency, *see* Distribution transparency
Remote desktop, 144
Remote evaluation, 172
Remote file service, 83
 remote access model, 84
 upload/download model, 84
Remote method invocation, 41, 205
Remote object, 63,64
 binding to, 63
 proxy, 63
 skeleton, 64
Remote procedure call, 38, 41,42, 84, 190, 192
 asynchronous, 205, 231
 at-least-once semantics, 511
 at-most-once semantics, 511
 client stub, 63
 deferred synchronous, 205
 exactly-once semantics, 511
 failure, 509
 multicast, 207
 one-way, 206
 synchronous, 231
Rendezvous node, 235, 308
Replicated object invocation, 436
Replication
 active, 431, 440, 474
 client initiated, 429
 invalidation protocol, 430
 mirror site, 426
 mirroring, 426
 partial, 457
 permanent replica, 426
 quorum based, 474
 sequencer, 441
 server initiated, 427

shared nothing, 427
update protocol, client-based, 431
update protocol, pull-based, 431
update protocol, push-based, 431
update protocol, server-based, 431
Replication transparency, *see* Distribution transparency
Representational State Transfer, 66
Request-reply, 79
Resource Description Framework, 375
Resource segment, 171
Resource sharing, 10
Resource virtualization, 127
REST, *see* Representational State Transfer
RESTful architecture, 66
Reverse proxy, 163
RMI, *see* Remote method invocation
Routing, 186
ROWA, *see* Read-One, Write-All
RPC, *see* Remote procedure call
RTP, *see* Real-Time Transport Protocol

SaaS, *see* Software-as-a-Service, 139
Safety, *see* Dependability, safety
Safety property, 482, 490, 502, 505
Sandbox, 147
Scalability
    administrative, 24, 27
    analysis of size scalability, 25
    geographical, 24, 26
    size, 24
Scalable Reliable Multicasting, 519
Scaling out, 28
Scaling technique
    asynchronous communication, 29
    caching, 31

hide latency, 29
partitioning and distribution, 30
replication, 31
Scaling up, 28
SCS, *see* Vserver, slice creation service
SCTP, *see* Streaming Control Transmission Protocol
Searchable encryption, 314
Secret key, 21
Secure channel, 22, 568
Secure Shell Protocol, 551
Secure Socket Layer, 583
Security
    proxy, 601
Security key, 21
Security mechanism, 548
    authentication, 548, 571
    authentication, continuous, 572
    authentication, electronic, 572
    authentication, multi-factor, 572
    authentication, single-factor, 571
    authorization, 548
    decryption, 21
    encryption, 21, 548, 555
    encryption, ciphertext, 555
    encryption, plaintext, 555
    full homomorphic encryption, 558
    homomorphic encryption, 558
    partial homomorphic encryption, 558
Security perspective, 10
Security policy, 547
Security principle, 549
    fail-safe defaults, 549
    least common mechanism, 550
    least privilege, 549
    open design, 549
    separation of privilege, 549
Security threat, 547
Selective routing, 310

Self-certifying name, 343
Self-configurable system, 18
Sensor, 43
Sensor network, 49, 295
Servant, 89, 156
Server, 24, 27, 60, 79
    concurrent, 150
    iterative, 150
    permanent state, 153
    session state, 153
    soft state, 152
    stateful, 152
    stateless, 152
Server stub, 195
Server-side script, 88
Service-level agreement, 98
Service-oriented architecture, 37, 64
Session key, 573
Session layer, 188
Shard, 554
Shared data space, 46, 69
    attribute, 71
    tuple, 69
SIDS, *see* Intrusion Detection System, signature based
SLA, *see* Service-level agreement
Smartphone, 2
SOA, *see* Service-oriented architecture
Socket, 208
Socket interface, 208
Software architecture, 56
    component, 57
    connector, 57
    event based, 70
    interface, 57,58
    layered, 57, 61
    microservice, 63
    object, 63
    publish-subscribe, 70
    service, 63
    shared data space, 70
Software-as-a-Service, 99, 129, 139

Space-filling curve, 381
Spanner, 259
SRM, *see* Scalable Reliable Multicasting
SSH, *see* Secure Shell Protocol
Starvation, 272
State machine replication, 264
Stateless execution, 66
Streaming Control Transmission Protocol, 187
Strong mobility, 173
Subscribe, 69, 72
Successor, 333
Super peer, 95, 293
Superserver, 150
Switch tree, 235
Sybil attack, 344, 586
Synchronization variable, *see* Lock
Synchronous, 504
Synchronous system, 469
System architecture, 56, 79
    three-tiered, 83
    two-tiered, 81
System calls, 129

TAI, *see* International Atomic Time
TCB, *see* Trusted Computing Base
TCP, *see* Transmission Control Protocol, 187
TCP handoff, 163
Thread
    context, 114
    many-to-many model, 120
    many-to-one model, 120, 122
    one-to-one model, 120
Thread-level parallelism, 124
TIB/Rendezvous, 308
    rendezvous daemon, 308
Time
    leap second, 252
    mean solar second, 252
    solar day, 251
    solar second, 251
    transit sun, 251

Time-to-live, 93
TLB, *see* Translation Lookaside Buffer
TLP, *see* Thread-level parallelism
TLS, *see* Transport Layer Security
TMR, *see* Redundancy, triple modular
Topology-based identifier, 337
TP monitor, *see* Transaction-processing monitor
Transaction, 38
    ACID, 38
    nested, 39
Transaction-processing monitor, 40
Transactional RPC, 38
Transient object, 154
Translation Lookaside Buffer, 113
Transmission Control Protocol, 59, 187
Transport layer, 187
Transport Layer Security, 551, 583
Transport-layer switch, 163
Trap, 131
Trapdoor, 314
Triangle inequality, 320
TrueTime, 259
Trust, 10, 21, 304, 586
Trust chain, 366, 588
Trusted Computing Base, 552
Trusted third party, 104
TTL, *see* Time-to-live
Tunnel, 551
Tuple space, 70

Ubiquitous computing system, 44
UDP, *see* Universal Datagram Protocol
Uniform Resource Identifier, 66
Uniform Resource Locator, 12, 86
Universal Datagram Protocol, 187
Universal Plug and Play protocol, 46
Unix
    namespaces, 134
Upcall, 57

handle, 58
UPnP, *see* Universal Plug and Play protocol
URI, *see* Uniform Resource Identifier
URL, *see* Uniform Resource Locator
UTC, *see* Coordinated Universal Time, 253
Utility computing, 98
Utilization, 26

Vector clock, 267,268
VFS, *see* Virtual File System
Virtual desktop environment, 82, 144
Virtual File System, 84
Virtual machine monitor
    hosted, 131
    native, 130
Virtual Network Computing, 144
Virtual organization, 35
Virtual private network, 550
Virtual synchrony, 523
    flush message, 528
    stable message, 527
Virtualization, 127
    guest operating system, 131
    host operating system, 131
    process virtual machine, 130
    virtual processor, 113
VM fork, 177
VNC, *see* Virtual Network Computing
VPN, *see* Virtual private network
Vserver, 136
    node manager, 137
    service provider, 137
    slice, 136
    slice authority, 137
    slice creation service, 137

WAN, *see* Wide-area network
War driving, 317
WAVE, 606

attestation, 606
entity store, 608
issuer, 606
map log, 608
operation log, 608
resource, 606
RTree, 606
RTree statement, 606
structural security, 608
subject, 606
Weak mobility, 172
Weak peer, 95
Web of trust, 570, 587
WebAssembly, 146
Wide-area network, 2
Window manager, 143
Worker task, 217
Worker thread, 125
Wrapper, 75
Write set, 416
Write-write conflict, 407

X kernel, 142
X protocol, 143
X Window System, 142
XML, *see* Extended markup language

Zeroconf, 46
ZeroMQ, 213
ZooKeeper, 280, 286, 422
ensemble, 286

BIBLIOGRAPHY

Abadi M. and Needham R. Prudent Engineering Practice for Cryptographic Protocols. *IEEE Transactions on Software Engineering*, 22(1):6–15, Jan. 1996. → 576.

Abbas N., Zhang Y., Taherkordi A., and Skeie T. Mobile Edge Computing: A Survey. *IEEE Internet of Things Journal*, 5(1):450–465, 2018. → 48.

Aberer K., Alima L. O., Ghodsi A., Girdzijauskas S., Hauswirth M., and Haridi S. The Essence of P2P: A Reference Architecture for Overlay Networks. In *5th International Conference on Peer-to-Peer Computing*, pages 11–20, Los Alamitos, CA., Aug. 2005. IEEE, IEEE Computer Society Press. → 89.

Acar A., Aksu H., Uluagac A. S., and Conti M. A Survey on Homomorphic Encryption Schemes: Theory and Implementation. *ACM Computing Surveys*, 51(4):1–35, 2018. → 558.

Adar E. and Huberman B. A. Free Riding on Gnutella. Hewlett Packard, Information Dynamics Lab, Jan. 2000. → 96.

Adelstein F., Gupta S., Richard G., and Schwiebert L. *Fundamentals of Mobile and Pervasive Computing*. McGraw-Hill, New York, NY, 2005. → 47.

Adve S. V. and Boehm H.-J. Memory Models: A Case for Rethinking Parallel Languages and Hardware. *Communications of the ACM*, 53(8):90–101, Aug. 2010. → 399.

Afanasyev A., Burke J., Refaei T., Wang L., Zhang B., and Zhang L. A Brief Introduction to Named Data Networking. In *IEEE Military Communications Conference (MILCOM)*, pages 1–6, 2018. → 386.

Agarwal A., George M., Jeyaraj A., and Schwarzkopf M. Retrofitting GDPR Compliance onto Legacy Databases. *Proceedings of the VLDB Endowment*, 15(4):958–970, Dec. 2022. → 554.

Ager B., Mühlbauer W., Smaragdakis G., and Uhlig S. Comparing DNS Resolvers in the Wild. In *10th Internet Measurement Conference*, pages 15–21, New York, NY, 2010. ACM Press. → 369.

Aguilera M. and Terry D. The Many Faces of Consistency. *Data Engineering*, page 3, 2016. → 395.

Ahlgren B., Dannewitz C., Imbrenda C., Kutscher D., and Ohlman B. A Survey of Information-centric Networking. *IEEE Communications Magazine*, 50(7):26–36, July 2012. → 385.

Aiyer A., Alvisi L., Clement A., Dahlin M., and Martin J.-P. BAR Fault Tolerance for Cooperative Services. In *20th Symposium on Operating System Principles*, pages 45–58, New York, NY, Oct. 2005. ACM, ACM Press. → 505.

Akgul F. *ZeroMQ*. Packt Publishing, Birmingham, UK, 2013. → 213.

Akyildiz I. F. and Kasimoglu I. H. Wireless Sensor and Actor Networks: Research Challenges. *Ad Hoc Networks*, 2:351–367, 2004. → 49.

Akyildiz I. F., Su W., Sankarasubramaniam Y., and Cayirci E. A Survey on Sensor Networks. *IEEE Communications Magazine*, 40(8):102–114, Aug. 2002. → 49.

Akyildiz I. F., Wang X., and Wang W. Wireless Mesh Networks: A Survey. *Computer Networks*, 47(4):445–487, Mar. 2005. → 49.

Albrecht J., Oppenheimer D., Vahdat A., and Patterson D. A. Design and Implementation Trade-Offs for Wide-Area Resource Discovery. *ACM Transactions on Internet Technology*, 8(4):1–44, 2008. → 383.

Alegre U., Augusto J. C., and Clark T. Engineering Context-Aware Systems and Applications: A Survey. *Journal of Systems and Software*, 117:55–83, 2016. → 45.

Ali W., Shamsuddin S. M., and Ismail A. S. A Survey of Web Caching and Prefetching. *International Journal of Advances in Soft Computing and Its Applications*, 3(1):18–44, 2011. → 453.

Allani M., Garbinato B., and Pedone F. Application Layer Multicast. In Garbinato B., Mirando H., and Rodrigues L., editors, *Middleware for Network Eccentric and Mobile Applications*, pages 191–214. Springer-Verlag, Berlin, 2009. → 233.

Allen R. and Lowe-Norris A. *Windows 2000 Active Directory*. O'Reilly & Associates, Sebastopol, CA., 2nd edition, 2003. → 379.

Allman M. Putting DNS in Context. In *Internet Measurement Conference*, page 309–316, 2020. → 369.

Alonso G., Casati F., Kuno H., and Machiraju V. *Web Services: Concepts, Architectures and Applications*. Springer-Verlag, Berlin, 2004. → 37.

Alvisi L. and Marzullo K. Message Logging: Pessimistic, Optimistic, Causal, and Optimal. *IEEE Transactions on Software Engineering*, 24(2):149–159, Feb. 1998. → 541, 542.

AMQP Working Group . AMQP, Protocol specification, Version 0-9-1, Nov. 2008. → 227.

Amza C., Cox A., Dwarkadas S., Keleher P., Lu H., Rajamony R., Yu W., and Zwaenepoel W. TreadMarks: Shared Memory Computing on Networks of Workstations. *Computer*, 29(2):18–28, Feb. 1996. → 33.

Andersen M. P. *Decentralized Authorization with Private Delegation*. Ph.D., University of California, Berkeley, 2019. → 606, 607, 608.

Andersen M. P., Kumar S., AbdelBaky M., Fierro G., Kolb J., Kim H.-S., Culler D. E., and Popa R. A. WAVE: A Decentralized Authorization Framework with Transitive Delegation. In *28th USENIX Security Symposium*, pages 1375–1392, 2019. → 606.

Andrews G. *Foundations of Multithreaded, Parallel, and Distributed Programming*. Addison-Wesley, Reading, MA., 2000. → 248.

Androutsellis-Theotokis S. and Spinellis D. A Survey of Peer-to-Peer Content Distribution Technologies. *ACM Computing Surveys*, 36(4):335–371, Dec. 2004. → 89.

Antonini M., Vecchio M., and Antonelli F. Fog Computing Architectures: A Reference for Practitioners. *IEEE Internet of Things Magazine*, 2(3):19–25, 2019. → 104.

Arkills B. *LDAP Directories Explained: An Introduction and Analysis*. Addison-Wesley, Reading, MA., 2003. → 376.

Attiya H. and Welch J. *Distributed Computing Fundamentals, Simulations, and Advanced Topics*. John Wiley, New York, 2nd edition, 2004. → 249.

Atxutegi E., Liberal F., Saiz E., and Ibarrola E. Toward Standardized Internet Speed Measurements for End Users: Current Technical Constraints. *IEEE Communications Magazine*, 54(9):50–57, Sept. 2016. → 454.

Avizienis A., Laprie J.-C., Randell B., and Landwehr C. Basic Concepts and Taxonomy of Dependable and Secure Computing. *IEEE Transactions on Dependable and Secure Computing*, 1(1):11–33, Jan. 2004. → 20, 466.

Awadallah A. and Rosenblum M. The vMatrix: A Network of Virtual Machine Monitors for Dynamic Content Distribution. In *7th Web Caching Workshop*, Aug. 2002. → 128.

Ayeswarya S. and Norman J. A Survey on Different Continuous Authentication Systems. *International Journal of Biometrics*, 11(1):67–99, 2019. → 572.

Azevedo L. G., Souza Soares E. F.de , Souza R., and Moreno M. F. Modern Federated Database Systems: An Overview. In *25th International Conference on Enterprise Information Systems*, pages 276–283, May 2020. → 427.

Babaoglu O. and Toueg S. Non-Blocking Atomic Commitment. In Mullender S., editor, *Distributed Systems*, pages 147–168. Addison-Wesley, Wokingham, 2nd edition, 1993. → 531.

Bader M. *Space-Filling Curves, An Introduction with Applications in Scientific Computing*. Springer-Verlag, Berlin, 2013. → 382.

Bailis P., Ghodsi A., Hellerstein J. M., and Stoica I. Bolt-on Causal Consistency. In *SIGMOD International Conference on Management Of Data*, pages 761–772, New York, NY, 2013. ACM, ACM Press. → 408.

Balakrishnan H., Kaashoek M. F., Karger D., Morris R., and Stoica I. Looking up Data in P2P Systems. *Communications of the ACM*, 46(2):43–48, Feb. 2003. → 90.

Baldauf M., Dustdar S., and Rosenberg F. A Survey on Context-aware Systems. *Int. J. Ad Hoc Ubiquitous Comput.*, 2:263–277, June 2007. → 46.

Baldoni R., Beraldi R., Quema V., Querzoni L., and Tucci-Piergiovanni S. TERA: Topic-based Event Routing for Peer-to-Peer Architectures. In *International Conference on Distributed Event-Based Systems*, pages 2–13, New York, NY, 2007. ACM Press. → 311.

Baldoni R., Querzoni L., Tarkoma S., and Virgillito A. Distributed Event Routing in Publish/Subscribe Communication Systems: a Survey. In Garbinato B., Miranda H., and Rodrigues L., editors, *Middleware for Network Eccentric and Mobile Applications*, pages 219–244. Springer-Verlag, Berlin, 2009. → 308.

Ballintijn G. *Locating Objects in a Wide-area System*. PhD thesis, Vrije Universiteit Amsterdam, 2003. → 338.

Banaei-Kashani F. and Shahab C. Criticality-based Analysis and Design of Unstructured Peer-to-Peer Networks as "Complex Systems". In *3rd International Symposium on Cluster Computing and the Grid*, pages 351–356, Los Alamitos, CA., May 2003. IEEE, IEEE Computer Society Press. → 237.

Baquero C. and Preguica N. Why Logical Clocks Are Easy. *Communications of the ACM*, 59(4):43–47, Mar. 2016. → 267.

Barborak M., Malek M., and Dahbura A. The Consensus Problem in Fault-Tolerant Computing. *ACM Computing Surveys*, 25(2):171–220, June 1993. → 504.

Barham P., Dragovic B., Fraser K., Hand S., Harris T., Ho A., Neugebar R., Pratt I., and Warfield A. Xen and the Art of Virtualization. In *19th Symposium on Operating System Principles*, pages 164–177, New York, NY, Oct. 2003. ACM, ACM Press. → 133.

Barron D. *Pascal – The Language and its Implementation*. John Wiley, New York, 1981. → 174.

Barroso L., Hölze U., and Ranganathan P. *The Datacenter as a Computer: An Introduction to the Design of Warehouse-Scale Machines*. Synthesis Lectures on Computer Architectures. Morgan and Claypool, San Rafael, CA, 3rd edition, 2018. → 129.

Baset S. and Schulzrinne H. An Analysis of the Skype Peer-to-Peer Internet Telephony Protocol. In *25th INFOCOM Conference*, pages 1–11, Los Alamitos, CA., Apr. 2006. IEEE, IEEE Computer Society Press. → 28.

Basile C., Whisnant K., Kalbarczyk Z., and Iyer R. K. Loose Synchronization of Multithreaded Replicas. In *21st Symposium on Reliable Distributed Systems*, pages 250–255, Los Alamitos, CA., 2002. IEEE, IEEE Computer Society Press. → 436.

Basile C., Kalbarczyk Z., and Iyer R. K. A Preemptive Deterministic Scheduling Algorithm for Multithreaded Replicas. In *International Conference on Dependable Systems and Networks*, pages 149–158, Los Alamitos, CA., June 2003. IEEE Computer Society Press. → 436.

Bass L., Clements P., and Kazman R. *Software Architecture in Practice*. Addison-Wesley, Reading, MA., 4th edition, 2021. → 56, 57, 79.

Bavier A., Bowman M., Chun B., Culler D., Karlin S., Muir S., Peterson L., Roscoe T., Spalink T., and Wawrzoniak M. Operating System Support for Planetary-Scale Network Services. In *1st Symposium on Networked Systems Design and Implementation*, pages 245–266, Berkeley, CA, Mar. 2004. USENIX, USENIX. → 136.

Beckers K., Heisel M., and Hatebur D. *Pattern and Security Requirements*. Springer-Verlag, Berlin, 2015. → 547.

Ben-Ari M. *Principles of Concurrent and Distributed Programming*. Prentice Hall, Englewood Cliffs, N.J., 2nd edition, 2006. → 33.

Bernstein P. Middleware: A Model for Distributed System Services. *Communications of the ACM*, 39(2):87–98, Feb. 1996. → 37, 74.

Bernstein P. and Newcomer E. *Principles of Transaction Processing*. Morgan Kaufman, San Mateo, CA., 2nd edition, 2009. → 38, 529.

Bernstein P., Hadzilacos V., and Goodman N. *Concurrency Control and Recovery in Database Systems*. Addison-Wesley, Reading, MA., 1987. → 535.

Bershad B., Zekauskas M., and Sawdon W. The Midway Distributed Shared Memory System. In *COMPCON*, pages 528–537. IEEE, 1993. → 404.

Bharambe A. R., Agrawal M., and Seshan S. Mercury: Supporting Scalable Multi-Attribute Range Queries. In *SIGCOMM*, pages 353–366, New York, NY, Aug. 2004. ACM Press. → 384.

Bhuyan M. H., Bhattacharyya D. K., and Kalita J. K. Network Anomaly Detection: Methods, Systems and Tools. *IEEE Communications Surveys & Tutorials*, 16(1):303–336,

2014. → 612.

Bilal S. M., Bernardos C. J., and Guerrero C. Position-based Routing in Vehicular Networks: A Survey. *Journal of Network and Computer Applications*, 36(2):685–697, Mar. 2013. → 319.

Bilge L. and Dumitraş T. Before We Knew It: An Empirical Study of Zero-day Attacks in the Real World. In *Conference on Computer and Communications Security*, pages 833–844, 2012. → 611.

Birman K. *Guide to Reliable Distributed Systems: Building High-Assurance Applications and Cloud-Hosted Services*. Springer-Verlag, Berlin, 2012. → 152, 507.

Birman K. A Response to Cheriton and Skeen's Criticism of Causal and Totally Ordered Communication. *Operating Systems Review*, 28(1):11 21, Jan. 1994. → 271.

Birman K. and Joseph T. Reliable Communication in the Presence of Failures. *ACM Transactions on Computer Systems*, 5(1):47–76, Feb. 1987. → 523.

Birman K. and van Renesse R., editors. *Reliable Distributed Computing with the Isis Toolkit*. IEEE Computer Society Press, Los Alamitos, CA., 1994. → 271.

Birman K., Schiper A., and Stephenson P. Lightweight Causal and Atomic Group Multicast. *ACM Transactions on Computer Systems*, 9(3):272–314, Aug. 1991. → 526.

Birrell A. and Nelson B. Implementing Remote Procedure Calls. *ACM Transactions on Computer Systems*, 2(1):39–59, Feb. 1984. → 192.

Bishop M. *Computer Security: Art and Science*. Addison-Wesley, Reading, MA., 2nd edition, 2019. → 547.

Bittencourt L., Immich R., Sakellariou R., Fonseca N., Madeira E., Curado M., Villas L., DaSilva L., Lee C., and Rana O. The Internet of Things, Fog and Cloud continuum: Integration and challenges. *Internet of Things*, 3-4:134–155, 2018. → 103.

Blair G. and Stefani J.-B. *Open Distributed Processing and Multimedia*. Addison-Wesley, Reading, MA., 1998. → 16.

Blake G., Dreslinski R. G., Mudge T., and Flautner K. Evolution of Thread-Level Parallelism in Desktop Applications. *SIGARCH Computer Architecture News*, 38(3): 302–313, 2010. → 124.

Blaze M. *Caching in Large-Scale Distributed File Systems*. PhD thesis, Department of Computer Science, Princeton University, Jan. 1993. → 429.

Bloom B. H. Space/time Trade-offs in Hash Coding with Allowable Errors. *Communications of the ACM*, 13(7):422–426, 1970. → 559.

Boneh D., Crescenzo G. D., Ostrovsky R., and Persiano G. Public Key Encryption with Keyword Search. In *International Conference Theory and Applications of Cryptographic Techniques*, volume 3027 of *Lecture Notes in Computer Science*, pages 506–522, Berlin, 2004. Springer-Verlag. → 314.

Bonnet P., Gehrke J., and Seshadri P. Towards Sensor Database Systems. In *2nd International Conference on Mobile Data Management*, volume 1987 of *Lecture Notes in Computer Science*, pages 3–14, Berlin, Jan. 2002. Springer-Verlag. → 50.

Bosch C., Hartel P., Jonker W., and Peter A. A Survey of Provably Secure Searchable Encryption. *ACM Computing Surveys*, 47(2), Aug. 2014. → 314.

Boyd R. *Getting Started with OAuth 2.0*. O'Reilly & Associates, Sebastopol, CA., 2012.

→ 605.

Braga D. D. S., Niemann M., Hellingrath B., and Neto F. B. D. L. Survey on Computational Trust and Reputation Models. *ACM Computing Surveys*, 51(5):1–40, 2018. → 586.

Brewer E. CAP Twelve Years Later: How the "Rules" Have Changed. *Computer*, 45(2): 23–29, Feb. 2012. → 506.

Budhijara N., Marzullo K., Schneider F., and Toueg S. The Primary-Backup Approach. In Mullender S., editor, *Distributed Systems*, pages 199–216. Addison-Wesley, Wokingham, 2nd edition, 1993. → 438.

Budhiraja N. and Marzullo K. Tradeoffs in Implementing Primary-Backup Protocols. Technical Report TR 92-1307, Department of Computer Science, Cornell University, 1992. → 438.

Buford J. and Yu H. Peer-to-Peer Networking and Applications: Synopsis and Research Directions. In Shen et al. [2010], pages 3–45. → 89.

Buford J., Yu H., and Lua E. *P2P Networking and Applications*. Morgan Kaufman, San Mateo, CA., 2009. → 89.

Bugnion E., Nieh J., and Tsafrir D. *Hardware and Software Support for Virtualization*. Synthesis Lectures on Computer Architecture. Morgan and Claypool, San Rafael, CA, 2017. → 129.

Bursell M. *Trust in Computer Systems and The Cloud*. John Wiley, New York, 2022. → 586, 593.

Cabri G., Leonardi L., and Zambonelli F. Mobile-Agent Coordination Models for Internet Applications. *Computer*, 33(2):82–89, Feb. 2000. → 68.

Cachin C., Guerraoui R., and Rodrigues L. *Introduction to Reliable and Secure Distributed Programming*. Springer-Verlag, Berlin, 2nd edition, 2011. → 248, 469, 475, 476.

Callaghan B. *NFS Illustrated*. Addison-Wesley, Reading, MA., 2000. → 83, 373.

Cantin J., Lipasti M., and Smith J. The Complexity of Verifying Memory Coherence and Consistency. *IEEE Transactions on Parallel and Distributed Systems*, 16(7):663–671, July 2005. → 406.

Cao L. and Ozsu T. Evaluation of Strong Consistency Web Caching Techniques. *World Wide Web*, 5(2):95–123, June 2002. → 453.

Carriero N. and Gelernter D. Linda in Context. *Communications of the ACM*, 32(4): 444–458, 1989. → 70.

Carzaniga A., Rutherford M. J., and Wolf A. L. A Routing Scheme for Content-Based Networking. In *23rd INFOCOM Conference*, Los Alamitos, CA., Mar. 2004. IEEE, IEEE Computer Society Press. → 310.

Carzaniga A., Picco G. P., and Vigna G. Is Code Still Moving Around? Looking Back at a Decade of Code Mobility. In *29th International Conference on Software Engineering (ICSE) (companian)*, pages 9–20, Los Alamitos, CA., 2007. IEEE Computer Society Press. → 168.

Castro M. and Liskov B. Practical Byzantine Fault Tolerance and Proactive Recovery. *ACM Transactions on Computer Systems*, 20(4):398–461, Nov. 2002. → 498, 501.

Castro M., Druschel P., Hu Y. C., and Rowstron A. Topology-aware Routing in

Structured Peer-to-Peer Overlay Networks. Technical Report MSR-TR-2002-82, Microsoft Research, Cambridge, UK, June 2002a. → 337.

Castro M., Druschel P., Kermarrec A.-M., and Rowstron A. Scribe: A Large-Scale and Decentralized Application-Level Multicast Infrastructure. *IEEE Journal on Selected Areas in Communication*, 20(8):100–110, Oct. 2002b. → 233.

Castro M., Rodrigues R., and Liskov B. BASE: Using Abstraction to Improve Fault Tolerance. *ACM Transactions on Computer Systems*, 21(3):236–269, Aug. 2003. → 501.

Castro M., Costa M., and Rowstron A. Debunking Some Myths about Structured and Unstructured Overlays. In *2nd Symposium on Networked Systems Design and Implementation*, Berkeley, CA, Mar. 2005. USENIX, USENIX. → 299.

Chandra T., Griesemer R., and Redstone J. Paxos Made Live: An Engineering Perspective. In *26th Symposium on Principles of Distributed Computing*, pages 398–407, New York, NY, Aug. 2007. ACM, ACM Press. → 484.

Chaudhari S. S. and Biradar R. C. Survey of Bandwidth Estimation Techniques in Communication Networks. *Wireless Personal Communications*, 83(2):1425–1476, 2015. → 454.

Cheriton D. and Mann T. Decentralizing a Global Naming Service for Improved Performance and Fault Tolerance. *ACM Transactions on Computer Systems*, 7(2): 147–183, May 1989. → 352.

Cheriton D. and Skeen D. Understanding the Limitations of Causally and Totally Ordered Communication. In *14th Symposium on Operating System Principles*, pages 44–57. ACM, Dec. 1993. → 271.

Cheswick W. and Bellovin S. *Firewalls and Internet Security*. Addison-Wesley, Reading, MA., 2nd edition, 2000. → 609.

Chisnall D. *The Definitive Guide to the Xen Hypervisor*. Prentice Hall, Englewood Cliffs, N.J., 2007. → 133.

Chondros N., Kokordelis K., and Roussopoulos M. On the Practicality of Practical Byzantine Fault Tolerance. In *Middleware 2012*, volume 7662 of *Lecture Notes in Computer Science*, pages 436–455, Berlin, 2012. ACM/IFIP/USENIX, Springer-Verlag. → 501.

Chou T. and Orlandi C. The Simplest Protocol for Oblivious Transfer. In *International Conference Cryptology and Information Security in Latin America*, volume 9230 of *Lecture Notes in Computer Science*, pages 40–58, 2015. → 566.

Chow R. and Johnson T. *Distributed Operating Systems and Algorithms*. Addison-Wesley, Reading, MA., 1997. → 538.

Chu Y., Rao S. G., Seshan S., and Zhang H. A Case for End System Multicast. *IEEE Journal on Selected Areas in Communication*, 20(8):1456–1471, Oct. 2002. → 234.

Clark C., Fraser K., Hand S., Hansen J. G., Jul E., Limpach C., Pratt I., and Warfield A. Live Migration of Virtual Machines. In *2nd Symposium on Networked Systems Design and Implementation*, Berkeley, CA, May 2005. USENIX, USENIX. → 175, 176.

Clark D. The Design Philosophy of the DARPA Internet Protocols. In *SIGCOMM*, pages 106–114, New York, NY, Sept. 1989. ACM, ACM Press. → 152.

Clement A., Li H., Napper J., Martin J.-P., Alvisi L., and Dahlin M. BAR primer. In

International Conference on Dependable Systems and Networks, pages 287–296, 2008. → 505.

Cohen B. Incentives Build Robustness in Bittorrent. In *1st Workshop on Economics of Peer-to-Peer Systems*, June 2003. → 96.

Cohen E. and Shenker S. Replication Strategies in Unstructured Peer-to-Peer Networks. In *SIGCOMM*, pages 177–190, New York, NY, Aug. 2002. ACM, ACM Press. → 94.

Comer D. *Internetworking with TCP/IP, Volume I: Principles, Protocols, and Architecture*. Prentice Hall, Upper Saddle River, N.J., 6th edition, 2013. → 187.

Committee on National Security Systems . (CNSS) Glossary. Technical Report 4009, Apr. 2015. → 552.

Contavalli C., van der Gaast W., Lawrence D., and Kumari W. Client Subnet in DNS Queries. RFC 7871, May 2016. → 364.

Conti M., Gregori E., and Lapenna W. Content Delivery Policies in ReplicatedWeb Services: Client-Side vs. Server-Side. *Cluster Computing*, 8:47–60, Jan. 2005. → 456.

Corbett J. C., Dean J., Epstein M., Fikes A., Frost C., Furman J. J., Ghemawat S., Gubarev A., Heiser C., Hochschild P., Hsieh W., Kanthak S., Kogan E., Li H., Lloyd A., Melnik S., Mwaura D., Nagle D., Quinlan S., Rao R., Rolig L., Saito Y., Szymaniak M., Taylor C., Wang R., and Woodford D. Spanner: Google's Globally Distributed Database. *ACM Transactions on Computer Systems*, 31(3):8:1–8:22, Aug. 2013. → 259.

Cordero C. G., Vasilomanolakis E., Mühlhäuser M., and Fischer M. Community-based Collaborative Intrusion Detection. In *International Conference on Security and Privacy in Communication Systems*, pages 665–681. Springer, 2015. → 612, 613.

Cristian F. Probabilistic Clock Synchronization. *Distributed Computing*, 3:146–158, 1989. → 255.

Cristian F. Understanding Fault-Tolerant Distributed Systems. *Communications of the ACM*, 34(2):56–78, Feb. 1991. → 466.

Cui S., Belguith S., De Alwis P., Asghar M. R., and Russello G. Collusion Defender: Preserving Subscribers' Privacy in Publish and Subscribe Systems. *IEEE Transactions on Dependable and Secure Computing*, 18(3):1051–1064, 2021. → 314, 315.

Culkin J. and Zazon M. *AWS Cookbook, Recipes for Success on AWS*. O'Reilly & Associates, Sebastopol, CA., 2022. → 66, 99.

Dabek F., Cox R., Kaashoek F., and Morris R. Vivaldi: A Decentralized Network Coordinate System. In *SIGCOMM*, New York, NY, Aug. 2004a. ACM, ACM Press. → 321.

Dabek F., Li J., Sit E., Robertson J., Kaashoek M. F., and Morris R. Designing a dht for low latency and high throughput. In *1st Symposium on Networked Systems Design and Implementation*, pages 85–98, Berkeley, CA, Mar. 2004b. USENIX, USENIX. → 338.

Damas J., Graff M., and Vixie P. Extension Mechanisms for DNS (EDNS(0)). RFC 6891, Apr. 2013. → 366.

Dannewitz C., Golic J., Ohlman B., and Ahlgren B. Secure Naming for a Network of Information. In *29th INFOCOM Conference Workshops*, pages 1–6, Los Alamitos, CA., 2010. IEEE Computer Society Press. → 344.

Day J. and Zimmerman H. The OSI Reference Model. *Proceedings of the IEEE*, 71(12):

1334–1340, Dec. 1983. → 183.

Deering S. and Cheriton D. Multicast Routing in Datagram Internetworks and Extended LANs. *ACM Transactions on Computer Systems*, 8(2):85–110, May 1990. → 330.

Deering S., Estrin D., Farinacci D., Jacobson V., Liu C.-G., and Wei L. The PIM Architecture for Wide-Area Multicast Routing. *IEEE/ACM Transactions on Networking*, 4(2):153–162, Apr. 1996. → 330.

DeJonghe D. *NGINX Cookbook*. O'Reilly & Associates, Sebastopol, CA., 2nd edition, 2022. → 163.

Demers A., Greene D., Hauser C., Irish W., Larson J., Shenker S., Sturgis H., Swinehart D., and Terry D. Epidemic Algorithms for Replicated Database Maintenance. In *6th Symposium on Principles of Distributed Computing*, pages 1–12. ACM, Aug. 1987. → 240, 243, 245.

Demirbas M. and Kulkarni S. Beyond TrueTime: Using Augmented Time for Improving Google Spanner. In *7th International Workshop on Large Scale Distributed Systems and Middleware*, New York, NY, 2013. ACM Press. → 260.

Dey A. Context-Aware Computing. In Krumm J., editor, *Ubiquitous Computing Fundamentals*, pages 321–352. CRC Press, Boca Raton, FL, 2010. → 46.

Dey A. and Abowd G. Towards a Better Understanding of Context and Context-Awareness. In *Workshop on the What, Who, Where, When, Why and How of Context-Awareness*, New York, NY, Apr. 2000. ACM, ACM Press. → 45.

Diffie W. and Hellman M. New Directions in Cryptography. *IEEE Transactions on Information Theory*, IT-22(6):644–654, Nov. 1976. → 565.

Dilley J., Maggs B., Parikh J., Prokop H., Sitaraman R., and Weihl B. Globally Distributed Content Delivery. *IEEE Internet Computing*, 6(5):50–58, Sept. 2002. → 165.

Dimou A., Iliopoulos C., Polytidou E., Dhurandher S. K., Papadimitriou G., and Nicopolitidis P. A Comprehensive Review on Edge Computing: Focusing on Mobile Users. In Nicopolitidis P., Misra S., Yang L. T., Zeigler B., and Ning Z., editors, *Advances in Computing, Informatics, Networking and Cybersecurity*, number 289 in Lecture Notes in Networks and Systems, pages 121–152. Springer-Verlag, Berlin, 2022. → 48.

Diot C., Levine B., Lyles B., Kassem H., and Balensiefen D. Deployment Issues for the IP Multicast Service and Architecture. *IEEE Network*, 14(1):78–88, Jan. 2000. → 232.

Donnet B., Gueye B., and Kaafar M. A Survey on Network Coordinates Systems, Design, and Security. *IEEE Communications Surveys & Tutorials*, 12(4), Dec. 2010. → 318.

Donovan A. A. and Kernighan B. W. *The Go Programming Language*. Addison-Wesley, Reading, MA., 2015. → 122.

Doorn J. H. and Rivero L. C., editors. *Database Integrity: Challenges and Solutions*. Idea Group, Hershey, PA, 2002. → 594.

Douceur J. R. The Sybil Attack. In *1st International Workshop on Peer-to-Peer Systems*, volume 2429 of *Lecture Notes in Computer Science*, pages 251–260, Berlin, Mar. 2002. Springer-Verlag. → 586, 588.

Droms R. Dynamic Host Configuration Protocol. RFC 2161, Apr. 1997. → 46.

Dubois M., Scheurich C., and Briggs F. Synchronization, Coherence, and Event Ordering in Multiprocessors. *Computer*, 21(2):9–21, Feb. 1988. → 398.

Dunagan J., Harvey N. J. A., Jones M. B., Kostic D., Theimer M., and Wolman A. FUSE: Lightweight Guaranteed Distributed Failure Notification. In *6th Symposium on Operating System Design and Implementation*, Berkeley, CA, Dec. 2004. USENIX, USENIX. → 508.

Duvvuri V., Shenoy P., and Tewari R. Adaptive Leases: A Strong Consistency Mechanism for the World Wide Web. *IEEE Transactions on Knowledge and Data Engineering*, 15(5):1266–1276, Sept. 2003. → 433.

Eastlake D. and Hansen T. Us Secure Hash Algorithms (SHA and SHA-based HMAC and HKDF), May 2011. → 585.

El-Sayed A., Roca V., and Mathy L. A Survey of Proposals for an Alternative Group Communication Service. *IEEE Network*, 17(1):46–51, Jan. 2003. → 233.

Elnozahy E., Alvisi L., Wang Y.-M., and Johnson D. A Survey of Rollback-Recovery Protocols in Message-Passing Systems. *ACM Computing Surveys*, 34(3):375–408, Sept. 2002. → 538, 543.

Elnozahy E. N. and Plank J. S. Checkpointing for Peta-Scale Systems: A Look into the Future of Practical Rollback-Recovery. *IEEE Transactions on Dependable and Secure Computing*, 1(2):97–108, Apr. 2004. → 540.

Elson J., Girod L., and Estrin D. Fine-Grained Network Time Synchronization using Reference Broadcasts. In *5th Symposium on Operating System Design and Implementation*, pages 147–163, Berkeley, CA, Dec. 2002. USENIX, USENIX. → 257, 258.

Erdös P. and Rényi A. On Random Graphs. *Publicationes Mathematicae*, 6:290–297, 1959. → 237.

Escriva R., Wong B., and Sirer E. G. HyperDex: A Distributed, Searchable Key-value Store. In *SIGCOMM*, pages 25–36, New York, NY, 2012. ACM Press. → 384.

Esposito C., Cotroneo D., and Russo S. On Reliability in Publish/Subscribe Services. *Computer Networks*, X(0):xxx, 2013. → 517.

Eugster P., Guerraoui R., Kermarrec A.-M., and Massoulié L. Epidemic Information Dissemination in Distributed Systems. *Computer*, 37(5):60–67, May 2004. → 240.

Evans D., Kolesnikov V., and Rosulek M. *A Pragmatic Introduction to Secure Multi-Party Computation*. NOW Publishers, Boston, MA; Delft, NL, 2018. → 566.

Feng B., Zhang H., Zhou H., and Yu S. Locator/Identifier Split Networking: A Promising Future Internet Architecture. *IEEE Communications Surveys & Tutorials*, 19 (4):2927–2948, 2017. → 329.

Ferguson N. and Schneier B. *Practical Cryptography*. John Wiley, New York, 2003. → 290.

Ferguson N., Schneier B., and Kohno T. *Cryptography Engineering: Design Principles and Practical Applications*. John Wiley, New York, 2010. → 557, 575.

Ferraiolo D., Kuhn D. R., and Chandramouli R. *Role-based Access Control*. Artech house, 2nd edition, 2007. → 595.

Ferraiolo D., Atluri V., and Gavrila S. The Policy Machine: A Novel Architecture and Framework for Access Control Policy Specification and Enforcement. *Journal of*

Systems Architecture, 57(4):412–424, 2011. → 598, 600.

Ferraiolo D., Gavrila S., and Jansen W. Policy Machine: Features, Architecture, and Specification. Technical Report NISTIR 7987, Revision 1, National Institute of Standards and Technology (NIST), Oct. 2015. → 598.

Ferrer A. J., Marquès J. M., and Jorba J. Towards the Decentralised Cloud: Survey on Approaches and Challenges for Mobile, Ad hoc, and Edge Computing. *ACM Computing Surveys*, 51(6):1–36, 2019. → 47.

Fiebig T., Lichtblau F., Streibelt F., Krüger T., Lexis P., Bush R., and Feldmann A. Learning from the Past: Designing Secure Network Protocols. In *Cybersecurity Best Practices*, pages 585–613. Springer-Verlag, Berlin, 2018. → 576.

Fielding R. *Architectural Styles and the Design of Network-based Software Architectures*. Ph.d., University of California, Irvine, 2000. → 66.

Fielding R. and Reschke J. Hypertext Transfer Protocol (HTTP/1.1): Message Syntax and Routing. RFC 7230, June 2014. → 188.

Fischer M., Lynch N., and Patterson M. Impossibility of Distributed Consensus with one Faulty Processor. *Journal of the ACM*, 32(2):374–382, Apr. 1985. → 503, 504.

Floyd S., Jacobson V., McCanne S., Liu C.-G., and Zhang L. A Reliable Multicast Framework for Light-weight Sessions and Application Level Framing. *IEEE/ACM Transactions on Networking*, 5(6):784–803, Dec. 1997. → 519, 520.

Fokkink W. *Distributed Algorithms: An Intuitive Approach*. MIT Press, Cambridge, MA., 2nd edition, 2018. → 248.

Foster I., Kesselman C., and Tuecke S. The Anatomy of the Grid, Enabling Scalable Virtual Organizations. *Journal of Supercomputer Applications*, 15(3):200–222, Fall 2001. → 36, 37.

Foster I. and others . The Open Grid Services Architecture, Version 1.5. GGF Informational Document GFD-I.080, June 2006. → 37.

Fowler R. *Decentralized Object Finding Using Forwarding Addresses*. Ph.D., University of Washington, Seattle, 1985. → 331.

Fox A. and Brewer E. Harvest, Yield, and Scalable Tolerant Systems. In *7th Worksop-Workshop on Hot Topics in Operating Systems (HotOS)*, pages 174–178, Los Alamitos, CA., Mar. 1999. IEEE, IEEE Computer Society Press. → 506.

Francis L. P. Privacy and Confidentiality: The Importance of Context. *The Monist*, 91 (1):52–67, 2008. → 553.

Franklin M. J., Carey M. J., and Livny M. Transactional Client-Server Cache Consistency: Alternatives and Performance. *ACM Transactions on Database Systems*, 22(3):315–363, Sept. 1997. → 443.

Fuggetta A., Picco G. P., and Vigna G. Understanding Code Mobility. *IEEE Transactions on Software Engineering*, 24(5):342–361, May 1998. → 171, 172.

Gamma E., Helm R., Johnson R., and Vlissides J. *Design Patterns, Elements of Reusable Object-Oriented Software*. Addison-Wesley, Reading, MA., 1994. → 75.

Garbacki P., Epema D., and van Steen M. The Design and Evaluation of a Self-Organizing Super-Peer Network. *IEEE Transactions on Computers*, 59(3):317–331, Mar. 2010. → 96.

Garcia-Molina H. Elections in a Distributed Computing System. *IEEE Transactions on Computers*, 31(1):48–59, Jan. 1982. → 283.

Garfinkel S. *PGP: Pretty Good Privacy*. O'Reilly & Associates, Sebastopol, CA., 1995. → 570.

Garman J. *Kerberos: The Definitive Guide*. O'Reilly & Associates, Sebastopol, CA., 2003. → 581.

Gazis A. and Katsiri E. Middleware 101: What to Know Now and for the Future. *ACM Queue*, 20(1):10–23, feb 2022. → 11.

Gelernter D. and Carriero N. Coordination Languages and their Significance. *Communications of the ACM*, 35(2):96–107, Feb. 1992. → 68.

Gentz R., Wu S. X., Wai H.-T., Scaglione A., and Leshem A. Data Injection Attacks in Randomized Gossiping. *IEEE Transactions on Signal and Information Processing over Networks*, 2(4):523–538, 2016. → 306.

Gerofi B., Ishikawa Y., Riesen R., and Wisniewski R. W., editors. *Operating Systems for Supercomputers and High Performance Computing*. Springer-Verlag, Berlin, 2019. → 34, 35.

Ghodsi A. Multicast and Bulk Lookup in Structured Overlay Networks. In Shen et al. [2010], pages 933–958. → 239.

Gifford D. Weighted Voting for Replicated Data. In *7th Symposium on Operating System Principles*, pages 150–162. ACM, Dec. 1979. → 441.

Gilbert S. and Lynch N. Brewer's Conjecture and the Feasibility of Consistent, Available, Partition-tolerant Web Services. *ACM SIGACT News*, 33(2):51–59, June 2002. → 505.

Gilbert S. and Lynch N. Perspectives on the CAP Theorem. *Computer*, 45(2):30–35, Feb. 2012. → 505.

Gkantsidis C., Mihail M., and Saberi A. Random Walks in Peer-to-Peer Networks: Algorithms and Evaluation. *Performance Evaluation*, 63:241–263, Mar. 2006. → 93.

Goel U., Wittie M. P., and Steiner M. Faster Web through Client-Assisted CDN Server Selection. In *14th International Conference on Computer Communications and Networks*, pages 1–10, 2015. → 166.

Goldreich O. *Foundations of Cryptography: Volume 2, Basic Applications*. Cambridge University Press, Cambridge, UK, 2009. → 553.

Gonzalez-Manzano L., Fuentes J. M. D., and Ribagorda A. Leveraging User-related Internet of Things for Continuous Authentication: A Survey. *ACM Computing Surveys*, 52(3):1–38, 2019. → 572.

Gray C. and Cheriton D. Leases: An Efficient Fault-Tolerant Mechanism for Distributed File Cache Consistency. In *12th Symposium on Operating System Principles*, pages 202–210, New York, NY, Dec. 1989. ACM, ACM Press. → 433.

Gray J. Notes on Database Operating Systems. In Bayer R., Graham R., and Seegmuller G., editors, *Operating Systems: An Advanced Course*, volume 60 of *Lecture Notes in Computer Science*, pages 393–481. Springer-Verlag, Berlin, 1978. → 529.

Gray J. and Reuter A. *Transaction Processing: Concepts and Techniques*. Morgan Kaufman, San Mateo, CA., 1993. → 38.

Gray J., Helland P., O'Neil P., and Sashna D. The Dangers of Replication and a Solution.

In *SIGMOD International Conference on Management Of Data*, pages 173–182, Montreal, June 1996. ACM. → 395.

Gropp W., Lusk E., and Skjellum A. *Using MPI-2, Portable Parallel Programming with the Message-Passing Interface*. MIT Press, Cambridge, MA., 3rd edition, 2016. → 220.

Guerraoui R. and Schiper A. Software-Based Replication for Fault Tolerance. *Computer*, 30(4):68–74, Apr. 1997. → 472.

Guerraoui R., Knežević N., Quéma V., and Vukolić M. The next 700 bft protocols. In *5th EuroSys (European Conference on Computer Systems)*, pages 363–376, New York, NY, 2010. ACM Press. → 501.

Guichard J., Faucheur F. L., and Vasseur J.-P. *Definitive MPLS Network Designs*. Cisco Press, Indianapolis, IN, 2005. → 155.

Guttman E. Autoconfiguration for IP Networking: Enabling Local Communication. *IEEE Internet Computing*, 5:81–86, 2001. → 46.

Hadzilacos V. and Toueg S. Fault-Tolerant Broadcasts and Related Problems. In Mullender S., editor, *Distributed Systems*, pages 97–145. Addison-Wesley, Wokingham, 2nd edition, 1993. → 466, 526.

Hahmy H. *Concepts, Applications, Experimentation and Analysis of Wireless Sensor Networks*. Springer-Verlag, Berlin, 2nd edition, 2021. → 49.

Hardt D. and others . The OAuth 2.0 Authorization Framework. RFC 6746, Oct. 2012. → 605.

Hassan W. U., Guo S., Li D., Chen Z., Jee K., Li Z., and Bates A. Nodoze: Combatting Threat Alert Fatigue with Automated Provenance Triage. In *Symposium on Network and Distributed System Security*, 2019. → 612.

Haynes T. Network File System (NFS) Version 4 Protocol. RFC 7530, Mar. 2015. → 83, 350.

Helder D. A. and Jamin S. End-Host Multicast Communication Using Switch-Trees Protocols. In *2nd International Symposium on Cluster Computing and the Grid*, pages 419–424, Los Alamitos, CA., May 2002. IEEE, IEEE Computer Society Press. → 235, 236.

Hellerstein J. M. and Alvaro P. Keeping CALM: When Distributed Consistency is Easy. *Communications of the ACM*, 63(9):72–81, Sept. 2020. → 410.

Henning M. A New Approach to Object-Oriented Middleware. *IEEE Internet Computing*, 8(1):66–75, Jan. 2004. → 156.

Herlihy M. and Shavit N. *The Art of Multiprocessor Programming*. Morgan Kaufman, San Mateo, CA., 2008. → 113.

Herlihy M. and Wing J. Linearizability: A Correctness Condition for Concurrent Objects. *ACM Transactions on Programming Languages and Systems*, 12(3):463–492, July 1991. → 400.

Herlihy M., Shavit N., Luchangco V., and Spear M. *The Art of Multiprocessor Programming*. Morgan Kaufman, San Mateo, CA., 2nd edition, 2021. → 33, 400.

Hintjens P. *ZeroMQ*. O'Reilly & Associates, Sebastopol, CA., 2013. → 213.

Hohpe G. and Woolf B. *Enterprise Integration Patterns: Designing, Building, and Deploying Messaging Solutions*. Addison-Wesley, Reading, MA., 2004. → 37, 41, 227.

Hong C.-H. and Varghese B. Resource Management in Fog/Edge Computing: A Survey on Architectures, Infrastructure, and Algorithms. *ACM Computing Surveys*, 52(5), 2019. → 103.

Hong J. The Privacy Landscape of Pervasive Computing. *IEEE Pervasive Computing*, 16 (3):40–48, 2017. → 103.

Horauer M. *Clock Synchronization in Distributed Systems*. Ph.D., University of Vienna, Department of Computer Science, Feb. 2004. → 253.

Horner L. J. Edge Strategies in Industry: Overview and Challenges. *IEEE Transactions on Network and Service Management*, 18(3):2825–2831, 2021. → 100.

Horowitz M. and Lunt S. FTP Security Extensions. RFC 2228, Oct. 1997. → 188.

Hosseini M., Ahmed D., Shirmohammadi S., and Georganas N. A Survey of Application-Layer Multicast Protocols. *IEEE Communications Surveys & Tutorials*, 9 (3):58–74, 2007. → 233.

Howard H., Schwarzkopf M., Madhavapeddy A., and Crowcroft J. Raft Refloated: Do We Have Consensus? *Operating Systems Review*, 49(1):12–21, jan 2015. → 289.

Hu V. C., Ferraiolo D., Kuhn R., Schnitzer A., Sandlin K., Miller R., and Scarfone K. Guide to Attribute Based Access Control (ABAC) Definition and Considerations. Technical Report NIST 800-162, National Institute of Standards and Technology, Jan. 2014. → 596.

Hu V. C., Kuhn D. R., Ferraiolo D. F., and Voas J. Attribute-Based Access Control. *Computer*, 48(2):85–88, 2015. → 596.

Huffaker B., Fomenkov M., Plummer D. J., Moore D., and Claffy K. Distance Metrics in the Internet. In *International Telecommunications Symposium*, Los Alamitos, CA., Sept. 2002. IEEE, IEEE Computer Society Press. → 454.

Hunt G., Nahum E., and Tracey J. Enabling Content-Based Load Distribution for Scalable Services. Technical report, IBM T.J. Watson Research Center, May 1997. → 163.

Hunt P., Konar M., Junqueira F. P., and Reed B. ZooKeeper: Wait-free Coordination for Internet-scale Systems. In *USENIX Annual Technical Conference*, 2010. → 280, 422.

Hutto P. and Ahamad M. Slow Memory: Weakening Consistency to Enhance Concurrency in Distributed Shared Memories. In *10th International Conference on Distributed Computing Systems*, pages 302–311, Paris, France, May 1990. IEEE. → 401.

Iqbal M. and Matulevičius R. Exploring Sybil and Double-Spending Risks in Blockchain Systems. *IEEE Access*, 9:76153–76177, 2021. → 587.

ISO . Open Distributed Processing Reference Model - Part 2: Foundations. International Standard ISO/IEC IS 10746-2, 1995. → 12.

Jakubeit P., Peter A., and van Steen M. The Measurable Environment as Nonintrusive Authentication Factor on the Example of WiFi Beacon Frames. In *5th International Workshop on Emerging Technologies for Authorization and Authentication*, Sept. 2022. → 572.

Jalote P. *Fault Tolerance in Distributed Systems*. Prentice Hall, Englewood Cliffs, N.J., 1994. → 443, 463.

Janic M. *Multicast in Network and Application Layer*. Ph.d., Delft University of Technology,

The Netherlands, Oct. 2005. → 232.

Janiga M. J., Dibner G., and Governali F. J. Internet Infrastructure: Content Delivery. Goldman Sachs Global Equity Research, Apr. 2001. → 455.

Jelasity M. and Kermarrec A.-M. Ordered Slicing of Very Large-Scale Overlay Networks. In *6th International Conference on Peer-to-Peer Computing*, pages 117–124, Los Alamitos, CA., Sept. 2006. IEEE Computer Society Press. → 300.

Jelasity M., Montresor A., and Babaoglu O. Gossip-based Aggregation in Large Dynamic Networks. *ACM Transactions on Computer Systems*, 23(3):219–252, Aug. 2005. → 297.

Jelasity M., Voulgaris S., Guerraoui R., Kermarrec A.-M., and van Steen M. Gossip-based Peer Sampling. *ACM Transactions on Computer Systems*, 25(3), Aug. 2007. → 241, 298.

Jesi G., Montresor A., and van Steen M. Secure Peer Sampling. *Computer Networks*, 54 (12):2086–2098, Aug. 2010. → 304, 306.

Jesi G.-P., Hales D., and van Steen M. Identifying Malicious Peers Before It's Too Late: A Decentralized Secure Peer Sampling Service. In *1st International Conference on Self-Adaptive and Self-Organizing Systems*, Los Alamitos, CA., June 2007. IEEE, IEEE Computer Society Press. → 588.

Johnson B. An Introduction to the Design and Analysis of Fault-Tolerant Systems. In Pradhan D., editor, *Fault-Tolerant Computer System Design*, pages 1–87. Prentice Hall, Upper Saddle River, N.J., 1995. → 470.

Josefsson S. *Shishi – Kerberos 5 Implementation*. Samurai Media Limited, Wickford, UK, 2015. → 581.

Joseph J., Ernest M., and Fellenstein C. Evolution of grid computing architecture and grid adoption models. *IBM Systems Journal*, 43(4):624–645, Apr. 2004. → 37.

Junqueira F. and Reed B. *ZooKeeper*. O'Reilly & Associates, Sebastopol, CA., 2014. → 280, 281, 287.

Kahn D. *The Codebreakers*. Macmillan, New York, 1967. → 556.

Karsten M. and Barghi S. User-level Threading: Have Your Cake and Eat It Too. In *International Conference on Measurements and Modeling of Computer Systems*, volume 4. ACM, Mar. 2020. → 122.

Kasera S., Kurose J., and Towsley D. Scalable Reliable Multicast Using Multiple Multicast Groups. In *International Conference on Measurements and Modeling of Computer Systems*, pages 64–74, Seattle, WA, June 1997. ACM. → 520.

Kaufman C., Perlman R., and Speciner M. *Network Security: Private Communication in a Public World*. Prentice Hall, Englewood Cliffs, N.J., 2nd edition, 2003. → 575, 580.

Kemme B., Jimenez Peris R., and Patino-Martinez M. *Replicated Databases*. Synthesis Lectures on Computer Architectures. Morgan and Claypool, San Rafael, CA, 2010. → 426.

Kermarrec A.-M. and Triantafillou P. XL Peer-to-peer Pub/Sub Systems. *ACM Computing Surveys*, 46(2):16:1–16:45, Nov. 2013. → 309.

Khormali A., Park J., Alasmary H., Anwar A., Saad M., and Mohaisen D. Domain Name System Security and Privacy: A Contemporary Survey. *Computer Networks*,

185, 2021. → 365.

Khoshafian S. and Buckiewicz M. *Introduction to Groupware, Workflow, and Workgroup Computing*. John Wiley, New York, 1995. → 226.

Khraisat A., Gondal I., Vamplew P., and Kamruzzaman J. Survey of Intrusion Detection Systems: Techniques, Datasets and Challenges. *Cybersecurity*, 2(1):1–22, 2019. → 612.

Kim M., Fielding J. J., and Kotz D. Risks of Using AP Locations Discovered Through War Driving. In *4th International Conference Pervasive Computing*, volume 3968 of *Lecture Notes in Computer Science*, pages 67–82, Berlin, May 2006. Springer-Verlag. → 318.

Kirsch J. and Amir Y. Paxos for System Builders. Technical Report CNDS-2008-2, John Hopkins University, Mar. 2008. → 480, 484.

Kleiman S. Vnodes: an Architecture for Multiple File System Types in UNIX. In *Summer Technical Conference*, pages 238–247, Atlanta, GA, June 1986. USENIX. → 84.

Kleppmann M. and Beresford A. R. A Conflict-Free Replicated JSON Datatype. *IEEE Transactions on Parallel and Distributed Systems*, 28(10):2733–2745, Oct. 2017. → 410.

Kohl J., Neuman B., and T'so T. The Evolution of the Kerberos Authentication System. In Brazier F. and Johansen D., editors, *Distributed Open Systems*, pages 78–94. IEEE Computer Society Press, Los Alamitos, CA., 1994. → 581.

Kopetz H. and Verissimo P. Real Time and Dependability Concepts. In Mullender S., editor, *Distributed Systems*, pages 411–446. Addison-Wesley, Wokingham, 2nd edition, 1993. → 18, 463.

Koren I. and Krishna C. M. *Fault-Tolerant Systems*. Morgan Kaufman, San Mateo, CA., 2007. → 463, 497.

Kotla R., Alvisi L., Dahlin M., Clement A., and Wong E. Zyzzyva: Speculative Byzantine Fault Tolerance. *ACM Transactions on Computer Systems*, 27(4), Dec. 2009. → 501.

Krakowiak S. *Middleware Architecture with Patterns and Frameworks*. Creative Commons, 2009. → 58.

Kreitz G. and Niemelä F. Spotify – Large Scale, Low Latency, P2P Music-on-Demand Streaming. In *10th International Conference on Peer-to-Peer Computing*, pages 266–275, Los Alamitos, CA., Aug. 2010. IEEE, IEEE Computer Society Press. → 28.

Kshemkalyani A. and Singhal M. *Distributed Computing, Principles, Algorithms, and Systems*. Cambridge University Press, Cambridge, UK, 2008. → 272, 493, 495.

Kucharski A. *The Rules of Contagion, Why Things Spread – And Why They Stop*. Profile Books, 2020. → 62.

Kumar K., Liu J., Lu Y.-H., and Bhargava B. A Survey of Computation Offloading for Mobile Systems. *Mobile Networks and Applications*, 18(1):129–140, 2013. → 168.

Lagar-Cavilla H. A., Whitney J. A., Scannell A. M., Patchin P., Rumble S. M., Lara E.de , Brudno M., and Satyanarayanan M. SnowFlock: Rapid Virtual Machine Cloning for Cloud Computing. In *4th EuroSys (European Conference on Computer Systems)*, pages 1–12, New York, NY, 2009. ACM Press. → 177.

Lai A. and Nieh J. Limits of Wide-Area Thin-Client Computing. In *International Conference on Measurements and Modeling of Computer Systems*, pages 228–239, New

York, NY, June 2002. ACM, ACM Press. → 144.

LaMarca A. and Lara E.de . *Location Systems: An Introduction to the Technology Behind Location Awareness*. Morgan & Claypool, San Rafael, CA, 2008. → 317.

Lamport L. The Part-Time Parliament. *ACM Transactions on Computer Systems*, 16(2): 133–169, May 1998. → 479.

Lamport L. Paxos Made Simple. *ACM SIGACT News*, 32(4):51–58, Dec. 2001. → 479, 480.

Lamport L. Time, Clocks, and the Ordering of Events in a Distributed System. *Communications of the ACM*, 21(7):558–565, July 1978. → 260, 441.

Lamport L. How to Make a Multiprocessor Computer that Correctly Executes Multiprocessor Programs. *IEEE Transactions on Computers*, C-29(9):690–691, Sept. 1979. → 397.

Lamport L., Shostak R., and Paese M. The Byzantine Generals Problem. *ACM Transactions on Programming Languages and Systems*, 4(3):382–401, July 1982. → 468.

Lampson B. How to Build a Highly Available System using Consensus. In Babaoglu O. and Marzullo K., editors, *12th International Workshop on Distributed Algorithms*, volume 1151 of *Lecture Notes in Computer Science*, pages 1–17, Berlin, Oct. 1996. Springer-Verlag. → 479.

Laprie J.-C. Dependability – Its Attributes, Impairments and Means. In Randell B., Laprie J.-C., Kopetz H., and Littlewood B., editors, *Predictably Dependable Computing Systems*, pages 3–24. Springer-Verlag, Berlin, 1995. → 547.

Laurie B. and Laurie P. *Apache: The Definitive Guide*. O'Reilly & Associates, Sebastopol, CA., 3rd edition, 2002. → 161.

Lawder J. and King P. Querying Multi-dimensional Data Indexed Using Hilbert Space-Filling Curve. *ACM Sigmod Record*, 30(1):19–24, Mar. 2000. → 381.

Levesque M. and Tipper D. A Survey of Clock Synchronization Over Packet-Switched Networks. *IEEE Communications Surveys & Tutorials*, 18(4):2926–2947, 2016. → 253, 257.

Levine B. and Garcia-Luna-Aceves J. A Comparison of Reliable Multicast Protocols. *ACM Multimedia Systems Journal*, 6(5):334–348, 1998. → 519.

Levine B. N., Shields C., and Margolin N. B. A Survey of Solutions to the Sybil Attack. Technical report, University of Massachusetts Amherst, Amherst, MA, 2006. → 588.

Lewis B. and Berg D. J. *Multithreaded Programming with Pthreads*. Prentice Hall, Englewood Cliffs, N.J., 2nd edition, 1998. → 113.

Li X., Jiang P., Chen T., Luo X., and Wen Q. A Survey on the Security of Blockchain Systems. *Future Generation Computer Systems*, 107:841–853, 2020. → 589.

Lilja D. Cache Coherence in Large-Scale Shared-Memory Multiprocessors: Issues and Comparisons. *ACM Computing Surveys*, 25(3):303–338, Sept. 1993. → 443.

Lin M.-J. and Marzullo K. Directional Gossip: Gossip in a Wide-Area Network. In *Proceedings 3rd European Dependable Computing Conf.*, volume 1667 of *Lecture Notes in Computer Science*, pages 364–379. Springer-Verlag, Berlin, Sept. 1999. → 244.

Lin S.-D., Lian Q., Chen M., , and Zhang Z. A Practical Distributed Mutual Exclusion Protocol in Dynamic Peer-to-Peer Systems. In *3rd International Workshop on Peer-to-Peer Systems*, volume 3279 of *Lecture Notes in Computer Science*, pages 11–21, Berlin,

Feb. 2004. Springer-Verlag. → 277, 278.

Ling B. C., Kiciman E., and Fox A. Session State: Beyond Soft State. In *1st Symposium on Networked Systems Design and Implementation*, pages 295–308, Berkeley, CA, Mar. 2004. USENIX, USENIX. → 153.

Liskov B. From viewstamped Replication to Byzantine Fault Tolerance. In Charron-Bost B., Pedone F., and Schiper A., editors, *Replication, Theory and Practice*, volume 5959 of *Lecture Notes in Computer Science*, chapter 5, pages 121–149. Springer-Verlag, Berlin, 2010. → 498.

Liu C. and Albitz P. *DNS and BIND*. O'Reilly & Associates, Sebastopol, CA., 5th edition, 2006. → 189, 359.

Liu C.-G., Estrin D., Shenker S., and Zhang L. Local Error Recovery in SRM: Comparison of Two Approaches. *IEEE/ACM Transactions on Networking*, 6(6):686–699, Dec. 1998. → 520.

Liu F. and Solihin Y. Understanding the Behavior and Implications of Context Switch Misses. *ACM Transactions on Architecture and Code Optimization*, 7(4):21:1–21:28, Dec. 2010. → 116.

Lo V., Zhou D., Liu Y., GauthierDickey C., and Li J. Scalable Supernode Selection in Peer-to-Peer Overlay Networks. In *2nd Workshop on Hot Topics in Peer-to-Peer Systems (HotP2P)*, pages 18–27, Los Alamitos, CA., July 2005. IEEE Computer Society Press. → 293.

Lua E., Crowcroft J., Pias M., Sharma R., and Lim S. A Survey and Comparison of Peer-to-Peer Overlay Network Schemes. *IEEE Communications Surveys & Tutorials*, 7 (2):22–73, Apr. 2005. → 32, 89.

Lui J., Misra V., and Rubenstein D. On the Robustness of Soft State Protocols. In *12th International Conference on Network Protocols*, pages 50–60, Los Alamitos, CA., Oct. 2004. IEEE, IEEE Computer Society Press. → 152.

Lv Q., Cao P., Cohen E., Li K., and Shenker S. Search and Replication in Unstructured Peer-to-Peer Networks. In *16th International Conference on Supercomputing*, pages 84–95, New York, NY, June 2002. ACM, ACM Press. → 93, 94.

Lynch N. *Distributed Algorithms*. Morgan Kaufman, San Mateo, CA., 1996. → 249, 283.

Lyu L., Yu H., Zhao J., and Yang Q. *Threats to Federated Learning*, volume 12500 of *Lecture Notes in Artificial Intelligence*, pages 3–16. Springer Nature, Cham, 2020. → 169.

Maassen J., Kielmann T., and Bal H. E. Parallel Application Experience with Replicated Method Invocation. *Concurrency & Computation: Practice and Experience*, 13(8-9): 681–712, 2001. → 436.

Madden S. R., Franklin M. J., Hellerstein J. M., and Hong W. TinyDB: An Acquisitional Query Processing System for Sensor Networks. *ACM Transactions on Database Systems*, 30(1):122–173, 2005. → 51.

Mahajan P., Alvisi L., and Dahlin M. Consistency, availability, and convergence. Technical Report TR-11-22, University of Texas at Austin, May 2011. → 408.

Malhotra A., Cohen I. E., Brakke E., and Goldberg S. Attacking the Network Time Protocol. In *Symposium on Network and Distributed System Security*, Feb. 2016. → 257.

Malone T. and Crowston K. The Interdisciplinary Study of Coordination. *ACM Computing Surveys*, 26(1):87–119, Mar. 1994. → 248.

Mao Z. M., Cranor C. D., Douglis F., Rabinovich M., Spatscheck O., and Wang J. A Precise and Efficient Evaluation of the Proximity between Web Clients and their Local DNS Servers. In *USENIX Annual Technical Conference*, pages 229–242, Berkeley, CA, June 2002. USENIX, USENIX. → 166.

Marzullo K. and Owicki S. Maintaining The Time in a Distributed System. In *2nd Symposium on Principles of Distributed Computing*, pages 295–305, New York, NY, 1983. ACM, ACM Press. → 259.

Mattern F. and Floerkemeier C. *From the Internet of Computers to the Internet of Things*, pages 242–259. Springer-Verlag, Berlin, 2010. → 44.

Mazouni K., Garbinato B., and Guerraoui R. Building Reliable Client-Server Software Using Actively Replicated Objects. In Graham I., Magnusson B., Meyer B., and Nerson J.-M., editors, *Technology of Object Oriented Languages and Systems*, pages 37–53. Prentice Hall, Englewood Cliffs, N.J., 1995. → 436.

Medina V. and Garcia J. A Survey of Migration Mechanisms of Virtual Machines. *ACM Computing Surveys*, 46(3):30, Jan. 2014. → 175.

Meling H. and Jehl L. Tutorial Summary: Paxos Explained from Scratch. In *17th International Conference on Principles of Distributed Systems*, pages 1–10. Springer, 2013. → 484.

Menasce D. and Almeida V. *Capacity Planning for Web Services*. Prentice Hall, Englewood Cliffs, N.J., 2002. → 25.

Menezes A. J., Oorschot P. C.van , and Vanstone S. A. *Handbook of Applied Cryptography*. CRC Press, Boca Raton, 3rd edition, 1996. → 568.

Merideth M. G. and Reiter M. K. *Selected Results from the Latest Decade of Quorum Systems Research*, pages 185–206. Springer-Verlag, Berlin, 2010. → 443.

Message Passing Interface Forum . MPI: A Message-Passing Interface Standard, version 4.0. Technical report, University of Tenness, Knoxville, June 2021. → 220.

Meyerovich L. A. and Bodik R. Fast and Parallel Webpage Layout. In *19th International World Wide Web Conference*, pages 711–720, New York, NY, 2010. ACM Press. → 124.

Mills D. Network Time Protocol (version 3): Specification, Implementation, and Analysis. RFC 1305, July 1992. → 257.

Mills D. L. *Computer Network Time Synchronization: The Network Time Protocol on Earth and in Space*. CRC Press, Boca Raton, FL, 2nd edition, 2011. → 257.

Milojicic D., Douglis F., Paindaveine Y., Wheeler R., and Zhou S. Process Migration. *ACM Computing Surveys*, 32(3):241–299, Sept. 2000. → 167.

Min S. L. and Baer J.-L. Design and Analysis of a Scalable Cache Coherence Scheme Based on Clocks and Timestamps. *IEEE Transactions on Parallel and Distributed Systems*, 3(1):25–44, Jan. 1992. → 443.

Mockapetris P. Domain Names - Concepts and Facilities. RFC 1034, Nov. 1987a. → 354, 359.

Mockapetris P. Domain Names - Implementation and Specification. RFC 1035, Nov. 1987b. → 354, 359.

Mohan C., Strong R., and Finkelstein S. Method for Distributed Transaction Commit and Recovery using Byzantine Agreement within Clusters of Processors. In *2nd Symposium on Principles of Distributed Computing*, pages 89–103, New York, NY, 1983. ACM Press. → 468.

Moll P., Shang W., Yu Y., Afanasyev A., and Zhang L. A Survey of Distributed Dataset Synchronization in Named Data Networking. Technical Report NDN-0053, UCLA, May 2021. → 386.

Mottola L. and Picco G. P. Programming Wireless Sensor Networks: Fundamental Concepts and State of the Art. *ACM Computing Surveys*, 43(3):19:1–19:51, Apr. 2011. → 49.

Moura G. C. M., Castro S., Hardaker W., Wullink M., and Hesselman C. Clouding up the Internet: How Centralized is DNS Traffic Becoming? In *Internet Measurement Conference*, page 42–49, 2020. → 365.

Mousazadeh M. and Ladani B. T. Gossip-based Data Aggregation in Hostile Environments. *Computer Communications*, 62:1–12, 2015. → 306.

Mühl G., Fiege L., and Pietzuch P. *Distributed Event-Based Systems*. Springer-Verlag, Berlin, 2006. → 69.

Muntz D. and Honeyman P. Multi-level Caching in Distributed File Systems. In *Winter Technical Conference*, pages 305–313, San Francisco, CA, Jan. 1992. USENIX. → 429.

Murty J. *Programming Amazon Web Services*. O'Reilly & Associates, Sebastopol, CA., 2008. → 66, 99.

Najafi A., Tai A., and Wei M. Systems Research is Running out of Time. In *Workshop on Hot Topics in Operating Systems (HotOS)*, page 65–71, 2021. → 249.

Naur P. and Randell B. Report on the NATO Software Engineering Conference 1968. Technical report, Scientific Affairs Division NATO, Brussels, Belgium, Oct. 1968. → 74.

Needham R. and Schroeder M. Using Encryption for Authentication in Large Networks of Computers. *Communications of the ACM*, 21(12):993–999, Dec. 1978. → 577.

Nelson B. *Remote Procedure Call*. Ph.D., Carnegie-Mellon University, 1981. → 514.

Neuman B. Proxy-Based Authorization and Accounting for Distributed Systems. In *13th International Conference on Distributed Computing Systems*, pages 283–291, Pittsburgh, May 1993. IEEE. → 601.

Neuman B. Scale in Distributed Systems. In Casavant T. and Singhal M., editors, *Readings in Distributed Computing Systems*, pages 463–489. IEEE Computer Society Press, Los Alamitos, CA., 1994. → 24, 28, 606.

Neuman C., Yu T., Hartman S., and Raeburn K. The Kerberos Network Authentication Service. RFC 4120, July 2005. → 581.

Ng E. and Zhang H. Predicting Internet Network Distance with Coordinates-Based Approaches. In *21st INFOCOM Conference*, Los Alamitos, CA., June 2002. IEEE, IEEE Computer Society Press. → 320.

Nguyen C. T., Hoang D. T., Nguyen D. N., Niyato D., Nguyen H. T., and Dutkiewicz E. Proof-of-Stake Consensus Mechanisms for Future Blockchain Networks: Fundamentals, Applications and Opportunities. *IEEE Access*, 7:85727–85745, 2019. → 292, 589.

Nissenbaum H. *Privacy in Context*. Stanford University Press, Stanford, CA, 2010. → 553.

Noble B., Fleis B., and Kim M. A Case for Fluid Replication. In *NetStore'99*, Seattle, WA, Oct. 1999. → 430.

Noveck D. and Lever C. Network File System (NFS) Version 4 Minor Verion 1 Protocol. RFC 8881, Aug. 2020. → 83, 350.

Nyers L. and Jelasity M. A Comparative Study of Spanning Tree and Gossip Protocols for Aggregation. *Concurrency & Computation: Practice and Experience*, 2015. → 522.

Nygren E., Sitaraman R. K., and Sun J. The Akamai Network: A Platform for High-Performance Internet Applications. *Operating Systems Review*, 44(3):2–19, July 2010. → 165.

OASIS . AMQP, Protocol specification, Version 1.0, Oct. 2012. → 227.

Obraczka K. Multicast Transport Protocols: A Survey and Taxonomy. *IEEE Communications Magazine*, 36(1):94–102, Jan. 1998. → 232.

Oikonomou K. and Stavrakakis I. Performance Analysis of Probabilistic Flooding Using Random Graphs. In *World of Wireless, Mobile and Multimedia Networks, 2007. WoWMoM 2007. IEEE International Symposium on a*, pages 1–6, June 2007. doi: 10.1109/WOWMOM.2007.4351694. → 237.

OMG . The Common Object Request Broker: Architecture and Specification, revision 2.4.2. OMG Document formal/00-02-33, Object Management Group, Framingham, MA, Feb. 2001. → 156.

OMG . UML 2.0 Superstructure Specification. OMG Document ptc/04-10-02, Object Management Group, Framingham, MA, Oct. 2004. → 57.

Ongaro D. *Consensus: Bridging Theory AND Practice*. Ph.D., Stanford University, Aug. 2014. → 479.

Ongaro D. and Ousterhout J. In Search of an Understandable Consensus Algorithm. In *USENIX Annual Technical Conference*, pages 305–319, Berkeley, CA, June 2014. USENIX, USENIX. → 289, 477, 479.

Onica E., Felber P., Mercier H., and Riviere E. Confidentiality-Preserving Publish/Subscribe: A Survey. *ACM Computing Surveys*, 49(2), June 2016. → 315.

Oram A., editor. *Peer-to-Peer: Harnessing the Power of Disruptive Technologies*. O'Reilly & Associates, Sebastopol, CA., 2001. → 32.

Otte P. Sybil-resistant Trust Mechanisms in Distributed Systems. Msc, Delft University of Technology, Dec. 2016. → 591.

Otte P., Vos M.de , and Pouwelse J. TrustChain: A Sybil-resistant Scalable Blockchain. *Future Generation Computer Systems*, 107:770–780, 2020. → 589, 590.

Özsu T. and Valduriez P. *Principles of Distributed Database Systems*. Springer-Verlag, Berlin, 4th edition, 2020. → 89, 426.

Pahl C., Brogi A., Soldani J., and Jamshidi P. Cloud Container Technologies: A State-of-the-Art Review. *IEEE Transactions on Cloud Computing*, 7(3):677–692, 2019. → 135.

Pai V., Aron M., Banga G., Svendsen M., Druschel P., Zwaenepoel W., and Nahum E. Locality-Aware Request Distribution in Cluster-Based Network Servers. In

8th International Conference on Architectural Support for Programming Languages and Operating Systems, pages 205–216, New York, NY, Oct. 1998. ACM, ACM Press. → 163.

Panzieri F. and Shrivastava S. Rajdoot: A Remote Procedure Call Mechanism with Orphan Detection and Killing. *IEEE Transactions on Software Engineering*, 14(1):30–37, Jan. 1988. → 515.

Pappas V., Massey D., Terzis A., and Zhang L. A Comparative Study of the DNS Design with DHT-Based Alternatives. In *25th INFOCOMConference*, Los Alamitos, CA., May 2006. IEEE, IEEE Computer Society Press. → 368.

Parecki A. *OAuth 2.0 Simplified: A Guide to Building OAuth 2.0 Servers*. Lulu Press, Inc, 2020. → 605.

Park S., Specter M., Narula N., and Rivest R. L. Going From Bad to Worse: From Internet Voting to Blockchain Voting. *Journal of Cybersecurity*, 7(1):1–15, 2021. → 592.

Parlavantzas N. and Coulson G. Designing and Constructing Modifiable Middleware using Component Frameworks. *IET Software*, 1(4):113–126, Aug. 2007. → 78.

Passarella A. A Survey on Content-centric Technologies for the Current Internet: CDN and P2P Solutions. *Computer Communications*, 35(1):1–32, 2012. → 165.

Pautasso C., Zimmermann O., and Leymann F. Restful Web Services vs. "Big" Web Services: Making the Right Architectural Decision. In *17th International World Wide Web Conference*, pages 805–814, New York, NY, Aug. 2008. ACM Press. → 66, 67.

Pease M., Shostak R., and Lamport L. Reaching Agreement in the Presence of Faults. *Journal of the ACM*, 27(2):228–234, Apr. 1980. → 468.

Perkins C. IP Mobility Support in IPv4, Revised. RFC 5944, Nov. 2010. → 47.

Perkins C., Johnson D., and Arkko J. Mobility Support in IPv6. RFC 6275, July 2011. → 47, 331.

Peterson L., Bavier A., Fiuczynski M. E., and Muir S. Experiences Building PlanetLab. In *7th Symposium on Operating System Design and Implementation*, pages 351–366, Berkeley, CA, Nov. 2006. USENIX, USENIX. → 136.

Pike R., Presotto D., Dorward S., Flandrena B., Thompson K., Trickey H., and Winterbottom P. Plan 9 from Bell Labs. *Computing Systems*, 8(3):221–254, Summer 1995. → 346.

Pinzari G. NX X Protocol Compression. Technical Report D-309/3-NXP-DOC, NoMachine, Rome, Italy, Sept. 2003. → 144.

Pitoura E. and Samaras G. Locating Objects in Mobile Computing. *IEEE Transactions on Knowledge and Data Engineering*, 13(4):571–592, July 2001. → 338.

Plummer D. An Ethernet Address Resolution Protocol. RFC 826, Nov. 1982. → 330.

Podling S. and Boszormenyi L. A Survey of Web Cache Replacement Strategies. *ACM Computing Surveys*, 35(4):374–398, Dec. 2003. → 453.

Popek G. J. and Goldberg R. P. Formal Requirements for Virtualizable Third Generation Architectures. *Communications of the ACM*, 17(7):412–421, July 1974. → 131, 132.

Popescu A., Constantinescu D., Erman D., and Ilie D. A Survey of Reliable Multicast Communication. In *3rd Conference on Next Generation Internet Networks*, pages 111–118, May 2007. → 517.

Popescu A. M., Tudorache G. I., Peng B., and Kemp A. H. Surveying Position Based Routing Protocols for Wireless Sensor and Ad-hoc Networks. *International Journal on Communication Networks and Information Security*, 4(1):41–67, Apr. 2012. → 319.

Poslad S. *Ubiquitous Computing: Smart Devices, Environments and Interactions*. John Wiley, New York, 2009. → 44, 46.

Postel J. Simple Mail Transfer Protocol. RFC 821, Aug. 1982. → 226.

Postel J. and Reynolds J. File Transfer Protocol. RFC 995, Oct. 1985. → 188.

Pourghassemi B. *Adaptive Tools for Performance Analysis of Large-scale Applications*. Phd, University of California at Irvine, 2021. → 146.

Pouwelse J. A., Garbacki P., Epema D. H. J., and Sips H. J. The Bittorrent P2P File-Sharing System: Measurements and Analysis. In *4th International Workshop on Peer-to-Peer Systems*, volume 3640 of *Lecture Notes in Computer Science*, pages 205–216, Berlin, Feb. 2005. Springer-Verlag. → 97.

Pradhan D. *Fault-Tolerant Computer System Design*. Prentice Hall, Englewood Cliffs, N.J., 1996. → 464.

Preguica N. Conflict-Free Replicated Data Types: An Overview. arXiv:1806.10254, 2018. → 410.

Prisco R. D., Lampson B., and Lynch N. Revisiting the Paxos Algorithm. In Mavronicolas M. and Tsigas P., editors, *11th International Workshop on Distributed Algorithms*, volume 1320 of *Lecture Notes in Computer Science*. Springer-Verlag, Berlin, Sept. 1997. → 479.

Qin H., Li Q., Speiser J., Kraft P., and Ousterhout J. Arachne: Core-Aware Thread Management. In *13th Symposium on Operating System Design and Implementation*, pages 145–161. USENIX, Oct. 2018. → 122.

Rabinovich M. and Spastscheck O. *Web Caching and Replication*. Addison-Wesley, Reading, MA., 2002. → 451.

Rabinovich M., Rabinovich I., Rajaraman R., and Aggarwal A. A Dynamic Object Replication and Migration Protocol for an Internet Hosting Service. In *19th International Conference on Distributed Computing Systems*, pages 101–113, Austin, TX, June 1999. IEEE. → 427, 428.

Radia S. *Names, Contexts, and Closure Mechanisms in Distributed Computing Environments*. Ph.D., University of Waterloo, Ontario, 1989. → 348.

Rajaraman V. Grid Computing. *Resonance*, 21(5):401–415, 2016. → 35.

Ramanathan P., Shin K., and Butler R. Fault-Tolerant Clock Synchronization in Distributed Systems. *Computer*, 23(10):33–42, Oct. 1990. → 253.

Ramirez W., Masip-Bruin X., Yannuzzi M., Serral-Gracia R., Martinez A., and Siddiqui M. A Survey and Taxonomy of ID/Locator Split Architectures. *Computer Networks*, 60:13–33, 2014. → 329.

Raynal M. and Singhal M. Logical Time: Capturing Causality in Distributed Systems. *Computer*, 29(2):49–56, Feb. 1996. → 262.

Rescorla E. and others . The Transport Layer Security (TLS) Protocol Version 1.3. RFC 8446, Aug. 2018. → 583.

Reynolds J. and Postel J. Assigned Numbers. RFC 1700, Oct. 1994. → 150.

Ricart G. and Agrawala A. An Optimal Algorithm for Mutual Exclusion in Computer Networks. *Communications of the ACM*, 24(1):9–17, Jan. 1981. → 274.

Richards M. and Ford N. *Fundamentals of Software Architecture*. O'Reilly & Associates, Sebastopol, CA., 2020. → 56.

Richardson T., Stafford-Fraser Q., Wood K. R., and Hopper A. Virtual Network Computing. *IEEE Internet Computing*, 2(1):33–38, Jan. 1998. → 144.

Risson J. and Moors T. Survey of Research towards Robust Peer-to-Peer Networks: Search Methods. *Computer Networks*, 50(17):3485–3521, 2006. → 93.

Rizzo L. Effective Erasure Codes for Reliable Computer Communication Protocols. *SIGCOMM Computer Communications Review*, 27(2):24–36, Apr. 1997. → 536.

Robbins K. and Robbins S. *UNIX Systems Programming*. Prentice Hall, Englewood Cliffs, N.J., 2003. → 113, 122.

Robin J. S. and Irvine C. E. Analysis of the Intel Pentium's Ability to Support a Secure Virtual Machine Monitor. In *9th USENIX Security Symposium*, pages 129–144, Berkeley, CA, 2000. USENIX. → 132.

Rodrigues L., Fonseca H., and Verissimo P. Totally Ordered Multicast in Large-Scale Systems. In *16th International Conference on Distributed Computing Systems*, pages 503–510, Hong Kong, May 1996. IEEE. → 441.

Rodriguez P., Spanner C., and Biersack E. Analysis of Web Caching Architecture: Hierarchical and Distributed Caching. *IEEE/ACM Transactions on Networking*, 21(4): 404–418, Aug. 2001. → 452.

Rosenblum M. and Garfinkel T. Virtual Machine Monitors: Current Technology and Future Trends. *Computer*, 38(5):39–47, May 2005. → 131.

Roussos G., Marsh A. J., and Maglavera S. Enabling Pervasive Computing with Smart Phones. *IEEE Pervasive Computing*, 4(2):20–26, Apr. 2005. → 44.

Rowe F., Baskerville R., and Wolff F.-C. Functionality vs. Security in IS: Tradeoff or Equilibrium? In *33rd International Conference on Information Systems*, 2012. → 566.

Rowstron A. and Druschel P. Pastry: Scalable, Distributed Object Location and Routing for Large-Scale Peer-to-Peer Systems. In *Middleware 2001*, volume 2218 of *Lecture Notes in Computer Science*, pages 329–350, Berlin, Nov. 2001. Springer-Verlag. → 233, 338.

Roy G. *RabbitMQ in Depth*. Manning Publications, Shelter Island, NY, 2018. → 227, 230, 231, 232.

Saad M., Spaulding J., Njilla L., Kamhoua C., Shetty S., Nyang D., and Mohaisen D. Exploring the Attack Surface of Blockchain: A Comprehensive Survey. *IEEE Communications Surveys & Tutorials*, 22(3):1977–2008, 2020. → 589.

Sagan H. *Space-Filling Curves*. Springer-Verlag, Berlin, 1994. → 382.

Sahoo J., Salahuddin M. A., Glitho R., Elbiaze H., and Ajib W. A Survey on Replica Server Placement Algorithms for Content Delivery Networks. *IEEE Communications Surveys & Tutorials*, 19(2):1002–1026, 2017. → 424, 425, 426.

Salaht F. A., Desprez F., and Lebre A. An Overview of Service Placement Problem in Fog and Edge Computing. *ACM Computing Surveys*, 53(3), June 2020. → 104.

Saltzer J. and Kaashoek M. *Principles of Computer System Design, An Introduction*.

Morgan Kaufman, San Mateo, CA., 2009. → 79, 546, 547.

Saltzer J. and Schroeder M. The Protection of Information in Computer Systems. *Proceedings of the IEEE*, 63(9):1278–1308, Sept. 1975. → 549, 550.

Saltzer J., Reed D., and Clark D. End-to-End Arguments in System Design. *ACM Transactions on Computer Systems*, 2(4):277–288, Nov. 1984. → 271.

Sambra A. V., Mansour E., Hawke S., Zereba M., Greco N., Ghanem A., Zagidulin D., Aboulnaga A., and Berners-Lee T. Solid: A Platform for Decentralized Social Applications based on Linked Data. *MIT CSAIL & Qatar Computing Research Institute, Tech. Rep.*, 2016. → 553.

Santoro N. *Design and Analysis of Distributed Algorithms*. John Wiley, New York, 2007. → 249.

Saroiu S., Gummadi P. K., and Gribble S. D. Measuring and Analyzing the Characteristics of Napster and Gnutella Hosts. *ACM Multimedia Systems*, 9(2):170–184, Aug. 2003. → 96.

Saxena D., Raychoudhury V., Suri N., Becker C., and Cao J. Named data networking: A survey. *Computer Science Review*, 19:15–55, 2016. → 386.

Saxena P. and Rai J. A Survey of Permission-based Distributed Mutual Exclusion Algorithms. *Computer Standards and Interfaces*, 25(2):159–181, May 2003. → 272.

Schlosser M., Sintek M., Decker S., and Nejdl W. HyperCuP – Hypercubes, Ontologies, and Efficient Search on Peer-to-Peer Networks. In *1st International Workshop on Agents and Peer-to-Peer Computing*, volume 2530 of *Lecture Notes in Computer Science*, pages 112–124, Berlin, July 2002. Springer-Verlag. → 238.

Schmidt A. Implicit Human Computer Interaction Through Context. *Personal and Ubiquitous Computing*, 4(2-3):191–199, June 2000. → 45.

Schmidt C. and Parashar M. Squid: Enabling Search in DHT-based systems. *Journal of Parallel and Distributed Computing*, 68:962–975, 2008. → 383.

Schmidt D., Stal M., Rohnert H., and Buschmann F. *Pattern-Oriented Software Architecture – Patterns for Concurrent and Networked Objects*. John Wiley, New York, 2000. → 76.

Schneider F. Implementing Fault-Tolerant Services Using the State Machine Approach: A Tutorial. *ACM Computing Surveys*, 22(4):299–320, Dec. 1990. → 264, 431.

Schulzrinne H., Casner S., Frederick R., and Jacobson V. RTP: A Transport Protocol for Real-Time Applications. RFC 3550, July 2003. → 187.

Schwarzkopf M., Kohler E., Frans Kaashoek M., and Morris R. Position: GDPR Compliance by Construction. In Gadepally V., Mattson T., Stonebraker M., Wang F., Luo G., Laing Y., and Dubovitskaya A., editors, *Heterogeneous Data Management, Polystores, and Analytics for Healthcare (DMAH 2019, Poly 2019)*, volume 11721 of *Lecture Notes in Computer Science*, pages 39–53, Berlin, 2019. Springer-Verlag. → 554.

Sebesta R. *Programming the World Wide Web*. Addison-Wesley, Reading, MA., 8th edition, 2015. → 87.

Sereno M. and Gaeta R. Generalized Probabilistic Flooding in Unstructured Peer-to-Peer Networks. *IEEE Transactions on Parallel and Distributed Systems*, 22(12):2055–2062, 2011. ISSN 1045-9219. → 238.

Servos D. and Osborn S. L. Current Research and Open Problems in Attribute-based Access Control. *ACM Computing Surveys*, 49(4):1–45, 2017. → 598, 601.

Seuken S. and Parkes D. C. Sybil-proof Accounting Mechanisms with Transitive Trust. In *International Joint Conference on Autonomous Agents and Multiagent Systems*, pages 205–212. ACM, 2014. → 590.

Shahrad M., Balkind J., and Wentzlaff D. Architectural Implications of Function-as-a-Service Computing. In *Annual IEEE/ACM International Symposium on Microarchitecture*, page 1063–1075, New York, NY, USA, 2019. Association for Computing Machinery. → 100.

Shapiro M., Preguiça N., Baquero C., and Zawirski M. Conflict-Free Replicated Data Types. In *13th International Conference Stabilization, Safety, and Security of Distributed Systems*, page 386–400, Berlin, 2011. Springer-Verlag. → 409.

Sharma P., Chaufournier L., Shenoy P., and Tay Y. Containers and Virtual Machines at Scale: A Comparative Study. In *Middleware 2016*, pages 1–13. ACM/IFIP/USENIX, Dec. 2016. → 138.

Shastri S., Banakar V., Wasserman M., Kumar A., and Chidambaram V. Understanding and Benchmarking the Impact of GDPR on Database Systems. *Proceedings of the VLDB Endowment*, 13(7):1064–1077, mar 2020. → 554, 555.

Shen X., Yu H., Buford J., and Akon M., editors. *Handbook of Peer-to-Peer Networking*. Springer-Verlag, Berlin, 2010. → 636, 642.

Sheth A. P. and Larson J. A. Federated Database Systems for Managing Distributed, Heterogeneous, and Autonomous Databases. *ACM Computing Surveys*, 22(3):183–236, Sept. 1990. → 427.

Shin M., Park M., Oh D., Kim B., and Lee J. Survey on the Clock Synchronization Schemes for Propagation Delay Measurement. *International Journal of Advanced Science and Technology*, 35:139–140, Oct. 2011. → 253.

Shoch J. Internetwork Naming, Addressing, and Routing. In *17th International Computer Conference*, pages 72–79, Los Alamitos, CA., 1978. IEEE, IEEE Computer Society Press. → 329.

Shooman M. L. *Reliability of Computer Systems and Networks: Fault Tolerance, Analysis, and Design*. John Wiley, New York, 2002. → 463.

Shriram A. and Kaur J. Empirical Evaluation of Techniques for Measuring Available Bandwidth. In *26th INFOCOM Conference*, pages 2162–2170, Los Alamitos, CA., 2007. IEEE, IEEE Computer Society Press. → 454.

Silberschatz A., Galvin P., and Gagne G. *Operating System Concepts*. John Wiley, New York, 10th edition, 2019. → 346.

Singhal M. and Shivaratri N. *Advanced Concepts in Operating Systems: Distributed, Database, and Multiprocessor Operating Systems*. McGraw-Hill, New York, 1994. → 537.

Sivasubramanian S., Pierre G., and van Steen M. Replicating Web Applications On-Demand. In *1st International Conference on Services Computing*, pages 227–236, Los Alamitos, CA., Sept. 2004a. IEEE, IEEE Computer Society Press. → 457.

Sivasubramanian S., Szymaniak M., Pierre G., and van Steen M. Replication for Web Hosting Systems. *ACM Computing Surveys*, 36(3):1–44, Sept. 2004b. → 453.

Sivasubramanian S., Pierre G., van Steen M., and Alonso G. Analysis of Caching and Replication Strategies for Web Applications. *IEEE Internet Computing*, 11(1):60–66, Jan. 2007. → 456.

Sivrikaya F. and Yener B. Time Synchronization in Sensor Networks: A Survey. *IEEE Network*, 18(4):45–50, July 2004. → 257.

Skeen D. Nonblocking Commit Protocols. In *SIGMOD International Conference on Management Of Data*, pages 133–142. ACM, 1981. → 534.

Skeen D. and Stonebraker M. A Formal Model of Crash Recovery in a Distributed System. *IEEE Transactions on Software Engineering*, SE-9(3):219–228, Mar. 1983. → 534.

Sletten B. *WebAssembly: The Definitive Guide*. O'Reilly & Associates, Sebastopol, CA., 2022. → 146.

Smart N. P. *Cryptography Made Simple*. Springer-Verlag, Berlin, 2016. → 557.

Smith J. and Nair R. The Architecture of Virtual Machines. *Computer*, 38(5):32–38, May 2005a. → 129, 130.

Smith J. and Nair R. *Virtual Machines: Versatile Platforms for Systems and Processes*. Morgan Kaufman, San Mateo, CA., 2005b. → 131, 132.

Smith M. and Howes T. Lightweight Directory Access Protocol (LDAP): String Representation of Search Filters. RFC 4515, June 2006. → 379.

Smith R. E. A Contemporary Look at Saltzer and Schroeder's 1975 Design Principles. *IEEE Security & Privacy*, 10(6):20–25, 2012. → 549, 550.

Soltesz S., Pötzl H., Fiuczynski M. E., Bavier A., and Peterson L. Container-Based Operating System Virtualization: A Scalable, High-Performance Alternative to Hypervisors. In *2nd EuroSys (European Conference on Computer Systems)*, pages 275–287, New York, NY, Mar. 2007. ACM, ACM Press. → 137.

Spector A. Performing Remote Operations Efficiently on a Local Computer Network. *Communications of the ACM*, 25(4):246–260, Apr. 1982. → 510.

Srinivasan S. *Kilim: A Server Framework with Lightweight Actors, Isolation Types and Zero-Copy Messaging*. Ph.d., University of Cambridge, Computer Laboratory, Feb. 2010. → 122.

Srisuresh P. and Holdrege M. IP Network Address Translator (NAT) Terminology and Considerations. RFC 2663, Aug. 1999. → 163.

Stallings W. *Crypotgraphy and Network Security*. Pearson Education, Englewood Cliffs, N.J., 7th edition, 2017. → 571.

Stanciu V., van Steen M., Peter A., and Dobre C. Privacy-Preserving Crowd Sensing and Analytics. In *17th International Conference Mobile and Ubiquitous Systems: Computing, Networking, and Services*, 12 2020. → 558.

Stankovic J. A. Research Directions for the Internet of Things. *IEEE Internet of Things Journal*, 1(1):3–9, Feb. 2014. → 44.

Stannat A., Ileri C. U., Gijswijt D., and Pouwelse J. Achieving Sybil-proofness in Distributed Work Systems. In *International Joint Conference on Autonomous Agents and Multiagent Systems*, pages 1263–1271, 2021. → 591.

Steiner J., Neuman C., and Schiller J. Kerberos: An Authentication Service for Open Network Systems. In *Winter Technical Conference*, pages 191–202. USENIX, 1988.

$\rightarrow$ 581.

Steinmetz R. and Nahrstedt K. *Multimedia Systems*. Springer-Verlag, Berlin, 2004. $\rightarrow$ 162.

Stevens W. *TCP/IP Illustrated, Volume 1: The Protocols*. Addison-Wesley, Reading, MA., 1994. $\rightarrow$ 59.

Stevens W. *UNIX Network Programming – Networking APIs: Sockets and XTI*. Prentice Hall, Englewood Cliffs, N.J., 2nd edition, 1998. $\rightarrow$ 123, 210.

Stevens W. *UNIX Network Programming – Interprocess Communication*. Prentice Hall, Englewood Cliffs, N.J., 2nd edition, 1999. $\rightarrow$ 113, 122.

Stevens W. and Rago S. *Advanced Programming in the UNIX Environment*. Addison-Wesley, Reading, MA., 2nd edition, 2005. $\rightarrow$ 115.

Stewart R. Stream Control Transmission Protocol. RFC 4960, Sept. 2007. $\rightarrow$ 188.

Stocker V., Smaragdakis G., Lehr W., and Bauer S. The Growing Complexity of Content Delivery Networks: Challenges and Implications for the Internet Ecosystem. *Telecommunications Policy*, 41(10):1003–1016, 2017. $\rightarrow$ 165.

Stoica I., Morris R., Liben-Nowell D., Karger D. R., Kaashoek M. F., Dabek F., and Balakrishnan H. Chord: A Scalable Peer-to-peer Lookup Protocol for Internet Applications. *IEEE/ACM Transactions on Networking*, 11(1):17–32, Feb. 2003. $\rightarrow$ 91, 333, 336.

Stratan C., Sacha J., Napper J., Costa P., and Pierre G. The XtreemOS Resource Selection Service. *ACM Transactions of Autonomous and Adaptive Systems*, 7(4), Dec. 2012. $\rightarrow$ 385.

Strauss J., Katabi D., and Kaashoek F. A Measurement Study of Available Bandwidth Estimation Tools. In *3rd Internet Measurement Conference*, pages 39–44, New York, NY, 2003. ACM Press. $\rightarrow$ 454.

Su A.-J., Choffnes D. R., Kuzmanovic A., and Bustamante F. E. Drafting Behind Akamai (Travelocity-Based Detouring). In *SIGCOMM*, page 435–446, 2006. $\rightarrow$ 166.

Sugerman J., Venkitachalam G., and Lim B.-H. Virtualizing I/O Devices on VMware Workstations Hosted Virtual Machine Monitor. In *USENIX Annual Technical Conference*, pages 1–14, Berkeley, CA, June 2001. USENIX, USENIX. $\rightarrow$ 132.

Sundararaman B., Buy U., and Kshemkalyani A. D. Clock Synchronization for Wireless Sensor Networks: A Survey. *Ad-Hoc Networks*, 3(3):281–323, May 2005. $\rightarrow$ 257.

Swamidass S. J. and Baldi P. Mathematical Correction for Fingerprint Similarity Measures to Improve Chemical Retrieval. *Journal of Chemical Information and Modeling*, 47(3):952–964, 2007. $\rightarrow$ 559.

Szymaniak M., Pierre G., and van Steen M. Scalable Cooperative Latency Estimation. In *10th International Conference on Parallel and Distributed Systems*, pages 367–376, Los Alamitos, CA., July 2004. IEEE, IEEE Computer Society Press. $\rightarrow$ 321.

Szymaniak M., Presotto D., Pierre G., and van Steen M. Practical Large-Scale Latency Estimation. *Computer Networks*, 52(7):1343–1364, May 2008. $\rightarrow$ 321.

Taiani F., Fabre J.-C., and Killijian M.-O. A Multi-Level Meta-Object Protocol for Fault-Tolerance in Complex Architectures. In *International Conference on Dependable Systems and Networks*, pages 270–279, Los Alamitos, CA., June 2005. IEEE Computer Society Press. $\rightarrow$ 436.

Taleb T., Samdanis K., Mada B., Flinck H., Dutta S., and Sabella D. On Multi-Access Edge Computing: A Survey of the Emerging 5G Network Edge Cloud Architecture and Orchestration. *IEEE Communications Surveys & Tutorials*, 19(3):1657–1681, 2017. → 103.

Tan S.-W., Waters G., and Crawford J. A Survey and Performance Evaluation of Scalable Tree-based Application Layer Multicast Protocols. Technical Report 9-03, University of Kent, UK, July 2003. → 235.

Tanenbaum A. and Bos H. *Modern Operating Systems*. Prentice Hall, Upper Saddle River, N.J., 5th edition, 2022. → 346.

Tanenbaum A., , Feamster N., and Wetherall D. *Computer Networks*. Prentice Hall, Upper Saddle River, N.J., 6th edition, 2021. → 183, 508.

Tanisch P. Atomic Commit in Concurrent Computing. *IEEE Concurrency*, 8(4):34–41, Oct. 2000. → 528.

Tarkoma S. *Overlay Networks, Toward Information Networking*. CRC Press, Boca Raton, FL, 2010. → 89.

Tarkoma S. and Kangasharju J. *Mobile Middleware: Supporting Applications and Services*. John Wiley, New York, 2009. → 47.

Tartalja I. and Milutinovic V. Classifying Software-Based Cache Coherence Solutions. *IEEE Software*, 14(3):90–101, May 1997. → 443.

Tel G. *Introduction to Distributed Algorithms*. Cambridge University Press, Cambridge, UK, 2nd edition, 2000. → 249, 283.

Terry D. *Replicated Data Management for Mobile Computing*. Synthesis Lectures on Data Management. Morgan and Claypool, San Rafael, CA, 2008. → 416.

Terry D., Demers A., Petersen K., Spreitzer M., Theimer M., and Welsh B. Session Guarantees for Weakly Consistent Replicated Data. In *3rd International Conference on Parallel and Distributed Information Systems*, pages 140–149, Los Alamitos, CA., Sept. 1994. IEEE, IEEE Computer Society Press. → 416, 420, 421.

Terry D., Petersen K., Spreitzer M., and Theimer M. The Case for Non-transparent Replication: Examples from Bayou. *IEEE Data Engineering*, 21(4):12–20, Dec. 1998. → 416.

Thomas R. A Majority Consensus Approach to Concurrency Control for Multiple Copy Databases. *ACM Transactions on Database Systems*, 4(2):180–209, June 1979. → 441.

TIBCO . *TIBCO Rendezvous Concepts, Release 8.3.0*. TIBCO Software Inc., Palo Alto, CA, July 2010. → 308.

Tourani R., Misra S., Mick T., and Panwar G. Security, Privacy, and Access Control in Information-Centric Networking: A Survey. *IEEE Communications Surveys & Tutorials*, 20(1):566–600, 2018. → 389.

Towsley D., Kurose J., and Pingali S. A Comparison of Sender-Initiated and Receiver-Initiated Reliable Multicast Protocols. *IEEE Journal on Selected Areas in Communication*, 15(3):398–407, Apr. 1997. → 518.

Trivedi K. *Probability and Statistics with Reliability, Queuing and Computer Science Applications*. John Wiley, New York, 2nd edition, 2002. → 26.

Tsafrir D. The Context-Switch Overhead Inflicted by Hardware Interrupts (and the

Enigma of Do-nothing Loops). In *2007 Workshop on Experimental Computer Science*, New York, NY, 2007. ACM Press. → 116, 117.

Tsui A. W., Lin W.-C., Chen W.-J., Huang P., and Chu H.-H. Accuracy Performance Analysis between War Driving and War Walking in Metropolitan Wi-Fi Localization. *IEEE Transactions on Mobile Computing*, 9(11):1551–1562, 2010. → 318.

Turek J. and Shasha S. The Many Faces of Consensus in Distributed Systems. *Computer*, 25(6):8–17, June 1992. → 503, 504.

Ulrich A., Holz R., Hauck P., and Carle G. Investigating the OpenPGP Web of Trust. In *European Symposium on Research in Computer Security*, pages 489–507. Springer, 2011. → 571.

Umar A. *Object-Oriented Client/Server Internet Environments*. Prentice Hall, Upper Saddle River, N.J., 1997. → 81.

UPnP Forum . UPnP Device Architecture Version 1.1, Oct. 2008. → 46.

Ur B., Bees J., Segreti S. M., Bauer L., Christin N., and Cranor L. F. Do Users' Perceptions of Password Security Match Reality? In *2016CHI Conference on Human Factors in Computing Systems*, pages 3748–3760. ACM, 2016. → 572.

Urdaneta G., Pierre G., and van Steen M. A Survey of DHT Security Techniques. *ACM Computing Surveys*, 43(2), June 2011. → 344, 588.

Uzunov A. V. A Survey of Security Solutions for Distributed Publish/Subscribe Systems. *Computers & Security*, 61:94–129, 2016. → 315.

van der Toorn O., Müller M., Dickinson S., Hesselman C., Sperotto A., and van Rijswijk-Deij R. Addressing the Challenges of Modern DNS: A Comprehensive Tutorial. *Computer Science Review*, 45:100469, 2022. → 359, 364, 365.

van Ede T., Aghakhani H., Spahn N., Bortolameotti R., Cova M., Continella A., van Steen M., Peter A., Kruegel C., and Vigna G. DeepCASE: Semi-Supervised Contextual Analysis of Security Events. In *International Symposium on Security and Privacy*. IEEE, 2022. → 612.

van Renesse R. and Altinbuken D. Paxos Made Moderately Complex. *ACM Computing Surveys*, 47(3):42:1–42:36, Feb. 2015. → 479.

van Rijn V. and Rellermeyer J. S. A Fresh Look at the Architecture and Performance of Contemporary Isolation Platforms. In *Middleware 2021*, pages 323–336. ACM/I-FIP/USENIX, Dec. 2021. → 139.

van Steen M. and Ballintijn G. Achieving Scalability in Hierarchical Location Services. In *26th International Computer Software and Applications Conference*, pages 899–905, Los Alamitos, CA., Aug. 2002. IEEE, IEEE Computer Society Press. → 342.

van Steen M., Hauck F., Homburg P., and Tanenbaum A. Locating Objects in Wide-Area Systems. *IEEE Communications Magazine*, 36(1):104–109, Jan. 1998. → 338.

Vaquero L. M., Rodero-Merino L., Caceres J., and Lindner M. A Break in the Clouds: Towards a Cloud Definition. *SIGCOMM Computer Communications Review*, 39(1): 50–55, Dec. 2008. → 98.

Vasilomanolakis E., Karuppayah S., Mühlhäuser M., and Fischer M. Taxonomy and Survey of Collaborative Intrusion Detection. *ACM Computing Surveys*, 47(4):1–33, 2015. → 612.

Vasudevan S., Kurose J. F., and Towsley D. F. Design and Analysis of a Leader Election Algorithm for Mobile Ad Hoc Networks. In *12th International Conference on Network Protocols*, pages 350–360, Los Alamitos, CA., Oct. 2004. IEEE, IEEE Computer Society Press. → 294, 297.

Velazquez M. A Survey of Distributed Mutual Exclusion Algorithms. Technical Report CS-93-116, University of Colorado at Boulder, Sept. 1993. → 272.

Viotti P. and Vukolic M. Consistency in Nontransactional Distributed Storage Systems. *ACM Computing Surveys*, 29(1), June 2016. → 395.

Vixie P. What DNS Is Not. *Communications of the ACM*, 52(12):43–47, Dec. 2009. → 369.

Vixie P. Rate-Limiting State. *Communications of the ACM*, 57(4):40–43, Apr. 2014. → 369.

Vogels W. Tracking Service Availability in Long Running Business Activities. In *1st International Conference on Service Oriented Computing*, volume 2910 of *Lecture Notes in Computer Science*, pages 395–408, Berlin, Dec. 2003. Springer-Verlag. → 507.

Vogels W. Eventually consistent. *Communications of the ACM*, 52(1):40–44, Jan. 2009. → 407.

Voigt P. and Bussche A.Von dem . *The EU General Data Protection Regulation (GDPR), A Practical Guide*. Springer-Verlag, Berlin, 2017. → 553.

Voorsluys W., Broberg J., Venugopal S., and Buyya R. Cost of Virtual Machine Live Migration in Clouds: A Performance Evaluation. In *1st International Conference on Cloud Computing*, volume 5931 of *Lecture Notes in Computer Science*, pages 254–265, Berlin, Dec. 2009. Springer-Verlag. → 176, 177.

Voronkov A., Iwaya L. H., Martucci L. A., and Lindskog S. Systematic Literature Review on Usability of Firewall Configuration. *ACM Computing Surveys*, 50(6):1–35, 2017. → 610.

Voulgaris S. and van Steen M. VICINITY: A Pinch of Randomness Brings out the Structure. In *Middleware 2013*, volume 8275 of *Lecture Notes in Computer Science*, pages 21–40, Berlin, Dec. 2013. ACM/IFIP/USENIX, Springer-Verlag. → 301.

Voulgaris S., Gavidia D., and van Steen. M. CYCLON: Inexpensive Membership Management for Unstructured P2P Overlays. *Journal of Network and Systems Management*, 13(2):197–217, June 2005. → 299, 304.

Voulgaris S., Rivière E., Kermarrec A.-M., and van Steen M. Sub-2-Sub: Self-Organizing Content-Based Publish and Subscribe for Dynamic and Large Scale Collaborative Networks. In *5th International Workshop on Peer-to-Peer Systems*, Feb. 2006. → 311.

Vu Q., Lupu M., and Ooi B. *Peer-to-Peer Computing, Principles and Applications*. Springer-Verlag, Berlin, 2010. → 89.

Vukolić M. *Quorum Systems: With Applications to Storage and Consensus*, volume 3 of *Synthesis Lectures on Distributed Computing Theory*. Morgan & Claypool Publishers, 2012. → 443.

Waldo J., Wyant G., Wollrath A., and Kendall S. A Note on Distributed Computing. In *2nd Workshop on Mobile Object Systems*, volume 1222 of *Lecture Notes in Computer Science*, pages 1–10, Berlin, July 1997. Springer-Verlag. → 15.

Walfish M., Balakrishnan H., , and Shenker S. Untangling the Web from DNS. In *1st Symposium on Networked Systems Design and Implementation*, pages 225–238, Berkeley,

CA, Mar. 2004. USENIX, USENIX. → 368.

Wams J. *Unified Messaging and Micro-Objects.* PhD thesis, VU University Amsterdam, 2012. → 15.

Welsh M. and Mainland G. Programming Sensor Networks Using Abstract Regions. In *1st Symposium on Networked Systems Design and Implementation*, Berkeley, CA, Mar. 2004. USENIX, USENIX. → 49.

Wendell P. and Freedman M. J. Going Viral: Flash Crowds in an Open CDN. In *11th Internet Measurement Conference*, pages 549–558, New York, NY, 2011. ACM Press. → 452.

Werbach K. *The Blockchain and the New Architecture of Trust.* MIT Press, Cambridge, MA., 2018. → 592.

Wessels D. *Squid: The Definitive Guide.* O'Reilly & Associates, Sebastopol, CA., 2004. → 452.

Wieringa R. and Jonge W.de . Object Identifiers, Keys, and Surrogates–Object Identifiers Revisited. *Theory and Practice of Object Systems*, 1(2):101–114, 1995. → 328.

Wierzbicki A. *Trust and Fairness in Open, Distributed Systems*, volume 298 of *Studies in Computational Intelligence.* Springer-Verlag, Berlin, 2010. → 586.

Wiesmann M., Pedone F., Schiper A., Kemme B., and Alonso G. Understanding Replication in Databases and Distributed Systems. In *20th International Conference on Distributed Computing Systems*, pages 264–274, Taipei, Taiwan, Apr. 2000. IEEE. → 395.

Wolff E. *Micrservices: Flexible Software Architecture.* Addison-Wesley, Reading, MA., 2017. → 65.

Wollrath A., Riggs R., and Waldo J. A Distributed Object Model for the Java System. *Computing Systems*, 9(4):265–290, Fall 1996. → 201.

Wolman A., Voelker G., Sharma N., Cardwell N., Karlin A., and Levy H. On the Scale and Performance of Cooperative Web Proxy Caching. In *17th Symposium on Operating System Principles*, pages 16–31, Kiawah Island, SC, Dec. 1999. ACM. → 451.

Wool A. Trends in Firewall Configuration Errors: Measuring the Holes in Swiss Cheese. *IEEE Internet Computing*, 14(4):58–65, 2010. → 610.

Wright G. and Stevens W. *TCP/IP Illustrated, Volume 2: The Implementation.* Addison-Wesley, Reading, MA., 1995. → 59.

Xiao Y., Zhang N., Lou W., and Hou Y. T. A Survey of Distributed Consensus Protocols for Blockchain Networks. *IEEE Communications Surveys & Tutorials*, 22(2):1432–1465, 2020. → 502, 503.

Xu X., Weber I., Staples M., Zhu L., Bosch J., Bass L., Pautasso C., and Rimba P. A Taxonomy of Blockchain-based Systems for Architecture Design. In *International Conference on Software Architecture (ICSA)*, pages 243–252. IEEE, Apr. 2017. → 108.

Yang B. and Garcia-Molina H. Designing a Super-Peer Network. In *19th International Conference on Data Engineering*, pages 49–60, Los Alamitos, CA., Mar. 2003. IEEE, IEEE Computer Society Press. → 95.

Yang K., Zhang K., Jia X., Hasan M. A., and Shen X. Privacy-preserving Attribute-Keyword Based Data Publish-Subscribe Service on Cloud Platforms. *Information*

Sciences, 387:116–131, 2017. → 314, 315.

Yang M., Zhang Z., Li X., and Dai Y. An Empirical Study of Free-Riding Behavior in the Maze P2P File-Sharing System. In *4th International Workshop on Peer-to-Peer Systems*, Lecture Notes in Computer Science, Berlin, Feb. 2005. Springer-Verlag. → 96.

Yellin D. Competitive Algorithms for the Dynamic Selection of Component Implementations. *IBM Systems Journal*, 42(1):85–97, Jan. 2003. → 78.

Yin M., Malkhi D., Reiter M. K., Gueta G. G., and Abraham I. Hotstuff: BFT Consensus with Linearity and Responsiveness. In *Symposium on Principles of Distributed Computing*, pages 347–356, 2019. → 502, 503.

Yousefpour A., Fung C., Nguyen T., Kadiyala K., Jalali F., Niakanlahiji A., Kong J., and Jue J. P. All One Needs to Know About Fog Computing and Related Edge Computing Paradigms: A Complete Survey. *Journal of Systems Architecture*, 98: 289–330, 2019. → 52, 100.

Yu H. and Vahdat A. Efficient Numerical Error Bounding for Replicated Network Services. In Abbadi A. E., Brodie M. L., Chakravarthy S., Dayal U., Kamel N., Schlageter G., and Whang K.-Y., editors, *26th International Conference on Very Large Data Bases*, pages 123–133, San Mateo, CA., Sept. 2000. Morgan Kaufman. → 446.

Yu H. and Vahdat A. Design and Evaluation of a Conit-Based Continuous Consistency Model for Replicated Services. *ACM Transactions on Computer Systems*, 20(3):239–282, 2002. → 410, 411, 455.

Zarrin J., Aguiar R. L., and Barraca J. P. Resource Discovery for Distributed Computing Systems: A Comprehensive Survey. *Journal of Parallel and Distributed Computing*, 113: 127–166, 2018. → 385.

ZeroC . *Distributed Programming with Ice*. ZeroC Inc., Brisbane, Australia, 2022. → 158, 159.

Zhang C., Xie Y., Bai H., Yu B., Li W., and Gao Y. A Survey on Federated Learning. *Knowledge-Based Systems*, 216:106775, 2021a. → 169.

Zhang F., Liu G., Fu X., and Yahyapour R. A Survey on Virtual Machine Migration: Challenges, Techniques, and Open Issues. *IEEE Communications Surveys & Tutorials*, 20(2):1206–1243, 2018. → 175, 176.

Zhang J., Ma M., Wang P., and Sun X.dong . Middleware for the Internet of Things: A Survey on Requirements, Enabling Technologies, and Solutions. *Journal of Systems Architecture*, 117, 2021b. → 49.

Zhang Q., Cheng L., and Boutaba R. Cloud Computing: State of the Art and Research Challenges. *Journal of Internet Services and Applications*, 1(1):7–18, May 2010. → 99.

Zhang Y., Xia Z., Afanasyev A., and Zhang L. A Note on Routing Scalability in Named Data Networking. In *International Conference Communications Workshops (ICC Workshops)*, pages 1–6, 2019. → 387.

Zhao F. and Guibas L. *Wireless Sensor Networks*. Morgan Kaufman, San Mateo, CA., 2004. → 49.

Zhu Z. and Afanasyev A. Let's ChronoSync: Decentralized Dataset State Synchronization in Named Data Networking. In *21st International Conference on Network Protocols*, pages 1–10, 2013. → 386.

Zhuang S. Q., Geels D., Stoica I., and Katz R. H. On Failure Detection Algorithms in Overlay Networks. In *24th INFOCOM Conference*, Los Alamitos, CA., Mar. 2005. IEEE, IEEE Computer Society Press. → 507.

Zogg J.-M. GPS Basics. Technical Report GPS-X-02007, UBlox, Mar. 2002. → 317.

Zolfaghari B., Srivastava G., Roy S., Nemati H. R., Afghah F., Koshiba T., Razi A., Bibak K., Mitra P., and Rai B. K. Content Delivery Networks: State of the Art, Trends, and Future Roadmap. *ACM Computing Surveys*, 53(2), 2021. → 165.

Zwicky E., Cooper S., Chapman D., and Russell D. *Building Internet Firewalls*. O'Reilly & Associates, Sebastopol, CA., 2nd edition, 2000. → 609.

GLOSSARY

BitTorrent: A distributed system for file sharing by which a file is partitioned into blocks and subsequently physically distributed among participants. A participant needs to copy and swap blocks with others (called tit-for-tat) to eventually gather all blocks to reconstruct the original file.

Blockchain: An append-only list of blocks of validated transactions. Each transaction and block can be replicated across all processes participating in the blockchain as they cannot be changed once published. The list is secured in the sense that *any* change to *any* transaction or block cannot go unnoticed.

Confidentiality: The property that information is disclosed only to authorized parties.

Consistency model (data centric): Describes what processes can expect concerning read and write operations from and to a logically shared data store that is physically distributed among the processes. In essence, a consistency model tells if and when local write operations are propagated to other processes, and the effects for local read operations.

Container: A special type of virtual machine, generally tailored to support only a specific operating system. A container provides an environment to an application suite, essentially mimicking the situation that this suite is being executed in isolation on a single machine. Where a virtual machine can host an operating system, a container can host only a suite of applications.

Critical region: A series of instructions to be executed by a process, which requires mutually exclusive access to specified resources.

Decentralized system: A networked computer system in which processes and resources are *necessarily* spread across multiple computers, usually caused by business constraints, lack of mutual trust, or geographical restrictions.

Dependable system: A system that provides availability, reliability, safety, maintainability, confidentiality, and integrity.

Distributed system: A networked computer system in which processes and resources are *sufficiently* spread across multiple computers, usually to meet performance and dependability requirements.

Distribution transparency: The phenomenon by which a distributed system attempts to hide the fact that its processes and resources are physically distributed across multiple computers, possibly separated by large distances.

Event matching: Typically occurs in publish-subscribe systems, where the publication of an event needs to be matched with all relevant subscriptions. A major problem is to support matching in a scalable manner.

Extensibility: Characterizes the extent to which a system can be extended (often without interrupting operations) with new functionality or components while avoiding affecting parts that are independent of those extensions.

Failure, error, fault: A system *fails* when it does not meet its specifications. A failure happens due to some *error*, such as a programming bug. The cause of an error is called a *fault*.

Fault tolerance: A system is fault tolerant when it can continue to provide its services according to specifications despite the presence of faults that influence its design, implementation, and execution.

Faults, errors, failures: A system is said to fail when it cannot meet its specifications. An error is a mistake that may need lead to a failure, such as a programming bug. A fault is the cause of an error.

Groupware: Distributed software to allow multiple users to collaborate from different locations through shared whiteboards, shared documents, etc.

Honest-but-curious: A server that behaves according to some protocol, but in the worst case keeps track of all the things it does.

Integrity: Ensures that alterations to the various assets of a system can be made only in an authorized way.

Interface Definition Language: A formal language for specifying the interfaces to various components of a distributed system. An IDL is used to generate code for different programming langauges that can subsequently be used to build applications making use of a component.

Interoperability: Characterizes the extent by which two implementations of systems or components from different manufacturers or development teams can co-exist and work together by merely relying on each other's services as specified by their respective interfaces.

Leader-election algorithm: A distributed algorithm that is executed among a group of processes such that, in the end, one of these processes can be designated as the leader of the group.

Logical clock: A system in which a group of processes keeps account of internal events, and also when messages are sent and received, to globally determine a consistent ordering of events.

Middleware: Software that constitutes a distributed system, implementing a myriad of mechanisms independent of any underlying system, as well as generally applicable for a wide range of applications.

Multiparty computation: The means for two or three parties to compute a value for which the data of those parties is needed, but without the need to actually share that data.

Open distributed system: A system that offers components that can easily be used by, or integrated into other systems. An open distributed system itself will often consist of components that originate from elsewhere.

Partial failure: A type of failure characteristic for a distributed system. Some process or resource, is not operating according to expectations, which, in turn, may have effects on other parts of the system. However, the system as a whole will continue to operate, albeit perhaps in unexpected ways.

Peer-sampling service: A service that operates in a potentially large distributed system, returning a (seemingly) randomly chosen peer from all available peers.

Perspectives on distributed systems: Due to the fact that a distributed system must meet so many different functional and nonfunctional requirements, which, in general, are mututal dependent, taking different perspectives on distributed systems allows for a more focused study. We distinguish perspectives on architecture, processes, communication, co-ordination, naming, consistency and replication, fault tolerance, and security.

Pervasive system: Systems consisting of a myriad of devices that are intended to blend into our environment naturally. Typical devices include smart-phones, smart watches, specific sensors and actuators, camera's, and so forth.

Portability: Characterizes to what extent an application developed for a distributed system A can be executed, without modification, on a different distributed system B that implements the same interfaces as A.

Remote procedure call: A communication mechanism that essentially mim-icks local procedure calls, yet where the execution of the call takes place at a remote server. In general, jsut as with local procedure calls, the caller waits until the procedure has been carried out fully.

Scalability: Refers to the extent that a system can scale in terms of its size, in terms of how geographically dispersed its components can be without seriously negatively affecting performance, or the extent to which a system can span multiple administrative organizations.

Scaling up or out: Scaling up is the process by which a machine is equipped with more and often more powerful resources so that it can better accommodate performance-demanding applications. Scaling out is all about extending a networked computer system with more computers and subsequently distributing workloads across the extended set of computers.

Separating policy from mechanism: Where mechanisms in a distributed sys-tem facilitate basic functionalities, such as storage, communication, processes, and so on, policies describe *how* those facilities are used. In general, separating facilities from the way how they are used is a good design principle, yet may overly complicate the configuration of a system.

Software architecture: The organization of distributed systems in terms of software components and their interaction.

System architecture: The actual realization of a distributed system requires that software components are instantiated and placed on real machines. A system architecture is the final instantiation of a software architec-ture.

Transaction processing monitor: A TP monitor is one of the first general-purpose mechanisms built into middleware. It is service that follows a standard protocol for executing a number of subtransactions, such that (1) each subtransaction adheres to the ACID properties, but (2) also the collection of subtransactions meets the ACID requirements.

Trusted Computing Base: The set of all security mechanisms in a (distributed) computer system that are necessary and sufficient to enforce a security policy.

Vector clocks: A system implementing logical clocks such that the logical time at which an event took place can be used to conclude that an event indeed took place before another event, thus capturing a potential causality between events.

Virtual machine: In general, a system providing its own interface to operating systems and applications, and implementing that interface for a specific instruction set or operating system. As a consequence, migrating or porting code across different architectures or operating systems becomes easier as long as the target environment provides the same interface the virtual machine is offering.

Virtual processor: A counterpart of a physical processor developed in software, providing a context in which the set of instructions of the physical processor are executed. A thread provides a minimal context for concurrent execution of instructions. An (operating system) process, in addition provides much stronger isolation guarantees between processes. For example, a process has its own, protected address space.

Made in the USA
Las Vegas, NV
21 February 2024

86037971R00374